# DANCE A WHILE

A Handbook for Folk, Square, Contra, and Social Dance

Tenth Edition

**Anne M. Pittman**
*formerly of Arizona State University*

**Marlys S. Waller**
*formerly of the University of Washington*

**Cathy L. Dark**
*Oregon State University*

WAVELAND PRESS, INC.
Long Grove, Illinois

For information about this book, contact:
Waveland Press, Inc.
4180 IL Route 83, Suite 101
Long Grove, IL 60047-9580
(847) 634-0081
info@waveland.com
www.waveland.com


Reissued 2015 by Waveland Press, Inc.

10-digit ISBN 1-4786-2698-4
13-digit ISBN 978-1-4786-2698-5



Printed in the United States of America

7 6 5 4 3 2 1

# Dedication

The Tenth Edition of *Dance A While* is dedicated to three women who have each made a major impact on recreational dance in the United States.

© Pasadena Ballroom Dance Association, Inc. All rights reserved.

**ERIN STEVENS, Social Dance**

Erin Stevens is one of the most dynamic individuals to help drive the revival in social dancing in our time. Growing up in a close-knit family in Pasadena, California, Erin has always danced. In 1983, Erin organized the Pasadena Ballroom Association with her sister, Tami, helping to turn Pasadena into one of the centers of social dance on the West Coast. Shortly after high school, Erin began to seek out the original innovators of popular and performance social dance on both coasts, studying and working with giants of an earlier time such as Dean Collins and Frankie Manning. Erin covers just about everything in the popular social dance realm, working in dance studios, film, video instruction, and performance. Her skill as a teacher is amazing; she has literally started thousands of people dancing. One of many peak events for Erin was dancing the Lindy Hop in a nationally televised performance at the White House in 1999 in front of President Bill Clinton and First Lady Hillary Clinton.

John Musemeche, photographer.

**VONNIE BROWN, Folk Dance**

Vonnie R. Brown, retired from the dance faculty of Louisiana State University, is the Artistic Director and Choreographer of the internationally lauded Karpaty Folk Ensemble of Baton Rouge, which she founded in 1972. Vonnie has long played a central role in Louisiana's recreational international folk dance scene and has taught at most of the major folk dance camps and festivals in the United States. She has also traveled widely for her dance research, and has taught in Japan and the Czech Republic. In 1986, Vonnie received the San Antonio Folk Festival annual award for outstanding contributions in folk dance. She was also honored by the National Folk Organization of the USA in 1993 for her contributions to the field. In addition, the Slovak government has officially recognized her for the work she has done in the preservation and promotion of the traditional dance and folklore of Slovakia.

Library of Congress, American Folklife Center Collection.

**MARGOT MAYO, Square Dance**

Margot Mayo is one of many women square dance leaders who were unsung heroes. Born in Commerce, Texas, she came to New York City in 1933 and attended several private schools including the Institute of Musical Art (now The Juilliard School), Martha Graham School of Dance, and Columbia University. As part of the folk revival movement, Margot formed the American Square Dance Group in 1934. In 1939, she founded the first folk dance magazine, *Promenade*, a collection of tunes, book reviews, and dances. In 1943, she published *The American Square Dance*, which was revised and expanded in 1948 and 1964. Although she was from the Southwest, her book—like many others of that period—focused on New England Squares, Quadrilles, Longway Sets, Running Sets, Play Party Games, and Round Dances. Margot also wrote brochures for Decca Square Dance Albums and recorded folk music from Kentucky, North Carolina, and Tennessee that is now deposited wih the Library of Congress' American Folklife Center. She was on the cutting edge of Ethnomusicology in American Folk Dance and American Folk Music. Like many women in the 1900s–1950s, Margot was best known nationally through her publications.

# Contents

Foreword xv

Preface xvi

- Changes in the Tenth Edition xvi
- Acknowledgments xvii

## 1 HISTORY 1

The Beginning 1

Forms 2

Music 2

Cultural Significance 3

- Religion 3
- Education 3
- Health 4
- Fertility 4

Dance in Today's World 4

- Artistic Dance 4
- Theatrical Dance 4
- Traditional Dance 5
- Social/Recreational Dance 5

## 2 EFFECTIVE GROUP INSTRUCTION 6

The Effective Instructor 6

Why Dance? 6

Purpose of Dance 7

Facilities 7

- Floor 7
- Acoustics 7

Equipment 7

- Sound Systems 7

Music 9

- Recordings 9
- Teaching with Recordings 10
- Live Music 10
- Teaching with Live Music 11

Planning Instruction 11

- The Total Dance Program Curriculum 11
- Dance Unit 12
- Daily Planning Instruction 12
- Objectives/Student Outcome 12
- Assessing Group Variables 13
- Content Selection 13
- Lesson Plan 13

Orientation to the Dance Class 16

- Setting the Stage 16
- Teaching Students with Special Needs 17
- First Class Meeting 19

Class Procedure 19

- Strategies for Selecting Material and Presentation 19
- General Teaching Points 20
- Teaching a Specific Dance 21
- Review 23
- Evaluation 23
- Enrichment Activities 24

*continues on page vi*

### Organizing Special Activities 25
- Family Dances 25
- Social Events 25
- Special Parties 26
- Theme Parties 26
- Senior Dances 27

## 3 DANCE FUNDAMENTALS

### Rhythm and Meter 28
- Rhythm 28
- Beat 28
- Note Values 29
- Accent 29
- Measure 29
- Meter 29
- Time Signature 30
- Line Values 30
- Phrase 30
- Tempo 30
- Rhythm Pattern 31
- Even Rhythm 31
- Uneven Rhythm 31
- Counting Rhythm 32

### Analysis of a Basic Rhythm 32

### Fundamental Locomotor Movements 32
- Walk 33
- Run 33
- Leap 34
- Jump 34
- Hop 35
- Sissone 35
- Assemblé 36
- Gallop 36
- Slide 37
- Skip 38
- Exercises for Fundamental Locomotor Movements 38

### Basic Dance Steps 38
- Shuffle, Dance Walk, or Glide 38
- Two-Step or Triple-Step 39
- Polka 39
- Schottische 39
- Waltz 40
- Mazurka 41

### Suggestions for Teaching Basic Dance Steps 41
- Analysis of Rhythm of Basic Step 41
- Method of Presentation 41
- Interdependent Factors Influencing Procedure 41

### Procedure for Teaching Basic Dance Steps and Turns 42
- Basic Dance Turns 42
- Schottische Turn Clockwise 42
- Two-Step Turn Clockwise 43
- Teaching Two-Step Turn Clockwise 43
- Progressive Two-Step 44
- Polka Turn 44
- Waltz 45
- Running Waltz 45
- Waltz Turns 45
- Pivot Turn 46
- Spin or Twirl 47

### Dance Formations 48

### Dance Positions 49

### Guidelines for Reading Dance Directions 54

### Music in Relation to Dance 54
- Listen to the Beat 54
- How to Recognize Music for Dance 55
- Rhythm Training and Appreciation 56

### Dance Style 56
- The Beautiful Dancer 56
- Ear and Ankle Alignment 57
- Good Posture—Key to Body Balance and Control 57
- Achieving Appropriate Style 57
- Teaching Style 58

## 4 AMERICAN DANCE SAMPLER 60

Dances from the European Courts to the American Ballrooms 61

The Unique Contributions of African Americans 61

The Spanish-Mexican Influence 62

Dance Styles of the People 62

Music 63

Dress 63

A Social Occasion 64

Revival of Folk Traditions 64

The Melting Pot versus Ethnic Identity 64

Play Party Games: Dances for Children 65

- BINGO 66
- BROWN-EYED MARY 67
- CAPTAIN JINKS 68
- LOOBY LOO 70
- POP GOES THE WEASEL 71
- SANDY LAND 72
- SHOO FLY 73
- SKIP TO MY LOU 74
- THE BEAR WENT OVER THE MOUNTAIN 74
- ALABAMA GAL 75
- NOBODY'S BUSINESS 76

A Selection of American Dances 77

- GRAND MARCH 78
- VIRGINIA REEL 80
- GRAND SQUARE QUADRILLE 82
- PAUL JONES YOUR LADY 84
- NINEPIN REEL 85
- PORTLAND FANCY 87
- OH JOHNNY 88
- RED RIVER VALLEY 89
- LEVI JACKSON RAG 90

Nonpartner Dances 91

- AMOS MOSES 91
- COTTON-EYED JOE (line dance) 92
- JESSIE POLKA 93
- POPCORN 94
- TEN PRETTY GIRLS 94
- TWELFTH STREET RAG 95

Mixers 96

- Gain or Exchange Partners 96
- Trade Dances 98
- Tags 98
- Elimination Dances 98

Partner Dances 99

- SCHOTTISCHE 99
- TEXAS SCHOTTISCHE VARIATIONS 101
- TEXAS SCHOTTISCHE FOR THREE 103
- SALTY DOG RAG 104
- BOSTON TWO-STEP 106
- HEEL AND TOE POLKA 107
- TETON MOUNTAIN STOMP 108
- COTTON-EYED JOE (couple dance) 109
- GARDEN WALTZ 111
- VARSOUVIENNE 112
- ALL-AMERICAN PROMENADE 114
- GLOWWORM MIXER 115
- JIFFY MIXER 116
- PATTY-CAKE POLKA 117
- MEXICAN MIXER 118
- TENNESSEE WIG WALK 119

Cajun Dance 120

- CAJUN WALTZ 121
- CAJUN TWO-STEP 122
- CAJUN ONE-STEP 122
- CAJUN JITTERBUG 123
- ZYDECO TWO-STEP 123

Country Western Dance 125

- Country Western Style 125
- Dance Hall Etiquette 125
- TRADITIONAL COUNTRY WESTERN SWING 126
  - Traditional Country Western Swing Rhythm 126


*continues on page viii*

Cowboy Swing Style 126
Cowboy Swing Variations 127
TRADITIONAL TWO-STEP 132
TEN-STEP 135
TRAVELING CHA CHA 136
COUNTRY WALTZ 138

Folk Dance from the Hawaiian Islands 140
History 140
Hula Fundamentals 141
Basic Foot and Floor Patterns 142
THE HUKILAU 143
KAHULI AKU KAHULI MAI 145
PUPU HINUHINU 147

5 SQUARE DANCE 150

History 150
Antecedents 150
Regional Influences 151
Early Leaders 153
Post–World War II 154
Standardization of Basic Movements 155
Square Dancing Moves into the Twenty-First Century 155

Teaching Square Dance 156
Which Road to Take, Choosing a Style 156
Teaching Approaches 156
Styling 157
The Caller and Calling 157
Calling Sequence 158
Calling Methods 158
Use of Prerecorded Calls 159

Big Circle Square Dance 159
GEORGIA RANG TANG 160
KING'S HIGHWAY 161
QUEEN'S HIGHWAY 161
SHOO FLY SWING 161
THE BASKET 161
BIRD IN THE CAGE 161
BOX THE GNAT AND BOX THE FLEA 162
BUTTERFLY TWIRL 162
DIVE FOR THE OYSTER 162
LADY 'ROUND THE LADY 162
MOUNTAINEER LOOP 162
POP THEM THRU 163
SHOOT THE OWL 163
TAKE A LITTLE PEEK 163

Basic Movements for Square Dances 164
Teaching Progression and Analysis for Basic Movements of Square Dance 164
Level 1A: Beginner Basics 1–8 165
Level 1B: Orientation to the Square 167
Level 2: Beginner Basics 9–18 168
Level 3: Beginner Basics 19–26 171
Level 4: Intermediate Basics 27–35 173
Supplementary Square Dance Patter 177

Organizing Squares and Changing Partners 178
Big Circle Mixers 179
Methods for Squaring Up 179
Methods for Changing Partners or Moving to a New Square 180

Square Dances: Patter and Singing Calls 181

Patter Calls 182
ANOTHER TRAIL 182
ARKANSAS TRAVELER 182
ARKANSAS TRAVELER WITH A CROSS TRAIL THRU 182
BEND IT TIGHT 182
BIRD IN THE CAGE: SEVEN HANDS 'ROUND 182
BOX THE GNAT: PULL BY 182
CATCH ALL EIGHT 183
COWBOY LOOP 183
DUCK THEN WHEEL AROUND 183
EASY BEND THE LINE 184
EASY SQUARE THRU 184
ENDS TURN IN 184

FORWARD UP AND BACK 184
FORWARD UP SIX 184
GENTS STAR RIGHT 185
GNAT AND FLEA 185
GO THE ROUTE 185
HALF SQUARE THRU COMBO 185
INSIDE ARCH AND OUTSIDE UNDER 185
NEW STAR THRU 185
OCEAN WAVE 186
PROMENADE THE OUTSIDE RING 186
PROMENADE THE RING 186
THE ROUTE 186
SALLY GOODIN' 186
SIDES DIVIDE 186
SPINNING WHEEL 187
SPLIT THE RING 187
SPLIT THE RING AND AROUND JUST ONE 188
STAR THRU: CALIFORNIA TWIRL 188
STAR THRU SQUARE THRU COMBO 188
TEXAS STAR 188
TEXAS WHIRLWIND 188

Singing Calls 189

ALABAMA JUBILEE 189
GENTLE ON MY MIND 189
HOUSTON 189
JUST BECAUSE 190
SMOKE ON THE WATER 190

6 CONTRA DANCE 192

History 192

English Country Dance Roots 192
The Rise of Longways Dances 193
Contra Dance in California before the Gold Rush 193
Country Dances Decline 193
Early Twentieth-Century Revivals 193
Post-World War II Years: The Ralph Page Revival 194
A New Generation Discovers Contras: "Dudley Dancers" 195
Live Music Takes Center Stage 195
The Country Dance and Song Society and Other Organizations 196
Contra Dance Research 196
Contra Dancing in the Twenty-First Century 196

Contra Dance Basics 197

Starting the Contra Dance Set 197
Formations in the Contra Dance 197
Progression 198
Music and Timing 199
The Role of the Caller 199
Dance Sources 199
Card File 200
Music Sources 200
Contra Dance Figures 200
Teaching Suggestions 201
Dance Levels and Teaching Progression 202
Contra Dance Tunes Composed by Ralph Page 203
AW SHUCKS! 204
BECKET REEL 205
BRIMMER & MAY REEL 206
BROKEN SIXPENCE 207
CDS REEL 208
CHAIN THE SWAIN 209
CHORUS JIG 210
CONTRA FOR MARGIE 211
DANCE GYPSY 212
DANCING SAILORS 213
DELPHINIUMS AND DAISIES 214
EASY DOES IT 214
HILLS OF HABERSHAM 215
HULL'S VICTORY 217
JED'S REEL 218
LADY OF THE LAKE 218
MORE AGAIN 219
THE NOVA SCOTIAN 220
THE OTHER MARY KAY 221
PETRONELLA 222
ROADBLOCK REEL 223

*continues on page x*

ROLL IN THE HEY 224
RORY O'MORE 225
SALMONCHANTED EVENING 226
SHADRACK'S DELIGHT 227
SMALL POTATOES 228
SO WHEN WAS THE WEDDING? 229
STARS OF ALBERTA 230
SUPERNOVA SCOTIAN 231
SYMMETRICAL FORCE 232
THORN STREET GYPSY 233
THE TOURIST 234
WEAVE THE LINE 235
WITH THANKS TO THE DEAN 236

# 7 INTERNATIONAL FOLK DANCE 238

## Introduction 238

Folk Dance in Industrialized Society 238

## Folk Dance Movement 239

Preserving Folk Dancing 239
Folk Dance in the United States 239
History of Folk Dance in American Education 240
Camps 240
Performing Groups 240
Research and Advanced Studies 241

## Understanding Folkways Enhances Dance 241

Eastern and Western Culture 241
Geography and Climate 241
Religion 241
Music 241
Folk Dancing Today: Three Main Styles 242
The Value of Folk Dancing 242
Teaching Approaches 243
Costumes 243
Holidays, Festivals, and Special Occasions 243

## Africa 244

The Continent 244
European Influence 244
Slave Trade 244
Traditional Dance 244
Art and Dance 245
Improvisation 245
Dance Instruments and Objects 245
Spiritual World 245
The Future 245
BORBORBOR (Ghanaian) 246
GAHU (Ghanaian) 247
PATA PATA (South African) 249

## Alpine Region: Switzerland, Austria, and Germany 250

Dance Characteristics 250
Folk Dancing in Switzerland 250
D'HAMMERSCHMIEDSG'SELLN (German) 252
DR GSATZLIG (Swiss) 254
KRÜZ KÖNIG (GERMAN) 256
MAN IN THE HAY (German) 258
SONDERBURG DOPPELQUADRILLE (German) 260
SPINNRADL ZU DRITT (Austrian) 261
Zwiefacher 263
DIE ALTE KATH (ZWIEFACHER) (German) 264
HOLDERBEERLI (ZWIEFACHER) (German) 265

## Balkan Countries 267

Introduction 267
Greece 267
Serbia, Macedonia, and Bosnia 268
Bulgaria 269
Roma Culture 269
ERSKO KOLO (Serbian) 270
HASÁPIKOS (Greek) 271
KOCANSKA GADA (Roma) 273
LESNOTO (Macedonian) 274
MISIRLOU (Greek-American) 276
PRAVO HORO (Bulgarian) 277
PLJESKAVAC KOLO (Serbian) 278
SARAJEVKA KOLO (Bosnian) 279

SAVILA SE BELA LOZA (Serbian) 280
ŠETNJA (Serbian) 281
SYRTÓS (Greek) 283
TROPANKA (Bulgarian) 284

## British Isles 285
Introduction 285
England 285
Ireland 287
Scotland 288
THE BRIDGE OF ATHLONE (Irish) 289
BUTTERFLY HORNPIPE (English) 291
FLOWERS OF EDINBURGH (Scottish) 292
GIE GORDONS (Scottish) 294
OSLO WALTZ (Scottish-English) 295
ROAD TO THE ISLES (Scottish) 296
SIAMSA BEIRTE (Irish) 297
THREE MEET (English) 298
THE WHITE COCKADE (Scottish) 299
WILLOW TREE (English) 301

## Canada 303
Discovery and Settlement 303
Population 303
Culture 303
Cape Breton 303
LA BASTRINGUE 304
THE SAINT JOHN RIVER 305

## China 307
ADMIRING THE MOON 308
GONG XI, HAPPY NEW YEAR 310

## Czech Republic and Slovakia 312
Background 312
Dance History and Characteristics 312
DOUDLEBSKA POLKA (Czech) 313
TANCUJ (Czech) 315

## France 316
Traditional French Music and Dance 316
A CROSSING BOURRÉE IN TWO TIME 318
BRANLE D'OSSAU 320
MON PÈRE AVAIT UN PETIT BOIS 321
RONDEAU DE GAREIN 323

## Guam 324
EL BAILE DEL PALO 324

## Hungary 329
Introduction 329
Dance Characteristics 330
HUNGARIAN MOTIFS 331
CSÁRDÁS PALOCOSAN 332
KISKANÁSZTÁNC 334
UGRÓS 335

## Israel 336
Clarification of Ethnic Names and Nationalities 336
Dance Characteristics 336
CHERKESSIYA 337
HAVA NAGILA 338
HINEH MA TOV 340
HORA 341
MA NA'AVU 342
MAYIM 343
VE' DAVID 345

## Italy 346
Background 346
IL CODIGLIONE 347
SICILIAN TARANTELLA 349

## Japan 351
Bugaku 351
Noh 351
Kabuki 352
HARUKOMA 353
TANKO BUSHI 354

## Lithuania 356
Background 356
KALVELIS 357
KLUMPAKOJIS 358

*continues on page xii*

Mexico 359
Dance in Mexico 359
EL JARABE TAPATÍO 361
LA CUCARACHA 363
LA RASPA 365
LA VARSOVIANA 366
LAS CHIAPANECAS 368
Philippines 370
TINIKLING 372
Poland 375
Dances of Poland 375
TRAMBLANKA—POLKA MAZURKA 377
WALCZYK "GES WODA" 379
Romania 380
Background 380
Music 380
ALUNELUL 381
HORA DE MINA 382
HORA PE GHEATA 383
ITELE 384
SIRBA DIN CIMPOI 385
Russia 387
Dance Characteristics 387
ALEXANDROVSKA 388
KOROBUSHKA 389
TROIKA 390
Scandinavia 392
Introduction 392
Denmark 393
Norway 393
Finland 394
Sweden 394
BITTE MAND I KNIBE (Danish) 395
DEN TOPPEDE HØNE (Danish) 396
FAMILIE SEKSTUR (Danish) 397
FAMILJEVALSEN (Swedish) 398
FJÄSKERN (Swedish) 399
HAMBO (Swedish) 400
NORWEGIAN POLKA (Norwegian) 402
SEKSMANNSRIL (Norwegian) 403
SNURRBOCKEN (Swedish) 404
TO TING (Danish) 406
TOTUR (Danish) 407
VOSSARULL (Norwegian) 408
South America 409
CARNAVALITO (Bolivian) 409
RANCHERA (Uruguayan) 410

8 SOCIAL DANCE 412
Introduction 412
Phases of Social Dance 413
Forms of Social Dancing 414
Dancesport 415
Teaching Social Dance 415
Trends in Vocabulary and Leading 415
Formations 415
Walk-Through 416
The Cue 416
Demonstration 416
Unison versus Free Practice 416
Dance Lesson Preparation 416
Style in Social Dance 417
Footwork in Social Dance 417
Dance Walk 418
Dance Positions 418
Closed Position 418
Techniques of Leading and Following 419
Following 420
Swing (Jitterbug) 421
Swing Rhythm 421
Swing Style 422
SINGLE-TIME SWING 423
TRIPLE TIME SWING 429
Swing Combos 431
WEST COAST SWING 431
West Coast Swing Rhythm 431
West Coast Swing Style 432

HUSTLE 435
Hustle with Partner 436
CHARLESTON 438
Charleston Rhythm 438
Charleston Style 439
Teaching Suggestions 439
Fundamental Charleston Steps 439
LINDY HOP 442

Line Dance 445
Teaching Tips for Line Dancing 446
Line Dance Style 446
ALL SHOOK UP 447
THE CONTINENTAL 448
COWBOY BOOGIE 448
FREEZE 449
HIP HOP DANCE 450
SATURDAY NIGHT FEVER (line dance) 452
Adaptations for Students with Disabilities 453
ELECTRIC SLIDE 454
SLAPPIN' LEATHER 455

Foxtrot 456
Foxtrot Rhythm 456
Magic Step (Bronze Basic) 457
Westchester Box Step 457
Foxtrot Style 457
Magic Step Series 458
Box Step Series—Westchester 463
The Pivot Turn 467
Foxtrot Combos 468

Tango 469
Tango Rhythm 469
Tango Style 469
Fundamental Tango Steps 470
Tango Combos 477

Waltz 478
Waltz Rhythm 478
Waltz Style 479
Fundamental Waltz Steps 479
Waltz Combos 485

Cha Cha 486
Cha Cha Rhythm 486
Cha Cha Style 486
Fundamental Cha Cha Steps 487
Cha Cha Combos 494

Mambo 494
Mambo Rhythm 495
Mambo Style 495
Fundamental Mambo Steps 495

Merengue 496
Merengue Rhythm 497
Merengue Style 497
Fundamental Merengue Steps 497
Merengue Combos 500

Rumba 501
Rumba Rhythm 501
Rumba Style 501
Fundamental Rumba Steps 502
Rumba Combos 508

Salsa 509
Salsa Style and Flavor 509
Fundamental Salsa Steps 509

Samba 513
Samba Rhythm 513
Samba Style 514
Fundamental Samba Steps 514
Samba Combos 518

## APPENDICES

Appendix A: Periodicals 519
Appendix B: Organizations and Resources 520
Appendix C: Record, CD, Cassette, and Video Sources—Distributors and Producers 523
Appendix D: Instructional Aids—Music and Videos 526
Music on the *Dance A While* CD 530

*continues on page xiv*

Bibliography 531

Glossary 539

Index of Mixer and Nonpartner Dances 556

Classified Indexes 557

Chapter 4: American Dance Sampler 557

Chapter 5: Square Dance 560

Chapter 6: Contra Dance 562

Chapter 7: International Folk Dance 564

Chapter 8: Social Dance 568

Subject Index 573

# Foreword

At their annual conference in February 2006, the National Folk Organization of the USA honored the four authors of *Dance A While,* for their many contributions to dance. While I am now retired as a participating author, I am thrilled with the additions and improvements to the book with each new edition. The authors are to be congratulated on consistently bringing new ideas to students and teachers. Cathy Dark, who has taken over leadership on the revisions to the book since my own retirement, is an active and enthusiastic dance teacher at Oregon State University, where she also directs a highly popular annual college student dance performance. After more than fifty years and many successful editions of *Dance A While,* Cathy is able to keep the book young and in tune with today's instructors, students, and dance enthusiasts.

A common theme we hear on the news these days is how more people of all ages are becoming more overweight and less active. Keeping dance a strong presence in the curriculum at all age levels can help combat this problem. Dance builds fitness, coordination, confidence, and social skills. Students who move to music in new ways, work with multiple dance partners, and experience a variety of rhythms acquire skills that help them socially as well as physically. *Dance A While* provides instructors with the tools they need to teach a fantastic variety of folk, square, contra, and social dances, and to instill a lifelong appreciation of these dances and the cultures that created them.

It has been an honor and a joy to work with the talented and dedicated team of authors over many years. I now wish the team the very best in keeping *Dance A While* such a fine contribution to the field of dance.

Jane Harris Ericson, MS (Retired)
*Dance Faculty*
*Washington State University*
Pullman, Washington

# Preface

In 1950, Marlys Swenson Waller, Jane Harris Ericson, and Anne M. Pittman published the 156-page first edition of *Dance A While,* never suspecting that it would grow to 580 pages and last more than fifty years. *Dance A While* is a true classic in the field. Like previous editions, the Tenth Edition of this best-selling introduction to recreational dance text offers guidelines for dance instruction and detailed directions for more than 260 individual dances from the United States and around the world, providing ample information for students and giving future dance instructors the background they need to be successful teachers.

Cathy Dark, who has been a part of the author team since the Eighth Edition, has led the way on this revision. Cathy has brought her enthusiasm for teaching and her passion for dance to the book once again, spearheading the major changes that make the Tenth Edition the most comprehensive, up-to-date, and user-friendly introduction to recreational dance available anywhere.

## Changes in the Tenth Edition

With every revision we strive to improve the book and keep it accessible and relevant for new generations of students. The revisions for the Tenth Edition reflect the many excellent and thoughtful suggestions of reviewers and colleagues. There are several exciting global improvements designed to make the book easier to use and apply to all levels of dance students. Written dance directions have been standardized so that the format is consistent within each style of dance. For instance, directions for folk dances are now laid out by counts within each measure of music. Sections at the beginning of each dance chapter explain how to interpret the directions for each particular style of dance. Each dance or dance move has been given a skill level, so an instructor will know at a glance if that dance or move is appropriate for his or her students. The level indications appear at the beginning of each section of dance directions and clearly indicate whether the dance is appropriate for Beginner 1, 2, or 3; Intermediate; or Advanced students. In addition, we have brought back, by popular demand, the classified indexes of dances, which appear on pages 557–572. These indexes group all like dances together by style and break them down by level, providing a practical resource for planning dance lessons.

We've also made updates and revisions to each dance chapter, adding new background information, teaching tips, cultural and historical details, and—of course—new dances. Chapter 4, American Dance Sampler, has been reorganized into clearer sections to group the dances by type. One brand-new section in this chapter is devoted to Play Party Games. These traditional dancing games are based on basic locomotor skills, making them appropriate for very young children. Elementary school teachers will find these activities ideal for their students. There is also a new Hawaiian Dance section, which includes the ever-famous Hukilau, as well as two other dances, Kahuli Aku Kahuli Mai and Pupu Hinuhinu.

Chapter 5, Square Dance, has a completely revised and streamlined history section, providing faster access to the fun historical facts and explanations of the regional style differences. The section "Teaching Square Dance" has been restructured, with truly beginner information added so that teachers otherwise unfamiliar with square dance can easily organize a square and provide a uniquely American cultural dance activity in their curriculum.

Chapter 6, Contra Dance, includes new historical background information that helps set the stage for classes. Contra dance has long been associated with New England and the East Coast, but it has come to be popular across the country. Three new dances from various regions are Chain the Swain, Stars of Alberta, and Thorn Street Gypsy.

Chapter 7, International Folk Dance, with its wealth of folk dances, is a fantastic resource for any instructor wishing to explore the dances of any of the over thirty different cultures represented. Chapter 7 takes an interdisciplinary approach, including geography, history, music, art, and social studies in the background information for the dances. Understanding the many diverse cultures that coexist on our planet facilitates better understanding, communication, and respect for all people in the world. New information on the Roma culture will, we hope, help eliminate the lingering prejudice toward the Roma people. We are proud to share a small part of their wonderful cultural heritage with the addition of the Kocanska Gada, a wonderful party dance for everyone. Another new dance in this chapter is a lively festival dance from Japan, the Harukoma.

Chapter 8, Social Dance, includes all the exciting dances that students see in the media today. Social dance has been gaining mainstream popularity with several new reality television programs and movies with dance themes. We have significantly upgraded the Salsa section, including more information about the background and many styles of Salsa. Four new moves have been added to provide what are considered the most common steps for a solid foundation in Salsa. Hollywood movies such as *Hairspray* have also spurred increased public interest in line dances, leading to the inclusion of The Continental, a 1960s line dance.

## Acknowledgments

*Dance A While* is a treasure because of the many teachers that have generously shared their material, expertise, and philosophy. We thank them all!

We are honored that Jane Harris Ericson, original coauthor and colleague, has written the Foreword. In addition, we would like to express our great appreciation for her extensive work in developing the format and content of *Dance A While* over many editions.

The new Hawaiian dance section in Chapter 4 was made possible by the work of Paula Luv, Lecturer and Performer at the University of Hawaii. We appreciate Dina Blade for sharing her Beamer Hawaiian material. Thank you to Olivia Steinhoff, president of Oregon State University Hawaiian Dance Club for sharing the Hukilau. Thanks also to longtime friend Henry "Buzz" Glass for his dances.

For Chapter 6, David Millstone contributed a fresh approach to the history of contra dance, including recognition of Ralph Page and Ted Sannella and the influence of Dudley Laufman. Penn Fix wrote the Contra Dance Basics section, which assists the beginning teacher in learning the rudiments of Contra dance. Thank you, Penn, for your work on presenting the progressions of contra dance and for introducing such a variety of wonderful dances ranging from Beginning to Advanced. We appreciate your efforts to single out creative contra dance choreographers from the past to the present-men and women who are talented representative leaders from all over the country.

We extend our gratitude to the many people who have contributed dances: Kathy Anderson, Don Armstrong, Fred Breunig, Mary and Fred Collette, Bob Dalsemer, Roger Diggle, Fred Field, Penn Fix, Herbie Gaudreau, Ralph Page, Graham

Hempel, Becky Hill, Tom Hinds, Erik Hoffman, Gene Hubert, Jim Kitch, Carol Kopp, Carol Ormand, Tony Parkes, Dan Pearl, Tanya Rotenberg, Ted Sannella, David Smukler, and Steve Zakon. The estate of Ralph Page has given *Dance A While* permission to include two original fiddle tunes composed by Ralph. Thank you Laura Page Wilson. The Country Dance and Song Society and the Lloyd Shaw Foundation have permitted *Dance A While* to include several dances from their publications.

Chapter 7, International Folk Dance, has two new additions. Thanks go to Šani Rifati for sharing his passion for his Roma culture through dance. Thank you also to Ryoichi Oikawa for his contribution of a new Japanese dance and for clarifications of Japanese dance steps. Over the years many specialists have contributed material about cultural characteristics and styles for international folk dances in *Dance A While.* Christina Wright has written a thoughtful article on French dance. Nelda Drury wrote the Dance in Mexico section. Karen Gottier has given valuable insight into the Folk Dancing in Switzerland section. Others include Kate Van Winkle Keller (English country dance), George A. Fogg (English country dance), Jacek Marek (Polish dance), Andor Czompo (Hungarian dance), and Gordon Tracie (Scandinavian dance).

*Dance A While* has enjoyed a rich collection of dances because so many teachers and students have generously shared their material with the authors. We wish to acknowledge the following: Vytanta Beliajus (Lithuanian dance), Sunni Bloland (Romanian dance), Laura Zanzi de Chavarria (Uruguayan dance), Richard Crum (Serbian dance), Pru Edwards (Canadian dance), Mihai David (Romanian dance), Jane Farwell (Swiss dance), Beatrice Feddy (Ghanaian dance), Klaus Fink (German dance), George A. Fogg (English country dance), May Gadd (English country dance), Madelynne Greene (French dance), Juan Guerrero (Guamanian dance), Michael Herman (various countries), Huig Hofman (German dance), Dvora Lapson (Israeli dance), Dick Oakes (Bulgarian dance), Una and Sean O'Farrell (Irish dance), Helfrid Rudd (Norwegian dance), and Marilyn Smith (French dance).

Chapter 8 has an expanded Salsa background section and several new Salsa moves thanks to Simona Boucek and Mike Eskeldson of Corvallis, Oregon. We are fortunate to have received materials from Gary E. Sanders of the University of Missouri, Kansas City.

National organizations, regular festivals, dance camps, and workshops are the glue that hold recreational dance together. *Dance A While* salutes and acknowledges the contributions made by the Arbeitgemeinschaft der Sing-, Tanz- und Spielkreise, the Country Dance and Song Society, Lloyd Shaw Foundation, and the Royal Scottish Country Dance Society.

We would like to thank those who provided the photos for the dedication page, especially John Musemeche of Baton Rouge for Vonnie's picture and Pasadena Ballroom Dance Association staff for Erin's picture. Thank you to Marc Green of Corvallis, Oregon for his wonderful words about Erin Stevens. Thanks to Rickey Holden for sharing his square dances in Chapter 5. Many thanks also to Jerry Graser for his encouragement, support, and wonderful technical advice about sound equipment for Chapter 3.

A very special thank you goes to Stew Shacklette, director of the Kentucky Dance Foundation, who has contributed his wonderful music for the CD. Stew's music and his dedicated work help to preserve and promote folk dancing and related arts, and we are very grateful for his collaboration and support.

Lynn Waller, Marlys's husband, offered valuable second opinions and constant support. *Merci!* Cathy would like to thank Mark and Kathi Tucker for their amazing support and help in keeping her sane. Thank you to Jennifer Morris of Tempe, Arizona and Mendy Gayler, Debi Rothermund, and Rena Thayer of Corvallis, Oregon for their invaluable deciphering and typing skills and their super-human ability to meet tight deadlines.

We would also like to thank our editors at Pearson Education, especially our amazing project editor, Robin Pille, for her infinite patience, wonderful support, good humor, and excellent coordination of *Dance A While.* We are also extremely grateful to Sharon Montooth for working her many production miracles. The Left Coast Group once again expertly turned our manuscript into the printed book. Thanks also to Martha Ghent, our talented copy editor, for saving us from ourselves on many occasions, and to Yvo Riezebos for his beautiful interior design.

Finally, we would like to acknowledge again those who have had special impact on this edition and the many fellow dance enthusiasts and teachers who have been loyal contributors over the many years.

*Anne M. Pittman*
*Marlys S. Waller*
*Cathy L. Dark*

# HISTORY

1

## THE BEGINNING

*Dance and the dancer have belonged to every age and culture since the beginning of time and thus have reflected the human condition and experience in each succeeding age. In the earliest human experience, dance was a functional means of survival. For ancient societies, dance was a psychological and physiological imperative.*

Among ancient peoples everywhere, religion was a highly developed notion of a world of unseen powers. Worship was an expression, in one form or another, of the dependence of humans on powers outside themselves. A universal dependence on nature for sustenance was a conspicuous element in ancient religion. Humans depended on natural phenomena—on the rain to grow plants, on the regular succession of seasons, and on the reproduction of animals. People feared sickness, death, hunger, drought, storms, and the spirits of the dead, both human and animal. The magic of rituals and ceremonies enabled them to communicate with and manipulate the unseen powers that controlled their lives. Ancient peoples created mimetic ceremonies and rituals from which the oldest of the arts has emerged: the dance.

Early people were one with their environment and, as such, were keen observers of the animal life around them. They reproduced with great fidelity the movements of birds and animals in the art of the period. These dancelike movements were unquestionably models for the mimetic movement used in ancient rituals. A common example in many cultures was the ceremony performed the evening before a hunt. Hunters would mimic the actions and movement of the animal about to be hunted. The ceremony was focused on praying to the gods or the spirit of the animal itself. These early dances were performed to ensure a successful hunt. The observation of the structured movements of bird and animal groups and individuals gave rise to

some of the earliest and oldest dance forms still in use today, namely, Circles, Chains, and Processionals.

## Forms

The *closed circle* is perhaps the most ancient of these forms and is believed to have derived from observation and imitation of the sun's rotation. In the early uses of the closed circle, dancers entered into the circle equally without regard for differences in gender or social position. Magic was generated by simple left-and-right movements around a central object that was the focus of the circle. Breaking the circle allowed the evil spirits out and the good spirits in, or vice versa, depending on the culture of the performers.

A second stage, in which the complexity of the circle increases, reflects the effect of cultural change. A dance for alternating genders or for only one gender indicates occupational differentiation. Movement directions, forward and backward and weaving in and out, also increase the complexity of the circle. The elaboration of the closed circle into the double circle with men on the inner circle, women on the outer circle, either facing center or each other, represents forms used for executing occupational dances and fertility rites.

The *chain* is derived from the closed circle (Figure 1.1). It first occurred, perhaps, when the closed circle was broken. Moving, or traveling the chain from one place to another, allows the magic or good luck engendered by the circle to be distributed over a larger area. Chain dances were generally gender free; that is, they could be danced by either gender or by a combination of genders usually placed alternately in line. The Lira vase, modeled and decorated 22 centuries ago by Indo-Europeans, depicts a group of four women linked with three men in a chain who are moving sideways in unison. The *carole*, a song-dance of the early Middle Ages, was danced in a chain formation. The *farandole*, a form of carole, was also danced in a hand-linked line or chain.

The *processional* consisted of a single or double file of dancers. The latter form was more common and consisted of couples, men in one file and women in the other. The processional, march, or promenade was once a complete dance; however, it was more commonly used to begin a program of dancing. The processional form is said to have originated from two important tribal customs, namely, to clean the community after a hard winter and to ensure its continued fertility. In England, whole communities dance the processional, moving through the town and in and out of houses, cleaning all before them with a May branch or a green broom. It is from the processional of couples that first the early Processional Court Dance, then the English Longways sets and their continental versions, and finally the Couple Dances developed.

FIGURE 1.1 Chain dance formation.

Throughout the ages, forms such as these have functioned to describe something about the society and culture of which they were a part. In the early stages of human development, the forms were as simple as humans imitating animals. As society became more complex, dance forms also became more complex. The effects of cultural changes on dance forms are particularly reflected in gender, occupational, and social-class distinctions. These prehistoric dance forms—the circle, chain, and processional—still exist in present contemporary dance sequences.

## Music

Music, the twin sister of dance, has, through the ages, been intimately related to all phases of life—birth, death, love, work, play, war, peace, and religion—and to a myriad of occurrences that arouse human emotions, be they joyous, comedic, or tragic. Because of this intimate relationship with all facets of the human experience, music has had a universal appeal.

Ancient music was spontaneous and improvised, and it was characterized by its nonaesthetic nature and lack of notation. In primitive cultures, music had a magico-functional purpose that served to carry out and perpetuate tribal traditions. The endless singsong of tribal chanters is reflected in early Christian chanting as well as in the droning rhymes of a child jumping rope.

The order in which the elements of music were developed is not known. It is tempting to surmise, however, that early humans were sensitive to the wealth of rhythm in their natural world. The rhythm of seasons, wind, water, and people's own physiological processes were constant cues. There is evidence that primitive people were keenly aware of the two sets of percussion instruments, hands and feet, provided by nature. It is equally tempting to surmise

FIGURE 1.2 Egyptian hieroglyphs depicting dance.

that they vented their feelings of joy and sorrow in bodily motions accompanied by rhythmic noises. These rhythmic patterns and raw snatches of melody enacted in pantomime or expressed in grunts and shouts were the antecedents of dance and song.

The origins of instrumental music can be projected on more solid grounds because practically all types of instruments existing today can be traced from ancient times. Three classes of instruments have evolved: percussion, wind, and string.

*Percussion instruments*, predominantly the drum, were used to accompany ritual dances and to communicate. In addition to the drum, rattles, seashells, twigs, bone scrapers, and gourds are examples of percussion instruments employed in ancient cultures.

*Wind instruments* in the form of flutes, trumpets, and reeds date back to the Stone Age. The flute and the trumpet are associated with magico-religious functions. The trumpet is also known to have been used as a signaling instrument in much the same way as it is used today.

In early cultures, the *string instruments* were the least developed. The predominant vocal and rhythmic character of primitive music did not require the use of melody or pitch. Cave paintings, dated 30,000 to 15,000 B.C., reveal a human disguised in an animal skin and apparently playing a bow. This gives rise to the possibility that the hunting bow could very well have been the progenitor of string instruments. Whether rhythm preceded melody, vocal music preceded instrumental music, or, in fact, it all happened simultaneously, music was born.

# Cultural Significance

Human history attests to the significance of dance as a serious and sacred activity. It was not a mere exuberant display of energy separated from the other institutions of a society. It was, indeed, the basis of the survival of the social system in that it contributed significantly to the society's functional and instrumental needs.

## Religion

Among pre-Christian civilizations, dance was a functional part of religion. In Egypt, dance was an essential part of every religious celebration. Worship was predominantly a ritualized concern for death and rebirth. Egyptian art has left lasting tributes to the importance of dance in wall paintings, reliefs, and literary hieroglyphs (Figure 1.2). The Egyptians were the first to describe dance movement on paper, and so they are the inventors of the art of choreography.

The Bible, particularly the Old Testament, gives abundant evidence of the importance and place of dance in ancient Hebrew religion. Dance was primarily an act of gratitude for victory or an accompaniment for a hymn of praise. Dances were generally joyous in nature and circular in form. Gratitude, joy, and praise are all found in David's dance in leading the procession of the ark and the canticle of the Israelites after the destruction of the Egyptians led by Miriam and "all the women" (Exodus 15.20), and David danced before the Lord with all his might (II Samuel 6).

## Education

Dance pervaded the life of ancient Greece, primarily in the form of worship and education (Figure 1.3). It also penetrated everyday life and achieved perfection as an art form in Greek drama. The Muse of Dance, Terpsichore, was one of the seven Muses. Ancient Greek philosophy defined the soul as the harmony of the body; thus, the aim of the Greeks was to develop equally all poses of the mind and the body. Dance, a chief branch of education, was the medium through which total integration of mind, body, and spirit could be achieved.

Dance as it is functionally significant to education has been recognized at various stages throughout human history. The Greeks considered dance a necessary part of education for all people. Plato proposed that all children, boys and girls, be instructed in dance from an early age. He wrote, "To sing well and to dance well is to be well educated" (Lawler 1964, 124). The Pyrrhic was the great Greek dance of war. It was accompanied by the flute and danced by armed warriors, who simulated warlike deeds with all the proper maneuvers for attack and defense. Sparta required every child over the age of five to learn the Pyrrhic and to practice it in a public place.

In New England, contrary to popular belief, settlers recommended that the young be taught to dance to learn poise, discipline, and good manners. John Locke, the great commonsense philosopher, wrote of dancing, "Nothing appears to me to give the children so much becoming confidence and behavior . . . as dancing" (Damon 1957, 3). Elsewhere in the New

FIGURE 1.3 Greek dancing.

World, Native American war dances and primitive hunting dances were occasions to teach and practice the skills necessary for war and hunting.

### Health

The preservation of health and the power to cure ailments through dance rituals are found in every culture. Among ancient people, the *Death Dance* was a united rhythmic effort to remove the ghost, dust the spirits from the house, quiet the emotions, and dispel the fears of those who remained. The fifteenth century European version of the Death Dance was strange in that it happened only in the minds of medical writers and artists. Paintings and woodcuts of the period depict the universality of death, the equality of death, and the vanity of rank and riches. All people, regardless of caste, eventually succumbed to the Death Dance. Death also appeared among the living in the form of a skeleton as a warning of impending death.

Captain Cook, of English naval fame, required his crew to dance the *Hornpipe* to ensure immunity from disease. In mid-fourteenth century Italy, the violent, nervous exercise of dancing was believed to relieve the harmful effects or the unreasonable fear of the bite of the tarantula spider.

Devil dances to drive out the ghost of a dead person are thought to be the basis for many funeral dances found throughout history. The Hopi Indians of Arizona use an ancient sand-painting ceremonial for curing purposes. During the four holy days following na ih es, the San Carlos Apache girl's puberty ceremony, the girl's power is believed to be strong enough to cure the sick (Basso 1966, 160). So great is the residual power of the dance in this ceremony that it has even been known to cure conditions such as bowed legs (Goodwin 1969, 443).

### Fertility

Dance in the form of fertility rites has been universally used by humans to propagate the species and to secure food. Initiation, courtship, marriage, and birth are themes represented by the dance in these rites. In the initiation rite, youth is danced into adulthood. Fertility of the fields and of humans is abduced by the power generated by encircling a maypole, a tree, or a sword. The three themes symbolized by the dance are (1) passage from one phase to another, as from youth to adulthood or from single to married status; (2) transfer of power (e.g., to carry or decorate with green or to encircle another person); and (3) purification, exemplified by leaping through or running around fire. "Sowing and copulating, germinating and bearing, harvesting and delivering are under one law" (Sachs 1937, 67).

Dance and the dancer have belonged to every age and culture since the beginning of time. It is evident that dance and the dancer have played a significant role in the evolution of mankind. In all ages, the human body, as an instrument moving in space and time, has made dance unique among the arts. It is this uniqueness that makes dance older than art and thus explains the antiquity and universality of dance.

## Dance In Today's World

The role of dance in the modern world is diminished compared to earlier times. Dance is not a focal point of contemporary culture, though its function in a modern society is manifested in several different ways. Organizing dance into four main areas may help students to understand the role of dance today: artistic, theatrical, traditional, and social/recreational. These classifications are one of many organizational approaches. They are not fully cross-cultural, but fit well in an industrialized society.

### Artistic Dance

Artistic dance is created to be performed and considered as *art*. This includes dance forms such as ballet and modern dance. Ballet performances can be based on traditional stories, such as the *Nutcracker*, or the work of many contemporary companies, like Dance Theater of Harlem and The New York City Ballet. Examples of modern dance companies are Merce Cunningham Dance Company, Pilobolus, and Mark Morris Company.

### Theatrical Dance

Theatrical dance is meant to entertain. Dance, including tap and jazz, from movies and Broadway musicals, are examples of theatrical dance. Classic examples of this style can be found in the movies *Seven Brides for Seven Brothers, Footloose,* and *Dance with Me,* or the Broadway musicals *Cats, Fosse,* and *Swing.*

## Traditional Dance

Traditional dances come from a specific culture and usually have a specific social function. For example, in traditional Romanian culture a special dance is performed before the spring planting at each farm. This dance is meant to scare away all the evil spirits in the ground and assure a bountiful crop. The Southwest Native American Rain Dance, which is a ceremonial prayer to the spirits for rain and fertility of the crops, is another example.

## Social/Recreational Dance

Ballroom, swing, square, contra, line, and international folk dancing are forms of dance enjoyed by people from all walks of life for recreational and social enjoyment. Demonstrations and performances of social dance styles typically share a culture or a passion with the audience. Many ballroom dancers refine their skill and technique for competitive performances, but initially most people start dancing for social and recreational enjoyment. It is the social and recreational forms of dance that are presented in *Dance A While*.

**DANCE TIMELINE** *Highlights of the history of dance*

| | |
|---|---|
| **China, 4000 BCE** | A Neolithic bowl depicting a line of dancers holding hands indicates that dance was part of the life of the Neolithic Yang-shao culture. |
| **Egypt, 3400–525 BCE** | Royalty use specially trained slaves to dance for entertainment. These slaves could be considered the first professional dancers. |
| **Greece, 428–347 BCE** | Plato declares dance a necessity for the ideal republic. |
| **Rome, 275 BCE–300 CE** | Pantomime, a form of interpretive dance-drama, is popular in the Roman theater. |
| **China, 206 BCE–220 CE** | During the Han dynasty, dancers undergo strict training, raising dance to a new artistic level. |
| **Japan, 794** | Bugaku, the forerunner of Kabuki, is developed as the first professional classic dance form. |
| **England,1300** | Couple dancing develops. The Morris dance is the most characteristic rural dance in England. |
| **Western Europe, 1424** | Inspired by the bubonic plague of the previous century, *Le Danse Macabre,* also called the Dance of Death, is an allegorical depiction of the inevitability of death. |
| **England, 1550** | Under the reign of Queen Elizabeth, social dance becomes an important part of court life. |
| **France, 1661** | Louis XIV founds the Académie Royale de la Danse, officially establishing ballet as an art form. |
| **England, 1651** | John Playford publishes *The English Dancing Master,* a dance manual with instructions and music for English country dances. |
| **Vienna, 1780** | The waltz becomes a popular social dance with the younger generation, shocking moralists with its "indecent" close embrace. |
| **USA, 1890s** | Ragtime music, with its syncopated rhythm, allows a greater freedom of movement. |
| **USA, 1903** | Isadora Duncan breaks away from the restraints of classical ballet and introduces a new concept in dance performance, modern dance. |
| **USA, 1998** | The Gap Khakis Swing commercials started a swing dance revival that is still going. |
| **Today** | There is a renewed interested in ballroom dancing, due in part to several movies and television programs. |

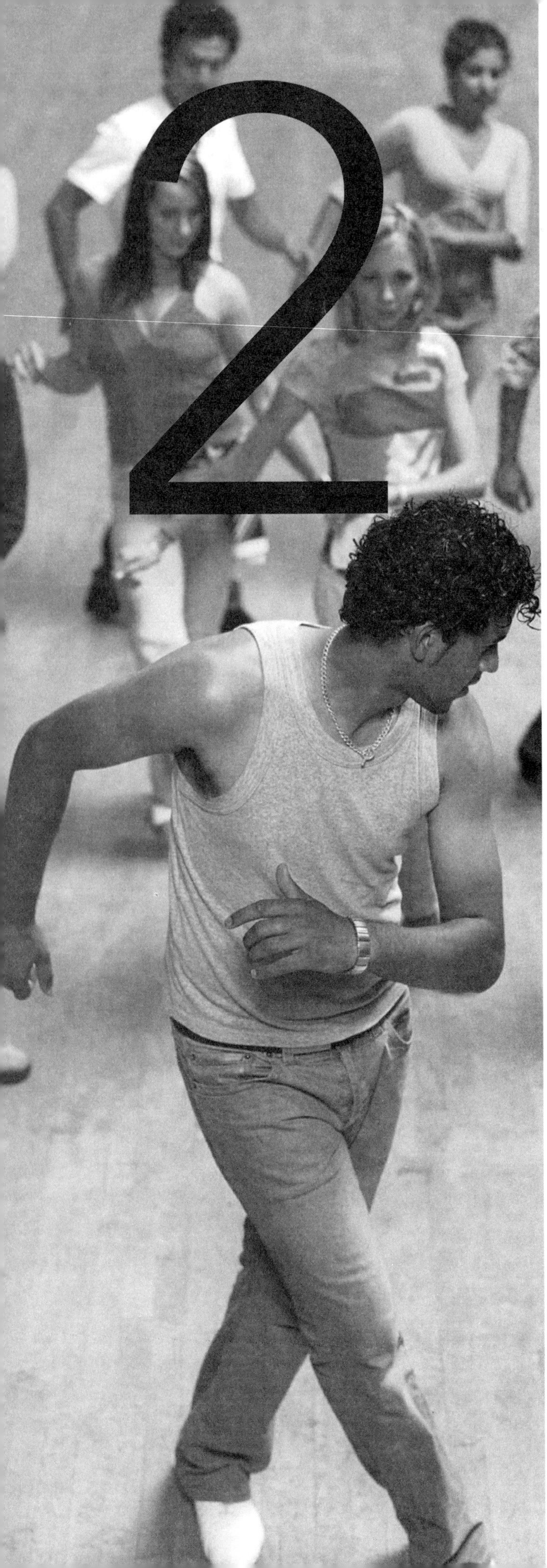

2

# EFFECTIVE GROUP INSTRUCTION

## THE EFFECTIVE INSTRUCTOR

*An effective dance teacher knows more than just dance steps. The instructor needs to be a dancer, teacher, sound technician, facility manager, musician, event coordinator, and most importantly, understand the purpose and value of dance in the curriculum.*

An instructor must learn to relate to the learner, the learning process, the dance context, and the demands of the culture. For effective group instruction, the instructor must be able to analyze and cope with variable learning skills and thoroughly understand the resources and dance material. This is often considered the pedagogy of teaching dance. The purpose of this chapter is to explain the varied features of dance instruction as encountered in a learning environment.

### Why Dance?

When dance is part of the curriculum, students often ask: "Why do we have to dance?" To respond to this question, the instructor must understand the value of dancing and how it serves the students. The following points[1] describe the major benefits of dance education.

1. *Social Interaction:* In the classroom, students interact as a group or with individual partners. At a dance, opportunities to meet new people are common.

1. Refer to the brochure *Dance Education—What Is It? Why Is It Important?* National Dance Association. www.aahperd.org online book store.

2. *Aerobic exercise:* Dancing increases your heart rate, providing cardiovascular benefit. Research at the Miami Human Performance Laboratory has shown that even the "stop and go" effect of ballroom-dance sequences is not a deterrent to receiving aerobic and fat-burning benefits.
3. *Increased exposure to rhythm:* Moving in rhythm facilitates the student's understanding of music.
4. *Alternative to sports (for nonathletes):* Not many students are part of athletic teams, but all students can participate in dancing.
5. *Improved balance and coordination:* Dance training provides body awareness and stresses good posture.
6. *Artistic form of self expression:* Dance allows the incorporation of personal styling, making movement unique to each dancer.
7. *A lifelong activity:* Dance is easily adaptable to all age groups.
8. *FUN!*

# Purpose of Dance

Classes in the community or at a school where dance is an elective attract students for many different reasons. The purpose can be learning to dance, improving dance skills, or understanding dance traditions. Once an individual demonstrates interest, the instructor has a unique responsibility to maintain and develop that interest.

Many dancers work to acquire dance skills that will enable them to join community dance groups, resulting in social relationships and an enjoyable pastime. Some dancers join groups for technical reasons, such as to acquire and/or increase their repertoire of dances, to develop a technical understanding of dance fundamentals, and to expand their performance skills. Either purpose is a viable reason for participating in a dance program, and both are important factors to be considered when preparing to teach dance.

# Facilities

A well-ventilated room with good acoustics, adequate lighting and heating, and sufficient floor space is essential. An area too small may limit the freedom of movement and type of dance. An area too large may generate acoustical problems that can distort the music and verbal instructions and destroy the spirit of the occasion. Also, dancers may feel uncomfortable with too much space; it is better to be slightly crowded.

## Floor

A preferred dance floor has a framed construction, known as a *sprung* floor, which provides dancers with a resilient surface. In contrast, an example of an inappropriate dance floor is concrete covered with wood or tile. Dancing for an hour on this surface is much more physically demanding. Avoid dancing on carpeted surfaces to prevent the transfer of static electricity.

Different dance forms require the surface (usually wood) of the floor to have varying degrees of slickness. This can be attained with different finishes and dance waxes.

For safety and facility maintenance, cleanliness is essential. Changing into dance shoes (shoes for inside use only) at the perimeter of the floor or outside the classroom will help keep dust and dirt off the floor. After each class, a quick sweep of the floor with a dust mop will also be beneficial.

## Acoustics

Permanent acoustical treatment is extremely expensive and is seldom found in the buildings used by dance groups. Since poor acoustics is a handicap to a dance group, the following practical suggestions have proven useful in improving the sound in halls and gymnasiums adapted to use for dance.

1. Drapes of any material (burlap, flannel, rugs, blankets) suspended from the ceiling can improve sound.
2. Acoustics in an ordinary gymnasium can be improved by hanging mats around the walls.
3. Ceilings can be lowered with crepe paper streamers or similar decorations.
4. Human bodies absorb sound. The sound system adjusted to an empty room is not always adequate when the room is filled with dancers. This fact should be kept in mind when the sound system is set up for a large crowd.

# Equipment

## Sound Systems

A wide variety of electronic equipment is available to dance professionals. This section will assist you in making better choices for your program. A basic sound system consists of a music playing device (CD player, MP3 player, or tape deck), microphone, amplifier or receiver and mixer, and speakers. The first three components plug into the amplifier, which sends the signal out to the speakers. This use of separate components is the most flexible approach: when one piece needs repair, the rest of the system is still functional. Also, upgrading and repair can be achieved one piece at a time. If a portable system is needed, several brands of reasonably priced karaoke machines (with a microphone jack) are available.

## Speakers

Good speakers are critical to a quality system. Placement should be in opposite corners of the room, at least *three feet above the dancers,* pointed toward their heads. If budget allows, having one speaker for each corner of the room creates an even distribution of sound. Speakers should be compatible with the amplifier output.

## Amplifier

A professional amplifier is equipped with several channels for individual volume controls. Each channel represents one component (tape deck, CD player, turntable, microphone). Two channels, or two components, can be operated at the same time: this allows the microphone to be used while playing music. Dance instruction is improved with this capability.

An amplifying device intended for home use is called a receiver, a combination of a radio receiver and an amplifier. In contrast to a professional amplifier, a receiver amplifies one component at a time. A mixer unit can be added to a receiver to use a microphone while playing music.

## Microphone

Microphones provide four distinct advantages for dance instructors: (1) vocal cord damage is minimized, (2) the learning environment is enhanced when the students can easily hear instructions, (3) professionalism is maintained when the instructor can talk rather than yell, and (4) regaining control of the class (when necessary) is facilitated. A couple of disadvantages should be noted: extra time is required to ensure that equipment is operational, and communicating through the microphone is not as personal.

Due to advances in technology, wireless mikes have become affordable. Sweat-resistant wireless microphones, developed for teaching aerobics, cost more than typically used wireless microphones. A wireless system has two parts: the receiver that plugs into the amplifier and the microphone itself. The microphone is connected to a power pack. Some power packs are meant to be worn on a belt. Always be prepared with a belt or strap on which to clip the power pack. Newer models have the power pack on the headset itself. This is highly recommended, as damage to the cord that goes from the headset to the power pack, when worn on a belt, is very common. The newer models use a rechargeable battery that saves money and helps keep toxic trash out of the landfill.

Three styles are available: lapel, handheld, and headset. The headset is slightly more expensive than the other two styles, but provides increased freedom of movement while teaching. Most power packs have a mute switch that allows the instructor to mute the microphone without walking over to the amplifier. This muting capability is ideal for individual instruction, without the whole class hearing the comments. Also, when leaving the room wearing the microphone, sound will not be inadvertently transmitted.

Covering the mike is a piece of foam called a windscreen. This allows the user to get closer to the mike. Each instructor should have an individual windscreen for hygienic purposes.

To test a microphone, do not blow into it. The sound is not pleasant, and transmitted moisture will eventually corrode the microphone. Counting "1, 2, 3, test, test" is a common way to adjust the volume. Standing in front of or in line with a speaker while wearing a microphone creates a squeal called *feedback.*

## Music Playing Devices

CD players are a fairly standard device for playing dance music in a class room setting. An essential feature of a CD player for teaching dance is pitch control[2] (variable speed control), which allows the instructor to adjust the tempo of the music to the students' ability. CD players allow the instructor to immediately go to any track, thus not making the students wait while filing through a list of songs. The CD player needs to be on a stand that will not be jarred by dancing feet, especially if the dance includes stamping.

MP3 Players have become quite popular for teaching dance. Their size and the amount of music that they hold makes them very convenient. Many MP3 players also have pitch control. This usually is accessed from the settings menu, and then selecting "play speed."

The use of the remote is becoming an important skill for dance teachers. The remote allows instructors to operate the equipment from the middle of the classroom, without running back and forth. The remote also has a fade control that provides an excellent transition from dancing back to teaching.

When working with CDs, it is recommended to make a teaching master with music from multiple

2. Equipment with pitch control usually needs to be ordered from a specialty equipment catalog.

artists in one specific dance style (waltz, swing, etc.). Using one CD will maximize the time for instruction rather than spending time changing CDs during the lessons. This same concept may be applied to MP3 players by creating files of music for specific dance styles.

### Transferring Music from Other Devices

Cassette tape decks and turntables are no longer in common use, but occasionally, music for a specific dance can only be found on a cassette tape or a vinyl record. It is possible to transfer this music to a computer using music transfer software. There is an *input* plug on the back of most computers that a cassette deck may be plugged into. Transferring music recorded on vinyl records requires the use of a pre-amp. The turntable is plugged into the pre-amp, and the pre-amp is plugged into the computer. Some software packages include a pre-amp.

When choosing a turntable to transfer music, there are several features to consider. Vinyl records are played in three different speeds: 33, 45, and 78 rpm (revolutions per minute). Therefore, a machine that has three speeds is desirable. The quality of the sound is directly related to the quality of the cartridge and needle. The magnetic cartridge gives a truer tone quality than the crystal type. A diamond needle will last longer than a sapphire needle.

### Care of Turntable and Records

Keeping the needle clean and changing it as needed are important. Taking care of the records will increase their longevity and maintain their sound quality. Store records in a vertical position in a case, and put dividers between each record. A thin foam cushion on the bottom protects rims, and a tight cover keeps dirt and dust out. The 45-rpm discs should be stored flat, in jackets.

### Video Recorder

There are dedicated video recorders, cameras with video options, and even some cell phones that are able to take short video clips. Videotaping a class and playing it back for them is a useful teaching tool. It allows the students to see exactly what they are doing and enables them to better understand how to work on their own styling. Sensitivity and care should be used so as not to embarrass anyone. Videotaping is especially good when working with a performing group.

# Music

## Recordings

Recordings on CDs are the primary sources of musical accompaniment for dance. Refer to Appendix C for lists of music sources. The recording industry for dance is in a state of flux and fewer companies are producing music for folk dancing. Thus, the availability of recordings to match one's equipment can be difficult to find. Copying music from someone and passing it along is increasing and raises serious ethical and legal questions. It is driving dedicated companies out of business. Recorded music of superior quality and variety is available, making it possible to have colorful and authentic music for instruction and participation. The wide variety of domestic and foreign recordings available makes it necessary for the teacher or the leader to be discriminating in choosing musical accompaniment. The following suggestions may assist in making appropriate choices:

1. The music should include an introductory passage so that the dancers can begin in unison.
2. A steady tempo is desirable unless a change is appropriate to a particular dance.
3. The music should be authentic; that is, if a dance is traditionally done to a special tune and the recording is available, it should be used.
4. The phrasing should be clear and definite.
5. The quality of the music is extremely important in generating enthusiasm and style in dancers.

The following suggestions are appropriate to the selection of recordings for dance areas included in *Dance A While*.

### Folk Dance

Several recordings are often available for the same folk dance. The version that corresponds in sequence to the direction for the dance should be selected. It is generally advisable to use the recording recommended by the dance reference. Since no list of suggested recordings can be kept completely up to date, it is advisable to ask the music shop or company to make a substitution when requested recordings are no longer available.

### Square Dance

The problems of selection in square dance center on finding recordings that are suitable to the caller's voice and have the desired tempo and rhythm. Callers should make selections only after listening and practicing to a variety of recordings. There are several advantages to recordings with calls: they can be used as models for learning to call, as supplements to live calling for calls not in the musical key or vocal range of the teacher, and as opportunities for a group to dance to a wide variety of callers.

### Contra Dance

Only a few of the contra dances require special music; for instance, Rory O'More uses the tune by the same name. Therefore, it is the teacher's choice to select appropriate music for the specific flow of figures (storyline) in a given dance. Some dances suggest a jig, others a reel, others a march. Finding a recording that arouses the dancers and the caller is the next step. Eventually the teacher will rely on certain tunes for specific dances, because they "fit like a glove."

### Social Dance

The criteria for selecting social dance music include finding recordings that have a definite beat and a regular tempo and that are appropriate for listening. For those who teach few or occasional classes, acquiring CDs or cassette tapes that have a variety of dance music styles is recommended. Today you can find a large selection of CDs and tapes with compilations of upbeat music for social dancing. Refer to Appendix C for lists of music sources. The specialist, however, needs greater variety in music. The radio is a continuous source of current and standard music. Jotting down the title and name of the recording artist aids in securing music from local shops and in keeping a current collection for teaching.

## Teaching with Recordings

1. Before using a recording in class, know the music and be familiar with the phrasing and the dance sequence. Humming or whistling the tune can be advantageous.
2. Occasionally, students may bring their own music to dance class. Review this music in private, since it may not be appropriate for the class in tempo, style, or lyrics.
3. All recordings for a particular class should be preselected and arranged in order of use. The class should not have to wait while the instructor finds a particular song.
4. Isolating a musical phrase on a recording to practice a certain movement is easily accomplished by noting time the phrase starts (e.g., the phrase starts 33 seconds into the song).
5. Play the music for the class to hear before presenting each part of the dance.
6. Practice ahead of time to give correct verbal cues synchronized to the music.
7. The starting signal (e.g., a hand movement) or cue should be matched to the introduction on the recording. Tell the class if the recording has no introduction.
8. An adjustable speed control (pitch control) allows practice at a variety of tempos. Without a pitch control, when you need to work with a specific recording, the dance should be practiced without music. The tempo of your verbal cues should be increased until reaching the tempo of the recording.
9. When teaching dances not associated with a single song and pitch control is not available, preselect recordings with several different tempos. This can be accomplished by varying the beats per minute (BPM) of each song. To establish the BPM of a song, count the number of beats that occur in a 6-second time frame and multiply by 10. As an example, with single time swing dancing, begin the music at 100 BPM and then gradually increase to 180 BPM. Dancing to the beat of a song is very difficult for many people. The problem is compounded if the tempo does not match their skill level.

## Live Music

There is a resurgence of live music for dancing. A live band or orchestra accents the color, flavor, and festive atmosphere of the occasion. The opportunity for recreational musicians to play enhances any dance. Many ethnic groups, such as Scandinavian and Slavic groups, have developed musicians' groups playing native instruments for their dances. Even in social dance, big-band sound, country western, and salsa, musicians are available.

The best musicians, colorful as they may be, should blend with the group. The dancers are the focal point of the dance and, although musicians should enter into the spirit of the occasion, they should not become a distraction. They need to limit their solos and interpretive music.

The instruments commonly used for square dance and contra dance are the fiddle, piano, banjo, bass violin, and guitar. The fiddle is sufficient for small groups if the fiddler is good. A combination of three to five instruments is most desirable.

The instruments used for international folk dance vary. Accordions, horns, reed instruments, and foreign musical instruments native to a particular country are used with more common combinations of instruments.

## Teaching with Live Music

Some dance teachers are fortunate to have a fiddler, an accordion player, or a trio to work with, although few institutions still have an accompanist. The primary advantage, in addition to the stimulation of live music, is the time saved by not having to attend to and adjust mechanical devices during the presentation of a lesson. Flexibility in applying music to the dance-teaching sequence is perhaps even more of an advantage than saving time. The accompanist can introduce music with the movement very early and make the rhythm clear and definite. The beginner can hear the beats of the music better. The introduction of accompaniment in the early stages trains dancers from the beginning to let the music help cue them in pattern and step changes, so counting is avoided.

For social dance, a three- to seven-piece band is usually adequate, depending on the talent of the group. Listening to an audition tape or attending a band rehearsal is advisable when an unknown band is being considered. Small bands or combos can sometimes be assembled from talent in the community or the school. In all cases, the band should be notified about the specific type and tempos of music planned. Rather than discussing how fast or slow a song is played, communicate with the musicians in terms of BPM. The type of music varies with the age and interest of the group to be entertained.

Dance musicians need an understanding of the dance itself and should realize that the character of the dance is influenced by the manner in which they play the tune. The tempo must be steady, and the length of the songs kept under three minutes. As they play, musicians need to watch the dancers and sometimes adjust the tempo or emphasize a phrase. Phrasing is extremely important for all dances. As the teacher and the accompanist work together, the accompanist will sense when to start playing while the group is practicing.

The working relationship between teacher and accompanist is important. They should begin by establishing certain vocal and hand signals. Most important, the teacher should stand at all times in view of the accompanist so that signals can be clearly seen or easily heard. Common vocal communications between the teacher and accompanist are "ready and" and "ready begin." Common hand signals are lowering the hand palm down to indicate a slow tempo, raising the hand palm up to indicate a faster tempo, nodding the head or raising the hand above dancers' heads to signal a stop at the end of the music, and waving the hand back and forth above the dancers' heads or saying "stop" to stop the music immediately.

The teacher can do a great deal to make the accompanist an integral part of the group. When the accompanist becomes a real part of the group, and not just a tool, everyone benefits because the involvement stimulates greater interest. The music should complement the activity; it should not dominate it.

Great care should be exercised in the selection of an accompanist. An accompanist should:

1. Have thorough musical training.
2. Play in a steady rhythm, accenting certain parts to help the dancers while they are learning a new dance.
3. Know the music well enough to be able to give attention to the group and the teacher during performance.
4. Rehearse all new music prior to the class.
5. Adjust the tempo to the dancers' ability or change the rhythm to accompany the teacher's analysis.
6. Know dance and be sensitive to ways in which cooperation between teacher, dancer, and accompanist can be enhanced.
7. Be able to develop and vary the music to make it interesting for the dancers because most folk music is noted simply.

# Planning Instruction

## The Total Dance Program Curriculum

In the formal school situation, the total dance program consists of a planned progressive sequence distributed throughout the entire school curriculum from first grade through graduation.

At any school level, the year's program is further subdivided into units of instruction and daily lesson plans. Each subdivision is organized systematically, with specific objectives, content, learning experiences, and appraisals in the form of evaluations. Each part of the total program should combine with the others to form one sequentially related dance program.

Materials selected for a specific unit should be related to the overall plan. The overall program should be flexible enough to allow for adaptation of materials in smaller units to meet specific or unique needs of a particular group within the total system. Evaluation of the individual units in terms of stated objectives should provide information necessary for revision of the sequential program in relation to the changing needs of students.

## Extracurricular Opportunities

The total dance program should not be an isolated experience to be participated in, in lockstep fashion, throughout the school curriculum. Ideally, the instructional phase of the total school program should be augmented by many extracurricular opportunities. Clubs, exhibition groups, festivals, and celebrations of special events and holidays are all opportunities for enriching formal learning sessions. In addition, dance may be integrated with other subject areas, for example, language courses or dramatic presentations such as operettas and musicals.

# Dance Unit

A *dance unit* is a period of time during which a planned sequence of learning experiences concentrates on a specific form of dance. The dance unit is a segment of the total dance program. Units should be planned and linked together to offer progressive experience in each dance area included in the total program. The dance unit is not an isolated learning experience but rather one of many stepping stones that provide sequential learning experiences in each dance area included in the total dance program. The following factors should be considered in planning a dance unit: (1) general purposes or objectives of the unit; (2) age, gender, skill, and dance experience of the participants; (3) facilities and equipment; (4) time allotment (class periods per week, continuous or divided, number of weeks per unit); (5) relationship of unit to school curriculum; (6) leadership experience and background; (7) relationship to community recreational program; and (8) enrichment activities.

## Goals

*Goals* are statements in broad terms that indicate what activities will be accomplished over a long term. The statement, "The student will be able to perform six traditional dance steps," is an example of a goal for a dance unit.

# Daily Planning Instruction

Planning for daily instruction must be planning with a purpose. Prior to teaching a dance class, the instructor should be able to answer the following questions: Who does what, how, when, where, and for how long? In answering these questions, an instructor should include information about:

1. Equipment.
2. Arrangement of students, number of students in a class and their grouping (e.g., partners, individuals, small groups), and location of students during instruction (line, circle).
3. Types and sequence of movements that will be taught. What will the instructor tell and demonstrate to students? (Plan to use complete yet concise instruction to ensure the shortest time possible spent on instruction with a longer period of activity/practice.)
4. Ways to provide students with the greatest chance for success.

A written outline of specific content and procedures to be presented in a given period of time is called a lesson plan. Using a lesson plan will ensure that activities are presented in a logical progression, which will allow for student success. A positive learning environment with fewer teacher frustrations and greater opportunities for student involvement will be created with the use of a lesson plan.[3] The following sections explain the makeup of a lesson plan; a sample lesson plan is shown on pages 14 and 15.

# Objectives/Student Outcome

In the lesson plan, the instructor should establish learning objectives. A learning objective is an act that the learner can do following observable and measurable instruction. An objective examines the potential outcome of the lesson. Objectives are implicit or explicit statements about what an instructor wants students to learn (in relationship to the three learning domains: psychomotor, cognitive, and affective). Well-stated objectives clearly identify what a student is to learn and/or perform as a result of instruction. An objective has three parts.

1. *Task:* What are students to accomplish?
2. *Situation:* What is "given" (e.g., with a partner, individually, or practice versus putting all the steps of the dance together in a performance[4])?
3. *Criteria:* What does the instructor need to observe to measure attainment of this objective? What are the critical elements or movements of the dance? Can students explain or demonstrate those elements?

The following statements illustrate how an objective is stated.

1. *Acceptable:* "The student will be able to dance the two-step." This identifies the task but does not indicate the situation under which the

3. Refer to Dr. Barbara E. Cusimano, *Rhythmic Activities*, p. 11, JOPERD, April 1989.

4. In sports instruction, playing a game is referred to as the performance component of the class. This use of performance should not be confused with a stage performance.

demonstration occurs or the critical elements that are to be observed.

2. *Better:* "The student will be able to dance the two-step with the beat of the music." The instructor can observe whether or not the student executes the two-step to the beat of the music (criteria), but there is still no description of the situation.
3. *Best:* "The student will be able to dance the two-step (task) with a partner around the dance floor for two minutes (situation) and demonstrate the ability to execute the critical element of the foot work, step together step with the beat of the music (criteria)." This objective is measurable and observable with all three parts identified.

## Assessing Group Variables

Assessing skills, knowledge, attitudes, and characteristics is an important first step in formulating objectives and selecting learning experiences. Some common group variations and suggested adaptations follow.

### Range of Skill and Motor Ability

Skill is seldom distributed evenly in a group. Although it may be clustered at one end or the other of a continuum, it will still represent a range. In an advanced group, the range is as apparent, although not as formidable, as in a beginning group. Materials should be selected to accommodate all skill levels and, at the same time, provide for sequential progression toward a minimum standard of accomplishment for all. Dances involving locomotor skills can keep the level of participation and incentive high until the skill range of a group is narrowed to a manageable range.

### Range of Experience and Association

Experience implies formal learning, such as a class or a club membership. Informal experiences like imitating dance movements without formal instruction and/or participation in rhythmic activities—such as marching in a band or a drill team, twirling a baton, or reacting to television or radio music—represent a type of association that constitutes a viable background for dance.

## Content Selection

After diagnosing group needs and formulating objectives, the teacher must search dance literature for specific dance materials with which to build content. The search for dance content is more efficient and need-serving when the teacher selects materials in terms of dance structure.

Dance structure refers to the component parts or basic elements that make up a dance. For most dance forms, these elements are basic step, position, formation, nationality, degree of difficulty, and musical meter. In square dance, these elements are patter, singing, basics, and figure type.

## Lesson Plan

An average dance lesson plan will include five sections:

1. *Warm-up Activities.* Have the music playing as the students enter the classroom, allowing them to begin dancing on their own. Start the class with as little instruction as possible, using simple (if applicable, non-partner) previously learned dances. A written prompt on a board close to the entrance may help to encourage students to start dancing. The primary purpose of the warm-up section is to give students immediate activity. At this time, the instructor should move around the classroom and interact with students. Greet them, reinforce students' behavior, and generally set the tone for the class. In addition, the instructor may take roll quickly and efficiently.
2. *Lesson Focus*
   a. *Review.* Review is a formal or informal coverage of previously learned materials. The review may be conducted as a formal part of the lesson by the instructor or it may be an informal student-participation session. The review serves two purposes: to refresh the students' memory of material from earlier classes, which often provides students with immediate success, and to help students who have been absent. Formal review does not necessarily have to be part of every lesson. Holding the review at the beginning of the class period is more of a tradition than a requirement. The review session may be integrated into the warm-up phases.
   b. *New Material.* This section of the lesson is for the introduction of material not covered in previous lessons. It is often a good idea to describe to the students the objectives (i.e., what they should be able to do as a result of this lesson) of the new material, which helps improve their focus on the tasks. This is a technique referred to as anticipatory set. Several anticipatory ideas for dance are listed under Setting the Stage, on page 16. New materials may be in the form of a fundamental step (such as the polka), a new square dance figure, a swing dance variation, or an entire folk dance. New materials may also appear in the form of an adaptation of a dance, such as the conversion of an individual routine to a partner dance. The new material section may be

## Lesson Plan Example: *Saturday Night Fever* Line Dance

**Equipment Needed**

Stereo, fitness cue CD, fitness cards, headset microphone, dance CD *(Staying Alive)*

**Page:** *1 of 2*

**Instructor:** K. Mucha

**Grade:** Upper Elementary/Middle School

**Date:** 2/4/15

**Lesson:** *2 of 5*

| | Expected Student Objectives/ Lesson Outcomes | Movement Content/ Experience | Organization/ Teaching Hints |
|---|---|---|---|
| **1. Warm-Up Activities** | Warming up the body and preparing mentally and physically to dance. | Using several different tempos of popular music, ask students to move to the beat. | *Grouping:* Scattered.<br>*Safety:* Students moving at safe speeds, in control of their bodies, keeping eyes up to watch for peers. |
| **2a. Lesson Focus: Review** | Review the steps of the *Electric Slide* and gain confidence in performing it. Prepare students to learn new material. | Quick verbal review of the *Electric Slide*. Perform similar dance movements to transfer skills students know into new dance. | *Grouping:* Students in lines, all facing forward.<br>*Safety:* Arm distance apart. |
| **2b. Lesson Focus: New Material**<br>**Anticipatory Set:** Last class we talked about rhythm and how to find and move to a beat in music. Today we are going to learn a new dance and practice moving on beat with the music. How many of you have seen the movie *Saturday Night Fever*? Some of the moves in the dance we will learn today are in that movie. You may remember that in the movie when the dancers are learning a new dance they count the beats aloud to help them stay on rhythm. Today when we are practicing the dance we are all going to count aloud to help us stay on beat. | Students will be able to perform the steps of the *Saturday Night Fever* line dance. | Steps to *Saturday Night Fever* line dance:<br>1. Walks forward and back (counts 1–16)<br>· back (1–4)<br>· forward (5–8)<br>· back (9–12)<br>· forward (13–16)<br>• Practice move 1 as a group.<br>2. Walks side, turn side (counts 1–16)<br>· walk right (1–4)<br>· walk left (5–8)<br>· turn right (9–12)<br>· turn left (13–16)<br>• Practice move 2 as a group.<br>• Practice moves 1 and two together.<br>*(Continue with steps 3–5 in the same manner.)* | *Grouping:* Students in lines, all facing forward.<br>*Safety:* Arm distance apart.<br>Continuous teacher scanning and adjusting to monitor student learning. |

## Lesson Plan Example: *Saturday Night Fever* Line Dance, continued

**Instructor:** K. Mucha

**Page:** *2 of 2*

| | Expected Student Objectives/ Lesson Outcomes | Movement Content/ Experience | Organization/ Teaching Hints |
|---|---|---|---|
| **3. Activity** | **Psychomotor Objective:** Students will be able to move on beat with the rhythm of the music while performing the *Saturday Night Fever* line dance. Assessed through teacher observation during practice. Do students move their body on the appropriate beat of the music for two moves of the dance (see next column for dance moves)? | Practice the *Saturday Night Fever* line dance in its entirety. | *Grouping:* Students in lines, all facing forward.<br>*Safety:* Arm distance apart.<br>Continuous teacher scanning and adjusting to monitor student learning. |
| **4 Closure** | **Cognitive Objective:** Students will be able to verbalize the sequence of five moves in the *Saturday Night Fever* line dance to a partner when prompted.<br>**Affective Objective:** Have students show their level of enjoyment of the rhythmic activity. | Ask students to turn to a partner and tell them the sequence of the five moves in a row for the *Saturday Night Fever* line dance.<br>Ask students to close their eyes and show their level of enjoyment with a thumbs up, down, or sideways. | Teacher notes informal assessment of learning objective. |
| **5. Lesson Reflection (Instructor)– Content**<br>How well did the content you planned and delivered match your students? Did the content challenge your students? In what ways? | Did all or most of your students meet your objectives? | Could they perform the task according to the criteria you set? | |

presented in any part of a class period. Beginning the lesson with new material is a means of varying class procedure and providing a longer segment of the class time for presentation and practice. Ending with new material is possible, if the material is short, energetic, and especially designed as a fun ending to the class period.

3. *Activity.* This is the section of the lesson plan in which the new material is practiced in its entirety, emphasizing fun and enjoyment, which encourages student development in the affective learning domain. Dancing for fun will help to ensure a feeling of success for both the student and teacher. This part usually takes place at the closing of the class. The students should leave with a sense of accomplishment and a feeling of anticipation for the next lesson. If the dance movement has been physically demanding (e.g., a fast swing or a high-paced folk dance) and the students are returning to other classes, ending with a calming dance (e.g., a slow waltz) is suggested.
4. *Closure.* The instructor should summarize the lesson, compare class performance to the objectives, and lead a closing activity. Closure may include a favorite dance or checking cognitive concepts. Instructors may evaluate students' progress based on their ability to meet class objectives. The students should leave with a positive feeling.
5. *Lesson Reflection.* When the lesson is over, the instructor can reflect on the content, programming, student interaction, and practice opportunities of the lesson. Did the students meet the planned objectives? What could have been done to increase their success?

### Procedure and Organization

The material from the five activity sections of a lesson plan can each be divided into three subcategories. Use columns to accomplish this task. The three subcategories are:

1. *Expected Student Objectives/Lesson Outcomes:* See the discussion under Objectives/Student Outcomes on pages 12–13.
2. *Movement Content/Experience:* This section lists the movement that will be taught in the lesson, critical elements and specific verbal cues, and the sequence of instruction and practice scenarios.
3. *Organization/Teaching Hints:* This section provides points for efficient delivery of the content, including class structure and groupings. Any notes or recommendations for the teacher can be placed here.

# Orientation to the Dance Class

## Setting the Stage

Dance is typically and culturally consistent when taught with traditional male/female roles. Participation and promotion should be encouraged by both male and female faculty. Group participation in planning the dance unit enhances understanding and creates greater enthusiasm.

Several items should be discussed prior to beginning the dance unit. Good preparation elevates student interest and helps maintain the flow of the class.

1. Emphasize to the students that they will be able to use their new skills at the next dance event.
2. Try to relate dancing to current movies, dancing on TV, or famous people. If they have seen it somewhere else, it helps to validate their opinion of dancing.
3. Discuss personal hygiene with all age groups. Nothing is more uncomfortable than dancing with or next to someone who has an unpleasant odor.
4. Let the students know that nonparticipating students (sick students or those with specific religious beliefs against dancing) will be assigned to do other tasks. They should not be allowed strictly to observe. Bored spectators can be disruptive.

### Etiquette

Simple good manners and courtesy are part of helping everyone in a group have a good time. It is the teacher's responsibility to create the kind of atmosphere that contributes to easy social adjustment and relationships among members of the dance group. Assisting members in becoming acquainted with each other and learning to mix are the most important social responsibilities, and they add to the fun and pleasure of the occasion. Etiquette is everybody's responsibility.

The teacher's language (his or her choice of words and phrases) can remind group members of simple courtesies. Gentle admonitions are helpful; for example, "thank your partner for the dance and invite another lady to be your new partner," "get together with the couple nearest you, introduce your lady and exchange partners," "escort your lady off the floor and introduce her to someone who is sitting out," and "there are a few extra ladies (men), and so between dances will the ladies (men) who are dancing take turns trading out so that everyone will get a chance to dance." These simple pleasant directions set the tone for interpersonal relationships necessary in the dance group.

The following are a number of techniques for bringing about social intermixing to provide opportunities that gradually develop into pleasant habits.

### Social Aids

The use of an attractive name tag helps people to get acquainted and feel at ease. Square dance and folk dance clubs use them with tremendous success. They are equally welcomed by students in a class.

Still another successful idea has been the appointment of a host and hostess for each session. They have the responsibility of seeing that everyone has a chance to dance, that name tags are ready, that visitors are included in the activities, and that guests are met and made to feel welcome. In a large group, members can take turns playing host or hostess so that everyone has an equal opportunity to participate in the dancing.

### Fun with Cutting In

In almost every mixer, there is a break during which an extra person can step in and steal a partner, which automatically puts someone out. This can be good fun if everyone gets into the spirit of it. If the leader shows the group how and encourages stealing partners during the mixers, the problem of extras in a group is reduced.

Cutting in is a fun technique also used in square dancing. However, it should be stressed that the skill of cutting in lies in the ability to cut the other person out and yourself in without breaking the continuity or rhythm of the figure.

In social dance, cutting in can also be made into a fun situation; for example, use one or two couples, give the girls a peach, the boys a lemon, and they cut in by passing the peach or lemon to another boy or girl.

### Uneven Numbers: Creating a "Ghost Partner"

For club and party dances, uneven numbers are a rather common occurrence and often are considered a problem. Event organizers need to be particularly alert and resourceful in handling this imbalance. An extensive repertoire of nonpartner dances, dances for threes, and simple partner-exchange mixers will allow everyone to participate.

During classroom instruction of traditional male/female partner dancing, people are commonly paired up with the same sex to balance out uneven numbers. This can be uncomfortable for some people and requires students to learn material that will not be used often. Using the concept of "Mr. or Ms. X" provides an efficient technique for working with uneven numbers. At the beginning of class, people without partners should be interspersed around the circle and assigned the "ghost partner" of Mr. or Ms. X. As the class proceeds, either males or females are selected to rotate (move around the circle to the next person, or "ghost partner") at intervals determined by the instructor. When a student encounters Mr. or Ms. X, he or she should be instructed to continue working on his or her own role. At the next rotation, the student returns to a real partner. Rotating partners fairly often ensures that no one student is with a ghost partner for very long.

When teaching traditional male/female partner dancing with same-sex classes, it is necessary to divide the class in half and assign lead and follow roles. The instructor can then refer to "lead" and "follow," rather than "male" and "female," positions and steps. Students should stay in their assigned role for the duration of the class.

## Teaching Students with Special Needs

*By Kristina Waller Golden, Laguna Hills, CA*

The prevailing philosophy in the consideration of individuals with disabilities in the United States is one of **inclusion,** the notion that all people have the right to be included with their peers in all age-appropriate activities throughout their lives. Educators may hear terms such as *mainstreaming, integration,* and *inclusion.* Each term has its origins in the aim to bring individuals with disabilities into environments with their typical peers, and each accomplishes that end, though the means may vary. In any event, regardless of what this "bringing together of all people" is called where you live, there will be people with disabilities that will participate in dance, and will want to learn.

One needs to consider vision, hearing, physical abilities, cognitive abilities, and behaviors. However, one needn't be a trained "special educator" to include people with disabilities in dance activities and have success. Therapeutic professionals use dance as one activity in the rehabilitation of certain disabilities. Objectives of rehabilitation programs can be to eliminate the physical disability, to reduce the physical disability, or to retrain the person to perform within his or her physical disability.

There are three key areas to consider: physical inclusion, social inclusion, and instructional inclusion. A teacher can ensure that inclusion will occur when planning addresses all three areas.

**Physical Inclusion** Is the learning environment physically accessible to everyone? Will a person with limited physical mobility need a helper? Are there safety issues for a person with limited vision, or, does everyone understand what a wheelchair can do when it spins around? Consider these kinds of points as you assess physical inclusion.

**Social Inclusion** Dance educators are often sensitive to this phenomenon, since it is natural in our culture for dance learners to feel excluded (e.g., those unsure of their physical abilities, those insecure with the opposite sex). Good dancers also tend to group or partner together, creating more exclusion of those less adept. Keep in mind that this may be compounded for a person with disabilities. Some peers may feel that a person with a disability is helpless or unapproachable. Of course this is not the case, and the teacher can be key in helping to promote interaction, even talking about the person's disabling condition in such a way to help everyone gain understanding, and thus opening the doors to social inclusion. Dance has a wonderful way of making people feel part of a group.

**Instructional Inclusion** As with any group, choose material that is appropriate to the class members' skill level and adapt the teaching as necessary so that everyone can participate. This may involve use of an interpreter for a hearing-impaired student, a buddy for the visually impaired, more copying the movements for those who are visual learners, pairing up a student with one who has already caught on. Let the students brainstorm ways to help include an individual in a dance. Allow for small successes and praise results. All participants experience a positive effect and benefit. It's a "win-win" for everyone. It is a helpful bridge to the real world in which we live.

## General Adaptations for Teaching Dance

*By Kelly Mucha, Portland, OR*

Good teaching is adaptive teaching! Adaptations are not just for people with disabilities; all individuals have unique needs. Progressing slowly and offering alternate steps to the class as a whole can help all learners as well as promote the inclusion of people with disabilities into the educational setting.

When adapting a lesson, consider its objectives. If you are teaching rhythms for fun, exercise, or social inclusion, it is probably not necessary to have all students perform the same steps. If the dance (e.g., a line dance) allows, invite your students to add their own character (adaptation) to the steps. Keep in mind that safety is an issue. Remind students that when adapting steps they need to be adequately coordinated with the rest of the class to avoid collisions.

Keep in mind that each individual is different. Not all adaptations will work for all individuals. *When in doubt, ask the student.* The student knows his or her body the best, and may have some ideas on adapting the dance to fit his or her abilities. Peers may also have suggestions for adapting the dance for a fellow student. This is inclusion at its best!

**Students With Visual Impairments** Rhythms are a great activity for people with visual impairments. The students can use the auditory cues and music to find the beat. They may also benefit from a tap on the shoulder to indicate the beat or direction of movement. These reminders can be offered by the teacher, teacher's aide, or peer tutors. Another consideration when teaching basic locomotor movements to people with visual impairments relates to body positioning: they may not feel comfortable raising their feet from the ground in a jump, hop, leap, etc. Instead, have the students mimic the motion without leaving the ground by bending their knees before raising up, or shuffling their feet across the ground. Students with visual impairments may also experience difficulties in balance.

**Students With Cognitive Disabilities** Students with mental retardation or dyslexia may have difficulty in following the direction of steps or following a fast-paced lesson. Take care in slowing the pace of instruction to allow the students to cognitively understand the movements. Check regularly to be sure they are accurately following the dance (e.g., "What is the next step after we walk forward 4 counts?"). If the direction of the movement or the side (right or left) of the body performing the movement doesn't make a large difference in the dance, simplify the dance by not specifying which direction or side to move. (Note: If performing a line dance, be sure the students have enough space to move in any direction without hitting a peer.)

**Students With Hearing Impairments** Students with hearing impairments may have difficulty in finding the beat of a dance because they may not hear the music or verbal cues well. At the beginning of the lesson, place students with hearing impairments where they can follow the movement of the teacher or a skilled student. Taps on the shoulder or upper back indicating the rhythm or tempo of the movement may also be helpful. For examples of a dance adaptation, see the Hip Hop or Saturday Night Fever line dance.

**Students Using Wheelchairs** Refer to Fundamental Locomotor Movements, Wheelchair Adaptations, pages 33–38.

## First Class Meeting

The first class should be carefully planned to convey the feeling that the student will successfully learn to dance and have positive social interaction. This important first contact should give the student confidence and a desire to continue with the class. Significant factors to be considered for the first meeting include the following.

1. Select short and simple dances (e.g., a line dance) that the majority of students will be able to master.
2. Because younger students are reluctant to hold hands, make their dance experience positive with a contemporary line dance. The Electric Slide and Saturday Night Fever Hustle are beginning-level line dances. Moving into dances with little physical contact like the Virginia Reel and the Tennessee Wig Walk provides a good introduction to partner dancing. One thing leads to another, and suddenly they are ready to swing.
3. Use music that reflects the students' interest, age, and cultural background. Music that students enjoy will facilitate their acceptance of dancing.
4. Use quick, easy sequences for forming sets of three, four, six, and eight. Dances may be arranged in the order of numbers involved, thus making it easy to change from one formation to another.
5. During the first lesson with partners, use the grand march or a similar technique to organize the students. At any age, asking someone to dance can be a traumatic experience. Students are typically more comfortable when partner selection is made at the instructor's direction rather than their choice. As students gain confidence with partner dancing, the instructor should integrate social etiquette into the lesson. Both male and female students need to know how to ask a person for a dance and how to thank their partners after the dance. As the class progresses, they may be allowed or encouraged to choose their own partners.
6. Rotate partners often.
7. Emphasize activity. Long waits or lectures can test students' attention spans. Keep activity high by talking less.
8. Give individual instruction only after the rest of the class is dancing.
9. End the lesson with an exciting hint about something special in the next lesson.

# Class Procedure

## Strategies for Selecting Material and Presentation

The suggestions that follow constitute rather specific guidelines for class procedures relevant to selecting materials, achieving variety within a class period, and using enrichment materials to make the class period a warm, friendly, and informative experience.

2

1. Materials should correspond to the skill level of the group.
2. Beginning activities should include the entire group. Nonpartner circle dances are recommended.
3. The warm-up dances should be simple and short.
4. Plan material in a teaching progression. When teaching motor skills or dance steps a teaching progression would begin with steps that are very simple, (walking) to more complex, easiest to most difficult. This will aid students in mastering the movements in a comfortable format. Reviewing steps before moving on to new material is also part of an instructional progression. New material should relate to and depend on the preceding part. There are many types of progressions such as tempo, movement, aerobic, part to whole, stylistic, and time signature.[5] See Table 2.1 for an example of walking dances taught in a teaching progression.
5. Mixers are a must, especially during the first few lessons. Include a generous number of nonpartner dances for uneven numbers of men and women. This eliminates the time for choosing partners and arranging formations and fosters more instruction and dancing.
6. Frequent partner changes should be used.
7. Plans should allow time and include opportunities for the group to be social.
8. Put new steps to use in the normal dance setting as soon as possible. Example: a ballroom dance step taught in a line or a circle formation should be danced in ballroom fashion as soon as possible.
9. Include new and review material in each lesson after the first lesson.
10. Arrange the lesson content to provide for periods of activity and rest, contrast in style and steps, and variety in formation. Examples: circles, lines, sets, and so on.

5. Graham Hempel, Associate Professor of Dance, San Diego State University, lecture notes.

**TABLE 2.1** *Walking dances taught in a teaching progression*

| Dance | Formation | Movement | Level |
|---|---|---|---|
| Electric Slide | Solo | Walking forward and backward | Beginning 1 |
| Tanko Bushi | Solo | Walking, adding some arm gestures | Beginning 2 |
| Šetnja | Line | Walking, skips and hops | Beginning Intermediate |
| Road to the Isles | Partner / Circle | Walks, hops, ½ turns | Beginning Partner |
| La Bastringue | Partner / Mixer | Walks, two-step, buzz turn | Intermediate Partner |

11. To stimulate interest, presentation of material should include cultural information about the dance. This adds meaning to the dance and enhances understanding of style.
12. Discuss the unique features of a dance to help dancers distinguish one dance from another.
13. Allow ample time for practice, questions, requests, and suggestions, so that you can give individual assistance.
14. Encourage creative sequencing of moves; more experienced social dancers are often anxious to be free from set routines.
15. Visual aids supplement teaching. Pictures, diagrams, maps, cartoons, articles, movies, and special demonstrations stimulate interest. Costume dolls and other bits of folklore add to the cultural understanding of the dance. Learning is enhanced when dance titles are posted so that dancers can check their spelling and pronunciation.

## General Teaching Points

In teaching any style of dance, the following concepts should be considered.

1. The instructor's top priority is to make dancing fun and nonthreatening. Students who have an unpleasant experience might not try dancing again.
2. The student's comfort/safety is also the instructor's responsibility. When students are crowded or close to a wall, the instructor, rather than a student, should tell them to move. With younger students, being close enough to intentionally bump into someone is always a possibility. This "clowning" can disrupt the class and even cause injury.
3. The instructor should move around the class and allow all students an opportunity to see the moves demonstrated.
4. Practice transitions from one move to another. The transition may be more difficult than the individual steps.
5. Reduce each move to its simplest form by breaking down each step. Once the basic step has been mastered, add more movement.
6. Build the movement sequence:

   Teach step A and practice.

   Teach step B and practice.

   Practice A and B together.

   Teach step C and practice.

   Practice A, B, and C together.
7. State directions as succinctly as possible, reducing the possibility of misinterpretation. For example, "Start by standing on your right foot." Does this mean that you start with your left foot free, or your left foot on top of your right foot? Use proper grammar in your instructions. Beware of initiating your comments with words like OK, umm, and, and so.
8. Rotate partners often. This will:
   a. Provide students with an optimum learning experience by encountering students of varying skill levels.
   b. Ensure that no single student will be dancing the entire period with a (socially) less desirable classmate.

c. Maximize student participation the majority of the time.

9. When teaching partner dancing for ballroom and swing style, the current trend is to avoid gender-based instruction through the use of the terms lead (traditional male role) and follow (traditional female role). The traditional terms *men* and *women* are still being used in square dance and folk dance communities.

10. Emphasize *cueing*, which can be defined as verbal instruction given "in rhythm" to aid the students with the movement or the beat. When a cue is not used, students are not sure what to do. When using introductory cueing with music, the cue should be given on count 5 of the previous measure. This will start the students on count 1 of the next measure.

    The use of these cueing techniques will enhance student learning:

    a. Introductory cueing (while stationary), to help start a dance.

       Examples of cues starting on count 5:

       1. "1, 2, ready, go"
       2. "5-6-7-8"
       3. "ready and"

       Examples of a cue starting on count 1:

       1. "uh-one, uh-two, you know just what to do"

    b. Movement cueing, as a prompt while dancing.

       Examples of cueing a basic schottische step:

       1. Steps: "run, run, run, hop"
       2. Feet: "step right, left, right, hop left"
       3. Direction: "diagonal, 2, 3, hop"
       4. Counting: "1, 2, 3, hop"
       5. Sounds: "ba, ba, ba, boom"
       6. Rhythm: "quick, quick, quick, quick"
       7. Style: "smooth, smooth, smooth, up"

    c. Lead cueing (warning cueing), to introduce the next move while dancing.

       Example of dancing a basic swing step and moving into an "Arch":

| CUES | WHAT THE STUDENTS ARE DANCING |
|---|---|
| One, two, rock step | Basic swing step |
| Do the arch (*next move*), go now | Basic swing step, hears the new move |
| Lady goes under (*now the arch is executed*) | Arch |

11. Make sure all students can hear the instructions. Use of a microphone can facilitate this requirement.

12. Dress the part. Teaching a basketball class wearing wing tips and a suit would not inspire the class any more than basketball attire would motivate dance students.

13. This is the most important aspect of dance instruction: make it FUN. Students should leave every class with a sense of accomplishment and enjoyment.

## Teaching a Specific Dance

### Teacher Preparation

The teacher's preparation to teach a specific dance should include:

1. Knowledge of the basic steps.
2. An understanding of the sequence of the step patterns and their relation to the music.
3. A knowledge of the music (introduction, sequence, and tempo).
4. The ability to demonstrate the steps accurately, with or without music.
5. An organization of all materials that makes the best possible use of class time.
6. Reviewing a cue (prompt) card for each dance or movement.

**Cue Cards:** Keeping a card file with one dance or movement per card is a quick way to review a dance. The card should include the name of the dance on top and a basic write-up of each section. The card may also be carried into the teaching area for an inconspicuous review of the steps if needed. Each person will have his or her own shorthand to write out the dance notes. Care needs to be taken in writing up the dance, so that a year later the notes are still helpful. Below is an example of what may be written up for the folk dance: Alunelul, in Chapter 7. Also refer to page 200 for example of a contra dance cue card.

ALUNELUL Romanian Circle Dance Beginning level

Part 1: Beginning with right foot, 5 steps right, 2 stamps, repeat to the left, X 2

Part 2: 3 steps right, 1 stamp, repeat to the left, X 2

Part 3: In place, step stamp right and left and double stamp R. Repeat to left.

Teaching points: (1) Teach in lines (2) Add shoulder hold (3) Move into small circles

## Presentation of the Dance

The analysis of each dance to be taught varies. However, many of the steps in the analysis are similar for all types of dance.

1. Give the name of the dance. Write it on the board. If it is unusual and uncommon, have the class pronounce the name.
2. Give the nationality of the dance and any background that will add interest and make the dance more meaningful. Such information need not be given all at once but can be interspersed here and there between steps.
3. Play a short part of the record, enough to give the class an idea of the character, the quality, and the speed of the music.
4. Arrange the group in the desired formation. It may be practical to do this first.
5. Teach the difficult steps or figures separately. Refer to the suggestions for teaching basic steps.
   a. Teach basic step patterns, such as the waltz or the polka, independently of the dance. They should be mastered before being used in a dance.
   b. If the dance has steps that can be learned better in a line or a circle formation, isolate these and teach them before starting to teach the dance.
   c. If a specific step and pattern are involved, teach the isolated step first, then the figure. Talk the step through while demonstrating it and then direct the entire class in the pattern at the same time.
6. For dances with short sequences, demonstrate the entire dance and cue students as they do it. For dances with long sequences, analyze the part, try it without music first, and then with music. This process continues for the entire dance.
7. Give a starting signal or an introductory cue. This is helpful in getting everyone to start together.
8. Demonstrate with a partner as each part is explained to the group. It is not necessary to have a special partner. For many dances, the teacher can select an alert member of the class. As the teacher explains the step and demonstrates and leads the action, the partner should be able to follow easily. For a more difficult pattern, the teacher should practice with the student a few minutes before class begins. Do not use the same student all the time.
9. Correct errors in the whole group first. Give individual help as it is needed later.
10. Start the music slowly and gradually speed it up to normal tempo. When working with a machine without a speed-control mechanism, gradually speed up the dance with verbal cues until it is the same tempo as the record. For additional ideas refer to Teaching with Recordings and Teaching with Live Music.
11. Use the blackboard to help explain and clarify rhythm patterns. Have the group clap difficult tempos and rhythms.
12. Teach the repeated part of a dance first. For example, teach the chorus and then the first verse. If the dance is long, it is not necessary to teach all the verses on the same day.
13. Give lead reminders to help the male student guide his partner into the figure or the pattern of steps.
14. Demonstrate and practice the style along with the step pattern. For example, the manner in which the foot is placed on the floor, the resultant body action, and the position of the arms is a total relationship that should be learned at one time. If it requires unusual coordination, style can be taught separately. For specific styling comments, refer to the directions given in Chapter 3, pages 42–47.
15. Cue the dance steps on the microphone until the dancers have had sufficient practice to remember the routine.
16. There are many dance movies and instructional DVDs on the market today. The Web also has many sites with video clips of dance competitions and performances. When a class is ready to perfect its style, a short video presentation gives the students a visual image for which to strive. Many students are also inspired by watching a professional performance.
17. Change plans if a dance is too difficult or a poor choice for the group. Select another dance.
18. Be confident in correcting your own errors in teaching. All teachers make errors now and then. It is wise to correct them immediately. This can be done with a sense of humor or a light touch.
19. Be generous with praise and encouragement to the group.
20. Show personal enthusiasm and enjoyment for the dance. A teacher's enthusiasm and genuine interest in teaching does much to help others enjoy it.

## Review

1. Review verbally, and have the class tell the sequence of the dance. Then try the dance with the music while cueing the important changes.
2. Pick out the spots that need review and practice them. Point out the details of style and leading. Repeat the dance.
3. Announce the dance several days later, play the recording, and see how far the dancers can progress without a cue.
4. Avoid letting the class form the habit of depending on a cue to prompt them. Cueing is only a teaching device.
5. Make recordings of the class music available for those who wish to practice. Have the music playing when students come into class to encourage them to practice and to establish an appropriate atmosphere.

## Evaluation

In the school situation where a final grade is required for each student in a dance class, some consideration must be given to a fair means of evaluating students. While some teachers feel that it destroys the recreational value of a class to conduct tests, most students are anxious to be graded if they feel that they have had a reasonable opportunity to show what they know.

Occasional tests serve to stimulate better learning, to show progression and accomplishment, and to serve as a booster to those who are slow or disinterested. From the teacher's point of view, they focus attention on the students who need special help or encouragement and on the material that needs review. Students are very interested in how grades are computed. They want to know the relationship (percentage of points) of written tests, practical tests, attendance, and improvement to the final grade. Students deserve a clear statement that coincides with the department's philosophy. There are two kinds of tests: the practical or skill test and the written test.

### Practical Test

A *practical test* assesses the student's ability to perform a dance skill, such as a test on the waltz, the schottische, or the polka; a test on the fundamentals of square dance or contra dance; or a test on the basic steps in social dance. The following are types of practical tests that have been used for dance with reasonable efficiency and success.

1. *Subjective rating.* A subjective rating is determined from scores on a prepared checksheet. Five students at a time can be checked as they perform a skill individually or with partners. The sheet is given to the student so that he or she may benefit from comments; afterward, he or she signs it and turns it in.
2. *Systematic use of an achievement chart.* Each student can be checked off on an achievement chart as a few at a time are observed during the last ten minutes of a series of class periods.
3. *Cumulative grade system through use of name tags or numbers.* The teacher circulates and writes down a grade for each of the students as they dance. This should be done several times so that an average grade can be taken. If the students wear name tags throughout the course, the teacher can jot down grades at frequent intervals and thereby keep a progress chart on each student. Improvement may be quite evident with this system of checking.
4. *Colored tags used for grading.* The teacher circulates and gives each student a colored tag that represents the teacher's opinion of the student's ability (blue–excellent, red–good, yellow–fair, green–poor, and white–no opinion). At the end of the period, each student writes his or her name on the tag and turns it in. This method is effective in grading ballroom dance and can be used for each type of dance, including the rumba, the tango, and the waltz.
5. *Student checklist.* Students check each other on a prepared checklist. For example: good rhythm, poor lead, inconsistent step, and so on. They can check five persons with whom they dance. The student should sign the checklist. The teacher can then draw up a summary of the opinions. This is very helpful in grading and also in knowing which students need extra help.

### Written Test

The knowledge test gives every student a chance to show what he or she has learned, even though he or she may perform the skill poorly. More than one written test should be given, so that the student has a better understanding of how the questions will be phrased. For many, this is a different vocabulary. Two kinds of written tests have proven most satisfactory for grading.

1. The *short quiz is* a five-minute test in which the student is asked to identify a fundamental step, a rhythm pattern, a specific style, a position, or a lead. It should require only a few words and should have a specific positive answer. These can be corrected in class.
2. The *objective test* is usually given as a final test. It should be given far enough in advance to get the

papers corrected, returned, and discussed in class, with time allowed for questions and corrections. The objective test in dance should be set up to include material on etiquette, fundamental steps, rhythm, position, style, and history. There should be several types of questions, including true or false, multiple choice, and identification. Directions should be clear so that students will not need to ask questions on procedures. The method of scoring should be indicated on the test paper.

2

### Grading the Class

Grading the class should be handled efficiently to avoid long periods of inactivity and subsequent loss of interest. All cards, tags, pencils, numbers, and other materials should be ready to use before class begins. A group that is prepared for the testing period in advance is usually cooperative and helpful. With proper motivation, the dancers should feel that they can have as much fun as usual even though they are aware of being graded.

Grading should not take up an entire period. Each class period should include some dancing just for fun, free from grading. This will restore the spirit and relieve the tension that is sometimes present during the grading time. Grading should be scheduled throughout the semester and not left until the end. All final grading should be finished before the last week so that the last two periods can be devoted to perfecting the dances and enjoying the activity as pure recreation.

## Enrichment Activities

### Class Projects

Whether the class is oriented to teacher preparation or a regular "service" class, the opportunity for projects is rewarding. It recognizes the enthusiasm of those who want to do more and offers an opportunity for the student who may not perform well but excels in other skills related to the subject.

1. Make arrangements for a guest teacher to come and prepare written instructions.
2. Prepare a research paper related to a specific aspect of the dance or its country.
3. Prepare an audiovisual presentation (video or PowerPoint) of a specific dance or dance event.
4. Teach one dance in class.
5. Plan and execute a Social event (see the next page for more information).

### Bulletin Boards

The class bulletin board is a place to share ideas and interests. It is a vital link between the teacher, the students, and the enrichment materials. This important teaching aid can be used effectively in three ways: instructionally, promotionally, and creatively. A bulletin board theme can be developed around any dance-related topics. Examples of these include: basic skills, national background, region or geographic location, age groups, instruction, recreation, promotion, manners and customs, proper dress or costume, international politics, ethnic groups, seasons, holidays, states, female names, and many more. For example: post state names, symbols, and dances (Oregon: Square dance; California: West Coast swing). Students could put up one bulletin board with all materials relating to this theme or make it a continuous project by putting up materials during the lesson or before the lesson in which the dance is taught. A teacher who maintains an informative and attractive bulletin board and brings interesting bits of information, pictures, clippings, and articles to the class is the teacher who turns the ordinary into the extraordinary and opens a whole new world of meaning and understanding.

### Culminating Activities

Interest and enthusiasm generated by a series of lessons or a season of dancing often culminate in the desire for a special event that appropriately celebrates the achievements in skills and fellowship attained by the group. The following suggestions assist in planning such an event.

1. Several beginning classes could be combined for a late afternoon or evening dance party.
2. A guest caller or teacher could be invited to make the last class session a special occasion.
3. The group could attend a convention, festival, or a jamboree together.
4. School groups could give a demonstration for a school assembly, a parent-teacher association, or a service club group.
5. An exhibition team could be invited to put on a performance for the group. The exhibition group could teach and dance at least one simple dance with the group.
6. Post a list of community dance opportunities on the bulletin board. The list could include classes, clubs, summer camps, workshops, clinics, festivals, and leadership training sessions.

### Community Resources

Ethnic groups, foreign students attending local high schools or colleges, square dance and folk dance clubs, museums, libraries, and art galleries are found in almost every community and can be involved in the school dance program in many ways.

Foreign students often can show regional or national costumes and musical instruments typical of their homelands and slides or movies of their homelands. Their presence in a community offers an obvious opportunity for cultural exchange.

Ethnic groups often carry on many of their former customs and can be invited to share and compare their culture in appropriate ways with the dance class. Many ethnic groups in the United States have forgotten specific dances but, because they retain their native language to a greater extent than other customs, they can share songs and music if not dances.

### Teacher Resources

The teacher must bridge the gap between the daily task of teaching dance skills and the vast amount of dance-related information if the instructional experience is to be more than a social and psychomotor experience. Keeping current is a constant task in the teaching profession; if the dance teacher is to keep current, reviewing periodic literature in dance and dance-related periodicals is both a necessity and an efficient means of keeping abreast of the field. Current magazines carry information about other literature, including books, films, records, and costumes and so make it possible for the teacher to be more selective about the materials to be reviewed in depth.

A teacher who participates in the dance groups and the related activities in a community enriches and improves his or her instructional skill in an enjoyable and pleasant manner. Encouraging students to attend concerts, foreign films, festivals, art shows, exhibitions, plays, and selected television performances is important, but it is equally important that the teacher also participate in these cultural opportunities.

Traveling abroad has been a tradition with American school teachers, and it is a valuable professional and personal experience. Traveling at home is equally important. In fact, getting to know one's state and region is important. Language, customs, dress, dances, songs, humor, and stories are different for every section of the United States. These regional differences are a rich part of our heritage and are the fabric of our culture. Visiting, talking, dancing, sightseeing, and sharing individual differences around a campfire, along a mountain trail, and across a tennis net are what learning and teaching are all about.

Refer to Appendix B, Organizations and Resources, for specific addresses; Internet addresses have been included.

## Organizing Special Activities

### Family Dances

Parents, especially those who have had their children later in life, yearn for a dance activity that involves the whole family. A sensitive leader and cooperative parents can make family dances work. Everyone looks forward to the occasion. *Arriving on time* is important since the easiest dances come first. But the committee (leader) needs to have some activities ready to go—blowing up balloons, moving chairs, mixing lemonade, drawing with color markers on butcher paper attached to the wall with a theme, i.e., "spring green." Parents need to participate, too, even in some table games. Two activities are enough until a sufficient number of people are present to "circle up" and dance. These are called "ice-breakers." Start with simple dances to peppy music, circle left and right, and play party games like Amos Moses, Jiffy Mixer, and Alabama Gal. Obviously the adults need to split up and dance with the children. Grand marches are excellent. Families need to agree on a length of time for the very elementary dances. The program depends on the ages, ability, and flexibility of the group. *A good program does not just happen.* It takes thought and planning, reaching out to the dancers' level of ability and accommodating odd numbers. Singing, playing games, eating, and creating skits are other activities to have in addition to dance.

There needs to be a clear understanding of purpose and a group effort for success. Those with children may leave after the first hour; some may want to have another activity available after the first hour for the restless, so that the rest of the family can dance a while longer. Some children will prance on the side of the stage, perfectly happy, as the group moves on to more complicated dances. Family dances are very rewarding.

### Social Events

A class barn dance, church dance mixer, wedding, or special celebration is the occasion for a one-night dance party. An experienced leader is often brought in from outside the group to conduct party games and run the program. Many unknown factors make planning difficult: the number of participants is often indefinite; the range of ability may vary; and the balance of genders, more often than not, may be uneven. The one thing the group has in common is a desire to have a good time. An effective leader should be guided by these principles.

1. People enjoy group participation if they are allowed to join in willingly and are not forced to take part.
2. Plan a simple, flexible program that can be quickly adjusted to the moods and the caprices of the situation.
3. Nonpartner dances, novelty activities, and mixers that are learned quickly are effective in these unpredictable groups.
4. Dances for threes or odd numbers are especially suitable when there are more of one gender than the other.
5. A high level of performance is not necessary. The group needs only to do the dances well enough to feel comfortable and have fun.
6. Careful planning includes getting the group active as soon as possible and moving from one activity to the next in well-planned transitions.
7. A dance or a mixer that has been particularly satisfying may be worth repeating. The group may even request a repeat. The leader can work request dances into the program when they are appropriate for the majority of the dancers.
8. A sensitive leader knows when to stop. Any single dance or mixer should not last more than five minutes. An hour of organized mixers and dances is generally sufficient. Square dance or ballroom dancing can be used to vary or extend the time. Other forms of social recreation—such as games, skits, stunts, and refreshments—can supplement the party.
9. Ballroom dance is an all-time favorite dance activity for single sessions. An evening of ballroom dancing requires a minimum of planning, and leadership for program direction is not necessary. The primary objective is to create an evening of easy, pleasant activity during which old and new friends can meet and dance. A few mixers are appropriate and useful. Mixers should be of an informal partner-exchange type, carried out when couples are arranged informally around the floor. This is preferable to the circle-patterned step mixers associated with square dance and round dance. The inclusion of a currently popular novelty dance provides a change of pace and adds to the fun of the evening. The planning committee should be cautioned to resist the temptation to turn this type of session into a grand mixer.

## Special Parties

The program for a special party for members of a regular dance group should include familiar dance favorites. It is not an appropriate time to teach new dances or techniques. The general fun and enthusiasm can be enhanced with skits, novelty mixers, and exhibition numbers by special guest performers. Added festivity can be achieved by planning the program, decorations, and refreshments around a theme.

## Theme Parties

Having a dance with a theme will add a special appeal to the event. Specific time periods, such as the fifties or sixties, swing or disco, Hawaiian or Latin, are examples of popular themes for dances. An example of planning a circus theme party is provided below.

*Occasion:* Last club meeting.

*Theme:* Circus.

*Promotion:* Appropriate posters based on circus slogans: "Under the Big Top," "Greatest Show on Earth."

*Costumes and decorations:* Provide construction paper, wallpaper, and crepe paper along with string, cellophane tape, and scissors, so that guests can construct clown hats to wear during the evening. Each guest can also make one item to hang on the wall for decoration.

*Name tags:* The guests' first names plus the name of a traditional circus animal organize the group into animal families for a special dance number, such as an animal square dance with each square made up of one type of animal. Examples: Gus Elephant, Diane Tiger, Willie Monkey, Jean Lion.

*Master of ceremonies:* The caller or the dance leader, depending on the type of dance group, leads the circus parade from outside in or around the dance floor. Followers mimic animal walks appropriate to their last names. Music should be a rousing circus march.

*Program:* Rename dances to fit the theme. For example: High-Wire Two-Step, Elephant Stomp, Trapeze Square, Tightrope Mambo, Tattoo Tango.

*Last dance of the evening:* All dancers gather in square dance sets or circles according to family name on name tag and, after the last dance, sit down on the floor in family groups.

*Refreshments:* A parade of animals, some juggling cookies or donuts and others carrying water pails of punch to fake dousing the guests, parade into the room led by the famous two-person horse. The horse is two dancers under a blanket or sheet, one as the head and the other as the rear end. A horse head can be made by simply drawing a likeness on a flat piece of posterboard.

After the parade antics are over, the guests are served from the pails and the cookie platters brought in by the animals.

## Senior Dances

A variety of Senior Dances are scheduled to meet different needs and interests. In general the seniors thoroughly enjoy dances that they did in the 1940s and 1950s. Ballroom dancing, especially the smooth jitterbug, Latin dances, and slow fox-trot brings seniors to the floor. They like a few mixers and pattern dances—not too many sequences to remember. Seniors enjoy the comfort of the familiar, limited new challenges, and the opportunity to repeat every week the dances they know. If the seniors live in rural areas or in an ethnic community, they might like other dances. For instance, the Scandinavians smile and dance when the schottische, Scandinavian Polka, or Hambo are played. If the seniors were especially active in square dance circles in the 1940s and 1950s, that's what they will seek out.

A leader needs to listen and be receptive to the seniors as they recall favorite dances. Find the music seniors like and include it. The chances are good that others know the dance or that the person would be willing to teach it. Seniors may prefer to come to events scheduled in the daytime since they may be reluctant to drive or take public transportation in the dark.

*Senior or community centers* will draw a regular following, even if events are once a week. Sometimes a group of retired musicians form a band and delight in playing for the gang regularly. Sometimes the local musician's union will sponsor a monthly dance for seniors with live music.

*Ethnic museums or lodges* sponsor senior dances.

*Retirement homes* may sponsor two types: a regular dance or a very modified program for seniors with limited ability to move. Dances are modified considerably to meet their ability. Some enjoy sitting in a chair (wheelchair) and moving their arms to different dance rhythms. The leader has to be creative and use ingenuity to appeal to the residents. Even the adapted movement will bring joy as they remember other days.

# 3 DANCE FUNDAMENTALS

*To an untrained eye, dancing looks like a fun, creative, artistic expression in the form of movement to music. While this is certainly true, there is also much more to dancing that may not be immediately obvious. Rhythm, meter, timing, steps, positions, formations, style—these are the building blocks of dance. This chapter focuses on recognizing, understanding, and teaching the fundamental components of dance, including everything from the ten basic locomotor movements to the elements of dance style. This chapter outlines and gives teaching strategies for basic steps and turns that will be used often in the individual dances introduced in later chapters. The concepts in this chapter will help dance instructors effectively lead and teach dancers of various levels.*

## Rhythm and Meter

### Rhythm

*Rhythm* is the regular pattern of movement and/or sound. It is a relationship between time and force factors. It is felt, seen, or heard.

### Beat

*Beat* is the basic unit that measures time. The duration of time becomes established by the beat, or the pulse, as it is repeated. It is referred to as the **underlying beat.**

## Note Values

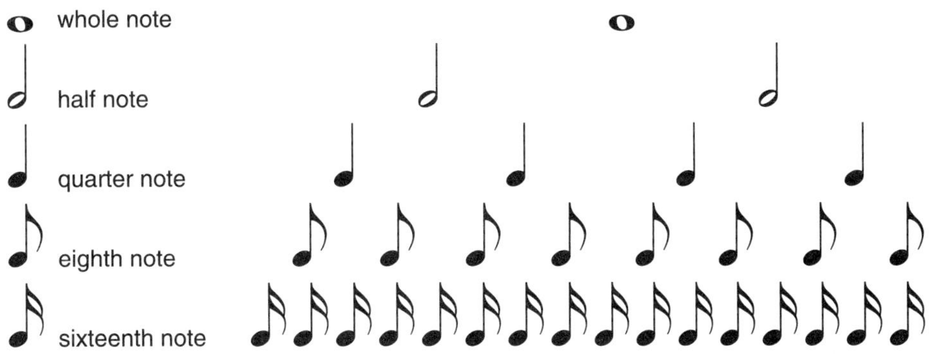


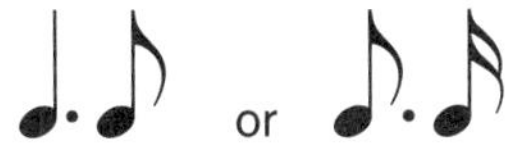


**dotted quarter or dotted eighth notes**
A *dotted note* increases the value by one-half. Therefore the dotted note equals one-and-a-half value of the original symbol. A dotted quarter note, then, is equal to a quarter plus an eighth; a dotted eighth is equal to an eighth plus a sixteenth.

**triplet**
A group of three notes played in the usual time of two similar notes. It would be counted *one-and-a* for one quarter note.

## Accent

**Accent** is the stress placed on a beat to make it stronger or louder than the others. The primary accent is on the first beat of the music. There may be a secondary accent.

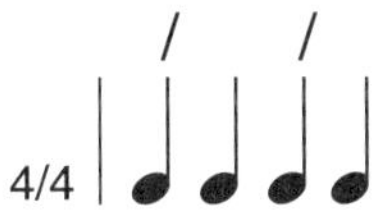


When the accent is placed on the unnatural beat (the off beat), the rhythm is *syncopated.*

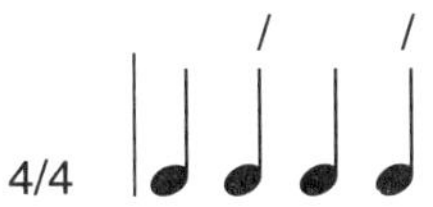


## Measure

A **measure** is one group of beats made by the regular occurrence of the heavy accent. It represents the underlying beat enclosed between two adjacent bars on a musical staff.

## Meter

**Meter** is the metric division of a measure into parts of equal time value and regular accents. Meter can be recognized by listening for the accent on the first beat.

## Time Signature

**Time signature** is a symbol (e.g., 2/4) that establishes the duration of time. The upper number indicates the number of beats per measure, and the lower number indicates the note value that receives one beat.

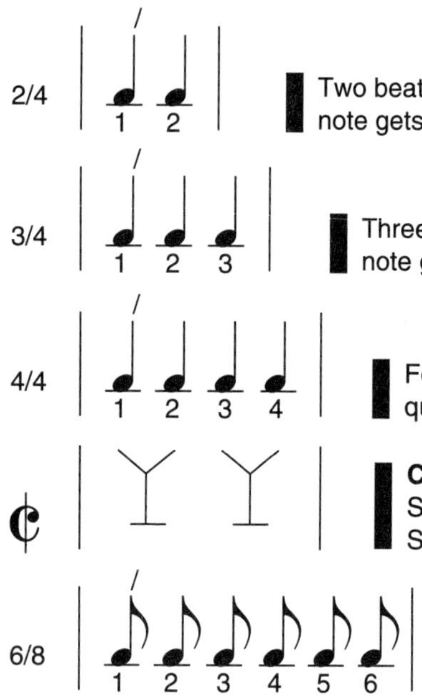


Two beats to the measure–accent on first beat–quarter note gets the beat.

Three beats to the measure–accent on first beat–quarter note gets the beat.

Four beats to the measure–accent on first beat–quarter note gets the beat.

**Cut time** plays the accented beats of the measure. Speed is often faster. Two beats to each measure. Same as fast 4/4 or 2/2 time.

Six beats to the measure–accent on first beat–eighth note gets the beat.

## Line Values

Whereas the musical notation establishes the *relative value of beats,* these same relative values can be represented by lines:

| | |
|---|---|
| one whole note | ________________________ |
| two half notes | __________ __________ |
| four quarter notes | _____ _____ _____ _____ |
| eight eighth notes | __ __ __ __ __ __ __ __ |
| sixteen sixteenth notes | _ _ _ _ _ _ _ _ _ _ _ _ _ _ _ _ |

## Phrase

A musical sentence, or **phrase,** can be felt by listening for a complete thought. This can be a group of measures, generally four or eight measures. A group of phrases can express a group of complete thoughts that are related just as a group of sentences expresses a group of complete thoughts in a paragraph. Groups of phrases are generally 16 or 32 measures long.

## Tempo

**Tempo** is the rate of speed at which music is played. Tempo influences the mood or the quality of music and movement. Sometimes at the beginning of the music or the dance, the tempo is established by a metronome reading. For example, metronome 128 means the equal recurrence of beats at the rate of 128 per minute.

## Rhythm Pattern

The **rhythm pattern** is the grouping of beats that repeat for the pattern of a dance step, just as for the melody of a song. The rhythm pattern must correspond to the underlying beat. Example: meter or underlying beat 4/4.

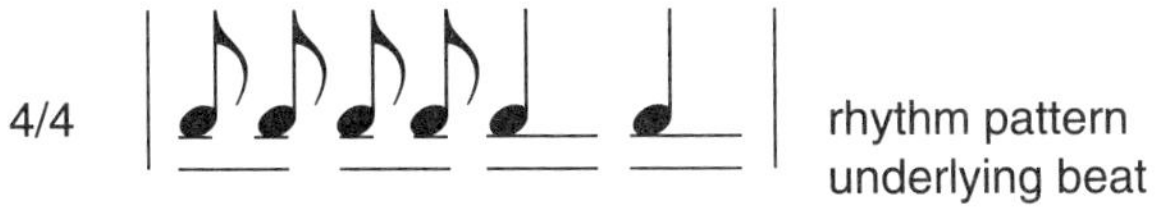


## Even Rhythm

When the beats in the rhythm pattern are all the same value (note or line value)—all long (slow) or all short (quick)—the rhythm is **even.** Even rhythms can be performed in movements such as, but not limited to, the walk, run, hop, jump, leap, waltz, and schottische.

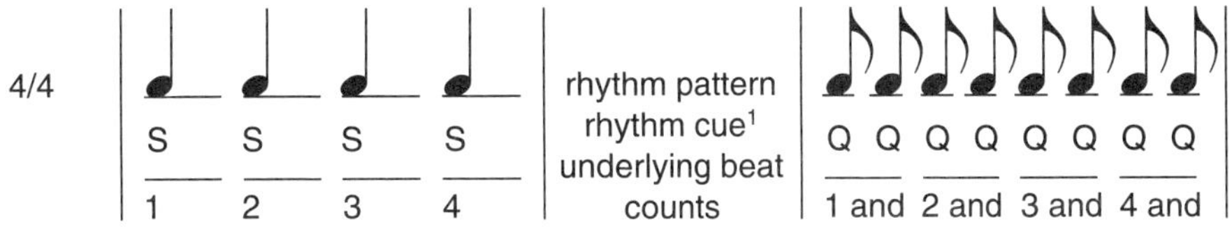


## Uneven Rhythm

When the beats in the rhythm pattern are not all the same value, but are any combination of slow and quick beats, the rhythm is **uneven.** Uneven rhythms can be performed in movements such as, but not limited to, the walk, run, jump, or leap, or in step patterns such as the two-step and the fox-trot.

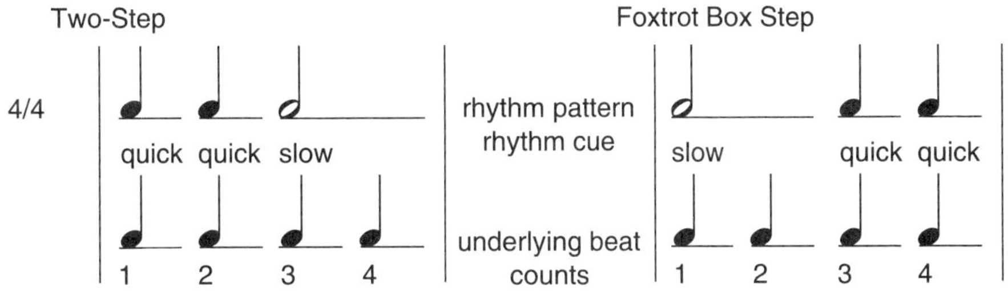


A *dotted beat* borrows half the value of itself again. Examples: skip, slide, gallop.

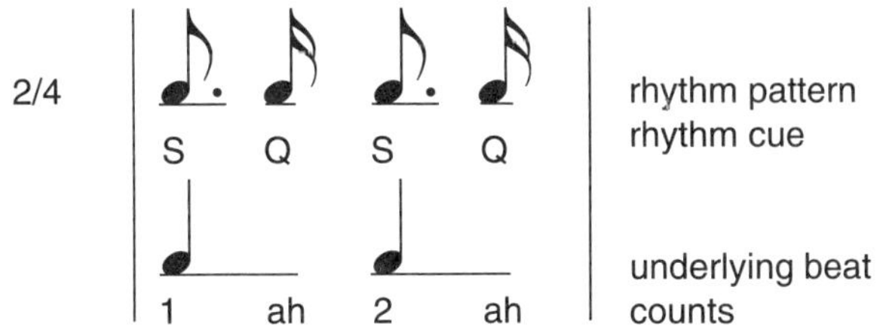


1. S = Slow; Q = Quick

When the note comes before the bar, it is called a *pick-up beat.*

Polka

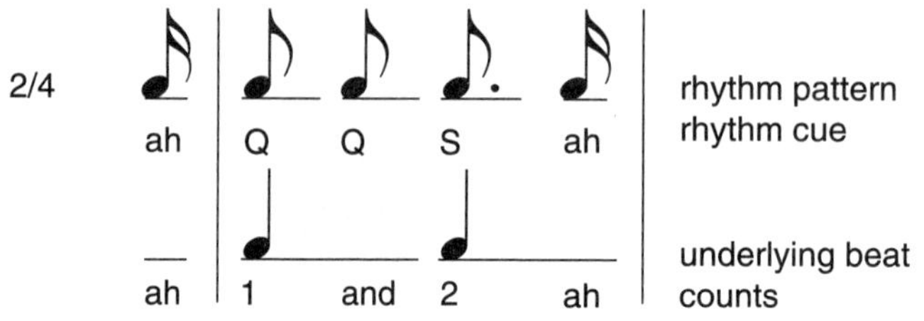


## Counting Rhythm

At times, listening to the teacher verbally count out the rhythm can be helpful. For each note, a number or sound should be made. The example below is for two quarter notes, two eighth notes, and four sixteenth notes.

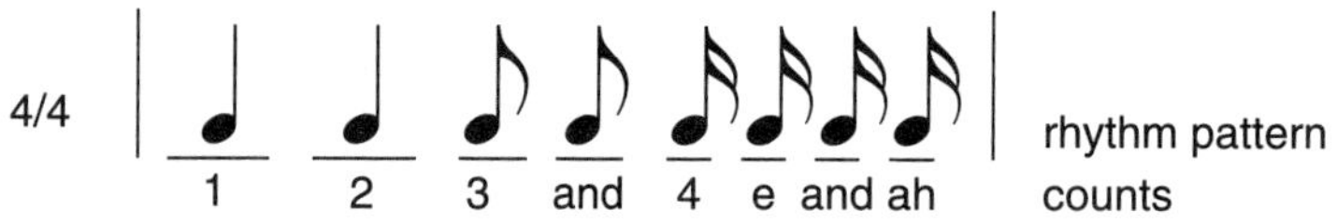


# Analysis of a Basic Rhythm

A teacher should thoroughly understand the complete analysis of each basic dance step to be taught. The following example shows the eight related parts of an analysis. Each basic dance step has been analyzed in this manner (including the basic steps of social dance in Chapter 8).

| | | | | |
|---|---|---|---|---|
| Two-Step | | | | name |
| 2/4 | | | | meter 2/4 |
| | / | | | accent |
| | step | close | step | step pattern |
| | ——— | ——— | ——— | rhythm pattern |
| | quick | quick | slow | rhythm cue |
| | ——— | | ——— | underlying beat |
| | 1 | and | 2 | counts |
| | | uneven rhythm | | type of rhythm |

# Fundamental Locomotor Movements

Easy movement has three variables: time, space, and force. *Time* involves the tempo or rate of speed, or duration (fast, moderate, or slow). *Space* involves the direction taken, distance covered, level, dimension (large, small), path (straight, twisted), and focus. *Force* involves the energy (power) expended, quality of movement; adjectives like brisk, quiet, hard, or gentle might apply.

Movement that travels through space is called *locomotor movement.* Movement that does not travel, like bending, twisting, pushing/pulling, is called *nonlocomotor movement.*

The following locomotor steps are simple ways to transfer weight in moving from one place to another. Combinations of locomotor movements form step patterns in folk, square, and social dance. Specific dances are listed for most locomotor movements. Sissone and Assemblé are ballet motifs and do not have dance examples. Wheelchair adaptations by Kelly Mucha.

## Walk

1. May be even or uneven rhythm.
2. A transfer of weight from one foot to the other, the weight rolling forward from the heel to the ball and toes on one foot, transferring to the heel, then the ball, toes of the other foot. In a **dance walk** the toes and ball of the foot strike first. *One foot is always in contact with the ground.*

| 4/4 | | | | |
|---|---|---|---|---|
| | / step | step | step | step |
| | R | L | R | L |
| | 1 | 2 | 3 | 4 |

even rhythm

**Dances:** Lesnoto—Chapter 7, Saturday Night Fever—Chapter 8

**WHEELCHAIR ADAPTATION** Slow, consistent pushes, allowing the student to glide forward or backward.

| 4/4 | | | | |
|---|---|---|---|---|
| | push | glide | push | glide |
| | 1 | 2 | 3 | 4 |

## Run

1. Fast, even rhythm.
2. A transfer of weight from the ball and toes of one foot to the other foot. During the weight transfer, both feet are off the ground.

| 4/4 | | | | | | | | |
|---|---|---|---|---|---|---|---|---|
| | / R | L | R | L | R | L | R | L |
| | 1 | and | 2 | and | 3 | and | 4 | and |

even rhythm

**Dances:** Troika—Chapter 7, Savila Se Bela Loza—Chapter 7

**WHEELCHAIR ADAPTATION** Short, fast pushes forward or backward, using both hands.

| 4/4 | | | | | | | | |
|---|---|---|---|---|---|---|---|---|
| | push | push | push | push | push | push | push | push |
| | 1 | and | 2 | and | 3 | and | 4 | and |

## Leap

1. Even rhythm.
2. A transfer of weight from one foot to the other foot, pushing off with a spring and landing on the ball of the foot, letting the heel come down, and bending the knee to absorb the shock. At one point, both feet are off the ground.
3. A leap may be compared to a run with a greater period of suspension in the air. Generally, a leap will travel.

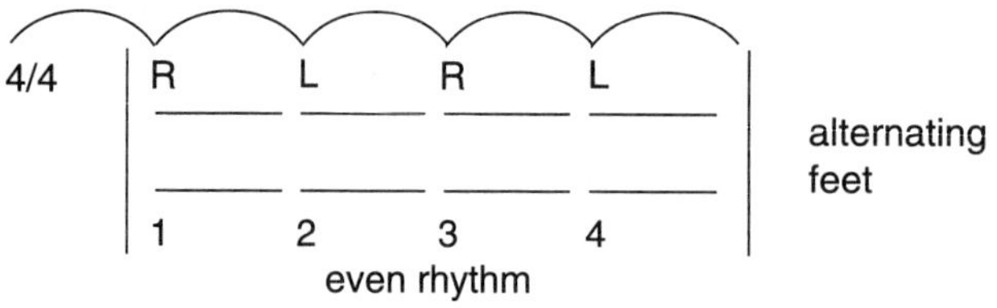


**Dances:** Hineh Ma Tov—Chapter 7, Tinikling—Chapter 7

**WHEELCHAIR ADAPTATION** Push to move with one hand and stop with the other hand.

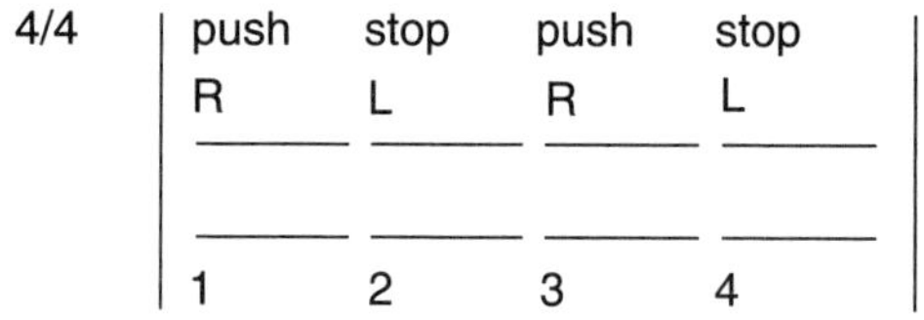


## Jump

1. May be even or uneven rhythm.
2. A transfer of weight with a springing action from both feet, lifting into the air, and landing on both feet.
3. Feet push off floor with strong foot and knee extension, the heel coming off first and then the toe.
4. On landing, the ball of the foot touches the floor first. Then the heel comes down, and the knees bend to absorb the shock of landing.

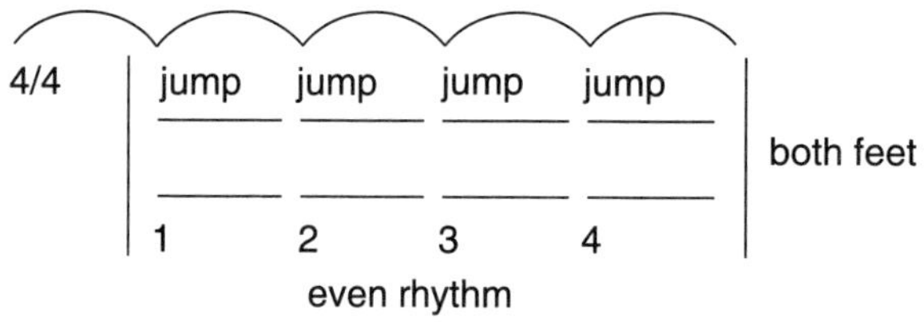


**Dances:** Jiffy Mixer—Page 116, Hip Hop Dance—Chapter 8

**WHEELCHAIR ADAPTATION** Strong pushes forward using two hands and stopping with two hands.

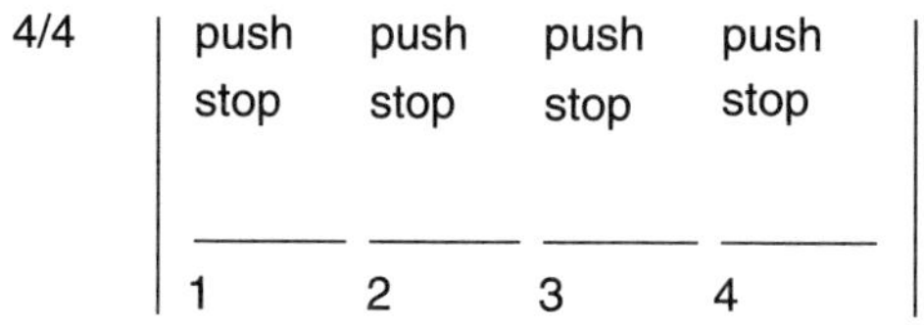

## Hop

1. May be even or uneven rhythm.
2. A transfer of weight by a springing action of the foot from one foot (push off from the heel/toe and land on ball then heel of foot) to the same foot.

| 4/4 | | | | |
|---|---|---|---|---|
| | /<br>hop | hop | hop | hop |
| | R | R | R | R |
| | ______ | ______ | ______ | ______ |
| | ______ | ______ | ______ | ______ |
| | 1 | 2 | 3 | 4 |

even rhythm

**Dances:** Mayim—Chapter 7, Korobushka—Chapter 7

**WHEELCHAIR ADAPTATION** Strong pushes forward using one hand and stopping with one hand. To move straight, the student will need to alternate between the right and left hand. To hop in a circle, the student may use the same hand.

| 4/4 | | | | |
|---|---|---|---|---|
| | push | push | push | push |
| | stop | stop | stop | stop |
| | ______ | ______ | ______ | ______ |
| | 1 | 2 | 3 | 4 |

## Sissone

1. Even rhythm.
2. A transfer of weight with a springing action from both feet, lifting into the air, and landing on one foot (a hop), sometimes referred to as a *JOP* (*J* for "jump," *OP* for "(h)OP").

Slow Sissone

| 2/4 | | |
|---|---|---|
| | both jump | hop L |
| | _____ | _____ |
| | 1 | 2 |

even rhythm

Fast Sissone

| 2/4 | | | | |
|---|---|---|---|---|
| | both jump | hop L | step R | both jump |
| | ______ | ______ | ______ | ______ |
| | ____________ | | ____________ | |
| | 1 | and | 2 | and |

even rhythm

**WHEELCHAIR ADAPTATION** Push with both hands and stop with one hand (the chair will turn slightly with each stop). To move in a straight line, the student will need to alternate hands.

| 2/4 | | | | |
|---|---|---|---|---|
| | push | stop | push | stop |
| | both | L | both | R |
| | ______ | ______ | ______ | ______ |
| | 1 | 2 | 1 | 2 |

## Assemblé

1. Even rhythm.
2. A transfer of weight with a spring from one foot, lifting into the air, and landing on both feet.

Slow Assemblé

| 2/4 | | |
|---|---|---|
| | spring L | land both |
| | 1 | 2 |

even rhythm

Fast Assemblé

| 2/4 | | | | |
|---|---|---|---|---|
| | spring L | land both | spring R | land both |
| | 1 | and | 2 | and |

even rhythm

**WHEELCHAIR ADAPTATION** Push with one hand, and stop with both hands (the chair will turn slightly with each stop). To move in a straight line, the student will need to alternate hands.

| 2/4 | | | | |
|---|---|---|---|---|
| | push L | stop both | push R | stop both |
| | 1 | 2 | 1 | 2 |

## Gallop

1. A combination of a walk and a run.
2. Uneven rhythm: (6/8 ♩ ♪ ♩ ♪ or 2/4 ♩♪♩♪♩♪) .
3. 2–1 ratio; long–short, long–short.
4. Movement forward, knee action, heel leading.
5. One foot maintains lead.

| 6/8 | | | | | | | | |
|---|---|---|---|---|---|---|---|---|
| | step R | run L | step R | run L | step R | run L | step R | run L |
| | 1 2 | 3 | 1 2 | 3 | 1 2 | 3 | 1 2 | 3 |

uneven rhythm

| 2/4 | | | | | | | | |
|---|---|---|---|---|---|---|---|---|
| | step R | run L | step R | run L | step R | run L | step R | run L |
| | 1 and | ah | 2 and | ah | 1 and | ah | 2 and | ah |

uneven rhythm

**Dances:** Ninepin Reel—Page 85

**WHEELCHAIR ADAPTATION** A long push with one hand, followed by a short push with the other hand.

| 2/4 | push | push | push | push |
|---|---|---|---|---|
| | R | L | R | L |
| | 1 | and ah | 2 | and ah |

## Slide

1. A gallop moving sideward, right or left.
2. Uneven rhythm: (6/8 ♩ ♪ ♩ ♪ or 2/4 ♫♩♩♫♩).
3. 2-1 ratio; long-short, long-short.
4. Movement sideward can go right or left.
5. A step to the side on the right foot on the slow beat, close the left foot to right, shifting the weight quickly onto the left foot on the quick beat.
6. One foot maintains lead.

| 6/8 | / step | close | step | close | / step | close | step | close |
|---|---|---|---|---|---|---|---|---|
| | R | L | R | L | R | L | R | L |
| | 1 2 | 3 | 1 2 | 3 | 1 2 | 3 | 1 2 | 3 |

uneven rhythm

| 2/4 | / step | close | step | close | / step | close | step | close |
|---|---|---|---|---|---|---|---|---|
| | R | L | R | L | R | L | R | L |
| | 1 and | ah | 2 and | ah | 1 and | ah | 2 and | ah |

uneven rhythm

**Dances:** Man In the Hay—Chapter 7, Willow Tree—Chapter 7

**WHEELCHAIR ADAPTATION** Sweep arms to the side and back in front of the body. Note that the student's chair is not moving during this motion. While performing a dance with several side-to-side movements, position students using wheelchairs in enough space to avoid collision.

| 2/4 | side | front | side | front |
|---|---|---|---|---|
| | R | | L | |
| | 1 | and ah | 2 | and ah |

## Skip

1. A combination of a walk and a hop.
2. Uneven rhythm: (6/8 ♩ ♪ ♩ ♪ or 2/4 ♩♩♩ ♩♩♩).
3. 1–2 ratio; short–long.
4. A step and a hop on the same foot. Alternate feet.
5. Timing: If the skip is high, the hop has two beats (the accent is on the hop while in the air); the step, one beat. If the skip is low, the step has two beats (the accent is on the step). The hop one beat.

| 6/8 | step | / hop | step | / hop |
|---|---|---|---|---|
| | R | R | L | L |
| | 1 2 | 3 | 1 2 | 3 |
| | uneven rhythm | | | |

| 2/4 | step | / hop | step | / hop |
|---|---|---|---|---|
| | R | R | L | L |
| | 1 and | ah | 2 and | ah |
| | uneven rhythm | | | |

**Dances:** Sicilian Tarantella—Chapter 7, La Raspa—Chapter 7

**WHEELCHAIR ADAPTATION** A long push with both hands, followed by a short push with both hands.

| 2/4 | push both | push both | push both | push both |
|---|---|---|---|---|
| | 1 and | ah ___ | 2 and | ah ___ |

## Exercises for Fundamental Locomotor Movements

1. Practice each movement while clapping or playing rhythm instruments.
2. Vary the energy, space, direction, and style.
3. Put three different movements together and repeat the combination four times. For instance: run, run, leap, run, run, jump. Repeat four times. Write the rhythm pattern in counts and lines.
4. Compose a two-part dance (A, B) for 16 counts. Clap the rhythm or use rhythm instruments.
5. Have relay races using locomotor movements.

# Basic Dance Steps

## Shuffle, Dance Walk, or Glide

1. An easy, light step, from one foot to the other, in even rhythm.
2. Different from a walk in that the weight is over the ball of the foot.
3. The feet remain lightly in contact with the floor.

| 4/4 | / step | step | step | step |
|---|---|---|---|---|

**Dances:** Virginia Reel—Chapter 4, All American Promenade—Chapter 4

## Two-Step or Triple-Step

1. 2/4 or 4/4 meter.
2. Uneven rhythm.
3. Step forward on left foot, close right to left, take weight on right, step left again. Repeat, beginning with right.
4. The rhythm is quick, quick, slow.

| 2/4 | | | |
|---|---|---|---|
| | / | | |
| | step | close | step |
| | L | R | L |
| | Q | Q | S |
| | 1 | and | 2 |

uneven rhythm

**Dances:** La Bastringue—Chapter 7, Cotton-Eyed Joe—Chapter 4

## Polka

1. 2/4 meter.
2. An energetic, lively dance step in uneven rhythm.
3. Similar to a two-step with the addition of a hop so that it becomes hop, step, close, step. The hop comes on the pick-up beat.

| 2/4 | | | | | | | | | |
|---|---|---|---|---|---|---|---|---|---|
| | | / | | | | / | | | |
| | hop | step | close | step | hop | step | close | step | hop |
| | L | R | L | R | R | L | R | L | L |
| | ah | Q | Q | S | ah | Q | Q | S | ah |
| | ah | 1 | and | 2 | ah | 1 | and | 2 | ah |

uneven rhythm

**Dances:** Doudlebska Polka—Chapter 7, Klumpakojis—Chapter 7

## Schottische

1. 4/4 meter.
2. Smooth, even rhythm (tempos will vary depending on the music).
3. Three running steps and a hop or a step, close, step, hop.

| 4/4 | | | | |
|---|---|---|---|---|
| | / | | | |
| | step | step | step | hop |
| | L | R | L | L |
| | Q | Q | Q | Q |
| | 1 | 2 | 3 | 4 |

even rhythm

4. The schottische dance form is four measures (step, step, step hop; step, step, step hop; step hop, step hop; step hop, step hop).
5. Common and popular variations are to hold, turn, or swing the free leg on the fourth count instead of hopping.

**Dances:** Korobushka—Chapter 7, Road to the Isles—Chapter 7

## Waltz

1. 3/4 meter–accent first beat.
2. A smooth, graceful dance step in even rhythm (tempos will vary depending on the music).
3. Ladder step consists of three steps; step forward on the left, step to the side with the right, close left to right, take weight on left.

| | | | | | | |
|---|---|---|---|---|---|---|
| 3/4 | / fwd | side | close | fwd | side | close |
| | L | R | L | R | L | R |
| | S | S | S | S | S | S |
| | 1 | 2 | 3 | 1 | 2 | 3 |

even rhythm

**Dances:** Bitte Mand I Knibe—Chapter 7, Spinnradl zu Dritt—Chapter 7

4. The *box waltz* is the basic pattern for the box waltz turn. Step left forward, step right sideward, passing close to the left foot, close left to right, taking weight left; step right backward, step left sideward, passing close to the right foot, close right to left, take weight right. *Cue:* Forward side close, back side close.

| | | | | | | |
|---|---|---|---|---|---|---|
| 3/4 | / fwd | side | close | back | side | close |
| | L | R | L | R | L | R |
| | S | S | S | S | S | S |
| | 1 | 2 | 3 | 1 | 2 | 3 |

even rhythm

5. The **running waltz** used so often in European folk dances is a tiny three-beat running step with an accent on the first beat, three beats to each measure.
6. *Canter waltz* rhythm is an uneven rhythm in waltz time with the action taking place on beats one and three. The rhythm is slow, quick; slow, quick or long, short. (Refer to **canter rhythm,** Chapter 8.)

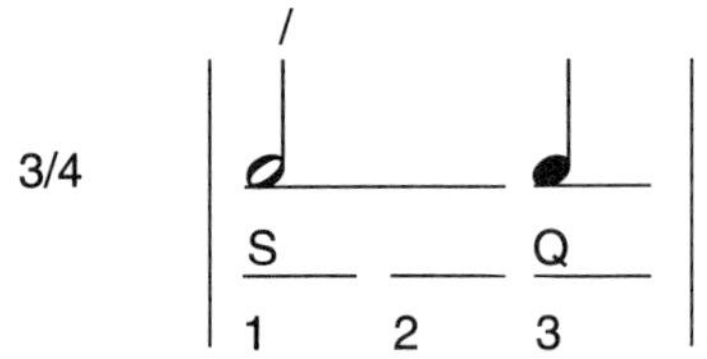


uneven rhythm

## Mazurka

1. 3/4 meter.
2. Strong, vigorous, even three-beat rhythm–accent second beat.
3. Step left, bring right up to left with a cut-step displacing left, hop right while bending left knee so that left foot approaches the right ankle. Repeat, left foot leading.

| 3/4 | | | | | | |
|---|---|---|---|---|---|---|
| | | / | | | / | |
| | step L | cut R | hop R | step L | cut R | hop R |
| | S | S | S | S | S | S |
| | 1 | 2 | 3 | 1 | 2 | 3 |

even rhythm

**Dances:** Krüz König—Chapter 7, Varsouvienne—Page 112



# Suggestions for Teaching Basic Dance Steps

The level of ability of the student and the degree of difficulty of the basic step will influence the manner in which a step is presented. The factors involved are interdependent and may be used in various combinations when the steps are being taught. The sequence of the factors and the starting point for teaching vary. Sometimes it is necessary to go back in the teaching process to an easier form. Several approaches may be necessary for everyone to learn the step.

Refer to the following section to see how these suggestions are applied in teaching basic dance steps.

## Analysis of Rhythm of Basic Step

Explain and discuss accent, time signature, even or uneven rhythm, and foot pattern in relation to rhythm.

1. Listen to music.
2. Clap rhythm with students.
3. Write out on blackboard.
4. Demonstrate action.

## Method of Presentation

1. Walk through with analysis and demonstration.
2. Practice.
3. Apply basic step in simple sequence.
4. Use basic step in simple dance.

## Interdependent Factors Influencing Procedure

1. Position of teacher in relation to group. Ideally the teacher should be a part of the group, standing in the circle, two steps inside the circle, or facing the line. Avoid standing in the middle because the teacher's back is to part of the group. The dancers cannot hear, and the teacher is unaware of whether they understand. In large groups, the teacher is on a platform, slightly above the group so that he or she may be seen and heard. Otherwise, a mike is necessary. A wireless mike affords more flexibility of position.

2. Demonstrations. When the teacher is facing lines of students, he or she should face the class and move as a mirror image, moving in the same direction as the students. If demonstrating in the circle, the demonstration should be given several times, moving to different locations, especially directly across the circle. Dancers tend to mirror what they see in a circle and forget to translate demonstration to the same foot and direction.
3. Formation of group for teaching.
   a. Line.
   b. Single circle.
   c. Double circle.
4. Position of people.
   a. Alone.
   b. With partner.
      1. Varsouvienne, couple, promenade, open, or conversation position.
      2. Closed or shoulder-waist position.
5. Accompaniment–with or without music.
6. Cue–with or without verbal cue.
7. Direction of movement.
   a. In place.
   b. Forward and backward.
   c. Sideward or diagonal.
   d. Turning.

# Procedure for Teaching Basic Dance Steps and Turns

## Basic Dance Turns

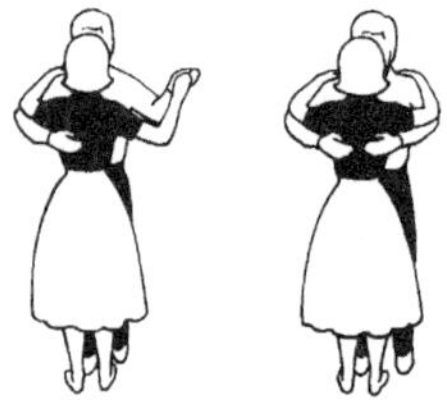

Using the fundamental dance steps, partners may turn clockwise or counterclockwise. Basically, if the man is leading with the left, the turn is counterclockwise; if he is leading with the right, the turn is clockwise. But in folk dance, the majority of the partner turns are clockwise. A successful turn actually starts with the preceding step, the man's back to center and his body moving into the turn. The man steps left backward in the line of direction, which allows his right foot to lead on the second step.

## Schottische Turn Clockwise

The schottische rhythm is even 4/4 meter. The pattern is step, step, step hop; step, step, step hop; step hop, step hop, step hop, step hop. The last two measures of four are used for the partner turn. The starting position for the turn is generally a closed position or a shoulder-waist position. By turning gradually, the couple can make only one turn clockwise on the four step hops, or, by turning a half-turn clockwise on each step hop, they can make two full turns. They progress forward in the line of direction on each step hop. When teaching the Schottische turn clockwise, practice the steps initially as an individual (single circle) and then as a couple (double circle). Directions are for man; woman's part is reverse.

1. *Single circle,* facing line of direction.
   a. Beginning left, take two schottische steps, moving forward in the line of direction. Rock forward on first step hop, rock backward on the second step hop, rock forward on the third step hop, and backward on the fourth step hop. Repeat.

b. Beginning left, take two schottische steps moving forward in the line of direction. Turn clockwise by rocking forward and backward twice to make one complete turn. Repeat. Discourage any body sway that may accompany the rock as soon as the pattern of turning is learned.

2. *Double circle,* take open position, facing the line of direction. Beginning left, take two schottische steps, moving forward in the line of direction. Take closed or shoulder-waist position. Turn clockwise by rocking forward and backward twice to make one complete turn. Repeat. Emphasize the importance of turning to face partner on the last schottische step so that the turn starts on the first step hop. Encourage more advanced dancers to make two turns.
3. Use a simple dance to practice the schottische step, for example, Schottische or Road to the Isles.



## Two-Step Turn Clockwise

The two-step rhythm is uneven 2/4 or 4/4 meter with a quick, quick, slow pattern. There is a half-turn on each measure (2/4 meter). The starting position is closed, with the man's back to center of the circle. *The turn is on the second count.*

| | LEFT-FOOT SEQUENCE (MAN) | RIGHT-FOOT SEQUENCE (WOMAN) |
|---|---|---|
| Count 1 | Step left sideward. | Step right sideward. |
| Count and | Close right to left, taking weight on right. | Close left to right, taking weight on left. |
| Count 2 | Step left around partner, toeing in and pivoting clockwise on the ball of the foot a half-turn around. | Step right forward between partner's feet and pivoting clockwise on the ball of the foot a half-turn around. |

**NOTE:** The man starts with the left sequence, the woman starts with the right sequence. After a half-turn, the woman then starts with the left sequence and the man with the right sequence. They continue to alternate. By this process of *dovetailing with the feet,* man and woman can turn easily without stepping on each other's feet. Couple progresses in the line of direction as they turn.

**STYLE:** The steps should be small and close to partner. The body leans back and aids in the turn. The turn is on the ball of the foot. Each partner must give the impetus for the turn by pivoting on his or her own foot.

**LEAD:** Closed position, the man should have a firm right hand on the small of the woman's back so that she can lean back against it. His right arm guides her as he turns.

**CUES:**

1. Left-foot sequence: side close around. Right-foot sequence: side close between.
2. Practicing together in closed position. Side close turn, side close turn.

## Teaching Two-Step Turn Clockwise

1. *Double circle formation,* man with his back to the center of the circle. Take closed position. Begin on man's left, woman's right.
   a. Moving toward the line of direction, take four slides, pivoting around clockwise on the last slide so that the man faces the center of the circle. Take four slides to the man's right still in the line of direction, pivoting on the last slide clockwise so that the man is back in original position. Repeat. Emphasize that the last slide is the pivot clockwise and that the man must lead the woman with his right arm as he goes around so that they can turn together.

b. Moving to the man's left (line of direction), take two slides and pivot clockwise halfway around on the last slide. Then, reaching in the line of direction, take two slides to the man's right and pivot clockwise to original position. Repeat.

2. Use a simple dance to practice two-step turn, for example, Boston Two-Step.

## Progressive Two-Step

1. The forward two-step can be taught simply by moving forward on the cue *step, close, step,* alternately left, then right.
2. Take couple position. Take the two-step face to face and back to back, progressing in the line of direction.

## Polka Turn

1. Step-by-step rhythm approach.
   a. *Single circle,* all facing line of direction.
      1. Analyze the polka very slowly and have class walk through the steps together in even rhythm (hop, step close step).
      2. Gradually adapt the rhythm until there is a quick hop and a slower step close step.
      3. Gradually accelerate the tempo to normal polka time. Add the accompaniment.

   b. *Double circle,* take promenade, Varsouvienne, or couple position, facing line of direction. Polka forward with partner.
   c. Use simple dance to practice polka step, for example, Klumpakojis, page 358; and Heel and Toe Polka, page 107.
2. Two-step approach.
   a. *Single circle,* facing the line of direction. Beginning left, Two-Step with music, moving forward in the line of direction. Gradually accelerate the tempo to a fast Two-Step and take smaller steps. Without stopping, change the music to Polka rhythm and precede each Two-Step with a hop. If musician is available, this rhythm change can be made with music. Otherwise, cue without music until step is learned and then use Polka recording.

   b. *Double circle,* take promenade, Varsouvienne, or couple position, facing the line of direction. Polka forward with partner.
   c. Use a simple dance to practice Polka step, for example, Klumpakojis, page 358.

### Polka Turn Clockwise

The **clockwise turn** is used almost always for a polka partner turn in folk dance. The polka rhythm is uneven 2/4 meter. The pattern is hop, step, close, step. With the addition of a quick hop (pick-up beat) before each two-step, all the directions described for the two-step turn can be applied to the polka turn. The starting position is generally a closed position or a shoulder-waist position.

1. Slide approach
   a. Moving toward the line of direction, take seven slides, a step and a hop-turn, moving around clockwise on the hop so that the man faces the center of the circle. Take seven slides, a step and a hop-turn, moving around clockwise on the hop so that the man's back is to the center of the circle. Repeat.
   b. Reduce to three slides and a step hop-turn.
   c. Reduce to one slide and a step hop-turn.
   d. Cue: Slide and step hop, slide and step hop. Then put the hop first and cue:

Hop, slide and step, hop, slide and step.

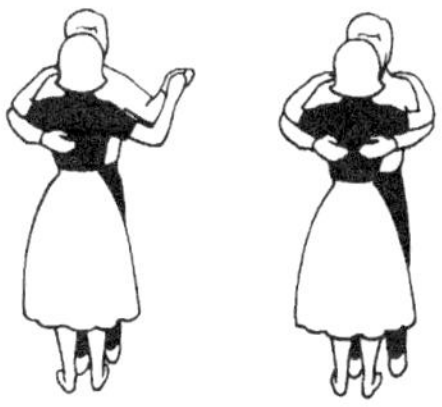

e. Practice individually and then with a partner. Dovetail feet as in the two-step turn. Emphasize that on the hop the man must lead the woman with his right arm as he goes around so that they can turn together.

f. Use a simple dance to practice polka turn, for example, Doudlebska Polka, page 313.

g. For style and lead, see two-step turn clockwise, page 43.

## Waltz

The waltz rhythm is even 3/4 meter. The basic waltz steps may be performed as a couple in several different styles or as an individual in several folk dances.

## Running Waltz

Single circle, hands joined. Move one step with each beat of the music. Accent first step of measure slightly.

## Waltz Turns

Three patterns are presented: the box waltz turn (turns clockwise and counterclockwise), and two traditional clockwise patterns, most often used in folk dances, step-side-close and step-step close.

### Box Waltz Turn

The box waltz turn is used in social dancing and in some American folk dances and can go either to the left in a counterclockwise turn or to the right in a clockwise turn, depending on which foot leads the turn. (These turns are described in detail under the waltz box turn, page 480.)

1. Learn box pattern individually.
2. Take closed dance position with partner. The man steps forward on the left and the woman backward on the right.
3. Practice turning left and right. Cue: Turn side close, back side close.

### Step-Side-Close Pattern

**LEFT-FOOT SEQUENCE (MAN):** Step left around partner, pivoting on the ball of the foot a half-turn clockwise (count 1). Step right sideward in line of direction (count 2). Close left to right, take weight left (count 3).

**RIGHT-FOOT SEQUENCE (WOMAN):** Step right forward between partner's feet, pivoting on the ball of the foot a half-turn clockwise (count 1). Step left sideward in the line of direction (count 2). Close right to left, take weight right (count 3).

1. Learn step pattern, turning clockwise individually. Sometimes to establish a complete half-turn, it is helpful to travel the length of the hall and indicate one wall to be faced on the first measure and the other wall to be faced on the second measure. The dancers try harder to complete one turn and always face the correct direction.
2. Partners take closed position and practice turn together.
3. Use a simple dance with a clockwise turn, for example, Familjevalsen, page 398.

**NOTE:** The man starts with the left sequence, the woman with the right sequence. After a half-turn, the woman starts with the left sequence and the man with the right sequence. They continue to alternate. By this process of dovetailing the feet, dancers can turn easily without stepping on each other's feet.

**STYLE:** The steps are small and close to partner. The pivot halfway around is on the ball of the foot on the first count. Each partner is responsible for supplying the impetus for the ball of the foot turn.

**LEAD:** The man has a firm right hand at the woman's back. She leans back and is guided into the turn by his firm right hand and arm.

**CUES:**

1. Left-foot sequence: around side close. Right-foot sequence: between side close.
2. Practice together in closed position. Turn side close, turn side close.

## Step-Step-Close Pattern

**LEFT-FOOT SEQUENCE (MAN):** Step left in the line of direction (toeing in, heel leads), pivoting on the ball of the foot and starting a half-turn clockwise (count 1). Take two small steps, right, left, close to first step, completing half-turn (counts 2 and 3).

**RIGHT-FOOT SEQUENCE (WOMAN):** Step right in line of direction (toeing out) *between partner's feet,* pivoting on the ball of the foot, starting a half-turn clockwise (count 1). Take two small steps, left, right, close to first step, completing half-turn (counts 2 and 3).

**NOTE:**

1. When the man steps backward left, the right foot leads the clockwise turn.
2. The man starts with the left sequence, the woman with the right sequence. After a half-turn, the woman starts with the left sequence and the man with the right sequence. They continue to alternate. When doing left-foot sequence, step backward in line of direction; when doing the right-foot sequence, step forward (but not as long a step as the first step in the other sequence). The dancers are turning on each count, but steps on counts 2 and 3 are almost in place. *Both feet are together on count 3.*

**LEAD:** The man has a firm right hand at the woman's back. She leans back and is guided into the turn by his firm right hand and arm.

**CUES:** Left-foot sequence: Back turn turn.
Right-foot sequence: Forward turn turn.

### *Reverse Direction of Turn*

*If turning counterclockwise, the left foot leads. If turning clockwise, the right foot leads.* To change leads from left to right or right to left, one measure (3 beats) is needed for transition. A balance step backward or one waltz step forward facilitates the transition. Or turning counterclockwise, after a left waltz step, immediately reverse direction with a right waltz step, turning clockwise (a more difficult maneuver). Eventually the lead comes back to a left one, and another transition occurs.

## Pivot Turn

The continuous pivot turn, used in folk dance and social dance, is a series of steps turning clockwise as many beats as desired and to different rhythms.

1. Slow, slow, slow, slow.
2. Quick, quick, quick, quick.
3. Slow, slow, quick, quick.
4. Slow, slow, quick, quick, quick, quick.

The man should be careful that he has room to turn, as the pivot turn progresses forward in the line of direction if done properly, and he should not turn so many steps as to make his partner dizzy. The principle involved in the footwork is the dovetailing of the feet, which means that the right foot always steps between partner's feet and the left foot always steps around the outside of partner's feet.

## Analysis of Pivot Turn

Take closed or shoulder-waist position. Preparation to start clockwise turn is the *preceding beat* of the pivot turn.

| RHYTHM CUES | STEPS |
|---|---|
| Slow | *Preliminary step.* Man steps right between partner's feet and leads into the turn by bringing his left shoulder toward his partner, increasing the body tension; shoulders become parallel and remain in that position for entire pivot. |
| Slow | Step left, toeing in across the line of direction and rolling clockwise, three-quarters of the way around the ball of the left foot. |
| Slow | Step right, between partner's feet forward in the line of direction, completing one turn. |

Last two steps repeat alternately.

**WOMAN:** The woman receives the lead as the man increases body tone. She maintains her body tone. She places her right foot forward in between his feet on the line of direction, left foot across the line of direction, right foot between, left across, and so forth.

**STYLE:** The hips and legs are closer together than most steps. They both must lean away, pressing outward like "the water trying to stay in the bucket." The concept of stepping each time in relation to the line of direction is what makes it possible to progress while turning as a true pivot turn should do.

**NOTE:**

1. In Scandinavian pivots, some have found it helpful to step on the right heel, transferring the weight to the sole of the foot; step left on the sole of foot, in effect pivoting on the right heel, left sole.
2. For further analysis, see the pivot turn section.

## Spin or Twirl

Whenever the woman is turned under her arm one or more turns (spins or twirls), it is important for the man to hold his left hand over the apex of her head; joined hands should be loose to allow turn.

3

# *Dance* FORMATIONS

These dance formations are representative of the dances in this book. There are many other variations.

## 1. NO PARTNERS

Single circle

Broken circle

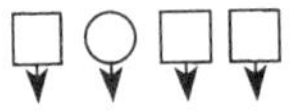

Line, side by side

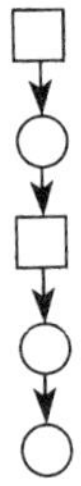

File, one behind each other

Key:

- □ Man
- ○ Woman
- ⟶ Direction facing
- △ Caller and/or music

Head couple is nearest to the caller and/or music.

## 2. COUPLES IN A CIRCLE

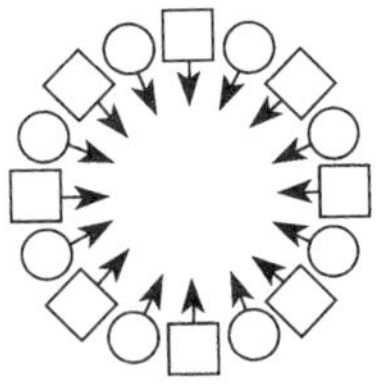

Single circle, facing center

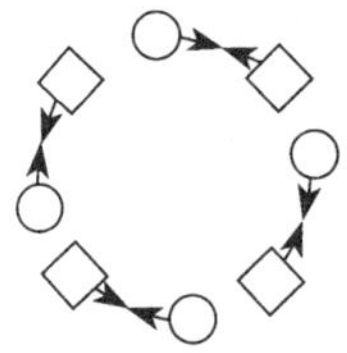

Single circle, man facing the line of direction, woman facing the reverse line of direction

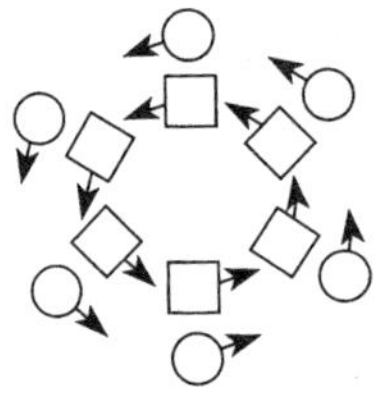

Double circle, couples facing the line of direction

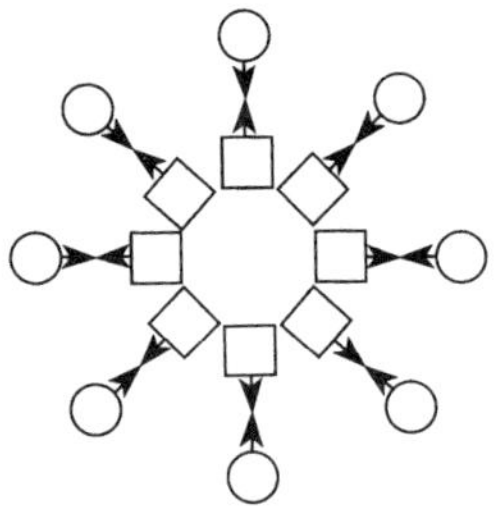

Double circle, partners facing, man's back to center

## 3. THREE PEOPLE

Set of three in a line, side by side

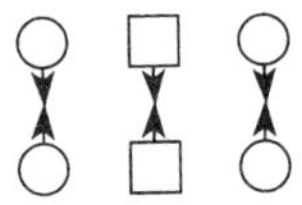

Set of three, facing set of three

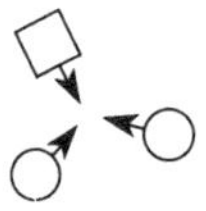

Single circle, facing center

## 4. TWO COUPLES

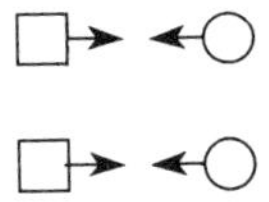

Set of two couples, partners facing

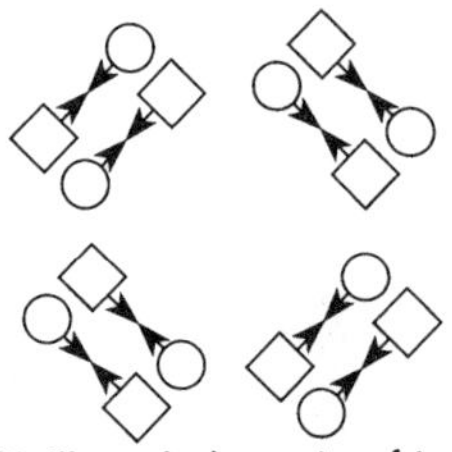

Sicilian circle, sets of two couples, couples facing

## 5. COUPLES IN A FILE DOUBLE FILE

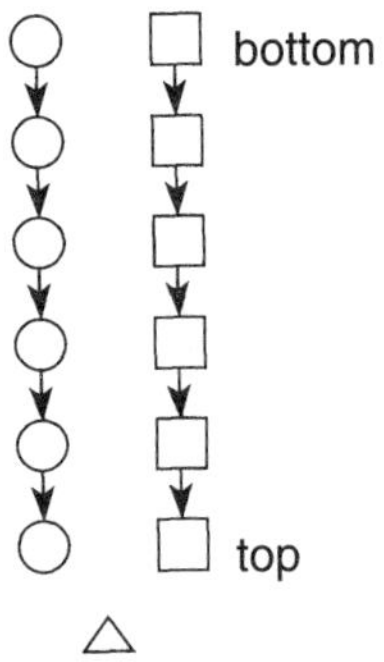


Longway or contra set, couples facing head

## 6. COUPLES IN A LINE

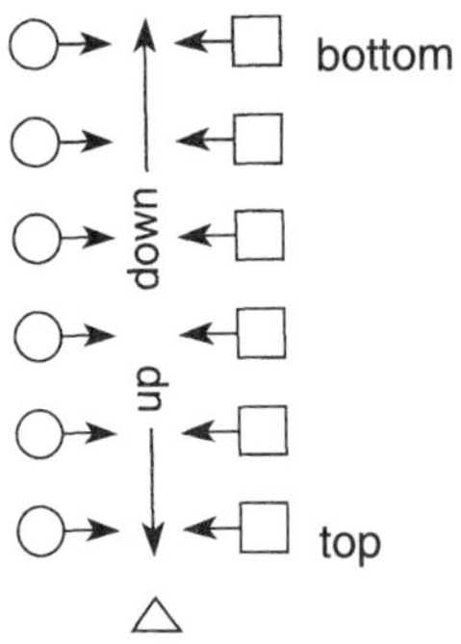


Longway or contra set, partners facing

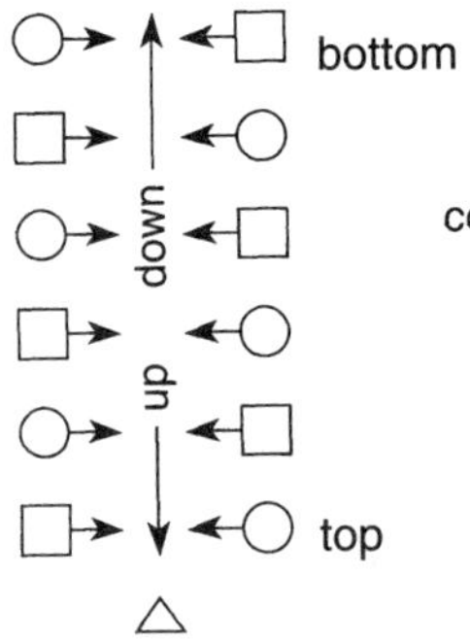


Couples 1, 3, 5 cross over contra set

## 7. FOUR COUPLES

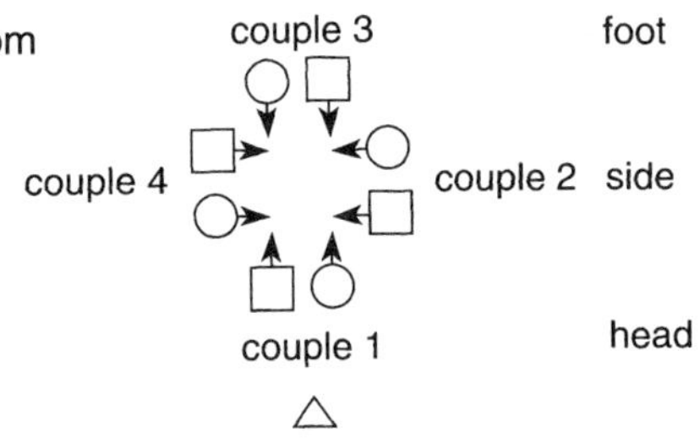


Set of four couples

# Dance POSITIONS

1. Back Cross

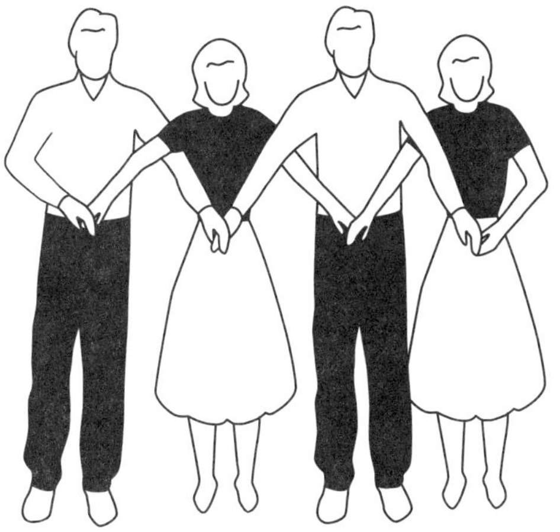

2. Basket Hold

3. Butterfly

4. Buzz Swing

5. Challenge Shine

6. Cross

7. Closed

8. Conversation Open

9. Cuddle

10. Escort

11. Face Off

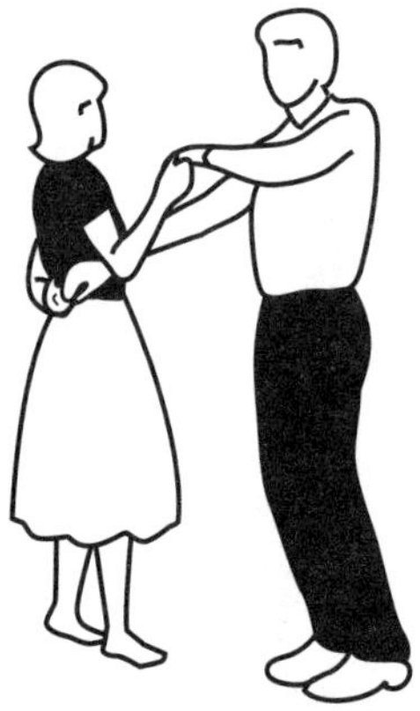

12. Hammerlock

13. Inside Hands Joined
Side by Side. Couple

14. Inside Hands Joined.
Ballroom style

15. Jockey

16. Latin Social

17. Left Parallel. Side Car

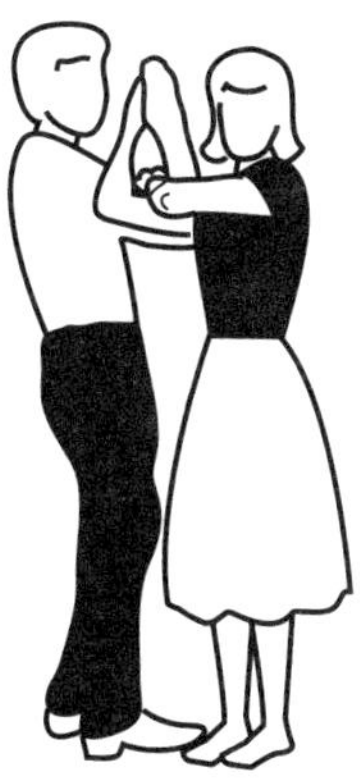

18. Little Window

19. Octopus

20. Ballroom Promenade
Open Position (Chapter 4)

21. Pigeon Wing
Right Hand Star

22. Promenade

23. Reverse Open

24. Reverse Varsouvienne

25. Right Parallel (Banjo). Outside Position

26. Semiopen

27. Skaters

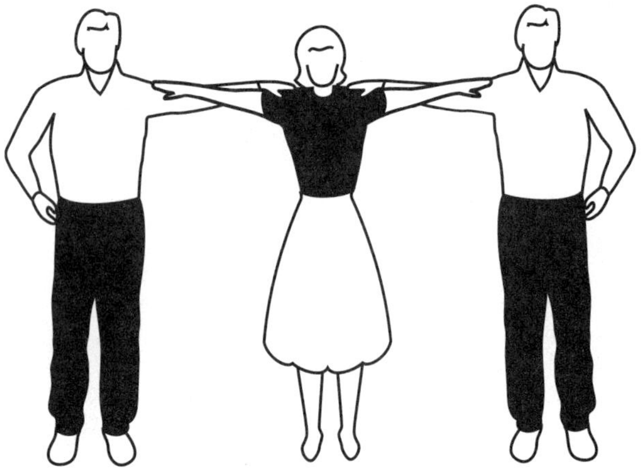

28. Shoulder Hold

29. Shoulder-Waist

30. Social Swing

31a. Swing Out. Flirtation

31b. Swing Out. Lindy Style

32. Two Hands Joined. Facing

33. "V" Position Handhold

34. Varsouvienne (Traditional) Sweetheart (Modern)

35. "W" Position Handhold

36. Yoke, Bridge

# GUIDELINES FOR READING DANCE DIRECTIONS

Written dance directions will appear for each dance covered in this book, but they will be structured differently depending on the type of dance because the structures of the dances themselves vary. In Chapters 4, 6, and 7, sections titled "Directions for the Dance" describe the movements of the dance with respect to the musical timing that is relevant for each dance style. For example, directions for folk dances in Chapter 7 are written according to counts for each measure of the music, while directions for contra dances in Chapter 6 are written according to the AABB parts of the music. In Chapter 5, Square Dance, the directions are given for individual figures performed by two to eight people at a time. In Chapter 8, Social Dance, the directions for each step are given separately with counts and cues. Each chapter will include more detail about how to interpret dance directions for that particular dance style.

Although written dance directions may be structured differently for different dance types, there are some common elements that appear across many styles. Each dance or dance step has a meter such as 4/4 or 2/4 and a level of difficulty. Many dances make references to directions such as "forward" or "back diagonal right." These directions are summarized in the figure below.

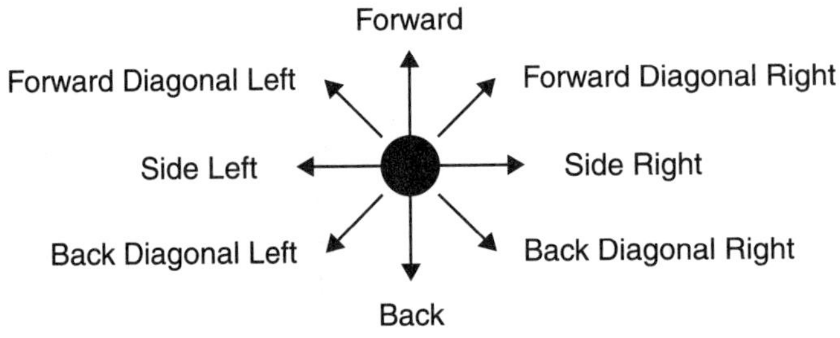


Forward refers to the direction a dancer is facing with the front part of the body (face, knees, toes). At any time, there are eight directions in which a dancer can move. The dancer can also perform a dance step without moving in any direction. Stepping underneath your center of gravity is referred to as "stepping in place."[2] In addition to movements and steps, a dance may also call for gestures, or movements done without transferring weight.

## Music in Relation to Dance

One problem that plagues the dance teacher more than any other is how to teach a student to hear and move to the beat of the music. A person who cannot hear the beat and constantly fumbles with all the relationships in movement that depend on being on the beat has a psychological handicap. Perhaps there are some basic understandings that can be learned and explored.

### Listen to the Beat

The underlying beat is usually carried by the string bass, the piano, and the drums. In Latin rhythms, the beat is carried by the bongo drum, the claves (sticks), or the wood block.

2. Ann Hutchinson, *Labanotation*, 1973, p. 35.

### The Beginner

The beginner should try to pick out a steady beat that is most dominant and synchronize his or her step with this downbeat. Quite often, people who think they have no sense of rhythm can clap a consistent pattern of beats but do not know what to listen for. If an individual can clap accurately to the basic beat and can depend on this beat to be consistent throughout a piece of music, he or she usually has the major problem solved. Regular practice moving with the beat brings confidence for dancing.

When an individual cannot clap to a regular beat and cannot hear a beat, the only way for him or her to learn is to:

1. Visually follow the clapping of the teacher or someone else in class.
2. Try to relate this with listening for the basic beat of a very obvious piece of square dance or march music. Mark time in place with the feet and then try to walk to this beat alone.
3. Gradually progress to other music that has a less obvious beat.
4. Walk with a good partner and try to feel the relationship of the movement to the beat until the individual can move with the beat.

The melody or the vocal can be very distracting to the individual who has difficulty with rhythm, and he or she tends to speed up or slow down. The more a dancer is concentrating on a dance step pattern, style, or lead, the easier it is to forget about listening to the music. A teacher can help in this case by calling attention to listening for the music. Thorough understanding and practice of the difficult step without music also permits greater freedom to listen to the music.

### The Dancer

When one has accomplished the hurdle of being able to dance to the beat of the music, the next step is to learn to listen to the rhythmic changes in the music.

1. The dancer should be able to recognize the beginning and the end of a phrase and anticipate this in his or her movement or call.
2. He or she should be able to recognize and adjust the movement to changes of tempo.
3. He or she should be able to identify the parts of a dance by the melodic changes in the music and therefore be able to make smooth transitions in movement or position.
4. He or she should be able to note the quality of the various parts of the music and be better able to interpret the appropriate style.
5. He or she should learn from experience with different types of rhythm to identify correctly one basic rhythm from another.
6. Finally, with experience, he or she should be able to interpret the music and in combining dance steps feel the relationship of the step to the music.

## How to Recognize Music for Dance

Certain facts must be learned to recognize music for specific dances.

1. Each dance rhythm is in a definite meter. For example, the dancer learns to recognize waltz music if he or she knows to listen to 3/4 meter with an accent on the first beat.
2. Each dance has a pattern of movement, the quality or feeling of which should identify with the quality of the music. For example, the dancer needs to know the rumba has a smooth, rolling Latin quality; the samba has a faster, bouncy, rocking quality; and the mambo has an offbeat, heavy, sultry quality. By trying to recognize this quality in the music, the dancer can usually identify the appropriate music.

3. Some types of dances have particular instruments that carry the bass or the melody. For example, the Latin American dances have the bongo drums, the sticks, the wood blocks, and the maracas, one or two of which carry the basic beat and another the rhythm pattern.
4. In folk dance, the music, the pattern of steps, and the style often relate to the meaning or the origin of the dance, and this association helps the dancer to remember and identify the music.

For more information, refer to Chapter 2, Music.

### Rhythm Training and Appreciation

There are different approaches for understanding rhythm. The Orff-Schulwerk process is one that is meeting success. It is a sequential approach to music education that uses all the elements of music (rhythm, melody, form, timbre, and harmony) in the development of conceptual understandings. Movement is one aspect. Teachers should explore a variety of approaches to this subject.

The teacher can contribute to rhythm training and appreciation through dance by following these guidelines.

1. Be thoroughly familiar with the music used for any specific dance, in order to
   a. Give verbal cues in the correct rhythm.
   b. Give the starting cue at the appropriate time.
   c. Cue the group with regard to the length of the musical introduction before the dance begins.
2. Direct the group to clap out difficult rhythms.
3. Point out rhythmic changes in the music and allow time for listening to the transitions from one part to another.
4. Point out and allow the class to listen to particular instruments or qualities in the music that help them remember the dance.
5. Provide frequent opportunities for student identification of music rather than announcing the dance.
6. Plan the program to include interesting cultural contrasts in music and dance.
7. Use words and meanings to folk songs that accompany dance.
8. Add significant authentic sounds to the recorded music, such as:
   a. Appropriate shouts or claps.
   b. Appropriate percussion instruments, such as tambourine or drum.
   c. Appropriate words or yodeling.
9. Explain meanings of music or dance and add highlights of folklore or background information.
10. Allow sufficient practice and review of dances so that the group can know dances well.

## Dance Style

### The Beautiful Dancer

A beautiful dancer is one of the most satisfying sights to watch. It is really not the intricate steps or figures that are noticed, but rather the rhythmical way the dancer seems to glide around the floor. There is an alertness, a vitality, a strength, and a beauty that transmits the feeling of complete control over the entire body.

The dancer receives more pleasure by continuously striving for the special style that makes each dance—square dance, tango, country western, Scottish reel—different.

It is as important to execute the style and mannerisms inherent in the dance of any country as it is to be able to dance the steps and pattern sequences. If twirls, whoops, and yells are added to every dance, the dances lose their individuality and become uninteresting. Without care, a fast clogging routine blurs into the intricate Slavic Kolos.

## Ear and Ankle Alignment

The subtle thought of maintaining ear and ankle alignment in an easy, natural way gives a person the poise and confidence so rightfully desired by all. The dancer who practices this secret of body balance will not tire as easily. Dancers who adopt the "ear to ankle lineup" as a slogan, whether dancing a favorite folk dance, in a square dance set, or on the ballroom floor, will have more assurance of what to do and how to do it, will wear their dress (costume) with greater charm and distinction, and will have a great deal more fun. The body carriage adds style to the dance pattern performed and gives the dancer that "finished look."

3

## Good Posture—Key to Body Balance and Control

1. Keep yourself upright—do not lean forward or backward. Do not stick out in the rear.
2. Keep your weight up—not dragging over your feet. This cultivates that "light on your feet" feeling.
3. Keep yourself a moving weight—alert all the way through your body—not planted on every spot you take.
4. Transfer weight smoothly and evenly from foot to foot without unnecessary motion of the hips from side to side or of the body up and down.
5. Move on a narrow base with the feet and legs close together.
6. Practice walking backward—the woman must learn to keep her balance when taking long, gliding steps backward.
7. Keep your eyes off the floor and the feet.
8. Bend the ankles, the knees, and the hips when executing a dip—not the back and head. The trunk is held erect.
9. Be at ease but in complete control of all parts of the body.
10. Relax, listen to the music, and *enjoy* dancing!

## Achieving Appropriate Style

One needs to make a conscious effort to develop style. Observation of dancers who have good style is a starting point; careful analysis and application must follow.

1. The expression on the dancer's face should reflect enthusiasm and a friendly, relaxed attitude. Dance with joy and pride.
2. Proper body mechanics are influenced by optimum posture. Age, body type, and personality influence the style, but still the goal is the same: smoothness, graceful carriage, and appropriate action for the dance. The position (contact) of the arms and hands for the different positions influence the style. *Resistance*, or "weight," is essential in partner dances. The tendency to stare at one's partner is uncomfortable for both, but occasional eye contact and focus toward partner or over partner's shoulder is important. Refer to dance walk, leading and following, and closed position in Chapter 8, Social Dance, for specific details as they are fundamental to style.
3. The blending of one step or figure to the next is important. The body position adjusts in preparation for a different step, figure, or direction. Smaller footsteps frequently solve some basic problems.

4. A study of different nationalities, their culture, and their way of life all give the dancer a broader understanding of the movement itself. Consider the influence of the costumes on the dance movement. For instance, tight jeans and large silver belt buckles have an influence on country western dance style.
5. Consider the movement of a particular ethnic group and look carefully at their method of walking and their body movement. Is the upper body flexible or rigid above the waist? Basic body movements tend to reflect basic feelings and attitudes. Do they move quickly or slowly? Are they "happy go lucky," temperamental, quiet, or reserved?

## Teaching Style

Some already have an innate sense of how to achieve style or have had a fair amount of dance training. Here the focus is making the dance style unique.

The average dancer has difficulty developing style and may feel that style is a nebulous thing or that the dance is for "fun" and is an end in itself.

1. The teacher must consciously incorporate the element of good style in his or her teaching, whether it's for a one-night stand, a class, or a performance.
2. The teacher, by virtue of his or her own posture, style of movement, and exemplification of different styles, sets an example—a visual one—that stimulates the dancer in an indirect way. A teacher should take every opportunity to attend workshops given by ethnic dance teachers to learn style firsthand. A live experience surpasses every written description.
3. The careful selection of music for each dance is important. A recording with native instruments, quality live music, and arrangements that are versatile and interesting all add flavor to the dance and encourage the dancer to aspire to better dancing.
4. In an atmosphere of gym shorts and tennis shoes, the teacher is challenged to promote appropriate style. All teachers know how much they may request students to bring shoes that will slide more easily and clothing that could be worn for informal dancing.
5. Special clothing frequently enhances the dance. Full skirts are very much a part of Mexican dances and square dances. The opanci—a soft, leather, moccasin-type shoe worn in Slavic dancing—allows for the rolling forward and backward action of the feet. This specific type of footwear allows the feet to respond closely to the Slavic style. The movement pattern of the dance frequently relates to the costumes of the period and nationality.
6. The teacher should experience greater success in developing style among dancers when only a few specific suggestions are made for each dance presented.
7. The teacher should point out the exact position of hands in relation to the waist and clothing; the action of hands and arms as in the manipulation of a skirt; any unusual body position, as in arching the upper torso in a draw step; the position and interaction of the individual in relation to partner and group; the details of footwork in terms of length of step, foot mechanics, and quality of step; the amount of energy expended in a movement; and the facial expression, including the focus of the eyes and the direction of the head.
8. The teacher should invite dance studio professionals, club dancers, foreign students, or community ethnic groups to dance with the students on special occasions or show films or videotapes of special styles. A visual experience with the real flavor of a dance often encourages dancers.
9. The use of mirrors and/or videotapes gives dancers an opportunity to see themselves and study specific movements.

10. Sometimes, if the teacher actually moves the dancers' arms or heads in the desired pattern, a kinesthetic sense of the movement is established, which is more meaningful than a verbal or a visual explanation.
11. The discipline that results from polishing a specific dance for an audience has a carry-over value for individual dancers as, subconsciously, they tend to apply better body control, precision, focus, and projection in their future dancing. Their attitudes and emotional responses are also different. To perform for others stimulates dancers to accept the demands of repetitive practice and achieve at a higher level. Even costuming excites and brings pleasure to the dancer.

# AMERICAN DANCE SAMPLER

*The dances covered in this chapter are those that the people—"the plain folk," "society," "young folk," "old folk," and "breadwinners"—enjoyed in the past for their own pleasure. Yesterday's social dances are today's folk dances.*

American dances come from several sources: the country dance tradition of England and Scotland, as evidenced by the contra dances; the square and circle dances of New England; the Kentucky running sets of Appalachia; the play party games; the dances of the French court; the Spanish-Mexican dances in the Southwest and early California; and the syncopated rhythms of the African Americans.

The dance scene in western Europe in the 1600s and 1700s was the foundation of American social dance tradition. English country dances, called *contree-danses*[1] by the French, were then the rage in England and France. The settlers brought these dances, the progressive longways for "as many as will" and the square formation, to the New World. There are records of morris and court dances, too.

Country dancing in the United States was the primary recreation for all classes. The majority of the settlers in the North were lower and middle class. In the South some had more money and also had the assistance of the slaves to work the land, which meant they

1. *Contree-danse* was shortened through usage to *contre. Contre* dances were square and longways. In those days a "contre dance" (country dance) could be either formation. In 1918, Elizabeth Burchenal's *American Country Dances* book reflects "twenty-eight Contra Dances," quadrille, longways, and Sicilian circle formation. Almost all the dances were from New England and reflected the notion that the terms *country dance* and *contra dance* were synonymous. At some point "contra dance" came to be applied only to progressive longway dances.

had more time for amusements. During the colonial period the upper class eventually began to dance the dances of the European courts.

# INFLUENCES ON AMERICAN DANCES

## Dances from the European Courts to the American Ballrooms

Historians refer to the period of seventeenth and eighteenth century as the Age of Enlightenment. Everything was ordered: for example, the architecture, the nomenclature of flora and fauna by Linnaeus, the box hedges and the formal gardens, and even the dances of the courts. France was usually thought of as the center of the Enlightenment, and French was the established language of international diplomacy, culture, and polite society. In matters of dress, literature, art, architecture, and home furnishings, London set cultural models and standards that were accepted by all the colonies. The wealthy colonists sent their children "home" to England to be educated. With this cultural flow, it was natural for the latest court dances to be very much a part of American society balls. Through mimicry, the bonded servants and slaves transplanted the court dances into their culture.

Before the advent of the waltz, the sophisticated, polished group dances with set figures, such as the minuet and cotillion[2] (sometimes referred to as the German dance), were the most popular dances at the balls. European music was commonly used in the American ballroom. The minuet, based on triple meter, appeared in many formations: two men and a woman, longway sets (Ford 1943, 96), quadrille sets (Ford 1941, 35), and later as a couple dance (Ford 1943, 112). Every action was studied. The stately, stylized posturing, promenading, deep bows, and curtseys of the minuet are an excellent example of how the dress of the day influenced a dance. The elaborate headdresses and powdered wigs, the heavy panniered skirts of the women, and the lace cuffs falling below the wrists and the brocade knee britches of the men reflected the style and the pattern of the minuet. The Oxford Minuet is one of the variations of the minuet still danced today. The gavotte, closely related to the minuet, preceded such familiar American round dances as the Badgers Gavotte and Glowworm Gavotte.

The waltz, the polka, and the Varsouvienne arrived from Europe on the social dance scene and sent couples whirling around the dance floor. The dancing master established his trade and traveled from town to town to teach the finer points of dance. During this period, books about dance were published in America, such as *The Art of Dancing*, written by Edward Ferrero and published by Dick Fitzgerald in 1859.

## The Unique Contributions of African Americans

In the history of European dance, Spanish-Moorish dances express African characteristics, as do the musical rhythms of tambourines, castanets, and stringed instruments. Some Catholic fiesta dances from the Middle Ages have links with Africa. Indirectly, the African influence was brought to the New World by the Europeans.

As a direct influence, consider the 8 million Africans who were imported as slaves during the seventeenth and eighteenth centuries. Africans in the South brought with them the most primitive instrument of all—the human body. Bare feet stomped, hands clapped, and voices sang, albeit aboard a slave ship, on the auction block, or on their white master's plantation. Dancing, whether by command or choice, furnished a meaningful link with the past and a temporary escape from the present.

Dancing depended on the whims of white owners. Some encouraged dancing and even provided the fiddle, thus recognizing dance as a means of entertainment for both the African Americans and their owners. A good fiddler was prized by his owner not only for his ability to play for plantation balls, but also for the higher price he brought at auction. It was common for African American musicians to furnish music for dancing at the Big House, and many times they also called out the dance figures.

Whereas Europeans traditionally accent the first beat of a measure, African Americans accent the second beat. Soon beats were skipped and the accent was placed on unexpected counts. This different accent is now labeled syncopation. As the result of an uprising in 1739, slaves were forbidden to use drums, so they transferred their rhythm to their feet, shook tambourines (perhaps acquired from the Spanish Creoles of the South), clacked bones (like castanets), and changed the African bonja (gourd with strings) to the banjo.

African American dancing was generally of two kinds: dance movements that pantomimed animals and highly acrobatic movements that required endurance and skill. The Pigeon Wing, Buzzard Lope, and Turkey Trot mimed animal movement and, as in the case of the Buzzard Lope, acted out the story of a buzzard seeking and finding food. The buck and the jig dances were of the individual acrobatic type

2. Although spelled *cotillon* in French, the preferred spelling of this word in the United States is cotillion and is the form used throughout *Dance A While*.

and were the objects of dance contests sponsored by the white owners. The Cake Walk, although used in contests, was mostly a festival dance common at harvest or crop-over times. Some of the dances were done with a container of water placed on the head—a continuation of the African custom of carrying burdens in this manner.

The house servants were the link between the Big House and the field hands in matters of manners and fashions. It was through them that the field hands learned the fashionable quadrilles, cotillion, reels, and big circles of the day. In the latter days of slavery, white influence was very apparent in black dance.

African Americans enjoyed dancing on special occasions such as Christmas, corn shucking, quilting bees, weddings, and funerals, but most of all on Saturday nights. Saturday night was a celebration of the end of the work week and was looked forward to and sung about in the fields all week in anticipation. Dances included set dances (squares), quadrilles, jigs, cutting the pigeon wings, Cake Walk, and Virginia Reel.

From the days before the American Civil War came such folk dances as Juba, Ole Aunt Kate, Jimmie Rose, Brother Eprum, Got Corn, and Gone On. Juba was quite famous in Georgia and the Carolinas. It was considered a simplified version of the African *Giouba.* The Shout and Ring Shout were sacred dances that remained on the plantations and in the Protestant churches. Shuffling, clapping, and singing in a ring that circled around and around was a way of retaining some vestige of their African heritage.

New dances continue to appear from the African American culture's never-ending creativity. African Americans have made a major contribution to American music and dance.

## The Spanish-Mexican Influence

The explorers and colonizers from Spain came across the Caribbean to Mexico and Central and South America and eventually to the American Southwest and California. Although they tried to colonize New Mexico during the 1500s, Spanish rule and culture were not established there until 1692. The New Mexican colonial dances, Spanish in origin, also reflect the influence of the native Pueblo Indians of the area. Although both the Spanish and the English claimed California, the first settlement, in San Diego in 1769, was Spanish and the Franciscan fathers soon established some 21 missions along the coast.

Two types of Spanish dance were brought to America: the classical dance by Spanish artists who set up schools in the East and the dances of the people brought along by the colonists, which were later influenced by the native Mexicans. The second type is seen mostly in the Southwest and California. The early isolation of these territories resulted in the dances becoming well established, thus retaining their European characteristics. The music and dance forms were the social dances of the settlers during this era. El Jarabe, El Fandango, La Bamba, and the minuet were some of the oldest dances. Song games such as El Burro and El Caballo, and the fandangos, *bailes,* and fiestas were all a part of this early tradition.

## Dance Styles of the People

As America was settled, the dance cultures blended together to form several "American" dance styles. The same dance steps from Europe took on an American flavor, while others transformed into something completely unique to America, such as Appalachian clogging. There is a great variety of dance styles, some traditional and others more contemporary. This section will give a brief overview of the great variety of American dances presented in *Dance A While.*

### Play Party Games

Play party games, sometimes referred to as folk games, are actually dances. They were developed mostly by the early settlers in Tennessee, Kentucky, West Virginia, and Ohio, and traveled westward with the pioneers. The dancers made their own music by singing the verses, and the people on the sidelines joined in the song, clapping their hands and stamping their feet to add to the merriment of the occasion. See page 65 for information on play party games.

### A Selection of American Dances

This section begins with the Grand March, a wonderful, nonthreatening way to organize partners, and then moves on into square and contra dances.

American square dance is truly a product of American culture, although it originated with the quadrilles of the French court and the country dances of England and Scotland. The became the caller who cued the dancers and established the rhythm of the dance with a running pattern of rhymes along with figure commands. See Chapter 5 for the history of square dance.

The English longway dances, Irish cross-road dances, and Scottish reels are the backbone of American contra dancing. Contra dancing was best known in New England. It is currently enjoying a surge of popularity all over the United States and the world. For the history of contra dance, see Chapter 6.

### Nonpartner Dances

Nonpartner dances like Ten Pretty Girls have dramatically increased in popularity since World War II, and even more so since the 1980s and 1990s.

Today the trend for line dances with set patterns to peppy tunes like Twelfth Street Rag, or dances like Amos Moses, the Hustle, and Cowboy Boogie, have all become a part of the scene.

### Partner Dances and Mixers

The American dancing public quickly adopted the waltz, the polka, the schottische, and the Varsouvienne as their favorites. From these couple dances, the popular round dance movement was born. Newly arranged dances done to popular tunes based on basic steps appeared regularly. After World War II, this practice mushroomed. A similar situation occurred in the 1600s: when John Playford's *English Dancing Master* first appeared, it contained 104 dances; 17 editions later, 918 dances were included. With the mass of newly composed American round dances, the prompter has again appeared on the scene to cue the dancers through the sequence. The old favorites persist and are referred to as old-time dances or pattern dances. The newly composed ones are here today, gone tomorrow.

### Cajun Dance

Cajun dance is an excellent example of a dance tradition whose roots go back to France. In 1604 the French colony of Acadie was established in Nova Scotia. Eventually the colonists were deported and a large number migrated to Louisiana. Cajun music and dance is a live tradition that has evolved from contact with the French, Spanish, English, black Creoles, East Texans, even rock and roll. Only a few dances remain, but they are very popular. Refer to Cajun dance on page 120.

### Country Western Dance

Country western dance is a natural, happy response to country western music. The dancers instinctively adapt old folk dances, square dance moves, and social dance patterns to the music. See page 125 for a more detailed discussion about country western dance.

### Hawaiian Folk Dance

Hawaii was the 50th state to be admitted to the Union. Hawaiian dance and music are based on poetic legends that continue to perpetuate Hawaiian history down through the generations. Basic movement patterns are presented along with dances that tell a story. See page 140 for a brief history of Hawaiian dance.

The diversity of American traditional folk dance continues to flourish as a means of understanding our heterogeneous heritage. And it allows countless opportunities for social exchange and recreation. Yes, American dance is alive and doing well!

## Music

The tunes for American dance came from the Old World, dance patterns blending with the new environment, variants and new dances arising with westward expansion, and transmission from generation to generation. Eventually, new tunes also were created for dance.

The violin (fiddle) has long been the traditional instrument for dance accompaniment. In New England the transverse or German flute was also used along with the violin in the late eighteenth century. The banjo, the guitar, the string bass, and the harmonica are frequently parts of the musical group. Different sections of the country favored special instruments, usually developed from the settlers' own creativity, for they were long accustomed to "makin' do" with whatever they had and using substitutes. The mountain folk of Appalachia made a corn-stalk fiddle for their children; a long-necked gourd became a "banjer"; and the mouth harp, a small whistle imitating a recorder, and the dulcimer were used. But the fiddle was their favorite. In the absence of musicians, the hand clapping and foot stomping of spectators and/or the patter rhymes of the caller established a rhythm and excitement for square dancers. Play party games illustrate a group of courting dances that move to the joyous singing of the dancers. Military brass bands were popular in America in the mid-1800s for fancy balls, but for the parlor or drawing-room a piano or a violin alone was preferred. A combination of two violins, flute, clarinet, cornet, and string bass was used, however, in larger rooms.

One way or another, if the people wanted to dance, they made their own music even when a musician was not present. The record player and tape recorder make it possible for more people to dance to good authentic recordings. But live music for recreational folk dancing is growing. It is vibrant and stimulating.

## Dress

The clothing that a particular class of people wore during a particular era is the clue to what they wore for dancing. The lower classes and the working classes have traditionally worn garments that fit more loosely and allow greater freedom of movement. The construction and the material of shoes determined the action of the feet (for example, the boots of a cowboy). Fancy ball gowns represent just one class of American society. Wigs and panniers were worn in colonial times, hoops in antebellum and Civil War times, and bustles in the 1870s and 1880s. The garments definitely restricted the movement of the dancers. Probably one of the greatest changes in style for women occurred when Irene

Castle wore clothing of lightweight material and full skirts, thus setting a casual style.

Today, almost anything goes as long as the dancer is comfortable. Whether dancers wear dresses, slacks, jeans, or shorts, they are more concerned about dancing for fun and are likely to wear what their peers do. But without a doubt, the graceful movement of a full skirt for women enhances many a dance.

## A Social Occasion

Dancing is a social occasion. It is a time to visit, to greet, to meet new people, to court, and to celebrate. Whenever people gathered together for barn raisings or quilting parties, the dancing began when the work was accomplished. Different parts of the country had their traditions, but, from the beginning, pushing back the furniture in the kitchen (New England) or dancing on the porch (Appalachia) was a common practice. Eventually, the school house, the Grange, the barn, and, in the warmer climates of California and the Southwest, the courtyard, allowed for more couples on the floor. To be sure, the upper level of society had their ballrooms and others had their dance halls and saloons. But for a large segment of America, dancing was a family affair. The stories of bundling children down at square dances on the frontier are common. With the advent of nightclubs, children were no longer part of the adult dance scene. Granges, community clubs, some churches, and some ethnic groups sponsor dances at which children are welcome.

Although the dancing masters helped to establish the etiquette of the period for the upper class, the plain folk were also concerned with courtesy in dance. It is interesting to note the presence of the "address, honor, and salute" in the dances of the court (minuets, lancers, quadrilles) and the absence of them in the Kentucky running set and play party games. "Honor your partner" is part of the square dance tradition; yet it is absent in the big circle, contra, and Sicilian circle.

The social dances are a vital part of the school recreational program. More churches today incorporate dancing activities into their recreational programs. And dance clubs and dance halls specialize in different kinds of social dance.

## Revival of Folk Traditions

Prior to World War I, folk traditions began to be revived. Folk dance was introduced in public schools and was encouraged by the efforts of Henry Ford and the activities of the WPA (Works Progress Administration) during the Depression. After World War II there was another surge of interest in international folk dancing and particularly square dancing. In the 1990s, ballroom dancing, especially swing, returned to popularity. Contra, country western, and line dancing became popular as well. Currently, Lindy Hop, salsa, zydeco, and hip-hop dancing are going strong.

*Country dancing* is a term that has returned to common usage. The cornerstone to the revival of old-time country dancing is live music. Contra and square dances dominate the program with a few round dances, ranging from a waltz to a lively polka, with mixers sprinkled in. Because dancing is definitely a social occasion, dancers change partners after every contra dance or after two square dances. The dancers enjoy variety but do not care to remember sequences from one week to the next. The caller gives a quick walk-thru and away they go.

More opportunities for the family to dance together are created. Dance programs and family camps consider the range of abilities. Adults who have had their children later like having the family dance together. More dances are scheduled for seniors. They enjoy the dances of the 1940s and also pattern dances.

## The Melting Pot versus Ethnic Identity

The colonists, the immigrants, the explorers, the slaves—each brought their culture and their dance with them, blending their ways with the New World as they established roots. Many were anxious to lose their Old World identity and their old languages and traditions and take on the new ways quickly. Yet others clung together, still holding fast to their traditions and continuing to pass these down to their children even while they learned the American way of life. The Greek communities illustrate this point well, particularly at their weddings and baptisms.

The concept of the melting pot dominated American thinking until around 1940. Then interest in ethnic identity, particularly among the minorities, began to grow. Native Americans, Hispanics, and African Americans have received in recent years considerable federal assistance to reinforce their ethnic heritages. As a result, other ethnic groups have found a rekindled interest in keeping their traditions alive and meaningful, including music, dance, dress, and art.

All Americans have benefited from this movement. Each group has greater pride and all Americans have gained a greater understanding and appreciation for the contributions that each group has made to society.

# PLAY PARTY GAMES: DANCES FOR CHILDREN

It would be difficult to find an activity that could provide more sociability than play party and singing games. These dances provide 100 percent opportunity for participation. They feature locomotor movements such as walking, running, skipping, and jumping instead of intricate steps that need to be learned before one can dance. Many require no partners; however, where partners are required, they provide frequent exchange, thus enhancing group sociability.

## Dance Me a Song

Play party and singing games were popular during pioneer days in the South and Midwest. Their natural habitat was Tennessee, Kentucky, Ohio, and West Virginia, and they were carried to the western states by migrating pioneers. They flourished, many in original form, in the Ozarks and Texas. Originally religion played an important part in the popularity of these dances. Many religious groups opposed dancing as wicked and the fiddle as an instrument of the devil. However, since parents and grandparents had enjoyed these activities during their "courting days," singing, clapping and stamping activities were considered free of their suspected evil.

The simplicity, the social interchange, and the opportunity for young people to "kick up their heels" all contributed to the spread of play party games, particularly in rural America where people had to rely on their own resourcefulness for their amusements.

The songs and figures of many play party games originally came from Scotland, England, Ireland, and Germany, where they were among the customs and traditions that the early settlers brought with them from the Old Country.[3] Similar types of dances, such as Old Dan Tucker, Paw Paw Patch, Bingo, Yan-kee Doodle, and Shoo Fly, are thoroughly American. They were passed from one generation to the next by word of mouth, and, of course, many versions of a song or a dance appeared for the same tune. Today, many of these same play party games are kept alive as children's dances in elementary schools or by fun-loving recreational leaders who incorporate them into events and parties for young people, suggesting some of the charm and dramatics that accompany the dance. With this spirit, modern dancers enjoy play party games just as much as the pioneers did and continue the tradition of passing them down from generation to generation.

Directions for the dances are given with the song verses. The dance movements are simple figures, for example, circle left or right as a group. It is a goal that everyone will sing and dance at the same time. At first, having a recording of the song to practice with is recommended. When students are comfortable with the movements, singing should be added.

3. For example: Ach Ja, Germany; Ja Saa, Norway; A Hunting We Will Go, England; Pop Goes the Weasel, England.

# Bingo

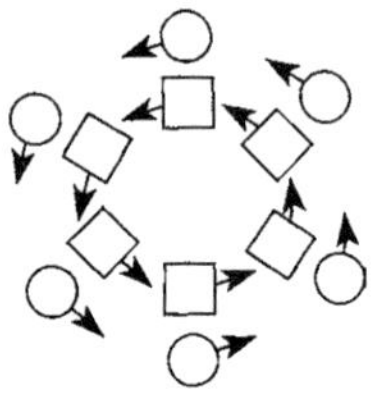

**CD:** Folk Dance Vol. 56

**Formation:** Couples in a double circle facing counterclockwise. Girls on boys' right.

**Level:** Beginning 1

## Directions FOR THE DANCE

| | *Verse* | *Action* |
|---|---|---|
| 1 | There was a farmer had a dog,<br>And Bingo was his name-o | Couples walk around the circle counterclockwise |
| 2 | (Spell out letters)<br>B-I-N-G-O!<br>B-I-N-G-O!<br>B-I-N-G-O! | Girls step in front of partner to face him. Girls are now facing clockwise, boys counterclockwise. Partners pass each other offering left hand to next oncoming dancer. Continue grand right and left spelling out the letters. On the last letter "O," keep this person as a new partner. |
| 3 | And Bingo was his name-o! | Turn to face original direction and repeat from the beginning. |

# *Brown-Eyed Mary*

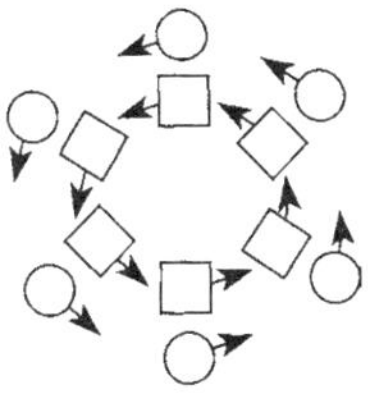

**CD:** Folk Dance Vol. 56

**Formation:** Couples in a double circle facing counter-clockwise. Girls on boys' right.

**Level:** Beginning 1

## Singing Call

**Brown-eyed Mary**

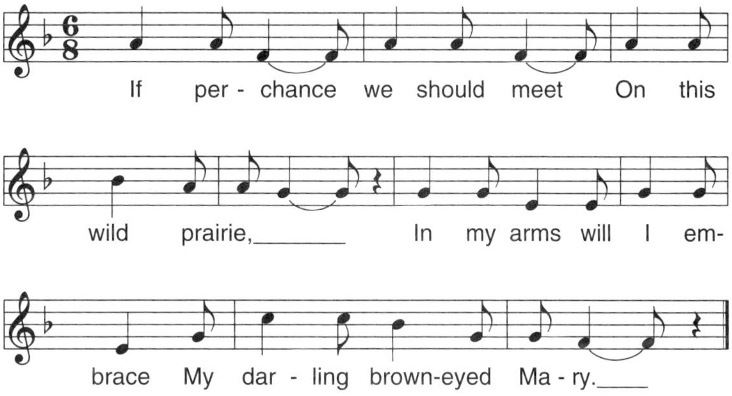


## *Directions* FOR THE DANCE

| | *Verses* | *Action* |
|---|---|---|
| 1 | If per-chance we should meet,<br>On this wild prairie,<br>In my arms will I embrace<br>My darling brown-eyed Mary. | Partners promenade around the circle. |
| 2 | Turn your partner halfway 'round. | Partners join right hands and turn halfway around so that boys face counterclockwise. |
| 3 | Turn your opposite lady. | Boys join left hands with the lady who was behind him and turn her completely around. |
| 4 | Turn your partner halfway 'round. | Join right hands with original partner, turn her completely around. |
| 5 | And promenade your right hand lady. | Take the lady behind as a new partner and repeat from the beginning. |

# Captain Jinks

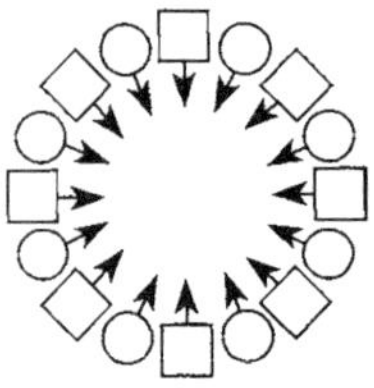

**CD:** Folk Dance Vol. 12
**Formation:** Couples in a single circle, facing center. Girls on partner's right.
**Level:** Beginning 1

## Singing Call

## *Directions* FOR THE DANCE

| | *Verses* | *Action* |
|---|---|---|
| 1 | When Captain Jinks comes home at night,<br>He claps his hands with all his might. | Clap hands. |
| 2 | Salute your partner, smile so bright,<br>For that's the style of the army. | All bow to partners. |

| | | |
|---|---|---|
| 3 | Join your hands and forward all,<br>Backward all, backward all<br>For that's the style of the army.<br>When Captain Jinks comes home at night, | Join hands in a circle and march forward and backward twice. |
| 4 | The gentleman passes to his right. | Gentlemen cross over in front of partner and take partner of man on the right. |
| 5 | Salute your partner, smile so bright,<br>For that's the style of the army | Swing the lady once around and keep her for a partner. |
| 6 | Join your hands and forward all,<br>Backward all, backward all,<br>Join your hands and forward all,<br>For that's the style of the army. | Promenade counter-clockwise until song is finished, than start over again. |

# Looby Loo

LOOBY LOO is about taking a bath in very cold water. The story goes that a little boy was used to taking a bath every Saturday night, but one night the water was very cold. His mother made a game of getting in one limb at a time to make taking a cold bath fun and possible!

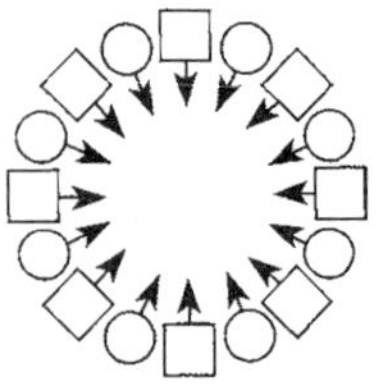

**CD:** Melody House Kim9126 CD
**Formation:** Single circle.
**Level:** Beginning 1

## Singing Call

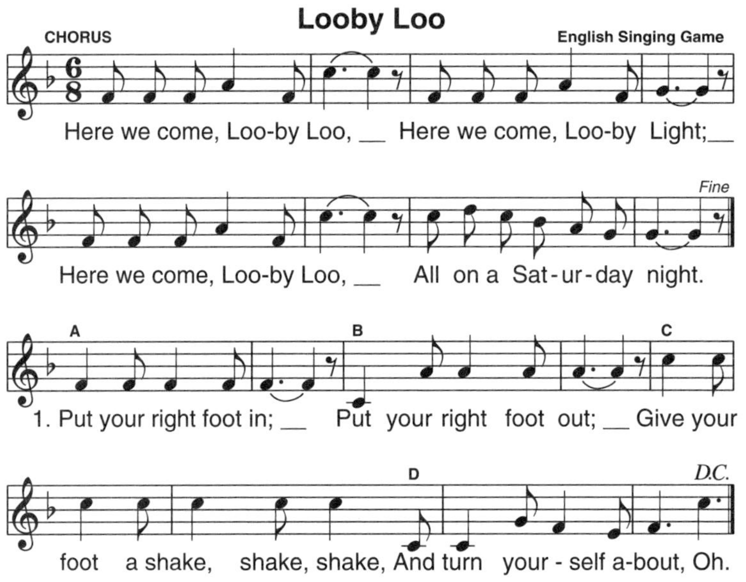


## *Directions* FOR THE DANCE

1. Dancers join hands and skip or walk around singing the chorus.
2. At the end of the chorus, dancers put their right foot forward in the circle, then backward out of the circle, toe touching floor, then shake foot vigorously and turn completely around, right arm leading.
3. Repeat chorus, and after each chorus vary the lyrics and motion as follows:
   Put your left foot in
   Put your right hand in
   Put your left hand in
   Put your head way in
   Put your whole self in

# *Pop Goes the Weasel*

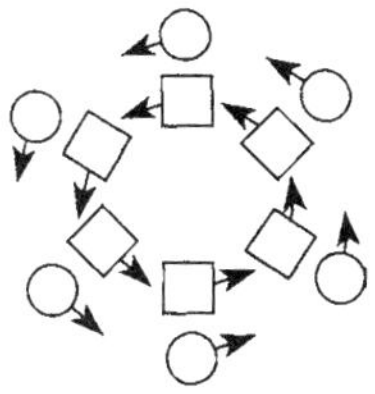

**CD:** Folk Dance Vol. 19

**Formation:** Single circle of couples, girls to the right of the boys. Extra dancers in the center.

**Level:** Beginning 1

*Lyrics:* A nickel for a spool of thread,
A penny for a needle;
That's the way the money goes,
Pop goes the weasel.

Mary's got the whooping cough,
Johnny's got the measles;
That's the way the money goes,
Pop goes the weasel.

You buy the baby clothes,
I'll buy the cradle;
That's the way the money goes,
Pop goes the weasel.

## *Directions* FOR THE DANCE

Couples circle left and on the last line, "Pop goes the weasel," all drop hands, hook right arms, and swing around in place. Extras in the center try to snatch a partner and take a place in the circle.

# *Sandy Land*

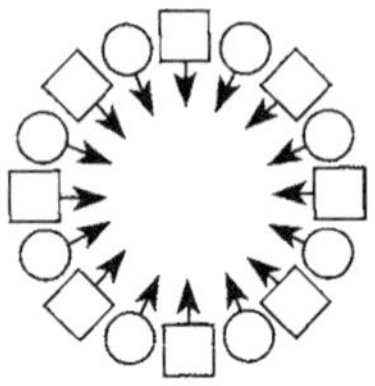

**CD:** At the Fiddler Knee
**Formation:** Single circle, by partners, facing in.
**Level:** Beginning 1

## Singing Call

*Verse 3*
Raise big taters in sandy land. (3 times)
If you can't dig'm I guess I can.
Chorus:
Make my living in sandy land. (3 times)
Ladies fare thee well.

How old are you, my pretty little miss?
How old are you, my honey?
She answered me with a ha, ha, ha.
"I'll be sixteen next Sunday."

*Verse 4*
One more river I'm bound to cross. (3 times)
'Fore I see my honey.
Chorus:
Will you marry me, my pretty little miss?
Will you marry me, my honey?
She answered with a ha, ha, ha.
"I'll run and ask my mama."

*Verse 5*
Humpback mule I'm bound to ride. (3 times)
'Fore I see my honey.
Chorus:
Hop come along, my pretty little miss.

## *Directions* FOR THE DANCE

Walk four steps to center of circle raising joined hands. Walk four steps away from center lowering hands. Repeat to center and back. Partners face and begin the grand right and left until partners meet. Hook right elbows, turn once around, and continue the grand right and left until partners meet. Take promenade position with partner and walk or skip around the circle.

# *Shoo Fly*

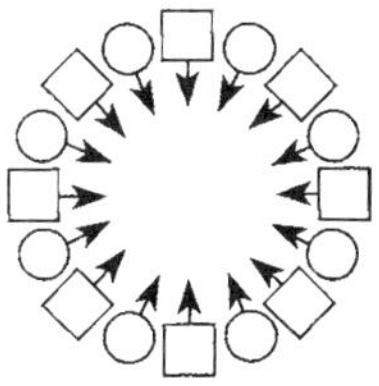

**CD:** Folk Dance Vol. 11
**Formation:** Couples form a single circle. Girls to the right of the boys.
**Level:** Beginning 1

## Directions FOR THE DANCE

| ***Lyrics*** | ***Action*** |
|---|---|
| Shoo fly don't bother me<br>Shoo fly don't bother me | Dancers take four steps to the center and back. |
| Shoo fly don't bother me<br>For I belong to somebody | Repeat to center and back. |
| I do, I do, I do, And I ain't gon-na tell you who, For I belong to somebody, | Partners join hands and turn around and back to place. |
| Yes, in-deed I do. | Boys drop right hands and turn the girl under his left arm to the boy on the left. All now have new partners for the repeat of the dance. |

*Alternate Lyrics*

Shoo fly don't bother me
Shoo fly don't bother me
Shoo fly don't bother me
For I belong to somebody
I feel, I feel, I feel
Like a morning star,
I feel, I feel, I feel
Like a morning star.

# Skip to My Lou

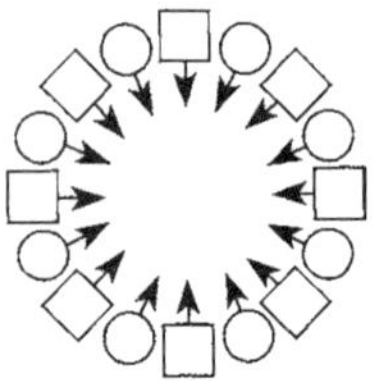

**CD:** Folk Dance Vol. 11

**Formation:** Single circle of partners facing center. Girls on partners' right. An extra dancer is in the center. Larger groups may have more extras in the center.

**Level:** Beginning 1

## *Directions* FOR THE DANCE

All sing and clap to a verse started by the center singles. Dancers in the center steal a partner and skip around the circle back to the stolen girl's (or boy's) place. Dancers whose partners were stolen immediately steal a new partner.

*Lyrics:*

I've lost my girl, now what'll I do?
(3 times)
Skip to my Lou, my dar – ling

I'll get another, a better one too; (3 times)
Skip to my Lou, my darling.

Cat's in the buttermilk, shoo, shoo, shoo
(3 times)
Skip to my Lou, my darling

Flies in the sugar bowl, shoo, shoo, shoo
(3 times)
Skip to my Lou, my darling

Little red wagon painted blue (3 times)
Skip to my Lou, my darling

Hurry up slowpoke, do, oh, do
(3 times)
Skip to my Lou, my darling

4

# The Bear Went Over the Mountain

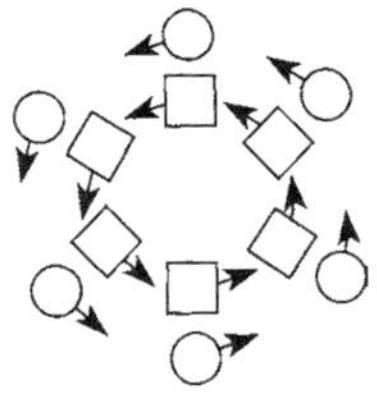

**CD:** KM-9510, or any recording of "We Won't Be Home 'Til Morning."

**Formation:** Couples in a double circle facing counterclockwise. Boys on the inside.

**Level:** Beginning 1

*Verse:*
The bear went over the mountain
The bear went over the mountain
The bear went over the mountain

*Chorus:*
To see what he could see
To see what he could see
To see what he could see

## *Directions* FOR THE DANCE

1. During singing of the verse couples walk around the circle
2. During singing of the chorus partners face, join right hands, and do a grand right and left.
3. At the end of the chorus dancers take new partners and repeat from the beginning.

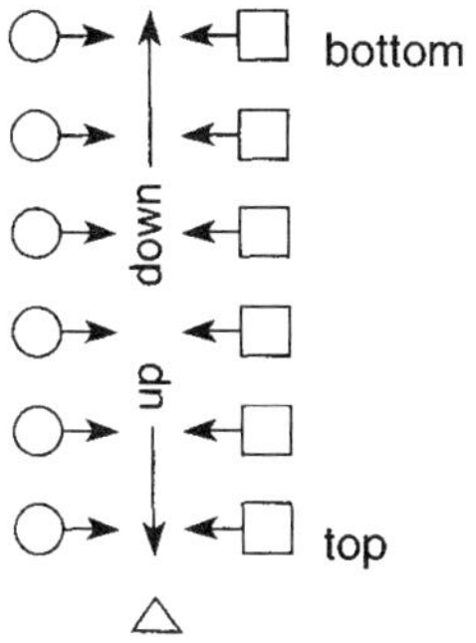


# *Alabama Gal*

ALABAMA GAL, a play party game, was taught by Jane Farwell at the Oglebay Folk Dance Camp, Wheeling, West Virginia, in 1948.

**CD:** Simple Gifts, Smithsonian Global Sounds.

**Formation:** Longway sets, men on left, ladies on right, partners facing. Large groups should be divided into sets of 16 couples or less.

**Level:** Beginning 1

## Singing Call

**Alabama Gal**

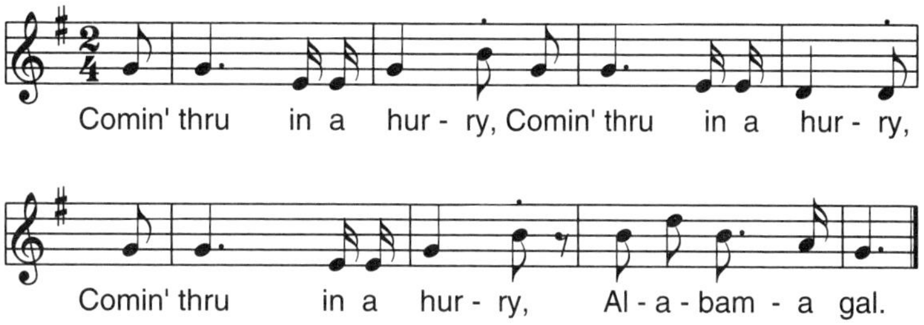


*Verse 2*
You don't know how how
You don't know how how
You don't know how how
Alabama Gal.

*Verse 3*
I'll show you how how
I'll show you how how
I'll show you how how
Alabama Gal.

*Verse 4*
Ain't I rock candy
Ain't I rock candy
Ain't I rock candy
Alabama Gal.

## *Directions* FOR THE DANCE

1. Everyone or just the caller sings the verses.
2. Head couple joins two hands, extending arms shoulder height. Slides down and back between two lines.
3. Head couple **reels** down the set by starting with a right-hand swing, once and a half. When the active couples reach the foot of the set, they join the lines.
4. As soon as all four verses have been sung, next couple starts to slide down center and back and reel. Therefore, each time the first verse is sung, a new couple starts "comin' thru in a hurry." The fun comes when a new couple begins to slide through the set while the reeling continues!

# *Nobody's Business*

NOBODY'S BUSINESS is a fun-loving American play party game. The tune is catchy and it is an excellent mixer.

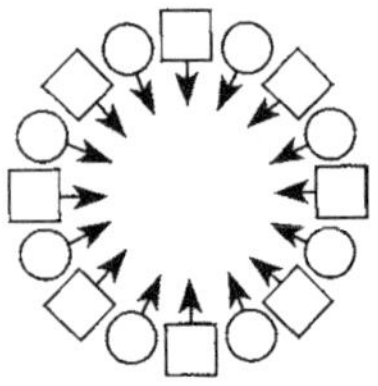

***Dance A While* CD:** "Nobody's Business."

**CD:** Folk Dance Vol #011.

**Formation:** Single circle, couples facing center, woman to right of partner, hands joined.

**Level:** Beginning 1

## Singing Call

**Nobody's Business**

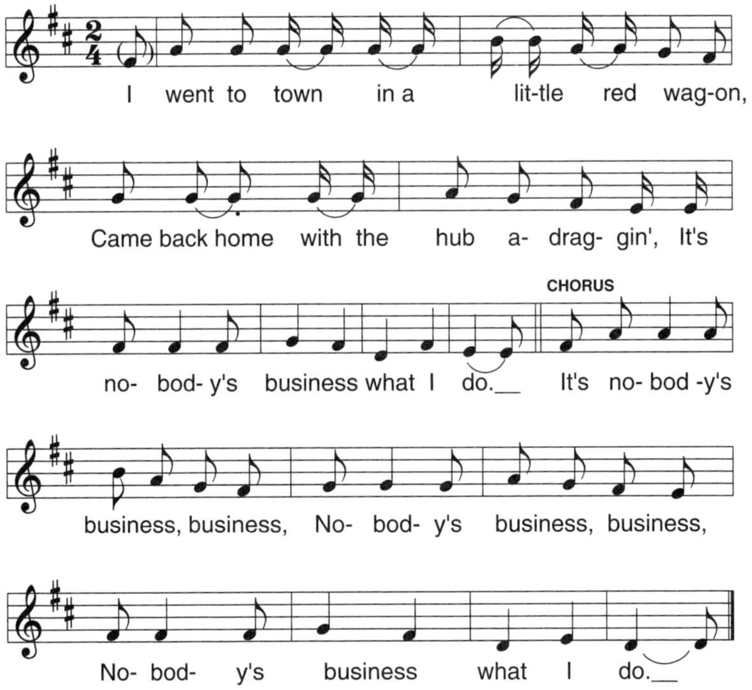


*Verse 2*
Way down yonder about a mile and a quarter,
Some old man's going to lose his daughter,
It's nobody's business what I do.

*Verse 3*
Butterbeans has killed my baby
Popcorn has killed the old lady,
It's nobody's business what I do.

*Verse 4*
I've got a wife and she's a daisy,
She won't work and I'm too lazy,
It's nobody's business what I do.

## *Directions* FOR THE DANCE

1. Everyone sings the verses with the chorus between each verse.
2. For each verse, all join hands and circle to the left, walking briskly.
3. For the chorus, release hands, partners face, ready for a grand right and left with an elbow swing. Partners hook right elbows and make one complete turn (each turn lasts one line of the chorus). Each meets the next person, men always progressing counterclockwise, women clockwise, with a left elbow swing; then the next with a right elbow swing. There are three elbow swings. Complete the last swing, men taking this one for their new partners.
4. For the next verse, all join hands and circle left. Continue alternating the action with each verse and chorus.

# A SELECTION OF AMERICAN DANCES

4

The following sampler of American dances is presented to illustrate cultural patterns, beginning in 1620 and continuing to the present. The dances included in this chapter are viable in that they trace a dance tradition, are still danced today in communities (in schools, recreational groups, and dance halls), and represent various dance formations and basic dance steps. At different times in history, each type has enjoyed great popularity in a particular area and with a special segment of society.

The dance directions for this section explain the figures that are performed as a group of people work and move together. For more information on teaching contra, refer to Chapter 6. For more information on teaching square dance, see Chapter 5.

# Grand March

LET THE DANCE BEGIN! The Grand March has long been a part of American dance tradition. At ceremonial occasions and balls, the instrumental groups would play a short concert prior to the dancing. Then the floor managers of the ball would signal for the dance to begin: the instrumentalists would play a march and the couples would begin a grand promenade around the room for the Grand March. Today, for special occasions, dance festivals, and one-night stand dance parties, the Grand March is part of the program. It may not be first; it may occur after the intermission. Dancers look forward to that moment of everyone dancing together, winding in and out from one pattern to the next.

The Grand March may be used as an end in itself, because it is impressive and stimulates group feeling, or it may be used as a means for organizing a group quickly for another activity. A Grand March is most effective when many people participate. Guests do not always arrive punctually; this fact should always be considered in scheduling a Grand March.

4

***Dance A While* CD:** "Grand March."

**Music:** Any lively march, two-step, or square dance tune.

**Position:** Escort.

**Formation:** Double circle, couples facing the line of direction, or two single files, men in one and women in the other.

**Steps:** Walk

**Level:** Beginning 1

## *Directions* FOR THE GRAND MARCH

### Leadership

The leader stands at either the front or the rear of the room. A change in pattern is indicated as the group nears the leader. It is helpful if the first two or three couples are familiar with the various figures to be used in the Grand March. Experienced couples will follow the leader's cues more easily and set the pattern for the others to follow. An assistant standing at the opposite end from the leader facilitates the flow.

### Beginning

A Grand March may be started either in couples or from two single files of individuals. The latter is particularly suited for groups not already acquainted.

1. **Two single files:** Men line up on one side of the room and women on the other. Both files face either the front or the rear of the room as indicated by the leader. **Note:** The leader must be careful to indicate the proper direction for the two files to face so that the women will be on the right side of the men when couples are formed. Each line marches toward the end of the room, turns, and marches toward the opposite line. The files meet, forming couples in escort position, ladies to the right of the men, and march down the center of the room.
2. **Couples in a double circle:** Couples in escort position form a double circle and march counterclockwise. One couple is selected as the leader and that couple, followed by the others, moves down the center of the room.

### Figures

These figures may be used in any order as long as they flow from one to the other.

1. **Single files**
   a. **Inner and outer circle.** When each couple reaches the front of the room, partners separate, men left and women right, and travel down the side of the room until they meet at the opposite end. Then the lines pass each other. The women travel on the inside, men on the outside, and go down the side of the room until they meet again at the front of the room. They pass again, the men traveling on the inside, women on the outside, and again go down the sides of the room.
   b. **The cross (X).** When each file reaches the rear corner, the leader of each file makes an abrupt turn and travels diagonally toward the front corner on the opposite side. Both files cross in the center of the room, lady crossing in front of partner. The files travel down the side of the room toward the rear corners. The diagonal cross is repeated, the man crossing in front of his partner.
   c. **Virginia Reel.** Couples move down the center in double file. When each couple reaches the front of the room, partners separate, men left, women right, and travel down the sides of the room to form two files about 10 to 15 feet apart. Both lines face each other. The head woman and the foot man meet in the middle and dance away. Then the head man and foot woman meet in the middle in like manner and dance away. This process is repeated until all have partners and are dancing.
2. **Couples**
   a. **Four, eight, or sixteen abreast.** When the couples marching down the center arrive at the front of the room, the lead couple turns to the right, marches to the side of the room, and back toward the rear of the room. The second couple turns left, the third right, and so on, and march to the side and back to the rear of the room. When they meet at the rear of the room, the two approaching couples march down the center of the room together, thus forming a group of four abreast. At the front of the room each group of four marches alternately to the right and left, down the sides and at the rear of the room they form a line eight abreast. The same procedure is followed to form lines of 16 or more abreast. After the group has formed lines of 16 abreast they may be instructed to mark time in place.
   b. **"Ring up" for squares.** If groups of eight are desired for the next activity, for example, a square dance, the couples mark time when they are eight abreast. Each line of eight then "rings up," or makes a circle.
   c. **Over and under.** When the couples are four abreast, the two couples separate at the front of the room, one turning right, the other left. When the couples meet at the rear of the room, the first couple of the double file on the right side of the room makes an arch. The first couple of the other double file goes under the arch and quickly makes an arch for the second couple they meet. All couples in both double files are alternately making an arch or traveling under an arch.
   d. **Snake out.** When the couples are eight or 16 abreast, the person on the right end of the front line leads that line in single file to the right of the column of dancers and in between lines two and three. As the person on the left end of the first line passes the person on the right end of the second line, they join hands and line two then follows line one. The leader then leads the line between lines three and four and again as the last person in the moving line passes the right end of the third line, they join hands and line three joins

*continues on next page*

with lines one and two. The moving line weaves in and out of the remaining lines and each time the person on the end of the moving line passes the right end of the next line they join hands and continue weaving in and out. After all lines have been "snaked out," the leader may lead the line in serpentine fashion around the room and eventually circle the room clockwise in a single circle, all facing the center.

e. **Danish march.** When the couples are in a double circle or double file, partners face and stand about 4 feet apart. The first couple joins hands holding arms out shoulder height and slides the length of the formation used. The second couple follows, and so on. When couples reach the end, they join the group. This may be repeated with partners standing back to back as they slide.

f. **Grand right and left.** When couples are in a single circle, partners face and start a grand right and left. This may continue until partners meet or until the leader signals for new partners to be taken for a promenade or other figure.

g. **Paul Jones.** When couples are in a single circle, any of the figures for a Paul Jones may be used. See page 84

## Ending

There is no set ending for a Grand March. However, the ending should be definite so that there is a feeling of completion and satisfaction. It may end with people in groups for the next activity or in a circle with everyone joining in a song or dancers may swing into a waltz, a polka, or some other planned activity.

# *Virginia Reel*

THE VIRGINIA REEL, known as Sir Roger de Coverley in England, was first published about 1685. This was one of many dances the colonists brought to America, and the name eventually changed to Virginia Reel. It was danced in the ballrooms and on the village greens, by all. The Virginia Reel is a contra dance that children today learn in school and fondly remember as part of their American heritage of dance. Adults enjoy the dance at one-night stands and family gatherings.

Virginia Reel is a traditional contra. It is a longways dance and there is progression (the top couple moves to the bottom at the end of the dance). The directions presented are for one of the common ways that recreational groups dance the Virginia Reel today because everyone is dancing most of the time.

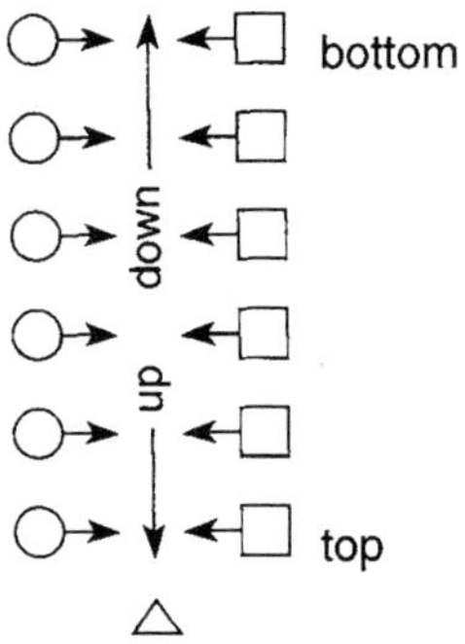


***Dance A While* CD:** "Irish Washerwoman (Virginia Reel)."

**CD:** Folkraft CD 2912-10.

**Music:** Irish jig tune such as "Irish Washerwoman."

**Formation:** Contra dance formation. Four to eight couples, partners facing.

**Steps:** Walk, slide (sashay).

**Level:** Beginning 1

## *Directions* FOR THE DANCE

Meter 6/8

| | |
|---|---|
| A1 | **Forward and bow** (8 counts). Lines walk forward, curtsey and bow to partners, and walk backward to place. |
| | **Forward and right hand 'round** (8 counts). Lines walk forward, partners join right hands, turn clockwise once around, and move backward to place. |
| A2 | **Forward and left hand 'round** (8 counts). Lines walk forward, partners join left hands, turn counterclockwise once around, and move backward to place. |
| | **Forward and two hands 'round** (8 counts). Lines walk forward, partners join two hands, turn clockwise once around, and move backward to place. |
| B1 | **Forward and do-si-do** (8 counts). Lines walk forward, partners do-si-do, and move backward to place. |
| | **Head couple sashays down the center and back** (8 counts). |
| B2 | **Head couple, right arm to partner and reels** (sequences of 8 counts). To reel, head couple hooks right elbows in middle of set and turn clockwise once and a half, separate; head man turns next woman counterclockwise in line, with left elbows hooked once around as head woman turns next man in line with left elbows hooked once around; head couple meets in middle of set, partners hook right elbows, turn clockwise once around. Head couple moves down set turning alternately next person in line with left elbow and then each other with right elbow, until they reach foot of set. |
| | **Head couple sashays back.** Partners turn each other a half-turn (now on original side), join two hands, slide to head of set. |
| | **Head couple casts off, forms an arch.** Partners separate and walk down outside of set, man left, woman right, to foot of set. Each person in line follows the head person, single file. Head couple join two hands to form an arch at foot of set. |
| | **Pass through and form your sets.** Partners join inside hands as they go through arch and promenade to head of set. Head couple is now at foot; original second couple is now head couple. |

Continue to repeat dance until couples are back to original positions. Wait for the beginning of a new phrase to repeat the dance.

**Note:** Although most figures are based on 8 counts, the number of couples in a set influences the length of the music for one complete round of the dance.

# *Grand Square Quadrille*

THE QUADRILLE ORIGINATED in the French court ballet, became established in the British Isles, and was very popular among the colonists in America. Quadrilles are still danced today, particularly in New England. The quadrille originally had six parts (Czarnowski 1950, 141), but later was shortened to five parts. A different piece of music is played for each figure, with a pause between figures for the dancers to catch their breath and an introduction of music before each figure. Eventually the quadrille was reduced to three parts. The numbering of couples differs from square dances in that the head couples are 1 and 2, side couples, 3 and 4. Quadrilles are traditionally *prompted;* that is, the caller gives the name of the figure.

Grand Square Quadrille is still danced today, particularly in New England. This version is based on a call by Bob Osgood of Sets In Order American Square Dance Society. Although the call *grand square* is known today by square dancers as one of the basics and is used as a break in square dance, the figure as such was part of many of the lancers, namely the fourth figure (Czarnowski 1950, 145).

**Music:** Any march music may be used.

**Formation:** Set of four couples in square dance formation. Couples are numbered as in square dancing today.

**Level:** Intermediate

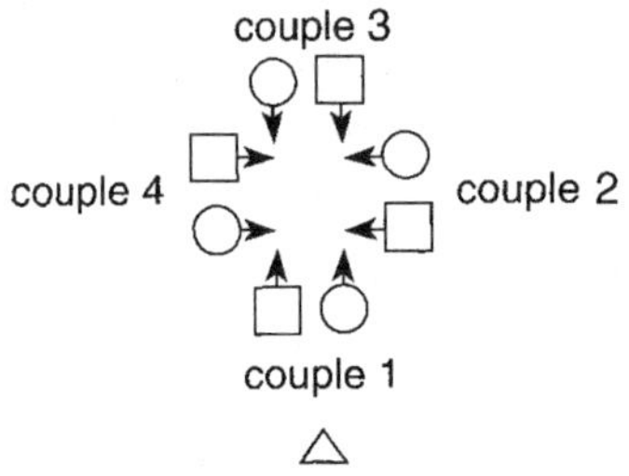


## *Directions* FOR THE DANCE

Meter 4/4

| ***Measures*** | |
|---|---|
| 1–2 | Introduction (8 counts): no action. |
| 1–8 | **Grand square** (16 counts). See Grand Square, page 173, for directions. |
| 1–8 | **Reverse grand square** (16 counts). |
| | **FIGURE I** |
| 9–12 | **Head couples right and left through and back** (16 counts). |
| 13–16 | **Side couples right and left through and back** (16 counts). |
| 9–12 | **Head couples to the right, right and left through and back** (16 counts). |
| 13–16 | **Side couples to the right, right and left through and back** (16 counts). |

**CHORUS**

1–8 **Grand square** (16 counts).

1–8 **Reverse grand square** (16 counts).

**FIGURE II**

9–12 **Head women chain over and back** (16 counts).

13–16 **Side women chain over and back** (16 counts).

9–12 **Head women to the right, chain over and back** (16 counts).

13–16 **Side women to the right, chain over and back** (16 counts).

**CHORUS**

1–8 **Grand square** (16 counts).

1–8 **Reverse grand square** (16 counts).

**FIGURE III**

9–12 **Head couples half-promenade and right and left home** (16 counts).

13–16 **Side couples half-promenade and right and left home** (16 counts).

Grand Square Quadrille, *continued*

9–12 **Head couples half-promenade right and right and left home** (16 counts). Couples 1 and 2 (couples 3 and 4) half-promenade with each other and right and left home.

13–16 **Side couples half-promenade right and left home** (16 counts). Couples 2 and 3 (couples 4 and 1) half-promenade with each other and right and left home.

**CHORUS**

1–4 **Grand square** (16 counts).

5–8 **Reverse grand square** (16 counts).

**Note:**

1. The caller prompts by giving the directions for the next maneuver on the last two to four counts of the preceding eight-count phrase.
2. Dancers dance to the music, using the exact number of beats to execute each maneuver, with action flowing from one pattern to the next.

# *Paul Jones Your Lady*

DURING THE NINETEENTH CENTURY, the group dances with set figures, like the quadrille, the lancers, and the Paul Jones, allowed for the interchange of partners. Paul Jones, formerly danced in the ballroom and frequently used as the first dance at a party, is still danced today as a lively mixer. In some parts of the West, the same dance is called Circle Two-Step or Brownee.

***Dance A While* CD:** "Boil 'Em Cabbage Down" and "Rag Time Annie."
**Music:** Any lively two-step.
**Position:** Promenade.
**Formation:** Double circle, couples facing line of direction.
**Steps:** Shuffle, two-step.
**Level:** Beginning 2

## *Directions* FOR THE MIXER

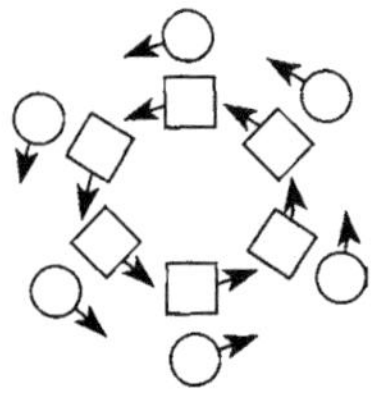

The leader calls out each figure and signals clearly. Each figure is danced briefly as it is merely a method of changing partners.

### I. PAUL JONES YOUR LADY OR PROMENADE

Couples promenade around room in one large circle.

### II. FIGURES

A. **Single circle.** Couples form a single circle, hands joined. Slide left, right, and/or shuffle to center and back. Each man takes his corner woman for a new partner.

B. **The basket.** Women form an inner circle, hands joined and slide left. Men form an outer circle, hands joined, and slide right. Both circles stop. Men raise joined hands. Women move backward through arches made by men and stand beside a man. Men lower arms. Everyone slides left, then right. Each man takes woman on right for a new partner.

C. **Across the circle.** Couples form a single circle, hands joined. Slide left, right, and shuffle to center, back, and center. Each man takes woman across the circle as a new partner.

D. **Grand right and left.** Couples form a single circle, hands joined. Slide left, right, and shuffle to center and back. Face partner and grand right and left around the circle. Each man takes woman facing him or lady whose hand he holds when leader signals for new partners.

E. **Gentlemen kneel.** Couples form single circle and face partners. Men kneel, women move in reverse line of direction, weaving in and out between kneeling men. Each man takes woman facing him when leader signals for new partners.

F. **Count off.** Double circle, couples facing counterclockwise. Women stand still and men move forward, counting off as many women as indicated by leader. Men may stand still while women move forward and count off in like manner.

### III. TWO-STEP

Couples in closed position, two-step about the room. Upon the signal "Paul Jones Your Lady," they again fall into a double circle and promenade counterclockwise around room until the signal for a new figure action is given.

# *Ninepin Reel*

NINEPIN REEL IS DANCED traditionally in America and England and was formerly known in Scotland. There are variations of figures but all have the common figure of five men circling in the center of the square and suddenly a break occurs; all choose a new partner; obviously, one is not able to claim a partner, and thus there's a new "ninepin." Some American versions have a caller who calls various square dance figures and when the call "ninepin" occurs, each man changes partners and once again there is a new "ninepin."

Elizabeth Burchenal in *American Country Dance* (1918, 61–62) has recorded two quadrille dances from New England with an extra man in the center: John Brown and Old Dan Tucker. There are dances for nine in Scotland, England, America, Germany, Sweden, and Finland with different names and many variations, from simple musical game types to very complicated figures.

This particular version was presented to Skandia Folkdance Society about 1952 by a Canadian couple attending summer school in Seattle, Washington. The pattern is similar to the English dance, Cumberland Square Eight.

***Dance A While* CD:** "St. Anne's Reel."

**Music:** Any reel music.

**Formation:** Set of four couples in square dance formation. Extra man or woman stands in middle of set and is referred to as "ninepin." In this case, directions assume "ninepin" is a man. If more than one set, arrange sets in file and line formation, so that couples sliding will dance through the neighboring sets and back.

**Steps:** Slide, buzz step, polka, shuffle.

**Level:** Beginning 2

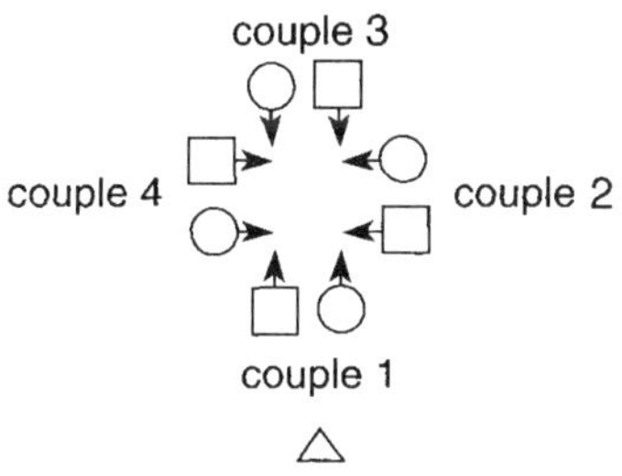


Square dance formation

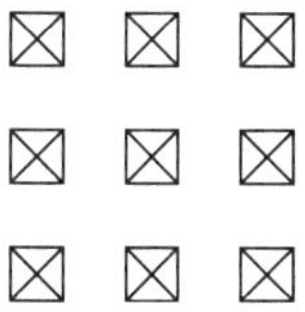

File and line formation

## *Directions* FOR THE DANCE

Meter 2/4 • Directions are the same for both woman and man, except when specially noted.

| ***Measures*** | |
|---|---|
| | **FIGURE I. SLIDES** |
| 1–4 | In closed position, head couples take eight slides (man beginning left, woman right) across set, exchanging places. Couples pass to the right of the "ninepin." If more than one set, couples may travel through |

*continues on next page*

| ***Measures*** | |
|---|---|
| | other sets in a straight line, always passing to the right of "ninepin." Couples do not turn at end of eight slides. |
| 5–8 | Head couples take eight slides (man beginning right, woman left) to return home, passing to *left* of "ninepin" (women's backs to "ninepin"). |
| 9–16 | Side couples repeat action of measures 1–8. |
| | **FIGURE II. CIRCLE LEFT AND RIGHT** |
| 17–24 | Head couples join hands in circle ("ninepin" in middle) and circle left, taking eight slides or four polka steps; circle right, taking eight slides or four polka steps. |
| 25–32 | Side couples repeat action of Figure II, measures 17–24. |
| | **FIGURE III. SWING** |
| 1–16 | "Ninepin" swings (waist swing, buzz step) woman of couple 1 (8-count swing). While "ninepin" swings, displaced partner moves to center of set and waits for each displaced partner to join him. At completion of swing, woman returns home; "ninepin" travels around set to each couple (2, 3, 4), swinging each woman and each displaced partner moves to center; women remain in home position. |
| | **FIGURE IV. CIRCLE** |
| 17–23 | At conclusion of last swing, "ninepin" travels to center to join the four men. All men join hands, circle left and right, taking polka steps or slides. *At any point, "ninepin," as he takes woman of his choice, calls "break."* Other men hurry to take new partner. Everyone swings to completion of musical phrase. Obviously, there is a new "ninepin." Couples take home position of woman to swing and to repeat dance. |
| | **FIGURE V. SWING** |
| 24–32 | All couples swing (see note 3 below). |

**Note:**

1. Ninepin Reel is obviously a rollicking, fun-loving mixer that absorbs extra people. Remember, the "ninepin" can be a man or a woman and each set can differ.
2. Everyone enjoys sliding (galloping) through more than one set, sometimes the length of the hall. Dance etiquette implies that one couple does not pass a preceding couple while galloping.
3. In Figures IV and V, if the "ninepin" is a real "swinger," he might call "break" after a couple measures of circling; whereupon there is a longer swing. On the other hand, the "ninepin" may prefer to complete the circling figure and call "break" at measure 24. The element of suspense created by the "ninepin" deliberately waiting until the last minute to indicate his choice of partner adds to the spirit of the dance.
4. Extra dancers on the sideline have been known to cut in when the "ninepin" calls "break," by casually waiting behind a couple. Someone from the original set must retreat to the sidelines or cut in on someone else at the earliest opportunity.

# *Portland Fancy*

PORTLAND FANCY is a traditional contra dance.

**CD:** Folkraft CD 2912-3.

**Music:** "Portland Fancy," Ford, Henry, *Good Morning*, 4th edition, p. 52; "Portland Fancy" and "Blackberry Quadrille," Page, Ralph, *An Elegant Collection of Contras and Squares*, pp. 78, 79.

**Formation:** Sets of four couples, contra formation, two couples facing two couples. Sets may be in a line or circle.

**Level:** Beginning 2

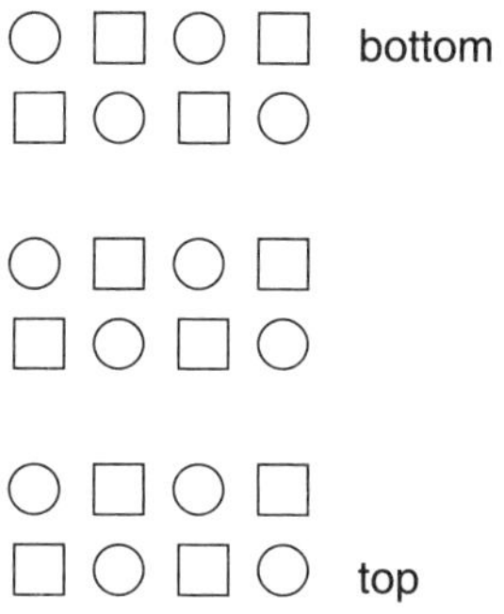


Line formation

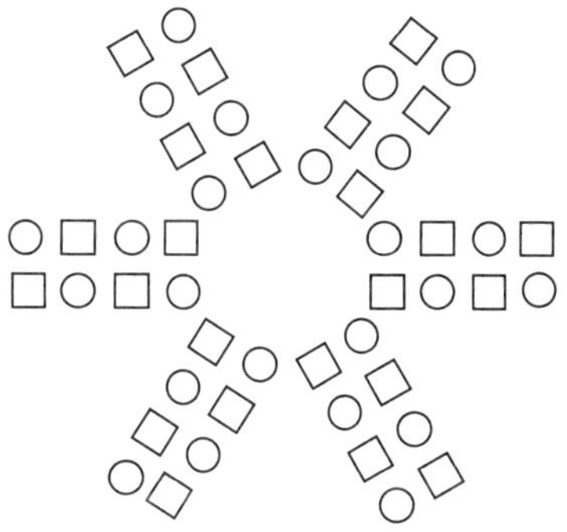

Circle formation

## *Directions* FOR THE DANCE

A1 **Circle left eight hands around** (16 counts).

A2 **Right and left thru, right and left back** (16 counts). Opposite couples, right and left.

B1 **Ladies chain over and back** (16 counts).

B2 **Forward and back** (8 counts). Join hands in line, take four steps forward and four steps back. **Forward again and pass thru and face a new foursome** (8 counts).

### Variation

Pass through two groups and face a new foursome.

# Oh Johnny

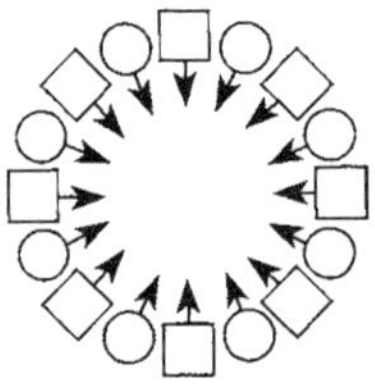

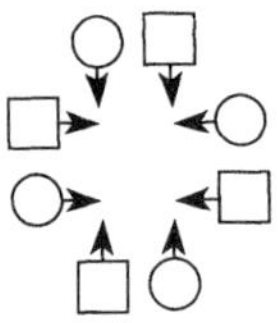

OH JOHNNY IS A POPULAR SINGING CALL that may be done as a square dance or large circle mixer.

**CD:** MACCD 2042 at www.dosado.com.

**Formation:** Single circle or square, couples facing center, woman to right of partner, hands joined.

**Steps:** Walk.

**Level:** Beginning 1

## *Directions* FOR THE MIXER

### Singing Call

**Oh, you all join hands and circle the ring.**
Circle moves clockwise.
**Stop where you are and you give her a swing.**
Men swing partners.
**Now swing that girl behind you.**
Swing corner woman.
**Go back home and**
**Swing your own if you have time.**
Swing with partners.
**Allemande left with your corner girl.**
Allemande left with corner.
**Do-sa 'round your own.**
Do-sa-do (sashay) around partner.
**Now you all run away with your sweet corner maid.**
Promenade counterclockwise with corner woman for a new partner.
**Singing, oh, Johnny, oh, Johnny, oh!**
Repeat call to end of recorded music.

4

# Red River Valley

**CD:** Folkraft CD 2911–4.
**Position:** Set of three, man between two women, arms linked.
**Formation:** Two sets of three, facing each other in large circle.
**Level:** Beginning 2

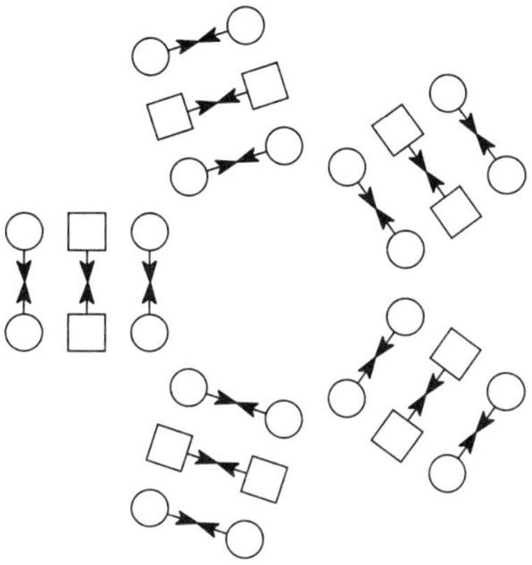

4

## *Directions* FOR THE MIXER

### Swinging Call

**VERSE 1**
**Now you lead right down to the valley.** Walk diagonally forward to right and pass opposite set to meet new set.
**Circle to the left, then to the right.** All join hands and circle left, then right.
**Now you swing with the gal in the valley.** Man swings (elbow or waist swing) right-hand woman.
**And you swing with your Red River gal.** Man swings left-hand woman.

**VERSE 2**
**Now you lead right on down the valley.** Each set links arms. Walk diagonally forward to right and pass opposite set to meet new set.
**Circle to the left, then to the right.** All join hands and circle left, then right.
**Now the girls make a wheel in the valley.** Four women make right-hand star, walking clockwise once around and return to place.
**And the boys do-sa-do so polite.** Two men do-sa-do, passing right shoulders.

**VERSE 3**
**Now you lead right on down the valley.** Each set links arms and passes opposite set as before to meet new set.
**Circle to the left, then to the right.** All join hands and circle left, then right.
**Now you lose your gal in the valley.** Two right-hand women change places crossing diagonally.
**And you lose your Red River gal.** Two left-hand women change places in same manner. Each man now has two new partners for repeat of dance.

# *Levi Jackson Rag*

*Levi Jackson Rag included by permission of Mountain Folk Festival, Berea College, Berea, Kentucky.*

The Levi Jackson Rag is an Anglo-American mixer for a five-couple set. It is a sprightly dance and ragtime-style tune by the late Pat Shaw; it was commissioned by the Mountain Folk Festival, Adult Section, of Berea College in 1975. The Adult Festival is held annually at Levi Jackson State Park near London, Kentucky.

Pat Shaw had a passionate interest in music and kept his interest in both folk song and dance centered in his life. He contributed significantly in the research, publication, and composition of music and dance and in the leadership of the folk dance movement.

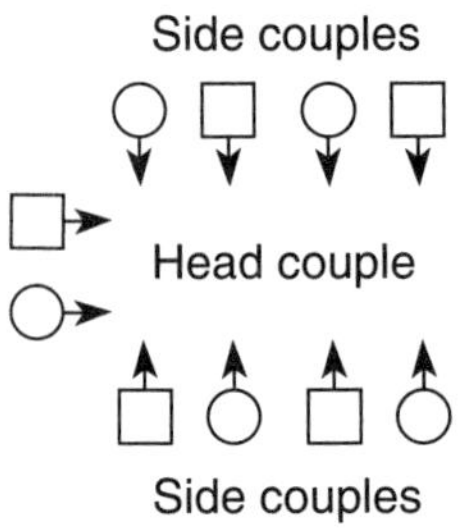


**CD:** Lloyd Shaw Foundation, Inc.

**Music:** "Levi Jackson Rag," Werner, Robert, *The Folklore Village Saturday Night Book,* p. 35.

**Formation:** Five-couple set, one head couple and four side couples.

**Steps:** Walk, swing.

**Level:** Intermediate

## Directions FOR THE MIXER

Meter 2/4

| | ***Measures*** | |
|---|---|---|
| | 1–4 | Introduction: no action (8 counts). |
| A | 1–8 | Side couples right and left through and back with opposite side couple. For measures 3–4, head couple, inside hands joined, walk halfway down center of set; for measures 7–8, continue to foot of set. |
| | 9–12 | Side couples join hands with opposites to circle four left once around, while head couple separates, casts back to home place. |
| | 13–16 | All partners do-si-do. |
| B | 1–4 | All five ladies chain to third man: right-hand star past partner and next man to third man, who turns woman with a courtesy turn. Head man should chain his partner around fairly fast, so that she may get back into the star that follows. |
| | 5–8 | All five ladies chain on two more places as above where they meet their new partners (their original corners). |
| | 9–10 | Promenade new partner in line of direction to next place, taking four steps. |
| | 11–12 | Balance partner right and left. |
| | 13–16 | All swing new partners in new places. |
| | | Repeat whole dance four more times, ending in original position. |

# NONPARTNER DANCES

This section includes contemporary folk dances, recently composed. Some follow a pattern from long ago; many are composed to popular tunes; some are line dances, which not only accommodate situations where there is an unequal number of men and women, but allow individuals "to do their own thing."

For further discussion and teaching tips for line dances, see Chapter 8.

# *Amos Moses*

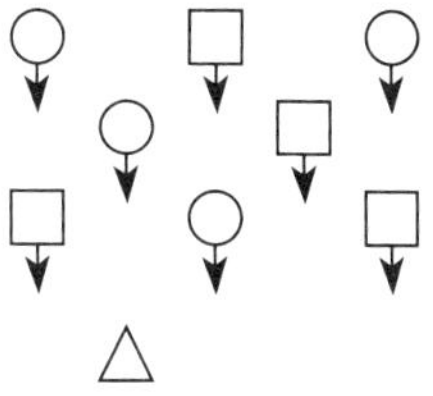

AMOS MOSES is a novelty dance with no partner.

**CD:** High/Scope RM8.
**Formation:** Scattered, all facing music.
**Steps:** Grapevine, stamp.
**Level:** Beginning 1

## *Directions* FOR THE DANCE

Meter 4/4 • Directions presented in counts.

| ***Counts*** | |
|---|---|
| 1–4 | Beginning right, place right heel forward, step right in place; place left heel forward, step left in place. |
| 5 | Grapevine in direction of music: pivoting a quarter turn left, step sideward right. |
| 6 | Step left behind right. |
| 7 | Step sideward right. |
| 8–9 | Turning right one-half turn, step left, right in place. |
| 10 | Stamp left foot, taking weight, and at the same time clap hands. |

**Note:** After each sequence all will face one-quarter turn to the right.

# Cotton-Eyed Joe (line dance)

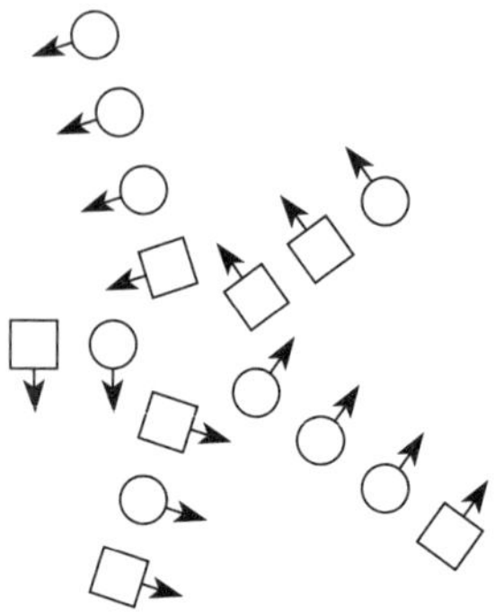

THIS IS THE LINE DANCE VERSION of the Cotton-Eyed Joe couple dance (page 109).

**CD:** Wagon Wheel Records *Folk Dance Now!* #13, "Cotton Eye Joe."

**Formation:** Lines of three, four, six, or as many as desired, arms around neighbor's waist, facing line of direction. Lines move like spokes in a wheel. Or lines of two in Varsouvienne or Promenade position.

**Steps:** Kick, two-step.

**Level:** Beginning 2

## *Directions* FOR THE DANCE

Meter 2/4 • Directions are same for man and woman.

| *Measures* | *Counts* | |
|---|---|---|
| | | **PART I. KICKER** |
| 1 | 1 | Beginning left, cross left foot in front of right knee. |
| | 2 | Kick left kick left. |
| 2 | 3–4 | Beginning left, step back taking one two-step. |
| 3–4 | 1–4 | Beginning right, repeat action of measures 1–2. |
| 5–8 | 1–4 | Repeat action of measures 1–4. |
| | 1–4 | |
| | | **PART II. TWO-STEP** |
| 9–16 | 1–8 | Beginning left, take eight two-steps in line of direction. |
| | 1–8 | |

Improvisation may take place in Part II, such as turning, backing up, or walking around.

# Jessie Polka

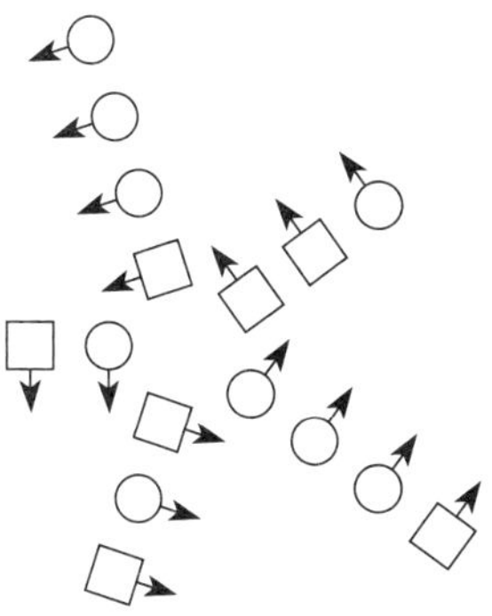

In country western dance, the Jessie Polka is also known as the Cowboy Polka or the Eight-Step Shuffle.

**CD:** Folkraft CD 2911-1.
**Music:** Any good polka.
**Formation:** Form groups of two or more in a line, with arms around each other's waists. Groups progress counterclockwise around the room.
**Steps:** Two-step or polka.
**Level:** Beginning 2

## Directions FOR THE DANCE

Meter 2/4

| *Measures* | *Counts* | |
|---|---|---|
| | | **PART I. HEEL STEP** |
| 1 | 1 | Beginning left, touch heel in front. |
| | 2 | Step left in place. |
| 2 | 3 | Touch right toe behind. |
| | 4 | Touch right toe in place, or scuff in place. |
| 3 | 5 | Touch right heel in front. |
| | 6 | Step right in place. |
| 4 | 7 | Touch left heel to left front diagonal. |
| | 8 | Touch left heel to the left side. Keep weight on right. |
| | | **PART II. TWO-STEP OR POLKA** |
| 5–7 | 1–8 | Beginning left, take four two-steps forward in the line of direction. Four polka steps may be used if preferred. |

### Variation

This dance may be done in a conga line, one behind the other, with the leader moving in a serpentine on the four two-steps.

### Mixer

Couples in line alternating woman and man. The woman may turn out to the right on the last two two-steps and come back in the line behind her partner. The woman at the end of the line rushes up to the head of the line.

# Popcorn

POPCORN IS A NOVELTY DANCE with no partner. It is also known as Alley Cat.

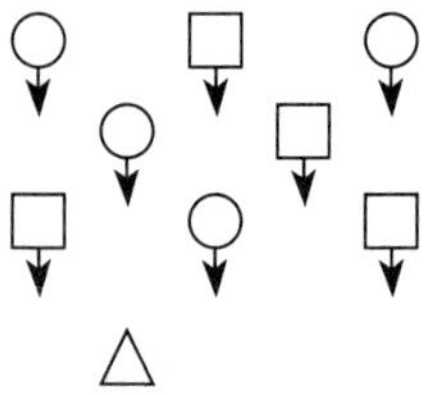

**CD:** Wagon Wheel Records *Dance for Fun and Fitness* #10, "Popcorn."
**Formation:** Scattered, all facing music.
**Steps:** Touch, kick, jump.
**Level:** Beginning 1

## *Directions* FOR THE DANCE

Meter 4/4 • Directions presented in counts.

| ***Counts*** | |
|---|---|
| | Introduction: no action. |
| 1–4 | Beginning right, touch right toe in front, then touch along side left. Repeat. |
| 5–8 | Beginning left, repeat action of beats 1–4. |
| 9–12 | Beginning right, touch right toe backward, then touch alongside left. Repeat. |
| 13–16 | Beginning left, repeat action of beats 9–12. |
| 17–20 | Kick right, knee up in front of left knee and return. Repeat. |
| 21–24 | Kick left, knee up in front of right knee and return. Repeat. |
| 25–28 | Repeat action of beats 17–24. Action is double time. |
| 29–30 | Clap both hands together once. |
| 31–32 | Jump and turn a quarter-turn to right. |
| | Repeat dance from beginning, making a quarter-turn to right at end of each sequence. |

**Note:** Introduction: "Popcorn" 24 beats; "Alley Cat" 1 beat.

# Ten Pretty Girls

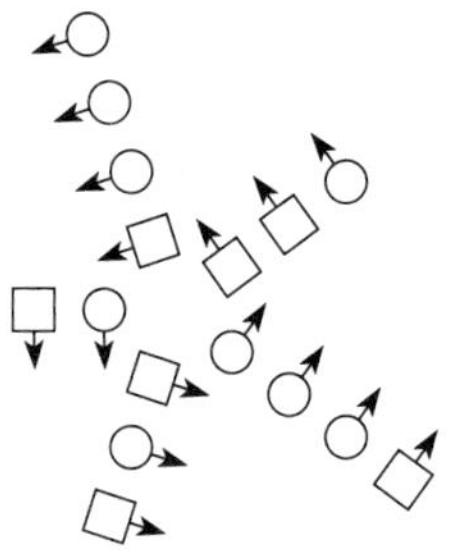

TEN PRETTY GIRLS is usually identified as originating in Texas. The schottische pattern of Ten Pretty Girls and that of the military schottische, one of the Texas schottische variations, are identical. According to Herb Greggerson (a well-known square dance caller and leader of the famous Blue Bonnet Set of El Paso, Texas[3]), the name of this dance is credited to the popular extravaganza producer, Bill Rose, who, upon seeing the dancers in El Paso, exclaimed, "Give me ten pretty girls and I'll use that dance at the Casa Mañana" (the 1936 Fort Worth extravaganza of the Frontier Centennial).

**CD:** Folkraft CD 2910-6.

**Formation:** Lines of three, four, six, or as many as desired; arms around neighbor's waist; facing line of direction.

**Steps:** Grapevine, walk.

**Level:** Beginning 1

## *Directions* FOR THE MIXER

Meter 4/4

| *Measures* | *Counts* | |
|---|---|---|
| 1 | 1–2 | Beginning left, tap left to side twice. |
| | 3 + 4 | Beginning left, grapevine to right stepping left behind right, right to side, cross left in front of right (quick, quick, slow). |
| 2 | 5–8 | Beginning right, repeat measure 1. |
| 3 | 1–4 | Beginning left, walk forward four steps. |
| 4 | 1–2 | Swing left forward, swing left backward. Body leans backward and forward with action of leg swing. |
| | 3 + 4 | Stamp three times in place (quick, quick, slow). |
| 1–4 | | Repeat the dance beginning right. |

4

# *Twelfth Street Rag*

Twelfth Street Rag is a novelty dance composed to a popular tune.

**CD:** High/Scope Vol. 5.

**Formation:** Single circle, hands joined; scattered; or lines of four to five, hands joined, facing line of direction.

**Steps:** Strut, Charleston, grapevine.

**Level:** Beginning 2

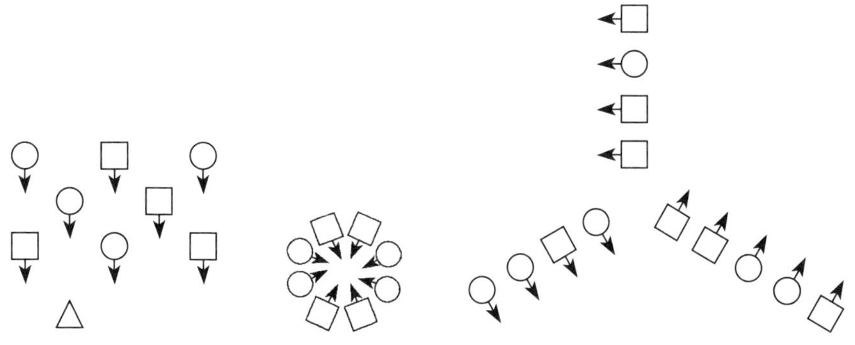

## *Directions* FOR THE DANCE

Meter 4/4

| ***Measures*** | ***Counts*** | |
|---|---|---|
| 1 | 1–4 | Beginning left, strut four steps forward. |
| 2 | 5 + 2 | Point left toe forward, then to side. |
| | 6–8 | Beginning left, take three steps backward. |
| 3–4 | | Beginning right, repeat action of measures 1–2. |
| 5 | 1–8 | Beginning left, take seven quick steps sideward to left. |
| | | Type of step options could be shuffle, step close, grapevine, and swivel steps. |
| 6 | 1–8 | Beginning right, take seven quick steps sideward to right. |
| 7–8 | 1–8 | Beginning left, take two Charleston steps in place. See pages 438–441 for break down of Charleston step. |
| | | Repeat dance. |
| | | **INTERLUDE** |
| 1 | 1–2 | Jump forward on both feet. |
| | 3–4 | Jump backwards on both feet, throwing hands back, turn and face the other way. |
| 2 | 5–8 | Turn individually to own right, taking three steps (strut right, left, right) and clap hands on the fourth count. Improvise during the interlude. |

4

# MIXERS

There are a variety of partner dances in this section. The set pattern makes these dances quick and easy to learn. The patterns take the pressure off of leading and following and allows beginning students to ease into more-complicated ballroom dance styles.

Many are mixer-type dances, which allow for changing partners. In the past some of these dances would be considered "ice breakers." The basic step is frequently the waltz, polka, schottische, or two-step. Refer to Chapter 8 for partner dance teaching tips.

The hardest element of partner dancing is asking someone to dance. Using a variety of activities to engage students in finding partners will reduce stress for the class. Many examples of these activities are listed below.

## Gain or Exchange Partners

1. **Upset the Cherry Basket:** When the music stops, the leader requests that everyone change partners. If couples are asked to change with the couple nearest them, everyone is involved, and no one walks to the side for the lack of a partner.

2. **Snowball, Whistle Dance, Pony Express, or Multiplication Dance:** One to three couples start to dance. When the music stops, each couple separates and goes to the sidelines and gets a new partner. This is repeated until everyone is dancing.
3. **Line Up:** The men line up on one side of the room, facing the wall; the women on the other side, facing the wall. When the signal is given, each line backs up until they gain a new partner.
4. **Arches:** All the dancers form a single circle and walk counterclockwise around the circle. Two couples form arches on opposite sides of the circle. When the music stops, the arch is lowered. Those caught in the arch go to the center of the circle, gain a partner, and go back to the circle to form new arches. Eventually, just a few dancers will be walking through the tunnel of arches. When all have partners, the dancing proceeds.
5. **Star by the Right:** Six men form a right-hand star in the center of a single circle formed by the group. The star moves clockwise, and the circle counterclockwise. As the leader gives the signal, six women hook onto the star; alternate genders are called out until all have hooked onto the star. A little spice is added if the last person on each spoke winks or beckons a specific person from the ring to join his or her spoke. When the star is completed the woman dances with the man on her right.
6. **Matching:** Advertising slogans (Ivory Soap–99.9 percent pure; it floats), split proverbs (a rolling stone–gathers no moss), famous couples (Romeo–Juliet), pairs of words that belong together (ham–eggs), playing cards (spades match with hearts for each number, clubs with diamonds), pictures cut in half (cartoons), or songs may be used for this mixer. Half of the slips of paper are given to the men, and the corresponding halves are distributed to the women. As the people circulate, they try to find the person with the corresponding half of their slogan, proverb, cartoon, or whatever has been selected to be matched. When everyone has found his or her partner, the dancing proceeds. If songs are used, each person sings his or her song until he or she finds the person singing the same song.
7. **Musical Chairs:** Set up a double row of chairs, back to back, almost the length of the room. Leave space between every group of four chairs so that partners can get together. The group marches around the chairs. When the music stops, each person tries to gain a seat. A man must sit back to back with a woman. These two become partners and proceed to dance while all the others continue to play the game until all have partners. When all are dancing, the next signal is given and partners separate and rush for a chair, thus providing a change of partners. **Musical knees:** Played like musical chairs, except that on a signal, the men get down on one knee and the women rush to sit on a knee. Those left out go to the side.
8. **Ice Cube Pass:** Double circle, men on the outside, women on inside. Pass an orange around men's circle; an ice cube around the women's circle. When the music stops, the man with the orange and woman with the ice cube step to center of circle or its outside and become partners. Repeat over and over, until all have partners. Several oranges and ice cubes may be passed simultaneously.
9. **Mexican Broom Dance.**[4] As couples are dancing, an extra man with a broom knocks the broom handle on the floor several times. Partners separate, women line up on left side of man with the broom and men on right side. The two lines are about five feet apart. All clap their hands while lining up and until they get a new partner. After everyone is in line, the man with the broom goes up and down the line and decides with which woman he wants to dance. When he has made his choice, he drops the broom and grabs his partner, while everyone else

4. Herb Greggerson, author of *Herb's Blue Bonnet Calls*, saw this mixer danced in Mexico and presented it for the first time at the Square Dance Institute at the University of Texas, April 1948. Directions were first printed in *Foot 'n' Fiddle*, editors Anne Pittman, Marlys Swenson, and Olcutt Sanders, May 1948, p. 4.

takes a partner, too, and dancing resumes. Then the extra man picks up the broom and the procedure starts all over again. More fun is added to the mixer if the man in going up and down the line pretends to drop the broom but actually keeps on looking for a different partner.

## Trade Dances

1. **Are You on the Beam?** While everyone is dancing, a spotlight is suddenly focused on a specific area. Those people standing in the rays of the light are requested to give a yell, sing a song, or trade partners.
2. **Hats Off!** Four hats are distributed among four couples. Each couple with a hat places it on one member of another couple. When the music stops, the couples with the hats must change partners.

## Tags

1. **Women's Tag or Men's Tag:** Certain dances may be designated as women's tag or men's tag.
2. **Similarity Tag:** Either a man or a woman may tag, but the person tagging can only tag someone who has a similar color of hair, eyes, shirt, shoes, and so on.
3. **"You Take the Lemon, I'll Take the Peach":** A few lemons or other designated articles are distributed among the men or the women. Anyone who holds the article may tag. Additional fun may be had by stopping the music periodically and anyone holding the article pays a forfeit. Later the forfeits are redeemed by performing a humorous stunt.

4

## Elimination Dances

1. **Number Please?** Each couple is given a number. Each time the music stops, a number is called out and the couple or couples having the numbers called sit down. Numbers are called out until only one couple remains.
2. **Lemon Dance:** An object—for example, a lemon—is passed from couple to couple. When the music stops, the couple with the object sits down. Eventually one couple is left.
3. **Dance Contest:** Determine the type of dancing for the contest, for example, waltz or jitterbug. It should be conducted in a casual manner with qualified judges. Gradually, the contestants are eliminated until one or two couples remain. Choosing two couples, instead of one, for the winners keeps competition from becoming too keen.
4. **Orange Dance:** Each couple balances an orange or a tennis ball between their foreheads and proceeds to dance. Slow music like a tango allows the dancers to concentrate on keeping the orange in position and still move to the music. When a couple drops the orange, they go to the sidelines. Eventually one couple is left and the rest have enjoyed the antics of those trying to keep the orange in position. Change the rhythm of the music to match the ability of the dancers.

# Schottische

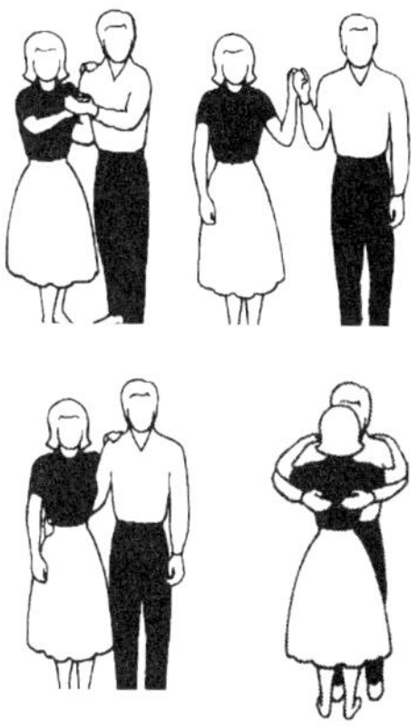

**Dance A While CD:** "Schottische."

**Music:** Any schottische. Schottische melodies and styles of arrangement relate to the quality of movement: a lively, bouncy one for step-hops; a smooth one for ballroom variations; and Texas Schottische variations.

**Position:** Open, couple, or conversation.

**Steps:** Schottische.

**Level:** Beginning 2

Refer to page 39 for schottische instruction.

## Directions FOR THE DANCE

Meter 4/4 • Directions are for man; woman's part reverse.

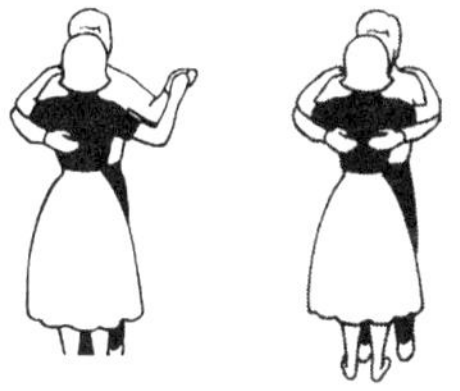

| *Measures* | *Counts* | |
|---|---|---|
| | | **BASIC** |
| 1–2 | 1–8 | Open position. Beginning left, move forward in line of direction with two schottische steps. |
| 3–4 | 1–8 | Closed position or shoulder-waist position. Turn clockwise with four step-hops. Progress in line of direction. |
| | | **VARIATIONS** |
| | | **I. WOMAN'S TURN** |
| 1–2 | 1–8 | Repeat action of measures 1–2 in basic schottische. |
| 3–4 | 1–8 | Four step-hops, man moves forward, while the woman turns clockwise under upraised left arm of partner. Woman may make one or two complete turns. Progress in the line of direction. |
| | | **II. MAN'S TURN** |
| 1–4 | | Directions are the same as for the woman's turn, except man turns clockwise under upraised right arm of woman. |
| | | **III. BOTH TURN** |
| 1–2 | | Repeat action of measures 1–2 in basic schottische. |
| | | Four step-hops, partners turn away from each other, man to his left, woman to her right. |
| | | Partners may make one or two complete turns. |
| | | **IV. DIAMOND** |
| 1–2 | | Man and woman take one schottische step diagonally forward away from each other. |

*continues on next page*

***Measures***

Man and woman take one schottische step diagonally forward toward each other.

Progress in the line of direction.

3–4 Repeat action of measures 3–4 in basic schottische.

**V. WRING THE DISH RAG**

1–2 Repeat action of measures 1–2 in basic schottische.

3–4 Partners face, join two hands and with four step-hops turn back to back (turning to man's left, woman's right) and continue roll until face to face. Join hands, and swing through between couple, below waist, and quickly overhead. The couple may make one or two turns.

**VI. ROCK**

1–2 Repeat action of measures 1–2 in basic schottische.

3 Step forward on left, take weight (counts 1–2). Step backward on right, take weight (counts 3–4). Rocking effect is produced by swaying body forward and backward.

4 Repeat action of measure 3.

**VII. BALLROOM SCHOTTISCHE**

1–2 Repeat action of measures 1–2 in basic schottische. On count 4, the hop is omitted and the free leg swings forward, toe pointed close to floor.

3–4 Closed position. Beginning left, pivot turn clockwise four steps, progressing in line of direction.

**VIII. SCHOTTISCHE FOR FOUR: HORSE AND BUGGY SCHOTTISCHE**

Two couples stand one behind the other, both facing the line of direction. Join inside hands with partner. The outside hands joined link the two couples together. The front couple is number one, the back couple is number two.

1–2 Repeat action of measures 1–2 in basic schottische.

3–4 Four step-hops. Couple 1 releases partner's hand and turning away from each other, man left, woman right, they move around couple 2 on the outside and come in behind them. Joining hands with partner, they therefore become the back couple and the couple 2 is now the front couple. Or couple 1 may take step-hops backward through the upraised arms of couple 2. This action will cause couple 2 to turn the dish rag in order to become straightened out. After turning, couple 2 becomes the front couple. These variations, if repeated, will return couples to starting position.

1–4 Repeat the entire action of measures 1–4 with couple 2 turning out or moving backward with step-hops, to return couples to original positions.

### Mixer

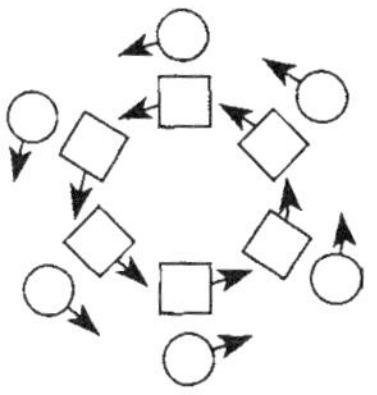

Double circle, couples facing line of direction. Dance basic schottische. The woman moves forward to a new partner on the second schottische step.

### Style

Three styles are used in this schottische: traditional–the schottische step is danced as a step, close, step, hop; barn dance–the schottische step is danced as a step, step, step, hop or run, run, run, hop; ballroom dance–step, close, step, lift. The hop is replaced by a slight lift of the body. Point toe of the free foot. The step-hops are replaced by a step-lift, with a rocking action forward and back.

The American style is to swing the free leg forward on the hop and the pattern is very smooth. The European style keeps the leg under the body and the hop has a bouncy action.

# *Texas Schottische Variations*

THE TEXAS SCHOTTISCHE was first seen by the authors as part of an exhibition danced and taught by Herb and Pauline Greggerson. The Texas Schottische was also referred to as the El Paso Schottische, because El Paso was home base for the Greggersons in those days. There are many Texas Schottische variations such as Douglas, Belen, and Scotch. As originally danced, these steps were not done in any special sequence.

***Dance A While* CD:** "Schottische, Bummel (Texas)"
**Records:** FD LP 4; MAV Album 4; Shaw E 23, or any smooth schottische.
**Position:** Varsouvienne.
**Steps:** Variations of grapevine, Schottische, and Two-step.
**Level:** Intermediate

## Directions FOR THE DANCE

Meter 4/4 • Directions are same for man and woman.

| *Measures* | *Counts* | |
|---|---|---|
| | | **I. MILITARY SCHOTTISCHE** |
| 1 | 1–4 | Point left toe in front of right foot (counts 1–2). Point left toe sideways to left (counts 3–4). |
| 2 | 5–8 | Step left foot behind right (count 1). Step right foot to right (count 2). Close left to right (count 3). Hold (count 4). |
| 3–4 | 1–8 | Beginning right, repeat action of measures 1–2. |

*continues on next page*



4

| *Measures* | *Counts* | |
|---|---|---|
| 5–6 | 1–8 | Beginning left, two walking steps forward followed by one two-step. |
| 7–8 | 1–8 | Beginning right, repeat action of measures 5–6. |
| | | **II. PETER PAN SCHOTTISCHE** |
| 1 | 1–4 | Step forward left (counts 1–2). Step forward right (counts 3–4). |
| 2 | 5–8 | Step forward left, right (counts 1–2), step left and pivot to own right (count 3), swing or lift right leg (count 4). Couple now faces in the reverse line of direction. |
| 3 | 1–4 | Moving backward, step right, lift left (counts 1–2). Step left, lift right (counts 3–4). |
| 4 | 5–8 | Step right, left, right, pivoting to own left (counts 1, 2, 3, 4). Couple now faces line of direction. |
| | | **III. McGINTY SCHOTTISCHE** |
| 1–2 | 1–8 | Step forward, slightly to left, with left foot, close right to left, step left, and swing right across left with a slight kick. Repeat stepping forward, slightly to right, with right foot. (Right, close, right, swing left across right with slight kick.) |
| 3–4 | 1–8 | Beginning left, take four step swings (kicks), moving forward in line of direction: step left and swing right across in front of left, step right in front of left and swing left across in front of right; repeat action. Body sways with a roll during the step swings. |
| | | **IV. BLUE BONNET** |
| 1 | 1–4 | Beginning left, take one schottische step to left, sideways, stepping left, step right behind left, step left, swing right in front of left as body rises and lowers on left foot. |
| 2 | 5–8 | Take one schottische step to right, sideways, woman rising and lowering on step swing. |
| 3–4 | 1–8 | Partners release left hands. Man and woman take 12 small steps in a quick, quick, slow rhythm (four times). Woman, beginning left, takes three small steps (quick, quick, slow), turns right to face partner, and moves so right arms are almost extended; woman travels around her partner, to man's right, behind him, to his left side, and back to orig-inal Varsouvienne position while taking three more series of small steps to the rhythm of quick, quick, slow. On the last quick, quick, slow, the woman turns clockwise under her right arm as she moves into her original position. As the woman is sweeping around the man, the man guides her, raising his right arm and circling his right hand above his head (lariat fashion); and the man takes 12 steps to the rhythm of quick, quick, slow, four times almost in place, moving slightly to assist the movement of his partner. See note 2 on the next page. |

**Note:**

1. In El Paso, Texas, McGinty is the name for a "big beer." In Lloyd Shaw's *The Round Dance Book* (1948), under Texas Schottisches, this variation is listed as Drunken Schottische.
2. Although *quick, quick, slow* is a two-step rhythm, the Greggersons did not two-step this figure; rather, they used a smooth travel of steps.

# Texas Schottische for Three

*Texas Schottische for Three included by permission of Jane Farwell, Folklore Village Farm, Dodgeville, Wisconsin.*

DURING WORLD WAR II, the Texas Schottische and Put Your Little Foot were the two round dances most frequently danced between square dances in the Southwest. Following the folk-transmission process, set patterns known as the California Schottische and Oklahoma Mixer have come from variations of the Texas Schottische. Jane Farwell adapted the Oklahoma Mixer and named it Texas Schottische for Three, partly to compensate for the man shortage during the war.

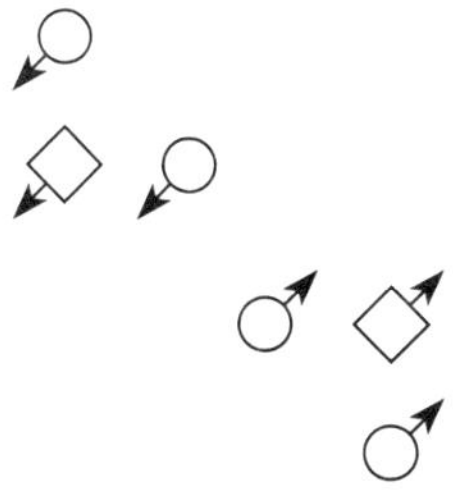

***Dance A While* CD:** "Schottische, Bummel (Texas)"

**CD:** Folkraft CD 2913-12.

**Music:** Any smooth schottische.

**Formation:** Group of three, facing line of direction; man in front of two women, man reaching back holds outside hand of each woman, women join inside hands behind man.

**Steps:** Two-step, walk, heel toe.

**Level:** Beginning 2

## Directions FOR THE DANCE

Meter 4/4 • Directions are same for man and woman.

| *Measures* | *Counts* | |
|---|---|---|
| 1–2 | 1–8 | Beginning left, take two two-steps, moving diagonally left, then right. |
| 3–4 | 1–8 | Beginning left, four walking steps forward. Each step takes two counts. |
| 5 | 1–4 | Place left heel forward, place left toe close to right instep. |
| 6 | 1–4 | Women release, inside hand. Man backs up three steps, pulling women around in front, as women take three steps (left, right, left) in line of direction, turning back to face reverse line of direction. Man faces line of direction, women face reverse line of direction. |

*continues on next page*

| ***Measures*** | ***Counts*** | |
|---|---|---|
| 7 | 1–4 | Beginning right, repeat heel, toe. Man gives a slight pull of hands, then releases hands |
| 8 | 5–8 | as all take three steps (right, left, right) forward. Man passes between the two women, and joins hands with new partners; women turn toward each other, pivoting on third step to face line of direction. |

**Notes**

1. A marvelous mixer for extra men to cut in, and, in Jane Farwell's words, "snatch two women" leaving another man to become one of the "thieves."
2. An excellent dance to teach the Schottische steps.

4

# *Salty Dog Rag*

THE SALTY DOG RAG is a novelty dance composed to a popular tune, based on the Schottische rhythm.

**CD:** High/Scope Vol. 9.
**Position:** Promenade.
**Steps:** Grapevine Schottische, step-hop.
**Level:** Beginning 2

## *Directions* FOR THE DANCE

Meter 4/4 • Directions are same for man and woman.

| ***Measures*** | ***Counts*** | |
|---|---|---|
| | | **PART I.** |
| 1–8 | 1–32 | Introduction: no action. |
| 1 | 1–4 | Beginning right, take one grapevine schottische step, moving diagonally forward right (step right, step left behind right, step right hop) |
| 2 | 5–8 | Beginning left, take one grapevine schottische step diagonally forward left (step left, step right behind left, step left hop). |
| 3–4 | 1–8 | Moving forward, take four step-hops (or step swings). |
| 5–8 | 1–16 | Repeat action of measures 1–4. |

| *Measures* | *Counts* | |
|---|---|---|
| | | **PART II.** |
| 1 | 1–4 | Dropping right hands, left hands remain joined, woman turns to face partner on her first step. Beginning right, take one grapevine schottische step sideways to own right (partners move away from each other). |
| 2 | 5–8 | Beginning left, each takes a three-step turn, turning left, toward partner. Begin impetus for turn by each pulling joined hands slightly, then drop hands to complete solo turn. |
| 3–4 | 1–8 | Catch right hands, shoulder height, elbows bent. Beginning right, take four step-hops (or struts), making one complete turn clockwise. |
| 5–8 | 1–16 | Repeat action of Part II, measures 1–4. On last step-hop, take promenade position and face line of direction. |
| | | **PART III.** |
| 1 | 1–4 | Beginning right, place heel forward, step right in place; place left heel forward, step left in place. |
| 2 | 5–8 | Rise on both toes swinging heels out (pigeon-toed); click heels together; stamp right, stamp left. |
| 3–4 | 1–8 | Beginning right, take four step-hops forward. |
| 5–8 | 1–16 | Repeat action of Part III, measures 3–4. |

**Note:** Many people dance Parts I and II alternately, omitting Part III.

# Boston Two-Step

The Boston Two-Step, of English origin, has become part of the American fabric of dance and is an old-time favorite still danced at the Grange halls and dance halls, where social dances (fox-trot, waltz) prevail. The dance programs feature occasional pattern dances like the Boston Two-Step.

**CD:** Folkraft CD 2913-4.

**Position:** Partners face, man joins woman's right hand with his left or join two hands.

**Steps:** Step swing, three-step turn, two-step.

**Level:** Beginning 2

## Directions FOR THE DANCE

Meter 2/4 • Directions are for man; woman's part reverse.

| ***Measures*** | ***Counts*** | |
|---|---|---|
| | | **PART I.** |
| 1 | 1–2 | Beginning left, step in place, swing right over left. |
| 2 | 3–4 | Step right in place, swing left over right. |
| 3–4 | 5–8 | Release hands. Traveling in the line of direction, take one three-step turn (man turning counterclockwise; woman clockwise) and swing right over left. |
| 5–8 | 1–8 | Join hands. Beginning right, repeat action of measures 1–4, three-step turn, moving forward in the reverse line of direction. |
| 9–12 | 1–8 | Join hands. Beginning left, repeat action of measures 1–4, three-step turn moving forward in the line of direction, *stamp right* (instead of last swing). Place weight on right foot. |
| | | **PART II.** |
| 13–16 | 1–8 | Closed position. Beginning left, take four Two-Steps, turning clockwise, progressing in the line of direction. |

### Variation

In Part II, a pivot may be substituted for the last two two-steps or for all four two-steps.

# Heel and Toe Polka

**Dance A While CD:** "Polka."
**Music:** Any lively polka.
**Position:** Closed or shoulder-waist.
**Steps:** Heel and toe polka, polka.
**Level:** Beginning 1

## Directions FOR THE DANCE

Meter 2/4 • Directions are for the man; woman's part reverse.

| ***Measures*** | ***Counts*** | |
|---|---|---|
| | | **PART I. HEEL AND TOE POLKA** |
| 1 | 1 | Hop right (count *and*), place left heel close to right instep. |
| | 2 | Hop right (count *and*), place left toe close to right instep. |
| 2 | 3–4 | With left foot, take one polka step to the left. |
| 3–4 | 5–8 | Repeat action of measures 1–2, beginning right. |
| 5–8 | 1–16 | Repeat action of measures 1–4. |
| | | **PART II. POLKA** |
| 9–16 | 1–16 | Take eight polka steps, turning clockwise, progressing in the line of direction. |

### Polka Variations

1. **Crossover polka:** Varsouvienne position. Man and woman both begin heel and toe polka by hopping right. Without releasing hands, woman crosses over to man's left on the hop step, close, step, man dancing almost in place. Woman crosses back to original position on second heel and toe polka. This action repeats. Part II, couple takes eight polka steps, moving forward in the line of direction.
2. **Crossover polka with three-step turn:** During the Crossover polka, Part I, woman makes a three-step turn to cross over and back. Heel toe, heel toe, release right hands and turn under left arm, stepping left, right, left; rejoin right hands. Repeat to right, releasing left hands for turn. Part II, polka forward.

3. **Slide polka:** Closed position, man's back to center of circle. Heel toe, heel toe, take four slides, traveling in the line of direction (the last slide is not completed in order to change direction). Repeat traveling in the reverse line of direction. Take eight polka steps, turning clockwise, progressing in the line of direction.

4. **Falcon Hop:** In 1950, at the after-parties of the National Folk Festival in St. Louis, it was fun to dance with the Polish-American dancers. To sprightly polka tunes, especially the Polish ones, in closed or shoulder-waist position, participants danced the Falcon Hop. The Falcon Hop is a small polka step, turning clockwise as dancers progress forward, but actually not traveling very far. The dancers appeared to "jiggle" as they hopped.

# *Teton Mountain Stomp*

The Teton Mountain Stomp was composed by "Doc" Alumbaugh, Alhambra, California. It was adapted from the old Buffalo Glide.

**CD:** Folkraft CD 2912-2; Wagon Wheel Records *Folk Dance Now!* #12, "Teton Mountain Stomp"; *Dance for Fun and Fitness* #6, "Teton Mountain Stomp."

**Position:** Closed.

**Formation:** Single circle, men facing in line of direction.

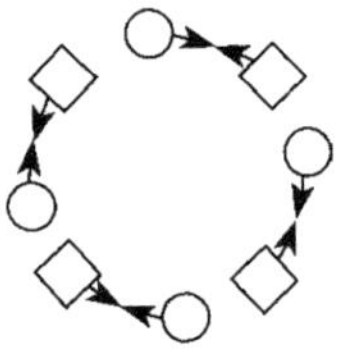

**Steps:** Walk, pivot, two-step.

**Level:** Begining 1

## *Directions* FOR THE MIXER

Meter 4/4 • Directions are for man; woman's part reverse.

The music is slow. Each step takes two beats, but it is easier to count it at one beat. The counts below will equal two beats.

| *Measures* | *Counts* | |
|---|---|---|
| | | **PART I. SIDE STEP AND STAMP** |
| 1–2 | 1–4 | Beginning left, step side left, toward center, close right to left, stepping on right, step left toward center, and stamp right next to left. |
| 3–4 | 5–8 | Beginning right, repeat action of measures 1–2, moving away from center of circle. |
| 5–6 | 1–4 | Step left to side left (count 1), stamp right beside left (count 2). Step right to side right (count 3), stamp left beside right (count 4). |
| | | **PART II. WALK** |
| 7–8 | 1–4 | Banjo position. Man walks four steps in line of direction (woman moves backward). |
| 9–10 | 5–8 | Turning to Side Car position. Man walks four steps backward in line of direction (woman moves forward). |
| 11–12 | 1–4 | Man takes half-turn to face line of direction and walks four steps forward to meet the second woman for new partner. Woman walks four steps forward in reverse line of direction to meet second man for new partner. |
| | | **PART III. TWO-STEP, PIVOT** |
| 13–14 | 1–4 | Closed position. Take two two-steps, turning clockwise. |
| 15–16 | 5–8 | Continuing in closed position, do four pivot steps. End with man facing line of direction. |

# Cotton-Eyed Joe (couple dance)

Dorothy Scarborough identifies "Cotton-Eyed Joe" as an authentic slavery tunesong in her book *On the Trail of Negro Folksongs.* One song antebellum blacks played and sang dealt with Cotton-Eyed Joe. Judging by the many verses—all in the same vein—he was a tantalizing, intriguing, and devilish character. The Cotton-Eyed Joe line dance found on page 92 emerged from this couple dance.

> Hadn't been for Cotton-Eyed Joe
> I'd 'a' been married twenty years ago
> With an old gourd fiddle and a cornstalk bow
> None could play like Cotton-Eyed Joe.

The fiddle tune, written in 2/4 meter, may be found in several references, one being Ira W. Ford's *Traditional Music of America.* Some references present the same tune in 4/4 meter.

According to Uncle Dave Dillingham of Austin, Texas, who learned the dance in Williamson County in the early 1880s, Cotton-Eyed Joe is nothing but a Heel and Toe "Poker," with fringes added. For the most part, the fringes, or variations, over and above the Heel and Toe Polka were originally clog steps, which required skill and extroversion on the part of the dancer.

Uncle Dave, at age 81 (1947), recalled the visits of Professor Whitehead, the visiting dancing master, who dealt with the finer points of ballroom dancing. The dancing master taught the Heel and Toe Polka in every community he visited, along with the waltz, and so forth. But the short duration of his visit, the scarcity of students, and the ability of dancers no doubt contributed to the fact that the Heel and Toe Polka was not mastered by the majority of the dancers. In addition to these difficulties, the fringes that really make the dance special were for the most part made up of clog steps, which not only require skill but also require an extroversion that is not a common trait attributed to the average dancer but is easy for the "Fancy Dan" who was, and still is, an exception on the dance floor. The dance as described is a simple version, commonly danced in Texas.

**CD:** Wagon Wheel Records *Folk Dance Now!* #3, "Cotton Eye Joe."
**Position:** Closed.
**Steps:** Polka, two-step, push step.
**Level:** Intermediate

## Directions FOR THE DANCE

Meter 2/4 • Directions are for man; woman's part reverse.

| ***Measures*** | ***Counts*** | |
|---|---|---|
| | | **PART I. HEEL AND TOE POLKA** |
| 1–2 | +1 | Hop right (count +), touch left heel out to the left (count 1). |
| | +2 | Hop right (count +), touch left toe behind right foot (count 2). |

Cotton-Eyed Joe, *continued*

| ***Measures*** | ***Counts*** | |
|---|---|---|
| 2 | 3–4 | Polka to left (counts +3, +4), in the line of direction. |
| 3–4 | 5–8 | Repeat measures 1–2 beginning with hop on left foot and travel in the reverse line of direction |
| | | **PART II. INDIVIDUAL TURN** |
| 5–7 | 1–6 | Starting left, take three two-steps left turning in a small circle. The man turns counterclockwise; the woman turns clockwise. |
| 8 | 7+8 | Facing partner, beginning left, stamp in place, left, right left. |
| | | **PART III. PUSH STEP** |
| 9–10 | 1 | With left, step side left, in line of direction. |
| | + | Place weight momentarily on right |
| | 2 | Push onto left foot, chugging left sideward again and flip right heel out to the side. |
| | + | Place weight momentarily on right. |
| 10 | 3–4 | Repeat measure 9. |
| 11–12 | 5–8 | Repeat action of measures 9–10, starting with the right foot, and moving to the right. |
| | | **PART IV. TWO-STEP OR POLKA** |
| 13–16 | | Four two-steps in closed dance position, turning clockwise, progressing in the line of direction. These may be polka steps. |

## Variations

The dancers perform the variations at random, measures 9–16. After the variation, the heel and toe polka and the individual turn are repeated.

1. **Two-step away and toward partner:** Moving away from partner, take four small two-steps; step left directly behind right (count 1), step right in place (count *and*), step left in place (count 2); step right directly behind left (count 1), step left in place (count *and*), step right in place (count 2); repeat. Moving toward partner, take four small two-steps.
2. **Hooking:** Partners grasp right hands, free left arm curved and raised shoulder height as each dancer hops on left, extending right foot to meet partner's right foot, hooking foot just back of partner's right ankle. Take eight hops, couple turning clockwise in place. Reverse direction, grasping left hands, hooking left ankles, and taking eight hops, beginning left. Couple turns counterclockwise. Partners lean away from each other, slightly offering resistance or counterbalance as they turn; hooked leg is straight.
3. **Jig steps:** These jig and clog steps are listed for historical significance and for the advanced dancer to pursue. They are not analyzed. Partners face each other and do jig or clog dance steps such as shifting sands, seven steps, grapevine twist, pigeon wing, double shuffle, buzzard loop, triple step, and rock the cradle. Uncle Dave Dillingham at 80 would dance these steps, doing a solo, while his partner marked the rhythm, moving ever so lightly in place, perhaps working her skirt "àla Square or Mexican" dance styling.

# Garden Waltz

THE GARDEN WALTZ is a German–American waltz for three dancers. It originated in New Braunfels, Texas. There are two rhythms, waltz and polka. It is also known as the Butterfly.

Ancestors of the Butterfly are: German, Schmetterlingtanz ("Butterfly Dance"); Czech, Zahradniček ("the gardener," from *Zahrada*, "garden"); Polish (Silesian), and Zasiale Górale ("The mountaineers sowed oats").

**Music:** iTunes, A Garden of Roses Waltz, Album: Waltz Favorites.

**Formation:** Set of three, man between two women, facing line of direction. Man's arms around women's waist, women's inside arm around man's waist, or hook elbows.

**Steps:** Hesitation waltz, waltz, polka, or two-step.

**Level:** Beginning 2

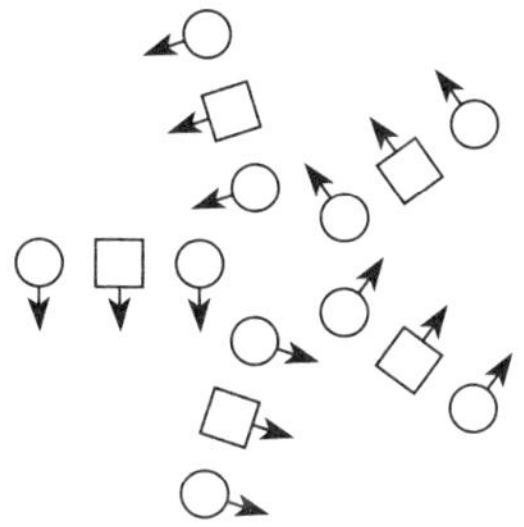

4

## *Directions* FOR THE DANCE

Meter 3/4 • Directions are same for man and women.

| ***Measures*** | ***Counts*** | |
|---|---|---|
| | | **I. WALTZ FORWARD** |
| 1–16 | 1–6<br>7–8 | Beginning left, take 16 hesitation waltz steps forward. Hesitation waltz step: Step forward left, knee slightly bent (count 1), bring right to left, rising on balls of both feet (count 2), end weight on left (count 3). Repeat beginning right. Styling: body falls count 1, body lifts counts 2 and 3, similar to body action in a step-swing. |
| Meter 2/4 | | |
| | | **II. POLKA TURNS** |
| 1–16 | 1–8<br>1–8 | Release hold. Beginning left, man takes 16 polka or two-steps, first hooking right elbows with right-hand woman, turning clockwise with four polka steps; then hooking left elbows with left-hand woman, turning counterclockwise with four polka steps. Turn right-hand woman, then left-hand woman again. If quick, turn each four times alternately. |

*continues on next page*

## Variation

Meter 3/4

| *Measures* | *Counts* | |
|---|---|---|
| | | **WALTZ TURNS** |
| 1–8 | 1–6<br>×–2 | Beginning left, take eight hesitation waltz steps forward. |
| 9–16 | 1–6<br>×–8 | Inside hands joined with man, raise arms. As man takes eight waltz steps forward, two women spin under raised arms away from man, right-hand woman counterclockwise, left-hand woman clockwise. Women may take eight waltz steps turning. |

Meter 2/4

| *Measures* | *Counts* | |
|---|---|---|
| | | **POLKA TURNS** |
| 1–8 | 1–8 | **Elbow Turns:** All dance eight polka steps as man hooks right elbows with right-hand woman, turn with four polka steps, then hooks left elbows with left-hand woman, turn with four polka steps. |
| 9–16 | 1–8 | **Arches:** All take eight polka steps: right-hand woman travels under arch made by man and left-hand woman, then back to place; man turns under his left arm; left-hand woman repeats. |

# *Varsouvienne*

The Varsouvienne is also known, especially in Texas, as Put Your Little Foot.

**CD:** Folk Dance CD Vol. 007.
**Music:** Lloyd Shaw, *Cowboy Dances,* p. 392.
**Position:** Varsouvienne.
**Steps:** Mazurka.
**Level:** Beginning 2

## *Directions* FOR THE DANCE

Meter 3/4 • Directions are same for both woman and man.

| *Measures* | *Counts* | |
|---|---|---|
| | 3 | Swing left heel across in front of right instep (count 3, pick up beat). |
| | | **PART I. LONG PHRASE** |
| 1 | 1–3 | Beginning left, step diagonally left, close right to left, weight ends on right (counts 1–2). Swing left heel across in front of right instep (count 3, pick up beat). |
| 2 | 4–6 | Repeat action of measure 1. |
| 3 | 1–3 | Beginning left, step left, right, left in place. |
| 4 | 4–5 | point right foot to right (counts 1–2). |
| | 6 | Swing left heel across in front of right instep (pick up beat). |
| 5–8 | 1–6 | Beginning right, repeat action of measures 1–4. |
| | 1–6 | |
| | | **PART II. SHORT PHRASE** |
| 9–10 | 1–6 | Repeat action of measures 3–4. |
| 11–16 | | Beginning right, repeat action of measures 9–10 through three times. |

### Variations for Measures 3–8 (Part I)

1. **Crossover:** Beginning left, the man moves the woman across in front of him to his left side with three steps. Beginning right, he moves her back to his right side.
2. **Turnback:** During the three steps, make half-turn clockwise and point in opposite direction. Beginning right, turn counterclockwise. *Note:* Forward or backward movements with a pivot on first or third step may be used.

### Variation for Measures 9–16 (Part II)

**Swing in and out:** Beginning left, repeat action of measures 3–4 as follows: Man: Take steps in place. Woman: Release man's right hand and take three steps toward center of circle to face reverse line of direction, out to the left and slightly in front of man. Beginning right, take three steps turning counterclockwise under man's upraised left arm and finish in original position. Repeat action toward center and back to original position.

### Mixer

On measures 15–16 in the swing in and out variation, woman may move in reverse line of direction to a new partner and turn counterclockwise into place beside him in Varsouvienne position.

**Note:** Because Parts I and II of the music vary on different records, the repetition of the action should vary accordingly.

# *All-American Promenade*

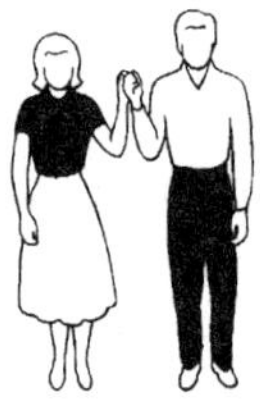

The All-American Promenade was composed by "Doc" and Winnie Alumbaugh, Alhambra, California.

**CD:** Folkraft CD 2911-19; Wagon Wheel Records *Folk Dance Now!* #17, "All-American Promenade."

**Position:** Inside hands joined.

**Formation:** Double circle, couples facing line of direction.

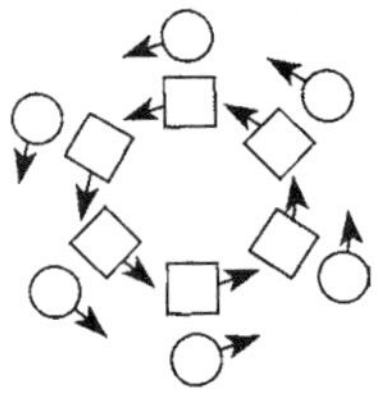

**Steps:** Walk, balance.

**Level:** Beginning 2

## *Directions* FOR THE MIXER

Meter 4/4 • Directions are for man; woman's part reverse.

| *Measures* | *Counts* | |
|---|---|---|
| | | **PART I. WALK STEP** |
| 1 | 1–4 | Beginning left, walk four steps forward, turn toward partner on fourth step to face reverse line of direction, join inside hands. |
| 2 | 5–8 | Back up four steps in line of direction. |
| 3–4 | 1–8 | Repeat action of measures 1–2 in reverse line of direction. |
| | | **PART II. BALANCE, EXCHANGE PLACES** |
| 5 | 1–2 | Beginning left, balance away from partner. Face line of direction during balance. |
| | 3–4 | Beginning right, balance away from partner. |
| 6 | 5–8 | Beginning left, man walks four steps behind woman to opposite side. Beginning right, woman takes one four-step turn counterclockwise in front of man to opposite side. Man assists turn with right hand, releases during turn and catches inside hand at end of turn. |
| 7 | 1–2 | Beginning left, balance toward partner. |
| | 3–4 | Balance away from partner. |
| 8 | 5–8 | Beginning left, man walks four steps, crossing behind woman, and moves forward to meet a new partner. Beginning right, woman takes one four-step turn to original side and meets new partner. |
| | | Repeat dance with new partner. |

### Variation

At measure 8, beginning left, man takes four steps diagonally forward to inside of circle to meet a new partner. Beginning right, woman takes one four-step turn, moving behind man to outside of circle to meet a new partner.

# Glowworm Mixer

**CD:** Folk Dances Vol. 56.
**Position:** Inside hands joined.
**Formation:** Double circle, couples facing line of direction.
**Step:** Walk.
**Level:** Beginning 1

## Directions FOR THE MIXER

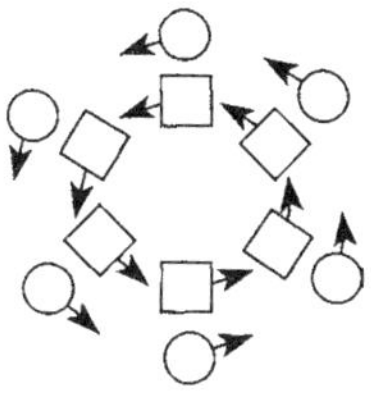

Meter 4/4 • Directions are for man; woman's part reverse.

| *Measures* | *Counts* | |
|---|---|---|
| | | **I. FORWARD** |
| 1 | 1–4 | Beginning left, walk four steps forward in line of direction. |
| | | **II. AWAY** |
| 2 | 1–4 | Partners face, beginning left, man walks backward into center of circle four steps as woman walks backward away from center of circle four steps. |
| | | **III. DIAGONAL LEFT** |
| 3 | 1–4 | Both man and woman face diagonally to their own left. Beginning left, walk four steps forward to new partner. |
| | | **IV. TURN FOUR** |
| 4 | 1–4 | Beginning left, hook right arms with new partner and turn around in four steps, ending in couple position. (The woman needs to spin around on the last beat to face line of direction.) |
| | | Repeat dance with new partner. |

**Note:** This may be danced to other four-beat music. It needs a newer tune now and then. For example: "Swedish Rhapsody," "Hello Dolly," "Hey Look Me Over," "Up with People," "A Spoonful of Sugar," "Hava Nagila," "Jingle Bells" (during the holidays), and current rock tunes.

# *Jiffy Mixer*

JIFFY MIXER was composed by Jerry and Kathy Helt, Cincinnati, Ohio.

**CD:** Wagon Wheel Records *Folk Dance Now!* #14, "Jiffy Mixer," *Dance for Fun and Fitness* #5, "Jiffy Mixer."

**Position:** Butterfly.

**Formation:** Double circle, man's back to center of circle.

**Steps:** Balance, walk, chug, step-close-step, heel and toe.

**Level:** Beginning 1

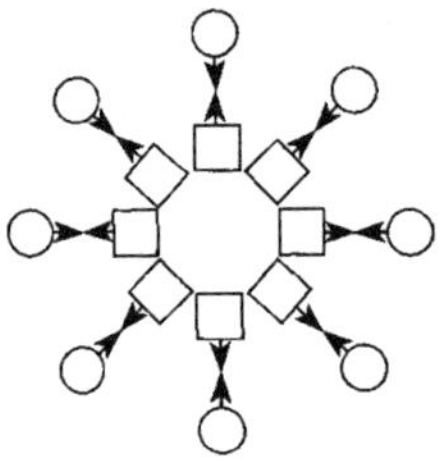

4

## *Directions* FOR THE MIXER

Meter 2/4 • Directions are for man; woman's part reverse.

| *Measures* | *Counts* | |
|---|---|---|
| 1–2 | 1–4 | Wait. |
| 3–4 | 5–8 | Beginning left, balance away from partner (step touch), balance together (step touch). |
| 1–2 | 1–4 | Beginning left, place left heel, toe, heel, toe, to side left. |
| 3–4 | 5–8 | Beginning left, step side left in line of direction, close right to left, step side left, touch right toe to left. |
| 5–8 | 1–8 | Beginning right, repeat the action of measures 1–4, moving in the reverse line of direction. |
| 9 –12 | 1–8 | Release hands. Backing away from partner, do four jumps. Clapping between each jump. Jump (count 1), clap (count 2). The clap is on the upbeat of the music. |
| 13–16 | 1–4 | Beginning left, take four swaggering steps (each step has 2 counts), diagonally right, each progressing to a new partner. The women move forward in the line of direction; men in the reverse line of direction. Take butterfly position to begin dance over. |
| | | Repeat dance from beginning with new partner. |

### Variation

An easier version, no partners, single circle, hands joined, all facing the center. Everyone begins the dance on the left foot, doing the same footwork. After the chug step, rejoin hands and travel in the reverse line of direction four slow steps *or* turn left, making a small circle, solo, four slow steps, to face center. Join hands and repeat dance.

# Patty-Cake Polka

**CD:** Folkraft CD 2912-8; Wagon Wheel Records *Folk Dance Now!* #21, "Patty Cake Polka Mixer"; *Dance for Fun and Fitness* #4, "Patty Cake Polka."

**Position:** Partners face, two hands joined.

**Formation:** Double circle, man's back to center.

**Steps:** Heel and toe polka, slide, walk.

**Level:** Beginning 1

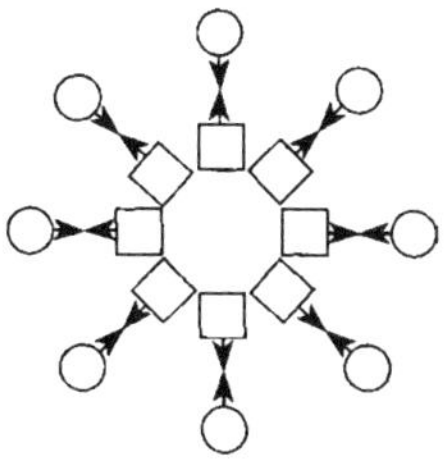

4

## *Directions* FOR THE MIXER

Meter 2/4 • Directions are for man; woman's part reverse.

| *Measures* | *Counts* | |
|---|---|---|
| | | **PART I. HEEL AND TOE POLKA AND SLIDE** |
| 1 | 1–2 | Beginning left, place left heel to left, place left toe to right instep. |
| 2 | 3–4 | Repeat measure 1. |
| 3–4 | 5–8 | Take four slides in line of direction. |
| 5–8 | 1–8 | Beginning right, repeat the action of measures 1–4, moving in reverse line of direction. |
| | | **PART II. CLAPS** |
| 8 | 1–2 | Clap own hands, clap partner's right hand. |
| 9 | 3–4 | Clap own hands, clap partner's left hand. |
| 10 | 5–6 | Clap own hands, clap partner's hands (both). |
| 11 | 7–8 | Clap own hands, slap own knees. |
| 13–14 | 1–4 | Hook right elbows and walk around partner and back to place. |
| 15–16 | 5–8 | Man moves forward in line of direction to new partner. Woman spins clockwise twice, as she moves in reverse line of direction to new partner. |
| | | Repeat dance with new partner. |

*continues on next page*

| ***Measures*** | ***Counts*** | |
|---|---|---|
| | | **VARIATION (Rhythm: quick, quick, slow)** |
| 9 | 1–4 | Clap partner's right hand three times. |
| 10 | 5–8 | Clap partner's left hand three times. |
| 11 | 1–4 | Clap partner's hands (both) three times. |
| 12 | 5–8 | Slap own knees three times. |

# *Mexican Mixer*

THE MEXICAN MIXER is a popular Texas–Mexican mixer dating from the French influence in Mexico. According to the noted Mexican dance authority Nelda Drury, San Antonio, Texas, the dance was introduced into Mexico during Maximilian's time and was danced to Viennese music.

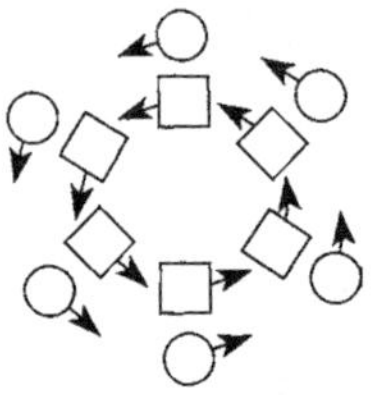

**CD:** High/Scope RM3 or any good Mexican polka.
**Music:** "Trompeta Magica," Werner, Robert, The Folklore Village Saturday Night Book, p. 24.
**Position:** Promenade.
**Formation:** Double circle, couples facing line of direction.
**Steps:** Walk, balance, step swing.
**Level:** Beginning 2

## *Directions* FOR THE MIXER

Meter 4/4 • Directions are for man, woman's part reverse.

| ***Measures*** | ***Counts*** | |
|---|---|---|
| | | **PART I. WALK AND GRAPEVINE** |
| 1 | 1–4 | Beginning man's left, walk forward four steps. |
| 2 | 5 | Face partner, give eye contact, hold right hands; man steps left to side left. |
| | 6 | Stepping with right behind left, |
| | 7 | Step with left to left side. |
| | 8 | Swings right across left or stamps right lightly, no weight. |
| 3–4 | 1–8 | Moving forward in the reverse line of direction, repeat action of measures 1–2. Man begins right. |
| | | **PART II. BALANCE AND TURN** |
| 5 | 1–4 | Single circle, man's back to center, woman faces center, partners' right hands joined, left hand to dancer on the left (corner). Beginning left, balance forward and back. |

| Measures | Counts | |
|---|---|---|
| 6 | 5–8 | Release left hands. Turn partner with right hand, hold halfway around with four steps. Now men face center, ladies face out. |
| 7 | 1–4 | With partners' right hands joined, man joins left hands with dancer on his left. Beginning left, balance forward and back. |
| 8 | 5–8 | Release right-hand hold, turn with left-hand hold half around counterclockwise with four steps. End with new partner in promenade position facing line of direction. |
| | | Repeat dance with new partner. |

Show enthusiasm by occasionally yelling or put tongue against upper teeth and make a continuous sound.

# Tennessee Wig Walk

THE TENNESSEE WIG WALK was composed by Harry and Dia Trygg, Tucson, Arizona, in 1954.

**CD:** Circle Dancing for Today, KEA 1146.

**Formation:** Double circle, couples, right-hand star position, men face line of direction, women face reverse line of direction.

**Steps:** Grapevine, walk.

**Level:** Beginning

## Directions FOR THE MIXER

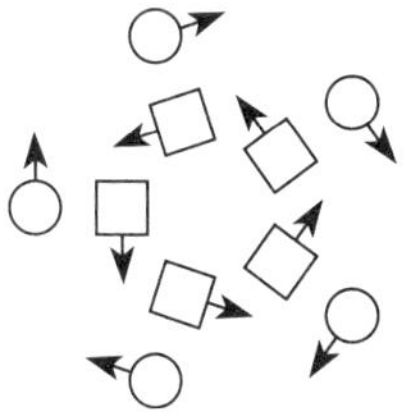

Meter 4/4 • Directions are for man; woman's part reverse.

| Measures | Counts | |
|---|---|---|
| 1–2 | | Introduction: no action. |
| 1 | 1–2 | Beginning left, point left toe forward in front of right. |
| | 2–4 | Point left toe to left side (slow, slow). |
| 2 | 5–8 | Exchanging places, grapevine, step left behind right, step right, cross left in front of right, hold (quick, quick, slow). |
| | | Man now on outside, woman inside, both facing original direction. Change to left hand star. |
| 3–4 | 1–8 | Beginning right, repeat action of measures 1–2 with opposite feet, returning to original position. |
| 5–6 | 1–8 | Right-hand star position. Turning clockwise, make one full turn, stepping left, right, left, brush right; right, left, right, brush left. End facing original direction. |
| 7–8 | 1–8 | Release hands. Leave partner and move forward with step, step, step, brush step, step, step, brush. Man progresses in line of direction, woman in reverse line of direction, passing first person on first "brush"; meeting next person on second "brush." Join right hands. |
| | | Repeat dance from beginning with new partner. |

# CAJUN DANCE

CAJUN DANCE, MUSIC, AND FOOD are very popular. In the 1980s Chef Paul Prudhomme of New Orleans attracted nationwide attention with his Cajun cooking and references to Cajun culture. Cajun culture suddenly bounced all over the United States. It exemplifies a true spirit of *joie de vivre.* The Cajun heritage is keyed to family, music, and the French language.

The word *Cajun* evolved from the word *Acadian* with the loss of an unstressed syllable (*cf.* "Injun" from "Indian"). The Acadians originally came from the French provinces of Normandy and Picardy along the English Channel. The first French colony, Acadie,[5] was established in 1604 in Nova Scotia, Canada. For political reasons the British deported the Acadians in 1755. Some migrated south, finally settling in the flatlands and bayous of Louisiana with other French immigrants. This coastal area, actually 22 of the 64 parishes of Louisiana, is referred to as Acadia, Acadiana, or Evangeline country.

From France the Acadians brought their seventeenth- and eighteenth-century culture to the New World. Their culture evolved and adapted with that of the French, English, Spanish, and African Americans. The white French-speaking people of Acadia are referred to as Cajuns; the black French-speaking people are Creoles (these are not the same Creoles who settled New Orleans).

Families have always gathered together for social occasions, first at homes and later at barns and dance halls. Music, French ballads, dancing, cards, and of course food were enjoyed. These gatherings were called *fais-dodo* ("go to sleep") because the children were bedded down in another room while the parties lasted till the wee hours. When the halls became night clubs, the children were excluded.

## Music

Originally the fiddle was the primary instrument and someone sang old French ballads. The interaction of the Acadians and Creoles influenced the music. The singing became less important as two fiddles played, one melody, one rhythmic backup. More French songs were lost in the 1880s when the German immigrants introduced the button accordion. By the 1920s, the accordion had displaced the fiddles. But during the 1930s and 1940s fiddles returned as the Cajun musicians were influenced by their Texas neighbors' country western music. Later Bob Wills's western swing, Nashville country western music, and rock and roll all touched Cajun music too. After World War II Cajuns returned home with a sense of pride and a rebirth of Cajun music took place. The folk festivals also encouraged traditional Cajun musicians to come forward. Michael Doucet is to be credited with his leadership in restoring interest in traditional Cajun music, encouraging acoustic playing, and playing outside the lounges.

Today the button accordion is the lead instrument and the accordion player also sings French songs. The fiddle and small triangle make up the band. In larger bands there are guitars, spoons, drums, bass, and sometimes brass. Of course there is electric amplification. Cajun music, sometimes referred to as "Chanky Chank" sounds, is a mix of sounds, styles, and cultural history.

A relatively new offshoot of Cajun music is *zydeco,* a combination of Cajun and rhythm and blues with a Caribbean musical pulse. Eighty years ago a song was written, "Zydeco es Pas Salee," which means "the snap beans have no salt." *Zydeco* is Cajun slang for the French *les haricots,* which means "green snap beans." Today zydeco means snappy music. Bands include a piano, accordion, and a rubboard (metal washboard or steel vest) strapped on the musicians who wear metal casings on the fingers to produce a myriad of sounds. The songs are in English or French. The rhythm is 4/4 with a strong 1–2, 1–2 beat.

5. Acadie, which the French called their settlement, was a descriptive word of the Micmac Indians, members of the Algonquin tribe.

### Music

Cajun: *Parlez Nous á Boire* (Two-step, swing, blues, waltz), CD 322; *Allon á Lafayette, Bayou Boogie,* Beausoleil; Vintage Beausoleil CDC-213; *Stir Up the Roux,* Bruce Daigrepont Zydeco: *Louisiana Blues and Zydeco.* Clifton Chenier. CD 329; *Motordude Zydeco,* A-2 Fay Records; *Pick Up On This,* CD 2129; and *My Name is Beau Jocque,* Beau Jocque, PCD-1031.

### Dance

The Acadian dance repertoire included the quadrille, lancer, polka, mazurka, play party types referred to as *danserond,* and contredanse. Many dances were performed without instrumentation during the 40 days before Lent, so they sang in French, which helped to keep the language alive. Young and old danced, especially those of a "marrying age." The contredanse was more like the Appalachian big circle, a country dance. In the late 1940s the Cajun round dance scene was very similar to that in Texas. It is almost a step back in time to watch the Cajuns dance the waltz, two-step, and one-step. Jitterbug is danced to two-step music. Zydeco is the latest dance. There are two-steps, one-steps, and a few waltzes. Zydeco and Cajun music affect the dancing styles. Cajun dance is smoother, more precise. Dancers circle the floor with more turns and the movement is horizontal. Zydeco dancers move in one spot with greater hip action. The syncopated zydeco beat generates a bouncy vertical style with few turns. The dancers move subtly, upright with bent knees and lower to the floor. The dance is flavored with small kicks.

# *Cajun Waltz*

**Position:** Closed
**Level:** Beginning 2

## *Directions* FOR THE DANCE

Meter 3/4 • Directions are for man; woman's part reverse.

**Forward Waltz:** Closed position. The man pulls the woman close, wrapping most of his right forearm around the woman's shoulder blades. Moving in the line of direction, step on each beat (left, right, left). The first step is longer, followed by a shuffle, shuffle. The man travels forward, woman backward, most of the time; minimal turning. Two measures (6 steps) to turn in place counterclockwise; may turn clockwise.

**Woman Turn:** Couple travels forward. Man releases right hand and steps slightly to left side (count 1) and forward (count 2, 3) as woman turns clockwise under his left arm, 3 steps. As she turns, she places her left bent arm behind her back. As she completes the turn, the couple resumes the closed position.

**Double Turn:** Couple travels forward and man releases right hand. Man takes three steps forward as woman turns with three steps clockwise under his left arm, places her left arm behind her back; woman continues to travel backward as the man turns counterclockwise three steps under his left arm; resumes the closed position.

### Style

The dance is smooth as if gliding on ice. A fluid movement is achieved by dancing on the balls of the feet and absorbing the movement with bent knees.

# *Cajun Two-Step*

**Position:** Closed
**Level:** Beginning 2

## *Directions* FOR THE DANCE

Meter 2/4 or 4/4 • Directions are for man; woman's part reverse.

The man pulls the woman close, wrapping most of his right forearm around the woman's shoulder blades. Progressing forward, the couple turns slowly counterclockwise, step-close-step touch. Step to the left side, and slightly forward, close right to left, step left in place, touch right to left instep (4 counts). May turn clockwise.

### Style

The dance is smooth. In some areas, dancers rock slightly side to side.



# *Cajun One-Step*

**Position:** Closed
**Level:** Beginning 1

## *Directions* FOR THE DANCE

Meter 4/4 • Directions are for man; woman's part reverse.

Travel forward stepping side to side on each beat (side touch, side touch). Turning counterclockwise, step side touch near instep, step side touch near instep, step side touch near instep, step side touch near instep.

Transition one-step to two-step or vice versa. The change of pattern is made when the feet are together.

# *Cajun Jitterbug*

CAJUN JITTERBUG is frequently danced to two-step music. The steps are smooth with many variations.

**Position:** Two hands joined.
**Level:** Beginning 1

## *Directions* FOR THE DANCE

Meter 2/4 • Directions are for man; woman's part reverse.

The basic step appears to be a "slight limp" with weight on right foot. Step left and lightly drag the right to the left, accent the second and fourth beats as the body drops (knees bend) ever so slightly. Step is smooth, not jerky or bouncy. Step close, step close (one *and* two *and*). The lead may change to right close, right close or during the moves, step alternately left, right on each beat like four-count swing, coming back into step close, step close. The arms push–pull like a parallelogram; arms held chest high, push to right side, pull left arm back, shift right side to right side and pivot clockwise using side close, side close or buzz step. Reverse to left side by side without losing a beat. The arms are never straight; sometimes referred to as "noodle arms."

The man leads the moves. All the figures are smooth, one leading to the next as the dancers cover a circular space. Refer to Swing for different figures.

# *Zydeco Two-Step*

**Music:** "Paper in My Shoe" by Boozoo Chavis; "Railroad Blues" by Lynn August; "Johnie Billie Goat" by Boozoo Chavis.

**Position:** Closed.

**Level:** Beginning 1

## *Directions* FOR THE DANCE

Meter 2/4 • Steps based on eight counts • Directions are for man; woman's part reverse.

| *Counts* | | *Cue* |
|---|---|---|
| 1 | Moving in place, step left | step |
| 2 | Bend knee (slight bounce) | drop |
| 3 | Step right | step |
| 4 | Step left | step |

*continues on next page*

Zydeco Two-Step, *continued*

| *Counts* | | *Cue* |
|---|---|---|
| 5–6 | Step right, bend knee (slight bounce) | drop |
| 7 | Step left | step |
| 8 | Step right | step |

**Note:** Move in place. Travel forward in line of direction, stepping forward on counts 1 and 5. Turn clockwise or counterclockwise on counts 1 and 5.

### Style

Keep steps small and controlled. Keep body accented downward, knees slightly bent, feet relatively flat on the floor with weight over the balls of the feet. Shoulders and arms are relatively still and parallel with the floor. The movements and gestures are smooth and subtle. The emphasis is more on the rhythm and footwork.

## Teaching Suggestions

Bounce in place eight or 16 counts before starting step. Start with slow music. Repeat any variations two or three times to establish the pattern. Increase tempo. Steps are quick and light.

### Variations

**Position:** Closed
**Level:** Beginning 2.

1. **Closed position, 1 basic step.** Repeat basic step, counts 1–6, then as man pushes left hand against woman's right hand (woman pushes right hand against man's left) man steps left foot behind his right, steps right in place and relaxes right hand (counts 7–8). Woman steps right behind her left, steps left in place.
2. **From closed position,** move into swing out position and continue basic step. Keep joined hands and arms firm as basic step continues. Return to closed position on count 1.
3. **Eat a beat:** Step on the toe, pivot or twist the heel in and out on counts 2 and 6.
4. **Brush (kick forward).** Step left, brush right forward, step right, step left. Step right, brush left forward, step left, step right.
5. **Closed position.** Step left turning clockwise, step right, left (slow, quick, quick). Open position. Step right, brush left forward, step left, step right (quick, quick, quick, quick). Turn on the first step. Take two sets to make one complete turn.

# COUNTRY WESTERN DANCE

COUNTRY WESTERN DANCE has been around for a long time; it is definitely a grass-roots dance. As country western music has increased in popularity, so has country western dance. Country western music, a twangy honky-tonk sound as played by Bob Wills and his Texas Playboys in the late 1930s, was just the beginning. The music is influenced by spirituals, Dixieland jazz, and the big band sound. The fiddle, steel guitar, and deep bass give country western music its character. The fiddle was part of the band. Wherever country western music is played, people dance. The dances are based on old folk dances, square dances, and social dances, topped off with a new look, called country western. Swing, one-step, two-step, schottische, waltz, and line dances are all part of the repertoire.

## Country Western Style

The country western look starts with cowboy or roper boots. Tight-fitting jeans are worn by both men and women. Large belt buckles adorn the dancers. Cowboy hats are commonly seen on the dance floor, though, for the last few years, younger men have been switching to baseball hats. In some settings, women may wear a western skirt instead of jeans. When dancers have a free hand, they hook the thumb near the belt buckle or into the closest pocket.

## Dance Hall Etiquette

At country western dances, several types of dancing may take place simultaneously. The perimeter of the dance floor is for round dances; the slower ones dance in the inside lane. Fast and slow dancers move counterclockwise around the floor. The swing dancers and line dancers split the center area, with line dancers closer to the band.

The man takes the woman's hand or arm or offers his arm to escort her onto or off the dance floor and to return her to her seat.

In western and Cajun dancing it is customary to leave the dance floor and return to your table or side of the room, even if you plan to dance the next dance with the same partner. The man still takes the woman's hand or arm and offers his arm to escort her onto and off the dance floor and to return to her seat.

Refer to Chapter 8 for skills in teaching partner dancing.

# Traditional Country Western Swing

## Traditional Country Western Swing Rhythm

Traditional country western swing is danced to a faster 4/4 time song, between 170 and 200 BPM. At times the traditional "cowboys" dance faster than the music, dancing with the music, not to the beat of the music. On popular country music TV programs and at many dance studios, the style of country swing performed is the East Coast Swing. The only difference from ballroom style is the music played.

## Cowboy Swing Style

The cowboys have a very smooth style. They slide their feet along the floor, almost never picking them up for a step. The emphasis of the dance is on the arm movements and the figures that are performed more so than the footwork. During many figures, the feet may not move at all.

Steps are small and arms are kept bent and close to the body. Two factors figured in the development of this style: (1) the fast tempo of music does not allow for large gestures, and (2) traditional dance floors were very small. Large steps or movement would cause a couple to bump into another couple.

Although from a distance, this style may look wild, with a good partner, the moves are very controlled and flow smoothly from one variation to another. There is a constant counterbalance between partners, allowing a "leaning" away (with a bend at the elbow joint) that is the characteristic mark of cowboy swing.

## *Directions* FOR THE DANCE

Meter 4/4

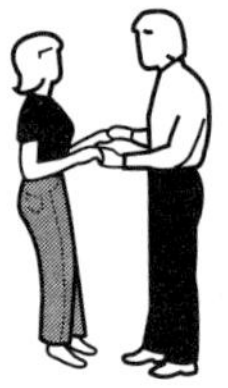

### Basic Step

**Position:** Two hands joined.
**Level:** Beginning 2

| *Counts* | *Steps* | *Step Cue* |
|---|---|---|
| 1 + | Step left, diagonal left forward | one |
| | Woman: Step right, diagonal left forward (crossing in front of her left foot) | |
| 2 + | Step right forward | two |
| 3 | Pivot 180° counterclockwise on right foot | together |
| + | Slide left to right foot, *keep weight on* right *foot* | one |
| 4 | Begin again | |

The basic must be done four times to start at the beginning of the next measure.

**Note:** Country swing music is 4/4 meter (4 beats to the measure) and the basic step takes 3 beats. Therefore there is a cross rhythm: 3 steps against a 4 beat measure. Repeating the step sequence four times brings one to the same starting point.

**Style:** The basic step is performed moving in a counterclockwise motion. Knees slightly bent and forearms are at the side with elbows bent. The man and woman lean away from each other (counterbalance). Letting go would cause a partner to fall backwards. Shoulders are slightly back and hips are over the heels. On the *together* step of the basic, some cowboys will touch their left foot to the side or slightly lift it off the floor for a little extra flair.

**Lead:** On count *1 and,* the man pulls the left side of his body back, guiding his partner to his right side. On count 3, the man brings both hands in front of him for a counterbalance with his partner.

## Cowboy Swing Variations

The man's hands must be able to rotate easily in woman's hands during any variation such as the Cowboy Arch, Cowboy Cross, Cowboy Cuddle, Walk Through (Brush Off), Octopus, and Pretzel.

### Cowboy Arch

**Position:** Two hands joined.
**Level:** Beginning 3

The man lifts up his left arm (forming the "arch") and goes under as the woman goes behind him, trading places. Prep: Man releases his right hand.

| *Counts* | *Steps* | *Step Cue* |
|---|---|---|
| 1 | Man steps diagonally left forward on left while raising left arm | man |
| 2 | Man steps right forward while turning one-quarter left (left shoulder back) | goes |
| 3 | Man lowers left arm and leans back over right foot, counterbalancing with his partner in a swing out position | under |
| | Finish move with woman's inside turn, page 424 | |

**Style:** As the man goes under his arm, he bends his knees so that he does not knock off his hat.

In the swing out position, the man is not facing his partner, but looks at her with his peripheral vision. "Real cowboys" look at their partners out of the corners of their eyes.

**Lead:** The man's left hand guides woman to his right side.

### Cowboy Cross

**Position:** Two hands joined.
**Level:** Beginning 3

The man lifts up both hands. Keeping them together, he leads the woman to his right side going under his hands, ending with arms in a "crossed" position.

*continues on next page*

Traditional Country Western Swing, *continued*

| *Counts* | *Steps* | *Step Cue* |
|---|---|---|
| | **CROSS** | |
| 1 | Man steps forward on left while raising both hands | cross |
| 2 | Man moves over his left foot and turns one-quarter right (right shoulder back) while taking both hands over the woman's head | woman |
| | Woman on right foot pivots counterclockwise one-half turn | |
| 3 | Man lowers both hands and leans back over left foot, counterbalancing with partner | under |
| | **UNCROSS** (feet do not move) | |
| | Man lifts both hands up, brings woman in front of him, turning her clockwise | uncross |
| | Man lowers both hands to belt level and leans over his right foot, counterbalancing with partner | turn through |
| | Man repeats cross and uncross | |
| | Finish move with woman's inside turn | |



**Style:** After the first step is taken, both the man's and woman's feet remain in place, pivoting on both feet to face toward partner. Both man and woman must keep their elbows bent on all counterbalances.

**Lead:** Man lifts both hands up and together and gently pulls the woman toward his right side to the cross position. The woman must allow the man's hand to twist in hers, as she goes under his hands.

## Cowboy Cuddle

**Position:** Two hands joined.
**Level:** Beginning 2

| *Counts* | *Steps* | *Step Cue* |
|---|---|---|
| | **CUDDLE IN** | |
| 1 | Man steps forward on left while raising his left hand | |
| 2 | Without releasing hands, the man will move his raised left hand across in front of her and up over her head as she is turning counter-clockwise one-half on her right foot | cuddle |
| 3 | Man lowers left hand as the woman finishes in the cuddle position close to him on his right side. Man leans forward over left foot, counterbalancing with his partner as she leans back over her left foot | in |
| | **CUDDLE OUT** (feet do not move) | |
| 4 | Man lifts left hand up and gently pushes with his right forearm against her back to start her turning clockwise one-half | cuddle |

| Counts | Steps | Step Cue |
|---|---|---|
| + | Man lowers left hand to belt level and leans back over his right foot, counterbalancing with partner | out |
| 1 + 2 + | Man repeats cuddle in and cuddle out | cuddle in<br>cuddle out<br>cuddle through |
| | Finish move with woman's inside turn page 424 | |

**Style:** After the first step is taken, both man's and woman's feet remain in place. The woman pivots on her feet to turn. Both man and woman must keep their elbows bent on the cuddle out counterbalance.

**Lead:** Man lifts left hand up and gently pulls the woman toward his right. The woman must allow the man's hand to twist in hers, as she goes under his hands. In the cuddle position, the man must be sure that his hands are at her waist level.

## Walk Through (Brush Off)

**Position:** Two hands joined.
**Prep:** Let go of your right hand.
**Level:** Beginning 3



The man moves through the space where the woman's left arm is, seemingly walking through the arm.

| Counts | Steps | Step Cue |
|---|---|---|
| 1 | Man steps diagonally left forward on left foot while turning counterclockwise (left shoulder back) | man |
| 2 | Man continues to turn and steps side on right foot. Release left hand when it is pulled against right side | turns |
| 3 | Man leans back over right foot. Bring left hand to left side (palm facing back) to catch woman's right hand | through |
| | Woman leans back over left foot and slides right hand along his waist to reconnect with his left hand (woman's palm up) | |
| | Finish move with woman's inside turn, page 424 | woman goes under |

**Style:** This move is often used at the end of a combination or to finish off a variation that has ended in the swing out position.

**Man:** Man using left hand, pulls partner forward toward right side.

## Octopus

**Position:** Two hands joined.
**Level:** Intermediate

| *Counts* | *Steps* | *Step Cue* |
|---|---|---|
| | **PART I** | |
| 1 | Man steps diagonally left forward on left foot | up |
| 2 | Woman steps diagonally left forward on right foot, ending right hip to right hip | |
| | Man swings both arms up and over both heads; lowering left hand behind head and right hand behind partner's head (octopus position) | and |
| 3 | Man lets go with both hands, and right hands slide along partner's right arm, turn one-eighth to right and lean away catching right hands (keep right elbow bent) | over |
| | **PART II** | |
| 4 | Man raises right elbow and pulls partner to right side; woman steps side right on right foot | change |
| 1 | Man turns woman left (counterclockwise) under right arm; man turns one-quarter counterclockwise (left shoulder back) (woman is behind man) and step side right on your right; he folds right arm behind his back and brings left hand to left side | hands |
| 2 | Man puts her right hand into his left hand (behind his back); continue turning one-quarter clockwise (right shoulder back); man leans back over right foot; woman leans back over left foot; man's left hand is holding woman's right hand | lean |
| 3 | Finish move with woman's inside turn, page 424 | turn the lady |

**Lead:** Pull your partner to your right side by raising both arms.

## Pretzel

**Position:** Two hands joined; the man's hands must be able to rotate easily in woman's hands.
**Level:** Advanced

The man moves through three different positions in one continuous move.

| *Counts* | *Steps* | *Step Cue* |
|---|---|---|
| | **PART I. MAN'S HAMMERLOCK** | |
| 1 | Man steps diagonally left forward on left foot while raising left arm | man |

| *Counts* | *Steps* | *Step Cue* |
|---|---|---|
| 2 | Man steps forward on right foot while turning counterclockwise one-quarter (left shoulder back) and goes under left arm (man must lower left elbow so he does not hit partner in the face); man folds right forearm to back in a hammerlock position | goes |
| 3 | Man pivots on both feet, continuing turning counterclockwise; extend left arm to left and in front of woman's waist | under |
| | Woman steps back onto right foot while turning clockwise one-quarter | |
| | **PART II. BACK TO BACK** | |
| 4 | Man raises left arm; pulling woman behind him with right arm while stepping left on left foot to a slightly wider stance | back |
| 1 | Man continues pulling partner to right. While passing back to back man raises right arm and lowers left arm | to |
| 2 | Partners are now right hip to right hip, with left arms behind the back | back |
| | **PART III. MAN TURNS, PULLS PARTNER FROM BEHIND** | |
| 3 | Man bends right elbow 90° | over man's |
| | Woman turns clockwise one-eighth while moving over right foot | |
| 4 | Man pivots on both feet counterclockwise one-quarter (left shoulder back); at the same time man brings right forearm over his head and lowers it to chest level, keeping left hand behind; woman is behind man | head |
| | Woman steps on left foot by man's left side while turning clockwise one-quarter | |
| 1 | Man releases his right hand while pulling left hand and partner from behind his back; man raises left arm to pull partner under his arm and in front of him | pull woman |
| 2 | Woman steps forward on right foot while passing under partner's arm; she pivots counterclockwise one-half (left shoulder back) and steps back on left foot (end in swing out position) | from behind |
| 3–4 | Finish move with woman's inside turn, page 424 | |

**Style:** This move must flow from one part to the next effortlessly. Once the man begins the Pretzel he does very little, if any, stepping. The woman must move around him as needed. This step is usually performed very quickly. Total control must be achieved before speed is increased.

**Lead:** In Part I, the man pulls right hand (palm facing back) back and down, guiding the woman to right side. The man continues to pull gently with right hand to woman's left shoulder to man's left shoulder.

# *Traditional Two-Step*

THE TRADITIONAL TWO-STEP is also known as the Shuffle. The dance is done in a smooth, flowing style. The rhythm—slow, slow, quick, quick, exactly like the FoxTrot Magic rhythm—is known as a *shuffle* beat.

Different two-step rhythms, noteworthy for their many regional variations, exist. The Texas Two-Step is an example. Although most common in Texas, this dance is popular throughout the United States and Canada. Texas Two-Step rhythm is quick, quick, slow, or step-together step. The Traditional Two-Step is normally danced to music between 75 and 95 BPM. The Texas Two-Step may be danced to faster music, up to 120 BPM.

In the mid 1990s, country western dance competitions became popular. A modern-style two-step, used for competitions, has a reversed rhythm; quick, quick, slow, slow. This style is favored in urban dance studios. Beginning variations on the first "quick" creates a snappier look. In rural areas of the country, where dance is considered a social activity, the traditional rhythm is maintained.



### Two-Step Rhythm

The music is written in 4/4 time. The step pattern takes a measure-and-a half of music. It is an uneven rhythm pattern—slow, slow, quick, quick.

| 4/4 | S | | S | | Q | Q |
|---|---|---|---|---|---|---|
| | 1 | 2 | 3 | 4 | 1 | 2 |

uneven rhythm

### Two-Step Style

The dance has smooth, controlled steps; there is no pumping of arms or bouncing. The closed dance position has several variations. The body has good posture alignment, with a straight back and knees slightly bent. Quite a bit of space should be left between partners in variations of the closed position. The man's left palm faces up and the woman's right palm faces down, resting lightly in man's left; man's right arm may be straight, right hand folding over woman's left shoulder. The position of the woman's left arm varies. The woman may fold her left hand over his right elbow; her elbow is down, her arm is limp, which gives a "careless look." Her left arm may be extended to rest on top of man's right arm. Or she may hook her thumb into one of the man's belt loops on his right side. They face each other squarely, shoulders parallel.

The dancers glide around the floor in a counterclockwise direction and cover a lot of territory. Although there are many variations, most dancers relax and move forward, with an occasional turn, or the man dances backward, but always they move in the line of direction.

## *Directions* FOR THE DANCE

### Basic Two Step

Meter 4/4 • Directions are for man; woman's part reverse

**Music:** Suggested tune, "Mercury Blue."
**Position:** Closed.
**Level:** Beginning 2

| *Counts* | *Steps* | *Rhythm Cue* |
|---|---|---|
| 1–2 | Step left forward | slow |
| 3–4 | Step right forward | slow |
| 1 | Step left forward | quick |
| 2 | Step right forward | quick |

**Style:** The forward steps should be long, smooth, gliding steps, straight ahead. The woman, moving backward, takes a long step, reaching from hip to toe. If the music is slow, for balance on the slow steps, dancers may step forward left, touch right to left (for balance), step forward right, touch left to right.

**Lead:** The body leads forward.

**Variations:** Over the past several years, many different variations have been added to the two-step repertoire. Some couples appear to be *swinging* as they move around the dance floor.

The basic footwork is maintained while executing the variations, which usually start on the first *slow*. Hands stay joined, except when noted. The man's hands must always be able to rotate easily in the woman's hands. Once in position, the man may decide to travel for a few basic steps before moving on to the next position.

### Varsouvienne

**Position:** Closed position.
**Level:** Beginning 3

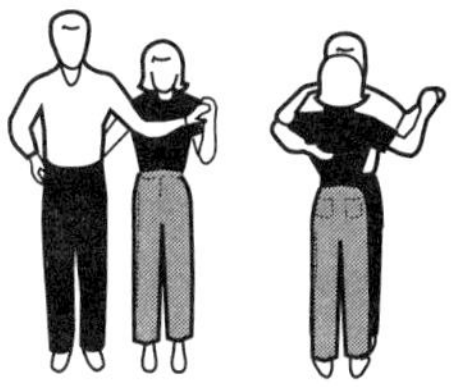

| *Counts* | *Steps* | *Rhythm Cues* |
|---|---|---|
| 1–2 | Man lifts left hand up and begins to turn woman counterclockwise 180° | slow |
| 3–4 | Man changes her right hand to his right hand continuing turning the woman 180° | slow |
| 1–2 | Man steps to woman's left side continuing turning her 180° (during the slow slow, quick quick the woman has turned one-and-a-half times); man and the woman join left hands ending in Varsouvienne position | quick, quick |
| 3–4 | Man lifts left hand and pulls down with right, causing the woman to turn clockwise 180° | slow |
| 1–2 | Man guides woman behind him | slow |
| 3–4 | Man lowers his left hand in front of woman. She steps up to his left side into a reverse Varsouvienne | quick quick |
| 1–2 | Man guides woman in front of him with left hand, starting to turn her clockwise 180° | slow |
| 3–4 | Man releases left hand and continues turning woman with his right hand 180° | slow |
| 1–2 | Man changes her right hand to his left, turning her 180° back to closed position | quick quick |

## Little Windows

**Position:** Varsouvienne position.
**Level:** Intermediate

| *Counts* | *Steps* | *Rhythm Cues* |
|---|---|---|
| 1–2 | Keeping right hand high, man raises left hand over woman's head, turning her clockwise 180° | slow |
| 3–4 | Man continues turning woman clockwise 180° with both hands | slow |
| 1–2 | Bring right arm to a 90° angle, man finishes turning woman clockwise 180°, ending in Little Windows; right hips together, man facing line of direction, woman facing reverse line of direction | quick quick |
| | This position may be reversed by turning the woman counterclockwise two-and-a-half times, until the left hips are together, man facing reverse line of direction and woman facing line of direction | |
| | Return to closed position by turning the woman clockwise one-and-a-half turns | |

## Yoke

**Position:** Varsouvienne position.
**Level:** Beginning 3

| *Counts* | *Steps* | *Rhythm Cues* |
|---|---|---|
| 1–2 | Man lifts his left hand up and over woman's head, gently turning her clockwise 180° | slow |
| 3–4 | Keeping left hand high, man moves right hand clockwise over woman's head, continuing turning her 180° | slow |
| 1–2 | Man lowers both hands behind neck, into a yoke position | quick quick |
| | This position may be reversed by turning the woman counterclockwise two turns in front of the man, guiding her to his left side | |
| | Return to closed position by turning the woman clockwise two turns | |

# *Ten-Step*

TEN-STEP IS ALSO KNOWN AS the Ten-Step Polka. A similar dance, 8 beats, is the Jessie Polka. Country western dancers call the Jessie Polka the Eight-Step Shuffle, or Cowboy Polka.

**Music:** Fiddle music; suggested tunes: "Uncle Pen," "Cajun Moon," "New Cut Road," "On the Road Again," "East Bound and Down."

**Style:** Review line dance style, page 446. Knees are slightly bent; keep the dance smooth.

**Position:** Couples in Varsouvienne position; woman's right-hand fingertips touch man's right for ease of turn; man's left hand reaches over (fingers down) woman's left, holding just above waist.

**Level:** Beginning 2

## *Directions* FOR THE DANCE

Meter 2/4 fast or 4/4 slow • Directions are presented in beats.

| ***Counts*** | |
|---|---|
| | **PART I.** |
| 1–2 | Beginning left–right knee bent–touch left heel forward, left foot turned to a 45° angle, and return; shift weight to left |
| 3 | Touch right toe backward |
| 4 | Brush (scuff) right heel as returning (no weight) |
| 5 | Touch right heel forward, right foot turned to a 45° angle |
| 6 | Sweep right, heel leading, across in front of left |
| 7–8 | Touch right heel forward, right foot turned to a 45° angle, and return, taking weight |
| 9 | Touch left heel forward, left foot turned to a 45° angle |
| 10 | Sweep left, heel leading, across in front of right |
| | **PART II.** |
| 11–18 | Beginning left, take four two-steps forward in line of direction (quick, quick, slow–four times) |

### Variations for Part II

**Level:** Beginning 3

Part I is referred to as "think steps" because the man decides what variation to do. During Part II partners may improvise with a wide variety of maneuvers. The number of two-steps may be increased by an even number.

1. The woman turns under man's left arm once or twice while moving forward.
2. Man lifts right hand over woman's head, woman taking four two-step turns toward the man, and moves to his left side to face line of direction in promenade

*continues on next page*

position. Repeat Part II; then man raises his right arm over his head like a lariat and woman takes four two-step travels behind the man. She starts to turn counterclockwise 360° (third two-step); her right shoulder comes to his right shoulder; man lifts his left arm up and extends his right arm down at his side, shoulder to shoulder; she pivots to face forward in original position (fourth two-step).

3. *The Train.* Taking four two-steps, woman moves in front of man, two hands still joined and resting on her shoulders. Repeat Part II in this position. The woman two-steps back to place.
4. Take two two-steps forward; on the next two two-steps, the man raises his right arm over her head, and the woman travels in front of man to face him. Arms are crossed, extended and firm, with right hand on top. Repeat Part II. Pivoting counterclockwise, take four two-steps. Repeat Part II. The man lifts right arm over his head as she travels around behind him, turning 360° as in variation 2 to face original position.
5. *Wheel Around.* In Varsouvienne position, take four two-steps; the couple turns counterclockwise, the man dancing almost in place as the woman travels forward. Or turn clockwise, the woman dancing almost in place, as the man travels forward.

# *Traveling Cha Cha*

**Counts:** 1 Slow, 2 Slow, 3 Quick, *&* Quick, 4 Slow

**Music:** "I Like It, I Love It" by Tim McGraw; "Big Heart" by The Gibson Miller Band; "I'm Not Strong Enough to Say No" by Blackhawk.

**Position:** Varsouvienne.

**Level:** Intermediate

## *Directions* FOR THE DANCE

Meter 4/4 • Directions are printed in beats.

| ***Counts*** | |
|---|---|
| | **PART I.** |
| 1–2 | Beginning left, rock forward and backward right |
| 3 + 4 | Cha cha cha; shuffle backward left, right, left |
| 5–6 | Rock backward right, rock forward left |
| 7 + 8 | Cha cha cha; shuffle forward right, left, right |
| 1–4 | Repeat action of beats 1–4 above |
| 5–8 | Repeat action of beats 5–8 above; on beats 7–8 raise right hands over woman's head while she turns one-half left to face man |

| Counts | |
|---|---|
| | **PART II.** |
| 1–4 | Man rocks forward left, backward right, cha, cha, cha; woman rocks forward left, backward right and on beats 3–4 cha, cha, cha turning one-half right under right hands to Varsouvienne position |
| 5–8 | Man rocks backward right, forward left, cha, cha, cha; woman rocks backward right, forward left, and on beats 7–8 cha, cha, cha turning one-half left to face man |
| 1–4 | Man rocks forward left, backward right, cha cha, cha; woman rocks backward left, forward right, cha, cha, cha turning one-half right on beats 3–4 to Varsouvienne position |
| 5–8 | Both rock backward right, forward left, cha, cha, cha |
| | **PART III. HALF TURNS** |
| 1 + | With left foot, step forward, count 1, pivot on left foot, turning clockwise 180 degrees end facing RLD. |
| 2 | With right foot, step forward |
| 3 + 4 | Starting with left foot, Cha Cha Cha forward |
| 5–8 | Repeat actions of counts 1–4 with opposite footwork, turning counter clockwise. |
| 1–8 | Repeat actions of counts 1–8 above |
| | **PART IV. TRAVELING CHA CHA** |
| 1–2 | With left foot, step forward, count 1, with right foot, step forward, count 2 |
| 3 + 4 | Starting with left foot, Cha Cha Cha forward |
| 5–8 | Repeat count 1–4 with opposite footwork, continuing to travel forward |
| 1–8 | Repeat actions of counts 1–8 above |
| | **PART V. SWITCHING PLACES** |
| | When stepping to the side, partners need to offset a little, so they do not step on each other. |
| | **Men's Part** |
| 1 | With left foot step side right, crossing behind on count 1. At the same time, release right hand hold and lower right hand to right side back |
| 2 | With right foot, step side right. At the same time, continuing to hold left hands with partner, lower left arm in front of women's waist |
| 3 + 4 | Starting with left foot, Cha Cha Cha in place. At the same time, rejoin right hands |
| 5 | With right foot, step side left, crossing in front of right foot. At the same time, release left hand and start to raise connected right hands |
| 6 | With left foot, step side left |
| 7 + 8 | Starting with right foot, Cha Cha Cha in place. At the same time, rejoin left hands in varsouvienne position |
| 1–8 | Repeat actions of counts 1–8 above |

# Country Waltz

**Dance A While CD:** "Ranchera," or any contemporary country western waltz (120 bpm).
**Beats:** Country waltz, a steady 3/4 beat.
**Slow:** "Alibis," Tracy Laurence CD: *The Best of Tracy Laurence Song.* 100 BPM
**Medium:** "Drift Off To Dream," Travis Tritt CD: *Country Club Song.* 120 BPM
**Fast:** "Five Dollar Fine," Chris Le Doux CD: *Stampede Song.* 130 BPM
**Position:** Closed position, man facing line of direction.
**Level:** Beginning 2

## *Directions* FOR THE DANCE

Meter 3/4 • Directions are for man; woman's part reverse.

| *Counts* | *Steps* | *Rhythm Cue* |
|---|---|---|
| 1 | Traveling forward, beginning left, step forward | long |
| 2 | Step right forward | short |
| 3 | Step left forward | short |
| 4 | Step right forward | long |
| 5 | Step left forward | short |
| 6 | Step right forward | short |

**Note:** Body position is important. Shoulders are always parallel. Man's right arm is firm, wrapped around the woman's back. The man steers (leads) with his left or right arm, pushing forward.

### Variations

#### Open Position

**Position:** Closed.
**Level:** Beginning 2

| *Counts* | *Steps* |
|---|---|
| 1–4 | Traveling forward step left, right, left, right |
| 5–6 | Change to open position, facing line of direction; step left, right |
| 1–4 | Traveling forward, step left, right, left, right |
| 5–6 | Resume closed position; man steps forward left, right; leading the woman to face the man with the woman's back to the line of direction |

#### Right Parallel Position

**Position:** Closed.
**Level:** Beginning 3

| *Beats* | *Steps* |
|---|---|
| 1–2 | Man moves into right parallel, stepping left, right |
| 3–6 | Both travel forward clockwise, stepping on each beat |
| 1–2 | Turning toward each other to left parallel position, left hips side by side |
| 3–5 | Travel forward counterclockwise |
| 6 | Man moves to closed position, facing line of direction stepping right |

### Turning Waltz Clockwise

**Position:** Closed.
**Level:** Advanced

Refer to page 45, Waltz Turns.

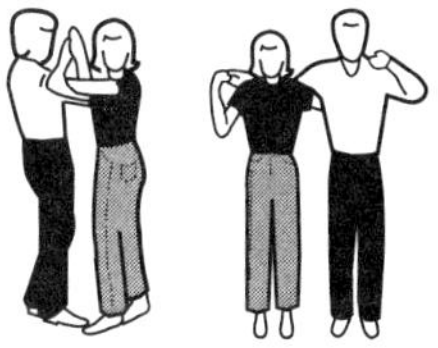

### Traditional Two-Step

Refer to pages 133–134 for various dance positions (Varsouvienne, Little Window, Yoke). These variations may be danced in the waltz, using 3/4 time.

# FOLK DANCE FROM THE HAWAIIAN ISLANDS

## History

Before European contact, music in Hawaii was a completely integrated system based on the use of poetry, rhythm, melody, and movement, which served the gamut of social needs from prayer to entertainment. Without a written history or literature to refer to, Hawaiians used musical poetry to call on the gods, honor their chiefs, lament the dead, tell of the creation, and perpetuate their history down through the generations. Poetry, therefore, was functional to their religious and social organization. Dance was an extension of poetry in the form of stylized visual accompaniment.

Traditional Hawaiian dance, unlike Asian and Indonesian forms, contained no theatrical or dramatic characterizations. Dance movement interpreted specific words of a poem or described a characteristic or thing mentioned in the poem. All hulas have a story background chanted by the dancers. Mele refers to the songs or words. Poetry was divided into two main types: all poetry not intended to be used with dance (oli) and poetry meant to be accompanied by dance (mele hula). The dancer's hands tell the story of the song, the hips maintain the rhythm. The hula is danced in bare feet.

Performers were trained in hula schools (halau) by a teacher (kumu) or a priest (kahuan) under a strict religious system imposed by the patron goddess (Laka) of hula. Hulas were performed, therefore, only by dancers who had graduated from a hula school. Although there were a great many taboos and religious rites connected with the training, many were anxious to learn since training was an entrée into the life of the courts of the chiefs. Schools were subsidized by the chiefs for reasons of prestige and entertainment. The primary functions of the hula dance at court were to honor the gods and sing praises of the chief and his ancestors.

The traditional hula was performed standing or seated. The seated version was more strenuous since the dancer raised and lowered as well as circled the torso from a kneeling position in which the dancer sat between the legs. In addition, the dancer often played an instrument. The standing hula was, as they are today, movements done while standing. Mele hulas or name chants were composed to honor a person. They became the property of that person and were passed down through generations. They told the story of the honoree in terms of his or her high birth, genealogy, or something for which the person was noted. The general structure of a performance consisted of music, usually percussion; reciting the poem, which was a two-line couplet; and movement or dance. Movement described specific words of the poem such as hands forming a flower or arms indicating the flight of a bird. If the dancer played an instrument, the body movements were used to convey the meanings.

Hulas are generally classified according to their instrumental accompaniment. The hula páhu (drum) is an important type danced to honor chiefs of high distinction. The hula pa ipu is danced accompanied by a gourd instrument struck by the hand or on the ground. The hula uli uli is a seated dance accompanied by a feathered rattling gourd. There are many hulas and instrumental combinations, including the unique hula páuimauna in which the chest and thighs are struck to generate two different sounds.

The modern-day hula is the result of Hawaiian contact with Western civilization. Captain Cook's visit in 1778 set in motion the change from a Neolithic society to one that integrated the cultural traits and values of Western civilization. Music and dance were most affected by the arrival of Christian missionaries in 1820. For a period of time after the influx of missionaries, Western values were represented on the one hand by sailors and on the other by missionaries. The contrast was at once bewildering if not at times humorous. The influence of the missionaries won; the dancers were clothed and the dance movements damned as lustful and evil. The dances, missionaries declared, not only violated Protestant values but took the Hawaiians from their work in the fields. The result was that the hula went underground.

In 1874 Kalakaua came to the throne and called hula teachers to his court to revive the dance and court dance troupes. The success of his effort culminated in an invitation for a Hawaiian dance group to perform at the 1993 World Columbian Exposition in Chicago. This was the first time the dance of Hawaii–the hula–was treated with the respect due an art form.

The revival of the hula was not without loss of the old and emergence of the new. The costumes became the "ti leaf" hula skirt and the long white frilly dress with fitted sleeves. The dance lost its religious restrictions and became open to everyone, not just trained professionals. Kalakaua's court marked the end of the traditional hula and the beginning of accultured dance and music.

For over half of the nineteenth century, Hawaiian music and dance was persecuted but was saved by the tenacity of a few conservative families. Traditional dance and music thus made its way into the twentieth century to be publicly recognized by a statewide program to study and teach the ancient hula. In 1970, some two hundred years after Western contact, only five individuals were known to be hula experts. Statewide conferences have since been held to revive and preserve the knowledge held by the remaining experts and to reinstate this ancient art form.

## Hula Fundamentals

*By the late Professor Billie Beamer of University of Hawaii*

The following fundamentals should not be regarded as the only "authentic" fundamentals. It must be pointed out that there were many hula schools in old Hawaii; each district or island had its own hula schools. These schools were separated by land and sea; therefore it was inevitable that there would be differences. If you were to analyze the dancers of modern Hawaii you would find differences in execution and in translation. It must be remembered that one version can be as authentic as the other. The old Hawaiians had a saying which in part reflects their philosophy, that is, that one can enjoy the creation of others as well as his own.

The method of working the hips as explained in the following fundamentals is commonly known in Hawaii as the "Beamer Method" or the "Heel-Hip Method." There are other groups or schools who use this technique besides the Beamers. Mrs. Louise Beamer was one of the first to use the terminology of "heel and hip" in her hula schools. While others may have been doing the same movement it was she who analyzed the movement and broke it down for teaching purposes.

### Ready Position or Waiting Position

Each dance is preceded by the dancer assuming this position. The right arm is extended (soft elbow) at the side at shoulder level, palm down, fingers extended. The left hand, palm down, fingers extended, is placed at the center of the chest with the elbow out at chest level. The right foot is pointed forward slightly in a tap position.

### Hula Bow

The dance is usually ended with a hula bow. The arms are extended forward (soft elbows) with hands crossed and palms down. The right foot pointed forward slightly, weight back on left.

### Gestures and Expression

Elbows should not be held close to the body. In most cases, the upper arms will be almost parallel to the floor. Position of the head is important to the total composition of a movement. The eyes should follow the leading hand with the head turned in the direction of the gesture. When both hands make the same gesture at the same level, the dancer looks first to the right then the left, then forward (slow gestures); if the gesture is fast, just look forward.

The wave of the hands should be a soft rippling movement rather than an exaggerated flexion of each individual finger. Above all do not grab with the fingers. The fingers are worked in unison.

## Basic Foot and Floor Patterns

Keep knees soft; they should never be hyperextended. This applies to all steps.

### Lewa (Sway)

**Position:** Ready position
**Level:** Beginning 3

| *Counts* | *Steps* |
|---|---|
| 1 | Beginning right, step in place, transferring weight and lifting left heel. |
| 2 | Push off with ball of foot to lift heel, allowing hip to raise softly. Keep shoulders level. Keep knees soft; they should never be hyperextended. This applies to all steps. |
| 1–2 | Repeat in the opposite direction; step left, right heel up. |

### Kaholo (Vamp)

**Position:** Ready position
**Level:** Beginning 3

| *Counts* | *Steps* |
|---|---|
| 1 | Beginning right, step to side transferring weight and lifting left heel. Do not bounce or rock. Step out. Do not drag feet. The length of the step is 4 counts depending on the individual and what is comfortable. The length of the step should permit a smooth and facile transference of the weight. If the tempo of the hula is fast, the steps must be shorter. |
| 2 | Close. Bring left foot next to right foot, transferring weight to the left and lifting right heel. |
| 3 | Step right to side, transferring weight and lifting up left heel. |
| 4 | Keep weight on right; just hold your last position. Hold same position as at end of third step for one count. Do not bring feet together or move them by turning in heels. |

**Note:** If pattern is to be repeated, repeat in opposite direction. It takes four beats to do a complete Kaholo pattern.

### Hela (Reach Tap)

**Position:** Ready position
**Level:** Beginning 3

| Counts | Steps |
|---|---|
| 1–4 | Flex knees before step begins, body on lower level. Weight is on left foot. (Reach Tap) Point right forward with leg extended, touching floor with toes and ball of (4 beats) foot. When pointing, the heel rotates in, toes rotate out slightly. The reach for the point should be comfortable. If dancer reaches out too far, movement will appear jerky or bouncing. |
| 1–4 | Bring right foot back next to left, transferring weight to right. Stay down on same level. Bend knee when bringing left foot back in place–this prevents straightening up and sitting down again. As foot is being placed, weight is shifting over gradually and smoothly. Foot is placed down flat on floor simultaneously with final shift of weight. |

# The Hukilau

A HUKILAU is a method of fishing invented by indigenous Hawaiians. The word comes from "huki," meaning "pull," and "lau," meaning "leaves." The fishing net was lined with leaves, which would help scare the fish into the center of the net. Hukilau Beach, in the town of Lā'ie on the island of O'ahu, is named after the technique, which has been used there for centuries. The Hukilau is now one of the first hula dances taught to local children in Hawaii, and is the most common hula dance taught to visiting tourists.

Special thanks to Olivia Steinhoff, president of Oregon State University Hawaiian Dance Club for sharing this dance. "The Hukilau Song" lyrics and music were composed and originally recorded by Jack Owens in 1948.

**CD:** Hukilau Hulas CD, Various Artists, Track 1 (available on *www.mele.com*)
**Formation:** Free formation, all facing front
**Position:** Ready position
**Level:** Beginning 2

## Directions FOR THE DANCE

Meter 4/4

Feet: Starting to the Right, Kaholo right and left through out the dance, unless otherwised noted.

Beginning level 1 adaptation: Starting with the right foot, step side right, bring left foot to right foot, step side right and touch left foot close to right, repeat to the left. Style: Arm movements are very fluid.

*continues on next page*

| *Words* | *Measures* | *Counts* | |
|---|---|---|---|
| | | | **PART I.** |
| Oh, we're going | 1 | 1–4 | Lift right arm up in front and bend at the elbow placing the thumb over the right shoulder twice. |
| to a hukilau | 2 | 5–8 | Reach with both hands to side left at waist height, pretend to grab onto a net and pull hands close to waist, repeat movement a second time. |
| A huki, huki, huki, | 3 | 1–4 | Repeat actions of measure 2 to the opposite side. |
| huki, hukilau | 4 | 5–8 | Repeat actions of measure 2. |
| | | | **PART II.** |
| Everybody | 5 | 1–4 | Arms extend forward at waist height with palms facing up, and than sweep out to the sides. |
| loves the hukilau | 6 | 5–8 | Repeat actions of measure 2. |
| Where the laulau is the kau kau | 7 | 1–4 | Place left arm in front, slightly bent at the elbow, palm up, fingers rounded as if holding a tennis ball. With the right hand take two fingers and pretend to scoop something out of the cupped hand and take the fingers to the mouth, as if eating. |
| at the luau | 8 | 5–8 | Repeat actions of measure 5. |
| | | | **PART III.** |
| We throw our nets | 9 | 1–4 | Bending at the elbows, place both hands by the right shoulder. Straighten out the arms, as if throwing out the nets. |
| out into the sea | 10 | 5–8 | Extend arms out about hip height, palms facing down. Bending at the elbow, lift right hand up approximately six inches. Lower right hand down, as left hand comes up. Repeat raising right and than left hand. |
| And all the ama ama come a-swimming | 11 | 1–6 | Place right palm on top of left hand. Thumbs out to the side. Move the hands up and down as if going over a wave. |
| to me | 12 | 7–8 | Lift elbows to side, tap thumbs to chest. |
| Oh, we're going<br>to a hukilau<br>A huki huki huki<br>hukilau | 13 -16 | 1–16 | Repeat action of Part II. |

| Words | Measures | Counts | |
|---|---|---|---|
| | | | **PART IV.** |
| What a beautiful | 1 | 1–4 | Lift arms chest height, bending at the elbow, place the left hand under the right elbow and the right hand on top of the left elbow. The arms are in a square formation. Rotating from the right elbow, lift the right hand up, keeping the right elbow on the left hand. |
| day for fishing | 2 | 5–8 | Move the right hand over the right shoulder and extend it out, as if throwing a fishing pole. |
| that old | 3 | 1–4 | Lower arms down to side. Lift them up from the side to just below shoulder height, bend at the elbow, and bring in to the upper chest. |
| Hawaiian way | 4 | 5–8 | Hold arm position. Feet: Stand with feet should width apart, Do several very small quick, hip circles counterclockwise. |
| Where the hukilau | 5 | 1–4 | Hold arms up with elbows bend and hands at upper chest. Feet: Continue with Kaholo step to the right. |
| nets are swishing | 6 | 5–8 | Lower arms down, elbows at side waist, forearms are parallel with the floor. From the elbow, forearms move right, left, right, left in a swishing motion. |
| Down in old Laie Bay | 7–8 | 1–8 | Lower arms to side. Keeping them straight, lift them up on the sides to just below shoulder height. Rotating from the elbow, turn the forearms down, so the back side of the hand is facing front. Bring the arms forward, as if holding a big exercise ball. |

The dance repeats from the beginning, matching the lyrics of the song.

# *Kahuli Aku Kahuli Mai*

KAHULI AKU KAHULI MAI is pronounced Ka-hoo-lee A-koo Ka-huu-lee Maee and means tree-shell there, tree-shell here. Paula Luv, Lecturer/Performer, University of Hawaii, Outreach College, Honolulu, Hawaii, taught this dance at Mainewoods Dance Camp 1997.

Kahuli Aku Kahuli Mai is a composition by Nona Kapuailohia Beamer, who is also a dancer and currently teaching Hawaiiana at Kamehamelu schools. Mahi Beamer, a tenor, specializes in the difficult high-register falsetto: a tradition in Hawaiian music from the time when women were forbidden by kapu to sing. Mahi is

*continues on next page*

assisted instrumentally by Ka'upena Wong and Kau'i Nohea playing the traditional instruments of the hula.

Dance courtesy of Nona Beamer, Beamer Hula Center and Marian Vasconcellos, University of Hawaii.

**CD:** Hawaii's Mahi Beamer
**Formation:** Free formation, all facing front.
**Position:** Ready position.
**Level:** Intermediate

*Lyrics:* (Traditional and Modern)

| | |
|---|---|
| Kahuli aku, kahuli mai | Hum a-far, hum a-near, |
| Kahuli lei ula, lei 'akolea, | A red lei of 'akolea, |
| Kolea, kolea, ki'i ka wai, | Plover, plover, fetch some dew, |
| Wai 'akolea, wai 'akolea. | Nectar from the 'akolea pond. |

Kahuli is the word for tree-shells and for the humming sound they make. Their chirping is similar to the sound of a cricket. The pond of the song is at Kalapana in Hawaii Island's Puna District. Play on words of the sort in this song (kolea: plover and 'akolea: fern) is much fancied by Hawaiians.

4

## *Directions* FOR THE DANCE

Meter: 4/4 • While dancing, chant the words. 4 measures.

| ***Words*** | ***Measures*** | ***Counts*** | |
|---|---|---|---|
| | | | **INTRODUCTION** |
| | | | Hula bow, hands shaped like a shell, waist level, palms down. |
| Kahuli aku | 1 | 1–4 | Kaholo beginning right. At waist level, right hand turns out, in, out using the wrists and HOLD. Progress forward with each turn |
| Kahuli mai | 2 | 5–8 | Kaholo beginning left. At waist level, left hand turns out, in out using the wrists and HOLD. Progress forward with each turn. |
| Kahuli lei ula | 3 | 1–4 | Hela right, then left. Wave forward, arms extended and parallel, point palms to chest, elbows out. |
| Lei'akolea | 4 | 5–8 | Hela right, then left. Put on lei around neck. Right hand forms a flower shoulder height, left hand low. |
| Kolea kolea | 5 | 1–4 | Lewa right, then left. Arms move like a bird flying right, then left. |
| Ki'i ka wai | 6 | 5–8 | Lewa right, then left. Fingers dive down at the waist twice to right, twice to left. |

| Words | Measures | Counts | |
|---|---|---|---|
| Wai 'akolea | 7 | 1–4 | Kaholo beginning right. Wave both hands parallel left then right; right hand forms flower high, left hand forms flower low. |
| Wai'akolea | 8 | 5–8 | Kaholo beginning left. Wave both hands parallel right, then left. Left hand forms flower high, right hand forms flower low. |
| Hum-m-m | 9 | 1–4 | Hela right. Wave both hands parallel left, chest level, two times; wave right hand at right diagonal and at chest. |
| Hum-m-m | 10 | 5–8 | Hela left. Wave both hands parallel right, chest level, two times; wave left hand at right diagonal and at chest. |
| | 11–30 | | Repeat measures 1–10 twice. |
| Hum-m-m | 31–34 | 1–16 | Hula bow. Wave both arms slowly, diagonally right, left, right and forward, arms extended center, hands crossed. |
| Hum-m-m | 35 | 1–4 | Hold everything. |

4

# *Pupu Hinuhinu*

PUPU HINUHINU is pronounced Poo-poo Hee-noo-hee-noo and means shell shiny. Paula Luv, Lecturer/Performer, University of Hawaii, Outreach College, Honolulu, Hawaii, taught this dance at Mainewoods Dance Camp 1997.

Pupu Hinuhinu is a composition by Nona Kapavailohia Beamer who is also a dancer and currently teaching Hawaiiana at Kamehamela Schools. Mahi Beamer, a tenor, specializes in difficult high-register falsetto: a tradition in Hawaiian music from the time when women were forbidden by kapu to sing. Mahi is assisted vocally by a group that includes his sister, Helen, and his Aunt Harriet; instrumentally by Ka'u-pena Wong and Kau'i Nohea playing the traditional instruments of the hula.

Dance courtesy of Billie Beamer, University of Hawaii.

**CD:** Hawaii's Mahi Beamer, Track: #7
**Formation:** Free formation, all facing front
**Position:** Sitting
**Level:** Intermediate

*Lyrics:*

| | |
|---|---|
| E Mahi'ai, 'auhea 'oe | O Mahi'ai, listen, |
| Komo mai e ku' aloha e | Come in my love, |
| Komo mai e himeni | Come in to sing, |
| Himeni i lohe au | Sing so I can hear |
| I kou leo nahenahe. | Your gentle voice. |

*continues on next page*

Mahi responds with Pupu Hinuhinu, Nona's song of the seashell: children find it on the beach, hear the sea in it, sing it to sleep, and go to sleep themselves.

## *Directions* FOR THE DANCE

Meter 4/4

| *Words* | *Measures* | *Counts* | |
|---|---|---|---|
| | 8 | 1–32 | Introduction: no action |
| | | | **VERSE 1** |
| Pu- | 1–4 | | Body leans forward as dancer claps hands gently, palms facing. |
| pu | 1 | 1–3 | Open palms out to side. |
| hinu | | 4 | Rise to knees, palms rise forward to head height, pivot out/in |
| | 2 | 1–2 | 1: Out/in, 2: Out |
| | | 3 | Sitting position, lower arms forward to lap height, palms facing. |
| Pu- | | 4 | Leaning slightly forward, clap hands gently forward. |
| pu | 3 | 1–2 | Sitting position, open hands to sides. |
| hinu | | 3+ | Rise to knees, hands move to head height, hands pivot out/in. |
| hinu | | 4+ | Out/in, |
| e | 4 | 1 | Out. |
| | | 2–3 | Sitting position, lower hands forward to lap height, palms facing |
| o ke | | 4+ | To left. |
| kahakal | 5 | 1+2 | Body leans slightly left, wave arms at left of lap, palms down. |
| | | + | To right. |
| kahakal | | 3+4 | Body leans slightly right, wave arms at right of lap. |
| e | 6 | 1 | Turn palms up. |
| | | 2–3 | Sitting position, left hand moves to left. |
| pu- | | 4 | Leaning slightly forward, clap gently, palms facing, forward. |
| pu | 7 | 1–2 | Sitting position, open palms to sides. |
| hinu | | 3+ | Rise to knees, hands rise forward to head height, pivot out/in, |
| hinu | | 4 + | out/in, |
| | 8 | 1 | out. |
| | | 2–4 | Body lowers slowly, arms lower slowly, forward. |
| | 9 | 1–3 | Palms facing. |
| | | 4 | To sitting position, hands to lap. |
| | 10 | 1–4 | Hold everything. |

| Words | Measures | Counts | |
|---|---|---|---|
| | | | **VERSE 2** |
| | 1–3 | 1–12 | Repeat the action from the beginning of Verse #1 through measure 3. |
| e | 4 | 1–2 | On knees, palms face out/in, HOLD. |
| | | 3 | Assume sitting position. |
| e | | 4 | Lower hands to left of head. |
| lohe ka– | 5 | 1–3 | Turn slightly to left, cup left hand over left ear. |
| kou | | 4 | HOLD. |
| e | 6 | 1–3 | Turn slightly to right, cup right hand over right ear. |
| | | 4 | HOLD. |
| | 7–11 | | Repeat the actions of Verse 1, measures 6–10. |
| | | | **VERSE 3** |
| | 1–3 | | Repeat the action from the beginning of Verse #1 through measure 3. |
| e | 4 | 1–2 | On knees, palms face out/in. HOLD. |
| | | 3 | Move to sitting position. |
| e | | 4 | Lower hands to left of face. |
| Mo–e | 5 | 1–3 | Leaning slightly left, rest hands on left cheek. HOLD. |
| | | 4 | Move hands to right of face. |
| Mo–e | 6 | 1–3 | Leaning slightly right, rest hands on right cheek |
| | | 4 | HOLD. |
| | 7–11 | | Repeat the action of Verse 1, measures measures 6–10. |
| | | | **VERSE 4** |
| | 1–3 | | Repeat the action from the beginning of Verse #1 through measure 3. |
| e | 4 | 1–2 | On knees, palms face out/in. HOLD. |
| | | 3 | Move to sitting position. |
| e | | 4 | Leaning slightly left forward, lower left hand slowly. |
| mo | 5 | 1–2 | To left of lap. |
| e | | 3 | To the ground. HOLD. |
| e | | 4 | Lower right hand slowly. |
| mo | 6 | 1–2 | To left of lap. |
| e | | 3–4 | To the ground. HOLD. |
| e | | + | Lower left cheek |
| mo | 7 | 1–3 | slowly to |
| e | | 4 | rest on hands. |
| e | 8 | 1–4 | Eyes close, sleep. |

# 5 SQUARE DANCE

## History

### Antecedents

The antecedents of modern American square dance are the English country dances and the French *contredanses—cotillion*[1] and *quadrille*. The English country dances—the *rounds, longways,* and *square for eight*—were introduced into France in the late seventeenth century. The round and square eight forms were transformed by the French into the *Contredanse Française* and a later form called the cotillion. The *contredanse* and the *cotillion* were dances for two and four couples in a square formation.

The word *cotillion* means "underpetticoat" and comes from a French peasant song to which it was danced. The *cotillion* was strictly a square in formation. Writers of the time used the terms *contredanse* and *cotillion* interchangeably, making it difficult to clarify the early development of these dance forms. Historians, however, agree that these forms were the antecedent of the *quadrille* and thus of our modern square dance.

The *quadrille* was a five-figure dance done by four couples in a four-sided figure or square. In its early form, the *quadrille* consisted of four of the most popular *contredanses* of the time. A fifth figure derived from the *cotillion—Le Final*—was added at a later date to make the traditional five figures of the dance. The five figures were *Le Pantalon, L'Ete, La Poule, La Frenis,* and *Le Final.* French *quadrilles* were for two, four, or any number of couples, and each remained vis-à-vis, dancing only with each other. In England, the quadrille was danced with only four couples. Quadrille music was as exciting as the many and varied dance figures. The French used semi-classical music, light opera tunes, and music composed especially for the quadrilles by well-known composers of the time.

Couple dances were also gaining in popularity at the same time the quadrilles were in vogue. The waltz,

1. Although spelled *cotillon* in French, the preferred spelling of this word in the United States is cotillion and is the form used throughout *Dance A While.*

polka, mazurka, and redowa were exciting new dances featuring daring dance positions and flying feet! The coexistence of the two resulted in combining quadrilles with couple-dance steps. Waltz quadrilles were especially numerous and popular.

The lancers was a very elegant and elaborate form of the quadrille. It must, therefore, be counted among the antecedents of our modern square dance. The lancers consisted of four couples arranged vis-à-vis, and the five figures were danced with the opposite couple. In reality, the lancers was a sequence of five square dances, each part danced to a different tempo. The fifth figure was usually a rousing military style 4/4 tempo. The well-known Grand March is actually the fifth figure of a long-forgotten lancers. Although a quadrille, the lancers was listed and thus distinguished from quadrilles on the dance programs of the day.

Lancers music was usually written by well-known composers of the time and played by live full orchestras. Many American lancers were danced to Gilbert and Sullivan melodies and some to Stephen Foster songs. Although known and danced in the early 1800s, lancers did not become popular until the mid- to late nineteenth century. In America, the French quadrilles were cast aside in favor of lancers in all the major urban areas of the time.

These were the dance forms flourishing in western Europe. And like all other parts of the culture brought by immigrants to the New World, they were subjected to the test of a radically different environment. Those dances that survived emerged irrevocably altered. Just as the individual identities of colonial Americans were being molded from, for example, Scotch-Irish to New York citizen to loyal American, so were dance forms being molded and shaped into new forms with new identities.

Colonial America inherited a rich dance tradition. It is no wonder that dance was one of the most significant features of colonial life. Indeed, dance was reported to be the chief amusement. Dance was not limited by social class or ethnic group, but was enjoyed by people of all stations.

## Regional Influences

The early part of the nineteenth century saw America becoming a dancing nation. Dancing masters were everywhere for hire; the new minister was welcomed at an Ordination Ball; even teachers and ministers doubled as dancing masters to augment their salaries. Plain folks danced everywhere and on all occasions, in taverns, town halls, and kitchens; at barn raisings, husking bees, and roof raisings.

Dance developed differently in the major regions of the country, New England, the South, the Southwest (Texas), and the West. Over time, the characteristics from these regions blended together to form a truly American western square dance. The following section covers the history and dance elements for each area.

### New England

New Englanders cast aside the five-part quadrille for the three-part quadrille.[2] The Singing Quadrille developed as a simpler, free-flowing adaptation. These "modern quadrilles" were set to such dashing American folk tunes as "Darling Nellie Gray," "The Girl I Left Behind Me," and "Hinkey Dinkey Parley Voo." A prompter cued both the quadrilles and square dances for the different figure movements. The prompter's title later changed to "caller," as he called out the dance figures.

The tunes, the dances, and the rhyming caller became widely popular. Singing calls by the hundreds were invented and flourished from New York to Maine. The French-Canadian populace of New England were especially enthusiastic participants, and they are credited with embellishing these modern quadrilles with the long count swing and buzz step.

The New England square dances consisted of an introduction, a primary figure interspersed with breaks, and an ending. The movements are usually keyed to eight beats and the movement starts at the beginning of a phrase. The cue precedes the movement.

Nineteenth-century singing quadrilles and squares settled comfortably alongside the New England contra to become widely known as New England-type dancing. Little did the average New Englander of the time suspect that this new American hybrid would be the basis for twentieth-century square dance.

### The South

The Running Set is a dance form of the people of Kentucky and the southern Appalachian Mountains who came to the New World from northern England and the lowlands of Scotland. They found, in the hills and valleys, an isolation that for many years permitted them to practice and thus preserve almost unchanged the customs and traditions of their homelands.

Cecil J. Sharp,[3] the noted English folklorist, came to the Appalachian Mountains in 1917 in search of

2. *Good Morning!* (Ford and Ford, 1943) chronicles New England quadrilles.
3. Cecil J. Sharp and Maud Karpeles, *The Country Dance Book* (1918), Part V.

early English ballads and songs. While there, he observed the dance form known as the running set. His scholarly observations and inquiries led him to conclude that it was, indeed, the earliest form of the English country dance. The absence of courtesies such as bowing, saluting, and honors indicated to him that the dances were uninfluenced by court manners and thus predated dances found in Playford's first dance book of 1650. He further suggested that the history of the running set might date back to seventeenth-century England and Scotland or even earlier to the May Day Rounds, a pagan quasi-religious ceremonial of which the Maypole Dance is the best example.

The running set was more in the tradition of the round eight than the square eight. The dance action moved around the square as opposed to across it. The running set was danced in a circle for as many couples as desired or, as was more typical, in a square or set for four couples. The typical dance action consisted of the first couple leading to the right, dancing a figure, then to couple three repeating the figure, and then couple four repeating it. As the action began with couple four, couple two began the "follow-up" action with couple three. The do-si-do, a staple of western square dance, was used to finish off the figures. The dance was long and very vigorous!

The characteristics of the running set as danced in Kentucky and the southern Appalachian Mountains make it the most immediate antecedent of the western brand of square dance and the Big Circle Square Dance (see page 159). The two most enduring characteristics are the use of a caller and the figure action of moving or visiting around the square.

In the running set, the caller either called from within the set, prompting the dancers, or from outside the set. If calling from outside the set, the caller would add folksy, rhythmic lines of "patter" to the directions for executing the figure. This was the forerunner of the colorful western patter calls of the early twentieth century.

The step used was a bouncing run that beat out the rhythm against the dance floor. Dancers appeared erect with loose jigging action of the arms. In early times, the sound of the rhythm of the feet was the music for the dance. Singing play party games, or dancing without fiddle music, was then an offspring of the running set.

The caller cues and uses rhyming patter as the dancers dance. The cue precedes the dancers' movement. Southern callers adjust their calls to where the dancers are in the musical phrase, whereas New England callers call at the beginning of the phrase.

## The West

The New England quadrilles and the Kentucky running sets are the forebears of western square dance. As settlers traveled westward and southward they brought their dances from New England, the Eastern Seaboard, the mountains of Allegheny, and Appalachia.

The desire for more freedom, more land, and a better life stirred settlers to travel onward to the West. The major waterways became avenues of migration.

During the western migration across North America there were several significant historical events: the Lewis and Clark Expedition of 1803, the War of 1812 with England, the Missouri Compromise of 1820, the issue of slavery, the California Gold Rush of 1849, and the Civil War beginning in 1861.

Settlers eventually crossed the Sierra Nevada mountains or followed the Oregon Trail to the West Coast.

Western square dance is characterized by the patter calling of the South and an independence of movements from the phrases of the music, which may be hoedowns, popular contemporary tunes, or country western music. Original western square dancing keeps the dancers together and is not dictated by the musical phrases. The caller cues before the action with steady rhyming of patter, but the cueing is dependent upon the position of the dancers. The figure is the dominant characteristic. The caller follows the figure, but may change and use any opener, break, or ending.

## Texas, the Southwest

Texas square dance heritage came largely from the South with the settlers who moved to the frontier after the Civil War. Settlers brought with them not only their love of dancing, but also their dance traditions: the visiting couple figures, do-si-do, and square dance caller.

Social life was patterned around ranching and the demands of ranch life rather than cotton farming. The sparseness of settlements and the distances to be traveled made social gathering rare but highly prized. In west Texas, the two most important ingredients of social life, women and fiddlers, were as scarce as "hen's teeth."

When an itinerant fiddler showed up in ranch country, a dance was arranged regardless of the day of the week. Fiddlers and their music were in short supply in west Texas, but the enthusiasm for dancing to the sounds of the "frisky fiddle" was not.

At social gatherings, there were usually three times as many men, even counting all the females from the youngest to the oldest. Women prided themselves on being able to dance all night without missing a set, and, more often than not, they would easily wear out their shoe soles in one evening. Social gatherings were so important to the cowboy that he thought nothing of riding a great distance to "squire" a woman to a dance. One cowboy is reputed to have ridden 10 miles to hire a buggy, 15 miles to get the woman, 15 miles to the dance, 15 miles back to the woman's home, 15 miles to return the buggy, and, finally, 10 miles on horseback to reach home—a total of 80 miles. Square dancing was serious business in Texas, and the conditions of frontier life made it possible for the square dance to become firmly embedded in Southwestern culture before the region began to suffer from the inroads of urban civilization.

Texas became the home and stronghold of the colorful patter call and the intricate dance figures that were created by the uninhibited imagination of the callers. Texas square dancing was the product of the oral rather than the written tradition. Calls were passed along and repeated as remembered. Unaware of the more traditional spelling of square dance terms, cowboy callers called them as they sounded; thus "dos-a-dos" became "do-see-do," "chassez" became "sashay," and "allemande" became variously "al-a-man" or "alamand."

## Early Leaders

In the early twentieth century, when square dancing was at a low ebb in other parts of the United States, folks in west Texas were working hard all day and dancing harder all night. One of the most important pioneers of this period was H. F. Greggerson, Jr., of El Paso, Texas, better known as Herb. Greggerson was a dancer, caller, and writer who used his feet carrying mail during the day and, in his leisure moments, dancing at a faster tempo at night. He was a strong force in helping El Paso build its reputation as the center of western cowboy square dancing. Before World War II, dancers by the hundreds attended Herb's "barn" to learn and dance to his directions, which were embellished by colorful patter and delivered with a twinkle in his eye.

Greggerson and his wife Pauline traveled and danced throughout west Texas and New Mexico collecting old-time calls and dances. The resulting collections were published in two books, *West Texas Square Dances* and *Herb's Blue Bonnet Calls,* the latter copyrighted in 1937.

In 1939 the Greggersons traveled with their exhibition group, The Blue Bonnet Set, as guests of the Highway 80 Association to the World's Fair in New York. The occasion was a showcase for different dance groups from all parts of the United States. The opportunity for fellowship and exchange between dancers and callers led to a greater appreciation and awareness of the status of square dance in America. Exhibitions at the Roosevelt Hotel in New York and at the Edgewater Beach Hotel in Chicago earned The Blue Bonnet Set the title of World Champion Square Dancers. The authors of *Dance a While* recognize the work of Herb Greggerson in collecting, teaching, and calling the traditional dances of the western cowboy as a major contribution to the history of square dance in America.

Lloyd Shaw and his wife Dorothy were two giants among the few of their kind in the early development of square dancing in the West. In addition to his talent as a teacher and writer, Shaw was more importantly an innovative and creative leader. Early in pursuit of his interest in square dancing, he envisioned a future in which all Americans would be square dancing. In the 1930s and 1940s, his Cheyenne Mountain Dance Group showed America the joy and spirit of American dance. He further ensured the success of his vision by spending his summers instructing hundreds from all walks of life on how to teach square dancing.

As school superintendent in Colorado Springs, Colorado, Shaw's first interest in dance came from searching for an adjunct to the school's athletic program. He began teaching European folk dance and, after winning over the football team, the dancers became an official group. The Cheyenne Mountain Dancers' first performing tour found them doing all European dance. Later they added some American dances from the Henry Ford *Good Morning!* (1943) collection of New England contras and quadrilles. It was not until Shaw became interested in the dances that were indigenous to the Colorado Mountains in which he lived that the Cheyenne Mountain Dancers became an all-cowboy dance group.

The Shaws' love of the mountains and the local activities made it a labor of love to research and collect from old-timers the dances of miners, prospectors, and cowboys in the Rocky Mountain West. Pappy Shaw related the pathway of western square dance to the tide going out (west) and returning (east). The dances they found had come along with settlers migrating West and were the offspring of the southern mountain running set, four-couple squares with patter calls and figures reflecting western ways in their titles. In 1939, Shaw published *Cowboy Dances,* his collection of calls and figures gathered in Colorado and the surrounding mountain area. This was followed in 1948 by the *Round Dance Book.* Getting

America interested in American dance was his vision, and it happened!

The Lloyd Shaw Foundation is an incorporated, nonprofit organization founded by former summer-class members to perpetuate his memory, his work, and his special philosophy. The foundation trains teachers and dance leaders, produces records and teaching materials, sponsors recreational dance weeks, publishes books and pamphlets, and collects and disperses dance material of historical interest.

## Post–World War II

The rapid growth and expansion of square dance after World War II was largely the outgrowth of population movements and technical advances in sound equipment. Population movements were of two kinds: movement to urban areas because of continued industrialization and population displacement associated with service in the armed forces and employment in defense-related industries. The technical improvements in the quality and availability of sound equipment made teaching and calling to groups of all sizes possible and effective. Portable equipment made ownership by schools, families, teachers, and callers a reality, thus multiplying the opportunities for dance experience. In addition, the durability and availability of properly recorded music provided the correct dance tempo and authentic sounds for dancing.

The American penchant for following the latest fad was also a factor. In the 1940s and 1950s, square dance hobbyists contributed greatly to the popularity of square dance through public performances and exhibitions that introduced nonparticipants to the dance. The precision and style of these exhibitions became a standard of performance for other dancers to emulate, thus raising the skill level of the dance. As an added bonus, the massive effort to serve the social needs of wartime America created a rich opportunity for developing leadership in square dance for the future. These are the factors that made it possible for thousands of Americans to be introduced to their own heritage, the American square dance.

The postwar years were characterized by mass participation in square dance. Classes for over a hundred at a time were common. Communities vied to host the largest and best jamborees, festivals, or square dance contests. Major public events, such as inaugurations, patriotic celebrations, and civic anniversaries, featured square dance as a main social event. Crowd estimates at these early dance events ranged from 5,000 to 10,000 people. This formerly quiet, predominantly rural form of recreation had suddenly become the mass mania of urban living.

Commercial ventures for square dancers included merchandising of current dress styles for men and women. Recording companies flourished by providing a wide assortment of recordings and sound equipment. Teaching materials in the form of books, pamphlets, and recorded teaching progressions became available. Former part-time teachers and callers became full-time professionals. Summer calendars began to be filled with institutes, workshops, and vacation-oriented opportunities to dance in exotic places. In 1970, a group known as Legacy (dissolved in 2002) was formed to provide a vehicle for communication between manufacturers, producers, publications, and square dance associations. Square dancing had arrived in the marketplace.

As dance skill and experience increased, dance moved from a mass activity into smaller organized units. The *dance club* became the heart of square dancing. Club calendars included classes, interclub exchanges, and travel to major special events. Associations were the outgrowth of club activities.

Solid growth of regional organizations in various parts of the country made the step to a national-level organization easy and logical. Annual national square dance conventions began in 1952, at a time when interest in the movement was on the upswing. Since the first convention, cities from north to south and coast to coast have hosted the national convention. Attendance figures for early conventions were between 15,000 and 20,000. Attendance figures for the 1970s exploded to between 40,000 and 50,000. It is estimated that between 1960 and 1979 6 million people were square dancing worldwide. American square dance is in vogue as an international form of recreation in Canada, Japan, Australia, England, Germany, and many other countries. In 1990, Legacy performed a survey and estimated that approximately 375,000 people were involved in club dancing in the United States. In 2003, it's estimated that the number of club dancers has dropped by half, and the numbers will continue to decline if traditional square dancing is not adapted to modern society.

Square dance is no longer a quaint cowboy or country hillbilly activity. Media coverage, movies, and television have been instrumental in making square dance a familiar activity to an extensive American audience. A commemorative stamp issued by the United States Postal Service in 1970 increased the visibility of square dance. The third week in September has been set aside as Square Dance Week and has been officially proclaimed by mayors and governors across the country. The spirit of square dancing is found in the simple cooperative effort of dancers dancing. Square dance is truly America's folk dance.

## Standardization of Basic Movements

The picture of square dance in its formative years was a mosaic of regional dance differences. The three dominant types were the prompt and the singing calls of the eastern states and the patter calls of the western states. The upsurge of interest in square dance led to a natural flow of dances from one section of the country to the other. Western square dance became popular in the East, while singing calls became popular in the West. Although the skilled and experienced dancer could travel and dance comfortably in any area, the regional differences in basic steps, promenade positions, dance tempos, type and duration of swings, balance steps, and stylings gave the square dance movement a "Tower of Babel" effect. There was no common vocabulary of dance terms understood and used by teachers, callers, or dancers. In effect, there was your way and my way, but no common or right way to perform basics. The increased number and mobility of square dancers within and between regions made this a major problem.

The widespread enjoyment of square dancing is largely due to the fact that dancers from coast to coast and overseas execute the same fundamental movements, called basics. The dance movements and steps, and the styling of hands, arms, and positions are all taught and executed in the same manner. The rationale behind this standardization of basics and learning progressions is to make it possible for dancers to learn calls in any given area and thus be skilled enough to dance to calls anywhere, across the country or overseas.

The guiding force behind the movement to standardize square dance movements and teaching procedures was Bob Osgood of Los Angeles, a teacher, caller, and long-time editor of *Sets In Order,* later known as *Square Dancing Magazine,* the official publication of the Sets In Order American Square Dance Society. As early as 1960, a booklet describing 30 basics was available from *Sets In Order.* The work was the result of a cooperative study Osgood made with the help of prominent callers across the country. The success and acceptance of this early work led Osgood to head a larger study in 1969, which resulted in organizational changes to facilitate the work of standardization. The work of standardization, adoptions, and changes was carried on by *Callerlab,* an arm of the International Association of Square Dance Callers. All standardized movements and plateaus, or ability levels, were published in *Square Dancing Magazine* as a joint venture with Callerlab.

The mainstream level of square dancing (as designated by Callerlab) consists of 68 movements. Advanced and challenge levels (again, designated by Callerlab) provide movements that serve the interests of highly skilled and dedicated dancers. The lists of movements are frequently evaluated and updated. A concerted effort is now focused on the mainstream level to sustain interest at a comfortable level, so dancers will not feel pressure to learn the latest "curlicue" in order to enjoy the pastime.

Other groups and publications, such as the American Callers Association and *Dance A While,* have composed lists of basic dance moves as well.

## Square Dancing Moves into the Twenty-First Century

Square dancing is alive and well! Dancing the squares of the 1940s and 1950s has made a comeback for the casual dancer.

### Traditional

A new generation is dancing traditional squares with patter calling, whether using Southwestern, cowboy western, Southern, or New England figures. Today's callers go to libraries and used bookstores to research books and periodicals from the period for their figures and patter. Traditional squares are on the program with contra dances. Dancers enjoy the diversity and are not encumbered with learning a new series of basics; they need only to know the moves that the caller uses. A quick walk-through enables them to perform the dance. There may be an element of "here today, gone tomorrow," but for the moment the dancer is having a "rip-snorting good time."

### Mainstream

The number of dancers who are dedicated to mainstream square dance, though still in the thousands, has dropped off at an alarming rate. Several years ago, Callerlab hired marketing professionals to assess the problem and determine what was needed to revitalize this type of square dancing. As a result, the "Phoenix Plan" and the "Arts Alliance Plan" were established. These plans focus on defining an entry-level program that has worldwide acceptance and can be taught in one season. If a community has a predominance of mainstream clubs, dancer participation should increase. The leadership of Callerlab forecasts a comeback for square dancing.

### Old Time

There is also a dedicated group of people, both young and old, interested in researching, preserving, and following the trail of square dance development in the United States. The correlation to music, recreation, and anthropological patterns provides a continuing awareness of square dance in American culture.

# Teaching Square Dance

## Which Road to Take, Choosing a Style

There are three choices: traditional square dance, modern western square dance with standardized movements (which uses basic combinations of movements), or a little bit of each.

### Traditional Square Dance

The caller cues the dancers and delivers rhyming patters with abandon. The caller selects a dance and chooses breaks to contrast and complement the main figure. Breaks should provide a smooth transition at the beginning and the end of the main figure and get dancers back to home position.

Traditional square dances use moves that are easily taught that evening, so that everyone may be involved. This style is wonderful to allow beginners to be involved. Today, this style is still danced at monthly county dances held at grange halls across the country. The emphasis is having everyone dancing, from grandparents to grandchildren.

### Modern Western Square Dance

Since the advent of standardized movements, whether by Callerlab, the American Callers Association, or *Dance A While,* square dances have changed, but the sequence for all groups is similar. As the caller (or teacher) works through the list, he or she prepares the dancers to dance at club program-designated levels. The dancers are then able to travel across the country dancing at festivals, workshops, or conventions, following the same square dance movements. They may also find square dance groups abroad that follow the same sequence and vocabulary. With this procedure the dances have no names. Each caller combines the basic movements, moving from one level to the next. There is a definite appeal to putting together combinations that flow well and keep the dancers on their toes, matching the caller's skill. Modern western square dance callers use singing calls as well, which of course become standardized through repetition. Modern western square dancing callers also employ sight calling.

## Teaching Approaches

Teachers may choose one of two approaches for teaching the beginning square dance basics. The *big circle approach* makes use of the single circle, double circle, and Sicilian circle for teaching and practicing basics that can be done without reference to the square formation. The *set approach* begins with the dancers in the square formation and teaches the basics in reference to positions and movement directions as they evolve from the use of a simple square dance call.

### Big Circle

The big circle approach is immediately attractive in that it allows all class members to be active at once; the teacher makes the class "odd or even" in numbers so there can be no extras. The single circle is particularly useful for demonstration. Dancers can see the mechanics and style of a basic move. Basics appropriate to the single circle are the shuffle (circling left, right, forward and back), do-sa-do, swing, allemande left, honor, twirl, single-file promenade, grand right and left, and forearm turns. The double circle is appropriate and useful in teaching promenade, California Twirl, you turn back, box the gnat, and wheel around. The Sicilian circle is a formation in which two couples face, one facing clockwise and the other counterclockwise. It is useful in teaching ladies chain, right and left thru, pass thru, box star position, square thru, star thru, or any basic movement requiring this set-up.

The big circle approach is useful for class warm-up and review. It allows all class members to be active, including the teacher, who may fill in if there is an extra dancer. It may also be used as part of a lesson to present and demonstrate new basics. The big circle approach is versatile and should be used throughout a series of lessons whenever appropriate and needed.

### Set/Square

The set approach combines maneuvering in the square with learning the basic movements as they occur in a given dance sequence. After all, the set is only a "square" in concept. Once dancers respond to a call, the set can become a single circle, double circle, or parallel lines. This is an exciting approach because it plunges the dancers into full square dance action. Their objective—to learn to square dance—happens in the first lesson and is not delayed by practice and drill on style and technique. In a short series of lessons, getting to the heart of the dancing motivates the dancer to listen and learn.

### Planning Units and Lessons

The basic movements in this text provide materials for beginners and intermediates. Beginning materials are covered in levels 1, 2, and 3. Intermediate materials are covered in level 4. In addition, there are ample dance call (figure) sequences and singing calls to provide practice in learning and combining movements for all levels.

Public schools and recreation groups may find it advantageous to divide the materials into a series of five or six lesson units progressively linked and scheduled throughout the year. Recreation groups and after-school clubs can easily cover the first 35 basic moves in one year.

A rule of thumb suggests that instruction should go slowly enough for dancers to learn and enjoy each lesson and fast enough to hold their interest and provide a challenge. Planning in relation to a specific "on the job" situation provides the best estimate of content and length of instructional period. The overall objective should be to provide a sound skill basis in an atmosphere of fun and fellowship and challenge enough for dancers to choose square dance as a lifetime recreational pursuit.

A daily lesson plan is a systematic checklist of progress toward the overall goal of learning the square dance. Mastering a few skills during each lesson may include:

1. Warm-up and review of basic movements in a circle to include all class members. Or dance a figure using previously learned basics.
2. Presentation of new basics. Isolate each one from any specific dance and include a walk-through and practice call.
3. Call and dance of one or more dances containing new basics with combinations of several previously learned dances. Or allow the class to request favorites.

## Styling

Dancing style begins with the dance step. The step should be a walking step on each beat of the music. The result is a smooth, flowing movement enjoyable to the individual and the dance group. From the first musical note, dancers should begin to respond to the rhythm by taking three small steps and a touch forward then backward. Dancers not involved in the call should maintain this rhythmic action to be ready to move into the call. An alternative is to take any combination of clogging steps. Clogging steps may be interjected as the spirit moves you, as well.

Styling results from executing basics in the proper number of counts or beats of music. Timing varies, but it is an important part of learning the basics. Women's chain over and back, including the courtesy turn, takes 16 counts. Women move across and courtesy turn in eight counts and repeat to home position in eight counts. Hand clasps, arm holds, wrist holds, and swing and turn positions are all part of the style, comfort, and logic of dance movement. Dancing the basics in the proper counts gives style and elegance to the dance action. Teach styling and timing techniques with each basic movement. Dancers will enjoy and take pride in making the right moves.

## The Caller and Calling

The caller is truly an American innovation whose role, particularly in the early days, was to keep the dance alive by passing along calls and figures from generation to generation solely by oral tradition. Today, the caller is a teacher and a group leader and, in like manner, the teacher is a caller and a group leader. The success of a series of square dance lessons depends upon creating a pleasant, friendly, and fun-filled atmosphere in a class or club setting. The caller-teacher must first be a trained teacher to select and present materials in an orderly progression. The caller-teacher must also be an accomplished dancer to demonstrate the movements and dance style effectively.



### Goals of the Caller

The ultimate objective of square dance calling, regardless of method, is to call sequences that are possible to execute, are logically linked and flow smoothly one to the other, stimulate the interest and enthusiasm of the dancers, and, finally, return dancers to their partners and home positions at the end of a sequence.

### Keys to Good Calling

*Clarity:* Enunciate clearly and emphasize the "action words" and short directive phrases: "*Ladies* star left," "allemande left."

*Rhythm:* Keep an active "patting foot" call on the beat of the music. Call the next movement while dancers are executing the last call. Be aware of musical phrases. Begin the call on the phrase or downbeat.

*Command:* Project calls out; do not swallow or mumble the calls. Call within the framework of dancers' knowledge and ability level.

*Judgment:* Adjust dance progressions and practice time to the ability level of the dancers. Review often and in interesting combinations of basics. Avoid endless walk- and talk-throughs without music.

*Enthusiasm:* Approach each lesson in a natural, sincere, and friendly manner. Display humor, reward progress, and encourage the better dancers to dance with and help upgrade the skills of other dancers.

## Calling Sequence

The basic movements are simply called one after the other without additional colorful rhymes or phrases. The calls sound similar to those of an auctioneer in that they are announced in rapid and clipped fashion. In putting together a sequence of calls or when calling ad lib, several rules apply. First, the movements must be possible to execute in the order called; that is, they must be linked and flow one from the other. Second, the first call must get the square into the formation needed to begin executing the sequence. Mainstream calls are executed from several line-type formations such as eight chain thru, two-faced lines, and ocean wave. Line formations begin and end all sequences. The ending line formation should put the dancers in position to execute an allemande left, thus allowing the dancers to move to home position with their original partner.

There are two general rules to remember. Basic calls or movements work in lines and the allemande left is the key call for resolving or terminating the sequence. Callers should have in mind several "get-out" calls that do indeed get dancers into the proper position should the free-wheeling calls they use not do so. The "get-out" is a short call that allows the caller to move gracefully from an improper sequence to a proper one.

## Calling Methods

### Prompt Calling

This is the simplest form of calling. The instructor needs only call out the name of the figure or movement in time with the music.

### Patter Calling

Patter calling features colorful rhyming phrases accompanying the call directions used in Western cowboy dance figures. The additional phrases allow time to execute the movements. With the advent of basic movements, the additional lines of patter were curtailed in favor of more directions and less color. The patter caller is still, however, free to call extemporaneously, thus retaining the competitive aspect of this method of calling.

### Singing Calls

The present-day singing calls are largely done in the same mode as in the past. The calls follow a set sequence and are arranged to the melody of a song. As in the past, dancers tend to memorize the dance action and are not wholly dependent upon the caller. Singing calls follow popular musical trends and are continually being choreographed to the latest hit tunes. This feature makes singing calls current in each succeeding generation of dancers.

**Examples of different styles of calling:**

| | |
|---|---|
| Prompt: | Promenade Home |
| Patter: | Hold that gal don't let her fall,<br>Promenade around the hall. |
| Singing: | Keep the lady and Promenade the ring, Promenade to Houston, Houston, Houston. |
| Sight: | Similar to patter. |

### Sight Calling

*Sight calling* gives the caller complete freedom to ad-lib and move dancers around with interesting combinations without attention to where any one individual dancer is during a call sequence. However, once the sequence is to be terminated, the caller must find four predetermined dancers and assess their positions to get them back to original home positions. This is due to the fact that most basic movements and all of the mainstream movements are danced symmetrically in lines. Dancers need to be in the proper order so that an "allemande left" call will return them to home positions. Should this not be the case, callers must know several "get-outs" to get dancers in position for an allemande left. The image system of calling requires the caller to have an affective mental image of the entire square while following a key dancer around the pattern as it changes. The caller thinks of himself as the key dancer. A good metaphor for this system is that the caller is in the "footprints" of the key man or that he is the "ghost" or "image" of that dancer.

There are three steps to sight calling:

1. Establish primary and secondary couples. The primary couple should be easily recognizable. The secondary couple should be the couple to the left of the primary couple. For insurance, select two couples in more than one square to offset the possibility of a breakdown during a call.
2. Call any sequence moving dancers around freely, but be aware of formations.
3. Terminate the call sequence by matching up the primary and secondary couples and putting the square in lines with their original partners. The square is thus ready for the call "allemande left," which moves dancers back to home positions.

### Tips for Sight Calling

1. The primary couple should be the one couple easiest to remember. They may be friends or acquaintances or simply have on colorful outfits. Tall couples are more prominent and visible and thus make good primary couples.
2. Establish primary and secondary couples in at least three squares. The odds of three squares breaking down are in the caller's favor.
3. Use squares in the front of the hall. The better dancers tend to gather there and are less likely to make mistakes.
4. Call several quick left allemandes, watching a different square each time, to reinforce the identity of the primary and secondary couples.
5. The sight calling system always works as long as the calls are symmetrical, so that the whole square moves to the call. It does not work when only half of the square is active.

### Cue Cards

There are a variety of methods for moving dancers through a sequence of calls and returning them to home positions in the set. The easiest method is the use of *cue cards,* or prearranged written sequences. The caller's emphasis on notes, however, negates his role as an attractive and entertaining caller. The *pure memory* caller must commit to memory volumes of materials. Although this method overcomes the cue card lack of eye contact between dancer and caller, calling from memory is inflexible and lacks variety in presentation. The *module caller* uses certain sequences of a few basics that are more or less rigidly learned. However, they can be put together rather spontaneously to provide fairly interesting sequences.

## Use of Prerecorded Calls

In public schools and recreational groups, the use of calls on cassettes, CDs, and videos serves to keep the class dance materials current, provides an opportunity to dance to professional calling, and serves as a model to upgrade the teacher-caller's live calling ability.

Overuse of recorded calls can restrict the class to one type of call and thus distract from the spontaneity and challenge of live calling. It can also contribute to poor preparation by the teacher-caller. Live calling reinforces knowledge of the call pattern and increases the teacher-caller's understanding of the many basic movements to be taught.

Using prerecorded calls presumes that the teacher knows and has danced the call and that all basics have been taught and used in other dances. A suggested teaching progression follows.

1. Play the new material to accustom the class to the sound of the caller's voice and the tempo. This also gives the class a preview of the basics involved in the dance.
2. Analyze and walk the class through the first segment of the call.
3. Call it live and up to tempo, with no music.
4. Dance to the recorded call and music.
5. Repeat steps 2 and 4 for the remainder of the dance.

**NOTE:** Modern equipment allows users to stop and start recordings at any point. This aids and reinforces instruction.

5

# Big Circle Square Dance/ Kentucky Running Set

Very much alive today in the southern Appalachian region and a variant of the Running Set is the Big Circle Square Dance, a dance known by many names, such as the Mountain Square Dance, Appalachian Big Circle, and Great Circle.

It is interesting to note that the concept of the big circle with sets of two couples (active and inactive couples, or odds and evens) is known throughout the United States. New England does a version referred to as the Circle, Sicilian Circle, or Cirassian Circle, which has traveled to the four corners of our country. In 1945, the big circle was a common dance, both as a traditional form in the community and as a teaching method for square dance.

The Big Circle Square Dance has much in common with the Kentucky Running Set. At this time, there is an effort to differentiate between the two. Glenn Bannerman, professor of recreation and outdoor education, Presbyterian School of Christian Education, Richmond, Virginia, has researched and assisted in keeping the western North Carolina style alive. The ideas presented follow this style.

The Big Circle Square Dance is a social occasion. The dancers come to see their friends, and during the big circle friends greet one another and quiet exchanges of news may go on during the dance. It differs from the Kentucky running set as follows: A walking step is danced even on the swing and is referred to as "smooth dancing," or single- and double-clog steps, by the spirited dancers; the Varsouvienne position is used for the promenade; and there are more people involved, maybe as many as 50 in a circle, all couples dancing and the figures changing frequently.

Some groups clog the entire dance when the spirit moves them. In the South there are groups that specialize in precision dancing (clogging) and perform exhibition dances to hoedown or pop music.

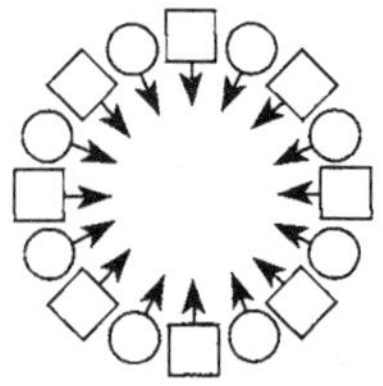

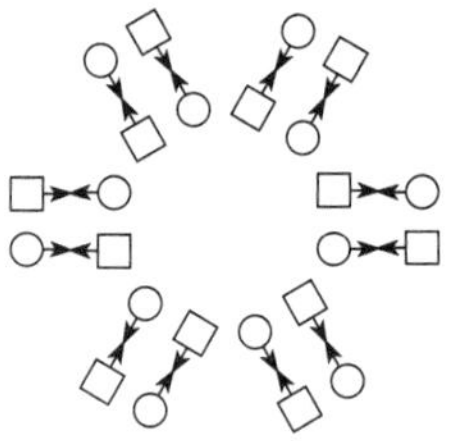

***Dance A While* CD:** This CD includes three musical selections that may be be used to practice any of the square dance figures presented in this chapter. They are: "Boil 'Em Cabbage Down," "Irish Washerwoman (Virginia Reel)," and "Rag Time Annie."

**Music:** "Old Joe Clark."

**Formation:** Couples, woman on partner's right, in large single circle. Even-numbered couples. Prior to dancing, determine head couple and number couples 1, 2, 1, 2, and so forth, so that at the call "odd couple out to the even couple," couple 1 moves into the circle (backs to center) to face couple 2 (face center). Couple 1 always progresses on the inside in the line of direction (counterclockwise) to the next couple; couple 2 progresses on the outside in the reverse line of direction (clockwise).

**Steps and style:** A walking step, even on the swing, swing position. When moving in one large circle or in small circles, joined hands are held at shoulder height. Promenade in Varsouvienne position.

**The caller:** Preferably the caller (lead man or woman of head couple) calls from the floor while dancing. If the group is large, then he or she stands by the musicians and uses a microphone.

## Directions FOR THE DANCE

The caller uses a variety of figures, one pattern leading to the next. The basic structure includes: an introduction (with the whole group in a large circle), a series of figures (with the group in small circles), and a ending (with the group in a large circle again).

### Introduction

Large-circle figures are called involving the whole group in a large circle. Any of the following large-circle figures may be called: circle left and right, promenade, swing partner, swing corner, promenade single file, grand and left, queen's highway, king's highway, shoo fly swing, and Georgia rang tang.

#### Georgia Rang Tang

**Circle left.**
**The other way back.**
**With the Georgia rang tang.** The man releases his left hand with his corner and travels through the arch made by his partner and her corner; then he continues to weave in and out through the arches made by each succeeding two dancers, his partner and other dancers following in and out. Do not let go of hands. The circle continues to move right until everyone has completed the figure. The leader may go on with endless rhyme such as:
**Make your feet go whickety whack.**
**Hurry, hurry, hurry.**

### King's Highway

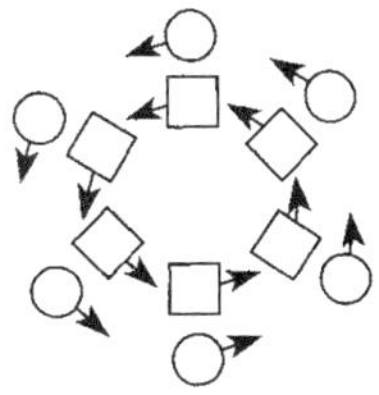

**Promenade.**
**Gents turn back on the king's highway.** The head man steps behind his partner, turns right, and travels in the reverse line of direction around the circle, followed in succession by the men behind; the women continue to travel forward.
**Promenade.** When each man meets his partner, he crosses to the inside of the circle, *behind* his partner, and they promenade in the line of direction.

### Queen's Highway

**Promenade.**
**Ladies turn back on the queen's highway.** The head woman turns right and travels in the reverse line of direction around the circle, followed in succession by the women behind; the men continue to travel forward.
**Promenade.** When each woman meets her partner, they promenade.

### Shoo Fly Swing

**Shoo fly swing around the ring.** The man of the head couple faces his partner (man's back to center of circle).
**Right to your own.** He swings his partner by the right hand.
**Left on the side.** She swings the man of the next couple (to the woman's right) by the left hand. Now back to own partner with the right, left to the next man (second couple to right), and so on around the circle. Her partner follows on the inside of the circle. After the first couple has passed three couples, the next couple starts the same pattern. Each couple continues until they are back home.

## Figures

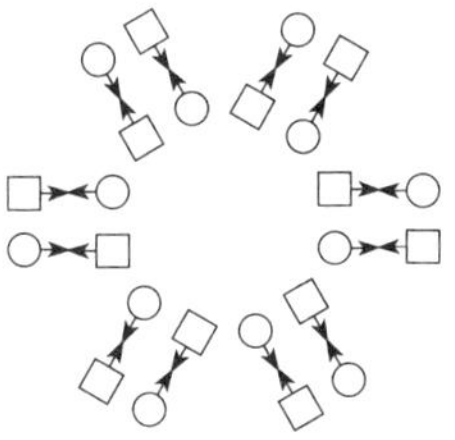

**Odd couples out to the even couples.** They join hands, circle four to the left until a small circle figure is called. Any of the following small circle figures may be called: circle left and right, right- and left-hand star, ladies chain, right and left thru, butterfly twirl, bird in the cage, take a little peek, lady 'round the lady, dive for the oyster, and shoot the owl. At the call "odds on to the next," the active couple moves forward on the inside to the next couple and circles four.

### The Basket

**Circle four hands around.**
**Ladies join your hands.**
**The men the same.** Women join two hands across, men join two hands above the women.
**Ladies bow the gents know how.** The men raise their arms over the heads of the women (women bow under) and lower them behind women's backs.
**The gents bow, the ladies know how.** The women raise their arms over the heads of the men and lower them behind men's backs.
**Circle left.** With right foot forward, scoot to the left with a modified buzz step.
**Break and swing your corner. And now your own. And on to the next.**

### Bird in the Cage

**Circle four hands around.**
**Cage the bird with three hands 'round.** Active woman steps in center. Inactive couple and active man join hands and circle around active woman.
**Bird flies out, crow hops in.** Active man steps in center as active woman joins circle with inactive couple.
**Ring up three and you're gone again.**
**Crow hops out and make a ring.**
**Swing your partner and on to the next.**

### Box the Gnat and Box the Flea

**Circle four.**
**With your opposite box the gnat.**
**Now box the flea.** Same person.
**Do–si–do.** Same person.
**Now swing that gal high and low.**
**And circle four.** Repeat call with own partner.
**And lead onto the next.**

### Butterfly Twirl

**Ladies twirl.** Women turn in place.
**Gents twirl.** Men turn in place.
**Everybody twirl a butterfly twirl.** Everybody turns in place.
**Now swing your corner girl.**
**And swing your own.**

### Dive for the Oyster

**Circle four.**
**Dive for the Oyster.** Without releasing hands, active couple moves forward through an arch made by the inactive man and woman back to face the inactive couple.
**Dive for the clam.** The inactive couple moves forward through an arch made by the active man and woman and then moves back into place, all four dancers holding hands.
**Dive for the sardine.**
**And take a full can.** The active couple moves through an arch made by the inactive man and woman, this time passing through to the other side, "wringing the dishrag." The dancers in the active couple move away from their partner, back to back. As they move back into the circle the active couple pulls the other couple through their raised hands. The inactive couple turns back to back as they go through the arch and then return face to face. All dancers face in and continue to circle left.
**Now circle four once around and on to the next.**

5

### Lady 'Round the Lady

**Lady 'round the lady and the gent solo.** The active woman leads, her partner following, and goes between the inactive couple; the woman goes behind the inactive woman, around her and in front, while her partner goes behind the inactive man, around him, and back to face the couple.
**Lady 'round the gent and the gent don't go.** The active woman goes between the inactive couple, travels behind and around the inactive man, and back to face the inactive couple; the active man stands in place.
**Now circle four once around and on to the next.**

### Mountaineer Loop

**Circle four.**
**Mountaineer Loop.** The even couple raise their arms for the odd couple to pass through. The odd couple releases man's right, woman's left, as they go through the arch; man turns left, woman right and travel back home, the even couple turning under their arch. Odd couple rejoins hands.
**And circle left.**

### Pop Them Thru

**Circle four.**
**Back with a left-hand star.**
**Then gents reach back and pop them through to a right-hand star.** Men reach across their chests with right hands (under left arm) for their opposites' right hand. All release star as men turn their opposite under their right arms and all form right-hand star.
**Gents reach back and pop them back.** Men repeat above action using left hand to form left-hand star.
**Swing your opposite on the same old track.** Men turn to swing the woman following them in the star.
**Swing your partner.**
**And onto the next.**

### Shoot the Owl

**Three hands 'round if you know how.** Active man circles three with inactive couple.
**When you get right, shoot the owl.**
**Two hands up, the gents shoot under.** Circle three once and one-half. Inactive couple "shoots" active man under arch to partner.
**Grab your partner and swing like thunder. Active couple swings.**
**Circle four and on to the next.**

### Take a Little Peek

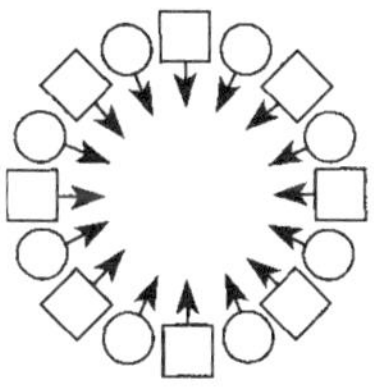

**Around that couple and take a little peek.** Active couple separates, woman peeks right, man peeks left around behind inactive couple.
**Back to the center and swing your sweet.** Active couple swings.
**Around that couple and peek once more.** Couple repeats "peeking" action.
**Back to the center and circle four.**
**Lead to the next.**

## Ending

Large circle figures are called involving the whole group in a large circle.

## Notes

1. When determining the active and inactive couples, always count around the circle counterclockwise. Also, do not let the couple to the left of the head couple start counting clockwise; it adds to the confusion, especially if there is an uneven number of couples present.
2. During the small circle figures, at the call "odds on to the next," the active couple moves forward to the next couple. They join hands and circle four to the left until a new figure is called.
3. If dancers become mixed up, call "find your partner, and everybody swing."
4. There is no end of figures that may be used, once the format of the Big Circle Square Dance is learned. The figures presented are just a few.

# Basic Movements for Square Dances

The square dance basics included in this text are aimed at the beginning, intermediate, and club dancer and teacher-caller.[4]

***Level 1A: Beginner Basics 1–8***

1. Walk/Clog
2. Honors
3. Do-Sa-Do
4. Promenade/Single-File Promenade
5. Twirl
6. Walk Swing/Buzz Step
7. Allemande Left
8. Grand Right and Left/Weave the Ring

***Level 1B: Orientation to the Square***

a. Forming the Square
b. Maneuvering in the Square
c. Practice Basics 1–8

***Level 2: Beginner Basics 9–18***

9. Split the Ring
10. Pass Thru
11. Separate Go Around One
12. Star Basics (Texas Star)
13. Forearm Turns
14. Sashay Family (Half Sashay, Roll Away to a Half-Sashay)
15. Courtesy Turn
16. Ladies Chain
17. Circle to a Line–Lines of Four
18. Bend the Line

***Level 3: Beginner Basics 19–26***

19. Right and Left Thru
20. Four Ladies Chain
21. Do Paso
22. All Around Your Left-Hand Lady–Seesaw
23. California Twirl
24. Dive Thru
25. Ends Turn In
26. U-Turn Back

4. The progression of the basic movements was arranged by Jane Harris Ericson, Anne M. Pittman, and Marlys Swenson Waller in 1978. Over the years different groups (e.g., *Sets In Order*, the American Callers Association, Callerlab) have established teaching progressions that are similar.

***Level 4: Intermediate Basics 27–35***

27. Cross Trail Thru
28. Grand Square
29. Box the Gnat/Box the Flea
30. Allemande Thar
31. Square Thru
32. Star Thru
33. Alamo Style
34. Wheel Around
35. Ocean Wave

## Teaching Progression and Analysis for Basic Movements of Square Dance

The basic movements of square dance have been arranged from simple to complex in a recommended teaching progression. Basics may be combined and called to practice interrelated movement patterns within the overall progression. The progression is designed to give the teacher-caller full information germane to each basic. The information includes: analysis or description of movement, specific teaching suggestions for each movement, diagrams for visual aid, calls for practicing basics as used in a dance, and recommended singing and/or patter calls using the basics in a dance figure.

### Basic Square Dance Formula

In creating a new square dance, the following formula may be used. Understanding this formula will also help in reading the directions for Singing Calls (pages 189–191).

| PART | WHO DANCES | POSSIBLE MOVES |
|---|---|---|
| Intro or Opener | All | Honor your partner |
| Break | All | Circle left, Grand Right and Left, Promenade Home |
| Main figure X 2 | Head couples active, then dance to change partner | Right and Left Thru. Head Ladies Chain, Promenade your corner. |
| Repeat Break (women across from home position) | | |
| Main Figure X 2 | Side couples active, then all dance to change partner. | |

| PART | WHO DANCES | POSSIBLE MOVES |
| --- | --- | --- |
| Repeat Break (women back with original partner.) | | |
| Ending | All | Wave to the girl across the hall. |

See pages 177–178 for examples of patter calls for openers, breaks and endings.

A very simple square dance would not follow this pattern. Some traditional formulas would have everyone repeating a main figure "Oh Johnny" is an example. Others might have each couple in turn be the active couple during the main figure.

## Level 1A: Beginner Basics 1–8

Regardless of class size, the beginning basics 1–8 should be practiced in a single circle so all class members are able to participate. The single circle formation allows for easy demonstration and viewing of class progress from the center of the circle. The teacher-caller may also "dance and call" from this formation or simply call out basics from the center of the circle.

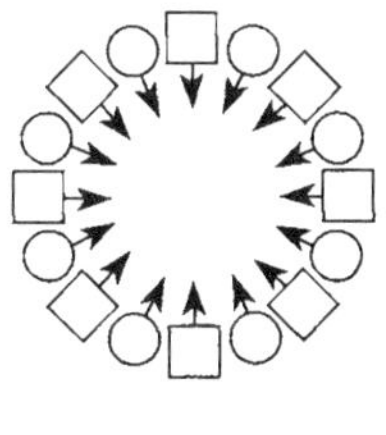

### 1. Walk

An easy, light, walking action in even rhythm, with the weight being transferred from heel to toe. A shuffle, weight on the ball of the foot, may be used. The action should be in time with the music. The body is held upright.

**TEACHING AIDS:** (a) Join hands in a single circle moving left, right, forward, and back. (b) Styling of hand clasp: man's palm up, woman's palm down. (c) Move with small steps, synchronize with partner, and step to the beat of the music.

### 2. Honors

Partners turn slightly to face each other while shifting the weight to the outside foot and pointing the inside foot toward partner. Often called Bow to Partner.

**TEACHING AIDS:** (a) One may dip slightly, keeping the back straight and the weight over the outside foot (man's left, woman's right). (b) The action can take four counts in all: shift weight and dip (count 1), hold (2), and recover facing the set (counts 3 and 4).

### 3. Do-Sa-Do

Partners face, pass each other right shoulder to right shoulder, move around each other back to back and return to original position facing partner.

**TEACHING AIDS:** (a) Dancers should learn to keep hands and arms down to the sides and slightly behind. (b) Dancers can turn slightly on a diagonal in passing so as to make it easier to get around without bumping.

**PRACTICE CALL** [1] (using first three basics)

**All join hands and circle left**
**Everybody go forward and back**
**Face your partner, do-sa-do**
**Bow to your partner.**

### 4. Promenade/Single-File Promenade

#### Promenade

Partners take **promenade position** and move counterclockwise around the circle.

**TEACHING AIDS:** (a) The joined right hands are on top. (b) The hands are joined (man's palm up, woman's palm down) at about waist level. (c) The man may take the initiative to lead slightly as they move forward. (d) A clockwise direction is called a **wrong-way promenade.**

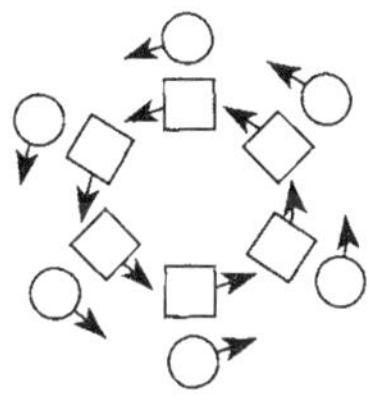

#### Single-File Promenade

Dancers turn to face counterclockwise and walk one behind the other single file around the circle.

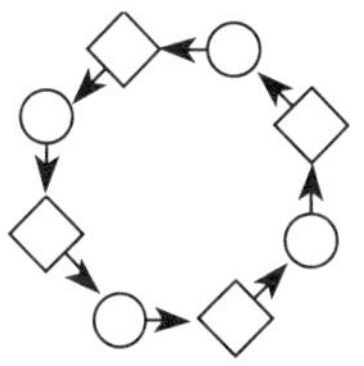

**TEACHING AID:** Dancers may go into single-file promenade from a promenade. The woman steps in front of the man, and they move one behind the other counterclockwise around the circle.

**PRACTICE CALL** [2]

**All join hands, circle left**
**Break, promenade single file**
**The other way back**
**Face the center, go forward and back**
**Honor your partner.**

**PRACTICE CALL** 3

**Bow to partner, promenade**
**Promenade single file**
**Home you go and do-sa-do.**

## 5. Twirl

Partners face, join right hands. Man lifts right hand, turning woman under man's right arm once clockwise. As woman completes turn, man takes her left hand. Couples resume promenade position or as directed by caller.

**TEACHING AIDS:** (a) Woman must move along line of direction while turning to stay slightly ahead of man who is following woman's turn. (b) A good demonstration helps dancers style the twirl. (c) Twirl is not always called. It is a styling movement done automatically.

**NOTE:** In practice call 4 the twirl may be done twice, once after each call "right to your partner, promenade."

**PRACTICE CALL** 4 (using the first five basics)

**All join hands and circle to the left**
**Now circle to the right**
**Everybody go forward and back**
**Do-sa-do your partner**
**Right to partner, promenade**
**All join hands to forward and back**
**Do-sa-do your corner**
**All join hands and circle to the left**
**Now circle to the right**
**Face partner, do-sa-do**
**Right to partner and promenade.**

## 6. Walk Swing/Buzz Step

### Walk/Swing

Partners take **swing position.** Dancers walk around each other, turning twice around clockwise in four or eight counts.

**TEACHING AIDS:** (a) Body erect, lean back from waist and look at each other. (b) Woman rolls off man's right arm to next position called or may twirl to a promenade position.

### Buzz Step

A more advanced swinging technique. Dancers are in the same position as they were for the walk swing. They turn twice around as before and open up facing the center of the square. The difference in the buzz step is that the rhythm is uneven. Instead of being an even beat shuffle (♪♪), it is a long-short-long-short (♩♪) rhythm.

**TEACHING AIDS:** (a) Each person places the outside of the right foot close to partner's right foot and turns the foot a little each time, pivoting around a center point between the two dancers. The right foot takes the long beat, and the left foot takes the short beat and acts in a pushing motion to propel the turn around. (b) Dancers should lean away from each other and take advantage of the centrifugal force. (c) Momentum must be stopped near the end of the turn so that they can make a controlled stop in place. (d) The buzz step should be very smooth. Avoid bobbing up and down.

## 7. Allemande Left

Corners take a left forearm grasp and turn each other once around and go back home.

**TEACHING AIDS:** (a) Left elbow is bent, dancers pull away slightly on the turn. (b) Grasp forearm with palm of hand rather than fingers.

**PRACTICE CALL** 5 (using basics 1–8)

**Honor your partner, swing your partner**
**All join hands and circle left**
**All to the center and back**
**Now swing your partner round and round**
**Promenade her single file**
**Join hands and circle left**
**All to the center and back**
**Allemande left your corner**
**Do-sa-do your partner, do-sa-do corner**
**Swing your partner**
**Bow to your partner and stand right there.**

## 8. Grand Right and Left/ Weave the Ring

### Grand Right and Left

Partners face and join right hands, move forward, pass partner, extend left hand to the next dancer, right to the next, and so forth, until dancers meet original partner. Men move counterclockwise; women move clockwise.

**TEACHING AIDS:** (a) Dancers release hand grasps quickly as they pass. (b) Dancers meet partner or person with whom they began the figure. Listen for next call; it could be "swing partner," "do-sa-do," or "promenade home." (c) To promenade, man should take woman's right in his right and turn woman clockwise into promenade position.

**PRACTICE CALL** 6

**Face your partner**
**Grand right and left**
**Meet partner, promenade.**

**PRACTICE CALL** 7

**Allemande left with your left hand**
**Right to partner, keep going**
**Right and left grand**
**Meet partner, promenade.**

### Weave the Ring

Same as grand right and left except that dancers do not touch hands when passing each other.

**TEACHING AID:** Dancers may turn slightly on a diagonal when passing so as to pass each other closely without bumping.

**PRACTICE CALL** 8

**All join hands and circle left**
**Break, reverse, go single file**
**When you get home, swing your partner**
**Allemande left and weave the ring**
**In and out 'til you meet your maid**
**Take the little girl and promenade.**

## Level 1B: Orientation to the Square

Dancers need to learn how to form a square and to understand and practice the movement possibilities based on its structure.

### A. Forming the Square

1. Four couples form a square. Each couple forms one side of the square. All couples face the center of the square, each man with his partner on his right. This is **home position** for each couple.

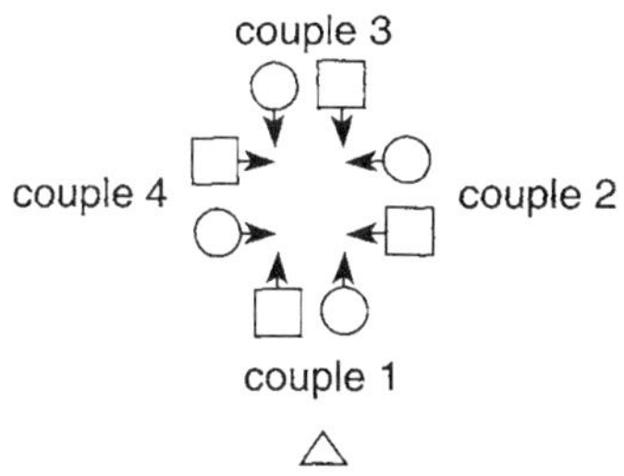


2. Couples are numbered counterclockwise or to the right around the square. Couple 1 always has their backs to the caller and music; couple 2 is to the right of couple 1; couple 3 is across from couple 1 and to the right of couple 2; couple 4 is across from couple 2 and to the left of couple 1.
3. Couples 1 and 3 are called **head couples** and are numbered 1 and 3 in most of the calls. Couples 2 and 4 are called **side couples** and are numbered 2 and 4. □ = man, ○ = woman, △ = caller.
4. The woman to the left of each man is the **corner lady.** The woman in the couple to the right of each man is the **right-hand lady.** The woman directly across from each man is the **opposite** lady.
5. Couples are called **active couples** when their number is called for an action. **Inactive couples** are those not called for an action, but they may be involved in an action by the active couples. The active couple is also called the **lead couple.**

Practice call 9 is designed to provide practice in learning home positions, couple numbers, individual numbers, and interaction with partner and corner. Basics 1–8 are used as they relate to the square formation. For full and complete practice, the call sequence should be: opener, main figure for women, break, repeat main figure for men, repeat break (gives extra allemande left practice), and add the ending.

**PRACTICE CALL** 9 (Two Little Sisters Form a Ring)

***Opener***

**Honor your partner, honor your corner**
**All join hands and circle left**
**Circle right the other way back**
**Into the center and give a little yell**
**Back right out and circle left**
**And home you go.**

***Main Figure***

**Two little sisters form a ring**
Women 1 and 2 join hands in center of square
**Circle left don't be slow**
Women 1 and 2 circle once around
**Home you go and do-sa-do (or swing)**
**Three little sisters form a ring**
Women 1, 2, 3
**Circle left don't be slow**
Circle once around
**Home you go and do-sa-do (or swing)**
**Now four little sisters form a ring**
Women 1, 2, 3, and 4
**Circle left don't be slow**
**Home you go and do-sa-do (or swing).**

***Break***

**Allemande left that pretty maid**
**Right to your partner and**
**Grand right and left.**
**Meet your partner and promenade.**
**Home you go there is more.**

Repeat figure for men.

***Ending***

**Honor your partner, corner too**
**Thank you folks, I'm all through.**

**NOTE:** Teachers may wish to teach basic 13 "forearm turn" and use it as a "single arm swing" rather than using the waist swing at this early stage of learning. This would be a good choice in classes that have more women than men. More important, there is less style and technique in the "forearm turn" used as a "single arm swing," thus allowing the class to go through the first eight basics and get to a whole square dance in the very first lesson.

## B. Maneuvering in the Square

Maneuvering in the square means learning to move in relation to eight dancers. This is a group action and therefore requires group timing to achieve smooth interaction and transitions. The following "traffic" rules will help dancers move as a group more efficiently.

*Rule 1:* Standard practice is to dance forward and back with three small steps and a touch on the fourth count.

*Rule 2:* While dancers are executing the first call, they should listen for the next call. The caller will overlap the action of the first call with the second. Remember that calls can be ad lib, or extemporaneous; dancers must listen!

*Rule 3:* The size of the square may be kept compact by the men promenading with left shoulders pulled in toward the center of the square. Distance to home is shortened and movement is better timed.

*Rule 4:* When a couple or individual dancers moves around the outside of the square, dancers should move to center as they pass.

*Rule 5:* Promenading around the square: Men should always promenade partners (own or new one) to the man's home position. A promenade may be called for less than once around. These fractional promenade distances may be danced outside or inside the square.

*Rule 6:* Dancers are always in home position with original partner at the end of a call sequence. It is the responsibility of the caller to make this happen.

*Rule 7:* The best solution to a breakdown in executing the call is to go to home position. This will allow the figure to become untangled and dancers may "pick up the call" and continue dancing in good order.

*Rule 8:* How far to promenade: The rule of thumb is to promenade home if the distance is one quarter or more to go. If the distance is less than one quarter (you are almost home), you should go full around to home position.

*Rule 9:* Lead to the right simply means couples move to the right of the square and stand in front of the appropriate couple. Example: Couples 1 and 3 move to the right and stand in front of couples 2 and 4.

*Rule 10:* Dancers should react to the various positions in the square rather than to "a person" who is supposed to be there. Example: Allemande left, dancer should move to the corner position and react with whomever is there.

*Rule 11:* Dancers are in sequence when they are in the original order in the square (i.e., as numbered 1 to 4 counterclockwise). Dancers are out of sequence when any two have changed places (i.e., couples 1 and 3 pass through or all couples pass through or as individuals change in a two ladies chain.

*Rule 12:* Swing the opposite lady: Men swing opposite by moving simultaneously, allowing the man on the left to pass across in front before reaching opposite woman. Or they may make a brief right-hand star in the center to reach the opposite in more orderly fashion. Men move right across in front of partner to swing right-hand lady, face center, and wait for next call.

## C. Practice Basics 1–8

Practice basics 1–8 in square formation.

**Easy square dances:** Split the Ring, Cowboy Loop, Sally Goodin', Bird in the Cage.

## Level 2: Beginner Basics 9–18

### 9. Split the Ring

The lead couple moves between the man and woman of the opposite couple.

**TEACHING AIDS:** (a) Couple being "split" moves sideways and apart to let lead couple through.
(b) After moving through, lead couple must listen for next call. Example: "Separate go around the outside ring, home you go and swing."

**PRACTICE CALL** 10

**First couple go down the center**
**Split the ring, separate,**
Move around the outside of the square
**Go back home**
**Everybody do-sa-do.**

*Repeat* for each couple.

**PRACTICE CALL** 11

**1 and 3 go forward and back**
**Forward again, face the sides**
**Split the ring, separate**
Move around the outside of the square
**Go back home, do-sa-do.**

*Repeat* for 2 and 4.

## 10. Pass Thru

Two couples face. Dancers move forward passing opposite dancer's right shoulder to right shoulder.

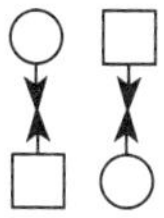

**TEACHING AID:** Dancers pass thru and listen for next call.

**PRACTICE CALL** **12**

> **1 and 3 pass thru**
> **Separate, come around two**
> **Right back home**
> **2 and 4 go forward and back**
> **Everybody do-sa-do.**

*Repeat* for 2 and 4.

## 11. Separate Go Around One

Men move left, women right to separate. Dancers then move around the nearest inactive dancer to face partner in center of square. Wait for next call.

**PRACTICE CALL** **13**

> **1 and 3 pass thru**
> **Separate, go around one**
> **Come in between the sides**
> **Go into the middle**
> **Pass thru, split the next two**
> **Separate, go around one**
> **Come down the middle**
> **Pass thru face partner**
> **Swing and square set.**

*Repeat* for 2 and 4.

**Square dance:** Split the Ring, Go Around One.

## 12. Star Basics (Texas Star)

The following basics are used in the dance figure Texas Star. However, they may be used separately in other combinations.

### Star Hand Formation

This is how dancers join hands in a basic star formation.

### Four Gents Star

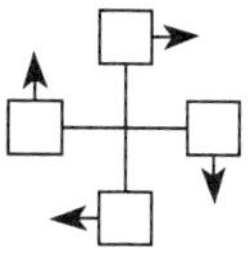

Men go to the center, touch hands, fingers up, and move around the center of the ring.

**TEACHING AIDS:** (a) The men make a right-hand star, turning clockwise, and a left-hand star, turning counterclockwise. (b) When changing from a right-hand star to a left-hand star, the men release with the right hand, make a right face turn, and form the star with the left hand. (c) The four women may form the star in the same manner.

### Star Promenade

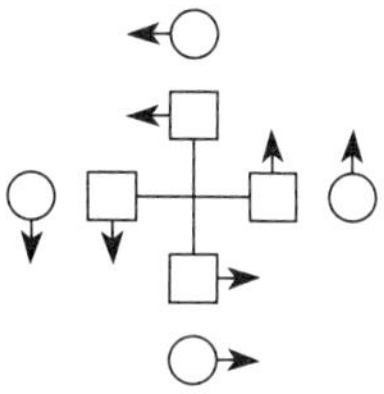

Four couples move in same direction. Men star with left hand moving counterclockwise. Women star with right hand moving clockwise.

**TEACHING AIDS:** (a) Each man puts right arm around partner's waist, woman's left arm should rest on man's upper right arm. (b) Woman needs to move toward man to be picked up to begin the star. Remember, men are holding hands in a left-hand star as they start the pickup.

### Gents Swing Out Ladies Swing In

Men break the star and back up, turning as a couple counterclockwise. Women move into center to form a right-hand star. The "swing out and in" may be a half-turn or a turn and a half to put the women in the star.

### Box Star Position

Dancer (man or woman) places right or left hand on the wrist of the dancer in front. This wrist hold is also called a *packsaddle*.

**Square dances:** Texas Star and Gents Star Right.

## 13. Forearm Turns

Forearm turns are a means of turning in place with the use of a forearm grasp. This basic may be used instead of or along with the waist swing as a "single arm swing." It is easy to learn and is useful in classes where there are more women than men, or vice versa.

**TEACHING AID:** Dancers should pull away slightly, keeping the elbow bent, the arm firm, and palm against the partner's arm.

**PRACTICE CALL** 14

**All face your partner**
**Turn partner right arm round**
**Men star left in the center**
**Meet your partner, do-sa-do**
**All join hands and circle left**
**Go once around and get back home**
**Now gents star right, one time around**
**Pass your partner, allemande left**
**Come back to partner and swing.**

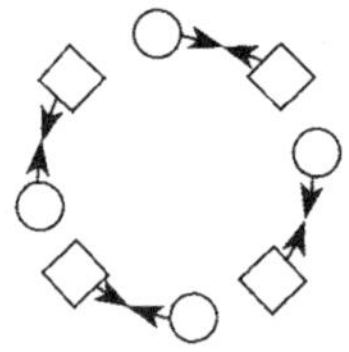

**Square dances:** Arkansas Traveler and Mañana.

## 14. Sashay Family: Half-Sashay, Roll Away to a Half-Sashay

### Half-Sashay

Partners are side by side, facing same direction, woman on man's right. Man moves behind, sideways to his right; woman moves sideways to her left.

**PRACTICE CALL** 15

**Join hands and circle right**
**Break the ring with a half-sashay**
**Join hands and circle more**
**Break the ring with a half-sashay**
**Join hands and circle right, listen to my call,**
**Swing the girl across the hall,**
**Now promenade home.**

### Roll Away to a Half-Sashay

*Source: Ed Gilmore in 1950*

Partners are side by side, facing same direction, woman on the man's right. The woman rolls across in front of the man to his left side. As she rolls, she makes one complete turn counterclockwise.

**TEACHING AIDS:** (a) The man guides the woman across with his right hand and simultaneously steps to his right so that they end up having exchanged places. (b) He will release her left hand and take her right in his left. (c) In star promenade position, the man will have his right arm around the woman's waist and will help her roll across in front of him to the other side. (d) Dancers learn to respond to this basic as half-sashay, roll away, or whirl away (synonymous terms).

**PRACTICE CALL** 16

**All join hands and circle left**
**Roll away with a half-sashay**
**Circle left in the same old way**
**Ring, ring, ring, I say**
**Roll away with a half-sashay**
**All you gents listen to my call**
**Swing the girl across the hall.**

## 15. Courtesy Turn

Couple faces in same direction. Man takes woman's left hand in his left, places right arm around waist. Couple turns as a unit, man backing up as couple turns counterclockwise to face original direction or as caller indicates.

**TEACHING AIDS:** Woman's right palm should rest lightly on her right hip over man's hand.

## 16. Ladies Chain

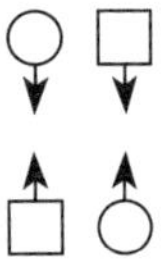

Two couples are facing each other. The two women take right hands and pull by and then give a left hand to the opposite man. The man takes her left hand in his left and does a courtesy turn, turning once around to face the other couple. The two women have changed partners. Repeat to home position.

**TEACHING AIDS:** (a) Couples 1 and 3 execute ladies chain across in the square formation. This acts as a demonstration for other couples. Repeat for couples 2 and 4. (b) Men should take two-step to the right after releasing women and reach out with left hand to receive new partner for courtesy turn. (c) Dancers may also practice all at once in a diagonal formation (i.e., couples 1 and 2 chain as couples 3 and 4 chain). (d) Use practice call 17 for all four couples to practice on the diagonal (i.e., couple 1 with 2 and couple 3 with 4). (e) Use practice call 18 in the set or square formation to teach and practice four ladies chain.

**PRACTICE CALL** 17

**Bow to your partner**
**Bow to your opposite**
**Two ladies chain across**
**Chain right back**
**All four go forward and back**
**Two ladies chain**
**Now chain 'em back.**

**PRACTICE CALL** 18

**Bow to your partner**
**Couples 1 and 3 promenade outside**
**Go all the way around**
**Couples 2 and 4 ladies chain**

**2 and 4 chain back**
**Couples 2 and 4 promenade outside**
**Go all the way around**
**1 and 3 ladies chain**
**1 and 3 chain back**
**All four ladies chain across the set**
**All four ladies chain right back**
**All join hands and circle left**
**Break and promenade single file**
**Home you go, everybody swing.**

## 17. Circle to a Line—Lines of Four

Couples 1 and 3 (or 2 and 4) lead to the right, circle two-thirds around; active man drops left-hand grasp and pulls the line out straight.

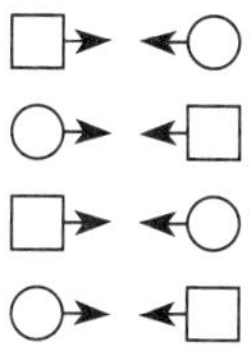

**TEACHING AIDS:** (a) To get the notion of couple positions in the line, simply have couples 1 and 3 (or 2 and 4) move over and stand beside couples 2 and 4. Men 1 and 3 will be opposite their home position. (b) Practice having 1 and 3 (or 2 and 4) move from home position, circle with 2 and 4 into position as in (a). The inactive women should turn counterclockwise under partner's right arm to move comfortably into position at end of line.

## 18. Bend the Line

From any line of an even number (usually four people), the line breaks in the middle, the centers of the line back up, and the ends of the line move forward until both halves of the line are facing.

**TEACHING AIDS:** (a) The center two people release hands and back up at the same time that the two end people move forward so that each half of the line pivots to face the other. (b) When two lines of four face each other, bend the line; the result is that two new lines of four are formed, facing each other in the new direction.

**PRACTICE CALL** 19

**1 and 3 lead to the right**
**Circle, break and form a line**
**Go forward up and back**
**Pass thru and bend the line**
**Go forward up and back**
**Pass thru and bend the line**
**Go forward up and back**
**Pass thru and bend the line**
**Go forward up and back**
**Pass thru and bend the line**
**Now all join hands and circle eight.**

*Repeat* for 2 and 4.

**Square dances:** Easy Bend the Line and Bend It Tight.

# Level 3: Beginner Basics 19–26

## 19. Right and Left Thru

Two couples face each other. Dancers join right hands and pull past opposite, passing right shoulder to right shoulder. Couples have backs to each other. Courtesy turn to face again and repeat to original place.

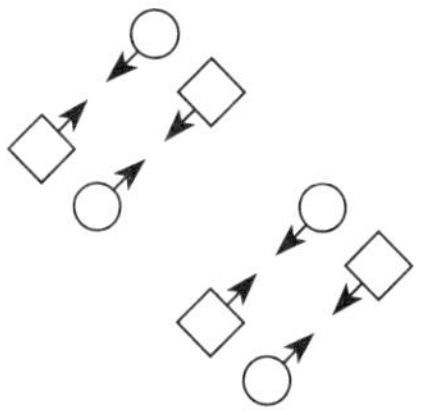

**TEACHING AIDS:** (a) Practice in square formation or on the diagonal as suggested for ladies chain. (b) The call is not necessarily followed by a "right and left back" call. Dancers must listen to caller for directions. (c) Use practice call 20 on the diagonal and call 21 in the square formation.

**PRACTICE CALL** 20

**Honor your partner**
**Honor your opposite**
**Go right and left thru**
**Right and left back**
**Do-sa-do your opposite gal**
**Go right and left thru turn your pal**
**Now do-sa-do opposite, don't be slow**
**Right and left thru and back you go.**

**PRACTICE CALL** 21

**Couples 1 and 3 go right and left thru**
**Couples 2 and 4 go right and left thru**
**Couples 1 and 3 go right and left back**
**2 and 4 go right and left back**
**Head ladies chain across**
**Side ladies chain across**
**All four ladies chain back.**

**Square dances:** The Route, Promenade the Outside Ring, Split the Ring Variations, and Old-Fashioned Girl.

## 20. Four Ladies Chain

All four women move to the center, touch right hands, and move clockwise to opposite man. Opposite man and woman courtesy turn, women move back into center, touch right hands clockwise to home position, and courtesy turn. Basic also called grand chain.

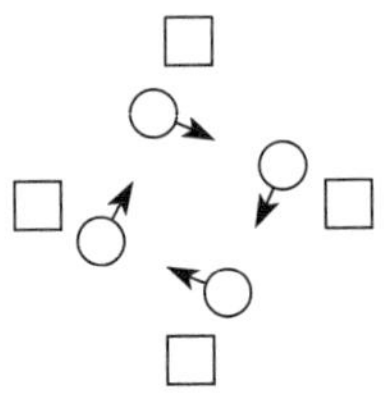

**TEACHING AID:** The four women need to keep track of where they are so they will only pass one man and be turned by the opposite. Use practice call 21.

## 21. Do Paso

*Source: Lloyd Shaw in 1947*

Starting position is a circle of two or more couples. Partners face, take a left forearm grasp, and turn each other counterclockwise until facing the corner. Turn corner with right forearm grasp until facing partner. Take partner with the left hand, and man turns woman with courtesy turn.

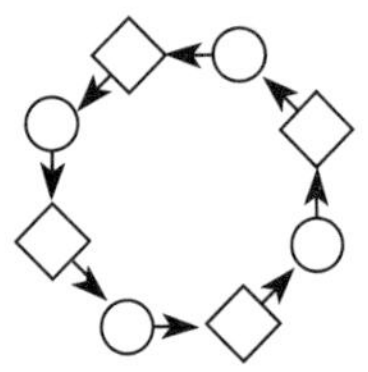

**TEACHING AID:** Practice first in circle of four or more couples, then practice in circle of two couples.

**PRACTICE CALL** 22

**All join hands, circle left**
**And around you go**
**Break into a do paso**
**Partner by the left, corner by the right**
**Now turn your own if it takes all night**
**Join hands, circle.**

*Repeat* all.

## 22. All Around Your Left-Hand Lady—Seesaw

Often used with seesaw your taw. Corners move one time around each other in a loop pattern, the man starting behind the corner, on around her and back to place, the woman starting in front of him and around him back to place. This completes half of the loop. Seesaw your partner is a similar action that completes the other half of the loop.

**TEACHING AID:** Dancers learn that these are companion figures, but the second loop does not always follow the first loop; it depends on the call.

**PRACTICE CALL** 23

**Walk all around your left-hand lady**
**Oh boy, what a daisy**
**Seesaw your pretty little taw**
**She's the best you ever saw.**

**Square dance:** Goodbye My Lady Love.

## 23. California Twirl

This is the same as the frontier twirl. This basic is used by a couple to reverse the direction they are facing. If they are facing out, they turn to face in, and vice versa. Partners join inside hands (man's right, woman's left). The man walks around the woman clockwise as he turns her counterclockwise under his right arm.

**TEACHING AIDS:** (a) The woman begins and ends on the man's right side. (b) They must let the hands slip easily around each other so as not to twist the wrist. (c) Both actually turn a half-turn.

**PRACTICE CALL** 24

**Head couples pass thru**
**California twirl**
**Side couples pass thru**
**California twirl.**

*Repeat* all.

## 24. Dive Thru

Two couples are facing each other. The couple whose back is to the center of the square makes an arch by joining inside hands. The couple facing them ducks under the arch and moves forward. The arching couple now facing out turns a California twirl.

**TEACHING AID:** The California twirl is done automatically from this position. The caller does not call it.

**PRACTICE CALL** 25

**Head ladies chain across**
**But don't chain back**
**1 and 3 lead to the right**
**Circle halfway 'round**
**Now dive thru pass thru**
**There's your corner**
**Allemande left.**

*Repeat* for 2 and 4.

## 25. Ends Turn In

*Source: Ed Gilmore in 1952*

Starting position is when two lines of four are facing out. The two persons in the center of the line form an arch, and the two persons on the ends of the line drop hands, walk forward, and go together under the arch, moving into the center of the square. The arching couple California twirls.

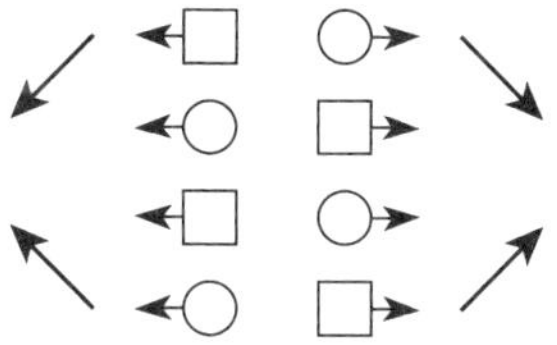

**TEACHING AID:** To practice, direct 1 and 3 men to stand next to corner women and 1 and 3 women stand next to corner men. The two facing lines move forward, pass thru and join hands; lines are facing out. Repeat practice for 2 and 4.

**Square dances:** Ends Turn In and Inside Arch Outside Under.

## 26. U-Turn Back

This is an individual turn or about-face to move in the opposite direction.

**PRACTICE CALL** 26

**1 and 3 pass thru**
**U-turn back**
**2 and 4 pass thru**
**U-turn back.**

*Repeat* all.

**PRACTICE CALL** 27

**1 and 3 roll away with a half-sashay**
**Up to the center and back that way**
**Pass thru and U-turn back**
**Right and left thru on the same old track.**

*Repeat* for 2 and 4.

**Square dances:** Roll Away Combo 1 and Gentle on My Mind.

# Level 4: Intermediate Basics 27–35

## 27. Cross Trail Thru

Two couples are facing each other. Each person passes by the opposite right shoulder to right shoulder and then the woman crosses to the left in front of the man. The man crosses to the right behind the woman. They all stop facing out, side by side, woman on left of man, and follow the next call.

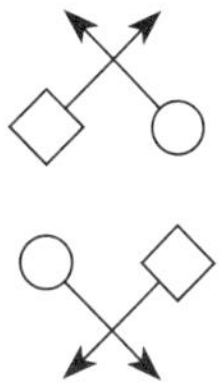

**TEACHING AIDS:** (a) Next call may be "go around two." (b) May be done from line formation; couples end up facing out. When facing out in a line, the two in the middle of the line are corners and will turn to face for allemande left. End dancers will find corners behind them on the end of the opposite line.

**PRACTICE CALL** 28

**1 and 3 cross trail thru**
**Separate and go around two**
**Home you go, pass by your own**
**Allemande left**
**Honor your partner at home.**

*Repeat* for 2 and 4.

**PRACTICE CALL** 29

**1 and 3 promenade the outside ring**
**Go just halfway round**
**Same two cross trail thru**
**Now allemande left with your left hand**
**Right to partner, shake her by the hand**
**And there you stand.**

*Repeat* for 2 and 4.

**Square dances:** Another Trail, Roll Away Combo 2, Arkansas Traveler with Cross Trail, and Split the Ring Variation 2.

## 28. Grand Square

This is a no-patter call. Dancers walk individually around a square pattern on the floor. Each side of square is four counts. Dancers move along each side with three steps and turn or hold as indicated.

**TEACHING AIDS:** (a) All dancers should practice action from the head couple and side couple positions. (b) Caller may cue with word cues as in practice call.

5

## Grand Square Figure

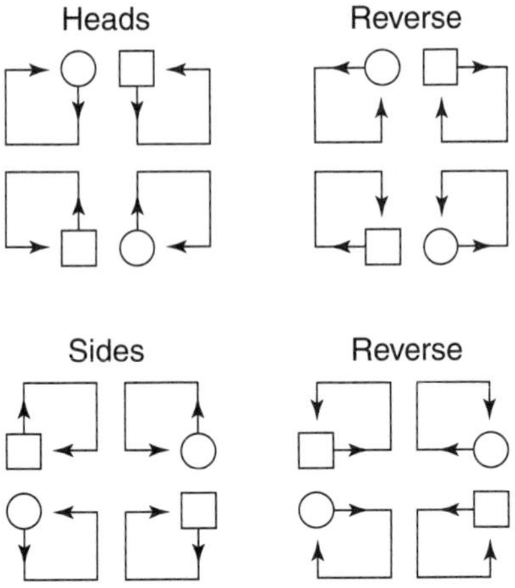


*Heads*

1. Go forward three steps and turn on fourth count to face partner.
2. Take opposite's hand beside you and back up three steps, turning on fourth count to face the person by your side.
3. Drop hands, back away from this person three steps, turning one-quarter on fourth count to face partner.
4. Move forward three steps toward partner and hold the fourth count (do not turn).

*Reverse*

5. Move backward away from partner three steps, turn one-quarter on fourth count to face the opposite person.
6. Move forward toward opposite three steps, turn one-quarter on the fourth count to face partner.
7. Take opposite's hand beside you and move forward three steps, turning on the fourth count to face opposite.
8. Drop hands, take partner's hands, back up three steps into home place, and hold the fourth count.

*Sides*
Start with 5, 6, 7, 8, 1, 2, 3, 4.

**PRACTICE CALL** 30

**Honor your partner—the lady fair** } A
**All get set for grand square**
**Walk 2 3 turn**
**Walk 2 3 turn**
**Walk 2 3 turn**
**Walk 2 3 reverse** } B
**Walk 2 3 turn**
**Walk 2 3 turn**
**Walk 2 3 turn**
**Walk 2 3 hold.**

A. "Honor your partner . . ." on last eight counts of phrase.

B. Start figure with new phrase, 32 counts of music.

**Square dances:** Gentle On My Mind using grand square for opener, middle break, and ending, or any previous square dance, using grand square as trim, or Grand Square Quadrille.

### 29. Box the Gnat/Box the Flea

#### Box the Gnat

Partners face, join right hands, and exchange places, as the woman turns counterclockwise under the man's right arm, man walks around woman clockwise. Partners end facing, having exchanged places.

**TEACHING AIDS:** (a) The hands are allowed to slip easily around each other so as not to twist the wrists. (b) Dancers should learn to listen for "box the gnat, pull by," in which they hold on with the right hand after box the gnat and use that hand to pull by that person. (c) Practice this first with partner, then with corner, and then use practice calls 31 and 32.

**PRACTICE CALL** 31

**1 and 3**
**Roll away to a half-sashay**
**Box the gnat across the way**
**Pull by for a right and left thru.**

*Repeat* for 2 and 4.

#### Box the Flea

Similar to box the gnat except that both man and woman use the left hand instead of the right. The lady is turned clockwise under the man's left arm; the man walks around her counterclockwise. They end up facing each other but have changed places.

**TEACHING AIDS:** (a) The hands slip easily. (b) Dancers should listen for a pull by to follow.

**PRACTICE CALL** 32

**Allemande left your corner**
**Meet partner, box the gnat**
**Pull by and with your corner**
**Box the flea, pull by**
**Swing your partner.**

**Square dance:** Gnat and Flea

### 30. Allemande Thar

*Source: Lloyd Shaw in 1938*

A star formation for all four couples in square. Dancers allemande left, back to partner with right, pull by to next with left forearm grasp. Men turn this woman a half-turn counterclockwise until men can make a box star (packsaddle) in center. Men travel backward in the star, women travel forward. On call "shoot the star," men release box star position, turn woman on left arm halfway around; women are facing clockwise, men counterclockwise. Dancers release arm position, move forward to the next with right hand, pull by, a left forearm grasp to the next, men turn as before into box star backing up. "Shoot the star" again and turn the woman halfway around, move forward to meet original partner and follow the next call.

**TEACHING AIDS:** (a) The key word to this basic is *thar.* (b) Men should let women set movement pace in box star. (c) Allemande thar star is used as a trim and as part of a patter call any time from a left-arm turn.

**PRACTICE CALL** 33

**Allemande left and allemande thar**
**It's right and left and form a star**
**Gents back up in a right-hand star**
**Now shoot that star to the heavens whirl**
**Go right and left to a brand new girl**
**And form that star again**
**Back 'em up boys but not too far**
**Shoot that star and find your own**
**Promenade, go right on home.**

## 31. Square Thru

Two couples are facing each other. Right square thru, starting with the right hand, will be described here. The square thru may be full square thru (four hands), three-quarters square thru (three hands), half square thru (two hands), or square thru five hands, as described below.

***Full Square Thru***

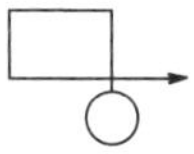

Face opposite, take right hand, pull by, turn one-quarter to face partner, give left hand, pull by, turn one-quarter to face opposite, give right hand, pull by, turn one-quarter to face partner, give left hand, pull by, and stop.

**TEACHING AIDS:** (a) Take four hands, right, left, right, left, hand over hand; the women travel counterclockwise around the center of the square; the men travel clockwise. (b) Drop the hand after pulling by. (c) Do *not* turn the last time. (d) Each person ends facing his or her corner.

***Three-Quarters Square Thru***

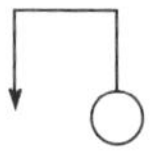

Take three hands, right, left, right.

**TEACHING AIDS:** (a) Do *not* turn the third time. (b) Each person ends facing out.

***Half Square Thru***

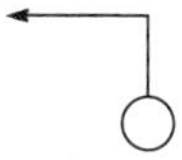

Take two hands, right, left.

**TEACHING AID:** Do not turn the *second* time.

***Square Thru Five Hands***

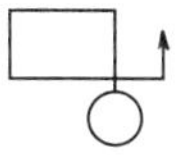

Take five hands, right, left, right, left, right.

**TEACHING AIDS:** (a) Do not turn the *fifth* time. (b) Will end facing out.

**NOTE:** A left square thru is executed in the same manner, beginning with the left hand.

**PRACTICE CALL** 34 (full square thru)

**1 and 3 square thru**
**Count four hands, right, left, right, left.**
**Then split the outside two**
**Go around one and come back home.**

*Repeat* for 2 and 4.

**PRACTICE CALL** 35 (full square thru)

**1 and 3 promenade halfway 'round**
**Same two square thru**
**Split the outside two**
**Come around one to the middle**
**Cross trail thru**
**Allemande left.**

*Repeat* for 2 and 4.

**PRACTICE CALL** 36 (three-quarters square thru)

**1 and 3 up and back**
**Square thru three hands 'round**
**Then separate, go 'round one**
**Into the middle**
**Square thru three-quarters 'round**
**That's what you do**
**Split the sides, go 'round one**
**Into the middle, cross trail**
**To a left allemande.**

*Repeat* for 2 and 4.

**PRACTICE CALL** 37 (half square thru)

**1 and 3 half square thru**
**Right and left thru with the outside two**
**Dive thru, pass thru**
**Allemande left.**

*Repeat* for 2 and 4.

**Square dances:** Easy Square Thru, Pitt's Patter 3, Half Square Thru Combo, A Fooler A Faker, and Don't Let the Good Life Pass You By.

## 32. Star Thru

When two couples are facing, each person works with the opposite. The man takes the woman's left hand in his right hand and turns her one-quarter counterclockwise as he walks around her one-quarter clockwise. They end up side by side. This woman is now his new partner on his right.

**TEACHING AIDS:** (a) The new couple has made a quarter-turn and ends up facing the other couple who were their original partners. (b) The fingers need to slip around each other's easily in order to feel comfortable.

**PRACTICE CALL** 38

> **1 and 3 go forward and back**
> **Star thru, star thru again**
> **Cross trail back and find the corner**
> **Allemande left.**
>
> *Repeat* for 2 and 4.
>
> **Square dances:** Star Thru California Twirl, Star Thru Square Thru Combo, New Star Thru, and Go the Route.

## 33. Alamo Style

*Origin: Rickey Holden*

A variation of grand right and left. All eight dancers do an allemande left, hold on to the corner, but shift to a hands-up position and take partner right with a hands-up position, making a complete circle with the men facing in and the ladies facing out (diagram a). Dancers balance a short step forward and a short step back. Release the left hand and turn partner with a right hand halfway around so that the men now face out, the women face in. Join hands in the circle (diagram b). Repeat balance forward and back. Release with the right hand and turn with the left hand halfway around. Rejoin hands in the circle. Repeat balance and right-hand turn. Repeat balance and left-hand turn. There is your partner, follow the call.

**TEACHING AIDS:**

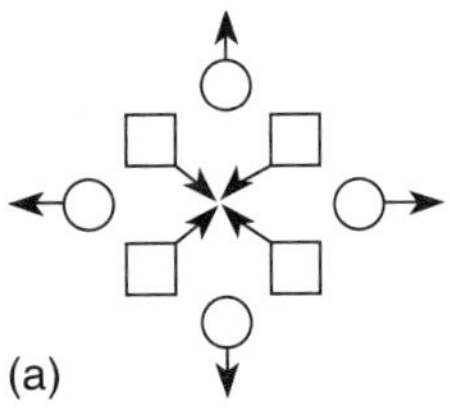

(a)

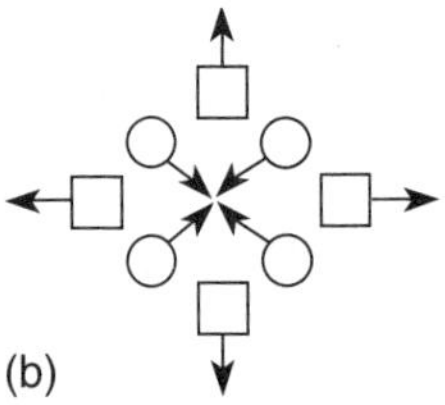

(b)

**PRACTICE CALL** 39

> **Allemande left, Alamo style**
> **Right to your own, balance a while**
> **Balance in and balance out**
> **Turn with the right hand half about**
> **Balance out and balance in**
> **Turn the left hand half about**
> **Balance in and balance out**
> **Turn with the right hand half about**
> **Balance in and balance out**
> **Turn with the left hand half again**
> **Swing your partner and promenade.**

## 34. Wheel Around

From a promenade, a couple will turn halfway around counterclockwise to face the couple behind them.

**TEACHING AIDS:** (a) Keeping the promenade position, the man will back up and the woman will move forward so that the move is a pivot in place. (b) The man who was on the inside for the promenade is now on the outside. (c) The dancers should learn to listen for the cue "promenade but don't slow down." (d) The caller may call "all four couples wheel around," in which case they will all be promenading the wrong way around with the woman on the inside. (e) The caller may call "1 and 3 wheel around," in which case 1 turns to face couple 4 and 3 turns to face couple 2. All should adjust slightly so that couples 1 and 2 are in line facing couples 3 and 4. If the caller calls "2 and 4 wheel around," then couples 2 and 3 are in line facing couples 4 and 1. (f) The next call might be "pass thru go on to the next," and couples will pass through the couple they are facing and proceed as a couple around the circle of couples in the direction they are facing, to meet the couple coming toward them.

**PRACTICE CALL** 40

> **Promenade but don't slow down**
> **First and third wheel around**
> **Go right and left thru**
> **Cross trail to an**
> **Allemande left.**
>
> *Repeat* for 2 and 4.

**PRACTICE CALL** 41

> **Promenade but don't slow down**
> **First and third wheel around**
> **Go right and left thru**
> **Pass thru to a brand new two**
> **Right and left thru**
> **Cross trail, there's your corner**
> **Allemande left.**
>
> *Repeat* for 2 and 4.

## 35. Ocean Wave

A line of dancers, usually four, facing in alternate directions.

**TEACHING AIDS:** (a) The call usually is "do-sa-do to an ocean wave." Two couples facing each other do-sa-do with opposite all the way around and step forward as if to pass thru and stop when they get four in line. (b) Note diagram. Man and woman of couple 1 face one direction and man and woman of couple 3 face opposite direction. (c) All join hands in line, hands up, elbows down.

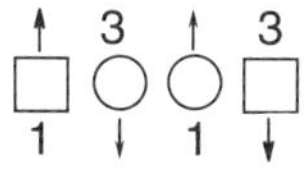


(d) All four balance forward (step touch) and backward (step touch). On the backward balance, dancers should reestablish relationships with their own partners by noting which one is facing the same direction as they are. (e) If the next call is right and left thru, they pull by the person who has their right hand and reach for partner with left for courtesy turn. (f) If the next call is box the gnat, it is done with the person who has their right hand in the line. (g) If next call is pass thru, release hands and move straight ahead. Same action for starting cross trail thru.

**PRACTICE CALL** [42]

**1 and 3 go forward and back**
**Now do-sa-do, go all the way 'round**
**To an ocean wave**
**Rock it up and back**
**Do right and left thru**
**And cross trail**
**To an allemande left.**

*Repeat* for 2 and 4.

**Square dance:** Ocean Wave.

## Supplementary Square Dance Patter

***Openers***

**Honor your partner, lady by your side**
**All join hands and circle wide**
**Break and trail along that line**
**The lady in the lead, the gent behind**
**Now you're home and now you swing.**

**Clap your hands**
**Now slap your knees** [twice]
**Bump-si-daisy if you please**
partners bump hips together

**Hi diddle, diddle**
**All eight to the middle**
**Back right out and swing your own**
**To the tune of the fiddle.**
**All jump up and never come down**
**Swing your partner 'round and 'round**
**And promenade, boys, promenade.**

***Endings***

**Honor your partner, corners all**
**Honor your opposite across the hall**
**And that is all.**

**Promenade—you know where**
**And I don't care**
**Take her out and give her air.**

**All you folks listen to the call**
**Thank you, ladies—that will be all.**

**Honor your partner and your corner too**
**Now wave at the gal across from you**
**Thank you folks, I'm all through.**

***Breaks***

**Allemande left, say what do you know**
**Back to your own and do-sa-do.**

**Allemande left as pretty as you can**
**Right to your honey**
**And a right and left grand.**

**Promenade around the ring**
**While the roosters crow and the birdies sing.**

**Here we go in a little red wagon**
**Rear wheel's broke and the axle's draggin'**
**Promenade, boys, promenade.**

**With your big foot up**
**And your little foot down**
**Promenade, go 'round and 'round.**

**Promenade, go 'round and 'round**
**Like a jaybird hoppin' on the frozen ground.**

**Allemande left with your left hand**
**Right to your partner**
**And a right and left grand**
**Promenade eight when you come straight.**

**Ace of diamonds, jack of spades**
**Meet your honey and all promenade.**

**Two, four, six, and eight**
**All promenade when you get straight.**

**Swing the girl across the hall**
**Go back home and swing your own.**

***Breaks for Fours***

*Half Square Thru*

**1 and 3 go forward and back**
**Now half square thru around the track**
**Right and left thru with the outside two**
**Dive thru, pass thru to an allemande left.**

*Square Thru*

**Heads go forward and back you do**
**Forward again and full square thru**
**Now count four hands is what you do.**
**Head two couples go square thru**
**Right, left, right, and pass a few**
**Partner left and now you're thru.**

*Star Thru*

**Heads go forward, back with you**
**Go forward again and pass thru**
**Around just one is what you do**
**Into the center and star thru**
**Cross trail thru, look out, gent**
**There's your corner, left allemande.**

***Breaks for Eights***

*Wheel Around*

**1 and 3 wheel around**
**Square thru three-quarters 'round**
**Go on to the next**
**Left square thru all the way 'round**
**Allemande left.**

**Promenade and don't slow down**
**Keep on walking that girl around**
**Heads back track and pass thru**
**Sides back track and follow those two**
**Lead two couples wheel around**

**Box the gnat with the two you found**
**Do a right and left thru**

**The other way back**
**Turn this girl, and**
**Cross trail thru.**

**Promenade, but don't slow down**
**First and third, wheel around**
**Right and left thru**
**Cross trail back to an allemande left.**

**Promenade, but don't be slow**
**1 and 3 wheel around**
**Star thru, square thru**
**Four hands count 'em too.**

*Gimmick for Bend the Line*

**Fourth couple bow and swing**
**Couple 1 promenade three-quarters to the right of number 4**
**Forward 4 and back**
**Couple 2 bow and swing**
**Up to the middle and split those four**
**Separate, go around two and line up six**
**Couple 3 promenade around one**
**Crowd into the line and make it eight.**

*Red Hot*

**Promenade red hot**
**Turn the right-hand lady, right arm 'round**
**Partner left, go all the way 'round**
**To your corner right, right arm 'round**
**Partner left, go once around**
**Promenade your corner as she comes 'round.**

*Do Paso*

**Eight hands up and away we go**
**Circle left and don't be slow**
**Break right out with a do paso**
**Partner left, corner right**
**Back to your partner**
**Turn that gal if it takes all night.**

*Double Back Track*

**Corn in the crib, wheat in the stack**
**Meet your honey and turn right back**
**Up the river and around the bend**
**Meet your honey turn back again**
**Meet your partner and promenade.**

**Listen folks to what I say**
**Meet your gal and go the other way**
**Whirl the rope and jerk the slack**
**Meet your partner and turn right back**
**Promenade, boys, promenade.**

**Meet your honey and sing a little song**
**Turn right back you done gone wrong**
**Meet your honey and sing once more**
**Turn right back as you did before**
**Meet your partner and promenade.**

## Organizing Squares and Changing Partners

Frequent changes of partners and sets are needed to help class members get acquainted and to establish a good rapport within the group. Mixers are of prime importance in dealing with extras and with groups in which the number of men and women is uneven. Random changes can serve to mix ability groupings and upgrade the overall dance-skill level. Meeting a variety of class members adds to the fun, sociability, and feeling of fellowship.

Mixing can also be a seemingly unintentional means of breaking up cliques and getting the attention of inattentive class members. Mixers can work as a gentle and even pleasant way to apply discipline, particularly when working with school and recreation groups. In any event, it is always wise to have a "pocket full of miracles" in the form of mixers when teaching dance.

Mixers to meet the demands of a variety of circumstances can be found in Chapter 4 under "Plain and Novelty Mixers" and "Paul Jones Your Lady." The following are samples of the kind that would accomplish the uses suggested in the foregoing discussion. All mixers should be done to musical accompaniment. Three square dance tunes are provided on the *Dance A While* CD. Square dance mixers should be called as illustrated by the following samples.

## Big Circle Mixers

1. Couples promenade counterclockwise. Men turn left and roll back to promenade their partner in the trailing couple.

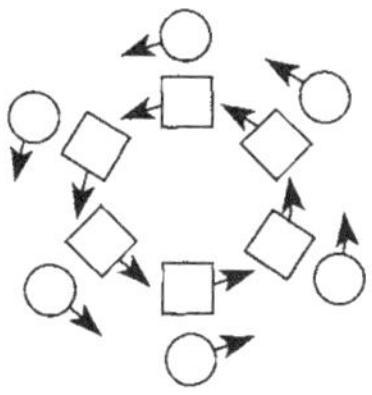

**Promenade go two by two**
**Gents roll back and promenade that gal behind you.**

2. Couples promenade counterclockwise. Men move forward to the next woman and promenade.

**Promenade this little pal**
**Now move up one and take a new gal**
**And all promenade**
**Promenade a little bit more**
**Move up one as you did before**
**And all promenade.**

## Methods for Squaring Up

1. **Grand March:** The Grand March is a traditional way of squaring sets. It serves chiefly as a mixer of couples rather than individuals. It is a particularly good and efficient way of organizing a large crowd into sets.

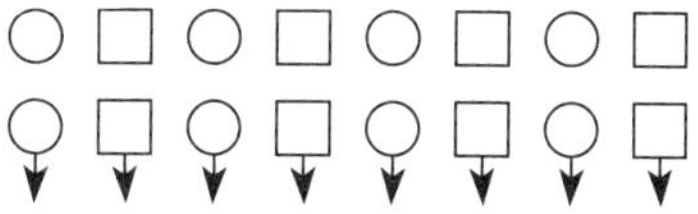

2. **Paul Jones:** This procedure will enable a group to get partners for forming sets. Women form a single circle facing out, circle to the left. Men form a single circle around the women, facing in, circle to the left. The larger group usually forms the outside circle. When the music stops, the men take the women directly opposite or nearest them for partners. Refer to Paul Jones Your Lady for additional variations.
3. **Circle Two-Step:** Once partners are secured, the leader may call out "circle four," "circle six," "circle ten," or any even number so that partners are not separated. Eventually "circle eight" may be called and sets arranged for dancing. Younger groups may enjoy this procedure: The leader blows a whistle or claps hands to indicate the number of couples he or she wishes to have form a circle.

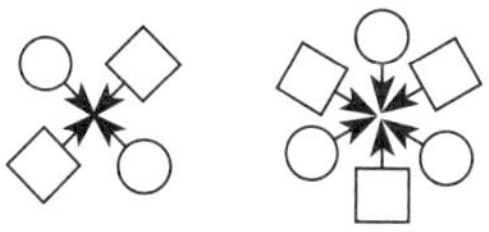

4. **Grand Promenade:** After partners are secured, the leader may use the following call to organize the group into sets.

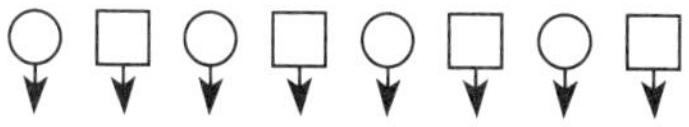

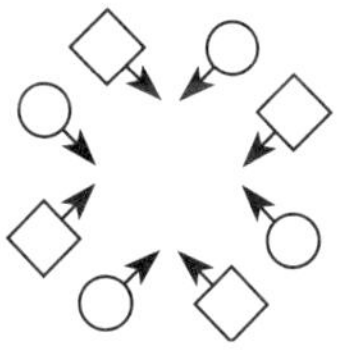

**Promenade go two by two**
**Now promenade a little bit more**
**Pick up two and make it four**
**Promenade and don't be late**
**Grab a four and make it eight**
**Line up now and keep it straight**
**Spread that line way out wide**
**And circle up eight on all four sides.**

5. **Promenade Around the Hall:** This call may be used at the beginning of the dance or at the end of any one call during the dance to arrange couples in different sets for the next call.

**Promenade one and promenade all**
**Promenade around the great big hall**
**Circle up four with any old two**
**Go 'round and 'round like you used to do**
**Now break that four and circle up eight**
**Hurry up gents now don't be late**
**Find your place right in that set**
**Stand right there, we ain't through yet.**

**VARIATION:** The following variation of the preceding call may be used to break up the sets and arrange the dancers in formation for a round dance.

**Break up your sets and promenade all**
**Promenade, go around the hall**
**Around the great big beautiful hall**
**Now stand right there upon the floor**
**Stand right there, we'll dance some more.**

## Methods for Changing Partners or Moving to a New Square

1. **Promenade Out of the Square:** During a call, usually where a trim or break is in order, the caller may change a couple or couples from one set to another and finish the call with new couples in every set. The following call indicates how this may be done.

**One and three–promenade**
**Right out of that square**
**And find yourself a brand new square**
**Promenade, go anywhere**
**Just find yourself a brand new square**
**Look for hands around the floor**
**Fill in there–they need two more**
**There's a spot–go over there**
**They need two more to make a square**
**One for the money, two for the show**
**All get set–'cause here we go!**

5

**VARIATION:** While the promenading couples are relocating, the caller may keep the other couples dancing by calling a ladies chain, right and left thru, or do-sa-do. The following call indicates how this may be done.

**One and three–promenade**
**Right out of that square**
**And find yourself a brand new square**
**Now two and four–while they are gone**
**Circle up four and carry on**
**Do-sa-do in the middle of the set**
**'Cause one and three ain't ready yet**
**Two and four go home to your places**
**And take a look at the brand new faces.**

2. **New Partner Calls:** The following may be used to secure new partners at the end of a call.

**Honor your partner and thank her too**
**Now swing the gal to the left of you**
**Swing your corner, that pretty little maid**
**Keep this gal and all promenade**
**Honor your partner, corners too**
**Swing that gal across from you**
**Swing that gal but not too hard**
**Stand right there with a brand new pard!**

3. **Directed Changes:** The leader may direct dancers to change places as follows.
   a. All women move one position to the right in the set.
   b. Each man takes his opposite, corner, or right-hand woman for a new partner.
   c. All the women or men move to the adjacent square and take the same positions in the new set.
   d. Women (men) leave the set and move anywhere around the room to a new square. Dancers should be in new square before the next dance call begins.

**Gents (ladies) to the center**
**And stand right there**
**Ladies (gents) run away to a brand new square**
**Sides (heads) to the center**
**And hold on there**
**Now the heads (sides) promenade right out of that square**
**Go anywhere I don't care**
**And find yourself a brand new square.**

4. **Scoot and Scat:** Scoot is the cue for the men and scat is the cue for the women. In general, the leader must explain the action to the group so that they will respond in the desired manner. The women or men may be directed to form a star in the center of the set; while the star is rotating, the leader calls "scoot" and the men leave the square and go to another one to form a star. If women are directed into a star figure, on the call "scat," they leave the square and get into another to form a star.

   Scoot and scat may also be called as part of the Texas Star. If the men are on the outside spokes of the star, "scoot" is called. The women continue to star and the men hook onto the spoke of the women's star in another set. When all squares have eight people, the caller continues the Texas Star. New partners promenade to the home position of the woman.

5. **Birdies in the Cage:** The following variation of the regular Bird in the Cage—Seven Hands 'Round (refer to page 182) may be used as a mixer.

**All four gents swing your right-hand lady**
**With a right hand around**
**Partner left with a left hand around**
**Corner lady with a right hand around**
**Now swing your partner with two hands around**

**And cage those birds as you come around**
**Now four hands up and away we go**
**The birds fly away through that open door!**

All four women are placed in the center of the set back to back. The men join hands and circle left around the women (birds). The men hold their hands up high, forming arches through which the women (birds) fly on the call, "The birds fly away through that open door." The call may be repeated with the "crows," the men, in the center and the women circling around with joined hands raised high. The "crows" fly away on the call, "The crows fly away through that open door." The "birds" or "crows" simply go to any new set and take a new partner for a repeat of the call.

# Square Dances: Patter and Singing Calls

The basics used in these dances are fully explained for teaching and calling purposes under Teaching Progression and Analysis for Basic Movements of Square Dance section on earlier in this chapter. Each basic in the teaching progression is accompanied by an analysis or a description of the movement, teaching aids, diagrams, and suggested dance figures using the basic. Basics are also analyzed in the Glossary.

The following chart lists square dances in levels. For a complete list, refer to the Classified Index of Square Dances.

| BEGINNING 1 | BEGINNING 2 | BEGINNING 3 |
|---|---|---|
| **Singing Calls** | | |
| Just Because | Alabama Jubilee | Houston |
| | | Smoke on the Water |
| **Patter Calls/Main Figures** | | |
| Bird in the Cage | Arkansas Traveler | Another Trail |
| Promenade the Ring | Bend It Tight | Forward Up and Back |
| Sally Goodin' | Catch All Eight | Inside Arch and Outside Under |

| INTERMEDIATE | ADVANCED |
|---|---|
| **Patter Calls/Main Figures** | |
| Easy Square Thru | Spinning Wheel |
| Go The Route | Texas Whirlwind |
| Sides Divide | |
| Star Thru: California Twirl | |

## Patter Calls

Only basic figures are presented in these dances. The caller must select an opener, break, and ending to choreograph a full square dance call. The figure is the dominant characteristic. The caller follows the figure but may change and use any opener, break, or ending. If the figure is long, breaks should be short; if the figure is short, breaks can be longer and more complicated. Breaks should be chosen to complement the formation the dancers are in at the time it is to be used. For example, when dancers are circling four, use a break for four.

The dances included in this section are representative of different figure types: symmetrical, double lead out, accumulative, and visiting couple figures. So now, "Buckle up your belly bands, loosen up your traces, all to your place with a smile on your face and let's do some old time square dancin.' "

## Practice Calls 1–42

These may be used for a complete dance. Each call brings the dancers back to a promenade or an allemande left position. If the dance ends with "promenade" or "allemande left," the caller must make up a continuity line to direct the dancers to home positions. When there are exceptions, a note will indicate to the caller where the dancers end up and how to repeat the call to bring them to home position. When the call is given for couples 1 and 3, it should be repeated for couples 2 and 4. When the call is given for couple 1, it should be repeated for all couples.

## Singing Calls

These dances are complete as they have an opener, basic figure, breaks, and ending.

# PATTER *Calls*

## *Another Trail*

**Basics:** Roll away to a half-sashay, right and left thru, cross trail thru.

**1 and 3 do a half-sashay**
**Up to the middle and back that way**
**Pass thru and U-turn back**
**Go forward and back on the same old track**
**Pass thru separate come into the middle**
**Pass thru split the ring, go 'round one**
**Come into the middle, right and left thru**
**Now cross trail thru, find your corner**
**Left allemande.**

## *Arkansas Traveler*

**Basics:** Forearm turns.

**1 and 3 go forward and back**
**Forward again**
**Turn your opposite right arm 'round**
**Partner left, left arm 'round**
**Corners right, right arm 'round**
**Partner left, left arm 'round**
**Promenade your corner as she comes around.**

**NOTE:** At the call "Partner left" (first time), the side couples may join in and start dancing. Man promenades the corner each time until he gets his original partner back. Called four times.

## *Arkansas Traveler with a Cross Trail Thru*

**Basics:** Forearm turns, cross trail thru.

**1 and 3 go forward and back**
**Sides do cross trail thru, separate**
**Go around the outside track**
**Heads go forward**
**Turn your opposite, right arm around**
**Partner left, left arm 'round**
**Corner right, right arm 'round**
**Partner left, left arm 'round**
**Promenade your corner as she comes around.**

**NOTE:** Couples 1 and 3 are doing the Arkansas Traveler figure, while 2 and 4 cross trail, separate, and go around the outside. At home, they must pass by partner to be ready to meet corner with right arm around.

## *Bend It Tight*

**Basics:** Split the ring, pass thru, bend the line.

**1 and 3 do a pass through**
**Split the ring and go around two**
**Hang on tight form two lines**
**Go forward and back keep in time**
**Pass thru and bend the line**
**Pass thru now and bend it tight**
**Circle up eight and keep it right.**

## *Bird in the Cage: Seven Hands 'Round*

**First couple bow, first couple swing**
**First get out to the right of the ring**
**Turn the right-hand lady right arm around**
**Back to your partner, left arm around**
**Opposite lady, right arm around**
**Partner left and left arm around**
**Corner lady right arm around**
**Swing your partner with two-hand swing**
**Cage that bird in the middle of the ring**
**Lady 1 whirls into center.**
**Seven hands up and circle left**
**All remaining dancers circle around bird.**
**The bird hops out and the crow hops in with bird**
**Gent 1 exchanges places with bird in the center.**
**Seven hands up we're gone again.**
**Crow hops out with an allemande left**
**All dancers allemande left.**
**Meet your partner and right and left grand.**

*Repeat* for men 2, 3, and 4.

## *Box the Gnat: Pull By*

**Basics:** Roll away to a half-sashay, box the gnat, right and left thru, ladies chain.

**Head 2 couples do a half-sashay**
**Come up to the middle and back that way**
**Right to opposite and box the gnat**
**Pull by for a right and left thru**
**Same two pass thru and separate go 'round one**
**Meet in the middle for a right and left thru**
**Same two pass thru and split the outside**
**Go around one to a line of four**
**Forward eight and back like that**
**Right to opposite box the gnat, pull by**
**Right and left thru**
**Ladies chain across the track**
**Chain back in the usual way**
**Roll away to a half-sashay**
**Join hands circle eight**
**Allemande left.**

## Catch All Eight

**First couple balance and swing**
**Down the center and split the ring**
Couple 1 goes across set and walks between (splits) couple 3.
**Lady go gee, gent go haw**
Woman goes right, man goes left.
**Meet your honey in the hall**
Couple 1 meets in home position.
**Catch all eight with the right, go halfway around**
All swing partner half-turn around clockwise with right forearm grasp.
**Back with the left go all the way around**
All swing partner one full turn counterclockwise with left forearm grasp.
**Swing your corner with a two-hand swing**
Join both hands with corner, turn once around clockwise.
**Meet your partner pass her by**
Pass partner's right shoulder.
**Pick up the next lady on the fly and promenade.**
Promenade new partner (right hand woman) to man's home position.

*Repeat* for couples 2, 3, and 4.

## Cowboy Loop

**First couple out to the couple on the right**
**Circle four with all your might**
**Break and trail that line to the next**
Man 1 breaks circle by unclasping left hand, leads line of four to couple 3.
**Two hands up and four trail thru**
Couple 3 raises joined inside hands, line of four passes under arch.
Couple 3 walks forward over line to position 1 in set.
**Turn right around and come back thru**
Man 1 pulls line around toward center of set and prepares to go under arch the second time. Couple 3 does California Twirl, walks back to position as line of four passes under arch to center of set.
**And tie that knot like the cowboys do**
Man 1 turns right and pulls the line through arch formed by last couple in line.
**Circle up four and away we go**
**Pick up two and make it six**
**Circle left till all get fixed**
Man 1 breaks circle with left hand and picks up couple 3 on left side.
**Break and trail that line to the next**
Man 1 breaks circle with left hand, leads line of six through arch formed by couple 4.
**Two hands up and six go thru**
Couple 4 raises joined inside hands, line of six passes under arch. Couple 4 walks forward over line to position 2 in set.
**Turn right around and come back thru**
Man 1 pulls line of six around toward center of set and prepares to go under arch the second time. Couple 4 turns around, walks back to position as line of six passes under arch to center of set.
**Tie that knot like the cowboys do**
Man 1 turns right and pulls the line through arch formed by last couple in line.
**Now circle up six and keep it straight**
**Pick up two and make it eight**
Man 1 breaks circle with left hand and picks up couple 4 on left side.
**Circle eight and here we go.**
Use any appropriate break.

*Repeat* calls for couples 2, 3, and 4.

## Duck Then Wheel Around

**Basics:** Roll away with a half-sashay, star thru, wheel around, ends turn in, cross trail.

**First and third go forward and back**
**Do a right and left thru across the track**
**Roll away with a half-sashay**
**Star thru and hear me say**
**Split the sides**
**Go 'round one and make a line of four**
**Forward eight and back you do**
**Forward again and pass thru**
**Join hands centers arch**
**Ends turn in**
**Go into the middle**
**Wheel around in the middle of the square**
**Do a right and left thru**
**With the outside pair**
**Dive thru**
**Right and left thru in the middle of the set**
**Pass thru**
**Split two go around to a line of four**
**Forward eight and back once more**
**Pass thru and join hands**
**Ends turn in—go into the middle**
**Wheel around in the middle of the square**
**Do a right and left thru**
**With the outside pair**
**Dive thru, pass thru**
**Split two and around one**
**Down the middle**
**Cross trail and find the corner**
**Left allemande.**

5

## *Easy Bend the Line*

**Basics:** Do-sa-do, bend the line.

**1 and 3 promenade three-quarters outside**
**Go 'round the ring**
**Line up four with 2 and 4**
**It's forward up and back**
**Do-sa-do across the way**
**Bend the line, that's what I say**
**Now do-sa-do in the center once more**
**Then circle eight, go 'round the floor.**

**NOTE:** Two lines face each other on the diagonal.

## *Easy Square Thru*

**Basics:** Right and left thru, dive thru, square thru.

**1 and 3 square thru**
**Right left right left**
**Right and left thru with the outside two**
**Dive thru, pass thru**
**Right and left thru with the outside two**
**Dive thru, pass thru**
**Allemande left.**

## *Ends Turn In*

*Source: Ed Gilmore in 1952*

**Basics:** Split the ring, pass thru, California Twirl, dive thru, ends turn in.

**1 and 3 go forward and back**
**Pass thru split the ring**
**Go around two and line up four**
**Forward eight and back with you**
**Pass thru, join your hands**
**Arch in the middle, the ends turn in**
**Circle four in the middle of the floor**
**Go one time around, same two**
**Pass thru, split the ring**
**Go around one and line up four**
**Forward eight and back with you**
**Pass thru, join your hands**
**Arch in the middle, ends turn in**
**Circle four in the middle of the floor**
**Go one time 'round, same two**
**Pass thru, watch out gent**
**Left to your corner left allemande**
**Right to partner, right and left grand.**

## *Forward Up and Back*

**Couples 1 and 3 go forward and back**
**Forward again and right and left thru**
**Right and left back in the same old track**
**Circle up four in the middle of the floor**
Break for circle of four.

**Couples 2 and 4 go forward and back**
**Forward again and right and left thru**
**Right and left back on the same old track**
**Circle up four in the middle of the floor**
Break for circle of four.

**Head ladies chain and chain right back**
**Side ladies chain and chain right back**
**Now all four ladies chain**
**Grand chain your ladies.**
Break for eight.

***Variation***

**1 and 3 right and left thru**
**2 and 4 right and left thru**
**1 and 3 right and left back**
**2 and 4 right and left back**
**Head ladies chain**
**Side ladies chain**
**Head ladies chain and chain 'em back**
**Side ladies chain and chain 'em back**
**All four ladies chain**
**Grand chain the ladies.**

## *Forward Up Six*

**First and third balance and swing**
**Now whirl your girl to the right of the ring**
Man 1 twirls woman 1 to man 2. Woman 1 stands to the left of man 2 to form a line of three, facing center. Man 3 whirls woman 3 to man 4. Woman 3 stands to the left of man 4 to form a line of three, facing center. Men 1 and 3 remain in home positions. Join hands in each line.
**Forward up six and back you go**
Lines of three go forward and back.
**Two gents loop with a do-sa-do**
Men 1 and 3 execute a do-sa-do.
**Now right hand up and left hand under**
Man 2 twirls the left-hand woman under the arch formed with right-hand woman to man 3. Right-hand woman is twirled outside and over left-hand woman to man 1. Man 4 twirls the women in the same manner with his left-hand woman going to man 1 and his right-hand woman going to man 3.
**Twirl those girls and go like thunder**
**Form new threes and don't you blunder**
Man 3 now has woman 4 on the right and woman 1 on the left. Man 1 has woman 2 on the right and woman 3 on the left. Two new lines of three are formed.

*Repeat* call three times beginning with "Forward up six and back you go," to return women to the right side of original partner. Then use any appropriate trim.

**NOTE:** Vary the call "Two gents loop with a do-sa-do" by calling "Two gents loop with a right elbow" or "Two gents loop with a left elbow."

## *Gents Star Right*

**Basics:** Star halfway 'round, preliminary basics.

**Gents star right, just halfway 'round**
**Turn your opposite left**
**Now star back home and here we go**
**Meet your partner do-sa-do**
**Now gents star left go all the way 'round**
**Meet your partner right, right arm 'round**
**To the corner, allemande left**
**Back to your partner, right and left grand**
**Hand over hand till you**
**Find your own, promenade**
**Come right on home.**

## *Gnat and Flea*

**Basics:** Box the gnat, box the flea.

**1 and 3 go forward and back**
**Right to opposite, box the gnat**
**Pull 'em thru and separate go 'round just one**
**Down the center, pass thru**
**Split the ring to 'round one**
**Come down the middle, left to opposite**
**Box the flea, pull 'em thru**
**Separate, go 'round one—come into middle**
**Swing your own right there at home.**

## *Go the Route*

**Basics:** Star thru, square thru, dive thru, bend the line.

**Head two ladies chain to the right**
**New side ladies chain across**
**Turn this girl is what you do**
**Now face the middle, star thru**
**Right and left thru and turn your Sue**
**Then pass thru, star thru to lines of four**
**Forward eight and back with you**
**Forward again, star thru**
**Then dive thru, pass thru**
**Square thru with the outside two**
**Four hands 'round, you go the route**
**Two lines of four, facing out**
**Now bend the line and star thru**
**Right and left thru and turn your Sue**
**Then dive thru and pass thru**
**Square thru with the outside two**
**Count four hands, you go the route**
**Two lines of four, you're facing out**
**Bend the line, go right and left thru**
**Allemande left.**

## *Half Square Thru Combo*

**Basics:** Right and left thru, dive thru, box the gnat, U-turn back, half-square thru.

**1 and 3 half-square thru**
**Right and left thru, outside two**
**Dive thru, pass thru**
**Right and left thru with outside two**
**Dive thru, half-square thru**
**Separate, go 'round one**
**Come into the middle, box the gnat**
**U-turn back**
**Left allemande.**

## *Inside Arch and Outside Under*

**Basics:** Dive thru.

**Couple one bow and swing**
**Lead to the right and circle half**
**Inside arch and outside under**
**Cross the hall and go like thunder**
**Some will arch, some dive under**
**Hurry up boys, don't you blunder**
**Lead to the next, circle half**
**Dive thru, lead to the next**
**Circle half and here we go**
**Inside arch and outside low**
**Dive thru, don't you blunder**
**Inside arch, outside under**
**Home you go and everybody swing.**

**NOTE:** Inside arch and outside under is continuous until the lead couple is in the middle of the set and can lead to couple 3. The side couples are opposite home. The repeat will take everybody home.

## *New Star Thru*

**Basics:** Star thru, cross trail thru, box the gnat, roll away to a half-sashay.

**1 and 3 go forward and back**
**Pass thru U-turn back**
**Now star thru**
**Right and left thru the outside two**
**Now dive thru, star thru**
**Right and left thru**
**Same ladies roll away to a half-sashay**
**New star thru across the way**
**Right and left thru with the outside two**
**Turn your girl**
**Dive thru, star thru**
**Right and left thru**
**Now cross trail thru go 'round one**
**Come into the middle**
**Box the gnat, pull her by**
**Allemande left.**

5

## *Ocean Wave*

**Basics:** Square thru, ocean wave.

**1 and 3 square thru**
**Count four hands that's what you do**
**Do-sa-do to an ocean wave**
**Balance forward up and back**
**Right and left thru turn your girl**
**Dive thru, pass thru**
**Do-sa-do to an ocean wave**
**Balance forward up and back**
**Right and left thru, turn your girl**
**Dive thru, pass thru**
**Allemande left.**

## *Promenade the Outside Ring*

**Basics:** Right and left thru, ladies chain, bend the line, promenade three-quarters, pass thru.

**1 and 3 promenade three-quarters 'round the outside ring**
**While the roosters crow and the birdies sing**
**Line up four with the sides**
**Diagonally now go forward and back**
**Go right and left thru**
**Right and left back**
**Two ladies chain, chain back**
**Forward eight and back in time**
**Pass thru and bend the line**
**Now right and left thru, you're doing fine**
**Forward eight and back once more**
**Pass thru and bend the line**
**Go right and left thru to your own land**
**Allemande left, go right and left grand.**

**NOTE:** "Line up four with the sides" means to go to the far side of the line nearest home.

## *Promenade the Ring*

**Basics:** Preliminary basics.

**Bow to your partner**
**Heads promenade go halfway 'round the outside ring**
**Sides up to the middle and back**
**Sides promenade go halfway 'round**
**Heads up to the middle and back**
**All join hands circle left**
**Go halfway 'round**
**When you get home face your own**
**Do-sa-do your partner**
**Same lady swing and promenade**
**Promenade single file**
**Go back home, face your own**
**Bow to your partner, corner too**
**Wave at the girl across from you.**

## *The Route*

**Basics:** Ladies chain, right and left thru.

**1 and 3 bow and swing**
**Lead to the right**
**Circle, break, and form a line**
**Forward eight and back you go**
**Forward again do-sa-do**
**Go right and left thru across the set**
**Right and left back, you're not thru yet**
**Chain those ladies across the hall**
**Turn and chain them down the line**
**Chain those ladies across the hall**
**Chain those ladies down the line**
**All join hands and circle left**
**And home you go.**

*Repeat* for 2 and 4.

**NOTE:** When women chain across hall and down the line, not all couples have the same amount of turn on the courtesy turn, so all need to adjust so that the timing works out right.

## *Sally Goodin'*

**First gent out and swing Sally Goodin'**
Man 1 swings right-hand woman Sally Goodin' with right arm around.

**Now your Taw**
Man 1 swings own partner left arm around.

**Swing that girl from Arkansas**
Man 1 swings opposite woman (Arkansas) with right arm around.

**Then swing Sally Goodin'**
Man 1 swings Sally Goodin' with left arm around.

**And now your Taw**
Man 1 swings own partner right arm around.

**Now don't forget your old Grandma**
Man 1 swings corner woman (Grandma) with left arm around.

**Home you go and everybody swing**
Swing with waist swings.

*Repeat* call with men 1 and 2 leading out and doing the figure simultaneously.

*Repeat* again with men 1, 2, and 3 leading out and dancing the figure simultaneously.

*Repeat,* fourth time, "All Four Gents" leading out and dancing the figure simultaneously.

## *Sides Divide*

**First four forward and back**
Couples 1 and 3.

**Forward again on the same old track**
**Swing in the center and swing on the side**

Man 1 swings woman 3, man 3 swings woman 1. Simultaneously couples 2 and 4 swing.

**Now swing your own and sides divide.**

Couples 1 and 3 swing own partners in center. Side couples separate, women go right, men left. Move one-quarter around set, meet opposite and swing.

**Circle four in the middle of the floor**

Couples 1 and 3.

**Sides divide and swing some more.**

Sides separate. Move one-quarter around set, meet partner and swing.

**Do paso and don't get sore.**

Couples 1 and 3 in center.

**Sides divide and swing some more.**

Sides separate. Move one-quarter around set, meet opposite and swing.

**Up the river and around the bend**
**Sides divide and swing again**

Sides separate, meet partners in original home position and swing.

**And promenade your corners all**

Men have new partners.

**Hold that gal don't let her fall**
**Promenade around the hall.**

Promenade new partner home.

*Repeat* call for couples 2 and 4.

*Repeat* from beginning until women are back in home positions.

## *Spinning Wheel*

*Spinning Wheel (as called) is included by permission of Rickey Holden, Brussels, Belgium.*

Original figure by Jere Long of Boise, Idaho.[5]

**Caller:** Rickey Holden

**CD:** Folkraft CD 2911-5

**Record:** Folkraft 1075[6]

**Head two couples, one and three, lead**
**Out to the right and circle half and**
**Don't you blunder, the inside arch and the**
**Outside under, right and left thru in the**
**Center and then turn back, two**
**Ladies chain in the middle of the floor then**
**Turn and chain with the outside four**
**Take that lady with a full turn around and you**
**Promenade in single file**
**Lady in the lead, Indian style, it's a**
***Spinning Wheel* so you spin it a while you**

The *Spinning Wheel* is a *left-hand star* for all eight people. Several grips are possible; one of the easiest is for each with left hand to grip the person in front (in the star) just above the elbow.

**Roll it along but you're going wrong! Go the**
**Other way back**

All eight people release left hands, turn half around and form a *right-hand star.*

**Gents reach back with your left arm, you**

Each man reaches back with left hand over own right shoulder to take free left hand of woman just in back of him (she now becomes his partner of the moment).

**Wind 'em up like a ball of yarn, [and] a**
**Do paso will do no harm**
**Do paso to beat the band then**
**Meet your partner with your left hand [and]**
**Promenade eight to the sandy land . . .**

## *Split the Ring*

**First couple out balance and swing**
**Down center and split the ring**

Couple 1 walks across set and between (splits) couple 3.

**Lady go gee and the gent go haw**

Woman 1 goes right, man 1 goes left, around outside of set back home.

**Swing when you meet**
**Swing at the head and swing at the feet**
**Side four the same**
**Down the center as you did before**
**Down the center and cast off four**

Couple 1 walks across set. Man 1 goes left between woman 3 and man 4. Woman 1 goes right between man 3 and woman 2. Walk outside of set back home.

**Swing when you meet**
**Swing at the head and swing at the feet**
**Side four the same**
**Down the center as you used to do**
**Down the center and cast off two**

Couple 1 moves forward to center of set. Man goes left and between (splits) couple 4. Woman goes right and between (splits) couple 2. Walk outside of set back home.

**Swing when you meet**
**Swing at the head and swing at the feet**
**Side four the same**

*Repeat* call for couples 2, 3, and 4.

5. Although Jere Long had moved to Boise, Idaho, at the time of this recording (1949) he lived and was calling in Phoenix, Arizona, when he created this figure. Therefore, this is a true Southwestern square dance figure.
6. As an illustration of phrasing, word command, voice command, and timing, see the complete call for Spinning Wheel, including introduction and ending, as called on record 1075 by Folkraft.

## *Split the Ring and Around Just One*

**Basics:** Pass thru, split the ring.

**1 and 3 bow and swing**
**Up to the center and back to the ring**
**Pass through, separate**
**Come around just one**
**Go down the middle, pass thru**
**Split the ring, separate**
**Go around one down the middle**
**Pass thru, separate**
**Come around one, pass thru**
**Meet your corner, left allemande**
**Right to partner, right and left grand.**

## *Star Thru: California Twirl*

**Basics:** U-turn back, box the gnat, California twirl, half-square thru, star thru.

**1 and 3 star thru**
**California twirl**
**Star thru**
**Right and left thru**
**Half-square thru**
**U-turn back**
**Box the gnat**
**Change hands**
**Allemande left.**

## *Star Thru Square Thru Combo*

**Basics:** Cross trail thru, star thru, square thru.

**Heads promenade just halfway 'round**
**Go down the middle, right and left thru**
**Then heads lead right—circle break**
**And make a line**
**Go forward and back—star thru**
**Square thru, four hands 'round**
**Now bend the line, then**
**Cross trail thru to allemande left.**

## *Texas Star*

**Basics:** Four men star, star promenade.

**Ladies to the center and back to the bar**
**Gents to the center and form a star**
**Right hand crossed**
**Back with the left and don't get lost**
**Meet your pretty girl, pass her by**
**Take the next gal on the fly (star promenade)**
**The gents swing out, ladies swing in**
**Form that Texas Star again**
**Break that star and everybody swing**
**Promenade home with the new little thing.**
Men have new partners.

*Repeat* three times until women are back to original partners.

## *Texas Whirlwind*

*Texas Whirlwind (as called) is included by permission of Rickey Holden, Brussels, Belgium.*

Original figure (titled Texas Tornado) by Fenton "Jonesy" Jones of Los Angeles, California.

**Ladies to the center and back to the bar**
**Gents to the center and form a star with a**
**Right hand across on the inside track a**
**Right hand star and the other way back**
**Left hand back and don't be late**
**Pass your honey and catch all eight with the**
**Next by the right and halfway 'round**
**Back with the left that half and all the way**
**'Round—your left hand lady with your**
**Right hand 'round, partner left go**
**All the way 'round, go once and a half, to your**
**Right hand lady with your right hand 'round**
**Partner left and all the way 'round**
**Gents to the center and don't fall down with a**
**Right hand across . . .**

*Repeat* three times.

**NOTES:**

1. Women do *not* progress. They get caught in the whirls but while the men are out starring the women stay home.
2. Once a man does *catch all eight* with a given woman, she is his "partner" from then on until he stars again and *"catches . . ."* another.
3. **Catch all eight:** Turn with right hand half around, release hands and turn with left hand once and a half around (actually in this dance, only once and a quarter), release hands, then turn corner with right hand once full around, turn partner with left hand once and one-half around, turn right-hand lady with right hand once full around, turn partner with left hand once and one-quarter.
4. **Thumb grip** is preferred for hand turns. For two people, right (or left) palms touching, elbows bent, thumb and forefingers clasping other person's thumb and other fingers also bent to clasp other person's hand naturally. This is the traditional grip used throughout the Southwest for their do-si-do (do paso).

# SINGING *Calls*

## *Alabama Jubilee*

**CD:** Alabama Jubilee CD Label No. BMVCD 3009 available from www. dosado.com/music.

**Basics:** Sashay, promenade, allemande left, grand right and left.

**Four little ladies promenade inside of the ring**
Women move in single file, counterclockwise, around inside of set.
**Back to your partner and give him a swing**
**Sashay 'round your corner girl**
Either sashay or do-sa-do.
**Bow to your partner boys, give her a whirl**
**Now four little gents promenade inside of the ring**
Men move single file, counterclockwise, inside of set.
**Sashay 'round your partner, give your corner a swing**
Either sashay or do-sa-do.
**You promenade just you and me**
Men promenade corner woman.
**To the Alabama Jubilee, yeah man**
**To the Alabama Jubilee.**

***Break***

**Turn the left-hand lady with a left hand 'round**
Turn corner once around. All turns with forearm grasp.
**A right to your partner go all the way 'round**
Turn partner once and a half.
**The right-hand lady with a left hand 'round**
Turn right-hand woman twice around.
**Now swing your little honey**
Waist swing.
**'Till her feet leave the ground**
**It's an allemande left, a right and left grand**
**Meet your little honey, take her by the hand**
**You promenade, just you and me**
**To the Alabama Jubilee, yeah man**
**To the Alabama Jubilee.**

*Repeat* figure and break three times until women are returned to original partners.

## *Gentle on My Mind*

**Caller:** Bob Ruff.

**Music:** Wagon Masters.

**CD:** Wagon Wheel Records Square Dance Now #1, "Gentle on My Mind."

**Basics:** Weave the ring, ladies chain, pass thru, right and left thru, roll away.

***Opener, Break, Ending***

**Allemande your corner**
**Do-sa-do your own**
**Four men make a left-hand star around**
**Turn your partner right**
**Your corner allemande**
**Partner do-sa-do**
**Weave the ring now**
**Meet partner, do-sa-do, promenade.**

***Figure***

**Four ladies chain**
**Turn your girl and then**
**1 and 3 go right and left thru**
**Turn your girl**
**Roll away—circle left**
**Four girls pass thru**
**Turn left, go single file**
**Men pass thru, swing**
**Promenade.**

**Sequence:** Opener, figure twice for 1 and 3, break, figure twice for 2 and 4, closer.

## *Houston*

**Caller:** Bob Ruff.

**CD:** Houston (Means I'm One Day Closer to You) Label no. FTCD115 available from www.dosado .com/music

**Record:** Wagon Wheel 924.

**Basics:** Allemande left, weave the ring, pass thru, star right, swing, do paso.

***Opener, Middle Break***

**Circle left and around you go**
**Circle left you do a do paso, your partner left**
**Turn your corner by the right**
**Partner courtesy turn, everybody circle left again**
**Circle left just a little bit more**
**Left allemande and weave the floor**
**In and out and when you meet her, you swing**
**Swing your lady and promenade the ring**
**Promenade to Houston, Houston, Houston.**

***Figure***

**1 and 3 (2 and 4) pass thru, separate go around 2**
**Home you go and do-sa-do your lady too**
**2 and 4 pass thru, separate around 2**
**Home you go and do-sa-do your lady too**
**All the men star right around the land**
**With your corner girl you go left allemande**
**Do-sa-do your partner, your corner swing**
**Keep this lady and promenade the ring**
**Promenade to Houston, Houston, Houston.**
**Twice for head couples, twice for side couples.**

## Just Because

**MP3:** "Just Because" Label no. MP3SMOKE1 available from www.dosado.com/music

**Basics:** Allemande left, allemande right, grand right and left, ladies chain, see-saw, star.

***Opener***

**Honor to your partners and to your corners all**
**Swing that opposite lady, she's the one across the hall**
**Now run away back home, swing and whirl your own**
**Thank your stars the bird ain't flown**
**Allemande left with the ol' left hand**
**Partner right and a right and left grand**
**Hand over hand around that ring**
**Right and left with the pretty little thing**
**Now promenade your partners, boys, shout and sing**
**Because, just because.**

***Figure***

**Now the two head ladies chain across, chain right over that ring**
**Send 'em right on back, take your own and give her a swing**
**Side two ladies chain across, chain right over that ring**
**Send 'em right on back, take your own and give her a swing**
**Allemande left your corner, allemande right your partner**
**Swing your corner lady around and around**
**Now promenade that corner, boys, shout and sing**
**Because, just because.**

***Break***

**It's all around your corner, that the gal we call Grandma**
**See-saw round your partner, she's the prettiest in the hall**
**All four gents center and star with the ol' right hand**
**Circle to your corner with a two-time allemande**
**Turn 'em once, turn 'em twice, back right off and bow real nice**
**Then a grand ol' right and left around the ring**

All four men step to center, form a right-hand star, walk all around new corner. Men take corners with left forearm hold breaking their star and walk two complete turns around with corners. At the end of the turns, men should all be facing counterclockwise around the set, women clockwise. Slip hands down from forearm hold to a hand hold, step back arms' length and bow, then take partners' right hand for the grand right and left.

**Now promenade that dear old thing,**
**Throw your heads right back and sing**
**Because, just because.**

On meeting partners across set, promenade home.

*Repeat* figure and break three more times.

## Smoke on the Water

**CD:** Smokecalls ("Smoke on the Water" CD with calls), Label no. SMKCALLSCD available from www.dosado.com/music

**Basics:** Allemande left, star, grand right and left, turn back, sashay, pass thru.

***I. Opener***

**Now you allemande left your corner**
**Then you walk right by your own**
**Right hand swing ol' Sally Good in'**

Right-hand lady

**Swing left hand there at home**
**Those four little ladies to the center**
**Make a star with your right hand**
**Then allemande left your corner**
**Partner right go right and left grand.**

***Break***

**There'll be "Smoke on the Water on the land on the sea"**
**Right hand to your partner, turn around and go back three**
**Let's do a left, a right, a left-hand swing**
**Go all the way around, right hand to your partner**
**Twirl her home and settle down**
Don't promenade, should be at home position

***II. Opener***

**Four gents center make a circle**
Circle left
**You turn it once around, go back home sashay your partner**
Pass right shoulders go back to back
**Gents star right when you come down**
**Turn that star out in the center**
**'Til your corner comes around**
**Then you allemande left your corner**
**Grand right eight go round the town**

*Repeat break:* "There'll be Smoke on the Water, etc."

***Figure***

**Head gents bow down to your partner**
**Swing that lady round and round**
**Pass right through right down the center**
**Separate go round the town**
Woman goes right men go left to home position
**Then you walk right by your corner**
**Sashay round your partners all**
All sashay partners passing right shoulders then back to back
**Then you allemande left your corner**
**Grand right eight go round the hall**

*Repeat break:* "There'll be Smoke on the Water," etc.
*Repeat II call:* "Four gents center," etc.
*Repeat figure* for "Side gents."
*Repeat break:* "There'll be Smoke on the Water," etc.
*Repeat opener:* "Now you allemande left," etc.
*Repeat break:* "There'll be Smoke on the Water," etc.

5

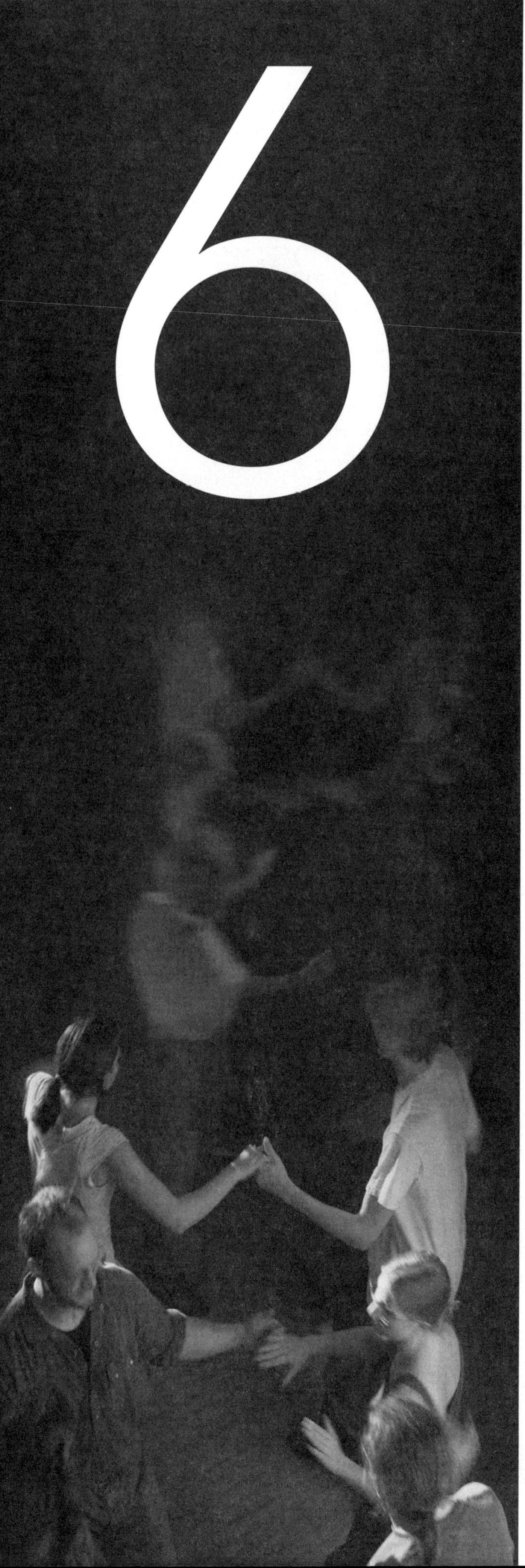

# 6 CONTRA DANCE

## History

*By David Millstone, Lebanon, NH*

### English Country Dance Roots

Contra dances are an American dance form that derive from earlier English country dances.[1] When early settlers from the British Isles arrived on this continent they brought their dances with them. The most important collection of such dances, John Playford's *The English Dancing Master*, first appeared in London in 1651 and went through eleven editions over the next 75 years. The books published by Playford, and then later by his son and numerous others, included specific tunes for each dance and provided a short review of the correct figures.

The English dances migrated across the English Channel to Holland and to France, where they were eagerly adopted by the royal courts. The French in particular were attracted to those country dances in square formation—four couples, one on each side—and these became the *Contredanse Française*, later the *cotillion*[2] and then the *quadrille*. When *contredanse* reappeared in English, it morphed into *contra dance*, which hints at opposites, two lines of dancers facing one another.

1 "Country dance" is a broad category that includes longways dances as well as squares and, sometimes, round dances. Most commonly, a country dance involves a pair of dancers who interact with a series of other couples in the course of the dance, repeating the same series of figures each time through the tune. Only within the last 30 years have contra dances formed the dominant part of an evening; historically, contras have been one part of a dance program that might include a combination of squares, English country dances, round dances, or international folk dances.

2 Although spelled *cotillon* in French, the preferred spelling of this word in the United States is cotillion and is the form used throughout *Dance A While*.

## The Rise of Longways Dances

Early editions of Playford included numerous "set dances" for two, three, or four couples in a variety of formations. Later editions, though, concentrated almost entirely on dances with men in one line facing their partners in another line, "longways for as many as will," the forerunner of the contra dance formation. In the first Playford edition, only about one-third of the dances were longways, but by the final edition, in 1728, about 98% of the dances were in longways sets. These are the dances that the English brought with them to the New World, where they were enjoyed in all the colonies along the Atlantic coast by people of all walks of life, from the ballrooms of Virginia to the kitchens of New England. Numerous written accounts document that social dancing flourished among the elite; we can only speculate about the dances done by common folk. The year 1788 marked the first publication in America of a collection of dances, assembled by dancing master John Griffiths from Providence, Rhode Island. Many of these dances appeared over the years in other publications as numerous dance manuals reprinted older dances and added new ones.

The settlers from England, Scotland, and Ireland came from cultures with deep music and dance traditions. English villagers kept alive a series of vigorous traditional dances that could still be collected in the twentieth century. In Scotland, Edinburgh and Glasgow hosted public dances as early as the 1720s and we know of reels being danced at weddings. The Irish, too, had their harpers and their pipers; many of the early tunes played by these skilled musicians found their way into English dance collections and later became mainstays of the contra dance repertoire.

Just as the language changed over time in its new home, so, too, did the music and the dances. The violins in elegant drawing rooms became fiddles in rough country kitchens and taverns. New tunes were brought by French-Canadians coming south to work in lumber camps and in New England textile mills and by the influx of Irish immigrants in the mid-1800s, with each group of immigrants bringing their own dance customs to be incorporated into the new nation's melting pot. For example, French-Canadian fiddle tunes are now used frequently for contras and one important Quebeçois dance influence is the long swing, 8 to 16 counts.

## Contra Dance in California before the Gold Rush

On the other coast, the Spaniards brought contra dance to the coastal ports of South America; the country dances–lancers, quadrilles, contras, Varsouvienne, waltz–came from the South, traveling northward up the California coast as far as Sonoma.

For example, *La Contradanza* was danced in Spain in the early part of the eighteenth century. Carl Vega gives a date of 1850 for its arrival in Buenos Aires; others give earlier dates spreading through South America and Mexico. Alfred Robinson describes *La Contradanza* at a *baile* in San Diego in 1829; it is a longways dance, with minor sets of two couples. As many as 18 figures were danced with a waltz chorus between each figure. Writing in 1950, Czarnoswki noted that *La Contradanza* was still performed for special fiestas in Santa Barbara and Monterey (Czarnowski 1950, 89–107)[3]. By the time the Americans from the East came to California by the overland routes, *La Contradanza* was out of fashion.

## Country Dances Decline

During the nineteenth century, country dancing fell victim to the rise of couple dances. The waltz, initially decried for its licentious embrace, was followed by the polka, a dance craze that swept Europe and America in the 1840s. By the early twentieth century, most forms of traditional dance, including both contras and squares, had largely disappeared from the cities of America, pushed out by more fashionable music and choreography, including the schottische, the Varsouvienne, the two-step, and numerous novelty dances.

However, small communities kept contras alive in northern New England and upper New York State. These rural areas, slow to adopt new ways, continued dancing the old contras at house parties called "junkets," "heel burners," "tunks," or "kitchen dances."

## Early Twentieth-Century Revivals

Several key individuals helped these dances find new enthusiasts. At the turn of the last century, Cecil Sharp's work sparked new interest in country dance as part of an English folk music revival. Sharp

3 Lucille Czarnowski was a Professor of Dance at the University of California, Berkeley, and Chairman of the Research Committee of the Folk Dance Federation of California. In the 1930s and 1940s, she collected oral histories, recorded music and songs of two generations, and researched extensively at libraries and museums the personal memoirs of travelers and pioneers and books of early California folklore. Her book gives an excellent description of the social setting on the great ranchos, mission pueblos, and presidio towns (1950, 17–25). The frequent social gatherings and Californians' passion for dancing are conveyed.

founded the English Folk Dance Society and in 1915 traveled to the United States and established an American branch of EFDS which in time became the Country Dance and Song Society.[4] (CDSS, in turn, became in later years a major promoter of contra dance and music through workshops at its camps at Pinewoods and other venues.) In later visits, Sharp spent nearly a year in Appalachia collecting traditional music, songs, and dances; his research popularized Appalachian square dances in particular.

At about the same time, a revival based in New York City and spearheaded by Luther Gulick and Elizabeth Burchenal saw the creation of a program of international folk dance adopted by the Playground Association of America; folk dance became part of a new physical education curriculum in American schools.

Country dancing–contras and squares alike–received another boost from automobile magnate Henry Ford. Incensed by what he saw as the musical and social degradations of ragtime and the Jazz Age, Ford sought to bring about a return to his vision of traditional American values. He imported dancing master Benjamin Lovett from Sudbury, Massachusetts, who became Ford's instructor at a new dance hall in Dearborn, Michigan, and taught the old New England contras to dancers in the Midwest. Ford insisted that his executives learn the rudiments of country dancing, and in 1926, he published the first edition of *Good Morning*, a collection of dances assembled by Lovett along with notes on etiquette. Ironically, while Ford promoted traditional music and dances, the automobiles emerging in vast numbers from his factories gave Americans new mobility that led to the gradual dissolution of the communities in which these rich traditions flourished.

The 1930s saw interest in American folk dancing in other parts of the nation. Lloyd Shaw, superintendent of the Cheyenne Mountain School, Colorado Springs, Colorado, began his research into "cowboy dances" of the Western frontier, an outgrowth of his earlier interest in international folk dance as promoted by Elizabeth Burchenal. By the end of that decade, Shaw sent his Cheyenne Mountain Dancers on tours around the United States, where their fancy choreography and energetic dancing sparked fresh interest in traditional dances. In later years, after Shaw's death and under the leadership of his widow, Dorothy Stott Shaw, the Lloyd Shaw Foundation continued teaching contras as part of their caller training classes.[5]

## Post-World War II Years: The Ralph Page Revival

On December 6, 1930, Ralph Page called his first dance in Stoddard, New Hampshire. From the 1930s until his death in 1985, Page became a well-known figure in the country dance world, ultimately respected as the "Dean of American dance callers." Page grew up in Munsonville, a tiny village in the remote, rural region around Mt. Monadnock in southwestern New Hampshire. The country folk came to dance squares, circles, lines, fox-trots, waltzes, and contras, and they called the occasion a "square dance." Commuting by train (he never learned how to drive) in 1943 Page started calling at a weekly dance at the YWCA in Boston, a series that lasted for some 25 years.

In early years, the crowd included soldiers stationed in the Boston area as well as college students involved in hiking and trips to the outdoors. (These Intercollegiate Outing Club Association dances are where callers such as Ted Sannella got their start, and Rickey Holden, another important dance leader, also started his dancing with Ralph Page in Boston.[6]) Ralph Page's programs were based on square dances—he would usually call three squares in a row—but he also included international folk dances and the longways contras that were part of the traditional New Hampshire repertoire.

Along with Mary Gillette and Philip Sharples, Page was one of the founders in 1945 of the New England Folk Festival Association (NEFFA). He enjoyed historical research and he resurrected many early American dances as well as composing tunes and dances of his own. He assembled a significant collection of dance music, old dance books and manuscripts, and he authored four books: *The Country Dance Book, The Ralph Page Book of Contras, Heritage Dances of Early America,* and *An Elegant Collection of Squares and Contras.* These provide us with a rich understanding of New England dance history. Page also published a magazine, *Northern Junket*, which

4. For contact information on these and other organizations, see Appendix B.
5. Englishman Frank Smith, an avid folk dancer, started the Christmas Country Dance School at Berea College in Kentucky in 1938 to train more Appalachian leaders to support Berea's Mountain Folk Festival; after only five years, the festival attracted thousands of spectators. In New York and at Pinewoods dance camp, May Gadd, a Cecil Sharp disciple from England, was busy directing the increased activities of the Country Dance and Song Society. All of these individuals and groups knew of and to some degree supported each other's work.
6. See the Bibliography for a list of titles by Holden and Sannella.

included editorials expressing his strong opinions an all matters related to folk music and dance:[7]

> I have insisted that the dancers act and behave like ladies and gentlemen! That a "ladies chain" should be done with a courtesy turn instead of a lot of spinning and twirling; that a "balance partner" is not an excuse for dust-raising pawing of the floor like a herd of lovesick buffalo; that wild, uncontrolled swinging should not be allowed. . . . I believe that you should treat the dances of our own country with respect and dance them with pride and a "wee bit of elegance."

Dancers flocked to Page's events and to camps where he taught, including his own New Hampshire dance weekends. He helped start a summer school to teach dancing and the art of dance calling; his graduates included contras along with squares in their repertoire. Page also recorded numerous albums, taught at folk dance camps from Maine to California, and toured Japan (sponsored by the U.S. State Department) and England.

After Ralph Page's death, Ted Sannella (1928–1995) became the best-known leader on the national contra dance scene. A skilled choreographer as well as a caller, he traveled across the United States and abroad, always promoting the highest quality of dance. Ted devoted enormous energy to the Ralph Page Dance Legacy Weekend and the future of contra dance, publishing several influential collections of contra and square dances along with suggestions for callers on how to teach them effectively. At this same time, caller Don Armstrong was actively promoting contras within the Lloyd Shaw Federation and similar groups based around square dancing; Armstrong also traveled abroad extensively, spreading interest in contras to such countries as Denmark, Germany, and the Czech Republic.

## A New Generation Discovers Contras: "Dudley Dancers"

If Ralph Page and other callers brought old contras and squares to a new audience in the years after World War II, it was Dudley Laufman who unleashed an enormous new wave of interest in country dancing in the late 1960s and early 1970s. A poet, musician, and farmer, Laufman began calling dances throughout New England, including an appearance at the 1965 Newport Folk Festival. Hippies and young back-to-the-landers flocked to rural New England and discovered the dances and the lively fiddle tunes. From Maine to Connecticut, hordes of dancers appeared at what were commonly called "Dudley dances." As these enthusiastic dancers learned that the longways dances were called "contras," by the mid-1970s some started calling the entire evening's program a contra dance.

Dudley also had a major influence on contra dance music. To be sure, over the centuries, as the dance changed, so did the music played for the dancing. A single fiddle around 1800 might be supplanted later in that century by an orchestra with several violins, cornet, clarinet, perhaps a flute or harp, with the rhythm being kept by a tuba or a string bass. Ralph Page's New Hampshire orchestra in the late 1940s included two fiddles, a string bass, piano, and accordion. Dudley's Canterbury Country Orchestra offered another model; there might be 20 musicians crowded on the stage, most of them sit-in musicians rather than hired professionals. In addition to playing tunes from the traditional repertoire, these musicians explored new tunes that Dudley introduced through his connections with the Country Dance and Song Society and English country dancing. Canterbury's first LP of contra dance music in 1972 spread New England dance tunes to folk musicians throughout the country.

The subsequent dissemination of contras can be traced directly to many "Dudley dancers" who with almost evangelical zeal carried an enthusiasm for country dancing as they moved from New England to other parts of the country. In the 1970s, dancers and musicians inspired by Dudley introduced contras to such far-flung locales as San Diego, Palo Alto, Berkeley, Portland, Missoula, Bloomington, St. Louis, and Dallas. By the 1980s, contras began to spread through Appalachia and the South; to the dismay of many who valued the region's traditions, Northern contra tunes often pushed out the old-time mountain fiddle tunes and indigenous square dances.

## Live Music Takes Center Stage

In many dance communities, recordings had started to replace bands for the dancing, a trend that was reversed with the Canterbury Orchestra and its many offshoots. Scores of musicians played with Dudley at one time or another, and they started forming their own bands. Brothers Rodney and Randy Miller released two important albums of "New England chestnuts," the contras that formed

7. The complete text of *Northern Junket* is now available online at the Library of Traditional Music and Dance website: http://www.izaak.unh.edu/dlp/NorthernJunket/pages/index.htm

the backbone of the traditional dance repertoire. In the Boston area, fiddler Donna Hébert joined Peter Barnes and Tony Parkes to form Yankee Ingenuity, and with Tony and Ted Sannella sharing the caller's microphone, they soon were attracting crowds of 300 for the Tuesday night dance. These musicians, joined by other groups such as Swallowtail and Wild Asparagus, began touring nationally, bringing the New England sound as far away as the West Coast. In the mid-1980s, Rodney Miller's two *Airplang* albums marked a pronounced shift away from the more traditional sound, opening the door to more influences from rock and roll, jazz, and Appalachian old-time tunes, helping lay the groundwork for musical innovations and variety which were to further influence the dancing. Today, there are bands in every part of the country, many of which tour extensively, and contra dancing almost everywhere is done to live music.

## The Country Dance and Song Society and Other Organizations

The Country Dance and Song Society (CDSS) was started in 1915 as a group solely concerned with English dances. Over time, however, square and contra dances were included. CDSS is the largest organization that offers many services to contra dancers and groups. It publishes a magazine, membership directories, books, and recordings. CDSS also sponsors dance camps and research, offers tax-exempt status and attractive insurance packages to groups, and maintains a research library.

Many organizations around the United States promote contra dancing and offer services. Some focus nationally, others serve a particular area; some are long established, while others are relatively new. Among them are the New England Folk Festival Association; the John C. Campbell Folk School in Brasstown, North Carolina; the Christmas Country Dance School in Berea, Kentucky; The Lloyd Shaw Foundation; and Folklore Village in Wisconsin. In addition, an Internet search of "contra dance" followed by the name of a city or state will provide numerous contacts.

## Contra Dance Research

The Library of Traditional Music and Dance at the University of New Hampshire, Durham, is the most complete collection related to contra dancing. It contains Ralph Page's personal collection of dance and music books, a similarly vast collection from Ted Sannella, papers and recordings from a dozen other figures in the country dance world, and the archives of the Country Dance and Song Society. All this information is available for researchers. UNH is also the venue each year for the Ralph Page Dance Legacy Weekend, whose organizers pay particular attention to the roots of traditional dancing. Many colleges have advanced degrees in folklore and encourage dissertations relating to dance.

## Contra Dancing in the Twenty-First Century

Within the last 30 years, contra dancing has made a big leap forward in popularity, both across the United States and internationally, including active groups in England, Denmark, Belgium, and the Czech Republic. Several factors have contributed to the increased enthusiasm. First among these is the central role of live music. Today's contra musicians bring fresh energy to traditional tunes; they also present newer compositions with lively arrangements. Choreographers are creating new dances at a rapid rate; today's contras usually involve all dancers moving at once, replacing the *actives* and *inactives* of an earlier era. In recent decades, some terminology has changed and new figures have been created or imported from other traditions. The *corner* or *the one below* is now referred to as a *neighbor;* the *gypsy* and the *hey* have come to contras from English country dancing, while *pass through to an ocean wave* or *pass the ocean* from modern Western square dancing has entered the contra lexicon. The increased number of specialized dance camps or dance weekends, and the continued mobility of leaders, dancers, and musicians have all added to the contra dance scene.

Today, although people will say they are "going to a contra dance," in actuality there may be a few square dances and round dances during the evening as well. Rather than take classes, as is the norm in club-style square dancing, newcomers can walk into most contra dances and learn what they need to know that night, in the company of friendly people and toe-tapping live music. Most groups encourage dancers to switch partners each dance, so singles find the contra dance scene a welcoming community. After a period when some dancers were only interested in contras, we now are seeing more interest in squares again, especially some of the more intricate dances of the 1950s and 1960s. In addition, contra dancers usually include round dances such as the waltz and add other dances to their repertoire like English country dancing, swing, Cajun, salsa, clogging, and even the hambo.

Contra dance enthusiasts still face some of the dilemmas that the square and round dance people had with standardization, proliferation of new figures, and burnout. Although talented musicians have more opportunities to play, only a few callers or musicians can make a living on this alone. Family dance camps offer increased possibilities for dancers who want to share their interests with their children, and while some dance communities have seen a resurgence of dancers in their teens or early twenties, others are seeing a graying of the dance floor.

Once again the tradition of contra dancing is firmly established. People enjoy dancing contras for the same reasons as long ago. The sense of community and fellowship is strong. It's part of our heritage. It's "good fun." Yes, contra dancing is full of life in the twenty-first century.

# Contra Dance Basics

*By Penn Fix, Spokane, WA*

## Starting the Contra Dance Set

A contra dance set consists of two lines of dancers facing about four feet across from one another. The caller and musicians are at one end of these lines, referred to as the **top of set.** The **bottom of set** is farthest away from the caller. In these two lines, partners are across from each other with the women in the line on the caller's left and men in the line on the caller's right.

A novice teacher of contra dances would benefit from dancing with a contra group first or studying a contra video suggested in Appendix D. Before teaching the dance, the caller announces, "Take hands four." The couple at the top of the set takes hands to make a circle of four with the next couple. Then the next two couples join hands in a circle, followed by the next and the next. The couple nearest the caller in each of these circles is referred to as the **active couple.** The other couple in each circle is the **inactive couple.** Note that a couple can start at the bottom of the set without another couple.

## Formations in the Contra Dance

Once the dancers have taken hands four, the caller then must align them in the correct formation. There are four major formations used in contra dancing.

### The Improper/Cross Over Formation (duple improper)

In the **improper formation,** the partners in the active couple in each circle change places with each other before the dance begins (Diagram 1). When couples have reached the top or bottom of the set and are waiting out as neutral couples, they must remember to change places with their partners before reentering the dance.

Diagram 1

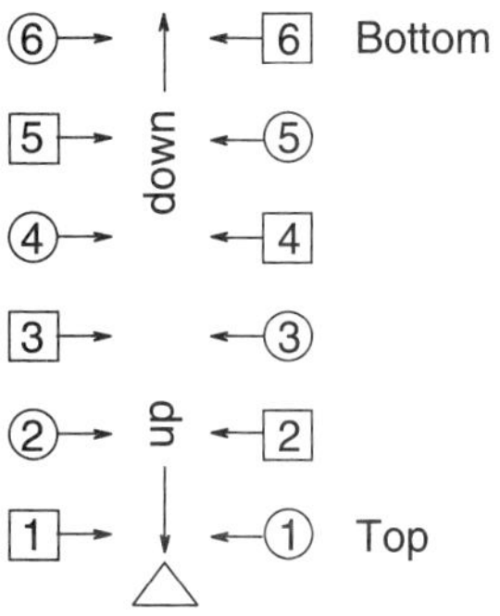


Improper
Cross Over
1, 3, 5 are active

### The Proper/Not Cross Over Formation (duple proper)

In the **proper formation,** the active couple in each circle does not change places before the dance (Diagram 2); while waiting out at the top or bottom, couples do not change places with their partners.

Diagram 2

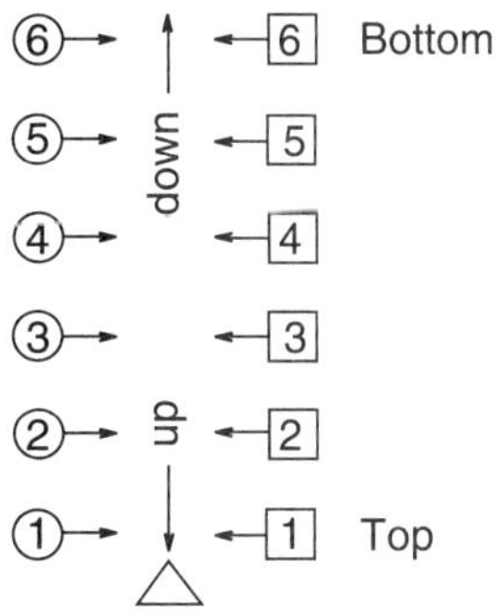


Proper
Not Cross Over
1, 3, 5 are active

### The Becket Formation

Partners are alongside one another to start the dance (Diagram 3) in the **Becket formation.** The couples in the line on the caller's left progress down while the couples in the line on the caller's right move up. There are no designated actives or inactives in this formation.

Diagram 3

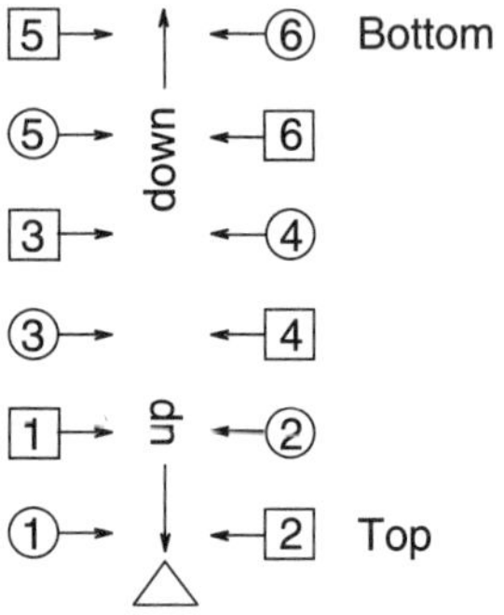


Becket

△ = Caller and Musicians

### The Triple Formation

In the **triple formation,** the active couple joins with two inactive couples in a circle of three couples. The call is "Take hands six." Triple contras are usually proper (Diagram 4). The inactive couple that has reached the top of the set must wait out *two sequences* of the dance. When ready to reenter as an active couple, there will then be two inactive couples below them. As an active couple nears the bottom of the set with only one inactive couple to dance, both couples continue the dance sequence with an imaginary third couple. After this sequence, the top couple is at the bottom and waits out just one sequence before reentering as an inactive couple.

Diagram 4

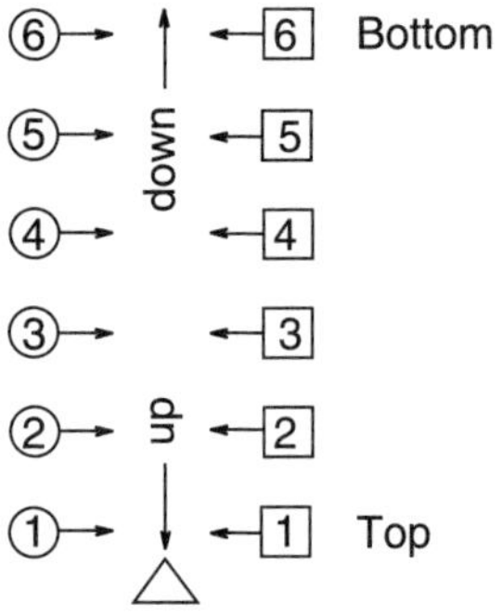


Triple Proper
Not Cross Over
1, 4 are active

## Progression

The active couple dances with the inactive couple below through a sequence of dance figures. A **progression figure** within the sequence will result in the active and inactive couples changing places. When the sequence begins again, the active couple is dancing with a new inactive couple. Eventually the active couple will reach the bottom of the set with no inactive couple with which to dance. Inactives will reach the top with no actives to dance. As **neutral couples,** they both will rest out at the top and bottom for a sequence, or one time through the contra dance. They then return in reverse roles: inactives are now actives, progressing down the set, and actives are now inactives, progressing up the set. See Diagrams 5–8 for a progression. The example is an improper dance.

Diagram 5

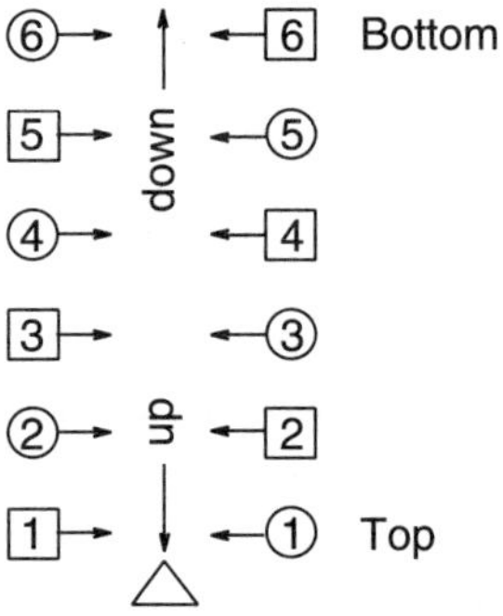


Improper
Cross Over
1, 3, 5 are active

Diagram 6

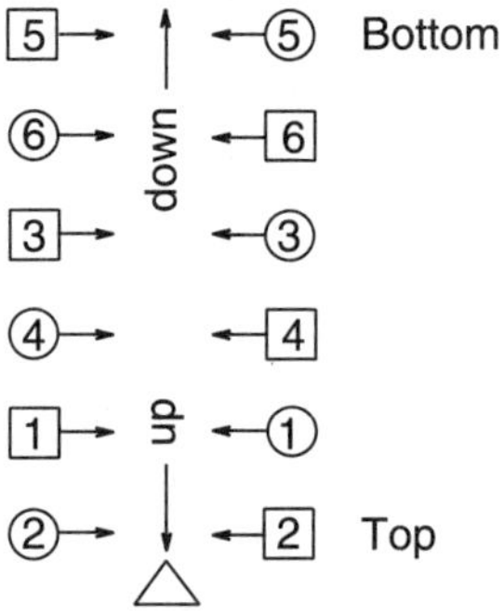


Diagram 7

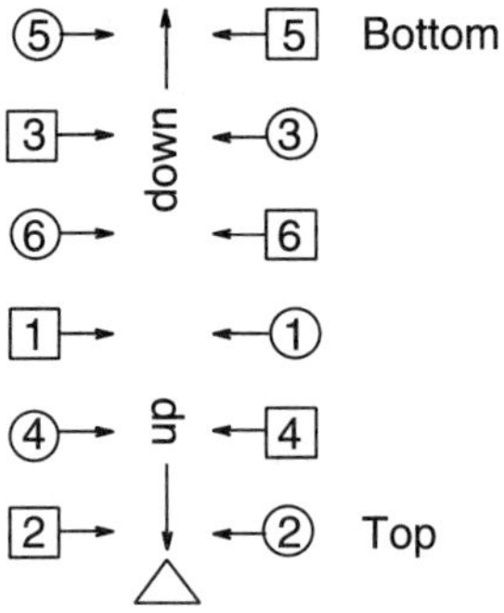


Diagram 8

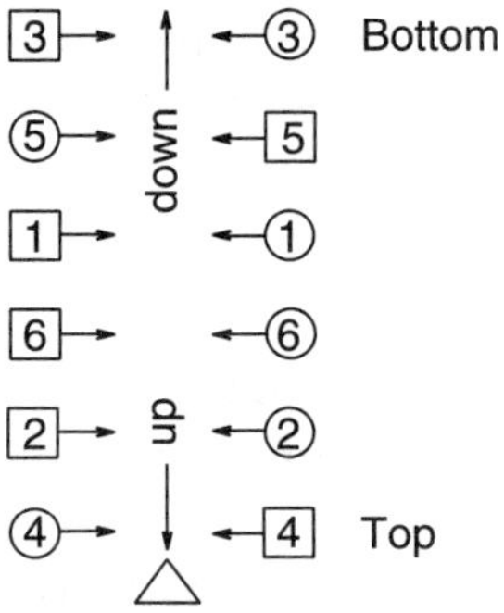

## Music and Timing

The contra dance and the music played for it are structurally married. Contra dance tunes have two parts, referred to as A and B. Each part has eight measures. For a contra dance, the tune is repeated twice in a sequence of AABB. The sequence of dance figures known as a contra dance is as long as a tune played AABB. When the tune repeats the AABB format, so too does the contra dance.

For dancers and caller alike, these tunes played in AABB sequence translate to 64 counts. Thus a sequence of figures is 64 counts long. Most of the contra dance figures have assigned counts of 16, 8, or 4 in length. These counts are the beats of the music. Dancers must execute each step on the beat of the music and use the proper number of counts for each dance figure. If done in this manner, the dancer remains in time with both the dance and the tune and thus is not late or early for the next figure.

## The Role of the Caller

The caller orchestrates the entire evening of dance and serves a variety of functions. He or she selects the dances, teaches the dances, acts in liaison with the musicians, sets the pace of the music, and signals to the band and dancers when to end the dance. The calls are cues that give direction to dancers with a minimal amount of rhyming patter. The caller's responsibility is to choose a dance appropriate for the group and sequence in the program and then teach it to the dancers. This teaching occurs during the walk-through before the music begins. During this time, the caller has an opportunity to teach specific figures if the dancers are unfamiliar with them and to make the dancers aware of the specific sequence of figures of this dance. After the walk-through, the caller returns the dancers to their original spots before starting the dance.

Once the contra is under way, the caller must rely on abbreviated cues. For example, a ladies chain may have to be taught during the walk-through but during the actual dance, the caller prompts by simply saying, "ladies chain."

The call itself must precede the actual movement so timing of the call is critical. It is essential for the caller to know how long figures take and how the figures fit the music. During the sequence of figures the caller must prompt two counts before the actual figure begins.

The calls are usually directed to the active couples in the set. In Becket formation dances where there are no actives or inactives, the call is directed to partners and neighbors.

The beginning of the dance can be the most difficult for a caller since the initial prompt must be done before the music starts. When working with musicians, the caller can request a short musical introduction, often referred to as "four potatoes." This two- or four-beat introduction allows the caller to prompt the first figure before the figure begins. When using recorded music, the caller must know the recording so as to cue properly because some recorded music does not have introductions.

The dance can be repeated 10 or even 20 times. If the dancers are new to contras, then shorter is better, maybe 10 times through the dance. If the dance is symmetrical with actives and inactives dancing the same figures at the same time, then fewer times through the dance is warranted. If the dance is asymmetrical, with the active couple doing all the swinging and the inactives having little action, then the dance should be repeated 15 or 20 times.

After the dancers become familiar with the sequence of a dance, the caller can prompt less or even stop prompting during that particular dance. Remember, dancers are cued not only by the caller but also by the music.

The ending of a dance can be a good deal easier if, before the evening begins, the caller and musicians agree to ending signals. As the contra dance is nearing the end, the caller signals to a previously designated member of the band, "Two more times." This signal means that the musicians will play the tune two more times through. This signal is usually made in the B2 part of the dance. The caller then calls the dance two more complete times. In the final B2, he can reinforce communication by turning to all the musicians and saying, "We are going out." The dance ends immediately after the B2. The caller invites the dancers to thank their partners and the band and find another partner for the next dance.

## Dance Sources

The caller draws from a number of sources for contra dances. True to its traditional nature, word of mouth and direct participation are two major sources for dances. Also, new dances are being composed almost daily. In the folk tradition, these new compositions are offered freely to the contra dance community. Although there are no restrictions in terms of user fees, acknowledgment of the composer when known is expected after the walk-through. This book offers a wide variety of resources in the Appendices and the Bibliography.

## Card File

Callers record dances in many ways, but the most popular remains a card file system. Note that the card (see card on next page) records the date and location that the caller-teacher learned the dance; the name of the person who taught the dance (in our example the teacher and originator of the dance are the same person, but both pieces of information are handy); proper, improper, triple, or Becket; and key cues, which are capitalized. On the back, any helpful information for teaching purposes and interesting facts are listed. It is wise to record the dance as taught because, in referring to it later, there is less error. The card may be carried to the dance and used for a quick refresher.

Lady of Lake '85

PIERCE'S HALL STROLL[8]

Duple, improper

A1:1 LADIES DO-SI-DO
2 GENTS DO-SI-DO left shoulder 1½ & go to PARTNER
A2:3 Everyone SWING your OWN on sides of set (16 counts)
4 (long swing) end (1s face down, 2s face up) escort position
B1:5 "STROLL" promenade along lines, turn as couple (8 counts)
6 And RETURN look for opposite couple (8 counts)
B2:7 RIGHT HANDS ACROSS turn 1½ round (8 counts)
8 GENTS DROP OUT to original side
Men will have progressed one position.
Ladies continue to turn right to LADIES CHAIN HALFWAY (8 counts)
Ladies chain away from partner to opposite. Women will be on original side and have progressed one position.

Community hall, East Putney, VT, where Fred Breunig calls dances.
Composed for the Sesquicentennial, 1982.

Note:
#2 Gents LEFT shoulder do-si-do 1½ to face partner on her side
#6 Must recognize opposite couple at end of promenade Star position—shake hands
#7 Emphasize turning STAR 1½, until gents get back to their original (improper) sides! Must turn star with DETERMINATION or Not on Time
#8 At end of ladies ½ chain, gents can direct (lead) ladies into their do-si-do of next lady
All couples are equally active.

## Music Sources

Today's contra dance revival is built squarely on the shoulders of musicians. Live music has powered the continued interest in contras.

Irish, Scottish, English, French-Canadian, and even some Southern and Western hoedown tunes have found their way into the repertoires of contra dance musicians. Most of these tunes are jigs, reels, hornpipes, and even marches written in 6/8, 2/4, and 4/4 meter. While the New England Chestnuts have tunes long associated with the dances, contemporary dances do not. Any tune can be played so long as it stays within the structure of 32 bars or 64 beats.

More important than the choice of tunes is the manner in which they are played. Musicians must play at a tempo that matches the walking step used by dancers. In addition they should phrase their music to help dancers associate the beginning and ending of the figures, which parallel the ending and beginning of the parts of the tune. Some tunes are chosen to match the character of the dance. Jigs are bouncy; reels energetic and flowing. The music should reflect the spirit and buildup of the dance. Musicians can make the music match the excitement as the dance builds up to a high point.

Callers may use recorded music. The *Dance A While* CD includes three musical selections that can be used to practice a wide variety of contra dances: "Irish Washerwoman (Virginia Reel)," "St. Anne's Reel," and "Miller's Reel." For even more music sources, see the Tune Books section in the Bibliography, and also Appendix D.

## Contra Dance Figures

### The Basic Step

A light rhythmic **walking step** to the beat of the music is used throughout the dance. Starting on the right foot is recommended. The arms hang freely at the side unless they are used to execute a dance figure.

### The Swing

Contra dancers live to **swing**! Almost all sequences have a swing and many crescendo into a swing. The hand holds vary in different parts of the country, but the swing position is the most common. Both dancers step into the swing on the right foot. A walk-around, right hips are parallel. If using a buzz step, right toes are almost touching, hips and shoulders are parallel. The action is clockwise. Knees are slightly bent. Counterbalance is important, with feet close together, upper bodies bowed. The length of the swing is often 12 or 16 counts and not less than 8.

8. Included by permission of Fred Breunig, Putney, VT.

### The Balance

The **balance** (4 counts) often comes before a swing. It was originally intended as an introduction or greeting. Preceding a swing, two dancers take hands (either both hands or right hands) and step forward toward each other, back from each other, and then directly into the swing. This figure has developed over the years to a step on the right foot moving forward and slightly to the right of the partner, lifting the free left foot in a kicking or swinging motion, followed by rising on the ball of the right foot. Weight is then transferred by stepping on the left foot, backing up slightly, and moving left of the partner. The right foot swings in front, followed by rising on the ball of the left foot. Often the stepping on the right and left feet is accompanied by heavy stomps, which once inspired Ralph Page to note the dancers sounded like "a herd of lovesick water buffalo."

A balance may also occur when dancers are joined by hand in a line of four or along contra lines.

### Other Contra Dance Figures

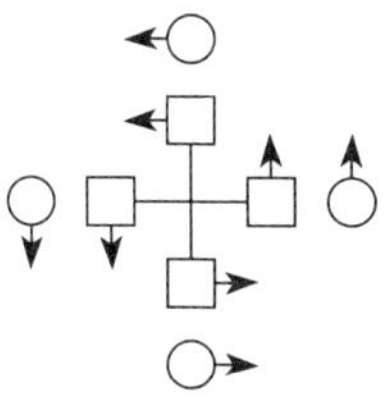

Common figures found in both traditional square dance and contra dancing include **ladies chain** (a full chain over and back, 16 counts), **half chain,** (over and courtesy turn but no return, 8 counts), **do-si-do** (8 counts), **promenade** (8 counts), **forward and back** (8 counts), **allemande** turns (4-6-8 counts), **right and left thru** (a full right and left over and back, 16 counts), **half right and left** (over and courtesy turn but no return, 8 counts), and **right hand star** (8 counts). See the Glossary for details on these figures.

## Teaching Suggestions

### Sicilian Circle

The movement up and down the contra dance set can be confusing at first. Many newcomers become disoriented while waiting out at the top or bottom of the set. Perhaps an easier way to teach the progression and transition from one contra sequence to the next is through the **Sicilian circle** formation. Couples face couples clock- and counterclockwise in a big circle. Men have their partner on their right side facing the other couple. Essentially, this formation is similar to an improper/cross over contra but without a top or a bottom. No one waits out a turn.

### The Role of the Active

In proper and improper contras, the caller prompts to the active couple. For example, "Swing the one below" directs the active man to swing the inactive woman and the active woman to swing the inactive man in their circle of four.

Becket contras have no active or inactive couples. The caller prompts to partners, men, and women. In a circle of four, *your neighbor* is the person of the opposite gender who is not your partner.

Because of the popularity of symmetrical dances in which every couple is dancing the same figure at the same time, the roles of active and inactive are less defined. In some instances, *your neighbor* has replaced *your inactive* in the call. For example, "Swing the one below," can be replaced with "Swing your neighbor."

### The Role of the Inactive

In asymmetrical contras, the actives will dance figures while the inactives either are watching or assisting. Because the calls are directed to the actives, the inactives must know what to do without being prompted. The inactives also play an important role in the management of the formation. For example, when the actives go down the center of the set, and before they can come back to cast off, the inactives can straighten the lines out by making sure they are not too far away from their partners across the set nor too far away from the next inactive up and down the set. In addition, some contras creep away from the top of the set. Inactives can help by taking one step up toward the caller each time the actives go down the center. The other role the inactives play is as assistants to the actives. They accept them in cast-offs and allemande turns in contra corners.

### Contra Corners

To start **contra corners** (16 counts), the active couple is below their original inactives in a proper/not cross over formation. Contra corners are across the set for each active person. The first contra corner is diagonally right from the active person; the second contra corner is diagonally left. For the call "turn contra corners," active partners meet in the center of the set and take right hands, turn halfway, and drop hands. They turn their first corner (the one diagonally right) with left hands all the way around and again drop hands. Active partners turn three-quarters around in the middle of the set with their right hands. They then turn the second corners (the one diagonally left) by the left hand all the way around and wait for the next call. In contra corners, the actives use their right and left hands, alternately; the corners always use their left hand to turn an active person. Each turn is 4 counts. See Diagram 9.

Diagram 9
Contra Corners

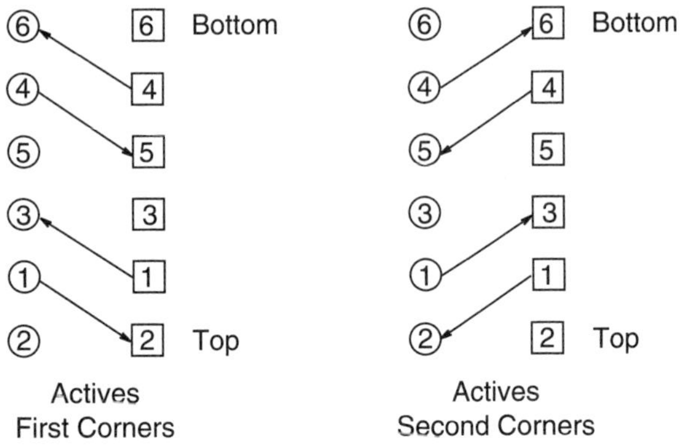


### Starting Becket Dances

An easy way to get dancers into the Becket formation is to start from a proper contra dance formation. Announce, "Take hands four and top couples in each circle cross over." Once couples are in the improper formation, then "Take hands four again and circle left one-quarter round." Now partners are alongside each other and are facing another couple across the set.

### The Gypsy

The **gypsy** (8 counts) can best be described as a do-si-do except that the two dancers always face each other, maintain eye contact, and never turn their backs to one another. In a right shoulder gypsy, the two move clockwise around each other; in a left shoulder gypsy, they travel counterclockwise.

### Hey for Four

In a **hey for four** (16 counts), four dancers are in a line going across the set; the center two are facing one another and the other two are on the outside facing the center of the set. They weave without touching hands, moving in a figure eight pattern with an additional loop in the middle. In the most common formation, the center two are women and the outer two are men. To begin, two women face each other and pass right shoulders. Traveling toward the opposite side, the women pass left shoulders with the approaching man. The women continue making a loop to left to face center, pass next man left; women pass right in center, pass man left, loop to the left to face center, pass next man left, and are back in original position. The men follow the path of the woman in front of them by passing left shoulders with the woman, right shoulders with the man in center, left with the other woman, and loop left to face center. Men return passing the woman left, men pass right in center, then woman left, loop left, and are home.

## Dance Levels and Teaching Progression

The contra dances selected in the following section are divided by ability levels: beginning, intermediate, and advanced. Because most students using this book are newcomers to contras, beginning dances are divided further into three categories. Beginning 1 dances introduce the basic figures. Beginning 2 dances build on the content learned and applied in a different manner. Beginning 3 dances include those with the hey figure. Intermediate dances introduce the Becket formation to students. And the advanced dances can challenge both teacher and students!

| BEGINNING 1 | BEGINNING 2 | BEGINNING 3 |
|---|---|---|
| Aw Shucks | Contra for Margie | Chain the Swain |
| Broken Sixpence | Jed's Reel | Delphiniums and Daisies |
| Easy Does It | Small Potatoes | Roll in the Hey |
| Lady of the Lake | Salmonchanted Evening | Stars of Alberta |
| The Nova Scotian | | Symmetrical Force |
| So When Was the Wedding? | | Thorn Street Gypsy |
| Supernova Scotian | | |
| The Tourist | | |

| INTERMEDIATE | ADVANCED |
|---|---|
| Becket Reel | Brimmer & May Reel |
| Chorus Jig | CDS Reel |
| Dance Gypsy | Dancing Sailors |
| Hills of Habersham | Hull's Victory |
| More Again | The Other Mary Kay |
| Pierce's Hall Stroll | Petronella |
| Roadblock Reel | Rory O'More |
| Shadrack's Delight | |
| Weave the Line | |
| With Thanks to the Dean | |

## Contra Dance Tunes Composed by Ralph Page

*Gone a Rovin', Patriot's Jig, and McQuillen's Squeezebox—all original tunes composed by the late Ralph Page—are included by permission of the estate of Ralph Page.*

### McQuillen's Squeezebox

### Patriot's Jig

# *Aw Shucks!*

*Included by permission of Carol Kopp, Streetsboro, Ohio.*

AW SHUCKS! is a contemporary contra composed by Carol Kopp. The inspiration for Aw Shucks! arose from the square Northern Lights as well as the need for an easy and interesting dance. The title was inspired by the spirit of the southern Appalachian mountains.

**Music:** Jig or reel.
**Contra Formation:** Duple, improper/cross over.
**Level:** Beginning 1.

## Directions FOR THE DANCE

A1 **Active couples sashay down the center** (8 counts). Actives take two hands and slide eight counts down the center. Inactives, in the meantime, move up the line to take the place left by the active next to them.

**Active couples sashay back to your neighbors** (8 counts). Actives stop between the original inactives below. Actives stay in the center facing their partner. Don't change sides. Stay crossed over.

A2 **Actives clap** (4 counts). Actives clap own hands, then partner's right hand, then own hands, and partner's left hand.

**Actives turn to face neighbors and clap** (4 counts). Turn away from partner to face the inactive behind you on the outside. With the inactive, clap own hands, then inactives' right hands, then own hands, and inactives' left.

**Actives swing neighbors** (8 counts). After clapping, swing the same. Men finish the swing with the women on the right facing down the set. Join hands with couples across the set.

B1 **Down the center four in line** (6 counts).

**Turn as couples** (2 counts). With the one you swung, turn as a couple to face up the set. Join hands four in line again.

**Come back up and bend the line** (8 counts). Return to place and bend the line.

B2 **Ladies chain over and back** (16 counts). After the chain, actives step into the center to sashay. Remember the next inactive to dance with is now below the actives.

# Becket Reel

BECKET REEL is an original dance by Herbie Gaudreau of Holbrock, Massachusetts. He named it "Becket Reel" in honor of Camp Becket in the Berkshire mountains of western Massachusetts, where he called this dance while attending Charlie Baldwin's square dance camp. In some parts of New Hampshire it is known as Bucksaw Contra or Reel. It is similar to Slaunch to Donegal.

This was the first dance using this formation. The name of the dance became synonymous with the name of this formation, the Becket formation.

**Music:** Any preferred traditional-type reel, "Reilly's Own," Cole, M. M., *One Thousand Fiddle Tunes;* "Reel a Pitou," Page, Ralph, *An Elegant Collection of Squares,* p. 91.

**Contra Formation:** Becket. Refer to page 198, Diagram 3.

**Level:** Intermediate.

## Directions FOR THE DANCE

A1 **Allemande left your corner once around** (4 counts). Corner is person alongside you who is not your partner. At the top and bottom, the corner is across the set. The corner remains the same person throughout the dance.

**Come back and swing your partner** (12 counts).

A2 **Opposite ladies chain over and back** (16 counts).

B1 **On the left diagonal right and left thru** (8 counts). Each couple does a right and left through with couple in opposite line on left diagonal. Courtesy turn partner to face middle of set. If there is no one to right and left thru, do not cross the set, but wait.

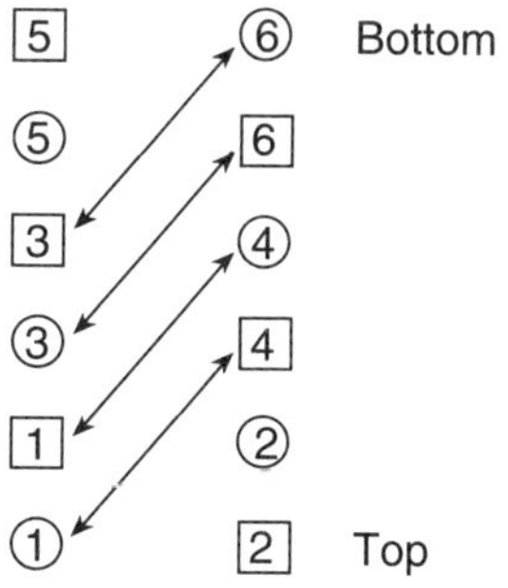

**Straight across, do a right and left thru** (8 counts). From lines, each couple does a right and left thru with couple directly opposite. Courtesy turn partner to face middle of set.

| | | | |
|---|---|---|---|
| [5] | ⟷ | ③ | Bottom |
| ⑤ | ⟷ | [3] | |
| [6] | ⟷ | ① | |
| ⑥ | ⟷ | [1] | |
| [4] | ⟷ | ② | |
| ④ | ⟷ | [2] | Top |

Straight across

| | | |
|---|---|---|
| ③ | [5] | Bottom |
| [3] | ⑤ | |
| ① | [6] | |
| [1] | ⑥ | |
| ② | [4] | |
| [2] | ④ | Top |

Ending position

B2 **Same two couples star by the left. Back by the right** (16 counts). As you come out of right-hand star, movement flows into left allemande at the beginning.

# *Brimmer & May Reel*

*Included by permission of Dan Pearl, Southborough, Massachusetts.*

BRIMMER & MAY REEL is a contemporary contra, composed by Dan Pearl in 1979. He had been dancing for about six months when he came up with this sequence, which owes a lot to Ted Sannella's "Patriot Jig." The Brimmer & May School was the site at that time of a large contra dance in the Boston area. This is the description of the dance as modified, for the better, by the folk process.

**Music:** Reel.
**Contra Formation:** Duple, improper/cross over.
**Level:** Advanced.

## *Directions* FOR THE DANCE

A1 **Swing the one below** (16 counts). Actives swing the inactives.

A2 **Right and left thru** (8 counts). Do not right and left back.

**Actives swing in the center** (8 counts). Finish the swing facing down the set with women on the right of their partners.

B1 **Down the center four in line** (4 counts). Join hands across the set. Actives are in the middle with two women next to each other and two men next to each other in line. Go down the set and then stop but continue facing down.

**Actives California twirl to their neighbor** (4 counts). Actives drop hands with their neighbors, California twirl (see Glossary), and make an arch with their partners. Then they face one another and pass right shoulders to face the one they swung in A1. Actives drop their joined hands.

**With the handy hand, actives turn their neighbor twice around** (8 counts). Active man turns inactive woman with left hands; active woman turns inactive man with right hands. After the actives have finished the turns, they face up the set as a couple; the inactive couple falls in behind them.

B2 **Up the center as couples, actives leading** (4 counts). Taking large steps, return two by two; actives are proper, not cross over and inactives are improper, cross over.

**Actives cast out below the original neighbors** (4 counts). Actives turn out one place to end below the original inactives; inactives have in the meantime moved up to take the position where the actives were before the cast-off. Inactives turn to face the original actives now below them. All join hands in a circle.

**Circle left halfway around** (4 counts). Couples are now back in their original cross over position.

**Pass thru up and down** (4 counts). Actives pass right shoulders with inactives onto the next couple to swing.

# Broken Sixpence

*Included by permission of Don Armstrong, Macks Creek, Missouri.*

BROKEN SIXPENCE is an original dance by Don Armstrong.

**Music:** Lively contra music.
**Contra Formation:** Duple, improper/cross over.
**Level:** Beginning 1.

## Directions FOR THE DANCE

A1 **Do-si-do the one below** (8 counts). Actives face down the set, inactives face up. Actives do-si-do the one facing.

**Men do-si-do** (8 counts). Men do-si-do in center of set.

A2 **Women do-si-do** (8 counts). Women do-si-do in center of set.

**Actives swing in the center** (8 counts). Swing in center of set, ending with woman on man's right, facing down the set. Active couple is between the inactive couple (couple below) in a line of four.

B1 **Down the center four in line** (6 counts). Join hands in line of four. Walk down the set.

**Turn alone** (2 counts). All four release hands, turn individually to face up the set.

**Come back home** (8 counts). Join hands. Walk up the set four in line. At home bend the line to form a circle.

B2 **Circle left once around** (8 counts).

**Star by the left** (8 counts). From left-hand star, turn away from the couple dancing with and move naturally into beginning of dance to "do-si-do the one below."

# CDS Reel

*Included by permission of Ted Sannella.*

CDS Reel is a contemporary contra. It is an original dance by Ted Sannella, composed in September 1984. The Country Dance and Song Society (CDSS) is the publisher of Sannella's books, *Balance and Swing* and *Swing the Next.*

**Music:** "Swinging on a Gate," Sannella, Ted, *Balance and Swing,* p. 69.
**Contra Formation:** Duple, improper/cross over.
**Level:** Advanced.

## Directions FOR THE DANCE

A1 **Swing your neighbor** (8 counts). Finish the swing with woman on the man's right facing across the set.

**All go forward and back** (8 counts). Join hands in line, move four steps forward, four steps back.

A2 **Big circle, all go left** (8 counts). Top couple joins hands and bottom couple joins hands to complete the *oval,* which moves left.

**Big circle, go right back to place** (8 counts). *Oval* moves right. *Note:* Each man locates his partner to form left-hand star, on call.

B1 **Left-hand star three-quarters with the opposite two** (8 counts). Active couple with original inactive couple above forms left-hand star, turn three-fourths around.

**All swing your partner** (8 counts). Men turn right to swing woman behind. Woman ends on man's right side.

B2 **Men allemande left, go once and a half** (8 counts). Two men allemande left, once and a half.

**Swing your neighbor** (8 counts). Men will swing the same person as the beginning; woman ends on man's right side. Active couples have progressed one position.

# Chain the Swain

*Included by permission of Becky Hill, Cleveland Heights, Ohio.*

CHAIN THE SWAIN was written in 1992 for a good friend, Dick Swain, who has since left Cleveland.

**Music:** Reel or Jig
**Contra Formation:** Duple, improper/cross over
**Level:** Beginning 3

## *Directions* FOR THE DANCE

A1 **Balance and swing your neighbor** (16 counts).

A2 **In long lines, go forward and back with a roll away** (8 counts). Lines go forward four steps. As they take four steps back, the man rolls the woman in his right hand across in front of him, while she twirls 360 degrees to his left side. He catches her on the other side in his left hand, her right. All end up facing into the center of the set.

**Half Gents Chain** (8 counts). Men give right hands to the man across, pull by and give left to his partner. She then courtesy turns him to face into the center of the set.

B1 **Men do-si-do** (8 counts). After the chain, men return to the center to either do-si-do or gypsy with one another.

**All swing your partner** (8 counts).

B2 **Circle left three-quarters round** (8 counts). After the swing, join in a circle with the other couple and circle just three-quarters around.

**Balance in the circle** (4 counts). Keep holding hands in the circle and balance together, first stepping on the right foot first.

**California Twirl** (4 counts). Men have their partners in their right hands. Turn your partner under changing places and at the same time facing the next couple. Couples are now progressed.

# Chorus Jig

Chorus Jig is a traditional contra, a "New England Chestnut." The tune, "Chorus Jig," is a reel (2/4), not a jig (6/8).

**CD:** "Chorus Jig," New England Chestnuts, Vol. 1 & 2 GMM 2005.

**Music:** "Chorus Jig," Page, Ralph, *An Elegant Collection of Contras and Squares,* p. 39; *Fiddler's Fakebook,* p. 68; *New England Fiddler's Repertoire,* No. 96.

**Contra Formation:** Duple, proper/not cross over.

**Level:** Intermediate.

## Directions FOR THE DANCE

A1 **Actives down the outside and back** (16 counts). Each active walks down the outside of the set, turning on counts 7–8, and returns to place.

A2 **Actives down the center and back, cast off** (16 counts). Active couples, holding inside hands, walk down the center, counts 1–6, turn alone, counts 7–8. Return to original position. Cast off, counts 5–8, arm around the inactive person, progressing one position down.

B1 **Turn contra corners** (16 counts).

B2 **Actives balance and swing** (16 counts). End swing facing up the set, moving to go down the outside below the person you cast off.

**Note:**
**Turn contra corners**—inactive person receives two consecutive turns, both left-hand turn, by two different people.

# *Contra for Margie*

*Included by permission of the estate of Ted Sannella and publisher, Country Dance and Song Society. Contra for Margie appears on p. 82, Sannella, Ted.* Swing the Next. *Haydenville, Massachusetts: Country Dance and Song Society, 1996.*

CONTRA FOR MARGIE is a contemporary contra composed on October 19, 1992, by Ted Sannella. Paul McCullough, a dear friend, had asked Sannella to write a contra for his girlfriend, Margie. Ted dedicated the dance to Margie Davis of Portland, Oregon.

**Music:** Jig or reel.
**Contra Formation:** Duple, improper/cross over–double progression.
**Level:** Beginning 2.

## Directions FOR THE DANCE

A1 **In long lines, go forward and back** (8 counts),

**Actives swing in the center** (8 counts). Finish the swing with women on the right of partner facing down the set. Actives join hands with the inactives who are on the outside.

A2 **Down the hall four in line, inside couple arch** (8 counts). Actives are in the center. Actives raise their joined hands to make an arch.

**Ends duck under, actives face up, come back up, two by two** (8 counts). Inactives duck under this arch to finish facing up the set as couples and return up the set. The actives retain joined hands, turn inward toward partner to face up and follow the inactives. The first progression occurs here.

B1 **Circle left once around with new neighbors** (8 counts). The actives turn to face the new couple below them and circle left.

**Do-si-do the same** (8 counts). Actives do-si-do the same inactives whom they circled in B1.

B2 **Balance and swing the same neighbors** (16 counts). Finish the swing with the women on the right facing across the set. The second progression occurs here. The actives will next dance with the inactives below. Join hands along the line.

# Dance Gypsy

*Included by permission of Gene Hubert, Graham, North Carolina.*

DANCE GYPSY is a contemporary contra composed by Gene Hubert of Graham, North Carolina.

**Music:** Jig.
**Contra Formation:** Becket. Refer to page 198, Diagram 3.
**Level:** Intermediate.

## Directions FOR THE DANCE

A1 **Down the center four in line** (6 counts). To start, as couples turn to face down the set, with the women on right of partner, join hands in line with couple across the set.

**Turn as couples** (2 counts).

**And return. Bend the line** (8 counts). Join hands.

A2 **Circle left three-quarters around** (8 counts).

**Swing your neighbor** (8 counts). Men are swinging the left-hand women. The swing occurs on the men's original side. Finish the swing facing a couple on the right diagonal across the set.

B1 **Ladies chain on right diagonal** (8 counts). If there is no couple on right diagonal, do not chain.

**Left-hand star straight across** (8 counts). Star with the couple straight across the set.

B2 **All balance and swing your partner** (16 counts). Partner is in the next left hand star up or down the set in B1. Couples swing on their original side. Finish the swing with women on right of their partners, facing down the set. Join in a line of four with couple across to start the dance again.

**Note:**
**Neutral couple** resting out remains as a couple in the line on the caller's right if at the top of the set and in the line on caller's left, if at the bottom. After the ladies chain, these couples with the new women from the chain should line up as if waiting to enter as an improper/cross over dance.

# *Dancing Sailors*

Dancing Sailors is a contemporary contra composed by Ed Shaw. Al Olson served as a consultant. Shaw and Olson had known each other as sailors, thus Ted Sannella suggested the name.

**Music:** Reel.
**Contra Formation:** Duple, proper/not cross over.
**Level:** Advanced.

## *Directions* FOR THE DANCE

A1 **Actives down the outside below two** (6 counts). Actives go down the outside of their own lines past the next two inactive couples.

**Actives go into the center** (2 counts).

**Meet in the center and return up the set** (6 counts). Actives come into the center to meet, face up as a couple, and go back up the center.

**Cast off** (2 counts). Actives cast off with their inactives (both turn). Finish in long lines facing across from partner. Actives are now below their inactives.

A2 **Turn contra corners** (16 counts). Man 5 has no first corner, woman 5 has no second corner. Actives finish the contra corners by turning with their second corners. Actives are now facing their partners in the center of the set.

B1 **Hey for four on left diagonal with second corners** (16 counts). This hey is done on a diagonal with the active couples and their second corners. Actives begin the hey passing right shoulders with partner. Note that the inactives are not dancing the hey with their partners.

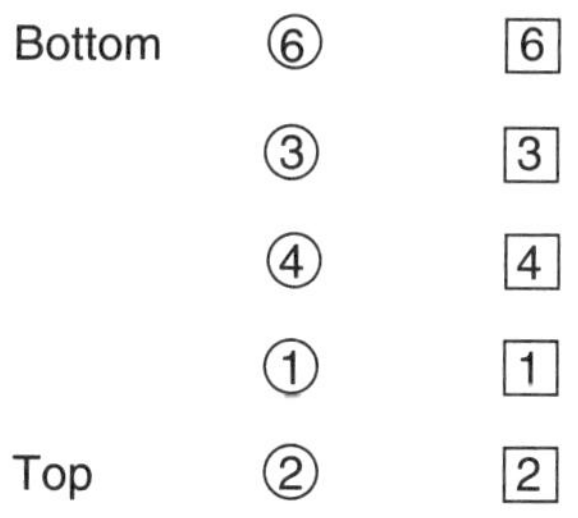

At start of contra corners

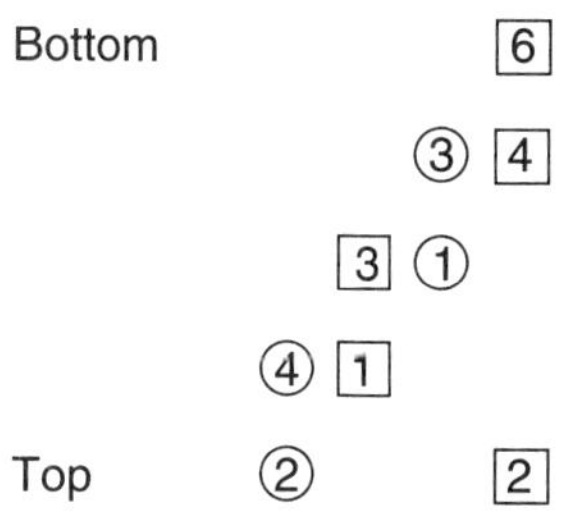

At start of hey with second corner

B2 **Swing your partner in the center of the set** (16 counts). Actives meet after the hey in the center to swing. Timing is important! The actives flow out of the hey into the swing. If late on the swing, a balance preceding the swing helps beginners to get the timing. After swinging, the actives must finish the swing facing up the set so that they are in the proper/not cross over formation. They then cast out to start the dance again. Remember, the inactives to cast off with are the new ones below.

# Delphiniums and Daisies

*Included by permission of Tanya Rotenberg, Philadelphia, Pennsylvania.*

DELPHINIUMS AND DAISIES is a contemporary contra, composed by Tanya Rotenberg of Philadelphia in 1985 for her parents on their 20th wedding anniversary. These flowers were used in her mother's wedding bouquet.

**Music:** Jig.
**Contra Formation:** Duple, improper/cross over.
**Level:** Beginning 3.

## Directions FOR THE DANCE

A1 **Allemande left the one below once and a half** (8 counts). Actives turn the inactives below. Women finish facing the center of the set.

**Ladies chain** (8 counts). Women chain to partner. Do not return.

A2 **Hey for four** (16 counts). Women begin by passing right shoulders in the center of the set.

B1 **All swing your partner** (16 counts). Couples swing on the side they first started the hey. Finish the swing with the woman on the right of her partner, both facing the couple across the set.

B2 **Circle left three-quarters around** (8 counts). Join hands with the couple across the set. It's the same couple you just completed the hey with. Circle left three-quarters, ending in original position.

**Allemande right the same one below once and a half** (8 counts). Actives turn the same inactives as in A1, and everyone progresses to the next to start the dance again.

6

# Easy Does It

*Included by permission of the estate of Ralph Page and publisher, The Lloyd Shaw Foundation. Easy Does It appears on p.16, Page, Ralph.* An Elegant Collection of Contras and Squares. *Denver, Colorado: The Lloyd Shaw Foundation, 1984.*

EASY DOES IT is a contemporary contra, composed by Ralph Page.

**Music:** Jig or reel.
**Contra Formation:** Duple, improper/cross over.
**Level:** Beginning 1.

## *Directions* FOR THE DANCE

| | |
|---|---|
| A1 | **Do-si-do the one below** (8 counts). |
| | **Swing the same** (8 counts). Men finish the swing with the women on their right facing into the center of the set. |
| A2 | **Ladies chain over and back** (16 counts). |
| B1 | **Promenade across the set** (8 counts). In promenade position with one you swung in A1, pass left shoulders with the couple across, turn as a couple, and face into the center of the set. |
| | **Right and left thru** (8 counts). Do not right and left back. |
| B2 | **Left-hand star** (8 counts). With the same couple star once around. |
| | **Right-hand star** (8 counts). Change hands and star in the opposite direction back to place. Then turn away to face the new couple to start the dance again. |

# *Hills of Habersham*

HILLS OF HABERSHAM is an original waltz contra dance by Mary and Fred Collette of Atlanta, Georgia. The Hills of Habersham refers to the mountains of north Georgia. The action of the dance is suggestive of the Chattahoochee River, winding its way to the Gulf. The tune is the ancient Irish melody, "The Bonny Cuckoo."

**Music:** "Star of Country Down" (3/4) and "Si Bheag, Si Mhor" (3/4), Werner, Robert, *The Folklore Village Saturday Night Book*, p. 53.

**Contra Formation:** Duple, proper/not cross over. Couples 1, 3, 5, and so on, active, do not cross over (duple, proper). In contra lines, hands joined, held at shoulder height, elbows V-shaped.

**Level:** Intermediate

**Note:** Instructions presented in measures, waltz rhythm. No call. Could prompt.

6

## *Directions* FOR THE DANCE

Meter 3/4

### Measures

| | |
|---|---|
| | Introduction: no action. |
| A 1–2 | Beginning right, take six steps; all move forward, partners passing right shoulders (drop hands and rejoin) to the opposite side. Now both lines face out from set. |

| | |
|---|---|
| 3–4 | Balance right and left, step swing or step touch. |
| 5–6 | Release hands. Beginning right, travel six steps clockwise, individually, in a circular pattern, about four feet in diameter, to face center of set. **Rejoin hands in lines.** |
| 7–8 | Repeat action of measures 3–4, balancing right and left. |
| 9–16 | Repeat action of measures A 1–8, returning to original position. |
| B 1–4 | Active couples, face up the set. Men turn left, women right, and travel down the outside of the set (twelve steps) passing two inactive couples. Cut through the line to meet partner in middle of set and join inside hands. |
| 5–6 | Moving up the set, active couple takes six steps to the inactive couple that was originally below them at beginning. Join hands in a line of four, facing up the set. |

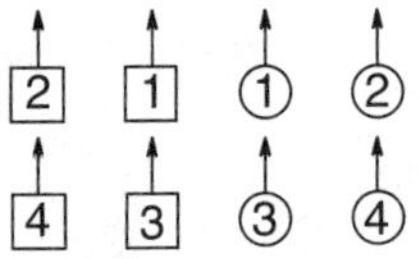


| | |
|---|---|
| 7–8 | All beginning right, balance right and left. |
| 9–10 | Inactives release actives' hands and continue to face up. Actives wheel around, man backing up, woman moving forward, taking six steps to face up. Line of four rejoin hands. |
| 11–12 | All beginning right, balance right and left. |
| 13–14 | Active couples release inside hands. Taking six steps, active person casts off with adjacent inactive person, hands still joined. Active is now below inactive, facing center. Both couples have progressed one position. |
| 15–16 | Rejoin hands in contra lines. Balance right and left. |

**Notes:**

1. Hills of Habersham was originally duple improper (actives crossed over). For beginners, this version (duple, proper) is easier to learn.
2. The balance of the original dance was step right, touch left toe, foot arched to right, body rising slightly on count 2, body lowering on count 3.
3. Dancers momentarily inactive balance right, then left alternately, keeping the waltz motion constant.

# *Hull's Victory*

HULL'S VICTORY is a traditional contra, a "New England Chestnut." This dance honors the battle in 1812 between the *USS Constitution*, commanded by Captain Isaac Hull, and the English ship, *HMS Guerriere*, commanded by Captain S. C. D'Acres.

**CD:** "Hull's Victory," New England Chestnuts, Vol. 1 & 2 GMM 2005.

**Music:** "Hull's Victory," Cole, M. M., *One Thousand Fiddle Tunes*, p. 103; Page, Ralph, *An Elegant Collection of Contras and Squares*, p. 57.

**Contra Formation:** Duple, proper/not cross over.

**Level:** Advanced.

## Directions FOR THE DANCE

A1 **Actives right hand to your partner, left hand across to the inactive** (4 counts). Active couples walk to center, join right hands, turn halfway and, still holding hands, join left hands with neighbor (inactive) across set. The inactive man has to make an adjustment stepping up the line and turning face down to accept the left hand of the active woman. Men face down the set, women up.

**Balance four in line** (8 counts). Balance four in line, step forward, touch; step back, touch.

**Allemande left your inactive twice around** (8 counts). Actives drop partner's hand, and allemande left neighbor twice around.

A2 **Allemande right your partner once around** (4 counts). Actives allemande right once around and form a line of four again.

**Balance four in line** (4 counts).

**Actives swing in center** (8 counts). End swing with woman on man's right facing down set. Join inside hands.

B1 **Down the center** (6 counts). Active couple walks down the set.

**Actives turn as a couple** (2 counts).

**Up the center, cast off** (6 counts). Couples walk up the set and cast off with original neighbor. Two men turn, arm around waist, as a couple; two women do same, to face center. Active couples have progressed one position.

B2 **Right and left thru over and back** (16 counts). Same two couples right and left thru over and back.

**Note:** Use pigeon wing position for balance and allemandes.

6

# *Jed's Reel*

*Included by permission of Penn Fix, Spokane, Washington.*

JED'S REEL is a contemporary contra, composed in 1983 by Penn Fix for his nephew.

**Music:** Reel.
**Contra Formation:** Duple, improper/cross over.
**Level:** Beginning 2.

## Directions FOR THE DANCE

A1 **Do-si-do the one below** (8 counts).

**Ladies do-si-do** (8 counts).

A2 **Men balance to each other** (4 counts). Men take right hands with one another and balance.

**Men do-si-do** (6 counts).

**Men allemande right once and a half** (6 counts). Finish this turn facing partners.

B1 **All balance and swing your partner** (16 counts). End the swing with the women on the right of their partners facing across the set.

B2 **Promenade across the set** (8 counts). Active couple passes left shoulder with inactives to change places. Turn as couples to face the center of the set. And join hands.

**Circle left three-quarters around** (6 counts).

**Pass thru up and down** (2 counts). Pass right shoulders with the original inactive onto the next.

6

# *Lady of the Lake*

LADY OF THE LAKE is a traditional contra, a "New England Chestnut."

**CD:** "Lady of the Lake," New England Chestnuts, Vol. 1 & 2 GMM 2005; Folkraft 2910-5.
**Music:** "Miller's Reel," Cole, M. M., *One Thousand Fiddle Tunes.*
**Contra Formation:** Duple, improper/cross over.
**Level:** Beginning 1.

## *Directions* FOR THE DANCE

A1 **Balance and swing the one below** (16 counts). Actives balance and swing the inactive below.

A2 **Actives balance and swing in the center** (16 counts). Actives swing their partner. Finish the swing facing down with active woman on the right.

B1 **Actives down the center** (6 counts). Active couples, inside hands joined, walk down the center.

**Turn alone** (2 counts). Turn alone to face up the set.

B2 **And come back, cast off** (8 counts). Join hands, return to original position, cast off, walk around inactive person, progressing one position down. Inactive does not turn.

**Ladies chain over and back** (16 counts). Ladies chain with original inactives.

# *More Again*

*Included by permission of Penn Fix, Spokane, Washington.*

MORE AGAIN is a contemporary contra composed by Penn Fix in 1996. It is a revision of an earlier dance of his called Settlement Swing. The dance is dedicated to his daughter Louise, who, at an early age, when wanting something in addition, would simply say "more again!"

**Music:** Reel.
**Contra Formation:** Duple, improper/cross over.
**Level:** Intermediate.

6

## *Directions* FOR THE DANCE

A1 **Do-si-do with the one below** (8 counts).

**Men face out and women face, join hands in wavy lines, and balance** (4 counts). After the do-si-do, dancers make long lines along their sides by taking one another's hands; men are facing out of the set and women are facing into the center.

**Turn the one on the right all the way around** (4 counts). Allemande right the person in your right hand once all the way around and back to the place where you started the turn.

A2 **Turn the one on the left all the way around** (4 counts). Allemande left the person who was in your left hand once all the way around and back to the place where you started the turn. For those couples at the top and bottom of the set, there may not be anyone to turn with. In that case, simply turn to face your original neighbor.

**All swing the one on the right** (12 counts). Swing your original neighbor; for the active couples this is the inactive neighbor below you.

B1 **Men allemande left once and a half** (8 counts). Men turn left with the dancer across the set. Men finish the turn facing their partner on the woman's side of the set.

**All swing your partner** (8 counts).

B2 **All promenade with your partner across the set** (8 counts). Change places with the couple across by passing right shoulders as a couple. Turn and face them again.

**Circle left three-quarters round** (6 counts). Finish the circle back in your original positions with the actives facing down and the inactives facing up.

**Pass thru onto the next** (2 counts). Couples pass right shoulders with their neighbors onto the next neighbors, moving smoothly into the do-si-do. They will turn the old neighbors by the left and the new ones by the right.

# *The Nova Scotian*

The Nova Scotian is an original dance by Maurice Henneger of Halifax, Nova Scotia, and was arranged by Ralph Page in 1954.

**CD:** Folkraft 2912; "Portland Fancy."

**Music:** "Speed the Plough," Cole, M. M., *One Thousand Fiddle Tunes.*

**Contra Formation:** Duple, improper/cross over.

**Level:** Beginning 1.

## *Directions* FOR THE DANCE

A1 **Allemande left with the one below** (4 counts). Active couples allemande left the inactives.

**Come back to the middle and swing your own** (12 counts). Active couples swing in center set. Finish the swing facing down with the active woman on the right.

A2 **Go down the center three in line** (6 counts). Active couple and inactive woman (active man has a woman on either side of him, partner on his right, inactive woman on his left) take six walking steps toward bottom of set.

**Right hand high, left hand under** (2 counts)**, return to place** (8 counts). Active man makes an arch with his right hand and his partner's left; left-hand woman walks under this arch as man's partner walks to other side, taking left-hand woman's place in line. Man now turns under his own right arm (2 counts). All are now facing up the set. Line of three returns to place with walking steps.

| | |
|---|---|
| B1 | **Ladies chain** (8 counts). Women chain to opposite side, courtesy turn. *Do not return.* |
| | **Circle left once around** (8 counts). Same two couples join hands and circle left. |
| B2 | **Right and left, over and back** (16 counts). Same two couples right and left through across the set and back. They then turn away from each other to face the next in line to start the dance again. |

# The Other Mary Kay

*Included by permission of Tom Hinds, Faber, Virginia.*

THE OTHER MARY KAY is a contemporary contra composed by Tom Hinds.

**Music:** Jig or reel.
**Contra Formation:** Becket. Refer to page 198, Diagram 3.
**Level:** Advanced.

## Directions FOR THE DANCE

| | |
|---|---|
| A1 | **Circle left three-quarters around** (6 counts). Join hands with couple across the set and circle so that couples are facing up and down the set. |
| | **Pass through up and down** (2 counts). Pass right shoulders with the original neighbor (1) and face the next neighbor (2). |
| | **With the next, do-si-do** (8 counts). With the new neighbor (2) do-si-do. Afterwards, turn to face the original neighbor (1). |
| A2 | **Star left with original neighbors** (8 counts). With couple that you circle with in A1, star once around back to the new neighbor (2). |
| | **Swing the new neighbor** (8 counts). Swing the neighbor you do-si-do with in A1. Finish the swing facing across the set. The rest of the dance is done with this second couple. |
| B1 | **Men allemande left once and a half around** (8 counts). Two men in the couples facing across from one another, turn by the left to face partners. |
| | **Half a hey for four** (8 counts). Men start by passing right shoulders with partners on the outside of the set. Women next go to the center and pass left shoulders; then pass the opposite partner on the other side of the set. |
| B2 | **All balance and swing your partner** (16 counts). All couples are swinging on the original side of the set. Finish the swing facing across the set. The couple you heyed with in B1 is the same couple you start the dance with again. |

**Note:** Neutral couple wait out as if it is an improper/cross over dance even though it is in Becket formation.

# Petronella

PETRONELLA is a traditional contra, a "New England Chestnut." It is an original dance introduced by Nathaniel Gow of Edinburgh, Scotland, in 1820. Gow's version danced a poussette; the American version is a right and left thru.

**CD:** "Petronella," New England Chestnuts, GMM 2005; Folkraft 2909-1.
**Music:** "Pat'nella," Page, Ralph, *An Elegant Collection of Contras and Squares,* p. 73.
**Contra Formation:** Proper/not cross over.
**Level:** Advanced.

## Directions FOR THE DANCE

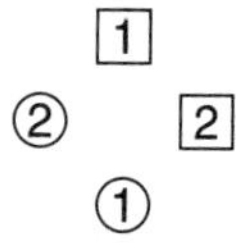

Diagram A
First Balance

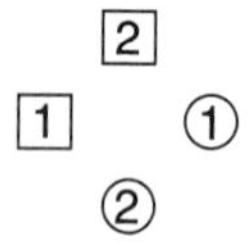

Diagram B
Second Balance

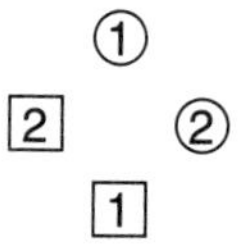

Diagram C
Third Balance

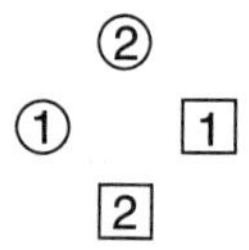

Diagram D
Fourth Balance

A1 **Active man drops between two, join hands** (4 counts) **and balance** (4 counts). To start, the active man turns into the center, between and just below the inactives. He is facing up the set. At the same time, his partner turns into the center, facing down. Then all four join hands to balance to the right and then to the left. See Diagram A.

**Turn to the right a quarter round** (4 counts) **and balance** (4 counts). All drop hands, turn individually clockwise 360° and moving a quarter around. All face in and join hands and balance right and left. See Diagram B.

A2 **Turn to the right a quarter 'round** (4 counts) **and balance** (4 counts). See Diagram C.

**Turn to the right a quarter 'round** (4 counts) **and balance** (4 counts). See Diagram D.

Starting with A1, actives turning into the center, the turn and balance is repeated a total of four times.

B1 **Down the center, turn alone** (8 counts). The inactive couple quickly moves into their original position so that the active couple may walk down the center. Each person turns alone, counts 7–8.

**Back to place and cast off** (8 counts). Active couple returns to original position, separate and walk around the one below and progresses down the set one position.

B2 **Right and left thru** (8 counts). Active couple and couple above right and left thru, two men passing right shoulders with opposite two women. No hands used in right and left thru. Two men and two women turn as a unit.

**And right and left back** (8 counts).

**Note:** In the original Petronella, the active couples had most of the action. Through the "folk process" the turn and balance was reversed so that the inactive couples were dancing more. The original Petronella is presented in the following variation.

Variation

**ORIGINAL PETRONELLA**

A1, A2 In **minor sets,** beginning right, active couples balance in the center of the set. Partners individually travel on a right diagonal, turn clockwise three-quarters, taking four steps (right, left, right, left) to face partner. Men will face up the set, women will face down.

Repeat three more times.

# *Roadblock Reel*

*Included by permission of Bob Dalsemer of Hayesville, North Carolina.*

ROADBLOCK REEL is a contemporary contra, composed by Bob Dalsemer.

**Music:** Jig or reel.
**Contra Formation:** Duple, improper/cross over.
**Level:** Intermediate.

## Directions FOR THE DANCE

A1 **In long lines, go forward and back** (8 counts).

**Pass thru across** (4 counts). Everyone changes places with their partners by passing right shoulders across the set. The actives turn to face the inactives below.

**Allemande right the one below** (4 counts). Once across the set, actives turn inactive below about three-quarters round. Finish this turn with women in the center. They join left hands and continue to hold right hands with their neighbors.

A2 **Across the set balance in line** (4 counts). In an **ocean wave,** balance to the right and left.

**Women allemande left halfway** (4 counts). Turn to face partners.

**All swing your partner** (8 counts). Finish the swing facing down the set with women on right of partner. Join hands with the couple across the set.

B1 **Down the center four in line** (6 counts). Actives are on the right side, inactives on the left.

**Turn alone** (2 counts). All drop hands, turn to face up and join hands again.

**Come back four in line** (6 counts). Bend the line (2 counts).

B2 **Circle left three-quarters round** (6 counts). After the circle, couples are back to where they started the dance in A1.

**Swing the original one below** (10 counts). Men finish the swing with women on their right facing across the set. This progression move occurs at the very end of the dance. Begin again by going forward and back and actives then dance with the next below.

# *Roll in the Hey*

*Included by permission of Roger Diggle, Madison, Wisconsin.*

Roll in the Hey is a contemporary contra, composed by Roger Diggle. This dance was composed in January 1985 with the idea of testing the transition, "hey for four passing right shoulders in the center, then circle left with someone new." The test has been successful. This contra is similar to the dance "The Bluemont Reel" by Warren Hofstra.

**Music:** Jig.
**Contra Formation:** Duple, improper/cross over.
**Level:** Beginning 3.

## Directions FOR THE DANCE

A1 **Circle left once around** (8 counts). Actives circle with inactive couple below.

**Swing the one below** (8 counts). Actives swing the inactives, finishing the swing with women on the right facing across the set.

A2 **Circle left three-quarters round** (6 counts). The same couples circle round. Finish the circle with partners on the men's original side.

**All swing your partner** (10 counts). Everyone swing your partner on the men's original sides. Finish the swing with the woman on the right of her partner facing across the set and join hands along the lines.

B1 **In long lines, go forward and back** (8 counts).

**Ladies chain** (8 counts). Do not return but finish with the women ready to return to the center of the set.

B2 **Hey for four** (16 counts). Women start the hey passing right shoulders in the center of the set. This hey ends after the men pass by the right shoulders in the center for the second time. Couples then progress to the next couple. Actives move down and inactives up to join in a circle with the new couples.

# Rory O'More

RORY O'MORE is a traditional contra, a "New England Chestnut." Samuel Lover, the grandfather of Victor Herbert, wrote the words and music of "Rory O'More."

**CD:** "Rory O'More," New England Chestnuts, Vol. 1 & 2 GMM 2005.
**Music:** Cole, M. M., *One Thousand Fiddle Tunes*, p. 62.
**Contra Formation:** Duple, proper/not cross over.
**Level:** Advanced.

## Directions FOR THE DANCE

A1 **Actives cross over and down the outside. Down below one** (8 counts). Actives take right hands, pass by, crossing to opposite side; walk down the outside of line, go around one person, and cut into middle of set to meet partner.

**Up the center, cross over. Cast off and actives join hands in the center** (8 counts). Walk up the center, release hands, cross to own side, woman crossing in front of partner; cast off, walk around the couple originally below the active couple, to face center. Active couples have now progressed one position down. Active couples move to center of the set, partners join right hands, and join left hands with adjacent active couple. Three lines will exist, two on the outside (inactive dancers) and one in the middle (active couples).

A2 **Balance right and left and slide right** (8 counts). Actives balance right and left. Release hands, take three slides and a step to right, past partner. Join left hands with partner and right hands with neighbor.

**Balance left and right and slide left** (8 counts). Actives balance left and right. Release hands, take three slides and a step to left, past partner.

B1 **Turn contra corners** (16 counts). Actives turn contra corners.

B2 **Actives balance and swing in center of set** (16 counts). At end of swing, dancers back into their own line, below the original inactives and ready to dance with the next inactive below.

# Salmonchanted Evening

*Included by permission of Steve Zakon, East Sullivan, New Hampshire.*

SALMONCHANTED EVENING is a contemporary contra, composed by Steve Zakon in March 1987. Zakon wrote the dance in honor of the band Fresh Fish, just before going on a three-week tour with them. Originally the dance was called "Not Tonight, I've Got a Haddock." Within a week it was renamed "Salmonchanted Evening"—a nonsense word, a delightful play on the words "some enchanted evening."

**Music:** Smooth tunes, well-phrased, such as jigs.

**Contra Formation:** Duple, improper/cross over.

**Level:** Beginning 2.

## Directions FOR THE DANCE

A1 **Allemande right below once and a half** (8 counts). Actives allemande with inactives once and a half. End with both men in center.

**Men allemande left once and a half** (8 counts). Men end on opposite sides facing partner on the other side.

A2 **All Gypsy partner on the side** (8 counts). **Gypsy** with partner by the right shoulder.

**All swing your partner** (8 counts).

B1 **Chain the ladies over and back** (16 counts).

B2 **Right and left thru** (8 counts). Right and left thru. *Do not return.*

**Circle left three-quarters** (6 counts). Join hands and circle left three-quarters. Active couples will face down the set; inactive couples will face up the set.

**Pass thru** (2 counts). Actives pass right shoulders with the inactives below and progress to the next inactive couple.

6

# Shadrack's Delight

*Included by permission of Tony Parkes, Billerica, Massachusetts.*

SHADRACK'S DELIGHT is a contemporary contra. It is an original dance by Tony Parkes. The dance was named for Betty and "Shadrack" McDermid.

**Music:** Scottish jig suggested. "Lamb Skinnet."
**Contra Formation:** Duple, improper/cross over.
**Level:** Intermediate.

## *Directions* FOR THE DANCE

A1 **Do-si-do the one below, go once and a quarter** (8 counts). End in a line of four across the set, actives face down the set, inactives face up the set.

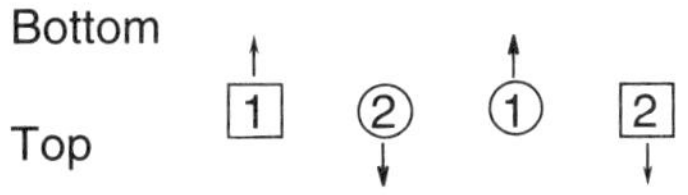


**Balance four in line** (4 counts). Begin balance to the right and then left (Ocean Wave). Look at the person in the direction of the balance.

**Turn half by the right** (4 counts). Turn neighbor by the right half-way, continue to hold hands with neighbor. Men meet in the center, take left hands. Actives end facing up the set, inactives facing down the set. Join hands in line of four.

A2 **Balance four in line** (4 counts).

**Men turn half by the left** (4 counts).

**All swing your partners** (8 counts). End with woman on right side of man, line of four, facing down the set, hands joined.

B1 **Down the center four in a line** (6 counts).

**Turn as a couple** (2 counts). Both men turn their partner so that the women remain on the right side of men and face up.

**Return to place, cast off** (8 counts). Cast off (4 counts); each couple, arm around waist, take four steps, turning out to face center.

B2 **Right and left thru across** (8 counts). Counter turn. Do not return. Active men will have progressed one position down.

**Same two ladies chain** (8 counts). Do not return. Women progress one position down, progression complete.

**Note:** Sometimes danced without the cast-off for a smoother transition in the women's line.

# Small Potatoes

*Included by permission of Jim Kitch, Phoenixville, Pennsylvania.*

SMALL POTATOES is a contemporary contra, composed by Jim Kitch.

**Music:** Jig or reel.
**Contra Formation:** Duple, improper/cross over.
**Level:** Beginning 2.

## Directions FOR THE DANCE

A1 **Balance and swing the one below** (16 counts). Actives swing with the inactive below, finishing the swing with woman on the right facing across the set.

A2 **Circle left once around** (8 counts). The circle starts and ends in this progressed position with actives below the original inactives.

**Ladies chain** (8 counts). Women chain to their partners but do not return.

B1 **Women do-si-do** (8 counts). Finish by turning to face partner.

**All swing your partner** (8 counts). Finish the swing with women on the right of the men facing across the set.

B2 **Circle left three-quarters round** (6 counts). Join hands with the couple across and circle back to original positions in A1.

**Pass thru up and down** (2 counts). Drop hands and pass right shoulders with original inactives onto the next couple.

**Actives do-si-do with your new neighbor** (8 counts). Begin the dance again with this same inactive couple by balance and swinging.

6

# *So When Was the Wedding?*

*Included by permission of Erik Hoffman, Oakland, California.*

So When Was the Wedding? is a contemporary contra composed by Erik Hoffman in 1991 to honor friends who were married at an earlier date. He called the dance at their reception and asked the question at the same time.

**Music:** Smooth flowing tunes, usually reels
**Contra Formation:** Duple, improper/cross over.
**Level:** Beginning 1.

## *Directions* FOR THE DANCE

A1 **In long lines, go forward and back** (8 counts).

**Swing your neighbor** (8 counts). Actives swing the inactives below and finish the swing with the woman on the right, facing across the set from their partner.

A2 **Women walk forward to partners** (4 counts). Men wait for women to come to them.

**Women pull partners back to women's place** (4 counts). Women take partners by two hands and back up to original side.

**All swing your partner** (8 counts). Finish the swing, face down the set with women on the right of men.

B1 **Go down the center four in line** (6 counts), **turn as couples** (2 counts).

**Return four in line** (6 counts), **bend the line** (2 counts). After bending the line, couples release connecting hands to face one another across the set.

B2 **Half right and left thru** (8 counts) with the couple you have been dancing with.

**Half ladies chain** (8 counts). Send your partner back to the other line. Actives will swing the inactive below.

# *Stars of Alberta*

*Included by permission of Carol Ormand, McFarland, Wisconsin.*

STARS OF ALBERTA is a contemporary contra composed by Carol Ormand in 1996 who has called frequently in the mid-west. This dance was written for four young very fine Canadian fiddlers during one of her trips north.

**Music:** Smooth flowing tunes, usually reels
**Contra Formation:** Duple, improper/cross over
**Level:** Beginning 3

## *Directions* FOR THE DANCE

A1 **Allemande right your neighbor once and a half** (8 counts).

**With the next below, star left** (8 counts). The allemande turn progresses couples to the next couple in line. With your partner, dance a star left with the next couple in line.

A2 **With the original neighbor, star right three-quarters** (6 counts). After completing the left hand star, look for the original couple you did the allemande with and form a right hand star.

**All swing your partner** (10 counts). Make sure to turn the star just three-quarters so that partners are o n the same side of the contra line.

B1 **In long lines, go forward and back** (8 counts). At the end of the swing, face in with the woman on the right of her partner.

**Half ladies chain** (8 counts). Chain your partner away from you.

B2 **Hey for four** (16 counts). Women begin the hey passing right shoulders in the center. This hey ends after the men pass by the right shoulders in the center for the second time. Couples then progress to the next couple.

6

# *Supernova Scotian*

*Included by permission of David Smukler of Syracuse, New York.*

SUPERNOVA SCOTIAN is a contemporary dance composed by David Smukler in 1993. Inspired by the Nova Scotian, this new contra reflects the more symmetrical nature of current contemporary dances.

**Music:** Smooth flowing tunes, usually reels.
**Contra Formation:** Duple, improper/cross over.
**Level:** Beginning 1.

## Directions FOR THE DANCE

A1 **Do-si-do your neighbor** (8 counts).

**Actives do-si-do** (8 counts). After the do-si-dos, the active woman goes into the center, faces down the hall, and takes her partner in her left hand and the inactive man in her right hand to face down the hall three in a line.

A2 **Down the hall, three in line** (6 counts). Remember the active woman is between the two men. The inactive woman remains back in her home place.

**Right hand high and left hand under and return to place** (10 counts). The active woman makes an arch with her right hand and the inactive man's left hand; her partner walks under this arch as the inactive man walks to the other side. The active woman now turns under her own right arm. All are now facing up the set. The line of three returns to place.

B1 **All balance and swing partners** (16 counts). Women are swinging on their own sides. Finish the swing facing into the center of the set with the women on the right of their partners.

B2 **Half right and left thru** (8 counts).

**Circle left three-quarters** (6 counts).

**Pass thru up and down** (2 counts). Pass right shoulders with original inactive and move onto the next inactive to start the dance again.

6

# Symmetrical Force

*Included by permission of Fred Feild, Tucson, Arizona.*

SYMMETRICAL FORCE is a contemporary contra, composed by Fred Feild in 1979. The founder of the Chicago Barn Dance Company, Feild incorporated southern Appalachian figures in this dance to interest contra dancers in squares and big circle dances.

**Music:** Reel.
**Contra Formation:** Duple, improper/cross over.
**Level:** Beginning 3.

## Directions FOR THE DANCE

A1 **Do-si-do inside first, then outside with the ones below** (8 counts). Also known as a mirror do-si-do, the actives start the do-si-do by both going down the center of the set, splitting the inactives and going around the outside of them back to place. The active man starts by passing left shoulders and active lady, right shoulders.

**Allemande the ones below *twice* around with the handy hand** (8 counts). Active man turns inactive lady with left hand while active woman turns inactive man with right hand. Finish with the actives in the center of the set.

A2 **Actives swing your partner** (16 counts). Actives end the swing facing down the set with woman on right of partner. Join hands with original neighbors on the outside of the line.

B1 **Down the center four in line** (6 counts). Actives are in the middle of the line of four.

**Actives back under own joined hands, while inactives turn in to face up** (2 counts). Without dropping any hands, the actives bring their joined hands over their heads, turn away from their partners, and bring their arms down in front of them. The arms end up crossed in front, forming two leaves of a clover.

**Come back up** (8 counts) in a line of four.

B2 **Inactives join hands on top and circle left** (8 counts). After returning four in line, the inactives join their free hands on top to complete the four-leaf clover. The circle of four then moves to the left.

**Inactives arch, actives go through, unwinding** (4 counts.) Inactives raise their joined hands and pull actives under their arch. All continue to hold joined hands in a circle.

**Actives then go under again to the next** (4 counts). Actives go through the arch of the inactives and thereby go down the center to the next inactive couple to start the dance again. Remember both active man and woman remain in the center of the set for the do-si-do.

# *Thorn Street Gypsy*

*Included by permission of Graham Hempel, San Diego, CA.*

THORN STREET GYPSY is a contemporary contra. It is an original dance composed by Graham Hempel on March 29, 1996. Hempel wrote the dance in honor of the San Diego Folk Heritage dancers that meet every week on Thorn Street in the North Park district of San Diego, where he regularly calls.

**Music:** Smooth flowing reels in a minor key.
**Contra Formation:** Duple, improper/cross over and double progression.
**Level:** Beginning 3.

## Directions FOR THE DANCE

| | |
|---|---|
| A1 | **All gypsy your neighbor** (8 counts). Actives gypsy the neighbor below (first neighbor). |
| | **All Swing that neighbor** (8 counts). Actives swing same neighbor and end facing across (first progression). |
| A2 | **Actives gypsy your partner** (8 counts). Gypsy in the center. |
| | **Actives swing your partner** (8 counts). End the swing facing down. |
| B1 | **Go down the hall four in line with the next** (8 counts). Actives step in between the couple below (second neighbors), form a line of four, and with them go down the hall (second progression). |
| | **Turn alone and come back up the hall** (8 counts). Turn around and in a line of four come back up the hall in a line of four. |
| B2 | **Circle to the left** (8 counts). Ends close in and form a circle of four; circle to the left. |
| | **Left hand star** (8 counts). Put your left hand in and turn a left hand star the other way back. Look for the next (third neighbor). |

**Note:**
In this **double progression dance,** the actives progress through two inactive couples during a single sequence and begin the dance sequence again with the third inactive couple.

6

# The Tourist

*Included by permission of Ted Sannella.*

THE TOURIST is a contemporary contra. It is an original dance by Ted Sannella, 1970. This version was arranged by Ralph Page.

**CD:** "Lamplighter's Hornpipe," Folk Dancer 18.
**Music:** "Lamplighter's Hornpipe," Cole, M. M., *One Thousand Fiddle Tunes.*
**Contra Formation:** Duple, improper/cross over.
**Level:** Beginning 1.

## Directions FOR THE DANCE

A1 **Down the outside of the set, turn** (8 counts). Active couples turn out and walk down outside of set, behind their own respective lines, eight steps. Each turns toward center of set on counts 7–8.

**Come right back** (8 counts).

A2 **Into the center with a do-si-do** (8 counts). Active couples step to middle of set and do-si-do.

**Circle four hands once around** (8 counts). Actives join hands with the active couple below, circle left once around.

B1 **Balance and swing the one below** (16 counts). Active balance and swing the same inactive as in A2. Finish the swing facing across the set, ready to ladies chain.

B2 **Ladies chain over and back** (16 counts).

6

# *Weave the Line*

*Included by permission of Kathy Anderson, Dayton, Ohio.*

WEAVE THE LINE is a contemporary contra, composed by Kathy Anderson.

**Music:** Jig or reel.
**Contra Formation:** Duple, improper/cross over–double progression.
**Level:** Intermediate.

## Directions FOR THE DANCE

A1 **Actives star left below** (8 counts). Actives star with inactives below.

**Circle left once around** (8 counts). Actives with the same inactives circle.

A2 **Weave the line past two couples** (8 counts). Holding inside hands with partner, progress past two couples. Actives move to the left to pass the first inactive couple, women passing right shoulders. Then moving to the right, they pass the second inactive couple, men passing left shoulders. Actives are now facing a third inactive couple. At the ends, neutral couples immediately turn as couples to face into the set and reenter.

**Actives as individuals do-si-do inactives 3** (8 counts). Drop hands with partners and do-si-do the inactive in the third group.

B1 **Actives balance and swing inactives 2** (16 counts). After the do-si-do with the inactive 3, everyone turn away to face the inactives 2 to balance and swing. Finish the swing, facing across the set and join hands along the lines.

B2 **In long lines, go forward and back** (8 counts).

**Actives swing your partner in the center** (8 counts). Actives finish the swing facing down the set to star left with the next couple who was originally inactive 3.

**Note:** In this **double progression dance,** the actives progress through two inactive couples during a single sequence and begin the dance sequence again with the third inactive couple.

# *With Thanks to the Dean*

*Included by permission of Steve Zakon, East Sullivan, New Hampshire.*

WITH THANKS TO THE DEAN is a contemporary dance composed by Steve Zakon in 1985. This dance salutes the dean of contra dancing, Ralph Page. Zakon wrote the dance in Page's memory to thank him for his efforts to keep contra dancing alive and vital for generations to follow.

**Music:** Smooth flowing tunes, usually reels.
**Contra Formation:** Duple, improper/cross over and double progression.
**Level:** Intermediate.

## Directions FOR THE DANCE

A1 **Allemande left below, go once and a half** (8 counts). Actives allemande left the one below, turn once and a half. End with women facing to the center.

**Ladies chain** (8 counts). Courtesy turn. Do not chain back.

A2 **Ladies allemande right** (4 counts). With right hand, women turn once round to face partner.

**All swing your partner** (12 counts). Everyone swings partner. Finish swing with women on right of partners, facing into the center of the set.

B1 **Circle left, once around** (8 counts). Join hands with the couple across the set and circle left once. All couples slide to the left (along the line), picking up the next couple (first progression). Men take responsibility to slide left with your partner.

| | | |
|---|---|---|
| Bottom | [5] | [6] |
| | ⑤ | ⑥ |
| | [3] | [4] |
| | ③ | ④ |
| | [1] | ② |
| Top | ① | [2] |

Start and finish of circle left once around.

**Couples move left along the line** (2 counts).

**Circle left with the next three-quarters round** (6 counts). Finish the circle with the actives facing down and inactives facing up, ready to do-si-do with one another.

| | | |
|---|---|---|
| Bottom | [3] | ⑥ |
| | ③ | [6] |
| | [1] | ④ |
| | ① | [4] |
| | | ② |
| Top | | [2] |

Start of circle left three-quarters around

| | | |
|---|---|---|
| Bottom | ⑥ | [6] |
| | [3] | ③ |
| | ④ | [4] |
| Top | [1] | ① |

End of circle left three-quarters round

B2 **Do-si-do the second inactive** (8 counts). With the ones you circled three-quarters, do-si-do.

**Allemande right the same once and a half** (8 counts). The active couple progresses one position down at the end of the allemande (second progression). The left hand is free to start the dance over with "Allemande left" with a new couple.

| | | |
|---|---|---|
| Bottom | ⑤ | [5] |
| | [3] | ③ |
| | ⑥ | [6] |
| | [1] | ① |
| | ④ | [4] |
| Top | [2] | ② |

# 7 INTERNATIONAL FOLK DANCE

## Introduction

*The dance of a cultural group is considered its folk dance, sometimes referred to as peasant or ethnic dance. It is the story of a people's culture expressed through movement. Folk dances are influenced by religion, music, costumes, and geography, and are used to reinforce a culture's sense of identity. They celebrate rituals (planting or harvest) or rites of passage (birth, death, marriage). Being an intimate part of a culture, folk dances provide a storehouse of tradition. Folk dances also reflect changing social conditions, and for that reason may be considered living history.*

### Folk Dance in Industrialized Society

By the 1800s, the impact of the industrial revolution in Europe and the United States threatened to blot out the natural flow of folk expression. For example, the dance ritual before planting in the spring was no longer needed to ensure a bountiful crop—science explained what made the seeds grow. Similarly, traditional village costumes were set aside as people began to wear modern city clothing.

The threatened disappearance of folkways, songs, music, costumes, and dances spurred governments, private individuals, and organizations to make concerted efforts to preserve these traditions. Organized efforts to revive interest in folk traditions began at different times in different countries, but in each the main thrust was to collect, note, and preserve in national repositories the finest possible examples of folk song, dance, music, costume, and art.

# Folk Dance Movement

## Preserving Folk Dancing

In Sweden, Arthur Hazelius created the Nordiskz Museet, or Northland Museum, to house rare folk dances and folk art. In 1893, the Friends of Swedish Folk Dance was formed. This and other organizations have worked to make this phase of Swedish culture known to every generation. The revival movement led to formation of the Danish Folk Dance Society in 1901. In 1911, Cecil Sharp, an English writer and musician, helped found the English Folk Dance Society. Branches of this society have been established throughout the British Commonwealth and America.

A series of events prior to the outbreak of World War II marked the revival of the folk dance movement in Europe. In 1928, the International Congress of Popular Arts was held in Prague; 31 nations attended the Congress, convened by the Assembly of the League of Nations. The purpose was to study the geographical distribution of the different artistic forms of folk life and to compile records and devise methods for encouraging and preserving the popular arts still in existence. In 1935, the English Folk Dance Society and the British National Committee on Folk Arts sponsored an International Folk Dance Festival in London. In 1939, a second Congress was held in Stockholm, Sweden. Some 3,000 delegates and officials attended. The program provided opportunity for presentation of papers, discussions, and dance demonstrations by the various national groups in attendance.

## Folk Dance in the United States

In the early 1900s, folk dancing was found in major U.S. urban areas, such as New York, Chicago, and San Francisco, preserved by ethnic groups for social events and festivals. People outside the cultural community came to the festivals as spectators. Schools made use of folk dancing, but folk dancing was seldom of interest as a community activity. Many organizations tried to integrate folk dancing into community recreational programs, but it remained a special exhibition event. Between 1930 and 1940 the Folk Festival Council of New York struggled to make folk dancing a popular recreational activity, with little result.

A major boost to international folk dance was felt in 1940 when the New York World's Fair and the San Francisco World's Fair introduced folk dance as an attraction for public participation. The enthusiastic response by the general public led to the formation of two major centers for the lay-folk dance movement: the Folk Dance House, founded by Michael and Mary Ann Herman in New York City, and Chang's International Dancers, formed by Soon Chang in San Francisco. The California Folk Dance Federation, Country Dance and Song Society (CDSS), New England Folk Festival Association (NEFFA), and Texas Folk Dance Camp (TFDC) have promoted folk dance. These East-West urban strongholds of international dancing have produced thousands of folk dancers who have, in turn, spread the fun and enjoyment of folk dance throughout America.

After World War II, many international folk dance performing groups traveled to share their culture around the world. Sol Hurok, a dance promoter, brought the Russian Moiseyev Dance Ensemble to the United States. He was the first to bring folklore to the theater. This heightened the general population's awareness of folk dancing and added greatly to the folk dance movement. By the end of the 1940s, communities and colleges throughout the United States boasted recreational and performance folk dance groups.

Although most folk dances in the 1930s and 1940s were couples dances, examples of line dances can be found. For instance, Michael Herman and Vyts Beliajus taught some kolos, line dances learned from eastern European immigrants. Then, in the 1950s, Dick Crum introduced dances from the Balkan region of eastern Europe. In 1951, Fred Berk started a weekly Israeli folk dance session in New York. These innovative programs changed the perception of international folk dancing away from European couple dances. Balkan and Israeli dances were mostly line and circle dances, and people could participate without worrying about having a partner. With the introduction of this style, recreational folk dancing grew significantly and was very popular from the 1960s to the 1980s, reaching its peak in the mid-1970s.

During this time, generalized folk dance teachers gave way to specialists who taught dances of a single nationality. These specialists would present new material at dance camps, workshops, and festivals throughout the United States. Traditional folk costumes were commonly part of the folk dancing events. Dancers wanting more information could go on guided tours to European dance festivals to see the dance performed in a truly ethnic form.

Many dancers were also drawn to the musical side of folklore. Perhaps resulting from the popularity of folk singers, dancers dusted off guitars and violins. Interest in playing ethnic instruments grew. Dancing to live music gave a burst of new enthusiasm to the folk dancing community.

However, as the 1980s drew to a close, younger generations were attracted to other types of music and dance, and interest in folk dancing declined. By 1990, colleges and universities changed physical education classes to electives, and most folk dance classes were discontinued.

Today, as at the beginning of the twentieth century, folk dance clubs are found mostly in big urban centers. International folk dancing is still strong where it is supported by local ethnic populations, and thousands of community recreational folk dance groups still exist. In contrast, only a few universities offer international folk dance classes or recreational dance programs. As trends and fads come and go, there may be a new spark that brings folk dancing back to mainstream public attention. An activity that supports understanding and tolerance of other cultures and has the extra benefit of aerobic exercise is worth the effort! *Dance A While* will be a valuable resource for anyone wanting to promote or take part in this valuable and healthy activity. To the next generation of folk dancers!

## History of Folk Dance in American Education

Educators and educational institutions have played a role in research, teaching, and fostering the use of folk dance in schools and recreation programs. Elizabeth Burchenal and C. Ward Crampton were two early researchers and collectors of traditional folk dances as they were being performed in European countries. By the beginning of the twentieth century, folk dance was widely used in physical education in secondary schools and colleges.

Elizabeth Burchenal's research and collection of dance materials from original European sources brought a wealth of folk dance materials to schools and recreation programs in the early 1900s. As chairman of the folk dance committee of the Playground and Recreation Association of America, she was instrumental in introducing folk dance to a wide audience and training many teachers over several decades. Burchenal became the first president of the American Folk Dance Society, which was formed in 1916.

Mary Wood Hinman, a physical educator of exceptional vision, worked to provide an appropriate and meaningful way for ethnic groups to perform and share their cultural heritage with other Americans. Her work resulted in a series of folk dance courses being offered at the New School of Social Research in New York City in 1933. The courses were designed to provide an opportunity for various ethnic groups to teach their native songs and dances to people of all backgrounds. With the same philosophy in mind, Hinman was instrumental in establishing Folk Festival Councils in other American cities.

Physical education departments at both public schools and colleges have influenced international folk dance by offering classes and research, maintaining performing groups, and sponsoring foreign teachers on the circuit.

## Camps

The *folk dance camp* became a popular vehicle for dancers and leaders alike to enjoy a total folk experience by learning about other cultures through dance, crafts, songs, games, costumes, and ethnic foods. They even provided a chance to celebrate a Swedish Christmas in July! Jane Farwell established the first such camp at Oglebay Institute in West Virginia in the early 1940s. Jane Farwell is easily the "Johnny Appleseed" of folk dance camps–she organized and conducted successful camps from Florida to Maine. The idea spread, and in the late 1940s and early 1950s camps influenced by her idea or led by her enthusiasm were in operation across America.

Today the folk dance camp is the prime vacation choice for thousands of folk-dancing Americans. Camps attract the top teaching professionals who represent specific ethnic groups. Camp programs include complete syllabi of material taught, adventures in gourmet foods from many nationalities, special classes in folk singing, expert guidance in making costumes, and more often than not all of this *and* college credits! Folk dance camps have come a long way since Jane Farwell and her campers "washed their faces in the May morning dew 'midst the fairy rings on a West Virginia hillside."

## Performing Groups

International folk dance performing groups are sponsored by different sources, such as colleges (for example, the Tamburitzans of Duquesne University) or specific ethnic groups. Performance demands have made it necessary for many groups to develop full-time professional staff to take care of their rehearsal and performance needs. Several of the more outstanding groups have become fully professional dance troupes. These highly skilled and brilliantly costumed groups give concerts and conduct classes and workshops in the communities in which they perform. Performing groups acquire extensive costume collections, acquire musical instruments unique to the nationalities they represent, and engage musicians for orchestral accompaniment. Members of the group actively participate in the research into the background of the dances and nationalities they represent. Groups travel extensively at home and abroad and are often invited to perform at important national festivals and events. For example, the Brigham Young University International Folk Dance Ensemble performed in the opening ceremony of the Salt Lake City 2002 Winter Olympics. Groups may perform in 100 or more concerts each year.

## Research and Advanced Studies

Academia and institutions like the Smithsonian and the Library of Congress are stimulating interest and research in folklore here and abroad. Tracing, preserving, and reexamining the early records of dance in the United States have opened up new areas of interest, careful research, and desire to preserve this information. Libraries are being established to house existing collections and correspondence. Advanced degrees are offered to folklorists with a focus on dance.

# Understanding Folkways Enhances Dance

## Eastern and Western Culture

Cultural influences in the form of borrowing and exchanging occur wherever two or more cultures meet along political or geographical boundaries. The Balkans are a historic example of an area that has for centuries been the meeting place of eastern and western culture. Of the many ethnic groups passing in and out, the major cultural influences came from the Slavs, who dominated from about the sixth century A.D. to the Middle Ages; the Romans, both pagan and Christian; and the Ottoman Turks, whose influence lasted into the nineteenth century.

## Geography and Climate

Worldwide, people have found homes in the desert, steppes, plains, river valleys, and mountains. Each of these settings influences lifestyle in its own unique manner. People who live in mountain terrains tend to be more isolated and less mobile, and they learn to make use of small spaces. It is under these conditions that traditions, folkways, and material cultures are most likely to be found intact and better preserved. The people of the southern Appalachian mountains in the southeastern United States are an example. In contrast, people living in river valleys or broad plains are more accessible and mobile. These groups, by virtue of their environmental setting, are more exposed to cultural exchange.

Climate is regarded as being a major influence on the quality of dance movement. Although it is a factor, it should not be regarded as an inflexible influence because climatic zones do not adhere to rigid lines of demarcation. Generally, dance movements of people living in a warm climate are fluid, flowing, and slow. They contain few strong, abrupt, or energetic motions. In extremely cold climates, dance movements are perceived to be strong, vigorous, and energetic, with sustained action. They often include acrobatic movements and contrary body actions. In temperate climates with a more gradual change in seasons and temperatures, dance movement is more balanced between vigorous and quiet sustained actions. The climate tends to prune out extraneous movements.

## Religion

Dance in the form of pagan rituals was ancient people's means of supplicating the gods. Rituals were performed to communicate with the unseen forces that were perceived to sustain and regulate human survival. With the advent of Christianity, pagan rituals lost their magical content but remained in form and structure to become the earliest known forms of folk dance. The Morris, Sword, and Maypole dances are examples.

## Music

Rhythm is important in folk dance music. Rhythm is the musical beat that drives dance movement. It is organized and structured sounds. Rhythm is the musical sound that catches the essential style and quality of movement in a folk dance. Authentic music and rhythm are important in keeping the ethnic flavor and spirit of a folk dance from being lost.

There are cultural variations in rhythm structure. Western culture is accustomed to 2/4, 3/4, and 6/8 meter with groupings of four, eight, and sixteen bars or measures. In eastern culture, the western-type meters are rare, except for 2/4. Irregular rhythms dominate, with 5/16, 7/8, and 11/16 being common. Musical phrases and dance phrases do not always coincide with groupings of three, five, and so forth, bars or measures.

The first musical instrument was the human voice; therefore no culture has been without music or some type of musical instrument. Musical instruments played a major role in the spiritual life and rituals of primitive societies.

The drum–a dried animal skin stretched over a hollow log and beaten to produce sounds–is believed by some to be the oldest nonvocal instrument. Others believe wind instruments, with a simple reed blown on to produce a tone, were first. Still others point to the hunter's bow, which produced a "twanging" sound when the arrow was released. In Africa, the drum was used for dance ritual and communication and was so important that it was referred to as "the pulse of life." The oldest music in America is that of American Indians. Their musical instruments–drums, rattles, bells, and rasps–are nearly as old as human society.

European instruments have counterparts in simple form in Africa and in more elaborate form in eastern countries. Instruments used for folk music and dance are largely those native to or invented by a particular national or ethnic group. The accordion, for example, was invented in Berlin in the 1820s by Friedrick Buschmann and has been a staple of German folk music and dance. In Sweden, the fiddle is the favorite instrument. For a period the accordion was played for old-time dances but once again the fiddle has returned for dancing. Philippine dance instruments reflect a diverse cultural background. Native rhythm instruments, sticks, bamboo poles, and coconut shells are used along with castanets and Spanish guitars. The study of musical instruments is fascinating, and it is significant in keeping the total background and spirit of folk dancing in perspective.

## Folk Dancing Today: Three Main Styles

There are three main styles of international folk dancing: traditional/ethnic, performance, and recreational.

### Traditional/Ethnic Folk Dance

These are folk dances that are performed in indigenous contexts, such as a village, with a purpose specific to the society. As late as 1986 in northern Romanian villages, dancing the Invîrtitia was still a significant part of the courtship ritual. Once a couple was married they did not perform that dance anymore; getting married fulfilled its function. With modernization, the people of the country have been exposed to modern ways of life, and the original function of their dancing has lost its importance. Today, in many ethnic communities, people will dance their traditional dances on special holidays or celebrations, not for the original purposes, but to preserve their traditions.

### Performance Folk Dance

Folk dances that are artistically choreographed for stage and demonstrations by amateur and professional groups are performance folk dances. Many countries, especially in Eastern Europe, have national folk dance ensembles devoted to performance folk dance.

### Recreational Folk Dance

These dances are enjoyed by people of various ethnic backgrounds not necessarily connected to the dance's background. They are performed as social and aerobic activities. Recreational folk dancing is also a means by which people learn about other cultures through dance.

Many recreational groups are going beyond just the steps of dancing. A weekend of folk dancing now would include traditional food, teaching of traditional instruments, and a live band to dance to. Live music is becoming much more prominent. Many younger people are starting to folk dance. They are intrigued by the amazing sounds and wonderful energy that comes from dancing to a live band. Less emphasis is put on complicated patterns of steps, giving way to more party dances, or dances that everyone can join in on.

## The Value of Folk Dancing

Folk dancing is an important part of a dance curriculum. It provides the benefits of aerobic activity, cultural understanding, and cultural preservation.

### Aerobic Activity and Increased Coordination

From the early 1920s, physical educators recognized the value of dance in human neuromuscular development, and utilized folk dance for the content of gymnastic dance routines. Movements from Irish jigs, Italian tarantellas, and the American Virginia Reel were incorporated into early gymnastic routines. Folk dance was also developing as a separate subject in physical education classes and the early playground movement. The movements performed in folk dancing increase heart rate, and learning step sequences and repeatedly practicing various steps increases student coordination and the ability to coordinate with the movements of others.

### Cultural Understanding

Interest in national cultural heritage has continued and accelerated into the new millennium. Efforts to preserve the knowledge and practices of the past have provided a wealth of information and artifacts from which dancers and dance scholars alike can draw for greater appreciation and understanding of dance's role in the cultural life of nations.

Folk dancing provides an opportunity to develop appreciation for the customs and traditions of other cultures, using the language of folk dancing as a common bond between people of all nations. One of the aims of many folk dance groups is to foster international understanding. Besides "painlessly educating" about other cultures, folk dancing develops good fellowship. Folk dancing is a recognized instrument for breaking down prejudices and for creating a spirit of good will toward all.

### Cultural Preservation

Many ethnic communities (Greek, Scandinavian, Filipino, Hispanic, Armenian, and Japanese, to name a few) promote their native dances through programs, classes, and performance groups for their young people. During festivals, performance groups may give a demonstration. Young and old may also dance at weddings and social events.

## Teaching Approaches

Teaching folk dancing encompasses several elements and may be cross linked to geography, the humanities, and other school subjects. World dance and cultural dance are other current terms for folk dancing.

Introducing the concept of different cultures and what that means will facilitate the students' understanding of folk dancing. Starting with the idea of different foods for different countries is one way to introduce this concept. Most students have eaten at a Mexican or Chinese restaurant and understand that Mexican food is different from traditional American food. The food of a country is only one small part of a culture. When the students understand this idea, references to other elements that help make up a culture may be introduced: language, music, clothing (costumes), and dance.

Visual aids help enhance understanding cultural difference. Bringing in a world map for students and having them find the countries that the dances are from is a fun activity. Sharing pictures of different costumes from travel brochures or books provides another visual element of a culture. Presenting students with a full spectrum of folk elements helps ready them for dancing.

### Reading Dance Directions

There are two main styles of written dance description in this chapter. Directions for dances that are made up of different figures, similar to contra or square dances, are given in measures. Directions for dances that have more individual footwork are written with counts and measures. Dance steps that were described in Chapter 3 are referred to by their name and not written out in this chapter. All major steps are defined in the Glossary.

Each of the dances included in this chapter contains bits and pieces of the culture from which it comes. The story behind the dance reflects the history, geography, climate, religion, lifestyle, and dance characteristics of the national group from which it is derived. Knowing the background and influence of these components of a dance gives depth and added dimension to teaching and performing. Learning folk dance, therefore, carries with it a greater responsibility than merely teaching or performing a physical skill. It is an opportunity to develop appreciation for the customs and traditions of other cultures, to discover that the language of folk dancing can be a common bond between people of all nations, and to learn that differences can become exciting adventures in discovering real similarities.

## Costumes

Costumes have an interesting and unique effect on the characteristic dance movements of the dancer. The style and range of movement is freed or restricted by the material and cut of the skirt, coat, or trousers. Headdress and footwear also have an interesting effect on qualities of movement. The effect costumes have on dance movement is an important element in studying the style and background of the dance.

Historically, costumes or clothing have served to protect from the elements, accommodate an occupational use, distinguish or give status, and represent a national or ethnological group. The folk dance costume is worn by national or ethnic groups and by members of international folk dance groups all over the United States. Costumes add an exciting and dramatic dimension to folk dancing.

## Holidays, Festivals, and Special Occasions

Dancing is a social event and, as such, is an integral part of the calendar of events in all cultures. Sundays and holidays are common times when work ceases and families and friends gather together for fun and fellowship, with music and dancing as a special way to express the joy of the occasion. Weddings are also times for the traditions and customs of a group to be shared, when all are made merrier by music and dance befitting the occasion.

Friends, neighbors, relatives, and often whole communities gather for cooperative work in the form of barn raisings, corn shuckings, or quilting bees. These occasions feature tables laden with potluck food and all the trimmings topped off with music and dancing until the wee hours of the morning.

Religious holidays are times of food, fiesta, and dancing. Celebrations may be in honor of a favorite saint and, as such, include mass, a festive parade, and music and dancing in the streets. In nonreligious groups, tribal or group tradition and custom may call for celebration by sacrificial offering to ancestral spirits and performance of ritual dancing.

Seasons are worldwide times of celebration. Christmas, harvest time, and midsummer are major times to bring out costumes, customs, decorations, food, and dance. Christmas is a time for elegant balls, caroling, and dancing around the Christmas tree. Harvest time, where older traditions still hold, is a community and family time to share work and play together. These are times when special traditions and customs are renewed.

# Africa

## The Continent

Africa is a vast continent and the home of some of the oldest evidence of human existence. As the twenty-first century opens, it has captured world-wide attention as a land of struggling governments.

The Sahara Desert naturally divides the continent into two parts. The north stretches from Morocco to Egypt, then up the Nile River to Ethiopia, the cradle of civilization. This area focuses on the Mediterranean Sea and is influenced by Arab culture. To the south, the barriers of the desert, mountains, and tropical forest serve to divide the northern Arab-oriented culture from the greater part of the continent called by the Arabs "*Bilad-as-Sudan*," or "land of the black people." This area makes up 20 percent of the world's total land area and is the poorest part of the world. It is divided into 40 countries and, except for South Africa, contains two-thirds of the world's least developed nations.

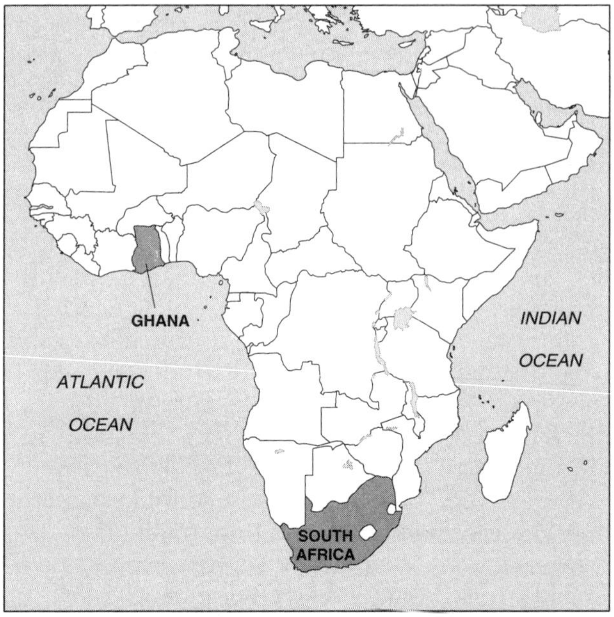


## European Influence

The desert, mountains, and tropical environment served as an impenetrable barrier to Europeans until the Portuguese landed at the Cape of Good Hope toward the end of the fifteenth century. Following this opening contact, Africa south of the Sahara was organized into spheres of influence for economic development by Great Britain, France, Spain, Belgium, Portugal, and Germany. Prior to this division the people affected had been organized into ethnic or tribal groups, many with semi-national status. These new boundaries cut across tribes and clans, leading to mutually antagonistic groups within one colonial entity.

## Slave Trade

National commercial expansion by European countries included not only exploitation of natural resources but, more tragically, the exploitation of human resources in the form of slaves. The importation of slaves to the New World was not the first incident of enslavement. The Portuguese are said to have begun African slave trading in 1441. Africans were enslaved by Europeans before the time of Columbus's voyage to find the New World. However, the stage was set, and by 1518 slaves were imported to the West Indies. By the end of the sixteenth century, it is estimated that the number of slaves in the West Indies numbered in the hundreds of thousands.

Contrary to some historians' assertions, these slaves brought with them a rich mythology, graphic and plastic art, and music with a highly developed rhythmic structure. Dance both secular and recreational was part of their heritage and a fundamental element in their aesthetic expression.

## Traditional Dance

The twenty-first century finds traditional African dance still an unknown and misunderstood art in the western world. Westerners generally regard it as a spontaneous expression producing gestures and movements lacking any technical mastery or regard for any system. Traditional African dance, on the contrary, has a complete mastery and respect for the precise rules perpetuated and passed down by the society of the Masques de Sagesse (Mask of Wisdom), which has preserved the richness and wisdom of the dance over the centuries.

Masks are not exclusively an African phenomenon. However, nowhere else is their use so widespread and varied. Masks are closely linked to religion, social life, and protection against evil spirits. Secret societies use them to make sure tribal traditions are upheld. Masks are almost exclusively used by males. In many tribes, under threat of punishment, females are not permitted to even set eyes upon them.

Dance is the pervasive and dynamic force in every aspect of African culture and is the living expression of the philosophy and memory of its evolution. Traditional African dance is the result of centuries of perfecting and cannot be danced or understood without the training of the Masques de Sagesse, who are the possessors and protectors of dance knowledge. It is they and they alone who pass this knowledge on to initiates by the centuries-old oral tradition.

## Art and Dance

The early twentieth century saw many conquests of non-European territories, particularly in Africa, which led to a greater exposure and understanding of African culture. In addition, it brought about a revolution in African arts, especially sculpture, and a rediscovery of the powerful force and unity of traditional dance. The general lack of knowledge of these many forms of art was mainly due to the tradition of an oral rather than a written means of communication. Statues and statuettes represented the material knowledge of everyday life and memory existed in the many forms of gestures. These were the manuals for choreographers of traditional dance.

## Improvisation

Improvisation is the chief characteristic of traditional dance. To achieve the freedom to improvise, traditional dance is taught and learned. Only after the basic movements, gestures, attitudes, and positions are learned is improvisation possible. Gestures learned according to tradition leave the dancer free within the technique to improvise and respond according to his inspiration, which is part of his dialogue with the cosmos. The dancer respects the traditional gestures as "words" of the dance but improvises and creates his own "phrases." The true superiority of African dance lies in the fact that the dance depends on repetition of basic movements and improvisation around these movements.

## Dance Instruments and Objects

Percussion is the basic rhythm for African dance. The most primitive of all percussion instruments is the stamping and clapping provided by the human body. Drums are the heartbeat of Africa. They both control and follow movement. They set the tempo and communicate the meaning of rituals and ceremonies. In addition, decorative objects carried or worn by the dancers help mark rhythm or beat time, and each carries its own meaning. These "dance objects" are essential to certain traditional dances, and it is considered a sacrilege to perform certain movements without them. The Bile, made from hair of the tail of a domestic or wild animal, is the oldest. The Gbon, usually a palm branch, is the most common. The Koou, a carved baton featuring scenes of everyday life, serves as a cane or third foot and represents old age. Together the instruments, dance objects, and movements enable African dance to express feelings and convey meanings without resorting to mime and pantomime.

## Spiritual World

Dance is an intricate part of daily life in every village. Children are cradled by the rhythm of walking, working, and dancing. Dance is the main avenue of communication and is the expression of life and all its emotions. Every dance tells something and is a link between body, earth, and sky. Its strength is that it draws its resources from the universe and thus recognizes the inseparability of man and the universe. To dance in the African manner is to understand that man is the divine spark indispensable to reaching and conveying the messages of the spiritual world.

The spiritual evolution of man, in African terms, is represented by three concentric circles. The larger or outer circle represents the world, the village, crowds, or body and is the seat of human values. The middle circle represents the intellect or intermediaries, those more detached from the world yet integrated into the world. They search for a more spiritual state. The inner or third circle represents the spiritual world. This is the world of initiates, the Masques. Dance is the common medium of each circle and the privileged form of exchange between the three circles.

As a major component of African culture, dance also depends upon the circle, which is the symbol of both spiritual and temporal life. The spectators represent the outer circle. The dancers represent the second circle and are the necessary intermediaries between the spectators and the spirit of the dance. Thus they are indispensable to reaching and conveying the message of the third circle of the spiritual world.

## The Future

For generations western civilization has been slowly creeping into this vast land and changing both its landscape and its people. As young Africans have become more accomplished in the manners of the West, knowledge and respect for the "old ways" of the "knowing ones" have diminished. Because dance is an integral part of the culture as a whole and daily life in particular, it can be a medium for protecting and preserving the cultural heritage of generations past.

# *Borborbor*

## Ghanaian

BORBORBOR, PRONOUNCED *bow-bow-bow,* means "bend down." Borborbor is danced mostly in the central part of the Volta region of Ghana. Dance was originally a medium of recreation, relaxation, and courtship. After a hard day's work and a big evening meal, young adults would gather in the open under the moonlight to dance away the day's toils. This gathering is also a place where single males look for future wives. Borborbor has evolved into a popular social dance. It is danced at funerals, outdoor events, weddings, church services, and parties. Beatric Feddy, PhD, Ghana, presented this dance during the Hoolyeh Folk Dance Festival in 1998.

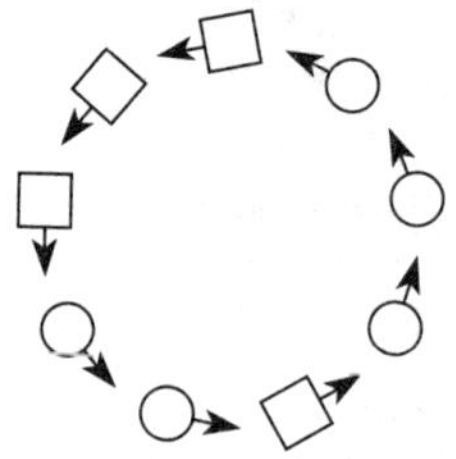

**CD:** "Saa Ml," by Ardey Allotey.[1]
**Formation:** Solo: single circle formation, facing line of direction.
**Props:** One handkerchief for each hand; tissue may be used as a substitute.
**Step:** Walk.
**Level:** Beginning 2

## *Directions* FOR THE DANCE

Meter 4/4

| *Measures* | *Counts* | |
|---|---|---|
| | | **PART I. THE WAVE** |
| 1 | 1–2 | Feet: With weight on the left foot, place the right foot diagonal right forward, bending down on the left knee at the same time. Shake hips on the down beat. |
| | | Arms: Raise right arm up as if waving (arm goes up, as the foot goes out). |
| | 3–4 | Feet: Bring right foot back to left, slightly straighten the legs. |
| | | Arms: Lower right arm as foot is brought back. |
| 2 | 1–4 | Repeat measure 1. |
| 3 | 1 | Step right forward. |
| | 2 | Step left forward. |
| | 3 | Step right forward. |
| | 4 | Jump on both feet in place. |
| | 4–6 | Repeat dance on left side. |
| | | Repeat measures 1–6 until the music changes. |

**PART II.**
**"Look at Him, Look at Her, Shaking His/Her Hips"**

Each dancer may choose which direction to travel (small steps and touches). There are three choices: Travel to another dancer and dance around him or her. Turn in place. Move in the line of direction.

1. CD available from Ardey Allotey. See Appendix C.

| Measures | Counts | |
|---|---|---|
| 1 | 1 | Step right in place. |
| | 2 | Touch left to left side, accent left hip to left side. |
| | 3 | Step left in place. |
| | 4 | Touch right foot to right side, accent right hip to right side. During this footwork hands are waist level, spinning clockwise around each other. |
| 2 | 1–4 | Repeat measure 1. |
| | | Repeat measures 1–6 until the music changes. |
| | | Repeat the dance from the beginning. |

### Style

Knees slightly bent, constantly moving the hips. Lean slightly forward from the waist.

# *Gahu*

## Ghanaian

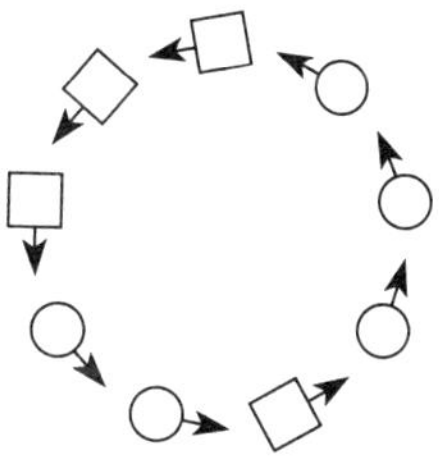

Solo

GAHU IS PRONOUNCED *ga-new.* Some sources support that *Gahu* literally means "money dance" (ga = money, hu = dance/drum). It is believed that *Gahu* originated from the Republic of Benin and spread to parts of Nigeria where Ghanaian fishermen adapted it from their Nigerian hosts. Today Gahu is a very popular communal entertainment danced by communities especially during celebrations. Beatric Feddy, PhD, Ghana, presented this dance during the Hoolyeh Folk Dance Festival in 1998.

**CD:** "Saa Ml," by Ardey Allotey. [1]

**Formation:** Solo: facing line of direction, single circle. Partner: double circle, hands not joined, facing line of direction.

**Props:** One handkerchief for each hand; tissue may be used as a substitute.

**Step:** Walk.

**Level:** Beginning 3

## *Directions* FOR THE DANCE

Meter 2/4 • Directions are the same for man and woman.

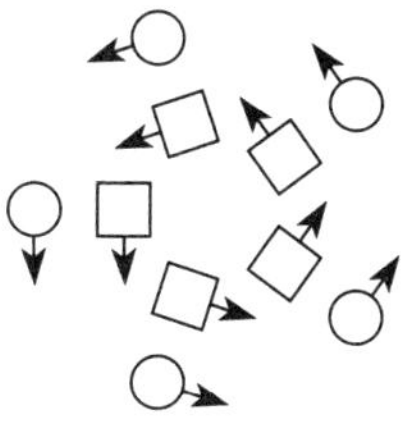

Partner

| Measures | Counts | |
|---|---|---|
| | | **PART I.** |
| 1 | 1 | Touch right foot diagonally right forward, leaning diagonally right forward, gesturing your right forearm diagonally forward, parallel with your right foot. Steps are small in length. |
| | 2 | Step with your right foot where you touched, gesturing elbow again. |

1. CD available from Ardey Allotey. See Appendix C.

| ***Measures*** | ***Counts*** | | |
|---|---|---|---|
| 2 | 1–2 | Repeat measure 1 on the left side | |
| | | Repeat measures 1–2 until the music changes. | |
| | | *Break:* Raise arms above your head, shake handkerchiefs, and say "Hoooo." | |
| | | Repeat Part I until the music changes. | |
| | | **PART II.** | |
| | | Partners face each other. While dancing Part II, arms are at your side with yours elbows bent. | |
| | | Move elbows back and forth, mimicking a wing movement of a bird. | |
| 1 | 1 | Step side right with right foot | |
| | 2 | Step right with left foot crossing in front of right | |
| 2 | 1 | Step side right with right foot | |
| | 2 | Lean a little right and slightly lift left foot | |
| 3–4 | 1–2, 1–2 | Repeat to the left | |
| | | Repeat measures 1–4 until the music changes. It will vary from song to song. | |
| | | *Break:* Raise arms above your head, shake handkerchiefs, and enthusiastically call out "Hooooo." | |
| | | **PART III.**<br>**"Show Your Money"** | **Vocals** |
| 1 | 1 | Facing slightly toward center and bending over a little at the waist, touch your right foot forward in line of direction. Pat your right hip with your right hand where a back pocket would be. | Mo– |
| | 2 | Step with right foot where you touched your right foot and pat your right hip again. | ney! |
| 2 | 1 | Facing slightly to your right, standing tall (knees still bent a little), touch your left foot forward in line of direction. Extend your right hand forward at waist level, palm facing up (to show the people sitting down the money you have taken from your pocket). | I have |
| | 2 | Step with left foot where you touched your left foot. | it! |
| | | *Break:* Raise arms above your head, shake handkerchiefs, and say "Hoooooo." | |
| | | Repeat the dance from the beginning | |

## Style

Knees slightly bent, constantly moving the hips side to side. Lean slightly forward from the waist.

# *Pata Pata*

South African

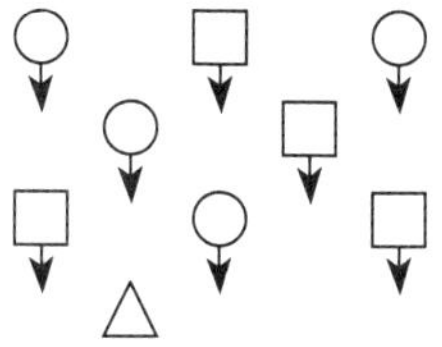

Pata Pata, pronounced *pah-ta pah-ta,* is a dance composed of African-type movements.

**CD:** High/Scope RM 6.

**Formation:** Scattered, all facing music. The last phrase includes a quarter-turn clockwise; therefore, each repeat faces a different wall.

**Style:** Many variations. Body, hand, and arm movements are improvisational.

**Steps:** Touch-step, walk, heel-toe swivel.

**Level:** Beginning 1

## *Directions* FOR THE DANCE

Meter 4/4

| ***Measures*** | ***Counts*** | |
|---|---|---|
| | | Introduction: No action. |
| 1 | 1 | Beginning right, touch toe diagonally forward and snap fingers. |
| | 2 | Step right beside left and clap. |
| | 3–4 | Repeat counts 1 and 2 using left foot. |
| 2 | 5 | With feet close together, weight on balls of feet, turn heels out and together, elbows bent waist high, turn elbows out and in. |
| | 6 | Weight on heels, turn toes out and in, hands out and in. |
| | 7–8 | Repeat action of counts 5 and 6. |
| 3 | 1 | Weight on left foot, lift right knee across in front of left leg, rotating right leg in. |
| | 2 | Touch right toe to right side. |
| | 3–4 | Repeat action of counts 1 and 2. |
| 4 | 5 | Step on right foot, pivoting one quarter-turn clockwise and kick left leg forward and clap. |
| | 6–8 | Facing a new wall, back up three walking steps (left, right, left). |

# Alpine Region: Switzerland, Austria, and Germany

## Dance Characteristics

Despite the differences in language, religion, politics, and geography, Switzerland, Austria, and Germany share many similarities in dance, particularly in the Alpine region. The most popular couple dances are the waltz, polka, and schottische. The ländler is a common dance with many variations. It is basically a courting dance in character: The man leads the woman through many figures in 3/4 or 4/4 time, and eventually the couple ends in closed position, revolving together around the dance floor. In 3/4 time, a flat-footed, even waltz (smooth) rhythm is maintained, and it is thought to be the forerunner of the Viennese waltz. The *Schuplatter* is also well known in the Alpine region as a part of the ländler or as a solo dance for men. Characteristically, the men stamp their feet and slap their knees, thighs, boots, or lederhosen to the rhythm of the music. The dance originated with the woodcutters in their free time, as a possible imitation of a grouselike wild bird during mating season.

The ritual dances are danced on special occasions, particularly at carnival time. Sword dances and dance-dramas such as the English ones are a part of carnival. Dance formations tend to follow the usual European patterns of longway sets, quadrilles, squares, or circles.

## Folk Dancing in Switzerland

*By Karin Gottier, Tolland, CT*

The dances of eastern Switzerland are very similar to those of Alpine Germany and Austria, while the dances of the western Swiss cantons are related to those of France, and in the south, to those of Italy. Most Swiss dances are couple or group dances using the steps of the popular ballroom dances of the nineteenth century: mazurka, waltz, polka, schottische, and gallop. Perhaps because of the austerity of the Calvinist period, few traditional dances survived, and many of the contemporary Swiss folk dances are reconstructions based on traditional dance figures that were collected and set either to traditional tunes or to melodies especially composed for these dances. Very few ritual dances have remained, and those are usually danced at "driving out winter" ceremonies, carnival, spring and harvest celebrations, and at the time of the ascent and descent of the cattle from the high pastures. There is literary evidence that Switzerland still knew "dances of death" until the middle of the last century. One such

ALB: Albania, BIH: Bosnia Herzegovina, HRV: Croatia,
MKD: Former Yugoslav Republic of Macedonia, MNT: Montenegro, SVN: Slovenia

source is Gottfried Keller. In his novel *Der grüne Heinrich*[1] he describes a funeral dance:

> We immediately hurried outside to where, on the corridor and stairs, the crowd began to pair off and form a procession, for without a partner no one was allowed to go up. I took Anna by the hand and fell into line which began to move, led by the musicians. They struck up a lugubrious mourning march, to the rhythm of which we marched three times around the attic, which had been converted into a ballroom, and formed a large circle. Hereupon seven couples stepped into the center and executed a lumbering old dance with seven figures and difficult jumps, kneefalls and intertwinings, accompanied by resounding clapping. After the spectacle had gone on for some time, the host appeared and went through the rows thanking the guests for their sympathy; here and there whispering into the ear of a young man–in such a way that all could hear–that he should not take the mourning too much to heart and to leave him (the host) now alone with his grief. Moreover, the host recommended that the youth should rejoice again in life. Whereupon he walked away and climbed down the stairs with lowered head as if they led directly to Tartarus. The musicians suddenly switched to a gay "Hopser," the older people withdrew and the young swept shouting and stamping across the groaning floor.

1. Gottfried Keller, *Der grüne Heinrich* (München: Willhelm Goldmann Verlag).

In character, Swiss dances are more sedate and earthbound than their German counterparts. Among folk dance groups, great emphasis is placed on precision of detail in the placement of hands and arms and in the holds between partners.

The Swiss folk dance movement has from its inception been a branch of the Swiss Costume Association (Schweizerische Trachtenvereinigung), which fosters and encourages the practice of all aspects of folk art. One of the pioneers in the field of Swiss folk dance was Luise Witzig. After having come into contact with the German and English folk dance movement, she recognized the importance of folk dance research and its significance to the work of the Swiss Costume Association. She began to conduct dance workshops in which she transmitted the results of her research work. This encouraged others to collect and notate existing material in their immediate areas. The Swiss Costume Association then made it its task to systematically collect old tunes and dance figures that were still to be found, especially in the Alpine areas. Because early researchers were able to find only fragments, many Swiss dances are reconstructions or new creations. By 1935 it was possible to publish the first collection of dance notations. Since then, this organization has released records, books, and pamphlets on the dances of all cantons. It also conducts annual folk dance leader training courses and folk dance workshops, always insisting on high standards of accuracy and precision.

Alongside the folk dance movement of the Swiss Costume Association, there exists the Association of Folk Dance Groups (Arbeitsgemeinschaft Schweizer Volkstanzkreise), which is a collective member in the Swiss Costume Association. This organization was formed in 1956 and consists of independent dance groups that practice all forms of European folk dancing and sponsor specialized workshops in the dances of a given country, conducted by an expert in that particular field. The objectives and practices of the Association of Folk Dance Groups are very similar to the recreational folk dance movement in the United States.

# *D'Hammerschmiedsg'selln*

## German

D'HAMMERSCHMIEDSG'SELLN, PRONOUNCED *duh-HAM-mair-shmeets-guh-sehln,* means "the journeyman blacksmith." This Bavarian dance was originally performed by men only. The intrigue of the clapping pattern has made it a popular dance. It was introduced by Huig Hofman from Belgium at Stockton, California, and Moorehead, Kentucky.

***Dance A While* CD:** "D'Hammerschmiedsg'selln."

**CD and Cassette:** High/Scope RM 7.

**Formation**: Set of four dancers, two couples, woman on partner's right (a) or four men, partners facing each other (b).

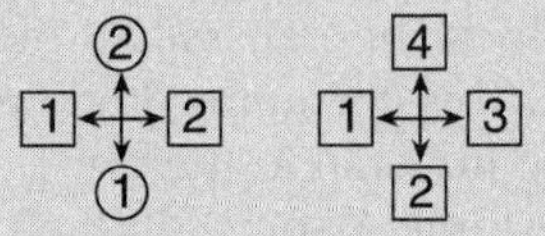


(a) (b)

**Steps:** Step–hop, waltz.

**Level:** Beginning 3

**Clap Pattern**

| Counts | Two measures = 6 counts |
|---|---|
| 1 | Both hands slap own thighs as knees flex slightly. |
| 2 | Clap own chest, body turning slightly left. |
| 3 | Clap own hands together. |
| 4 | Opposites clap right hands. |
| 5 | Opposites clap left hands. |
| 6 | Opposites clap both hands. |

## *Directions* FOR THE DANCE

Meter 3/4 • Directions are same for both man and woman, except when specially noted.

Couples that start on measure 1, count 1:

If two male–female couples, the men start clap pattern; if four men, man 1 and man 3 start. If four people, couple A, or person 1 and 3 start.

| *Measures* | *Counts* | |
|---|---|---|
| | | Introduction: no action. |
| | | **CLAP PATTERN** |
| 1 | 1–3 | Couple A start clap pattern. |
| 2 | 4–6 | Couple B start clap pattern. |
| 3–16 | | Both A and B continue through measure 16 |

| *Measures* | *Counts* | |
|---|---|---|
| | | **FIGURE I. CIRCLE** |
| 17 | 1 | All four join hands facing counterclockwise; with left foot step forward left. The circle will move counterclockwise. |
| | 2 | Hop on left foot. |
| | 3 | Hold. |
| 18 | 1 | With right foot, step forward. |
| | 2 | Hop on right foot. |
| | 3 | Hold. |
| 19–23 | | Repeat actions of measures 1–2. |
| 24 | 1 | With right foot, step forward. |
| | 2 | Hop on right foot, turning clockwise to face reverse line of direction. |
| | 3 | Hold. |
| 25–31 | | Repeat measures 1–7 of Figure I, Circle, moving clockwise. |
| 32 | 1 | With right foot, step forward. |
| | 2 | Hop on right foot, turning to face center. |
| | 3 | Hold. |
| | | **CLAP PATTERN** |
| 1–16 | | Repeat action of measures 1–16. |
| | | **FIGURE II. STAR** |
| 17–23 | 1–21* | Form right-hand star. Beginning left, take eight step-hops, star revolving clockwise. |
| 24 | 8 | With right foot, step forward. |
| | 2 | Hop on right foot, turning clockwise to face reverse line of direction. |
| | 3 | Hold. Form left-hand star. |
| 25–31 | | Take eight step-hops, star revolving counterclockwise. |
| 32 | 1 | With right foot, step forward. |
| | 2 | Hop on right foot, turning to face center. Release Star hand formation. |
| | 3 | Hold. |
| | | **CHORUS, CLAP PATTERN** |
| 1–16 | | Repeat action of measures 1–16. |
| | | **FIGURE III. LARGE CIRCLE** |
| 17–24 | 1–24* | Circles of four open out to form one large circle. Beginning left, take eight step-hops, circle moving clockwise. Reverse direction on the last step hop. |
| 25–32 | 1–24 | Take eight step-hops, circle moving counterclockwise. At the end, face center and bow. |

*continues on next page*

*Counting is best accomplished by saying the measure # for 1 and then 2–3. i.e., 123, 223, 323, 423, etc.

### Variation (Mixer)

| | |
|---|---|
| 1–16 | Clap pattern. |
| 17–24 | Figure I or II repeat circle left or right-hand star. |
| 25–32 | Take corner for new partner. Closed position. Man beginning left, woman right, take eight waltz steps, turning clockwise, dancing anywhere. Form a new set with a new couple to start clap pattern. |

### Notes

1. During circle figure, arms should be firm and dancers should lean slightly back, using centrifugal force, which adds zest to the dance.
2. The inner action of partners and couples in the precision of performing the clap pattern adds to the fun-loving spirit of the dance.

# *Dr Gsatzlig*

*Included by permission of Jane Farwell, Folklore Village Farm, Dodgerville, WI.*

## Swiss

DR GSATZLIG MEANS "exactly" and is from Appenzell, Switzerland. Jane Farwell learned this dance there and introduced it across the United States in 1954. Later, Farwell corrected one of the figures slightly, which accounts for two different versions. Although the music is written in 2/4 meter, it has the quality of a schottische.

**Music:** L. Witzig and A. Stern Pub. Hug and Co., Zurich 12 *Schweitzer Tanze.*

**Position:** Closed, man's back to center of circle, man's left, woman's right arms extended toward line of direction.

**Steps:** Side step, schottische, two-step.

**Level:** Beginning 3

## *Directions* FOR THE DANCE

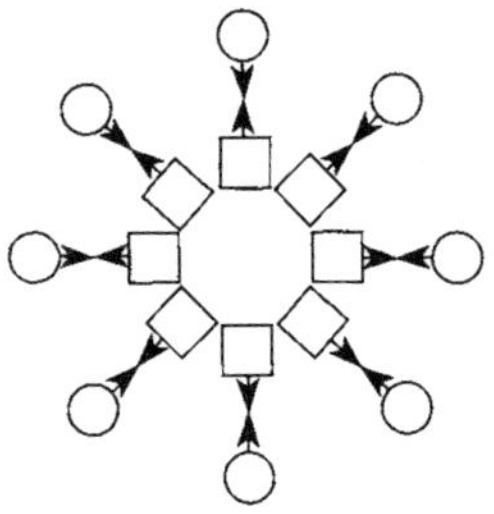

Meter 2/4 • Directions are for man; woman's part reverse.

| | ***Measures*** | |
|---|---|---|
| | 1–4 | Introduction. |
| | | **PART I. DR GSATZLIG (SIDE STEP)** |
| A | 1–2 | Beginning left, take four side steps, moving in line of direction. On last side step, keep weight on left. |
| | 3 | Beginning right, take two side steps in reverse line of direction, swinging joined hands sharply up, elbow bending, upper arm shoulder high. On last side step, keep weight on right. |

| | Measures | |
|---|---|---|
| | 4 | Take two side steps in line of direction, arms extended toward line of direction. Joined hands always point in the direction traveling. |
| | 5–8 | Beginning right, repeat action of measures 1–4, traveling in reverse line of direction. |
| A | 9–16 | Repeat action of measures 1–8. |
| | | **PART II. HEEL AND TOE SCHOTTISCHE** |
| B | 1 | Open position. Beginning left, take one heel and toe. |
| | 2 | Take two side steps in line of direction. Weight remains on left. |
| | 3–4 | Swinging joined hands sharply up, elbow bending, upper arm shoulder high, face reverse line of direction. Beginning right, repeat action of measures 1–2, moving in reverse line of direction. |
| | 5–8 | Closed or shoulder-waist position (latter preferred). Beginning left, take four slow two-steps (Swiss schottische steps) turning clockwise, progressing in line of direction. |
| B | 9–16 | Repeat action of measures 1–8. |

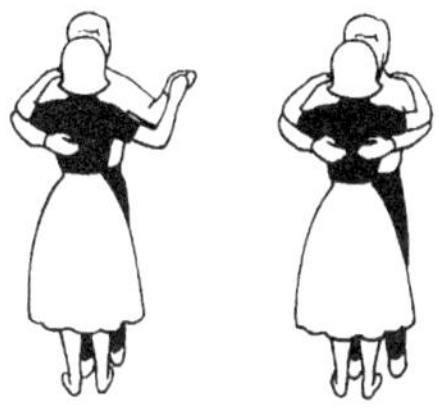

| | Measures | |
|---|---|---|
| | | **PART III. DR GSATZLIG (SIDE STEP)** |
| A | 1–8 | Repeat action of Figure I, measures 1–8. |
| | | **PART IV. SCHOTTISCHE** |
| C | 1–2 | Man faces line of direction, crossed arms held on chest; woman faces man, back to line of direction, hands on hips, knuckles toward body. Beginning left, take two schottische steps (step-close step-hop) (Swiss polka) in line of direction. Both move diagonally toward center, then away from center, always progressing forward. |
| | 3–4 | Take four slow step-hops in line of direction, man stamping left on first step, woman turning clockwise twice. |
| | 5–8 | Repeat action of measures 1–4. |
| C | 9–16 | Repeat action of measures 1–8, with right hands joined, free hand on hip. The woman turns clockwise under man's raised arm. |
| | | **PART V. DR GSATZLIG** |
| A | 1–8 | Repeat action of measures 1–8. |

## Routine

AABBACCAABBACCA. The record, Folk Dancer MH 1114, allows for this sequence.

## Style

The Swiss dance movements are small and precise. Keep the steps simple without much extension of the knee or foot. The side steps are little steps; do not scrape the foot, but lift each foot. Turn head and focus eyes on the direction of travel during the side steps. The abrupt change of direction and focus of a large group is very effective. Keep free hands on hips. Keep step-hops low and subdued. Jane Farwell refers to it as a "leisurely dance."

### Notes

1. It is fun to sing "la-la-la" during the specific tune for Dr Gsatzlig.
2. Add a few shouts "ya'hoo'hoo'hooy" any time.
3. In Switzerland, they call a polka a schottische and a schottische a polka. Because this book is used primarily in the United States, the terms schottische and polka as defined in American usage are used.

# *Krüz König*

*Krüz König directions translated by Karin Gottier, Tolland, CT.*

## German

"KRÜZ KÖNIG" IS A GERMAN dialect expression for *Kreuz König*, which means "king of clubs." Heinrich Dieckelmann, a German folk dancer and pianist, composed the tune and made a present of it to his friend Ludwig Burkhardt in 1924. Burkhardt immediately contacted folk dance groups in Hamburg and Berlin for ideas. Four couples in a square was very common in northern Germany. There was a desire for dances with more vivacity and more difficult figures. One day the dance was born, with no claim to steps or figures of ancient origin. Krüz König was a new folk dance. Ludwig Burkhardt was well known for his leadership in teaching German folk dance to young people and teachers and for his early publications of German folk dance. He described his dance in *Kneveler, das Tanzbuch mit "Krüz-König,"* Bärenreiter Verlag Kassel, 1927.

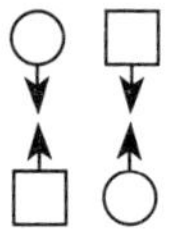

***Dance A While* CD:** "Krüz König."

**Music:** Herman, Michael, *Folk Dances for All*, p. 89.

**Formation:** Set of two couples facing, woman to right of partner, hands joined in a circle of four.

**Steps:** Run, step-hop, mazurka, Achtervör steps: step left foot to left, step right foot close behind left, step left foot to left and right across left. *Note:* This is like a grapevine step, but is *not leaped*. It is danced very close to the ground.

**Level:** Intermediate

## *Directions* FOR THE DANCE

Meter 3/8 • Directions are the same for man and woman except when specifically noted.

| ***Measures*** | |
|---|---|
| 1–4 | Introduction: No action. |
| | **FIGURE I. CIRCLE OF FOUR** |
| 1–4 | Beginning left, circle left with one Achtervör step and eight running steps. |
| 5–8 | Repeat measures 1–4. |

***Measures***

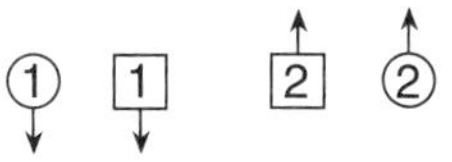

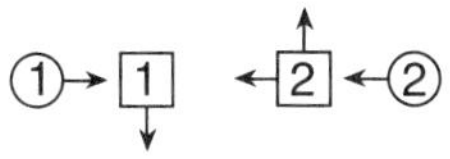

**FIGURE II. WINGS**

1–8 repeat — Partners take conversation position. Men hook left elbows to form a line of four.

Formation turns counterclockwise with 24 running steps. At the end of this figure, men release hold and women take a small step to the right to face center.

**FIGURE III. STRAIGHT CHAIN**

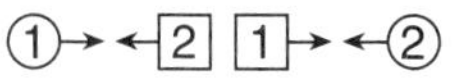

9–10 — With two step-hops men change places by giving left hands. Women dance two step-hops in place. Each man is now facing the opposite woman.

11–12 — With two step-hops men change places with women by giving right hands. The women are now on the inside of the set.

13–14 — With two step-hops women change places by giving left hands to each other while men dance two step-hops in place. Women are now facing their original partners.

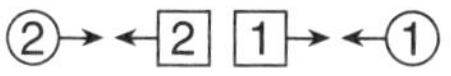

15–16 — Original partners give right hands and change places with two step-hops. Men are now on the inside of the set.

9–14 repeat — Repeat measures 9–14, returning to original place. Women are still on the inside.

15–16 repeat — With extended right-hand grasp, man pulls partner with momentum and half-turn counterclockwise to his right side to place. At the same time, men release women's right hand and take their left. All join hands to form a circle of four.

## Note

This figure should be executed with well-stretched arms and a large floor pattern.

**FIGURE IV. CIRCLE OF FOUR, CIRCLE OF TWO WITH MAZURKA**

17–20 — Beginning left, all dance four mazurka steps clockwise. Release hold with corner.

21–22 — Take two-hand hold with partner. Continue to turn clockwise with two mazurka steps.

23–24 — Without changing hold or direction, couples turn twice clockwise with six running steps.

17–22 repeat — Repeat four mazurka steps in circle of four and two mazurka steps turning with partner.

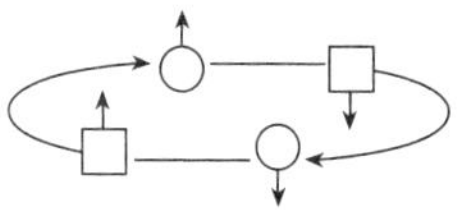

23–24 repeat — Repeat the six running steps turning partner; however, turn only once with three running steps and change to a right-hand hold. Men lead their partners to the center with right arms well extended, so that women stand in the center *right shoulder to right shoulder,* facing in opposite directions. Men take corner woman's left hand in their own left.

**FIGURE V. "KING OF CLUBS"**

25–28 — **Women on inside:** The two men run 12 steps clockwise, turning the two women, who form the center axis, with them.

*continues on next page*

***Measures***

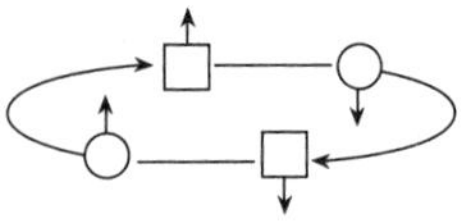

29–32 **Men on inside:** Left hand is released. With six running steps, man leads woman by the right hand outward to his place, taking her place in the center, standing right shoulder to right shoulder with the opposite man. Each woman takes the left hand of corner man into her own.

They run clockwise with six steps, turning the men, who form the axis of the formation, with them.

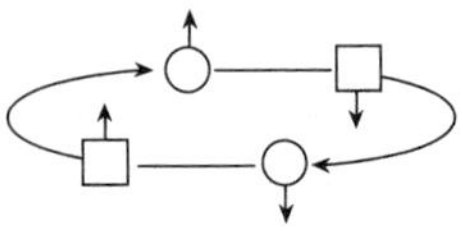

25–28 repeat **Women on inside:** With six running steps women release left-hand hold and lead their partners by the right hand outward, taking men's place in the center. Both men take left hand of corner woman in own left and continue to turn the set clockwise with six running steps.

29–32 repeat **Men on inside:** Repeat measures 29–32 with women dancing on the outside and men on the inside. During the last measure, men make half a jump-turn clockwise and join hands in a circle of four. Men will have their original partner on their left and the corner woman, who is now their new partner, on their right. The dance is repeated one more time with the new partner.

## Styling Note

The last figure should be danced with well-stretched arms. Dancers on the outside of the formation need to pull away from center of the set with their left arms. All stand very tall. In circle figures, the momentum is established by pulling away from the center of the set, or from partner. The character of the entire dance is one of restrained energy and controlled strength.

# *Man in the Hay*

German

MAN IN THE HAY IS DANCED to the tune of an old German folk song "A Farmer Had a Pretty Wife." The song is well known in Scandinavia.

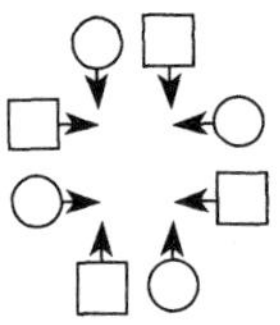

***Dance A While* CD:** "Man in the Hay."
**CD:** High/Scope RM 3.
**Music:** Burchenal, E., *Folk Dances of Germany*, p. 28.
**Formation:** Set of four couples in square dance formation.
**Steps:** Skip, slide.
**Level:** Beginning 1

## *Directions* FOR THE DANCE

Meter 6/8 • Directions are same for man and woman, except when specially noted.

***Measures***

1–4 Introduction: All join hands and swing arms forward and back briskly, standing in place. The movement is small and staccato. Keep elbows straight and stand in close formation.

| | *Measures* | |
|---|---|---|
| | | **FIGURE I. CIRCLE** |
| A | 1–16 | Beginning left, take 16 skips clockwise. Repeat counter-clockwise. |
| | | **Chorus** |
| B | 9–10 | Head couples take closed position. Man beginning left, woman right, take three slides to center and pause or stamp. |
| | 11–12 | Man beginning right, woman left, take three slides back to place and pause or stamp. |
| | 13–16 | Man beginning left, woman right, take six slides across set to opposite side, men passing back to back. Step left, bring right foot to left and hold. Do not turn. |
| | 17–20 | Repeat action of measures 13–16, returning to home position, woman passing back to back. Man leads with right foot, woman left. |
| | 9–20 | Side couples repeat action of measures 9–20, B. |
| | | **FIGURE II. WOMEN'S CIRCLE** |
| A | 1–8 | Four women join hands in circle. Beginning left, take 16 skips clockwise. Men clap. |
| | | **Chorus** |
| B | 9–20<br>9–20 | Repeat action of measures 9–20, 9–20, B. |
| | | **FIGURE III. MEN'S CIRCLE** |
| A | 1–8 | Four men join hands in circle. Beginning left, take 16 skips clockwise. Women clap. |
| | | **Chorus** |
| B | 9–20<br>9–20 | Repeat action of measures 9–20, 9–20, B. |
| | | **FIGURE IV. BASKET** |
| A | 1–8 | Head couples form circle, men's arms around women's waists, women's arms around men's shoulders. Beginning left, take 16 skips or slides clockwise. A brisk buzz step may be used here with the right foot in front of the left and so vigorous the women are swept from their feet. Keep basket hold firm and lean back. |
| | | **Chorus** |
| B | 9–20<br>9–20 | Repeat action of measures 9–20, 9–20, B. |
| | | **FIGURE V. BASKET** |
| A | 1–8 | Side couples repeat action of Figure IV, measures 1–8, A. |
| | | **Chorus** |
| B | 9–20<br>9–20 | Repeat action of measures 9–20, 9–20, B. |

*continues on next page*

Man in the Hay, *continued*

| | ***Measures*** | |
|---|---|---|
| | | **FIGURE VI. CIRCLE** |
| A | 1–8 | Take 14 skips clockwise and end with a bow to the center of the circle with hands still joined. |

## Variation

Arrange all the squares so that they are directly behind and beside another square, so that the couples may slide through several squares and return to original position during the chorus.

Measures 13–16, B, man beginning left, woman right, take eight slides across set and on through as many sets as they can go, men passing back to back. Measures 17–20, B, repeat action of measures 13–16, returning home, women passing back to back.

# *Sonderburg Doppelquadrille*

German

SONDERBURG DOPPELQUADRILLE IS a German variant of the Danish dance based on the dance description by Paul and Gretel Dunsing (Dunsing and Dunsing, 1946).

**MP3:** Dancilla.com

**Music:** Dunsing and Dunsing, *Dance Lightly,* p. 16.

**Formation:** Two lines facing each other, four couples in each line. Head couples are two couples on each side of line nearest head of set. Foot couples are two couples on each side of line forming remainder of set.

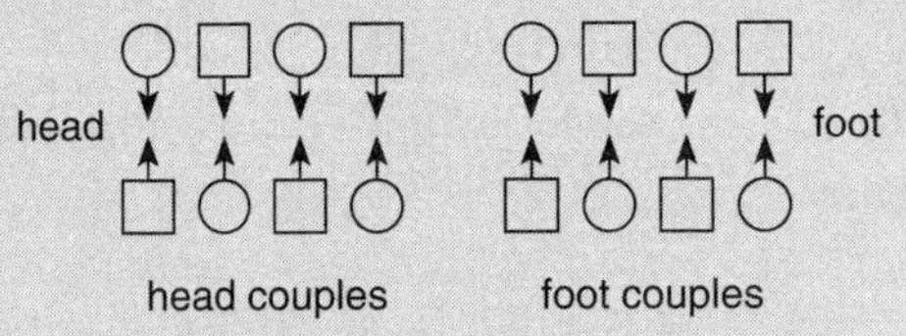


**Steps:** Walk, polka.

**Level:** Intermediate

7

## *Directions* FOR THE DANCE

Meter 2/4 • Directions are same for man and woman, except when specially noted.

| ***Measures*** | |
|---|---|
| | **PART I. TWO CIRCLES** |
| 1–16 | Head couples and foot couples join hands and form two separate circles. Beginning left, take 16 walking steps to left, circle moving clockwise; then take 16 walking steps to right, circle moving counterclockwise, ending in original formation (two lines). |

| *Measures* | |
|---|---|
| | **PART II. HEADS DOWN CENTER** |
| 1–4 | Head four join inside hands with opposite dancer and take eight walking steps moving down center of set (toward foot) and on eighth step turn individually to face reverse line of direction. Join inside hands and take eight walking steps forward to return to place. |
| 5–8 | Foot four repeat action of measures 1–4, moving toward head of set and back to place. |
| | **PART III. FOUR CIRCLES** |
| 1–8 | Opposite couples join hands. Take 16 walking steps, moving to left, and take 16 walking steps moving to right, ending in original position. |
| | **PART IV. CHAIN** |
| 1–8 | Opposite couples execute grand right and left in small circles, four dancers each. Opposite dancers join right hands, pass, left hand to partner, and so forth, ending in place and bowing to partner. |
| 9–16 | Repeat action of measures 1–8. |
| | **PART V. POLKA** |
| 1–16 | Couples take closed position or shoulder-waist position. Man beginning left, woman right, take 16 polka steps turning clockwise, progressing in line of direction around oval circle formed by two lines, back to place. |

### Variation

Measures 1–8, Part IV, opposite couples may execute right and left through across the set, then back to place, instead of grand right and left.

# *Spinnradl zu Dritt*

*Directions translated by Karin Gottier, Tolland, CT.*

## Austrian

VARIOUS FORMS OF THIS DANCE were collected in the Alpine regions of Bavaria, Austria, and the German settlement areas of Czechoslovakia. The most widely danced variant was collected by Hermann Derschmidt in 1924 in Klaffer, Upper Austria, and published by him and Erna Schützenberger in their five-part collection, *Spinnradl-unser Tanzbuch. Spinnradl* means "spinning wheel."

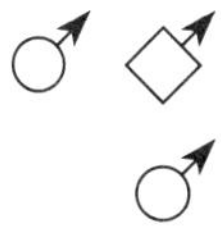

***Dance A While* CD:** "Spinnradl zu Dritt."

**Formation:** One man between two women. He holds their outside hands, while they join their inside hands behind his back. All face line of direction, left shoulder to the center. Arms are loosely stretched.

**Steps:** "Dreierschritt" (triple-walking step): a smooth, unaccented walk in 3/4 time. One triple-walking step requires three walking steps. Jump, light running steps.

**Level:** Beginning 2

*continues on next page*

## *Directions* FOR THE DANCE

Meter 3/4 • Directions are the same for man and woman.

| ***Measures*** | |
|---|---|
| 1–4 | Introduction |
| 1–8 | Beginning left, all move forward with eight waltz steps. These steps are danced close to the ground, smoothly and unaccented. Man looks alternately at the left and right woman. |
| 9 | On count 1, man pulls women forward. As their joined hands pass over his head, he bends his knees briefly and immediately stands up again. The joined hands of the women are now in front of him. On counts 2 and 3 the right woman turns once counterclockwise with two steps. She now stands between the man and left woman. (All hands should be held closed together. *Do not* release hold.) |
| 10 | As man and left woman form arch by lifting their joined hands, right woman slips under the arch by bending her knees briefly on count one. She continues moving to the right side of man. On counts 2 and 3 the left woman begins to make a clockwise turn. |
| 11 | While left woman continues to turn under her own arm to the right on count 1, the man begins to turn left on counts 2 and 3. All are back to the beginning position. |
| 12–14 | Repeat measures 9–11. This time the left woman slips through the arch, which is formed by man and right woman. The right woman turns out counterclockwise and the man clockwise. |
| 15 | All move forward with three short, light running steps. |
| 16 | All execute a *silent,* soft jump on both feet. Repeat measures 9–16. |

### Note

*At no time do the dancers back up.* The action moves forward over the head of the turning person. The movements of measures 9–16 flow into each other. The dancers do not remain in place but continue to move slightly forward in the line of direction. The character of the dance is smooth and flowing. The steps are danced close to the ground with no accent. The jump is soft, elastic, and silent.

Hermann Derschmidt writes in the collection *Spinnradl-unser Tanzbuch:*

> The man must see that the "ducking under" does not occur backwards, rather through the pulling of joined hands over head by the other two partners . . . the "ducking under" must occur exactly on the first count, during the second and third count each partner in turn prepares to duck under. (Schützenberger and Derschmidt, 1974, p. 15)

7

# *Zwiefacher*

ZWIEFACHER ARE TURNING COUPLE DANCES that alternate between even and uneven rhythms in regular and irregular intervals.[1] The earliest documentation of this musical form is from the mid-sixteenth century.

The music and dances come from a regional culture primarily from the Danube River drainage basin, which extends from Bohemia in the east, diagonally across the German-language area to the northwest, into Bavaria, Frankonia, Swabia, Rhineland-Palatine, and Alsace. The ethnic origin is uncertain, but it illustrates the transmigration of cultures.

The zwiefacher are known by many names. In the Black Forest a zwiefacher category is named a *Heuberger/Lange*. The term *Schweinauer* is used more to the east in the Ries region, which is close to Bavaria. Heuberg and Schweinau are names of a mountain and a village, respectively, and *lange* means "long ones." However, this does not seem to be of significance to the type of dance. In the Palatine region zwiefacher are known as *Bayerischer;* in the Upper Palatine as *Eintreter*, and *Grad und Ungrad* in the Bavarian Forest.

The dance alternates between pivots and waltzes or pivots and two-steps. Like the waltz, the zwiefacher are considered a social dance, not just a folk dance. The dance position varies from closed to adapted shoulder-waist positions. A couple may turn in one spot or whirl forward in the line of direction. Learning the sequence is complex. Karin Gottier suggests that speaking or singing the words to the melody may help one learn the patterns. As you learn, relax and enjoy this smooth, elegant turning dance.

1. The Zwiefacher background information is based on the article "About Zwiefacher" by Karin P. Gottier, in *Gauzeitung* 10, no. 2 (December 1996).

# *Die Alte Kath (Zwiefacher)*

German

DIE ALTE KATH IS A BAVARIAN DANCE. "Kath" is short for Katharina or Katherine. The title means "Old Katherine." The "old" may stand for "old friend." In the lyrics she is asking for another dance and the answer is "wait a while, you'll get it." The interpretation may be that she's not after a dance, but a man.

***Dance A While* CD:** "Die Alte Kath (Zwiefacher)."
**Position:** Closed or shoulder-waist.
**Steps:** Waltz, pivot turn.
**Level:** Advanced

## *Directions* FOR THE DANCE

Meter 3/4 • Directions are for man; woman's part reverse.

| ***Measures*** | |
|---|---|
| 1–2 | Beginning left, take two waltz steps, turning clockwise, progressing in line of direction. |
| Meter 2/4 | |
| 3–4 | Pivot clockwise, taking two steps, progressing in line of direction. Repeat action of measures 1–4 for the remaining music. Take two waltz steps and pivot, two steps, alternate. |

### Lyrics

Unsa oite Kath–möcht aa no–aa no, unsa oite
Kath möcht aa no oan;
Wart no a bissl–wart no a bissl–kriagst scho–kriagst scho,
wart no a bissl–wart no a bissl–kriagst schon oan

Unsa oite Kath–dö hat jetz–hot jetz, unsa oite
Kath–hot jetz an Mo
schiaglt a bissl–hinki schon a weng–tuats grod
tuats grod, schiaglt a bissl, hinkt schon a weng,
tuats grod no!

Our old Katie would still also, still also, our old Katie would still also like one (a man)
Wait a little–wait a little–you'll get–
You'll get,
Wait a little–wait a little–you'll yet get one

Our old Katie, has now–has now–our old
Katie–has now a man
is a little cross-eyed, limps already a bit–just about does it,
just about does it, is a little cross-eyed, limps already a bit, just about does it yet!

7

# *Holderbeerli (Zwiefacher)*

*Included by permission of Arbeitsgemeinschaft der Sing- Tanz- und Spielkreise in Baden-Württemberg e.V., Stuttgart, Germany.*

German

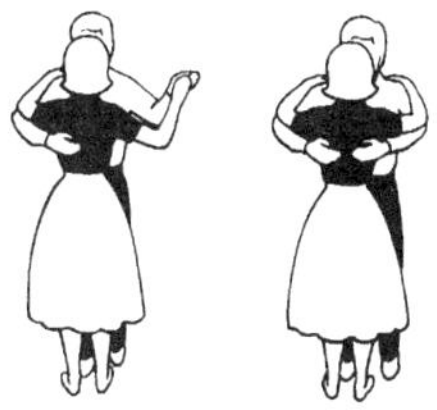

HOLDERBEERLI IS FROM THE BLACK FOREST. It is a traditional song and melody, recorded in the village of Langenschiltach. It means "elderberries." Holderbeerli was presented by Klaus Fink at the 10th Folk Dance/Folklore workshop of the North American Federation of German Folk Dance Groups, in Walla Walla, WA, July 2003.

**Music:** Holderbeerli.
**Position:** Closed or shoulder-waist.
**Steps:** Waltz, pivot turn.
**Level:** Advanced

## Directions FOR THE DANCE

Directions are for man; woman's part reverse.

| ***Measures*** | |
|---|---|
| Meter 2/4 | |
| | **PART I.** |
| 1–2 | Beginning left, pivot clockwise, taking two steps, wherever there is space or progress in line of direction. |
| Meter 3/4 | |
| 3–4 | Take two waltz steps turning clockwise, wherever there is space or progress in line of direction. |
| 5–8 | Repeat action of measures 1–4, pivot two steps, two waltz steps. |
| 1–8 | Repeat action of measures 1–8. |
| Meter 2/4 | |
| | **PART II.** |
| 9 | Beginning left, pivot clockwise, taking one step. |
| Meter 3/4 | |
| 10 | Beginning right, take one waltz step, turning clockwise. |
| Meter 2/4 | |
| 11 | Repeat action of measure 9. |
| Meter 3/4 | |
| 12 | Repeat action of measure 10. |
| Meter 2/4 | |
| 13–14 | Beginning left, pivot clockwise, taking two steps. |
| Meter 3/4 | |
| 15–16 | Take two waltz steps, turning clockwise. |

## Notes

1. Couple may turn clockwise or counterclockwise in place or progress in line of direction. Advanced dancers may reverse direction during any sequence.
2. P = pivot; W = waltz

| | | |
|---|---|---|
| Part I, measures 1–8, 1–8: | PP WW PP WW | PP WW PP WW |
| Part II, measures 9–16, 9–16: | P W P W PP WW | PW PW PP WW |

## Holderbeerli

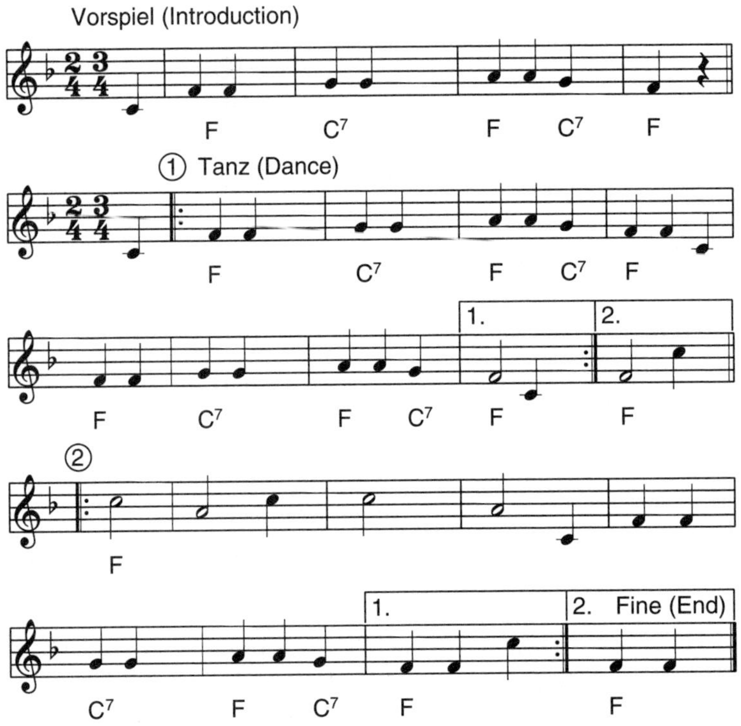


### Lyrics

| | |
|---|---|
| Die Holder, Holderbeerli sin zittig | The elder, elderberries are early |
| die Holder, Holderbeerli sin reif | the elder, elderberries are ripe |
| Die Holder, die Holder | The elder, the elder |
| die Holder, Holderbeerli, sin reif | the elder, elderberries are ripe |

# Balkan Countries

## Introduction

The Balkan Peninsula includes the former Yugoslavia grouping of Croatia, Bosnia, and Serbia, along with Bulgaria, Greece, and Albania. Originally occupied by Slavic tribes, the area has seen a steady flow of outside influences, including the Greeks, Romans, Crusaders, and Turks. Different areas have come under the influence of pagan, Roman Catholic, Greek Orthodox, Bulgarian Orthodox, and Islamic religions. As different countries have emerged from Ottoman Turkish control, boundaries have been established and national unification developed.

The long period of domination meant isolation from cultural movements going on in western Europe, and it caused the Balkan people to turn to their native folklore for identity and inspiration. Isolation worked to enrich their cultural heritage and served to make the Balkans an extensive storehouse of folk materials.

The Balkan Peninsula is rich in folk art, music, dance, and tradition. The fact that these countries have remained more agrarian for a longer period of time than other western European countries has made it possible to visit villages in remote areas and find people still wearing their native dress daily and performing traditional dances.

The folk dance tradition is a living one. The Sunday hora, a social get-together including dance, is a common custom in small and large communities. Each village has one or several places set aside for a dance: the square, the threshing circle, a barn or a hall for inclement weather, the wide porch of a home, or a level clearing or meadow.

The *chain dance* (circle), open or closed, is the common dance among the Balkans, but it is referred to by different terms and with different spellings: *kolo,* Serbia; *hora,* Romania; *horo,* Bulgaria; *oro,* Macedonia; and *xopos,* Greece (pronounced *hó-rohs*). The same words are used for the social occasion and the dance. There are many old tunes and songs for the hora, and newly composed tunes still use the complex rhythms that are associated with Balkan music. The rhythm of the songs relates to the length of syllables and goes back to Greek poetry and drama.

Some of the dances originated with the craft guilds; for example, the Butcher's Dance, the Shepherd's Dance, and the Tailor's Dance. Others were named for the place of their origin, and the ritual dances frequently were related to pagan ceremonies that were adapted to another religion. Originally, the chains were for men or women alone. The men's movement is more exuberant and dynamic, and the opportunity for the leader to show off is always present. Women have traditionally kept their movement more restrained, with feet closer to the floor and eyes downcast.

ALB: Albania, BIH: Bosnia Herzegovina, HRV: Croatia, MKD: Former Yugoslav Republic of Macedonia, MNT: Montenegro, SVN: Slovenia

Such couple dances as the waltz, schottische, and polka did not begin to appear until after 1876, when the western style began to influence the peasant dances. Today, it is common to include kolos (horos) with the ballroom dances.

## Greece

### Dance Characteristics

Dance was a common theme on ancient vases and frescoes in Byzantine monasteries. The Greek word *chorus* means "dance." The chorus in the tragedies sang and danced. The continuity of dance tradition among the Greeks persists through their history, from ancient Greece, through Byzantium, 400 years of slavery to the Turks, the uprisings, the establishment of Greece as a sovereign kingdom, the European influence, and the social and political reforms following World Wars I and II.

Greek dance has always been an integral part of the people's lives. It is characterized by the display of human emotions, expressing great joy, exuberance, sorrow, aspirations, and hopes. It is a living tradition that may be found at cafés, bars, and religious celebrations, wherever people meet.

Modern folk dancing in Greece can be classified in a variety of ways. One is according to rhythm.

There are the Syrtos or Kalamatianos, 7/8 meter; the Tsamiko, 3/4 meter; and the Hasápikos (sometimes referred to as the Butcher's Dance), 2/4 meter. Some folk dances are remnants of ritual drama, such as the survival of the hobby horse during carnival. Sometimes they are classified according to formation: circular, pair, or solo.

Most of the dances follow the circle or the broken circle formation; although men and women used to dance alone, they now dance together without partners. In the broken circle, the leader (traditionally a man, unless it is a women's dance) is on the right-hand end, holding two handkerchiefs, one in his right hand, away from the body, to wave and signal variations in step, and the other joining the leader to the next person in the line. The leader improvises steps in time with the music, displaying his ingenuity and skill. As the leader, he encourages the group to become one as they keep the basic step going. In small villages, the leader may use this opportunity to display his personality to the opposite sex. The element of competition among leaders is always present, as one attempts to surpass another. A second dancer can join the leader in improvisation. Occasionally the leader moves to the opposite end and the next person in line becomes the leader.

The body is firm and upright. The women traditionally move in a simple and dignified manner, with footwork close to the ground and eyes downcast. The man is more exuberant in his dance style, leaping, twisting, and turning, but always in time to the basic rhythm. The different regions have definite styles and traditions.

### Music

Greek folk music is a monophonic mixture of ancient Greek scales and Byzantine church music. Only the music of the Ionian Islands reflects western music. Usually the rhythms are 5/4 or 5/8, 7/8, or 9/8 (which are the rhythms of the tragedies). The dance steps are slow and quick, corresponding to the length of syllables of words, rather than to the beat. Musical meter was based on poetic meter.

The dances are performed with the accompaniment of the dancers' singing or folk instruments. String instruments are the lyre, the violin, the lute, the santouri (dulcimer), the mandolin, and the bouzouki. Wind instruments are the pipiza, the come-musa, the clarinet, the pastoral flutes, the gaida (bagpipe), and the zurna. Percussion instruments include drums, bells, triangles, défi (small tambourines), krotala (wooden spoons), and finger cymbals.

The musicians, not more than four or five, usually stood in the middle of the dancers and responded to the mood of the occasion. Certain instruments and combinations were typical of specific regions.

## Serbia, Macedonia, and Bosnia

### Dance Characteristics

In 1945, the Federal Republic of Yugoslavia was established. It was comprised of six republics (Serbia, Croatia, Slovenia, Macedonia, Montenegro, and Bosnia-Herzegovina) and was surrounded by seven nations (Austria, Hungary, Romania, Bulgaria, Greece, Albania, and Italy); it included four nationalities (Serbs, Croatians, Slovenics, and Macedonians), three main languages (Serbo Croatian, Slovenian, and Macedonian), three main religious traditions (Eastern Orthodox, Roman Catholic, and Islam), and two alphabets (Latin and Cyrillic). The great diversity that this represents speaks dramatically for the turmoil of this section of Europe.

The music, dance, and art of this region have much in common. The kolo is danced in all parts of the former Yugoslavia, but variations exist because of past influences. In predominately Muslim areas, women may not be visible; in Croatia, Slovenia, and North Serbia, as the result of western influence, the men and women may alternate; the silent kolos have resulted from the Turkish prohibition of native song; and where the Austro-Hungarian Empire dominated the northern section, the influence of the Catholic church and the church calendar and western music and dance are seen.

### Style

Kolos combine the Slavic dance traits of liveliness, gaiety, quickness, and gymnastic footwork. The dancers are relaxed from head to foot. The leader frequently carries a handkerchief, waving it to signal step changes or in rhythm to the music. The leader passes it to the next person to relinquish the position.

Serbia emerged as a nation at the end of the seventh century. The clans were fighting each other within; the Greek church and the Roman Catholic church each were struggling for domination in the Balkans; and the Turks, Russians, and Austrians were pressing from the outside. The Serbian culture is rich with influence from Turkey. Serbian dances usually move to the right. The steps are quite small, the upper body is "quiet," with most action below the knee. The soft leather, moccasin-type shoe, called *opanci,* allows for the rolling forward and backward action of the foot.

Macedonia is divided into three parts. Of the total population, 40 percent are Macedonian, 50 percent Greek-Macedonian, and 10 percent are Bulgarian-Macedonian. Located in the high mountains, the people are separated by streams and rivers; yet they share common traditions. Rich in timber, wheat, and minerals, Macedonia controls the route from central Europe down the valleys to the

Aegean Sea. Enemies have always desired Macedonia because of this pathway.

### Music

The tone of this region's music reflects intense feelings from sadness to gaiety. Occasionally a dancer will shout, expressing momentary emotion. The basic instruments are the svrala or frula (shepherd's pipe), the gaida (bagpipe), the gusle (fiddle), and the drum.

## Bulgaria

### Dance Characteristics

Although the area was originally occupied by Slavic tribes, the Bulgars, a Finno-Ugrian nomadic tribe, became established. Eventually the Slavic princes were driven out, but the ancient Slavic culture, including the language, persisted as the Bulgars settled and intermarried. Bulgarian music and dance reflect the influence of Greece, the Roman Empire, and the Ottoman Empire. Yet, in the mountainous regions, dance and rituals exist that show little influence of the invaders and are almost identical to those of Yugoslavia and southeast Russia.

The social aspect of Bulgarian dance tradition is a part of the Sunday horos, festivals, and country fairs. The customs (Joukowsky 1965) and dance are closely interrelated. The chain dances (horos) are the most popular. The Bulgarians dance with "devotion and dignity" and in general appear solemn as they move through complex rhythms. The upper body is "quiet," with most of the action in the feet. The skillful dancer is very light on his or her feet, almost "not touching the ground." The footwork is very precise. One word in the name of a dance frequently describes the character of the dance, for example, Tropanko Horo (stamped). There is great variety in steps, and the opportunity for the dancer to improvise and add personality is inherent. Although most horos move to the right, some move to the left; some move forward and backward with slight movement to the right or left. The tempos vary from slow to fast.

Through the various names for horos, it is suggested that the dance may be of Bulgarian, Romanian, or Turkish origin. Over the years, the horos have changed to meet the dancing tastes of the people of specific places and times. The chain dances used to follow very definite forms (closed, broken, led from one or two ends, straight line dance, crooked, and so on). There are also solo and couple dances, Ruchenitsa being the most common and the liveliest.

### Style

Different styles are associated with different regions. In southwest Bulgaria, dances are small-stepped and lively; in the north, they are more free, with humor and gaiety. Thracian dances are slower and more solemn and yet they are punctuated with stamps; the Drobrudza dances display more emotion, with the dancer's whole body moving at a moderate tempo and knees slightly bent.

Then there are the ritual dances. Some relate to nature, emphasizing the belief in the magic that certain dances are said to hold; others relate to religious holidays, marriage, and so forth. In Bulgaria, carnival dances and customs occur the week preceding Lent and at other feast days in the year.

Only recently has modern ballroom dancing reached the villages.

### Music

Singing, mostly by women, while dancing the horo is very common. The words express a wide range of moods. In some areas, antiphonal songs are common, with two or three singing and two or three others responding. Sometimes the folk instruments in various combinations are used as accompaniment. The instruments include three kinds, wind instruments like the gaida (bagpipe), various pipes, and the common whistle; string instruments like the gudulka, the gusla (a mandolin type), and the lute; and percussion instruments, including various sizes of drums and tympans. In place of folk instruments, orchestras of clarinets, violins, and drums are be coming popular, as is the use of military bands in small villages.

The most common meter is 2/4. But Bulgarian rhythms of unequal beats (5/16, 7/16, 9/16, and 11/16 meter) are characteristic of their music.

## Roma Culture

The Roma people moved from the East Indian region of Punjab during the twelfth century to all parts of Europe, including the Balkans. Roma people are often referred to as gypsies, a term that is considered derogatory. They are still thought of as a nomadic society. Today they live in permanent communities with their own rich culture of music and dance. The discrimination and prejudice toward the Roma as a race kept them autonomous. Only very recently has their wonderful music and dance started to move into the rest of the world's view.

# *Ersko Kolo*

## Serbian

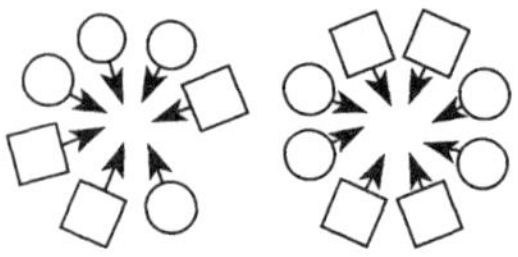

*Included by permission of Richard George Crum.*

ERSKO KOLO, PRONOUNCED *AIR-skoh KOH-loh,* was introduced at the University of the Pacific folk dance camp in 1955 by Richard Crum, who learned it in Yugoslavia.

> ***Dance A While* CD:** "Ersko Kolo."
>
> **Formation:** Open or closed circle, dancers facing center, hands joined in *V* position.
>
> **Steps:** Walk, run.
>
> **Level:** Beginning 1

## *Directions* FOR THE DANCE

Meter 2/4

| ***Measures*** | ***Counts*** | |
|---|---|---|
| | | **PART I. SLOW** |
| 1 | 1 | With right foot, step side right. |
| | + | Step left foot behind right. |
| | 2 | Step side right. |
| | + | Step left foot behind right. |
| 2–7 | | Repeat actions of measure 1 six more times, continually moving to the right while facing the center of the circle. (Counts: 3 + 4 + 5 + 6 + 7 + 8 + 1 + 2 + 3 + 4 + 5 + 6 + ) |
| 8 | 7 | With right foot, stamp right foot and take weight. |
| | 8 | With left foot, stamp left foot, do not take weight. |
| 9–16 | 1–8 | Repeat actions of measures 1 to 8 with opposite footwork. |
| | | **PART II. SCHOTTISCHE** |
| 1–2 | 1–3 | Turning one-quarter right to face line of direction, beginning right, take three running steps in line of direction on counts 1, 2, and 3. |
| | 4 | With weight on right foot, hop on count 4. Lift left knee up on hop. |
| 3–4 | 5–7 | Beginning left, take three running steps backward (clockwise) on counts 1, 2, and 3. |
| | 8 | With weight on right foot hop in place, turning one-quarter left, to face center. |
| 5–6 | 1–3 | Beginning right, take three running steps toward the center on counts 1, 2, and 3. |
| | 4 | With weight on right foot, hop. |
| 7–8 | 5–7 | Beginning left, take three running steps backward (out of center) on counts 5, 6, and 7. |
| | 8 | With weight on right foot hop in place, turning one-quarter right to face line of direction on count 8. |
| 9–16 | | Repeat actions of Part II, measures 1–8. |
| | | Repeat dance from beginning. |

### Styling

In Part I, be sure to keep facing straight towards center, while moving sideways. Always lift knee up on hop in Part II.

# *Hasápikos*

## Greek

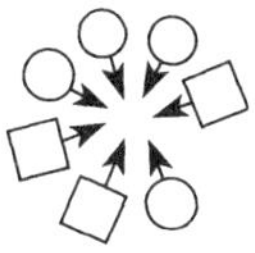

HASÁPIKOS MEANS "BUTCHER'S DANCE." Whereas the Americans call this dance Hasápikos, the Greeks refer to it as Serviko and reserve the word Hasápikos for the slow Hasápiko. This dance, known by different names, is common throughout the Balkans, the character of the variations differing.

**CD:** High/Scope RM 4.

**Formation:** Broken circle, arms extended, resting on adjacent dancer's shoulder (right in back of adjacent dancer's left), T position.

**Steps:** Walk, slide, step swing, pas de basque, skip, hop.

**Level:** Beginning 2

## *Directions* FOR THE DANCE

Meter 2/4

| ***Measures*** | ***Counts*** | |
|---|---|---|
| | | **PART I. BASIC STEP** |
| 1 | 1 | Line always progresses to right. With right foot, step to right side. |
| | 2 | With left foot, step side right behind right foot. |
| | | STEP SWING, measures 2–3. |
| 2 | 3 | With right foot, step side right. |
| | 4 | Lift left knee. |
| 3 | 5 | With left foot, step side left. |
| | 6 | Lift right knee. |
| | | **BASIC VARIATION: Cross in front.** |
| 1 | 1 | With right foot, step to right side. |
| | 2 | With left foot, step side right, crossing in front of right |
| 2–3 | 3–6 | Repeat step swing, measures 2–3. |
| | | **PART II. TURN** |
| 1 | 1 | Release arms and raise over head; with right foot, step to the right, point right foot toward the side right, beginning to do a full turn clockwise. |
| | 2 | Pivoting clockwise on right foot, ending with back to center, with left foot step side left, in line of direction. |
| | + | Pivoting clockwise on left foot, turn to face center. |
| 2–3 | 3–6 | Arms back to shoulder position, repeat actions of step swing, measures 2–3, Part I. |

*continues on next page*

| ***Measures*** | ***Counts*** | |
|---|---|---|
| | | **PART III: Progressive Turn** |
| 1 A | | Leader makes one turn while others in line dance basic step. |
| 1 B | | Leader and second dancer make one turn and then two step swings, while others dance basic step. |
| 1 C | | Or the leader may call oli ("all turn"). |
| | | **PART IV. SLIDE** |
| 1 | 1 | With right foot, step side right, starting a slide. |
| | 1+ | With left foot, bring left foot to right foot and take weight. |
| | 2 | Repeat actions of count 1. |
| 2–3 | 3–6 | Repeat actions of measure 1, two times. Toward end of musical phrase, take smaller steps to change pace back to basic step. |
| | | **PART V. SLIDE–STEP SWING** |
| 1 | | Repeat actions of measure 1, Part IV. |
| 2–3 | | Repeat actions of step swing, measures 2–3, Part I. |
| | | **PART VI. LEAP PAS DE BASQUE** |
| 1 | 1 | With right foot, leap side right. |
| | 2 | With left foot, leap side right, behind left foot. |
| 2–3 | 4–6 | Take two pas de basque steps in place. |
| | | **PART VII. TWISTING STEP** |
| 1 | 1 | With feet together, weight on heels, pivot and move toes side right. |
| | 2 | With feet still together, weight on toes, pivot and move heels side right. Knees slightly bent, body twists with each pivot. Repeat action as long as desired. |
| | | **VIII. SKIP PAS DE BASQUE** |
| 1 | 1–2 | Face slightly right. Beginning right, take two skipping steps in line of direction. |
| 2–3 | 4–6 | Face center and take two pas de basque steps in place. |

## Notes

1. The Greeks in the cafés cross in front and the folk dancers cross behind.
2. The leader indicates the order of figures.
3. The leader holds a kerchief in his or her right hand, arm raised, elbow bent, hand about the level of head, and signals change by twirling the kerchief.

## Style

The dancer's movement responds to the music. The step swing is more of a step lift, the knee bending slightly and straightening (body rises slightly) on the step. If the leader is a man, he shows his virtuosity by performing fancy acrobatic steps in time with the music, still leading the line. They are not as vigorous as Tsamiko.

# Kocanska Gada

*Permission to use Kocanska Gada courtesy of Šani Rifati, Sonoma County, California.*

## Roma

Šani learned Kocanska Gada while he was growing up in a Roma neighbor in Kosovo, southern Serbia. In order to share this dance with others, Šani agreed that it could be written down. The Romas' traditions are passed orally from one generation to the next. Children learn by dancing next to relatives at family celebrations. The following dance description is only a framework with which to start. The dance can be started at any point. Personal feelings and style may be added to this dance and are encouraged.

**Music:** Voiceofroma.com website.

**Formation:** Open circle that starts moving in line of direction, but snakes around the room as the dance progresses. Hands joined, held down in "V" position. The leader has a handkerchief in his free hand.

**Level:** Beginning 3

## Directions FOR THE DANCE

Meter 2/4

The dance can start anytime after the music begins. Arms swing forward and back on the beat. Watch the leader and follow any changes that might be done.

| *Measure* | *Counts* | |
|---|---|---|
| 1 | 1+ | Left foot step forward count 1. Right foot steps in place count 1+. |
| | 2+ | Left foot steps back count 2. Right foot steps in place count 2+. |
| 2 | 3+ | Left foot step forward count 3. Right foot steps in place count 3+. |
| | 4+ | Left foot steps next to right count 4, holding for 4+. |
| 3 | 1+ | Right foot steps forward count 1. Left foot steps in place count 1+. |
| | 2+ | Right foot steps back count 2. Left foot steps forward count 2+. |
| 4 | 3+ | Turning to face line of directions, left foot does a slight lift, almost a hop count 3. Right foot steps forward count 3+. |
| | 4+ | Right foot does a slight lift, almost a hop count 4. Left foot steps forward count 4+. |
| 5 | 5+ | Left foot does a slight lift, almost a hop count 5. Turning to face center, right foot steps side right count 5+. |
| | 6 | Left foot steps back count 6. |
| | + | Right foot steps in place count 6+. |
| | | Repeat the dance from the beginning. |

### Style

Small steps, with a bounce feeling.

# Lesnoto

## Macedonian

Lesnoto, or Lesno, is a common dance type in the regions of Macedonia and former Yugoslavia. Prior to World War II, the Macedonians traditionally danced it in separate lines, one for men and one for women. Currently, men and women dance together, particularly in the city, and when only the basic steps are performed.

***Dance A While* CD:** "Lesnoto."

**Formation:** Broken circle, hands joined, held at shoulder height, *W* position.

**Steps:** Walk, step swing.

**Level:** Beginning 1

## Directions FOR THE DANCE

Meter 7/8 • Directions are same for man and woman.

Commonly, the 7/8 rhythm is counted out in words, slow (counts 1–3), quick (counts 4–5), quick (counts 6–7).

| ***Measures*** | ***Counts*** | |
|---|---|---|
| | | **PART I. BASIC PATTERN LINE TRAVELS RIGHT.** |
| 1 | 1–3 | Face slightly right. With right foot, step side right (slow). |
| | 4–5 | Lift left knee across right (quick). |
| | 6–7 | Left foot step side right (crossing in front of right foot) (quick). |
| 2 | 1–3 | Facing center, step right foot so side right (slow). |
| | 4–7 | Lift left knee (quick, quick). Men lift left knee in front so that thigh is parallel to ground. Women lift left foot just off the ground and touch toe lightly in front of right foot. |
| 3 | 1–7 | Repeat actions of measure 2 to the left. |

Variations

| | | |
|---|---|---|
| | | **PART II. TURN** |
| 1 | | Release hand hold. Turning once clockwise, step right to side, pivoting to face out of circle (slow) step left, pivoting to face the center of the circle (quick, quick). Line continues to travel right. Men crouch slightly while turning. Rejoin hands. |
| 2–3 | | Repeat action of measures 2–3 of the basic pattern. |
| | | **PART III. SQUAT (MEN ONLY)** |
| 1 | | Repeat action of measure 1 of the basic pattern. |
| 2 | | Facing center, men squat with weight on balls of both feet, almost sitting on heels; knees face forward (slow), body rises, weight on right, lifting left knee as in basic pattern, measure 2 (quick, quick). |
| 3 | | Squat with weight on balls of both feet (slow), body rises, weight on left, lifting right knee as in basic pattern, measure 3 (quick, quick). |

**PART IV. COMBINATION**

1–3 Variations II and III may be combined with both men and women turning on measure 1; and on measures 2–3, men dance squats and women dance the basic pattern.

**PART V. STEP–HOP**

If the tempo is fast, add a step-hop on measures 2–3 with the knee lift.

## Notes

1. No introduction. Start dancing at the beginning of a phrase.
2. The variations may be introduced in any order at the discretion of the leader.

## Style

When men and women dance in same line and join hands at shoulder level, with right elbow bent downward and right palm facing upward, holding next dancer's left hand, left arm is held diagonally out to left side, with left palm facing downward and held by next dancer's right hand. Men (only) form separate line, using a shoulder hold; women use hold described above. Leader on right end holds handkerchief in right hand above head for signaling changes. The step is very simple; the subtlety of body movement reflects the Macedonian interpretation of the music and mood. The following suggestions will enable dancers to "catch the flavor" of the dance:

1. Hold the hands in the *W* position, slightly in front.
2. The footwork in Macedonia is light, close to the ground; not really bouncy or on "tippy toe."
3. In measures 2–3, during step lift of knee, there is a subtle double bounce following the step. The knee flexes slightly twice after the step. **Cue:** Slow quick quick, slow quick quick. Step flex flex, step flex flex.
4. Leader signals the variations by waving a handkerchief in a circle above head, anticipating a variation. To signal the turn, the right hand moves in front of the chest on the step left, swing right. This cues the line that a two-step turn follows.

# Misirlou

## Greek-American

The origin of Misirlou is most interesting inasmuch as it originated at Duquesne University in Pittsburgh (Holden and Vouras 1965). In 1945, Professor Brunhilde Dorsch, hoping to find a Greek dance for a program, contacted a Greek-American student, Mercine Nesotas, who taught several Greek dances to the dance group. The group enjoyed the dance Syrtos Haniotikos the most; Miss Nesotas called it the Kritikos. Because the appropriate music was not available, someone suggested that the steps be adapted to a slower piece of music, Misirlou. This dance was taught by Monty Mayo of Pittsburgh at Oglebay Folk Dance Camp, Wheeling, West Virginia, in 1948. It is danced all over the world now—even by Greeks.

***Dance A While* CD:** "Misirlou."

**CD:** High/Scope RM 8.

**Music:** "Misirlou," by M. Roubanis, Colonial Music Publishing Company, 168 West 23rd Street, New York, NY.

**Formation:** One large broken circle, joined hands held down, V position. Lead dancer at right end of line.

**Steps:** Two-step, grapevine.

**Level:** Beginning 3

## *Directions* FOR THE DANCE

Meter 4/4

| *Measures* | *Counts* | |
|---|---|---|
| 1 | 1 | Right foot steps in place, pointing left toe. |
| | 2 | Hold. |
| | 3 | Point left toe forward with a straight leg. |
| | 4 | Move left foot in a low circle counterclockwise, describe as an arc, to left and back toward right heel. |
| 2 | 5 | Left foot steps behind right. |
| | 6 | Right foot steps side right. |
| | 7 | Step left to right, crossing in front of right. |
| | 8 | Pivot counterclockwise a half-turn on left to face reverse line of direction. |
| 3 | 1-3 | Beginning right and moving clockwise, take one two-step. |
| | 4 | Hold. |
| 4 | 5 | Step back on left foot. |
| | 6 | Step right to side right, body facing center. |
| | 7 | Step left to side right, crossing in front of right. |
| | 8 | Hold. |

### Note

The dancer at the right end of the broken circle leads the line in serpentine fashion, coiling it counterclockwise, then reversing and uncoiling it clockwise, while executing the dance pattern.

### Variation

Measure 4: Beginning left, take one two-step backward, moving counterclockwise, and on last step pivot right on ball of left foot to face center.

# Pravo Horo

## Bulgarian

*Permission to use Pravo Horo courtesy of Dick Oakes, International Folkdance Instructor, Phantom Ranch, CO.*

PRAVO HORO IS PRONOUNCED *PRAH-voh hoh-ROH* and is translated as "straight (or direct) dance." The Pravo is found throughout eastern Europe and in the Balkans; it is called the national dance of Bulgaria, Albania, and Macedonia. There are many different variations of the basic step, and the order of the dance is freestyle, with the leader calling out different variations. Within that structure, individuals may also insert other variations, sometimes coordinating with two or more adjacent dancers for more enjoyment. This version flows in movement with the other dancers' steps.

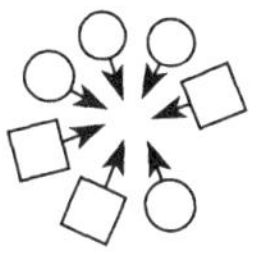

***Dance A While* CD:** "Pravo Horo."

**CD:** Any traditional Bulgarian music.

**Formation:** Open circle, hands joined in V position. When danced in short lines, dancers may hold neighbors' belts in a crossed arm position (right arm under).

**Style:** The style is rather heavy, with the knees always slightly bent.

**Level:** Beginning 1

## Directions FOR THE DANCE

Meter 2/4

| ***Measures*** | ***Counts*** | |
|---|---|---|
| | | Introduction: No action, or at the whim of the leader. |
| | | **BASIC STEP** |
| 1 | 1–2 | Facing center, step right sideways right and slightly diagonal forward on count 1. Step left near right on count 2. |
| 2 | 1–2 | Step right sideways right and slightly diagonal on count 1. Hold on count 2. |
| 3 | 1–2 | Step toward center with left, turning body so that left shoulder is somewhat toward center on count 1. Hold on count 2. |
| 4 | 1–2 | With right foot, step back from center on count 1. Step left foot next to right on count 2. |
| 5 | 1–2 | With right foot, step back again on count 1. Hold on count 2. |
| 6 | 1–2 | With left foot, step side left and slightly back on count 1. Hold on count 2. |
| | | **STAMP VARIATION** |
| 1 | + 1–2 | Facing center, stamp without weight on count *and,* step right sideways and slightly diagonal forward on count 1. Step left near right on count 2. |
| 2 | + 1–2 | Stamp without weight on count *and.* Step right sideways right and slightly diagonal on count 1. Hold on count 2. |
| 3–6 | | Repeat basic step. |

7

# *Pljeskavac Kolo*

## Serbian

*Dance arranged from the dance description by Michael Herman and reproduced here by permission of Folk Dance House, New York.*

PLJESKAVAC KOLO, PRONOUNCED *PLYE-skah-vahts KO-lo*, means "clapping kolo." It is a Serbian folk dance, a quick, easy, and charming introduction to the kolo.

> ***Dance A While* CD:** "Pljeskavac Kolo"
> **Formation:** Broken circle, joined hands held down, V position.
> **Steps:** Walk, stamp.
> **Level:** Beginning 1

## *Directions* FOR THE DANCE

Meter 2/4

| *Measures* | *Counts* | |
|---|---|---|
| | | **PART I. WALK, STEP IN PLACE** |
| 1 | 1–2 | Right foot steps diagonally right forward, left foot moves diagonally right forward. Circle moves counterclockwise. |
| 2 | 3+ | Step right, left, in place. |
| | 4 | Step right in place, pivoting one half-turn to left. |
| 3–4 | 5–8 | Repeat actions of measures 1–2, opposite directions. |
| 1–4 | 1–8 | Repeat actions of measure 1–4. |
| | | **PART II. STAMPS AND CLAPS** |
| 5 | 1–2 | Face center. Beginning right, take two walking steps (slow, slow) toward center. |
| 6 | 3–4 | Stamp three times right, left, right (quick, quick, slow). |
| 7 | 5–6 | Beginning left, take two walking steps (slow, slow) backward, away from center. |
| 8 | 7–8 | Clap hands three times (quick, quick, slow). |
| 5–8 | 1–8 | Beginning right, repeat action of measures 5–8. |

### Notes

1. Each walking step is done with a bounce and tremble of the entire body.
2. The leader may use a skip step instead of a walking step. Dancers follow the leader and use skip step too.
3. Spontaneous kolo shouts ("Veselo" . . . "hoopat svp–hup, hup, hup, tss, tss, tss," . . . or "ceceya") add to the interest of this dance.

# *Sarajevka Kolo*

## Bosnian

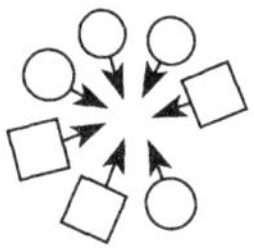

*Included by permission of Michael Herman, director of Folk Dance House, New York.*

SARAJEVKA KOLO IS PRONOUNCED *SAH-rah-yev-kah KO-lo*. The dance was introduced in this country by Michael Herman.

**CD:** Folkraft CD 2905.

**Formation:** Broken circle, joined hands held down, V position. Dancer at each end of circle places free arm behind back, fist clenched.

**Steps:** Step-hop, grapevine, pas de basque, walk, step-touch.

**Level:** Beginning 2

## *Directions* FOR THE DANCE

Meter 2/4

| | ***Measures*** | |
|---|---|---|
| | | **PART I. FAST MUSIC** |
| A | 1–2 | Face slightly right. Beginning right, take two step-hops, line moving right. |
| | 3 | Facing center, step right to right side, step left behind right (grapevine). |
| | 4–6 | Beginning right, take three small pas de basque steps (right, left, right). |
| | 7 | Face slightly left. Beginning left, take two walking steps to left. |
| | 8 | Step-hop left, turning on hop to face slightly right. The hop is a lift, ball of foot does not quite leave the floor. |
| | | Repeat action of Part I, measures 1–8 three times. |

Meter 4/4

| | | |
|---|---|---|
| | | **PART II. SLOW MUSIC** |
| B | 1 | Beginning right, take two slow walking steps, line moving right. |
| | 2 | Facing center, step right to right side, step left behind right, step right, touch left near right. |
| | 3 | In place, step left, touching right near left; step right, touching left near right. |
| | 4 | Beginning left, take three walking steps, line moving left. Pivot on left (count 4) to face right. |
| | 1–4 | Repeat action of Part II, measures 1–4. |

### Notes

1. As there is no introductory music, dancers may wait through the fast music and begin dancing with Part II, slow music.
2. The sequence of the music is AABBAAAABBAAAA, and so forth.

# Savila Se Bela Loza

Serbian

*Included by permission of Richard George Crum, Santa Monica, CA.*

Savila Se Bela Loza is pronounced *SAH-vee-lah say BAY-lah LOH-zah*, and means "a (grape) vine entwined in itself." The dance comes from Sumadija, Serbia. Dick Crum and Dennis Boxell introduced this dance to the United States.

> ***Dance A While* CD:** "Savila Se Bela Loza."
> **Formation:** Broken circle, joined hands held down, V position.
> **Steps:** Run, schottische, step–hop.
> **Level:** Beginning 1

## Directions FOR THE DANCE

Meter 2/4

| *Measures* | *Counts* | |
|---|---|---|
| | | **PART I.** |
| 1–9 | 1–18 | Face slightly right. Beginning right, take 18 small running steps. Line moves right (counterclockwise). |
| 10 | 19–20 | Jump on both feet. |
| 11–20 | 1–20 | Face slightly left. Beginning left, repeat action of measures 1–10. Line moves left (clockwise). |
| | | **PART II.** |
| 21–22 | 1–4 | Beginning right, take one schottische step, moving right. Or, facing center, step right, step left behind right, step–hop right. |
| 23–24 | 5–8 | Beginning left, take one schottische step, moving left. Or, facing center, step left, step right behind left, step–hop left. |
| 25–32 | 1–8 | Repeat action of measures 21–24 two times. |

### Variations

1. Measures 21–22: Face center, step right slightly forward, step left in place, step right beside left; hop right.

   Measures 23–24: Beginning left, repeat footwork.

   Measures 25–32: Beginning right, repeat action of measures 21–24 of variation 1.
2. Part II, a hop, step, step, step–hop may be substituted for the schottische step, traveling right and left or facing center and moving in place.

### Notes

1. No introduction. Music for Part I usually serves as an introduction, and dancers begin with Part II.
2. During Part I, measures 1–10, the leader on the right end may lead line anywhere, winding or coiling the line in a *counterclockwise* direction, even through an arch made by two of the dancers in the line. Measures 11–20, the dancer on the left end may lead line anywhere in a *clockwise* direction. The dancer on the left end never initiates the coiling; he coils only if the leader has coiled on measures 1–10. Neither the leader nor the end dancer should ever lead the line so that dancers will have their backs to one another.

### Lyrics

Singing these words while dancing adds a natural zest.

*Verse I*

| | |
|---|---|
| A. Savila se bela loza vinova<br>Uz tarabu vinova (repeat two times)<br>(Repeat A) | A pretty grapevine entwined itself<br>Along a fence, a grape (vine) |
| B. Todor Todi podvalio<br>Triput curu poljubio<br>(Repeat B twice) | Todor tricked Toda<br>Kissed the girl three times |

*Verse II*

| | |
|---|---|
| A. To ne beše bela loza vinova<br>Uz tarabu vinova (repeat two times)<br>(Repeat A) | It was not a pretty grapevine<br>Along a fence a grape (vine) |
| B. Todor Todi podvalio<br>Triput curu poljubio<br>(Repeat B twice) | Todor tricked Toda<br>Kissed the girl three times |

*Verse III*

| | |
|---|---|
| A. Vec to beše dvoje mili i dragi<br>Dvoje mili i dragi (repeat two times)<br>(Repeat A) | It was, rather, two lovers,<br>Two lovers |
| B. Todor Todi podvalio<br>Triput curu poljubio<br>(Repeat B twice) | Todor tricked Toda<br>Kissed the girl three times |

# Šetnja

7

## Serbian

*Šetnja included by permission of Richard George Crum, Santa Monica, CA.*

ŠETNJA IS PRONOUNCED *SHAYT-nyah* and is from Sumadija, Serbia. This dance is frequently done at Serbian festive occasions. A young man pays a Gypsy musician to play and he gathers his friends to join his line as they dance around the area. Dick Crum introduced this dance to the United States in 1955.

*continues on next page*

**CD:** Folkraft CD 2964.

**Formation:** Broken circle, left forearm held at waist level; right hand hooks and rests on left forearm of neighbor during slow music; joined hands held down, V position, during fast music. Leader at right end of broken circle.

**Steps:** Walk, step-hop.

**Level:** Beginning 2

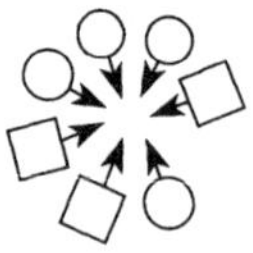

## *Directions* FOR THE DANCE

Meter 2/4

| ***Measures*** | ***Counts*** | |
|---|---|---|
| | | **PART I. WALK, SLOW MUSIC** |
| 1 | 1–2 | Facing line of direction. Beginning right, take two walking steps (slow, slow) in line of direction. |
| 2 | 3+ | Take two more walking steps (quick, quick,) moving in line of direction. |
| | 4 | With right foot, step right and face center (slow). |
| 3 | 5–6 | Step left behind right (slow), step right behind left (slow). |
| 4 | 7+ | Step backward left (quick), step right next to left (quick). |
| | 8 | Step left across in front of right (slow). |
| 5–8 | | Repeat action of measures 1–4 for slow music. |
| | | **PART II. STEP-HOP, FAST MUSIC** |
| | | Joined hands, held down |
| 1 | 1–2 | Face line of direction. Beginning right, take two step-hops in line of direction. |
| 2 | 3+ | Moving in line of direction, take two steps (quick, quick). |
| | 4 | Step-hop right, turning to face center on hop. |
| 3 | 5–6 | Step-hop left behind right, step-hop right behind left. |
| 4 | 7+ | Step backward left (quick), step right next to left (quick). |
| | 8 | Step-hop left across in front of right. |
| | | Repeat action of Part II, measures 1–4, until end of music. |

### Notes

1. No introduction. Start action with the beginning of a phrase.
2. During Part I, the manner is quite casual, with flexing knees. Part II is more exuberant as the dancer runs, taking the step-hops and two-steps.

### Lyrics

These words may be sung while dancing.

1. Dodji, Mile, u naš kraj, pa da vidiš, šta je raj. (repeat)
   Hej, haj, u naš kraj, pa da vidiš šta je raj. (repeat)
2. Prodje, Mile propeva, i volove protera. (repeat)
   Hej, haj, propeva, i volove protera. (repeat)

# Syrtós

## Greek

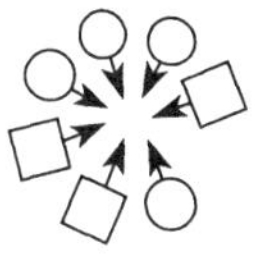

Syrtós is the most traditional folk dance in Greece. Basic footwork is always the same but varies in styling. The music may be 2/4, 4/4, or 7/8 meter. Kalamatianos, a Syrtós from Kalamata, is 7/8 rhythm. Whatever the meter, it is counted slow, quick, quick. Syrtós means "to pull or lead," which is characteristic of the dance movement.

***Dance A While* CD:** "Syrtós."

**CD:** Folkraft CD 2901. Most Greek albums include a good Syrtós.

**Formation:** Broken circle, hands joined, shoulder high, elbows bent, W position. Dancer at either end of broken circle may place free hand on hip, fingers pointing backward, or arm extended, snapping fingers.

**Step:** Walk.

**Level:** Beginning 2

## *Directions* FOR THE DANCE

Meter 2/4

Slow, Quick Quick is a good way to cue this rhythm.

| *Measures* | *Counts* | |
|---|---|---|
| 1 | 1 | Face center. Beginning right, step side right (slow). |
| | 2 | Step left behind right (quick). |
| | + | Step right to side right (quick). |
| 2 | 1 | Step left crossing in front of right (slow). |
| | 2 | Step right to side right (quick). |
| | + | Step left crossing in front of right (quick). |
| 3 | 1 | Step side right (slow). |
| | 2 | Touch ball of left foot slightly forward toward center (slow). |
| 4 | 1 | Step left backward (slow). |
| | 2 | Touch ball of right foot slightly behind left (slow). |
| | | Repeat pattern throughout the dance. |

### Style

The leader may be a man or a woman. A kerchief is usually held between the first and second dancers in line. This allows the leader greater freedom to execute variations. The second dancer gives the needed support to the leader to perform acrobatic moves. The dancers continue the basic step.

### Variations for Leader

1. Measure 4: Leader makes one solo turn counterclockwise, spins on left, touches right.
2. Measures 1–2: Leader steps right (slow), makes two solo turns clockwise (quick, quick, slow, quick), and steps left (quick).
3. Measures 1–2: Leader makes three solo turns clockwise (slow, quick, quick, slow, quick, quick) and joins the group on measure 3, step point.

# Tropanka

Bulgarian

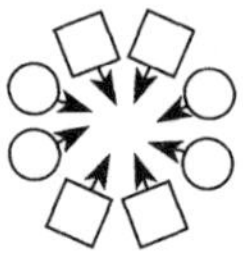

THIS LIVELY STAMPING DANCE is ideal for beginning an evening of fun with folk dancing for novice groups.

***Dance A While* CD:** "Tropanka."

**Formation:** Single circle, nonpartner dance. Joined hands, shoulder height, *W* position.

**Steps:** Walking, step-hop, stamp.

**Level:** Beginning 3

## *Directions* FOR THE DANCE

Meter 2/4

| *Measures* | *Counts* | |
|---|---|---|
| | | **PART I. WALK AND STAMP** |
| 1–2 | 1–4 | Beginning right, move with five quick walking steps (shuffle-like) counterclockwise, stamp left foot twice and pause. |
| 3–4 | 5–8 | Repeat beginning left, moving clockwise, stamp right foot twice. |
| 5–8 | 1–8 | Repeat measures 1–4. |
| | | **PART II. STEP HOP AND STAMP** |
| 1–2 | 1–4 | Face center, step-hop on right, swing left slightly across right. Step-hop on left, swing right slightly across left. Step on right in place and stamp left foot twice and pause. |
| 3–4 | 5–8 | Repeat measures 1–2, beginning left, and end stamping right twice and pause. |
| 5–8 | 1–8 | Repeat measures 1–4. |
| | | **PART III. TO CENTER AND BACK** |
| 1–2 | 1–4 | Beginning right, step-hop twice toward center, step on right and stamp left twice. |
| 3–4 | 5–8 | Repeat measures 1–2. Moving backward, begin left. |
| 5–8 | 1–8 | Repeat measures 1–4. |

### Note

During the move to center, joined hands are raised as dancers move in and lowered as they move out.

# British Isles

## Introduction

The British Isles were settled by the Celts, who came across from the Continent, by the Milesians, a nomadic Celtic tribe who came to Ireland from northern Italy (Lombardy), and then by invaders from the Basque country (Gallicia). Scotland was settled by the Picts (of uncertain origin) and the Scots, who came from Ireland. Subsequent invading tribes (Romans, Angles, Saxons, Normans, Danes) influenced the culture of the British Isles. The Celts practiced Druid rites, which included dancing, and some of the pagan rites were retained during their conversion to Christianity. A constant exchange of culture existed among the English, the Irish, and the Scottish as the result of natural migration, war, and travel by sailors from one country to another. Hugh Thurston (Thurston 1964, 5) has commented that the figures and the steps of the country dances during the period of 1720–1800 were so similar, with national characteristics lacking, that a particular dance could not be identified as English, Scottish, or even American.

ALB: Albania, BIH: Bosnia Herzegovina, HRV: Croatia, MKD: Former Yugoslav Republic of Macedonia, MNT: Montenegro, SVN: Slovenia

## England

### Dance Characteristics

England's Morris and Sword dances are two ritual dance forms, performed for renewal and continuance of life, that have survived over the centuries. The third form is the country dance, a term that covers a variety of social dances. According to Douglas Kennedy, "These English country dances came directly from the folk in the form of rounds and squares and longways and contras. Having established themselves as fashionable ballroom forms, they continued through the times of the Stuarts, Commonwealth, the Restoration, Queen Anne and the Hanoverian line right into our own century" (Kennedy 1964, 112).

### Morris Dance

Morris dance for centuries has been part of the spring Whitsuntide festival. Whit-Monday was the day for the Morris men to perform, a custom that was little known outside rustic villages in the English countryside until the nineteenth century. In 1899 Cecil Sharp observed an out-of-season Morris dance performed by six men dressed in white shirts, adorned with ribbons and padded leg bells, as they pranced and "footed" it in the snow of winter on the outskirts of Oxford. From that experience, Sharp was inspired to delve into the music, dance steps, and history of the Morris. The result was *The Morris Book*, a five-part publication that has been an invaluable source of information concerning this ancient ritual.

The origin of the name Morris is shrouded in the mist of history and is speculative at best. The Whitsuntide custom goes back to before the Norman conquest. Whether the dance had a name then is not known. In addition, the Morris has been estimated to have been in existence since the twelfth century. Scholars can only theorize about the name; however, the Moorish or Spanish origin of the name has generally been discounted.

In its early form the Morris included character actors such as the squire, clown, and fool, any one of whom would act as the leader depending on the region and/or Morris tradition from which they came. Other characters taking part in this ancient dance-drama were the hobby-horse, animal-men, and Maid Marion or "Betsy." During these early times the men dancers played a subsidiary role to the actors. In more recent times, the actors have become secondary to the dancers, who entertain with their spectacular athletic feats.

During its long history the Morris was plagued by ecclesiastical restrictions issued from Rome and Canterbury. In addition, the Puritans waged a vigorous campaign against this traditional rustic pastime. They succeeded in destroying so many of the countryside customs that not even Charles II could restore

7

all the Morris customs and all the Maypoles! This attitude came with the Puritans across the ocean to the colonies where, as occurred in some American southern communities, the word "dance" had to be replaced with the word "game."

The last 50 years has seen a revival of the Morris in America. Contemporary times even find the Morris danced by women. Today there are three organizations: the Morris Ring for men only, the Women's Morris for women only, and the Open Morris for men and women. At present no federation of Morris teams is based in the United States or Canada. Communication between groups and about group events is facilitated by the *American Morris Newsletter*, published in Silver Spring, Maryland.

## Sword Dance

The English Sword dance is a technically intricate, exciting, and dramatic dance form handed down by example and oral tradition from the remote past. The dance, coupled with the play or dramatic action, has a half-magic and half-religious aura.

The Sword Dance Play consists of two aspects, dancers who blacken their faces or wear masks, and a retinue of characters consisting of (depending on region and tradition) the hobby-horse, clown, the woman Beson Betty or Dirty Bet, and often a king, queen, lord, lady, and a quack doctor with his Jack. Although performed at other times of the year, the Sword dance's season traditionally was midwinter on Plough-Monday. It was through the absorbing and diligent work of Cecil Sharp that the details of this fast-dying dance tradition and the content and materials of the drama associated with it have been preserved. Sharp's three-part publication of *The Sword Dances of Northern England* remains today the invaluable source for information concerning this ancient custom.

The Sword dance is distinguished by the type of instrument used. The Yorkshire tradition consisted of a long rigid sword made of wood or iron. The Northumberland and Durham version, which was shorter and more flexible, was called a rapper. The dance is commonly referred to as the "Long Sword" or "Rapper" dance.

The rapper was fitted with handles at each end and a swivel at the hilt so that the blade could twist and turn within the hand. This turning feature coupled with the shorter blade allowed the dancers to twist and turn as individuals or for the whole group to literally turn inside out. *Stepping*, a highly skilled dance movement, was used to change patterns, alternating with the weaving of the swords in a figure. The Rapper dance style was acrobatic and breathtakingly exciting.

The very nature of the long sword with its more rigid blade eliminated the acrobatic elements found in the Rapper performance. The Long Sword dance thus is more elaborate and ceremonial in nature yet still dramatic and fascinating. Common to both performances, however, were the "dramatis personae" of the ancient Plough Play, the "lock," knott (sic), or rose, and the "calling on" stage by accompanying actors or characters.

The Long Sword dance always finished with a "lock." In some traditions the "lock" is tied around the neck of one of the accompanying characters, who then dies dramatically. In other traditions the beheaded actor simply gets up, brushes himself off, and leaves, thus signaling the end of the play. In still other traditions the beheading begins the dramatic part of the play. A mock doctor appears, accompanied by his Jack, to undertake a cure of the dead and restore him to life. The symbolism is that of fashioning new life from the ashes of the old, a repeated theme in Sword dance-dramas thought to be associated with the Mummers' plays.

The Rapper dance tradition seems to be found mostly in the coal mining districts of northern England. Versions of the Rapper dance vary little, which is thought to be a consequence of its existence in closely knit coal mining societies. The design of the sword, its length, and versatility are thought to be a product of the iron workers of antiquity.

## Country Dances

*By Kate Van Winkle Keller, Darnestown, MD, and George A. Fogg, Boston, MA.*

English country dances came to notice in the late 1500s as group dances performed at court and in sophisticated private gatherings. The first publication was in 1651 when John Playford gathered up more than 100 country dances then currently popular in London society. They were in a number of forms: rounds, squares, two- and three-couple, and longways sets; some were very simple ("Rufty Tufty"), others, more complex ("Chelsea Reach"). By 1690 when an eighth edition of his hugely popular book, called *The Dancing Master*, appeared, most of the old dances had been dropped in favor of a longways progressive formation in which couples stand in parallel lines, men in one line facing their partners in the other. This formation persists today in traditional and contra dances.

Longways country dances are performed in small groups within a larger set, the first couple in each "minor" set leading the figures. The dance has six or eight figures, such as back-to-back, hand-turn, circle, or lead through, that are arranged to fit the music and move the leading couple down one place. Each time the dance is repeated, the leading couple performs the figures again with a new subgroup in the set. The popularity of country dancing hinges on the repetitious nature of the figures and its flexibility. In the seventeenth and eighteenth centuries, steps were optional and were chosen by the leading couple to suit the company. The specific dance was also chosen for the occasion–those with more complex figures for elite dancers in public assemblies, simpler ones for dancers in barns and taverns.

Country dances served as an important cultural vehicle in British, European, and New World social settings between 1660 and 1800. Over this period, old court-oriented societies were replaced by materialistic middle-class people who displayed gentility and manners on the dance floor as badges of achievement. Country dances faded from view in the early nineteenth century as behavior and appearance ceased to be a defining social standard.

English Country Dancing Today English country dances flourish again today as a living tradition. In the nineteenth century, once it was acceptable to hold your partner in your arms in polite company, the waltz and the polka took over the ballrooms. Dancing was no longer something just to look at and admire, but something to enjoy physically, regardless of who was watching. But country dances persisted among country folk and were taught by rural dancing masters long enough to be remembered by the older generations when Cecil J. Sharp learned about them in the early 1900s. He collected and published a number and then sought their history in libraries. He interpreted old dance terms that had long gone out of use and took the lead in bringing English country dances back into vogue.

Since that time, modern dancing masters have created many new dances within the country dance form to fit the social mores of their day. Today, on both sides of the Atlantic Ocean, many follow Sharp's lead, seeking out and interpreting interesting old dances published by Playford, Bray, Walsh, Neal, and the Thompson family. Some are creating new material in the old forms, and others, such as Pat Shaw, have composed dances that synthesize traditional English, Scottish, and American idioms.

The earliest country dances were danced with Renaissance steps such as single, double, and perhaps some steps from the showy galliard. In the eighteenth century, elite dancers adopted French steps such as *pas de bourrée,* minuet, *contretemps,* rigadoon, and *balancé.* Today most country dances are performed with a smooth dance-walk, bouncy sets, and occasional slipping steps or skipping.

Music Country dances are composed to popular tunes of all kinds: old ballad tunes, marches and arias by Purcell and Handel, elegant dances from the theater, and joyful fiddle tunes from countryside. English country dances are tied to their tunes and the same tune is played throughout the dance. Tunes usually comprise two or three repeated eight-bar phrases in duple or triple meter. Present tastes in the United States lean toward triple meter tunes, and many new and old dances in triple time are found on ball and class programs.

Although it is impossible to define a typical country dance tune, some qualities can be observed. Smooth melodic motion, distinct cadences, and harmonic and rhythmic drive are present in the most satisfying tunes. Because each phrase is usually repeated, full modulations are seldom present, although tunes in AABA form often do modulate in the B strain, setting up a dramatic return to A ("La Belle Catherine").

Instruments to accompany early country dancing varied from a pipe and tabor (played by one person) to a full orchestra plus pipe organ, as found at assemblies in eighteenth century Bath. Over the years, the fiddle was probably the most commonly used instrument. Today, dances are usually accompanied by combinations of three or four instruments such as concertina, fiddle, flute, piano, accordion, harp, cello, and many others.

## Ireland

### Dance Characteristics

Despite a common background with the other British Isle countries, Ireland's dance and culture tend to be very different from Scotland's and England's. There are three types of Irish folk dances: jigs, reels, and hornpipes. Jigs and hornpipes are characterized by clog and tap steps, and reels by shuffle or gliding steps. The dances follow traditional formations of solos, couples, and groups or sets. The specially trained solo dancers perform step dances based on clog or shuffle steps. The popular dances are jigs and reels (simple steps) in round, square, and longways formations.

The tradition of Feis (a celebration of competitions among the poets, singers, musicians, storytellers, and dancers held after harvest in November) dates back to 1300 B.C. It has been suggested that it was originally a form of Thanksgiving. Different Celtic countries had a similar tradition but referred to it by other names. In the Feis contests, women were allowed to compete, and the minstrel in that period had more status than the warrior. The strong tradition of Feis is credited with keeping Irish folk music and dance alive. Despite difficult times when the Irish came to the United States, immigrant minstrels perpetuated their heritage, which has become a part of American folk music.

When the famous dancing schools–such as those at Limerick, Kerry, and Cork–were established, a polished style evolved and natural expressions were eliminated, with emphasis placed on the footwork. Some of the spontaneity of expression was lost. But the dance schools and competitions are to be credited with keeping the Irish dance tradition vibrant.

### Style

Characteristics of the Irish people, such as their keen sense of humor, happiness, wit, imagination, and superstition, prevail in their dances and music. The dancer is erect, hands at the sides, and face rather impassive. The range of movement is minimal. The distinguishing characteristic is the intricate and exact footwork. In the most difficult dances, there are about 75 taps per quarter minute. The control of the various sounds produced by the taps of heels and soles on the floor and against each other is of utmost importance in competitive dancing. Although the dances are based on five simple steps, improvisation and elaboration of steps are delightful characteristics of Irish dance.

### Music

Originally, the fife and harp were used for dance accompaniment. Today, fiddles, flutes, violins, and accordions are popular. Irish music is very lilting. The secondary rhythm of the tapping feet combines with the melody to create an interesting effect.

## Scotland

### Dance Characteristics

The unbroken history of Scottish dance has long been preserved as part of Scotland's strong national pride. The practice of regimental troops dancing to relieve tension before battle or to celebrate victories is one aspect of the Scottish heritage. After the 1745 rebellion when the English tried to end the clan system and suppress the Highland culture, the Scottish ways of dress, dance, and music became even stronger when they were forced underground. When the ban was lifted in 1782, Scotland's fierce national pride was stronger than ever. The Highland battalions, moving abroad and eventually around the world, wore their kilts and continued their ceremonies and dance traditions.

Another tradition, the Highland games, continues to stimulate interest through dance, bagpipe, and athletic contests. The Scottish Country Dance Society is to be credited with standardizing steps and techniques, setting up a system of exams and certificates, and publishing many Scottish dances.

Almost all Scots can dance several of their traditional dances. Today, during an evening of social dancing, a waltz country dance, a petronella, a skip the willow, or a highland schottische are usually included.

### Style

The Scots are very enthusiastic about dance and have always entered into it with a great deal of zest. Highland solo dancing or competitive dancing, such as the Highland Fling and Sword dance, are intricate and athletic. The carriage of the body is very erect and the supporting leg is kept straight. The toes are pointed at all times. Arms are used for balance. The hand and arm positions are exact; either the fists are at the hips, the arms curved over the head, with thumb and third finger touching, or one arm is held above the head and the other is held at the hip. The body movement is upward, with hopping or jumping off one or two feet on the first beat. This is referred to as *snap*. The feet beat in the air soundlessly. The body is propelled back upward into the air when the heel touches the floor. Elaborations of steps occur while the body is in the air.

### Music

Scottish Highland dances have been performed traditionally to the music of the bagpipes, which have a nine-note scale. The lilting rises and falls of the tunes influence the dance style. The snap occurs when a sixteenth note is followed by a dotted eighth. Although the first note, the first beat, is light and gives impetus to the next note, which is stressed and louder, the intake of breath when playing the bagpipe has become the snap or sixteenth note. Only the bagpipe can express the peculiar quality and rhythm of Highland dance music. The fiddle and piano are now played in many parts of Scotland for reels and jigs.

# The Bridge of Athlone

## Irish

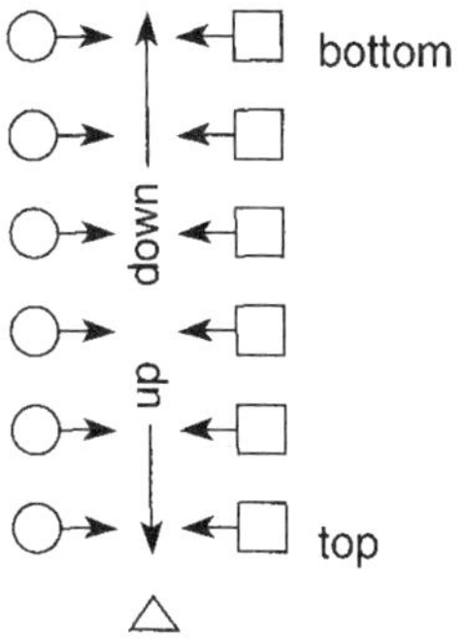


THE BRIDGE OF ATHLONE IS AN Irish dance that contains a figure representing the Bridge.

**CD:** Folkraft 2909.
**Music:** *Rakes of Mallow*; any good reel.
**Formation:** Longways set, even number of couples, facing each other, women on left side from the top.
**Steps:** Walk, side step (sevens and two threes).
**Level:** Beginning 1

## Directions FOR THE DANCE

Meter 2/4 • Directions are the same for man and woman.

| ***Measures*** | |
|---|---|
| 1–8 | Introduction: No action. |
| | **PART I. ADVANCE AND RETIRE** |
| 1–4 | Hands joined in a row. Beginning right, two lines walk toward each other and back up. |
| 5–8 | Repeat action. |
| | **PART II. SIDE STEP** |
| 1–4 | Hands still joined, side step to own right. (See side step analysis at end of dance.) |
| 5–8 | Repeat side step to left, now in original position. |
| | **PART III. DOWN THE CENTER AND BACK** |
| 9–10 | Couple 1, join both hands crossed, face to face, dance "seven" down the center. |
| 11–12 | Turning clockwise a half turn, dance "two threes." |
| 13–16 | Returning to top of set, dance "seven" and repeat half turn clockwise, dancing "two threes." |
| | **PART IV. CAST OFF** |
| 9–16 | Couple 1 casts off around the outside, walking sprightly, man left, woman right, to the bottom of the set. Other dancers follow the leaders. |

*continues on next page*

***Measures***

**V. THE BRIDGE**

1–8 Couple 1 joins two hands to form an arch at the bottom of the set. The other couples join two hands, go under the arch, and return to the top of the set.

Couple 2 will now be at the top of the set; couple 1, at the bottom. When they reach this position, all face their partner and raise two hands to form bridges the length of the set.

1–8 Couple 1 releases hands. Woman walks up the set under the bridges, the man walks up the outside (men's line).

9–16 At the top, the man walks to the bottom under the bridges, the woman goes down the outside (women's line). When they reach the bottom, they face each other and become the bottom couple.

The dance is repeated (without the introduction) until all have had an opportunity to be couple 1.

**SIDE STEP**

Meter 2/4 • Made up of two parts: "sevens" and "two threes."

**Sevens**

1–2 Moving sideward to the right, with a little jump (both feet off the ground), land on the toes, right heel over left toe (count 1). Step right a short step to the right (count 2). Step left toe to right heel (count 3). Step right a short step to the right (count 4). Step left toe to right heel (count 5). Step right a short step to the right (count 6). Step left toe to right heel, right foot lifted slightly (count 7). Hold (count 8). Repeat to the left, reversing the movements.

**Two Threes**

Each measure is counted: "one, two, *three*."

1 Beginning right, step on toe behind the left heel, lifting the left foot slightly (count 1). Step left in place and lift right foot slightly (count 2). Step right behind left and lift left foot slightly (count 3–actually 2 counts).

2 Repeat action of measure 1, beginning left.

The step may begin right or left. The step may be done in place or sideways.

# *Butterfly Hornpipe*

*Directions and permission to publish courtesy of George A. Fogg, Boston, MA.*

## English (Warwickshire)

THE BUTTERFLY HORNPIPE WAS PRESENTED by George A. Fogg at the Third Annual English Country Dance workshop at Lost Pines Dance Hall, Bastrop, Texas, in fall 1992.

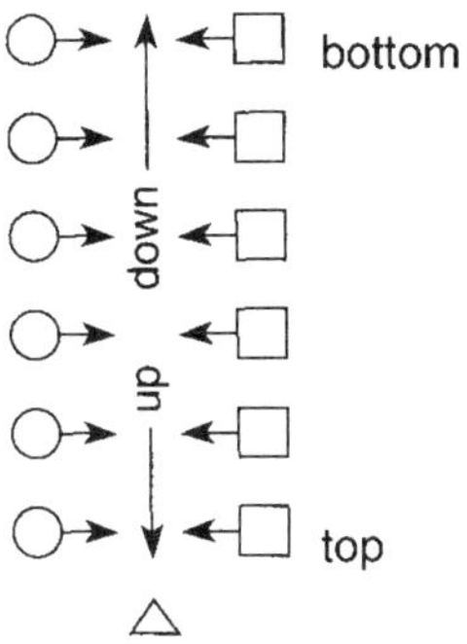


**Source:** *Community Dance Manual 1; Country Dances of Today 1* and Sharp, Cecil, *Country Dance Book 1.*

**Original:** Collected by Cecil J. Sharp.

**Music:** Any good hornpipe such as Manchester or Rickett's, also found in *Community Dance Manual 1* and *Country Dances of Today 1.*

**Formation:** Duple minor longways. Number couples 1, 2, 3, 4, 5, 6.

**Step:** Jaunty walking low easy schottische, two step.

**Level:** Beginning 3

## Directions FOR THE DANCE

Meter 4/4 • Directions are same for man and woman, except where specially noted.

***Measures***

**PART A1.**

1–8 Right-hand star and left-hand back, walking or easy schottische.

**PART A2.**

1–8 Arching (over and under), walk or easy schottische. (Ones over twos; then twos over ones and repeat.)

**PART B.**

1–8 In closed position, dance (two-step or schottische) one and one-half times around each other to change places.

Odd couples (1, 3, 5) move down the set one place and repeat dance with new couple below (couple 1 with couple 4, couple 3 with couple 6, and couple 2 and couple 5 inactive).

# *Flowers of Edinburgh*

## Scottish

*This dance is used by the permission of the Royal Scottish Country Dance Society, 12 Coates Crescent, Edinburgh, Scotland, EH3 7AF. Patron—Her Majesty The Queen; President—The Earl of Mansfield; Secretary—Miss M. M. Gibson. Permission granted April 16, 1986. [From Preston, 24 New Country Dances for the Year 1797.]*

DANCES WITH JACOBITE[1] NAMES, like Flowers of Edinburgh, may have been composed by the many fiddlers in Scotland. After the 1745 rebellion, the pipes were banned. The chiefs had their own fiddlers and the dances usually depict a famous battle, event, or, in many instances, a place name.

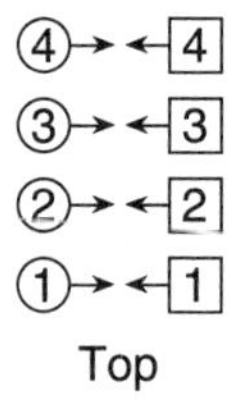


**CD:** Folkraft.

**Formation:** Longway reel-time dance. A four-couple set involving three couples in each 32-bar repetition. Top of set is indicated by left shoulder of first man.

**Steps:** Skip change step, pas de basque, poussette.

**Level:** Intermediate

## *Directions* FOR THE DANCE

Figure 1

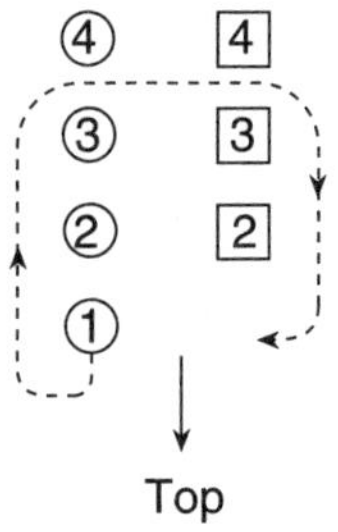


Figure 2

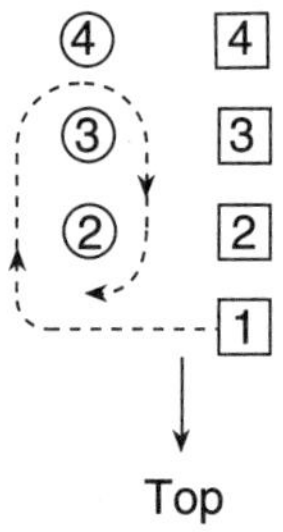


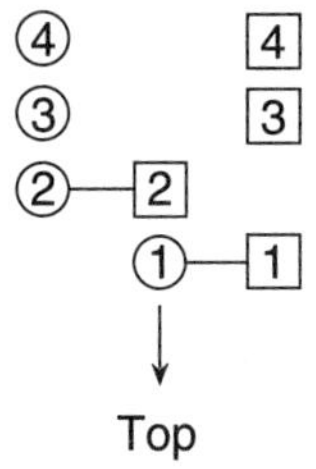


Meter 2/4 • Directions are same for man and woman, except where noted.

| ***Measures*** | |
|---|---|
| 1–6 | Dance begins with honors: men bow, women curtsey. |
| | First woman turns around by the right, and casts off two places (i.e., dances down behind second and third woman, then crosses over and dances up behind second and third man to her partner's original position, Figure 1). At the same time, first man follows his partner, crossing over and dancing behind second and third women, then up the middle to his partner's original position, Figure 2. (Six skip change steps.) |
| 7–8 | First couples set to one another. Two pas de basques. |
| 9–14 | Repeat bars 1–6, but first man leads as in Figure 1, and first woman follows, as in Figure 2. First couples finish in original position. (Six skip change steps.) |
| 15–16 | First couple set to one another. (Two pas de basques.) |
| 17–24 | First couple lead down the middle and up again. (Eight skip change steps.) |
| 25–32 | First and second couples poussette. (This is the progression sequence). **Notes:** Men begin with left foot. Repeat, having passed a couple. |

1. Jacobites were a political force attempting to establish the house of Stuart as the rightful heirs to the throne of England.

### Scottish Steps and Formations

**Skip Change Step:** Begin in first position. Skip (hop), on left foot while extending right foot forward, knee straight and toe pointed. Step on right foot, keeping leg straight and firm. Close left to right in third rear position (remain on toes). Step forward onto right foot. **Cues:** Skip (hop), step, close, step.

**Pas de Basque:** Push off left foot and leap sideways onto right, weight on ball of foot. Close left foot into third position front and change weight onto ball of left foot. Step back (shift weight onto right foot, keeping weight on ball of foot as left foot is extended forward in fourth intermediate position, toes down. **Cues:** Leap (count 1), step across (count 2), step in place (count 3). Step, beat, beat.

**Poussette:** Both hands joined at shoulder level, elbows at side, hands held firmly. Men begin with left foot. Couples dance eight pas de basque steps. The two couples change places by dancing along the sides of a square, couple 1 down the man's side, couple 2 up on woman's side. Couples dance one step away from center (measure 1); both quarter-turn on corner of square, pull with right hand–men now have backs to top of set. They are on sideline of set (measure 2); both travel up or down the set (measure 3); both quarter-turn, pull with right hand–men have backs to woman's side of set (measure 4); both dance to center of set (measure 5); both turn around to own sides (measure 6); all dancers fall back to sidelines. Dancers have now changed places (measures 7 and 8). *Note:* Pas de basque is used as a traveling step, moving forward and back. **Cues:** Away from center quarter-turn, up or down quarter-turn, dance into center turn half around, and fall back, fall back.

**Set or Setting:** Two pas de basques in place as directed.

# Gie Gordons

## Scottish

**_Dance A While_ CD:** "Gie Gordons."

**CD:** Folkraft CD 2908.

**Music:** _Folk Dancer,_ Volume 7, No. 4, p. 11.

**Position:** Varsouvienne.

**Steps:** Walk, two-step, pas de basque.

**Level:** Intermediate

## Directions FOR THE DANCE

Meter 2/4 • Directions are same for man and woman, except where noted.

| ***Measures*** | |
|---|---|
| | **PART I. WALK** |
| 1–2 | Beginning left, walk four steps forward in line of direction. On fourth step, pivot clockwise to face reverse line of direction. Woman is now on man's left. |
| 3–4 | Continue walking backward four steps in line of direction. |
| 5–8 | Repeat action of measures 1–4 in reverse line of direction. |
| | **PART II. TWO-STEP** |
| 9–12 | Man beginning left, takes four two-steps in line of direction, as woman, beginning right, turns clockwise under man's right arm four two-steps. Or man, beginning left, woman right, pas de basque out and in and man takes four walking steps in line of direction as woman turns twice clockwise under man's right arm. |
| 13–16 | Closed position. Man beginning left, woman right, takes four two-steps turning clockwise, progressing in line of direction. Or takes two two-steps turning clockwise, then man walks four steps forward, progressing in line of direction as woman twirls under raised right arm. Assume Varsouvienne position. |

### Note

This dance may be done with inside hands joined instead of Varsouvienne position.

7

# Oslo Waltz

Scottish-English

THE OSLO WALTZ IS a lively family-type waltz mixer. It is of Scottish-English heritage, set to a Norwegian folk song.

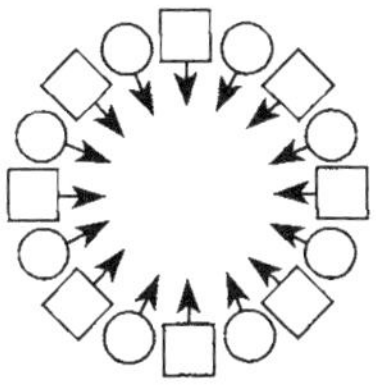

**Music:** Waltz.

**Formation:** Single circle, couples facing center, woman to the right of partner, all hands joined.

**Steps:** Waltz, waltz balance, three-step turn.

**Level:** Beginning 3

## Directions FOR THE DANCE

Meter 3/4 • Directions are for man; woman's part reverse.

| ***Measures*** | |
|---|---|
| | **PART I. WALTZ BALANCE AND LADY TURN** |
| 1–2 | Man begins left; all take one waltz balance forward. Man begins right; all take one waltz balance back. |
| 3–4 | Man begins left, takes waltz balance steps in place as he guides left-hand woman from his left to his right side. Woman makes one clockwise turn in two waltz steps as she crosses over. |
| 5–16 | Repeat measures 1–4 three times. |
| | **PART II. STEP-SWING, THREE-STEP TURN** |
| | Single circle, partners face in butterfly position. Man's new partner is woman on his right. |
| 1–4 | Man begins left, steps left to side, swings right across left. Steps right to side, swings left across right. Dropping hands, couples three-step turn individually toward center. |
| 5–8 | Man begins right; couples repeat step-swings and three-step turn to place. |
| | **PART III. DRAW, WALTZ** |
| 1–4 | Butterfly position: Man begins left; couples take two step-draws toward center. Repeat two step-draws away from center. |
| 5–8 | Closed position: Man begins left; couples take four waltz steps, turning clockwise, progressing counterclockwise around the circle. |
| | Repeat dance from the beginning. |

# Road to the Isles

## Scottish

Road to the Isles is a favorite marching song of the pipe bands. The tune called "Bens of Jura" was composed by Pipe Major MacLellan about 1890 with words by Dr. Kenneth McLeod. The original words are very similar to the song "Border Trail." The dance is relatively new in composition and is similar to the Scottish Polais Glide and the Douglass Schottische.

**CD:** High/Scope RM 5.

**Music:** Rohrbough, Lynn, Cooperative Recreation Service, *Sing it Again, Handy II*, p. 16.

**Position:** Varsouvienne.

**Step:** Schottische.

**Level:** Beginning 2

## Directions FOR THE DANCE

Meter 2/4 • Directions are same for man and woman.

| *Measure* | *Counts* | |
|---|---|---|
| | | **PART I. POINT, GRAPEVINE** |
| 1 | 1–2 | Point left toe forward, diagonal left. |
| 2 | 3–4 | Step left behind right (count 3), right to right side (count 4). |
| 3 | 5–6 | Left in front of right (count 5), and hold (count 6). |
| 4 | 7–8 | Point right toe diagonal, right forward. |
| 5–6 | 1–4 | Step right behind left (count 1), left to left side (count 2), right in front of left (count 3), and hold (count 4). |
| 7–8 | 5–8 | Point left toe forward (body leans backward), point left toe back (body leans forward). |
| | | **PART II. SCHOTTISCHE** |
| 9–10 | 1–4 | Beginning left, take one schottische step in line of direction. |
| 11–12 | 5–8 | Continue with a right schottische step. Without releasing hands, turn clockwise on hop (count 8) to face reverse line of direction. Woman is now on man's left. |
| 13–14 | 1–4 | Beginning left, take one schottische step in reverse line of direction. Without releasing hands, turn counterclockwise on hop to face line of direction. Woman is now back in original position on man's right. |
| 15–16 | 5–8 | Stamp in place right, left, right. |

### Style

The Scottish flavor may be added by precise and petite foot movement. Kicking the heel up on the hop of the schottische step so as to flick the kilt is characteristic.

# *Siamsa Beirte*

Irish

SIAMSA BEIRTE, PRONOUNCED *SHI-um-suh BEHR-ti*, means "a frolic for two." Siamsa Beirte is a 2/4 hornpipe time, *not* a reel. Una and Sian O'Farrell introduced Siamsa Beirte at the Stockton Folk Dance Camp in 1956.

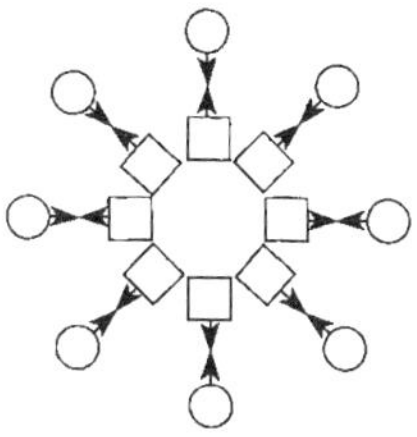

***Dance A While* CD:** "Siamsa Beirte."

**Music:** "Bluebell Polka," *Country Dancer,* May 1951, p. 16, or any evenly phrased Irish hornpipe.

**Formation:** Double circle, partners facing, man's back to center, right hands joined at shoulder height and left hand hanging relaxed by side.

**Steps:** Threes, rock, schottische.

**Level:** Intermediate

## *Directions* FOR THE DANCE

Meter 2/4 • Directions are for man; woman's part reverse.

| ***Measures*** | |
|---|---|
| 1–8 | Introduction: No action. |
| | **"THREES" AND ROCK** |
| 1 | Beginning right, hop in place, step to left on left, step right almost behind left, step left (counts *and* 1 *and* 2). Do not dip on second step. |
| 2 | Beginning left, repeat action in other direction (counts *and* 1 *and* 2). |
| 3–4 | Beginning right, hop in place; bringing left behind right, step on left, hop left; bringing right behind left, step on right, hop right; bringing left behind right, step on left; rock to side on right, rock to side on left (count *and* 1 *and* 2 *and* 1 *and* 2). The rock is side to side with feet close together, the right foot crossed in front of the left. Raise weight onto ball of foot and rock. The woman begins on the left foot but steps one foot behind the other as does the man. |
| 5–8 | Beginning with *left hop,* repeat action of measures 1–4 in reverse line of direction. |
| | **"THREES" AND CHANGE OVER** |
| 9 | Repeat action of measure 1. |
| 10 | Beginning with *left hop,* take one schottische step to change places. Man moves around woman as she turns counterclockwise under joined right hands. |
| 11–12 | Repeat action of measures 9–10 and return to original position. |
| | **IRISH TURN** |
| 13–16 | Take both hands, crossed so that man's right joins woman's right on top and man's left joins woman's left underneath. Hold at shoulder height, elbows bent. Man pulls right hand toward him and down and under the left, rolling up so that the woman's forearms are resting on |

*continues on next page*

him. Beginning with right hop, take four polka steps, turning clockwise, progressing in the line of direction. Irish folk dance teachers refer to this polka (hop 1–3) as "turning threes." Both pull away slightly, remaining in a true facing position for this turn.

### Style

The body is held erect but not stiff, with the head high; the steps are small, lively, and clean cut, with the toes pointing down.

### Note

The rhythm hop, step, step, step is taken in even rhythm (and 1 and 2) even though it is referred to as a polka.

# *Three Meet*

## English

*Dance arranged from the dance description by May Gadd,* Country Dances of Today, Book 2, *Country Dance Society of America, May 1951.*

THREE MEET IS A DANCE of greeting from northern England and Northumberland.

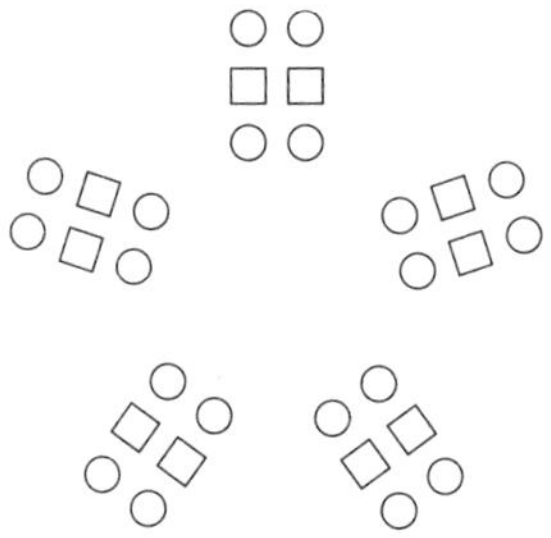

**CD:** Folkraft.

**Music:** Gadd, May, *Country Dances of Today, Book 2,* p. 15; Kennedy, Peter, *Fiddler's Tune Book 1.* Tune: "When Daylight Shines," p. 42.

**Formation:** Sets of three, two women and a man, or vice versa, arms linked, facing another set of three. All sets form large circle; alternately, one faces line of direction, the other reverse line of direction.

**Steps:** Running step, buzz step.

**Level:** Beginning 2

## *Directions* FOR THE DANCE

Meter 4/4

***Measures***

| | |
|---|---|
| | **PART I. FORWARD, BACK, AND CHANGE SIDES** |
| 1–4 | Take four steps, moving forward, four steps moving backward. Take eight steps on a diagonal to right, passing opposite set and turning counterclockwise a half-turn to face same set on opposite sides. |
| 5–8 | In new place, repeat action of measures 1–4 to return to original place. |
| | **PART II. ELBOW SWING** |
| 9–10 | Taking eight steps, the middle dancer turns right-hand partner with right elbow swing twice around in place. |

| ***Measures*** | |
|---|---|
| 11–12 | Middle dancer takes eight walking steps, turning left-hand partner with left elbow swing twice around. On last two steps, the three in set cuddle up (arms reach around each other, middle dancer's arms underneath) to form a basket of three. |
| | **PART III. BASKET IN LINE OF THREE** |
| 13–16 | In cuddle position, sets progress diagonally to right passing each other, while turning clockwise with a buzz step (right foot crossed in front of left), and meet new set coming in opposite direction. |
| | Repeat dance, each set dancing with new set. |

### Note

The English country dancers are particular about attacking each new phrase of music on time.

### Style

The English running step is a light, bouncy, dignified half-walk and half-run step. The body is in a dignified easy posture. The free hand of each outside dancer in the set hangs free to the side. The middle dancer holds the arms of the two partners in closely to his or her sides so that the threes can move easily as a unit. As a dance of greeting, the spirit is as light-hearted as the music. The dancers enjoy visiting around the circle to each new set of three.

# *The White Cockade*

## Scottish

*This dance is used by the permission of the Royal Scottish Country Dance Society, 12 Coates Crescent, Edinburgh, Scotland, EH3 7AF. Patron—Her Majesty The Queen; President—The Earl of Mansfield; Secretary—Miss M. M. Gibson. Permission granted April 16, 1986. [From Preston, 24 New Country Dances for the Year 1797.]*

THE WHITE COCKADE,[1] like the Flowers of Edinburgh on page 292, is another example of a dance from Scotland with a Jacobite name.

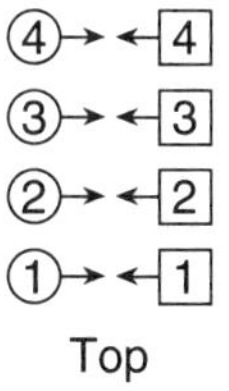


**Music:** Any eight-time 32-measure reel in 4/4 meter.

**Formation:** Longways reel-time dance. A four-couple set involving three couples in each 32-measure repetition. Top of set is indicated by left shoulder of first man.

**Position:** Feet in first position, hands by side.

**Steps:** Skip change step, pas de basque, slip step, setting.

**Level:** Beginning 3

1. Cockade is a rosette or a knot of ribbons usually worn on the hat as a part of a uniform or as a badge of recognition.

*continues on next page*

## *Directions* FOR THE DANCE

Figure 1

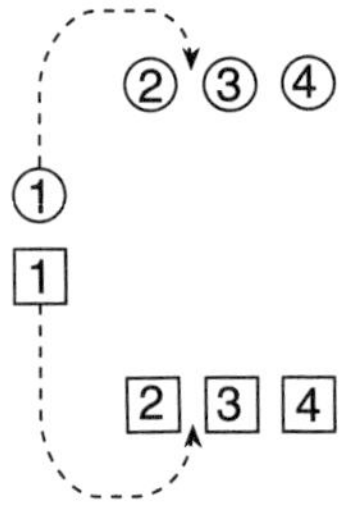

Figure 2

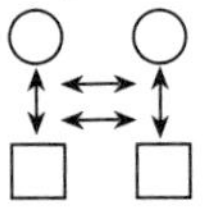

Meter 4/4 • Directions are same for man and woman.

| ***Measures*** | |
|---|---|
| 1–8 | Dance begins with honors to partner: men bow, women curtsey. First, second, and third couples set and cross over with two skip change steps giving right hands, then set and cross back with two skip change sets to original places, again giving right hands. |
| 9–16 | First couple leads down the middle and up again to top place in the middle of the dance. (Eight skip change steps.) |
| 17–20 | First couple casts off to second place on own side. Second couple steps up on measures 19–20. (Four skip change steps.) See Figure 1. |
| 21–24 | First and third couples dance four hands around to left. (Eight slip steps.) |
| 25–32 | Second and first couples dance rights and lefts with eight skip change steps. See Figure 2. |
| | Repeat, having passed a couple. |

### Note

Dance is repeated from second position, now involving third and fourth couples. Couple at the top stands and waits. At the end of the second sequence (32 measures), original first couple slips below the fourth couple, who now moves up. A new top couple starts the next 32 measures, or the third sequence. Once at the bottom of the set, the top couple becomes the new first couple.

### Scottish Steps and Formations

**Set or Setting:** Two pas de basques in place facing as directed.

**Skip Change Step:** Begin in first position. Skip (hop) on left while extending right foot forward, knee straight and toe pointed. Step on right foot, keeping leg straight and firm. Close left to right in third rear position (remain on toes). Step forward onto right foot. **Cues:** Skip (hop), step, close, step.

**Right and Left:** Each dancer extends right hand to partner and changes places across the line; each dancer faces up or down the line, gives left hand to other man or woman dancer, and changes places in line; each dancer gives left hand to other man or woman and finishes in original place. **Cues:** Across the line, up or down the line, across the line, up and down the line.

**Slipping Step:** This is used in all circles danced in reel or jig time, and in dances where the dancers join both hands to slip down, up, or across the dance. The step is started from first position (i.e., heels together, feet turned out at right angles, with heels raised; take a step sideways with left foot (second position), bring right foot to left foot with heels touching (first position). **Cue:** step, together; step, together. Movements normally done in circles to the left and right.

# *Willow Tree*

## English

WILLOW TREE WAS COMPOSED by Hugh Rippon, formerly with the English Folk Dance and Song Society, in 1968. It is based on the Dutch folk dance Gort Med Stroop.

**Music:** Medley of "Willow Tree," (6/8) "Wabash Cannonball" (2/4), "Golden Slippers" (2/4); Werner, Robert, *The Folklore Village Saturday Night Book,* p. 37; *English Dance & Song* Autumn 1963; *English Folk Dance & Song Society, Everyday Dances,* p. 14.

**Formation:** Longways set, eight couples. Head and foot couples are active; *do not* cross over.

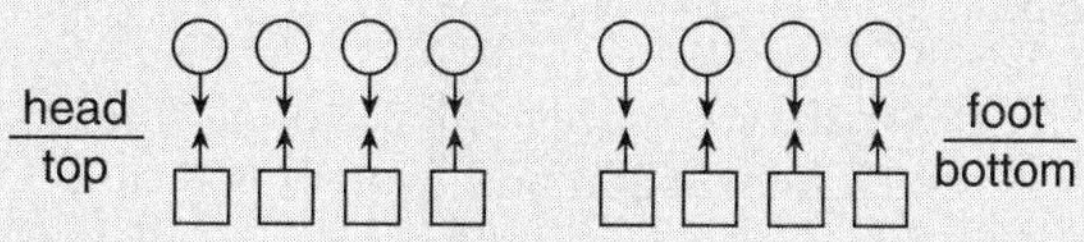


**Steps:** Slides, walk, buzz step swing.

**Level:** Beginning 2

### Note

No call. Could prompt.

## *Directions* FOR THE DANCE

Introduction: No action (4 counts).

A1, A2 **Partner change** (32 counts). Head couple, two hands joined, takes eight slides to foot of set (8 counts). Others clap hands. Head man leaves his partner at the foot, joins two hands with foot woman, and they take eight slides to head of set (8 counts). Foot man and woman 1 join two hands and take eight slides to head of set (8 counts). Foot man leaves woman 1 at the head of set and takes his original partner, two hands joined, and takes eight slides to return to original position (8 counts).

B1, B2 **Elbow Reel** (32 counts). Active couples, head and foot couples reel, hooking right elbows with partner in middle of set, and turn clockwise once and a half, separate. Active men turn counterclockwise next woman in line, with left elbows hooked, once around as active women turn next man in line with left elbows hooked once around. Head couples move down, foot couple up the set turning alternately next person in line with left elbow and then partner with right elbow until active couples meet in middle of set (between couples 4 and 5). Each dancer is on original side. Head and foot couples join hands to form a ring of four, raise hands to form four arches.

C1 **Cast Out and Promenade** (16 counts). The remaining three head couples (2, 3, 4) face up the set; the remaining three foot couples (5, 6, 7) face down the set. Couples 2 and 7 individually cast out, walk down the outside of the set to the middle of set, move through arch made by head and foot couple; meet partner in center of ring of four, join inside

*continues on next page*

hands. Couple 2 faces up, couple 7 faces down, move through the other arch, returning to head or foot of set. *(See diagram.)* Single-file, couples 3, 4, 5, and 6 move to head or foot of set, cast out, move through arches and promenade up or down set to next position.

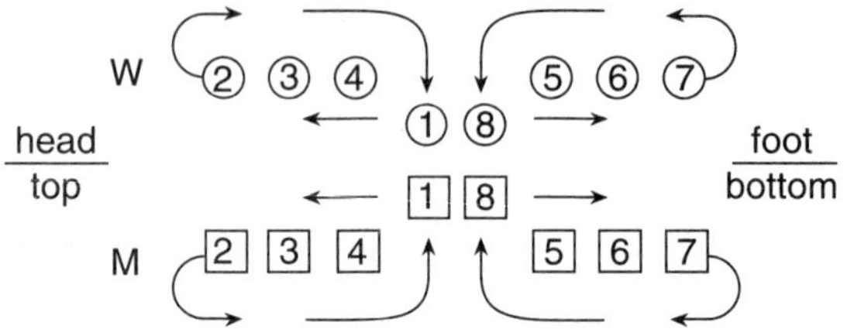


C2 **Swing** (16 counts). All couples swing. Couples 2, 3, and 4 have moved up one position and couples 5, 6, and 7 have moved down one position. Couples 1 and 8 are now in the middle of the set.

## Notes

1. Repeat dance until all couples have been active once or twice.
2. Forearm grasp may be used for reel.
3. Eight couples work best, but adjustments for six to ten couples are possible. Divide set in half; e.g., three couples and four couples. The reel can move faster or slower to complete.
4. The first figure must be danced to the proper music. The swing may be shortened or eliminated to accommodate those that are behind.

7

# Canada

## Discovery and Settlement

The Norse voyager Lief Ericson is purported to have sighted the east coast of Canada about A.D. 1000. Nearly 500 years later, in 1497, the Italian navigator John Cabot, sailing under the sponsorship of King Henry VII of England, landed on the northeast coast of North America. A second voyage in 1498 took him as far south as Cape Cod.

French exploration of the Bay of Fundy, Nova Scotia, and the Gulf of St. Lawrence began in the early 1500s. Jacques Cartier ascended the St. Lawrence as far as present-day Montreal and established a colony at Quebec. Settlers from Normandy and Picardy, along the English Channel, established Acadia in Nova Scotia in 1604.

In the ensuing 250 years, the French and English colonized the eastern seaboard of North America (Canada and the United States) and brought with them their culture, including music and dance. The last half of the eighteenth century (1750–1800) saw the French lose their foothold in Canada, and their governance in North America was removed to Louisiana. The English held on to northeastern Canada, but lost out to the revolutionaries of the Thirteen Colonies.

The early part of the nineteenth century (1800–1840) saw a great influx of Scots to eastern Canada, settling in Prince Edward Island, Cape Breton, and Nova Scotia.

## Population

Ninety percent of the Canadian population has settled mainly along the border of the United States. The cultural and ethnic origins of the population are represented primarily by British (English, Scottish, Irish, and Welsh), French, and German groups, followed next by people of Ukrainian, Italian, Dutch, Scandinavian, Polish, Jewish, and Russian backgrounds. Other groups include Native Americans, Eskimos, Asians, East Indians, other Europeans, and Africans.

## Culture

The three main cultural influences–English, French, and Scottish–have shaped the current traditions. The settlers who came to the New World brought with them their love of dancing seventeenth and eighteenth-century dances. Scottish Highland dancing, Scottish country dancing, Cape Breton step dancing, and French Canadian dance are very dominant. There is also a wide variety of European square dances and contra dances similar to that in the United States.

## Cape Breton

Cape Breton was originally inhabited by the Mi'kmaq Indians and in the eighteenth century was sparsely settled by the French. The present culture was influenced by the arrival of 30,000 Scots from the Highlands and western isles of Scotland, forced to leave between 1800 and 1850. This was a result of the Highland Clearances. Cape Breton became a stronghold of Gaelic culture. Its musical heritage, particularly a unique style and tradition of Scottish fiddling, thrives (Dunlay and Greenberg 1996).

The interrelationship of Cape Breton step dancing and rhythmic fiddle music is important in the preservation of each. An unbroken tradition of step dancing, solo form and social dancing, traces back to the earliest settlers from Scotland. The strathspeys and reels from Scotland were the original social dances. The introduction of the lancer and quadrille sets replaced the Scottish dances. It is an interesting course of Scottish country dancing both in Scotland and Cape Breton, coming, going, disappearing. The traditional Cape Breton fiddle music suited the new dances (lancer and quadrille), which thus survived. Today, step dancing has received great interest beyond Cape Breton. The tradition is kept alive by the explosion and interchange of recordings, publications, new compositions, traveling teachers, and musicians.

# La Bastringue

## French-Canadian

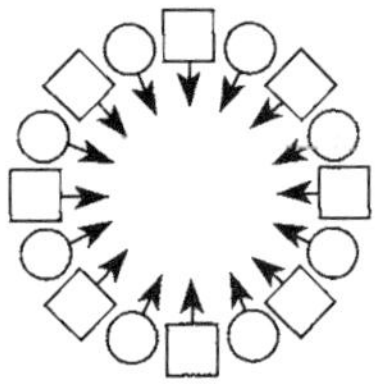

La Bastringue is a French Canadian mixer.

**Dance A While CD:** "La Bastringue."
**Formation:** Couples in a single circle, man's partner is on his left.
**Hand hold:** W position.
**Steps:** Walk, two-step, and buzz swing.
**Level:** Beginning 3

## Directions FOR THE DANCE

Meter 2/4 • Men and women use the same footwork.

| *Measures* | *Counts* | |
|---|---|---|
| | | **PART I. WALKS** |
| | | Introduction: 20 counts |
| 1–2 | 1–4 | Beginning right, take three steps to the center, counts 1–3. On count 4 tap left foot next to right. |
| 3–4 | 5–8 | Beginning left, take three steps back, counts 1–3. On count 4 tap right foot next to left. |
| 5–8 | 1–8 | Repeat action of measures 1–4. |
| | | **PART II. TWO-STEP (Keep arms in W position).** |
| 1–4 | 1–8 | Beginning right, take four two-steps in reverse line of direction. |
| 5–8 | 1–8 | Four two-steps in line of direction. |
| | | **PART III. SWING** |
| 1–2 | 1–4 | Man lifts his left arm up and woman turns under clockwise. |
| 3–8 | 5–12 | Swing position. Man beginning left, woman right, buzz step clockwise for 12 counts. |
| | | **PART IV. TWO-STEP WITH PARTNER** |
| 1–7 | 1–8<br>1–6 | Open position, forward hands released and arms (man's left, woman's right) hanging at the side, facing line of direction, beginning right, take seven two-steps forward, progressing in line of direction. |
| 8 | 7–8 | Turning one quarter-turn counterclockwise (man backing up, woman moving forward), take one two-step left to face center. Join hands in *W* position around the circle and repeat the dance from the beginning. |
| | | Man has new partner on his left. |

7

# *The Saint John River*

## Canadian

THE SAINT JOHN RIVER was composed by Prudence Edwards in 1966. This Scottish country dance won first place in a contest to commemorate Canada's Centennial in 1967. Pru Edwards was a member of the Fredericton Scottish Country Dance Group, New Brunswick, and now lives in Galiano, British Columbia.

**Music:** 32-bar strathspey. *Brave of Balquidder,* Singing Birds; *The Bonnie Lass o' Bon Accord;* Mary Hamilton.

**Formation:** Four couples in a four-couple set. All face center of set.

**Step:** Strathspey.

**Level:** Intermediate

## Directions FOR THE DANCE

Meter 4/4

| ***Measures*** | |
|---|---|
| Chord | Arms relaxed at sides, men bow from the waist. Women lift skirt slightly, right foot behind left, and curtsy. Arms are relaxed at sides unless specifically noted. The strathspey step is used throughout the dance; man and woman always begin with right foot. |
| | **PART I. THE STREAM** |
| 1–8 | First woman casts behind the second woman, crosses the set and casts behind the third man, crosses the set, casts behind the fourth woman, crosses the set and finishes below the fourth couple on the opposite side. The woman glances coquettishly back at her partner occasionally to be sure he is following. First man follows his partner to finish below the fourth woman on the opposite side. |
| | **PART II. THE BRIDGES AND THE SALMON POOLS** |
| 9–16 | First couple, inside hands joined, dances up under the two-hand arch formed by the fourth couple (measures 9–10); join two hands (arms graceful above waist–not stiff–man aiding the woman) and dances four strathspey steps, turning once and a half clockwise; inside hands joined, dance up under arch formed by the second couple (measures 15–16), finishing in original position. |

*continues on next page*

***Measures***

**PART III. THE REVERSING FALLS**

17–24 First couple, man's right hand joins woman's right hand, dances down the middle and up, followed by the second, third, and fourth couples. At the bottom, the first man and woman turn toward each other and dance up the set. The second couple individually dance one step up, turn toward each other, man takes partner's right hand with his right hand and dances two steps down the middle. They separate and turn out two steps up, turn toward the middle, and join right hands and one step home. The third couple follows the second couple, two steps up, turns, join right hands in the middle, goes down two steps, separates and turns out, two steps up, turns and goes down two steps home. The fourth couple individually dances four steps on the outside to the top, touches hands *briefly* (almost a push away), turns out and dances four steps back to place.

The first and fourth couples must be alert to complete their path.

25–28 In straight lines, facing center, all four couples pass partner's right shoulders, dance back to back (do-si-do).

**PART IV. THE RIVER MEETS THE SEA**

29–32 First couple dances a right-hand hey on own side to the bottom of the set; changing places with the second couple with right hands, third couple with left hands, and fourth couple with right hands to finish in fourth place facing center. First man and fourth woman make polite turns on last step (an extra quarter-turn).

Repeat dance with new top couple.

Bow to partner at the end of the dance.

## Notes

1. The Saint John River forms a portion of the border between New Brunswick and Maine and flows into the Bay of Fundy. On occasion, high tides flow upstream.
2. The figures reflect the various portions of the Saint John River as it moves through New Brunswick.

   *The Stream* (measures 1–8) describes the meandering course of the river as the man chases the woman.

   In *The Bridges and the Salmon Pools* (measures 9–16), couple one dances under an arch (bridge) and circles (as if in a pool).

   *The Reversing Falls* (measures 17–24) describes the action of the ebb tide as the river runs downstream over a shallow waterfall; the flow reverses with the incoming high tide.

   *The River Meets the Sea* (measures 29–32) has a wavelike back-to-back movement, and the head couple wends down the set as the Saint John River disappears into the sea.

# China

China is a vast country encompassing a civilization dating back more than 4,000 years. Discoveries of late Stone Age sites on the Loess Plateau along the Yellow and Wei Rivers indicate that the Chinese civilization did indeed develop independently of South Asian and Western cultures.

Scholars trace the first Chinese state to the Shang dynasty (ca. 1766–1122 B.C.). Priests, scholars, officials, and artisans of the Shang dynasty developed agriculture, formalized religion, set up government and legal systems, produced writing and literature, began the tradition of dynasties, and developed handicrafts and metallurgy. All of these accomplishments clearly distinguished China from other cultural systems of the same period. A common means of communication in the written literature has always been a unifying factor between past and present in Chinese culture.

China is a gigantic multinational country made up of the Han, the Chinese people, who represent approximately 90 percent of the population, and more than 50 national minorities. It is this mix and the influence they had on one another that created the common cultural tradition of the Chinese people. The bulk of dance before and after liberation has come from the minorities.

China experienced its first multinational unified state during the Han dynasty. Unification led to stability, economic progress, and frequent contacts between nationalities within and outside the borders. Under these circumstances literature, art, and dance flourished. A board of music was established to collect and improve folk song and dance. Variety shows became the vogue for performing and entertaining. These shows included acrobatics, martial arts, comic acts, recitals of music, song, and dance as well as other folk arts. The widespread popularity of the variety shows drew audiences from hundreds of miles around.

During the more than 400 years of the Han dynasty artists created many dances. Dancers underwent strict training during this time and were successful in raising dance to a new artistic level. However, the low social status of the dancer was such that only the figurines and stone engravings buried with the feudal nobles remain to tell the story of their work.

Music and dance were the main performing arts during the Tang dynasty. Although based on traditional dance, the choreography was bold and innovative and embraced many national folk dances as well as those introduced from abroad. It is said that whenever the Chinese adapted anything from abroad it was as if they had taken it as a prisoner to do with as they pleased. Tang arts absorbed everything, and given fairly stable political and economic conditions, a golden era in the development of dance in China's feudal society was created.

The Ming and Qing dynasties were the final stages of China's feudal system. Popular thought and action at this time bore the seeds of capitalism and a thriving city life spurred a boon in the arts. Traditional opera, singing, and story telling flourished while dance performances alone were rare. Dances at local festivals at this time were widespread. The traditional Lantern Festival held on the fifteenth day in the first month of the lunar calendar was a particularly joyous occasion for song and dance. Homes and streets were festooned with lanterns, fireworks were set off, drums and gongs sounded, and the Lion Dance and the Monk with the Big Head Dance were traditional attractions. Chinese literature in the form of books, poems, accounts, and recollections attest to the continued popularity of dance among the populace at festival times.

In the intervening years after the dynasty system became history and the Republic exited to Taiwan, some efforts were made to collect and arrange folk dance materials but the major effort was left to be done after liberation. Almost immediately the Chinese government seized on folk dance as a means of fostering national spirit and to present the people as happy and cheerful members of the new Chinese society.

National minority dances played an important role in the overall mosaic of Chinese folk dance. Their work, life, love, and customs were bound up in their dance, which was largely passed along by oral tradition. Handwritten historical documents carried few records of their dances. The most influential were the Mongol, Tibetan, Uygar, Miao, Korean, Yao, and Dai minorities. The following are some examples of the style and type of minority dance that was popular in central China.

In 1951, two years after liberation, a large celebration of song and dance called "Great Unity of the People" was held in Tiananmen Square. It was an opportunity for national minorities to demonstrate their dances as well as a national review of the achievements of professional dancers from the folk art tradition of old China. In 1952 the performance toured all areas of China to demonstrate unity and exuberance for the new society.

Under a policy adopted by the Chinese Communist Party and the central People's Government, national minority art and literature was to be developed. This policy led to extensive research, study, and rearranging of many of the traditional dances throughout China. Specifically, folk dance disciplines were set up in dance schools, dance teachers collected and arranged dance materials, and studies of dance in classical Chinese opera were undertaken aided by older performers in the opera. In the mid 1950s Chinese dance leaders created a national dance with a distinct style based on the study of national, traditional, and foreign dance forms. The result was "The Precious Lotus Lamp," the first large-scale dance-drama. A second large-scale dance-drama, "The East Is Red," which was especially supported by Premier Zhou Enlai, required some 3,000 dancers. This epic covered the various stages of the Chinese revolution.

Suddenly the Gang of Four headed by Jiang Qing came to power and brought to a virtual halt all the work in dance and other arts. During the 10 years of their influence artists, dancers, singers, and musicians were cruelly treated; they were executed, imprisoned, or sent to the country to do manual labor. In 1976 this foursome was ousted and national art was liberated for the second time. Since the mid 1970s, the national art movement has regained its momentum and is once again teaching, practicing, researching, and staging mammoth and spectacular performances for audiences in China and abroad.

China is presently awash in dance. Dances are created in villages, cities, communes, schools, factories, and professional dance schools. It is seen in parks, courtyards, plazas, indoors, and outdoors. A festival held in Beijing in 1972 was reported to have had more than 2,000 amateur groups performing. Performers, even eight- and eleven-year-olds, are polished, technically adroit, and project theater-quality proficiency.

Dance in China is an expression by and of the people. It is about them and exists for them. The frames of reference are contemporary situations, historical events, revolutionary themes showing workers, peasants, and soldiers as heroes and heroines, and stories of the crimes of the old society. Movement styles come from minority nationality forms, work techniques of the field and factory, old dances of the Tang and other dynasties, and even a touch of Wu Shu, a traditional style of physical culture. Regardless of the style or content, the dance is always presented in a joyous, happy, and exuberant mode.

The new China is clearly allowing for the fullest expression of people's ideas and feelings through dance. Just as the ancient "Book of Odes" suggests, "If words do not suffice, then sigh; if sighing fails, then sing; if singing is not enough, then let your arms and legs dance it" (Wang 1985, 1).

# *Admiring the Moon*

## Chinese

*A special thank you to Jimmy Ho, Oregon State graduate student, for help with background information. This dance is referenced from Viltis, Vol. No. 33, 6, March, 1975.*

ON THE FIFTEENTH DAY of the eighth lunar month (late October to early November), Chinese people celebrate the mid-Autumn festival, Yué-Ping (Loaves of the moon). Work is suspended and there are great parties and celebrations. After a special ceremony that honors the Moon Goddess, families sit together eating moon cakes while admiring the moon in its perfect splendor. It is thought that this dance is part of the mid-Autumn festival.

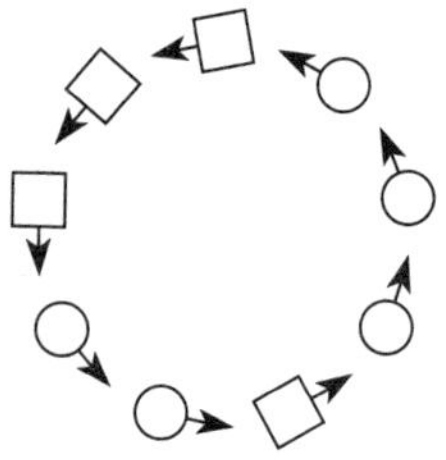

**Music:** Traditional Chinese folk music.
**Formation:** Single circle, hand joined in *V* position.
**Steps:** Walk, grapevine, hop.
**Level:** Beginning 2

## *Directions* FOR THE DANCE

Meter 4/4

| ***Measures*** | ***Counts*** | |
|---|---|---|
| | | **PART I. GRAPEVINE** |
| 1 | 1–4 | Beginning right, cross right foot in front of left on count 1. This should be accented with a small bend in the knee. Step side left on count 2. Cross right foot behind left on count 3 and step side left with left foot on count 4. |
| 2–6 | | Repeat measure 1 five more times. |
| | | **PART II. MOON SEQUENCE 1** |
| | | (Directions are for arm movements, hands move flowing, as if moving through water.) |
| 7 | 1 | Facing center, feet shoulder width apart, knees slightly bent. Slap thighs. |
| | 2 | Raise arms up to high right side. |
| | 3 | Slap thighs. |
| | 4 | Raise arms up to high left side. |
| 8 | 1 | Counts 1–3 are done, bending from the elbow. |
| | | Lower hands to left. |
| | 2 | Swing hand to right. |
| | 3 | Swing hand to left. |
| | 4 | Raise hand to high left side. |
| 9–12 | | Repeat actions of measures 7 and 8 two more times. |
| | | **PART III. MOON SEQUENCE 2** |
| | | (Side closes. Join hands in a circle. Measures 15 and 18 are only 2 counts.) |
| 13 | 1 | Beginning right side step to right. At the same time, keeping arms straight, swing them back, almost parallel to the floor. |
| | 2 | Step left foot next to right foot for a close. Lowering arms down at the same time. |
| | 3–4 | Repeat counts 1 and 2. |
| 14 | 1–4 | Repeat measure 13. |
| 15 | 1 | Step side right. |
| | 2 | Pivoting clockwise on right foot, release hands and turn to face out of circle. Swing left leg around to aid in the turn. Note, next sequence will begin with left foot. |
| 16–18 | | Rejoin hands. Repeat action of measures 13–15 with opposite footwork, still moving in the circle counterclockwise. |
| 19 | 1–4 | Beginning right, step to right. Bring left foot to right on count 2. Step to right on count 3 and touch left foot next to right on count 4. |
| 20 | 1–4 | Repeat actions of measure 19 with opposite foot work. |

*continues on next page*

7

| *Measures* | *Counts* | |
|---|---|---|
| | | **PART III. MOON SEQUENCE 3** |
| | | (Chinese hop turns. Release hands, left arms shoulder high, bend elbows on a horizontal plane and grasps opposite elbow with hands. Arms stay in this position throughout Part III.) |
| 21 | 1 | Beginning right, step side right, dipping arms to right. |
| | 2 | Step left foot to right and close, dipping arms to left. |
| | 3–4 | Repeat counts 1–2. |
| 22 | 1–3 | Repeat counts 1–3, measure 21. |
| | 4 | Hop on right foot, turning clockwise to face out of the circle. |
| 23–24 | 1–8 | Repeat measures 21–22 using the opposite foot work, moving counterclockwise in the circle. On last hop, turn to face center of circle and rejoin hands and repeat dance from beginning. |

## Note

Helpful cue for Part III: 1 *and* 2 *and* 3 *and* 4 *and* pivot out. 1 *and* 2 *and* 3 *and* 4 *and* pivot in. With variations in traditional folk music, adjust steps and order to fit music as required.

# *Gong Xi, Happy New Year*

## Chinese

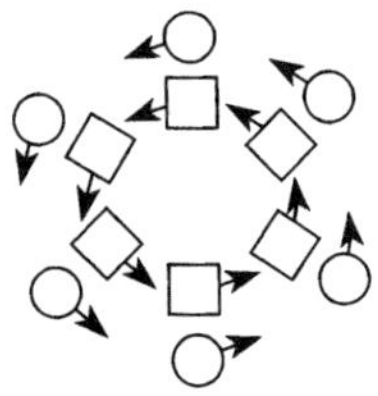

*Special thanks to Earl Lee, Oregon State University graduate student, and his parents for their help in gathering information of this dance. This dance is referenced from* Viltis, *Vol. 33, 6, March, 1975.*

Gong Xi is pronounced *kung-shi,* means "congratulations," and is used, for example, when someone wins an award. It is also the name of a very popular Chinese New Year's song. When used in this context, the phrase translates to "wish you a happy Chinese New Year." Gong Xi is sung during school productions and at New Year's celebrations. While people are singing it, they might perform a bowing motion and wave their arms up and down. There are several forms for this New Year's celebration dance.

**CD:** Melodies for New Year's Greetings, ChinaSprout, MFM011.

**Formation:** Couple in a single circle, women to right of partner, inside hands joined.

**Steps:** Walk.

**Level:** Beginning 3

## Directions FOR THE DANCE

Meter: 4/4 • Directions are for the man, women part is reverse, except when specifically noted.

**PART I. WALKING AND HEEL TOE**

| *Measures* | *Counts* | |
|---|---|---|
| 1 | 1–4 | Beginning left, take three step forward, counts 1–3, holding on count 4. |
| 2 | 5–8 | With weight holding on left foot, place heel of right foot forward, toe pointing up, on count 5, hold count 6. Place toe of right foot back on count 7, hold count 8. |
| 3–4 | 1–8 | Repeat action of measures 1–2, using reverse footwork. |

**PART II. TURNING AND BOWS**

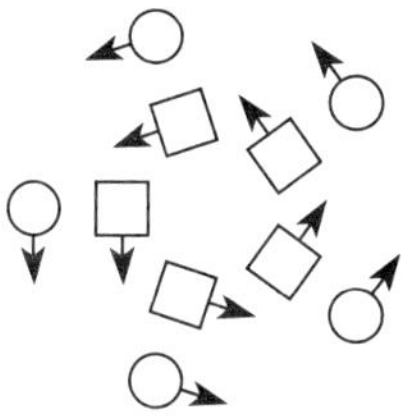

| *Measures* | *Counts* | |
|---|---|---|
| 5 | 1–4 | Releasing partner's hand, beginning with left foot, take four walking step in a small circle, turning counterclockwise (women turn clockwise), away from partner, counts 1–4. By count 4, the man's back should be to the center of the circle, facing his partner |
| 6 | 5–8 | Man bows: Man makes ball of his right hand and covers it with his left hand and places both hands on his chest. Man lowers hands towards partner on counts 5 and 6 and raise them back to his chest on counts 7 and 8.<br>Woman bows: Places left hand on left hip, palm down, and places right hand on left hand, palm down. Woman places right toe behind heel of left foot. She bends her knees slightly, counts 5 and 6, going down, and straightens her legs, counts 7 and 8. |

**PART III. RIGHT HAND STAR, BOW AND SINGING**

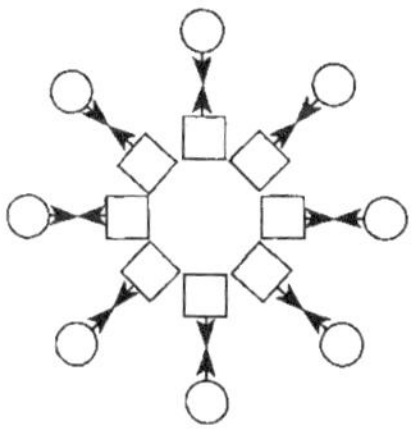

| *Measures* | *Counts* | |
|---|---|---|
| 7–8 | 1–8 | Joining right hands, man beginning left, partners walk eight steps around each other, ending where they started, feet together, facing partner. |
| 9–10 | 1–8 | Release hands and repeat measure 6 two times, singing "Gong Xi, Gong Xi, Gong Xi, Ni" (count 1, Gong; count 2, Xi; repeat two more times then count 7, Ni; nothing on count 8). |

**PART IV. CHANGING PARTNERS**

| *Measures* | *Counts* | |
|---|---|---|
| 11–12 | 1–8 | While bowing and singing, as described in measures 9 and 10, man and woman, beginning left, take a side step on count 1, bring right foot to left foot on count 2, repeat for counts 3 and 4. Ending facing a new partner and finish bowing and singing, counts 5 through 8.<br>Repeat dance from beginning with new partner. |

### Style

Steps are light and lively.

# Czech Republic and Slovakia

## Background

As 1992 turned into 1993, the country known as Czechoslovakia dissolved its unity, and by virtue of a "velvet divorce" peacefully became two separate political units, the Czech Republic and Slovakia. Despite the political separation, many common threads remain. The Czechs are of Slavic origin and speak a common Slavic language. In addition, the two political units inherited the historical and cultural legacy of Bohemia, Moravia, and Slovakia, which in the seventeenth century were part of the Austro-Hungarian Empire. Historically, and according to their folklore and folk art, Bohemia and Moravia can be divided into approximately 11 regions and Slovakia into nine regions. It is from these regions and their villages, although not well defined by geographical lines, that the abundance and variety of folk art is generated.

ALB: Albania, BIH: Bosnia Herzegovina, HRV: Croatia, MKD: Former Yugoslav Republic of Macedonia, MNT: Montenegro, SVN: Slovenia

## Dance History and Characteristics

The Chodsko region in Bohemia is noted for the gaiety and teasing nature of its songs and round dances performed in three-quarter time, and its tradition of bagpipe music. Folk art and dancing is highly developed in the mountainous Wallach region of Moravia, following its pastoral traditions and culture. In the Moravake Slovacko region, the folk traditions are so rich that each village has its own typical dances, songs, and embroidery on the national costume. Thus in the town market one can tell what village women come from by the way they dance, the manner in which they wear their national costume, and especially by the color of the embroidery on their blouses and kerchiefs.

Folk dances from this area did not originate in any one historical period but they can be traced back to various eras, from dances and customs that preserved elements of paganism to more recently created dances. The dances can be divided into several periods according to the dance elements they contain. The most ancient dances are the ceremonial dances, such as carrying out death, "Moreno" or "Merena"; spring dances performed around St. John's Eve; bonfires; dances of maidens welcoming spring; and some masked dances at the time of Mardi Ores.

Solo dances called "leaps" are for male dancers. They express strength, agility, courage, and daring. Working implements that can be used as weapons are frequent accessories in the dances. The most famous "leap" is the fiery Slovacko Verbunk, a dance for young men just entering military service.

Pair dances, or *whirls,* originated in the seventeenth century and are in three parts: the introductory vocal part, group whirling, and an improvisational part in which the men circle around the women, dancing in many varied figures. The sequence is dance, singing, dance.

Couple dancing in a closed circle, most often accompanied by bagpipe, is typical in some regions of Bohemia. These dances are performed one song to a dance and have a set number of figures. A typical round dance has marked rhythm expressing some traits of Czech nature such as humor, optimism and/or mischievousness.

During the first half of the twentieth century, close contact between town and country life changed traditional country dances into the social dances of the towns. Dances such as the polka, mazurka, schottische, waltz, quadrille, and lancer found a home in the newly created countries of the Czech Republic and Slovakia, and have taken on special national form and spirit.

Regional and national folk art festivals and competitions have been and still are important to the development of Czech and Slovakian folk art, song, and dance. In addition, they bring the beauty and traditions of the cultural heritage, and the patterns that have been added by each generation, to thousands of spectators who are justly proud of the richness and variety of their countries' folk art.

## Music

The oldest native instruments are the kobza (like a lyre), the viol, the lucec (hurdy-gurdy), the bagpipe, and the drum. A typical Slovakian folk band also includes a dulcimer and a violin. In southern Bohemia, the bagpipe is played alone or with a violin, and, in eastern Bohemia, the bands are composed of clarinets, violins, double basses, horns, and trumpets.

# Doudlebska Polka

## Czech

*Dance arranged from the dance description by Michael Herman and reproduced by permission of Folk Dance House, New York.*

DOUDLEBSKA POLKA, PRONOUNCED *DOH-dleb-ska,* is a simple mixer learned in Czechoslovakia by Jeannette Novak and introduced to American folk dancers through Folk Dance House, New York.

***Dance A While* CD:** "Doudlebska Polka."

**Formation:** Couples in closed position form one large circle or several smaller circles. Directions are for one large circle.

**Steps:** Polka, walk.

**Level:** Beginning 3

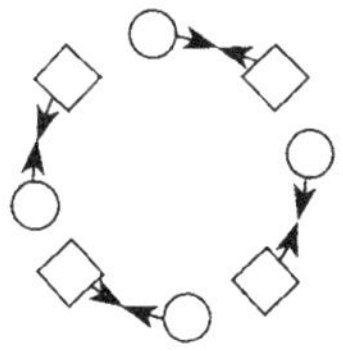

## Directions FOR THE DANCE

Meter 2/4 • The directions are for man; woman's part reverse, except where noted.

| ***Measures*** | |
|---|---|
| 1–4 | Introduction: No action. |
| | **PART I. POLKA** |
| 1–16 | Beginning left, take 16 polka steps turning clockwise, traveling in line of direction. |
| | **PART II. WALK AND CIRCLE** |
| 17–32 | Open position, woman's free hand on hip. Man stretches left arm out to place hand on left shoulder of man in front as couples take 32 walking steps moving in line of direction. This action moves dancers toward center to form a ring of couples. As ring revolves counterclockwise, everyone sings "tra-la-la," and so forth. |

*continues on next page*

***Measures***

| | |
|---|---|
| | **PART III. MEN CLAP, LADIES CIRCLE** |
| 33–48 | Men face center of circle and clap hands throughout figure as follows: clap own hands (count 1), clap own hands (count *and*), clap hands of man on both sides, shoulder high (count 2). Women with hands on hips, take one half-turn clockwise to face reverse line of direction and take 16 polka steps, progressing forward in reverse line of direction around men's circle. |
| | On last measure, each woman steps behind a man, and men turn around and begin dance again with a new partner. |

## Variations

1. Measures 1–16, for beginners a heavy two-step and the Varsouvienne position or inside hands joined may be substituted.
2. Measures 33–48, the men may slap a thigh occasionally, duck down, or cross their own hands over when they clap neighbors' hands.
3. Measures 17–32, if group is large, form several small circles.
4. Measures 33–48, if more than one circle is formed, ladies may "cheat" by moving from one circle to another.

## Notes

1. Those without partners go to the center (the "lost and found" department) and meet the other one without a partner.
2. If there are extra people, extra men without a partner may join dance during star figure, and extra women may join ring as women polka around outside.
3. Encourage group singing during the march, especially loud. It makes the dance fun!

# Tancuj

Czech

A CZECH FOLK DANCE pronounced *ton-tsooy.*

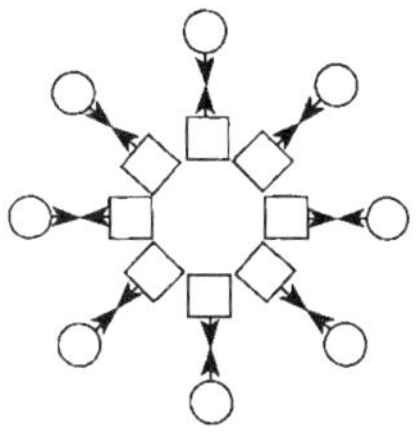

**Dance A While CD:** "Tancuj."
**Formation:** Double circle, couples facing, hands joined. Men's backs to center of circle, women face center.
**Steps:** Two-step, run, hop, step-swing.
**Level:** Beginning 2

## Directions FOR THE DANCE

Meter 2/4

| *Measures* | *Counts* | |
|---|---|---|
| | | **PART I. STEP TOGETHER STEP, SWING** |
| 1–2 | 1–4 | Moving to men's left, women's right. Men step sidewards left, close right to left, step left, and swing right across left. Women: step sideward right, close left to right, step right and swing left across right. |
| 3–4 | 5–8 | Repeat, moving in opposite direction. (**Note:** Swing joined hands vigorously.) |
| 5–16 | 1–8 ×3 | Repeat measures 1–4 three times. |
| | | **PART II. RUN** |
| 1–8 | 1–16 | Partners take a right hip position. Place right hand on partner's left hip, hold own hand on own hip. Run clockwise 16 steps. |
| 9–16 | 1–16 | Change to left hip-to-hip position and run 16 steps counterclockwise. |
| | | **PART III. STEP TOGETHER, STEP–SWING** |
| 1–16 | | Repeat Part I, Step together, step-swing. |
| | | **PART IV. HEEL AND TOE** |
| 1–8 | 1–16 | Partners move away from each other, men to center, women away from center. Hop on left, place right heel down, hop on left, place right toe down. Repeat hopping on right. Dance eight "heel-toe" movements away from partner. |
| | | **PART V. RUN** |
| 1–16 | | Repeat Part II, clockwise and counterclockwise run. |
| | | Repeat dance from the beginning. |

# France

## Traditional French Music and Dance

*By Christina Wright,*[1] *Seattle, WA, member of the Over the Water Hurdy-Gurdy Association*

### A Brief History

What is known today as traditional French music and dance existed as a normal facet of rural community life until the turn of the twentieth century. Dances were not explicitly taught; children naturally learned the dances and were incorporated into the community of dancers and musicians as they grew up. When the community gathered to dance, people may have chosen to wear their best clothes, but they were clothes of that time, unrelated to a nostalgic costume. The range of dances was narrow; communities danced "their own" dances in "their own" styles. It is probable that the rural community dances evolved over generations, taking on new forms, accents, steps, and styles. These changes were gradual, unaffected, and took place well within the original context of the dances. The dances were not recorded or notated, because they were taken for granted in everyday life. In other words, knowing the community's dances was effortless, a birthright of sorts. The dances were considered ordinary and unremarkable, and not worth the effort of writing down.

At some point–experts estimate sometime between World Wars I and II–the practice of indigenous traditional dance died out completely in France, as the culture in which traditional dancing had been commonplace gradually evaporated. For this reason, the practice of traditional French dance is said to be discontinuous. Because tradition died out as its natural "habitat" disappeared, that which is now called traditional music and dance is considered a *revival* of the tradition.

During World War II, when much of France was occupied by the Germans, the authorities outlawed any practice of traditional music and dance in an effort to subdue the people and suppress whatever vestiges of national pride resided in these traditions. This was a wonderful inducement for the French population to turn to its elders and eagerly request that the ancient repertoire be resurrected! In the atmosphere of secrecy and danger of the *bals clandestins,* young people learned the dances from what their seniors could dredge up from their memories. Ironically, it was these youths who became the bearers of the tradition.

1. Christina Wright wishes to acknowledge her reliance on Yves Guilcher (1998).

ALB: Albania, BIH: Bosnia Herzegovina, HRV: Croatia, MKD: Former Yugoslav Republic of Macedonia, MNT: Montenegro, SVN: Slovenia

Thirty years later, in the 1970s, as the current revival was gaining momentum, the only people remaining as informants on the practices of traditional dance had not lived within the context of that tradition. The direct link had been broken by time, war, and modernity.

### Many Regions

During the era when French traditional dances were part of the natural fabric of rural daily life, the regions of France were quite isolated from one another, and their music and dance traditions are quite distinct. Two interrelated factors defined the borders of the ancient regions within France: geography and language. A number of the ancient languages have persevered, and in many communities the language tradition *has* been continuous.

Therefore, when speaking of the traditional music and dance of France, we are not referring to a single culture or language, and the differences in languages and cultures are important. Many people of Brittany speak both French and Breton. In Brittany, the *bal chantée* is an active practice, in which two singers take turns singing verses as the dancers dance. These songs are sung in Breton. The people of the Pays Basque, an ancient country that predates both France and Spain, live with the border of those two nations running through the center of their homeland. The Basque language is alive and well. In fact, many Basques continue to reject the notion that they are French, even though they live within the official borders of France. In the Pays Basque, there is a dance leader who calls the steps to the *sauts* (a collective name for a type of Basque dance, literally, "jumps") in the Basque language.

## Instruments

The instruments of traditional French music vary greatly from region to region. One common theme, though, is the use of the bagpipes, or *cornemuses*. There are estimated to be 19 different types of bagpipes native to France. In Brittany, one popular bagpipe is the *biniou*. In Central France, the cabrette or musette is popular. As a group, French bagpipes are sweet, lyric instruments that have much in common with the sound of a contemporary oboe. In Brittany, a double-reed, short, flared horn known as a *bombarde* is often played in alternate choruses with bagpipes. The instrument requires intense lung pressure and produces a thrilling, loud, unmistakable call.

Another typical instrument in traditional French music is the hurdy-gurdy, or *vielle à roue*. To make the hurdy-gurdy sound, the player turns a crank on the end of a two-foot, resonating wooden "pod" shaped like a lute or guitar. As the player turns the crank, it turns a wheel, which serves as a kind of bow, coming in contact with six fixed strings. If the player knocks the instrument gently as she goes, she will add a percussive sound to the melody, which is played with the left hand on a keyboard resembling a short piano.

The diatonic accordion is also a popular instrument. The accordion is the modern addition to the ancient instruments described above, and made its appearance on the French music scene comparatively recently, in the mid-nineteenth century.

Regional instruments provide distinctive sounds to the traditional music of an area. In Béarn there are drums that consist of tuned strings that are struck to the beat with one hand while the other hand plays a straight flute. In the southeast, near Italy, the violin is quite common.

## Le Bal Folk (The Folk Ball)

There is an energetic and popular revival of traditional music and dance under way in contemporary France. At festivals, workshops, and gatherings throughout France, people are attending dances known as *bals folks*. A contemporary *bal folk* is an exciting and demanding event. Dancers are not motivated by a shared desire to preserve traditional dance, and they wear no regional costumes of yesteryear. Contemporary musicians are contributing new music in the meter and structure of the traditional tunes, and these original tunes are steadily being absorbed into the repertoire.

At a typical *bal folk* the range of dances is quite broad and might include *andros* and *hanter dros* from Brittany, two- and three-time *bourrées* from Berry and the Auvergne, *rondeaux* from Gascogne, a *branle* from the central Pyrénées and the *carnival de Lance* and *les septs sauts* (the seven jumps) from the Pays Basque. But there is more! The popular dances of the nineteenth century, the waltz, the mazurka, and the schottishe (called *Scottish* in France), as well as other favorites from abroad, are also part of this shared repertoire.

The complexity of the contemporary *bal folk* has created the need for instruction. Dancers want to become competent in all the dances they see being done. Most of the dancers did not learn these dances as children, or, if they did, they want to learn the nuances of these dances. This has created an inevitable conflict. Because the dance tradition is not continuous, who are the experts? What is the authentic version of these dances? As done where? When? As these questions are being debated by dance scholars in France, the dancing continues, unabated.

# A Crossing Bourrée in Two Time

## French

*Notated by Christina Wright, Seattle, WA.*

Bourrée is pronounced *boor-AY.* This is a version of the two-time bourrée as observed and learned by Christina Wright during trips to Central France from 1995 to 2002. This popular form of the dance is shared by literally thousands of people at public festivals. This particular style and form of the bourrée seems to have originated in Central France.

The bourrée matches its music exactly, taking 32 measures to complete, repeated as many times as the musicians choose to play it. Bourrées are composed of two 16-measure sections. With some shifts in emphasis, the same combination of steps can also serve for a three-time crossing bourrée.

**Music:** Any tune titled "Bourrée à Deux Temps"; Ton Ruban Bleu.

**Formation:** Long lines, partners facing, men on right side. Distance between lines about 5 feet.

**Basic Bourrée Step:** The bourrée step is defined by its rhythm. The knees are springy, but there is no hopping. The upper body is upright, natural, and relatively still, arms at sides, relaxed, moving freely with the rhythm. The bourrée step sequence runs throughout the dance, whether traveling or in place. The step sequence takes two measures.

**Level:** Beginning 2

### *Basic* BOURRÉE STEP

Meter 2/4 • Directions are the same for man and woman.

| *Measures* | *Counts* | |
|---|---|---|
| | | **PART I.** |
| 1 | 1–2 | Beginning left, step forward (count 1), pause with weight remaining on left foot (count 2). |
| 2 | 3–4 | Step right near left and shift weight to right (count 3), shift weight onto ball of the left foot (count *and*), shift weight onto right foot (count 4), pause, keeping weight on right (count and), ready to begin sequence again on left foot. The French call this part the "little steps." **Cue:** Step, ball, step. |
| | | **PART II. PIVOT** |
| 1 | 1–2 | Beginning left, step forward (count 1), pivot on left (count *and* 2), pause (count *and*) with weight remaining on left foot. Pivot begins slightly earlier than count 2. |
| 2 | 3–4 | Finish with the little steps: shift weight right, left, right, pause. **Cue:** Step, ball, step. |

## *Directions* FOR THE DANCE

| ***Measures*** | ***Counts*** | |
|---|---|---|
| | | **PART I.** |
| 1–2 | 1–4 | Beginning left, dancers step forward toward partner, taking one bourrée step, face to face, almost touching; shoulders remain parallel. Finish the step sequence with the little steps in place. |
| 3–4 | 5–8 | Still facing one another, reach backward with left, take one bourrée step. Finish with the little steps in place. |
| 5–16 | 1–8 | Repeat action of measures 1–4 three times, moving alternately forward and backward. |
| | | **PART II.** |
| | | Partners will be changing places by stepping forward, meeting briefly in the center, and staying to the right as they pass (passing left shoulders). |
| 1–2 | 1–4 | Beginning left, step forward (count 1), pivot one quarter-turn to left (counterclockwise) (count *and* 2), pause (count *and*). At completion of turn, all dancers have momentarily formed one line in center, facing partner, looking up and down set. Once in center, complete bourrée little steps (right, left, right, pause) in place, facing one another, shoulders parallel. |
| 3–4 | 5–8 | Dancers move to occupy partner's former place. Beginning left, step across right, pivoting a three-quarter turn to right (clockwise). At completion of three-quarter turn, dancers are facing one another. End with the little steps in place; shift right, left, right, pause. |
| 5–8 | 1–8 | Repeat measures 1–4 as dancers return to their original places. |
| 9–16 | 1–8<br>1–8 | Repeat Part II, measures 1–8. |

### Ton Ruban Bleu

Bourrée à deaux temps

Traditional French

# Branle d'Ossau

French

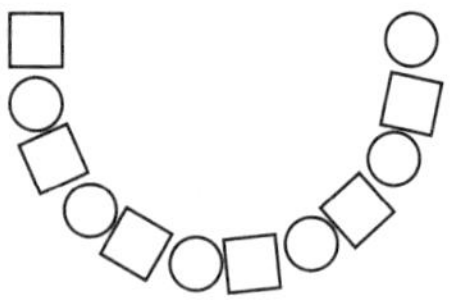

*Dance description and permission to use Branle d'Ossau courtesy of Marilyn M. Smith, Santa Rosa, CA.*

THIS IS AN OPEN CIRCLE DANCE from Gascogne Pyrénées: Vallée d'Ossau in Béarn. Marilyn M. Smith learned this dance from Pierre Corbefin in the summer of 1989.

**Music:** Marc Castanet et Michel Le Meur: *Raccord Duo Swing.*[1]

**Formation:** Open circle, traveling left (clockwise), hands joined in V position, arms down, men and women alternate positions.

**Step:** Rocking step.

**Level:** Beginning 1

## Directions FOR THE DANCE

Meter 2/4 • Directions are the same for man and woman.

| *Measures* | *Counts* | |
|---|---|---|
| | | Introduction: Dancers may begin at the beginning of any musical phrase. |
| 1 | 1–2 | Traveling to the left, dancers face center: Step left (count 1), hop slightly on left bringing right leg over in front of left (count 2), step across on right in front of left (count *and*). |
| 2 | 3–4 | Backing up slightly in line of direction, step left, right, left (counts 3, 4, *and*). |
| 3 | 1–2 | Dancing in place, step on the right slightly behind the left (count 1), hop slightly on right while bringing left leg behind right (count 2), step on left slightly behind right, end facing the center (count *and*). |
| 4 | 3–4 | Facing center, step on right in front of left (count 3), step back on left in place (left foot is behind right) (count 4), step on right in place (in front of left) (count *and*). The movement resembles a "rocking step" in place. |
| | | Repeat dance from beginning. |

1. CD available from Marilyn M. Smith. See Appendix C.

# *Mon Père Avait un Petit Bois*

## French

MON PÈRE AVAIT UN PETIT BOIS, pronounced *mohn pair ah-veh tanh puh-tee bwah*, means "my father had a little woods." This dance is a branle, a sixteenth-century court dance. Branle comes from *branler*, to shake, and is also known as "brawls." This branle was introduced at Mendocino Folk Lore Camp in 1963 by Madelynne Greene; it was taught to her in Normandie, France, in 1962 by Madame Jeanne Messager, leader of the Ethnic Dance Group in Caen.

**Music:** "Branle Normand," Folkraft 337-002.
**Formation:** Single circle, joined hands held down, *V* position. No partners.
**Steps:** Walk, step-hop, branle.
**Level:** Beginning 2

## Directions FOR THE DANCE

Meter 4/4 • Directions are the same for man and woman.

| *Measures* | *Counts* | |
|---|---|---|
| 1–2 | | Introduction: no action. |
| 1–2 | 1–8 | Beginning right, take four walking steps (slow, slow, slow, slow). Circle moves counterclockwise. |
| 3 | 1–4 | Facing center of circle, step forward on right (count 1); hop on right, swinging left leg with knee bent backward (count 2); step left (count 3); hop on left, swinging right leg straight forward (count 4). Arms swing backward and body bends forward (counts 1–2), arms swing forward and body leans backward (counts 3–4). |
| 4 | 5–8 | Repeat action of measure 3. |
| 5–8 | 1–8 × 2 | Repeat action of measures 1–4. |
| 9–12 | 1–8 × 2 | Beginning right, take eight branle steps. Branle step: Step right in place, left foot comes behind and just below right calf, softly touching (count 1), hop on right (count 2). Hands remaining joined, thrust right hand out to right, left elbow bending (count 1), maintaining arm position (count 2). Reverse footwork and arms for branle step, beginning left (counts 3–4). Shake hands right and left. |

### Lyrics

This dance is frequently done to the singing of the song, unaccompanied.

1. Mon per'avait un petit bois
   d'ou venez-vous bell'promener avec moi
   Il y crossait bien cinq cents noix
   d'ou venez-vous belle D'ou venez-vous donc
   d'ou venez-vous promener-vous promener la belle
   d'ou venez-vous bell'promener avec moi.
2. Il y crossait bien cinq cents noix
   d'ou venez-vous bell'
   Sur les cinq cents j'en mangais trois
   d'ou venez-vous bell'.
3. Sur les cinq cents j'en mangais trois
   d'ou venez-vous bell'
   J'en fus malade au lit des mois
   d'ou venez-vous bell'.
4. J'en fus malade au lit des mois
   d'ou venez-vous bell'
   Tous mes parents m'y venaient voir
   d'ou venez-vous bell'.
5. Tous mes parents m'y venaient voir
   d'ou venez-vous bell'
   mais non et n'y venais pas
   d'ou venez-vous bell'.

1. My father had a little woods
   Where do you come from, pretty (girl), stroll with me.
   There grew at least 500 nuts
   Where do you come from, pretty girl, where do you come from.
   Where do you come strolling from, pretty girl.
   Where do you come from, pretty girl, stroll with me.
2. There grew at least 500 nuts
   Where do you come from, pretty girl
   Out of the 500, I ate three
   Where do you come from, pretty girl.
3. Out of the 500, I ate three
   Where do you come from, pretty girl
   I was sick in bed for months
   Where do you come from, pretty girl.
4. I was sick in bed for months
   Where do you come from, pretty girl
   All my relatives came to see me
   Where do you come from, pretty girl.
5. All my relatives came to see me
   Where do you come from, pretty girl
   But no, and don't come
   Where do you come from, pretty girl.

# *Rondeau de Garein*

## French

*Dance description and permission to use Rondeau de Garein courtesy of Marilyn M. Smith, Santa Rosa, CA.*

THIS A LINE DANCE from Gascogne as learned by Marilyn M. Smith in Toulouse in the summer of 1986.

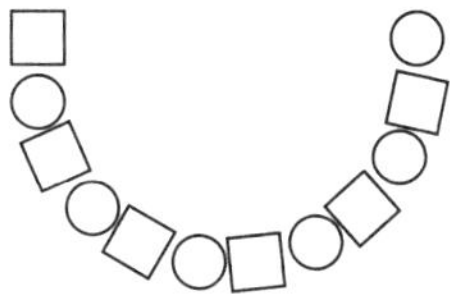

**Music:** "Suite des Rondeaux," *Bal Folk en Californie* by Le Soleil.[1]

**Formation:** Line leading to left (clockwise), hands joined, arms down at side or raised and bent at the elbow, right forearm folded across chest, left forearm of neighbor rests on top of dancer's right forearm. Preferable to alternate position of men and women along the line.

**Step:** As analyzed in dance description.

**Level:** Beginning 1

## *Directions* FOR THE DANCE

Meter 2/4 • Directions are same for man and woman.

| *Measures* | *Counts* | |
|---|---|---|
| | | Introduction (4 measures) |
| 1 | 1–2 | Facing center, lift slightly on right (preparatory left count *ah*), step to left on left (count 1), step on right beside left (count *and*), step slightly to left on left (count 2). |
| 2 | 3–4 | Facing center, step on right crossing over in front of left (count 3), step to left on left (count *and*), step on right crossing over in front of left (count 4). |
| 3 | 1–2 | Step in place on left (count 1), bounce twice in place on left, kicking right forward slightly from the knee, (knee is bent) and retract right foot slightly (counts 2 *and*). |
| 4 | 3–4 | Step back slightly on right (count 3), with slight preparatory lift on right (count *and*), close left to right with left heel next to right toes turned slightly out to the left (count 4). |
| | | Repeat dance from beginning. |

1. CD available from Marilyn M. Smith. See Appendix C.

## Guam

Guam, located in the Pacific Ocean's Micronesia, is a dynamic island whose cultural identity derives from its indigenous inhabitants, the Chamorros, as well as a variety of other influences, including the Spanish, Americans, and Japanese. While it is culturally diverse, much of Guam's traditional Chamorro identity continues to flourish through folkloric legends, customary dishes, colorful adornment, and most importantly, through music, song, and dance. Traditional instruments, such as the belembaotuyan, a stringed instrument made from a hollow gourd, produce rhythms and tunes that fill the air and add to the already thriving cultural arts scene. The following dance is an example of the vibrant culture of Guam.

# *El Baile del Palo*

El Baile del Palo translated literally means the "dance stick." El Baile del Palo, or the Guam Stick Dance, as it is commonly referred to since its introduction in the United States, is done by two dancers. Each dancer holds two sticks, one in each hand, and, in a rhythmic staccato of sharp striking sounds, they dance around each other alternately striking the ground, their own sticks, and the sticks of their partner. As the dance progresses, the dancers assume more difficult and unique positions that rhythmically demonstrate their nimbleness and great sense of timing, producing an exciting and beautifully coordinated series of figures. The significance and meaning of the dance has been lost over the long period of time consumed by passing it from one generation to another.

The dance was brought to the United States and introduced on the campus of Arizona State University, Tempe, Arizona, by Juan C. Guerrero, a student from Barrigada Village, Guam. The dance was learned by Guerrero from members of his family. Guerrero, with the assistance of Anne Pittman of the Women's Physical Education Department, arranged the dance notations.

In Barrigada Village, the dance is equally shared and enjoyed by women and men alike, although the striking action and direction of the sticks make it more readily appropriate for men. Couples may be composed of two men, a man and woman, or two women. Modern Barrigada women simply slip on a pair of slacks and join in the fun. Wearing slacks or shorts is advisable or the action of the dance will lose its effectiveness.

The rhythmic sound of striking the sticks provides the music for El Baile del Palo. The soft strumming of a guitar often accompanies the dance but is background music in reality; the striking of sticks is very effective alone. The count is an even 4/4 meter rhythm. It is quite possible to perform the sequence of figures in 3/4 time by double striking sticks each time the directions call for the dancers to cross strike their own sticks.

The sticks should be approximately 30 inches long; longer sticks may be used, depending on the height of the dancer. Sticks should be at least 1 inch thick and preferably round and smooth. This diameter is more sturdy and less likely to break under frequent use; it also produces a sharper and more audible sound, thus giving the dance its basic charm and effectiveness. Dowel rods are readily available at hardware and lumber supply stores.

### Special Notes on Performance:

1. At all times, the sticks must be struck together sharply! Each dancer must swing, not hold, the stick so that each count or beat makes a sound. Make free use of wrist action in operating the sticks.
2. Body weight should shift naturally and easily with the action of the sticks. There is no set foot pattern to follow when dancers move around each other

with walking steps; they simply move naturally and smoothly with the rhythm and action of the dance. Jerky motions and undue emphasis on getting in position on the turns tends to distract attention from the very intricate and effective action made by the sticks.

3. At all times, the distance between dancers should be sufficient to allow for easy striking. Under-reaching causes the dancers to look stiff and off balance. The distance between the dancers is the length of the stick.
4. The dance sequence is continuous from one figure to the other. Therefore, it is best to practice and learn a figure for at least two counts beyond its end in order to transition smoothly from one figure to the next. Perfect this much before adding another figure. In this way the dance becomes progressively easier to do.
5. *A*'s stick is swung parallel with tip slightly up. *B*'s stick is held at an angle and is swung so that it makes an arc downward.
6. In general, the right-hand stick should cross over the left-hand stick except where the crossing seems awkward or unnatural.
7. Dancers strike the ground with the ends of the sticks. When striking the ground, the sticks are parallel to each other and at a 45-degree angle with the striking surface.

**Formation:** Couples stand side by side, facing forward. The dancer on the left is the lead dancer and is referred to as *A*; the partner is *B*. The lead dancer is responsible for cueing and counting repeats in each figure as well as throughout the dance.

**Level:** Intermediate

## *Directions* FOR THE DANCE

Meter 4/4

| ***Counts*** | |
|---|---|
| | **FIGURE I. STRIKE GROUND, CROSS STRIKE STICKS** |
| | Dancers strike the ground with the ends of the sticks. When striking the ground, the sticks are parallel to each other and at a 45-degree angle with the striking surface. Dancers then cross and strike their own sticks. The sticks are clearly off the ground when cross striking one's own sticks. The body is slightly bent forward during the routine. Do not stand up to cross strike own sticks. Sticks barely leave the floor to cross. The action is similar to "cross sticks" in hockey. The action as is follows: |
| 1 | Strike the ground. |
| 2 | Cross strike your own sticks. |
| 3 | Strike the ground. |
| 4 | Cross strike your own sticks. |
| 5 | Strike the ground. |
| 6 | Cross strike your own sticks. |
| 7 | Strike the ground. |
| 8 | Cross strike your own sticks. |

*continues on next page*

| ***Counts*** | |
|---|---|
| | **FIGURE II. LEG SWING, CROSS STRIKE** |
| 1 | Swing right leg forward, cross strike sticks under right leg. |
| 2 | Stand erect, cross strike sticks in front of body below waistline. |
| 3 | Swing left leg forward, cross strike sticks under left leg. |
| 4 | Stand erect, cross strike sticks in front of body below waistline. |
| 5 | Stand erect, swing sticks behind hips and cross strike. |
| 6 | Stand erect, cross strike sticks in front of body below waistline. |
| 7 | Strike near stick of partner. As a strike is made, *A* makes a half-turn clockwise to face opposite direction. Dancers are now standing side by side with left shoulders almost touching. |
| 8 | *A* holds stick parallel to surface as *B* holds stick up at slight angle. Cross strike own sticks. |
| | **FIGURE III. ALTERNATE LEFT AND RIGHT SHOULDER IN OPPOSITION** |
| 1 | Step to own left into stride position, strike sticks between knees. Swing right hand stick between own knees; swing left-hand stick through partner's knees from behind. Cross strike sticks. |
| 2 | Step to own right, standing erect with feet together, cross strike own sticks. |
| 3 | Strike near stick of partner. *A* holds stick parallel to surface as *B* holds stick up at slight angle. |
| 4 | Cross strike own sticks. |
| 5 | Step to own left, stand erect in a back-to-back position. Swing sticks down and to the right and left sides of body to contact partner's sticks below waist level. Cross strike sticks. |
| 6 | Step to own right, standing erect with feet together, cross strike own sticks. |
| 7 | Strike closest stick of partner. As this strike is made, both dancers make a half-turn counterclockwise, ending right shoulders in opposition. |
| 8 | Cross strike own sticks. |
| 1–8 | Repeat action of count 1–8, Figure III to the opposite side. |
| 1–16 | Repeat Figure III to left and right side. |

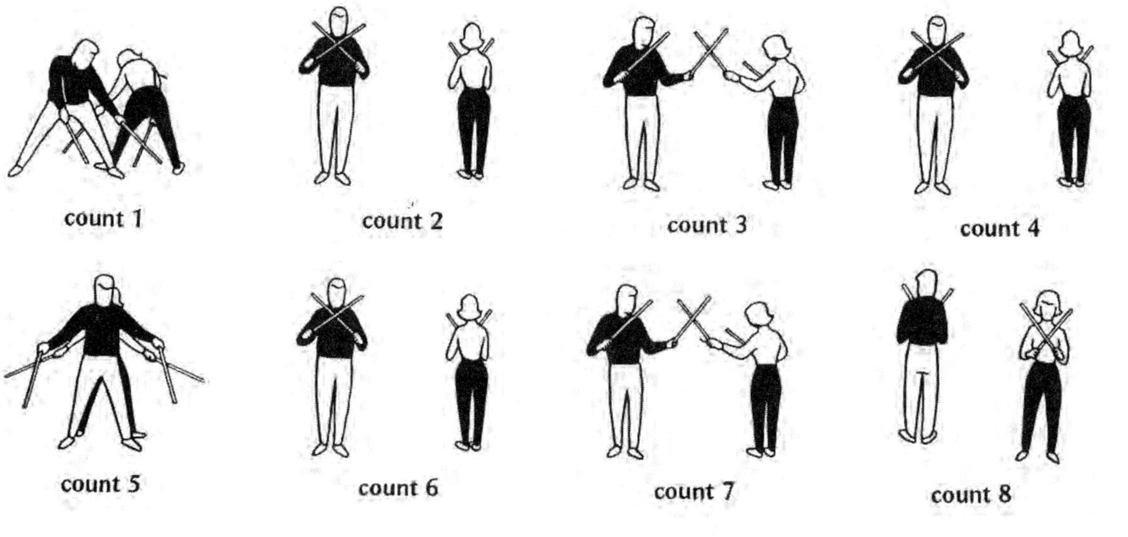

| *Counts* | |
|---|---|
| | **FIGURE IV. WALK, STRIKE, CIRCLE COUNTERCLOCKWISE** |
| | Dancers circle counterclockwise around each other and back to original positions by walking in semi-crouched position as they take small steps. The walk should be smooth and even as the dancers follow the natural rhythm and action of the beats. |
| 1 | Strike end of sticks to ground. |
| 2 | Cross strike own sticks. |
| 3 | Strike closest stick of partner. |
| 4 | Cross strike own sticks. |
| 5–8 + 1–4 | Repeat count 1–4 two more times. |
| 5 | Couples side by side, left shoulders in opposition. *A* kneels on right knee as sticks strike ground. *B* remains standing as sticks strike ground. |
| 6 | Cross strike own sticks. |
| 7 | Strike near stick of partner. *A* holds sticks up at slight angle as *B* swings stick parallel to surface for strike. |
| 8 | Cross strike own sticks. |
| | **FIGURE V. KNEEL, STRIKE, TURN, STRIKE** |
| | Couples maintain Figure IV ending position. *A* should kneel facing toward *B*'s left side for best results in executing the action required. |
| 1 | *A* swings left stick parallel and across in back of *B*'s legs, as *B* steps slightly sideways left into stride position and swings right-hand stick down between knees to contact *A*'s stick. |
| 2 | Cross strike own sticks. |
| 3 | Strike near stick of partner. |
| 4 | Cross strike own sticks. |
| 5 | *A* swings left stick parallel across in back of and to outside of *B*'s legs, as *B* steps slightly sideways left and swings right stick down to right of body to contact *A*'s stick. This contact is made outside and slightly back of *B*'s right knee. |
| 6 | Cross strike own sticks. |
| 7 | Strike near stick of partner. As strike is made, *B* makes a half-turn counterclockwise to face opposite direction. *A* remains in kneeling position but may shift slightly to left for greater comfort. |
| 8 | Cross strike own sticks. |
| 1–8 | Repeat action of counts 1–8 in Figure V to opposite side. |
| 1–16 | Repeat action of counts 1–16, Figure V. |
| 1–16 | Repeat actions of Figure IV, reversing the last 4 counts, having *B* kneel on right knee with *A* remaining standing. |
| 1–32 | Repeat actions of total Figure V with B kneeling. |
| 1–16 | Repeat action of Figure IV, except this time they face each other standing erect as dancers complete the fourth repeat. |

*continues on next page*

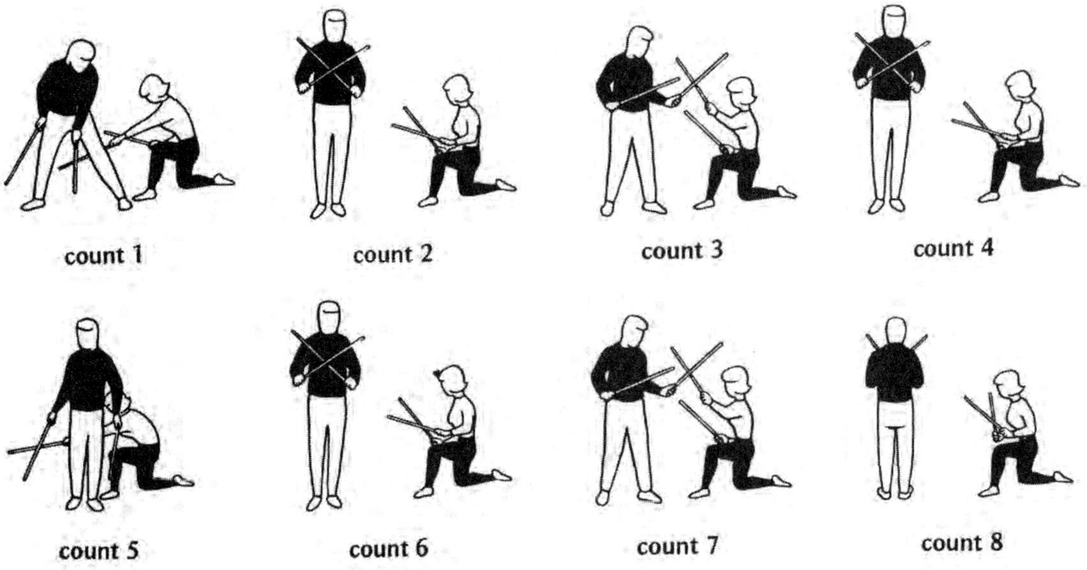


***Counts***

### FIGURE VI. DANCERS FACE, TWIST AND STRIKE, LEFT AND RIGHT

Dancers stand facing each other a comfortable distance apart. Without stepping to face right or left, twist at the waist and strike sticks to floor to right or left side, as directions indicate, cross strike own sticks, then strike partner's near stick as they twist to repeat action on other side.

| | |
|---|---|
| 1 | Twisting to own left, strike sticks to ground. Sticks are parallel to each other. |
| 2 | Cross strike own sticks, starting to stand erect. |
| 3 | Twisting to right, strike closest stick of partner. |
| 4 | Cross strike own sticks to right side of body. |
| 5 | Strike ground on right side. |
| 6 | Cross strike own sticks, starting to stand erect. |
| 7 | Twisting to left, strike closest stick of partner. |
| 8 | Cross strike own stick to left side of body. |
| 1–7 | Repeat counts 1–7. |
| 8 | *A* twisting left to face audience, *B* taking a quarter-turn clockwise to face forward, strike closest stick of partner. |

### FIGURE VII. ENDING

| | |
|---|---|
| 1 | Strike sticks to ground; sticks are parallel to each other. |
| 2 | Cross strike own sticks. |
| 3 | Strike closest stick of partner. *A* holds stick parallel with surface as *B* holds stick up at slight angle. |
| 4 | Cross strike own sticks. |
| 5–12 | Repeat action of counts 1–4 twice. |
| 13–15 | Repeat action of counts 1–3. |
| 16 | Cross sticks, without making sound, in front of chest. |

# Hungary

## Introduction

*By Andor Czompo, Professor Emeritus, Williamsburg, VA.*

Hungarian folk dances can be grouped into five major categories: herdsmen's dances (Pásztor táncok), leaping dances (Ugrós táncok), maidens' round (Leány karikázó), recruiting dances (Verbunk), and the Csárdás. To establish these categories, certain principles of classification were applied, based on the analysis of the spatial, technical, musical-rhythmical, and functional characteristics of the dances. Each of these dance types also represents different historical periods reflecting certain socio-cultural conditions. Although these dances comprise the living dance repertory of the Hungarian peasantry, their existence and popularity vary greatly within Hungary, and show not just functional differences but varied geographical distributions as well.

The old layer of the Hungarian folk dances includes the herdsmen's dances, the leaping dances, and the maidens' rounds. They date back to the Middle Ages and show similarities with other European folk dances of the same period. In addition to the maidens' rounds, which are always danced in a closed circle with varied handholds and accompanied by singing, the boundaries of the other older dances are not always clear. Their formations in particular show great variety from male solo to group and mixed couple variations. The dance tunes that accompany these dances also belong to the old layer of Hungarian dance music as defined by Béla Bartók. Other ancient and common characteristics are the lack of physical contact (or maybe just a handshake hold) between the partners in couple dances and the unstructured, improvised mode of performance. In the dance repertory of the village folk in the twentieth century, these dances reached the last stage of their natural existence. They are performed on rare occasions at weddings, family gatherings, or other festivities.

The recent, newer style of Hungarian folk dances, the Verbunk and the Csárdás, evolved and developed during the 18th and 19th centuries. Assuming a national character, they became the representative Hungarian dances both in Hungary and abroad.

The Verbunk (from the German word *werben*: recruiting) is the result of the eighteenth-century military recruiting practice, when musical entertainment and jollification were used to attract the attention of the young men and induce them to join the military service. The early Verbunk hardly differed from the male solo leaping and swineherd's dances; the technique, formation, and musical accompaniment adjusted later. In western Hungary a semicircle and circle form developed with a regulated structure, and often a dance leader was in charge. In eastern Hungary the dance maintained a solo form with a rich, highly improvised movement repertory of heel clicks, leg swings, and rhythmical boot-slapping. The earlier "Old Style" dance music, notated in 2/4 meter, changed to a more stately 4/4 beat with regular accents. This new style of music became very popular both in folk and national art music and continued in the popular Csárdás music well into the twentieth century. Although it lost its military significance, the Verbunk is still danced on special occasions. During regularly organized dance events, the Verbunk is the first dance of the dance order, followed by a general couple Csárdás.

ALB: Albania, BIH: Bosnia Herzegovina, HRV: Croatia, MKD: Former Yugoslav Republic of Macedonia, MNT: Montenegro, SVN: Slovenia

The Csárdás (from the word *csárda*, a roadside inn) is the most recent, the most popular, and the most widely known Hungarian dance. It developed during the nineteenth century from earlier couple dances by adopting some western European couple dance components, such as shoulder-waist and waltz positions for closer physical contact, and some turning elements. Improvised and unstructured, the Csárdás is usually danced in two parts. It begins with a Lassú (slow) section, where a two-step-like motif is dominant, performed mainly sideways. This is followed by a shorter Friss (fast) part, where turns and vertical movements dominate. The partners occasionally separate, providing an opportunity for the male to dance a solo, using motifs and patterns from the Verbunk.

After World War II the traditional lifestyle of the Hungarian peasantry changed drastically. The survival of the folk dances shifted to an institutionalized movement, emphasizing stage performance. During the 1970s and 1980s a new trend emerged, the so-called Táncház (dance house) movement. This is mainly an urban phenomenon. Devotees gather in clubs and youth centers to dance traditional folk dances to live music provided by village-style orchestras. The emphasis is on enjoyment, reestablishing the original purpose and function of folk dancing. There are still many well-known village folk ensembles, guarding traditional forms and principles with a conscious effort. The video *Hungarian Recreational Folk Dances* demonstrates a number of Hungarian folk dances.[1]

## Dance Characteristics

### Style

Hungarian folk dances comprise many stylistic traits depending upon their established types and are influenced by functional, emotional, spatial, and other specifics.

The maidens' rounds are usually serene and lyrical, with an increased dynamic range during the faster running part of the dance. The leaping dances are light and playful due to their more individualistic and improvised nature. The herdsmen's dances express control and skill, especially in the handling of implements. The recruiting dances in circle form show a more regimented and disciplined style, while the soloistic, improvised form preserved the earlier, light leaping dance character. In the Csárdás, which is basically a couple dance, the partners use technical synchronization and varied handholds with close physical contact to express the courting nature of the dance. Occasional separation and rejoining of the partners during the dance further enhance the teasing-flirting (*csalogató*) character of the Csárdás.

### Music

In the traditional village setting, Hungarians preferred a small band of musicians to provide accompaniment for general dancing. Often these musicians were gypsies; however, their music and melody repertory represented the traditional taste and preference of the peasant population whom they served. L. Gulyas, former musical director of the Hungarian State Folk Ensemble, points out the significant difference between the village and city gypsy musicians: "While the repertory of the urban musicians includes nineteenth century popular music as well as international drawing-room pieces and dance music, the rural gypsy musician is the depository of the specific peasant culture which surrounds him, particularly in instrumental folk dance music." The instruments used by the small village bands are the violin, viola, double bass, and sometimes a small dulcimer (cimbalom). The larger city gypsy orchestras use several violins and violas, cello, double bass, a large cimbalom, and a clarinet.

Traditional Hungarian folk instruments were used in the villages primarily as solo instruments providing music for small family or other gatherings. They were popular to accompany old types of dances. Such instruments were the duda (bagpipe), the citera (zither), the furulya (flute), and the nyenyere (hurdy-gurdy). These old instruments are enjoying a new revival and popularity in today's Táncház.

1. This video is available from Andor Czompo. See Appendix C.

# *Hungarian Motifs*

*Motifs arranged and permission to use courtesy of Andor Czompo, Williamsburg, VA.*

TECHNICAL EXERCISES USING basic Hungarian folk dance motifs and their combinations are very useful in increasing the skill level and agility needed to perform Hungarian dances. The exercises may be done in a "follow the leader" style. First try each motif several times in the order listed, making changes at the half point or end of melodies. Later, leaders may arrange their preferred patterns and create new and interesting combinations.

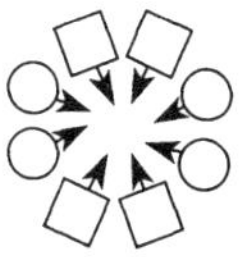

**Music:** Any good medium tempo (quarter note = 140–160 beats per minute) Verbunk, Csárdás, or Kanász-ugrós music in duple meter. Example; Hungaroton LPX 13031–32; Szatmári Verbunk or Dunántúli Ugrós or AC Special #3; Lassú Csárdás.[1]

**Formation:** Circle with a simple side-low handhold or let individual dancers hold hands on hips and face the center of the room.

## Motifs

1. **Knee Bends**

   Bend both knees slightly (counts 1–2), straighten both knees (counts 3–4). Note: The knee bends can be done in first position (feet together parallel) or second position (feet apart sideways parallel). Repeat the same way.

2. **Knee Bounces**

   Before count 1 bend both knees slightly. Straighten both knees with a slight accent (count 1), bend both knees slightly (count 2). Repeat the same way. (*Note:* The preliminary knee bend is necessary only at the beginning. The knee straightenings coincide with the primary accent of the music.)

3. **Side Close Step** (Single Csárdás step)

   Step on the right foot to the right side (counts 1–2), close the left foot to the right (no weight) (counts 3–4). Repeat with opposite footwork and direction.

4. **Double Csárdás Step**

   Step on the right to the right side (count 1), step on the left in place (beside right) (count 2), step on the right to the right side (count 3), close the left to the right (no weight) (count 4). Repeat with opposite footwork and direction.

5. **Step-Hop**

   Step on the right in place (count 1), hop on the right in place (count 2). Repeat with opposite footwork.

6. **Cifra**

   Leap on to the right side (count 1), step on the left in place (count *and*), step on the right in place (count 2). Repeat with opposite footwork and direction.

1. Music available from Andor Czompo. See Appendix C.

### Variations

**Cifra (Pas de Basque):** Leap onto the right foot to the right side (count 1), step on the left in front of the right (count *and*), step on the right behind the left (count 2). Repeat beginning leap to left.

**Back Cross Cifra:** Leap onto the right foot to the right side (count 1), step on the left behind and across the right (count *and*), step on the right in front of and across the left (count 2). Repeat beginning leap to left.

7. **Leap Hop Kick**

   Leap onto the right in place with a slight knee bend. At the same time lift the left in the back so the left lower leg is close to parallel with the floor (count 1); hop on the right in place. At the same time kick the left to forward-low position (count 2). Repeat beginning to the left.

8. **Run and Click**

   Take two running steps, right and left in place (counts 1–2), close the right to the left with accent (slight heel-click) (count 3), pause (count 4). Repeat the same way.

9. **Heel-Click**

   Bend both knees slightly. At the same time open both heels (pigeon-toed) (counts 1–2), straighten both knees. At the same time close the heels together with a slight accent (counts 3–4).

### Note

May be performed with these counts or twice as fast. Repeat the same way.

10. **Cross Jump Heel-Click**

    Jump into a "crossed position" (right foot in front of left) (count 1), jump into second position (feet apart and pigeon-toed) (count 2), jump into first position (feet together parallel, knees straight) (count 3), pause (count 4). Repeat the same way.

# *Csárdás Palócosan*

## Hungarian

*Description and permission to use Cárdás Palócosan courtesy of Andor Czompo, Williamsburg, PA.*

CSÁRDÁS IN PALÓC STYLE is from north-central Hungary. This version is arranged by Andor Czompo.

**CD:** Rounder 5005, "Play the Bagpipe, Uncle John."[1]

**Formation:** Independent couples. Partners face and join in a shoulder-shoulder position.

**Motifs:** Double Csárdás, turning Csárdás, two-step.

**Level:** Beginning 3

1. Music available from Andor Czompo. See Appendix C.

### Motifs

1. **Double Csárdás (♩♩♩♩)**

   Step on the right, to the right side (count 1), step on the left beside the right in place (count 2), step on the right to the right side (count 3), close the left to the right with partial weight (count 4). Repeat beginning left.

2. **Turning Csárdás (♩♩♩♩)**

   Step on the right in place turning one quarter to the right (count 1), step on the left in place (count 2), step on the right in place turning one quarter to the right (count 3), close the left to the right with partial weight (count 4).

3. **Two-Step (♫♩)**

   Step on the left forward (count 1), step on the right in place (count *and*), step on the left forward (count 2). Repeat beginning right.

## Directions FOR THE DANCE

Meter 4/4 • Directions are for man, woman's part reversed.

| ***Measures*** | |
|---|---|
| | Introduction: One note. |
| 1–2 | Double Csárdás twice starting to the man's right. Woman follows with opposite footwork. |
| 3 | Man executes the Turning Csárdás. Woman, following the man's lead, walks with three steps clockwise about halfway around the man (left, right, left) closing the right to the left with partial weight on the fourth count. |
| 4 | Double Csárdás to the man's left. |
| 5–8 | Repeat measures 1–4. |
| 9 | Double Csárdás to the man's right. |
| 10–12 | Two-step three times. During two-step partners release hands and separate. Man makes a small circle to his left; woman with opposite footwork circles to her right. At the end they rejoin in Csárdás position. |
| | Repeat the dance from the beginning four times. |

# *Kiskanásztánc*

## Hungarian

*Description and permission to use Kiskanásztánc courtesy of Andor Czompo, Williamsburg, VA.*

KIS MEANS "SMALL, SHORT." Kanásztánc is a swineherder's dance. This dance is a short version of a type of dance known as Kanásztánc. Although the majority of these dances are done with an implement (stick, shaft, small ax with a long handle), this version utilizes motifs that can be done without those implements. There are many sources for this dance. This arrangement is by Andor Czompo.

**Music:** Any good moderate tempo Kanásztánc or Ugrós: AC #3, CD.[1]
**Formation:** Solo, i.e., single dancer, hands on hips.
**Motifs:** Steps and hop, back cross cifra, close and step.
**Level:** Beginning 3

### Motifs

1. **Steps and Hop** (♩♩♩♩)

   Step on right toward a right forward diagonal into a small knee bend (count 1), step back on the left (count 2), step on the right forward into a small knee bend (count 3), hop on the right, turning about one-quarter to the left, at the same time swing the left lower leg forward (count 4). Repeat beginning left.

2. **Back Cross Cifra** (♫♩)

   Small leap onto the right to the right side (count 1), step on the left behind the right (count *and*), step on the right in front of the left (count 2). Repeat beginning left.

3. **Close and Step** (♩♩)

   Starting position: Weight is on the left in a small knee bend. The right foot is right-side-low with a slightly bent knee. Close the right to the left with accent (heel click). At the same time straighten both knees (count 1). Small step on the right forward into a small knee bend. At the same time lift the left to the left-side-low position with a slightly bent knee. Repeat beginning right.

   Individual dancers have hands or fists on hips. Start the dance at any time with the music.

## *Directions* FOR THE DANCE

Meter 2/4

| ***Measures*** | |
|---|---|
| 1–4 | Dance the steps and hop motif twice. |
| 5–6 | Dance the back cross cifra motif twice. |
| 7–8 | Dance the close and step motif twice. |
| | Repeat this sequence several times until the end of the music. |

### Note

For those who like to improvise, each motif may be done any number of times or in a different order.

1. Music available from Andor Czompo. See Appendix C.

# Ugrós

## Hungarian

*Description and permission to use Ugrós courtesy of Andor Czompo, Williamsburg, VA.*

THIS IS A CONTEMPORARY recreational folk dance in Hungarian Ugrós style arranged by Andor Czompo.

**CD:** Rounder 5005, "For a Birthday."[1]
**Formation:** Solo, i.e., a single dancer, hands on hips.
**Motifs:** Touch and step, back cross cifra, lift and step with claps, heel-click.
**Level:** Beginning 3

### Motifs

1. **Touch and Step** (♩♩): Touch the right heel forward on the floor (leg straight) (count 1), step on the right in place (count 2). Repeat beginning left.
2. **Back Cross Cifra** (♫♩): Small leap onto the right to the right side (count 1), step on the left behind the right (count *and*), step on the right in front of the left (count 2). Repeat beginning left in opposite direction.
3. **Lift and Step with Claps** (♩♩): Lift the right knee forward and hit the right thigh with the right hand (count 1), step on the right in place. At the same time clap the hands together in the front (count 2). Repeat beginning left foot and hand. Note: Man can lift the leg forward with bent and turned out knee and hit the inside of the lower leg (boot top).

### Variations on the Clap

Replace the single clap with a double (♫) or triple clap. (♫♩)

4. **Heel-Click** (♩♩♩𝄽): *Starting position:* Weight on left. The right foot is right-side-low with a slightly bent knee. Close the right to the left with slight accent (knees are straight) (count 1), bend the knees and at the same time turn out (open) both heels (pigeon-toed) (count 2), close the heels together with accent and straighten knees (count 3), pause (count 4).

## *Directions* FOR THE DANCE

Meter 2/4

Individual dancers face the music or the center of the dance floor. Hands are on hips. During the dance individual dancers can turn and change facing direction at will.

| ***Measures*** | |
|---|---|
| | Introduction: The first full melody. |
| 1–2 | Dance the touch and step motif 1 twice (right and left). |
| 3–4 | Dance the back cross cifra motif 2 twice (right and left). |
| 5–8 | Repeat measures 1–4. |
| 9–10 | Dance the lift and step motif 3 twice (right and left) with single claps. |
| 11 | Dance the lift and step motif 3 with double or triple claps. |
| 12 | Dance the lift and step motif 3 with left foot and hand. |
| 13–14 | Dance the back cross cifra motif 2 twice (right and left). |
| 15–16 | Dance the heel-click motif 4 one time. |
| | Repeat the dance from the beginning. |

1. Music available from Andor Czompo. See Appendix C.

7

# Israel

## Clarification of Ethnic Names and Nationalities

The advent of the nation of Israel in the late 1940s has led to some confusion as to the origin of dances from that country and region. "Dances named 'Palestinian' are pre-Israel-Jewish. During that (pre-Israel) era the Palestinians were the Jews; the Arabs were Arabs. Now the Arabs are the Palestinians and the Jews are Israeli."[1]

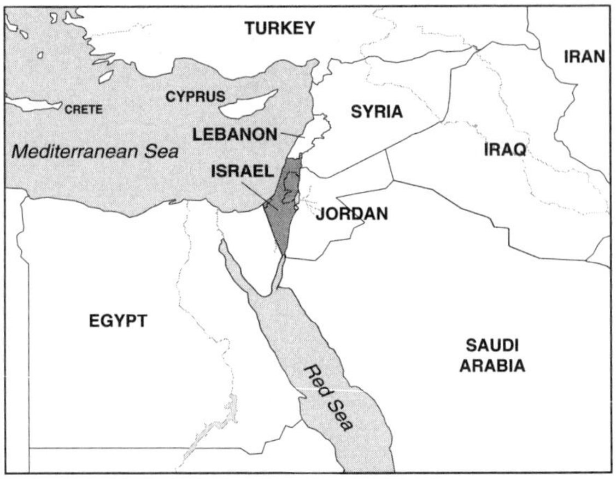


## Dance Characteristics

Since Biblical times Jewish dance (Beliajus 1968) has been spiritual in nature and very much a part of the religious experience. As thc Jews wandered about the world, they assimilated the culture of each new home into their own tradition. Dance has always been a part of the Jewish child's education and family life. During the Middle Ages, the popular "tanzhaus" (dancing hall) was established in the ghettos of France, Poland, and Germany, and Jewish dance leaders developed.

About 1736 Israel Baal Shem Tov, a young mystic who came from the Carpathian Mountains, inspired a new Jewish religious movement known as Chassidism (also spelled Hassidism). The movement flourished in the ghettos of Poland and eastern Europe. Baal Shem encouraged dance movement and singing with prayer to realize the nearness of God. A new ritual of dancing and humming in worship took place. Improvisation of dance "arose as a conscious attempt to create human joyousness out of misery" (Berk 1972, 1975).

With a long tradition of dance, the Jews immigrated to the new state of Israel (formed in 1948), bringing with them many diverse cultures and traditions. Today's Israeli folk dances are dances Jews have brought from other cultures, like eastern European ones. But a large number of the currently popular folk dances have been created by choreographers such as Gurit Kadman, Sara Levi, Yoav Ashriel, Rivka Sturman, Dvora Lapson, and Dani Dassa. Using German interpretive dance techniques and old and newly composed tunes, they have blended dance movements from the Yemenites, the Arabs, the Druzi, the Kurds, and the Hassidim (the largest impact being that of the Yemenites).

The Yemenites, Jews originally from the southwest corner of Arabia, started immigrating to Palestine about 1910. Although the Yemenites had many things in common with the Arabs, their religion was different, and they could read and write. The Yemenites were a link with the Biblical Hebrews. They had maintained old religious and cultural patterns, songs in the language of the Bible, and dances of Oriental rhythm. Their dances were slow and gentle, gradually accelerating as danced to drumming, hand clapping, and singing. Their basic dance forms inspired a new trend in Israeli dances and the Yemenite step in many variations became a basic step. A group of well-known dances (Dodi Li and Ma Na'avu) came from the Song of Songs.

Bukhara Jewish dance emphasizes hand movements (Beliajus 1962). Their melodies are mostly in 3/4 and 6/8 meter and sound like a ländler; therefore, people frequently mistake them for Bavarian dances.

The newly created folk dances involve a variety of themes: Biblical (Shibbolet Bassedeh, a harvest festival), the great need for water (Mayim Mayim), experiences that have occurred in modern times (Sisu Yerusalyim, choreographed after the Six-Day War, celebrates the joy of being in Jerusalem again), and discotheque dance (Shir Hashalom), referred to as "The Madison Avenue Dance" by Israelis. The movement in the dance rarely pantomimes its theme.

Line, circle, and couple dance formations are used. It is interesting to note that the Jewish square dance differs from European quadrilles in that the women of the side couples stand on the left side of their partners so that two women or two men are at each corner. The woman was not to touch a "strange man."

Characteristically the total body is involved in movement, frequently with a fluid, undulating movement; the knees and ankles are flexible; hand movements may be reaching upward, clapping hands symbolic of clapping cymbals in ecstasy, or reaching behind the back in a mood of restraint.

The music, also a blend of many cultures, may be tunes from other lands or newly composed ones. The music on Israeli recordings could be identified as German, illustrating the many cultures that Israeli dance represents. The melodies have a strong rhythmic pulse.

1. Following the publication of the 7th edition of *Dance A While*, Vyts Beliajus wrote the authors the above statement of clarification in a letter dated January 22, 1994.

# *Cherkessiya*

## Israeli

TSCHERKESSIA OR CHERKESSIYA is a dance for men from Circassia. They were followers of the Mohammedan faith, who sought religious freedom in the czarist days of Russia. They left southeastern Russia and migrated to Palestine and Syria. The Circassians were noted for their horsemanship. The rhythmic movement of the dance portrays either horses or riders.

**CD:** High/Scope RM 2.

**Music:** Beliajus, V. F., *Dance and Be Merry*, Vol. I, p. 12; Chochem, Corinne, and Roth, Muriel, *Palestine Dances*, p. 31; Lapson, Dvora, *Dances of the Jewish People*, p. 34.

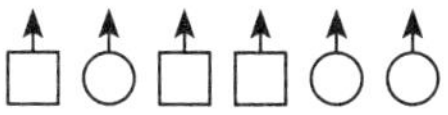

**Formation:** Groups of four to six dancers in a line, arms linked about one another's waist, or any number of dancers in a single circle.

**Steps:** Scissor kick, skip, shuffle.

**Level:** Beginning 1

## *Directions* FOR THE DANCE

Meter 2/4

| | *Measures* | *Counts* | |
|---|---|---|---|
| | | | **PART I. GRAPEVINE** |
| A | 1–2 | 1–4 | Keeping the left foot in place, step right across left, step left in place, step back right, step left in place. As cross step is taken, body leans forward, left knee bends to give flexibility to movement. As backward steps are taken, body should lean back as far as possible. |
| | 3–8 | 1–4 ×3 | Repeat action of measures 1–2 three times. |
| | | | **PART II.** |
| B | 9 | 1–2 | Line or circle moves to the right. Beginning right, step to the side, step left behind right. |
| | 10–16 | 3–16 | Repeat action of measure 9 seven times. |

### Variations for Part II

1. 16 scissor kicks (cut steps) in front.
2. 16 scissor kicks (cut steps) in back.
3. Combination of scissor kicks in front and back.
4. Eight slow skips to the right (one per measure).
5. Keep feet together, move both toes, then both heels to the right.
6. Semicrouch position, execute a shuffle step, moving to the right.

### Note

The action described in Part II may be used each time or a different action selected from the variations may be used for each repeat of the B music. The dance should be started in a slow tempo. Each repetition becomes faster until a climax of great excitement is reached. If done in a line, each group moves independently, allowing the action of Part II to carry it anywhere on the floor.

# Hava Nagila

## Israeli

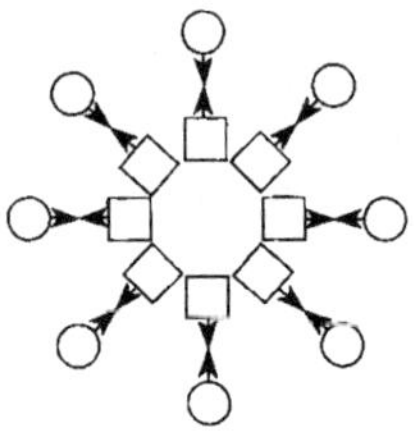

*Dance arranged from the dance description by Dvora Lapson, (1954, p. 19).*

HAVA NAGILA MEANS "come let us be joyful." This couple dance is done to an old hora melody, "Hava Nagila."

**CD:** High/Scope RM 4.

**Music:** Lapson, Dvora, *Dances of the Jewish People,* 1954, p. 18.

**Formation:** Double circle, partners facing, man's back to center, two hands joined. Partners stand close together, elbows bent, and hands joined.

**Steps:** Walk, leap, hop, jump, running step.

**Level:** Beginning 1

## *Directions* FOR THE DANCE

Meter 4/4 • Directions are for both man and woman, except when noted.

| | *Measures* | *Counts* | |
|---|---|---|---|
| | | | **PART I. PULL AWAY AND CIRCLE** |
| A | 1 | 1–4 | Beginning right, take four steps backward, knees bending slowly, taking body into crouch position by fourth step. Back remains fairly straight. |
| | 2 | 5–8 | Beginning right, take four steps forward, moving immediately into left reverse open position (count 5). Stand straight with left elbow bent and close to body, right arm is straight across in front of partner. Turn clockwise in reverse open position (counts 6–8). |
| | 3–4 | 1–8 | Repeat action of measures 1–2. |
| | 5–8 | 1–8 | Repeat action of measures 1–4. On fourth measure, partners face line of direction and take back cross position. |
| | | | **PART II. LEAP AND TURN, BALANCE AND RUN** |
| B | 1 | 1–4 | Beginning right, leap forward, body bending forward (count 1), step left beside right (count 2), step right back, body straightens (count 3), step left beside right (count 4). |
| | 2 | 5–8 | Repeat measure 1. |
| | 3 | 1–4 | Drop left hands. Beginning right, take four steps, woman making three-quarter turn to face man who turns one-quarter clockwise to face her. Partners join left hands under right. |
| | 4 | 5–8 | Beginning right, take four steps, woman in place, man turning a full turn clockwise under their joined upraised hands. Now in original starting position, with joined hands crossed. |

| | Measures | Counts | |
|---|---|---|---|
| | 5–6 | 1–8 | Man beginning left, woman right, take four balances to side. (Man–left, right, left, right; woman–right, left right, left.) |
| | 7–8 | 1–8 | Hook right elbows and extend left arm diagonally upward and outward. Take eight running steps around each other, turning clockwise once around to face original starting position. Drop hands and move apart about three feet. |
| | | | **PART III. CLAP, HOP, AND TURN** |
| C | 1 | 1–4 | Bend over to right and clap hands to one's own right side about knee level (counts 1–2). Repeat bending to left (counts 3–4). Sing "Uru Uru Achim." |
| | 2 | 1–4 | Bend forward and clap in front (count 1), gradually raise hands to outstretched arm position, in three upward lifts (counts 2–4). Head follows hand positions. Sing "Uru Uru Achim." |
| | 3 | 1–4 | Hands on hips. Jump in place (count 1). Take three hops on right, extending left foot forward (counts 2–4). |
| | 4 | 1–4 | Repeat action of measure 3, hopping on left foot and extending right. |
| | 5–6 | 1–8 | Repeat action of measures 3–4. |
| | 7 | 1–4 | Repeat action of measure 3, letting left foot trail behind while turning clockwise around in place once on three hops. |
| | 8 | 1–4 | Repeat action of measure 4, letting right foot trail behind while turning counterclockwise around in place once on three hops. |

## Lyrics

| | |
|---|---|
| A. Hava Nagila | Let's be joyful |
| Hava Nagila | Let's be joyful |
| Hava Nagila Venismecha | Let's be joyful |
| Repeat A | |
| B. Hava Neranena | Let's sing |
| Hava Neranena | Let's sing |
| Hava Neranena Venismecha | Let's sing and be joyful |
| Repeat B | |
| C. Uru Uru Achim | Wake up, wake up, brothers |
| D. Uru Achim Belev Sameach | Wake up, brothers, with a happy heart |
| Repeat D three times | |
| E. Uru Achim | Wake up, brothers |
| Uru Achim Belev Sameach | Wake up, brothers, with a happy heart |

# *Hineh Ma Tov*

## Israeli

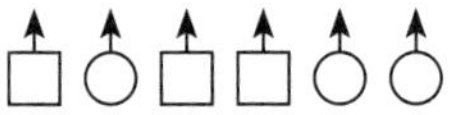

THE WORDS *HINEH MA TOV* ("How good it is to dwell together as brethren") are taken from the Bible and admonishes people to live in the world as brothers, friends, and good neighbors. The dance was choreographed by Rivka Sturman.

***Dance A While* CD:** "Hineh Ma Tov."

**Formation:** Nonpartner, broken circle. Lines may be composed of four to eight dancers, joined hands held down, V position, moving freely in any direction.

**Steps:** Walk, twinkle, yemenite.

**Level:** Beginning 2

## Directions FOR THE DANCE

Meter 2/4

| *Measures* | *Counts* | |
|---|---|---|
| | | **PART I.** |
| 1–2 | 1–4 | Beginning right, move counterclockwise four walking steps. Flex knees during slow walk; hold hands down and straight. |
| 3–4 | 5–8 | Beginning right, continue counterclockwise, run lightly eight steps. Stepping on counts 5+ 6+ 7+ 8+. Run in a quick, prancing style. |
| 5–8 | 1–8 | Repeat measures 1–4. |
| | | **PART II.** |
| 1 | 1–4 | Face center, raise joined hands to shoulder level. Leap softly onto right and bring joined hands down (counts 1–2). Step back on left (count 3), step right, crossing over left (count 4). |
| 6 | 1–4 | Step forward on left (counts 1–2). Stamp right softly beside left (counts 3–4). |
| 7 | 1–4 | Weight remains on left. Raise arms up high. Yemenite: Step right to side (count 1), shift weight back to left (count 2), step right across left (count 3). Hold count 4. |
| 8 | 1–4 | Repeat to left: Step left to left side (count 1), shift weight to right (count 2), step left across right (count 3), stamp right softly (count 4). Weight remains on left. |
| 1–8 | 1–16 | Repeat Part II |
| | | Repeat dance from the beginning. |

### Words

Hineh ma tov, uma naim (*hee-nay ma tov, ooma nayim*).
She-vet a chim gam ya chad (*sheh-vet akim gahm ya khad*).

# *Hora*

## Israeli

THE JEWISH PEOPLE, dispersed over the earth for many years, have kept their religion alive, but many of the folk traditions have become broken or lost. When the people returned to Israel, they brought dances from their former homelands. The Sephardic Jews, who left Spain during the Inquisition, settled in the Balkan area. They danced the Balkan Hora, adopting it and incorporating it into their festivities.

The word *hora*, a Croatian-Serbian word, means "tempo" or "movement." Although the earlier Hora dances were probably a part of primitive agricultural rites (the leaps and high jumps in the dance suggest and were supposed to induce high growth of corn); the Hora became more subdued and restrained as the people danced it indoors in small spaces. As danced in Israel today, it has absorbed the flavor of the people living there and is once again danced outdoors.

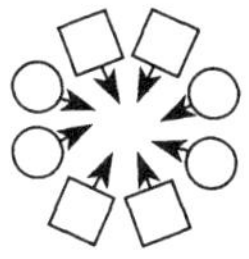

**Music:** Chochem, Corinne, and Roth, Muriel, *Palestine Dances*, p. 15; Beliajus, V. F., *Dance and Be Merry*, Vol. I, p. 37.

**Formation:** Single circle, hands on shoulders of person on either side, arms straight.

**Steps:** Step-hop, kick.

**Level:** Beginning 1

## *Directions* FOR THE DANCE

Meter 4/4

| *Measures* | *Counts* | |
|---|---|---|
| 1 | 1–2 | Moving counterclockwise, step right to side right. |
| | 3–4 | Step left to side right behind right. |
| 2 | 1–2 | Step right to side right. |
| | 3–4 | Kick left in front of right while hopping on right. |
| 3 | 1–2 | Step left to side left. |
| | 3–4 | Kick right across left while hopping on left. |
| | | This same pattern is repeated throughout the dance. |

### Note

Begin the Hora slowly to establish the rhythm, keep the tempo slow and the music soft, and then gradually accelerate the rhythm and increase the volume. If the group is large, it is interesting to have several concentric circles, some circles beginning with the right foot, moving clockwise, and others beginning with the left foot, moving counterclockwise.

### Style

If the movement of the dance begins mildly, with a tiny hop, it can build gradually to a larger hop as the tempo increases.

If dancers extend arms and lean back, keeping head up, the momentum is easier. Dancers should hold up their own arms, not press down on shoulders of the person to each side.

# *Ma Na'avu*

## Israeli

Ma Na'avu is a lovely nonpartner circle or line dance. The lyrics are from the Bible, Isaiah 52–57. The music was composed by Joseph Spivak, and the dance was choreographed by Rajah Spivak.

**CD:** High/Scope RM 6.

**Formation:** Single open circle or single line, hands joined, held down in V position.

**Steps:** Touch, grapevine, rocking, Yemenite.

**Level:** Beginning 2

## *Directions* FOR THE DANCE

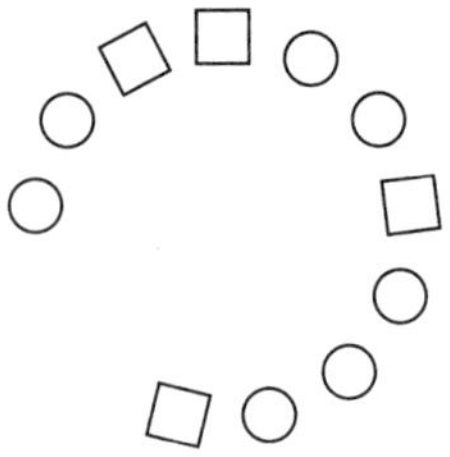

Meter 2/4

| *Measures* | *Counts* | |
|---|---|---|
| | | **PART I.** |
| 1 | 1–4 | Touch: Beginning right, touch right forward (count 1), touch right to side right (count 2). Step right behind left (count 3), step left to left side (count and), step right across left in front of left (count 4) (quick, quick, slow). |
| 2 | 1–4 | Rock: Rock weight back onto left (count 1 and), rock weight forward onto right (count 2 and), rock weight back onto left (count 3), step right forward in place (count and), close left to right (count 4). Lift body upward as if taking a deep breath, lower (count and) weight ends on right for repeat. |
| 3–4 | | Repeat action of measures 1–2 beginning left. |
| | | **PART II.** |
| 5 | 1–4 | Yemenite: Step right to side right (count 1), step left next to right (count and), step right forward and across left (count 2), turn to face counterclockwise by pivoting slightly on the right (count and). Move counterclockwise three steps left, right, left (counts 3 and 4). Bring joined hands to shoulder level during the three steps. End facing forward. |
| 6–8 | | Repeat action of measure 5 three times. |
| | | Repeat dance from the beginning. |

# *Mayim*

## Israeli

*Dance arranged from the dance description by Dvora Lapson (1954, p. 8).*

MAYIM IS A JEWISH FOLK TUNE. Translated, mayim means "water." The dance movements express the joy of finding water in arid land and emulate the motion of waves as they break on the shore. The dance originated in a kibbutz on the shores of Galilee.

***Dance A While* CD:** "Mayim."
**CD:** High/Scope RM 5.
**Music:** Lapson, Dvora, *Dances of the Jewish People,* p. 8.
**Formation:** Single circle, hands joined, held down in *V* position.
**Steps:** Grapevine (tscherkessia), run.
**Level:** Beginning 2

## Directions FOR THE DANCE

Meter 4/4

| *Measures* | *Counts* | |
|---|---|---|
| | | **PART I. GRAPEVINE (TSCHERKESSIA)** |
| 1 | 1–4 | Moving clockwise, cross right in front of left (count 1), step left to side (count 2), cross right behind left (count 3), step left to side with a light springy step, accenting step (count 4). |
| 2–4 | 5–8, 1–8 | Repeat measure 1 three times. |
| | | **PART II. TO CENTER AND BACK** |
| 5 | 1–4 | Beginning right, move to center with four running steps. Lift joined hands gradually above heads as dancers move to center, clap hands together on count 4. Sing "Mayim, Mayim, Mayim, Mayim" while moving to center. |
| 6 | 5–8 | Beginning right, repeat action of measure 5, moving away from center. Lower joined hands gradually down to sides. |
| 7–8 | 1–8 | Repeat action of measures 5–6. |

7

*continues on next page*

| ***Measures*** | ***Counts*** | |
|---|---|---|
| | | **PART III. RUN, TOE TOUCH, CLAP** |
| 1 | 1–4 | Beginning right, move clockwise with three running steps; hop on count 4 and turn to face center. |
| 2 | 1–4 | Hop right and touch left across front to right side (count 1); hop on right, touch left to side (count 2); hop on right, touch left in front to right side (count 3); hop on right, touch left to side (count 4). |
| 3 | 5–8 | Repeat actions of measure 2, counts 1–3. Hop on right, bring left foot to right, feet together (count 8). |
| 4 | 1–4 | Hop left, touch right in front to left side and clap hands directly in front at arm's length (count 1); hop on left, touch right to side and swing arms out to sides shoulder high (count 2); hop on left, touch right in front to left side and clap hands directly in front at arm's length (count 3); hop on left, touch right to side and swing arms out to sides shoulder high (count 4). |
| 5 | 5–8 | Repeat action of measure 4, Part III, rejoining hand in a circle (count 8). |
| | | Repeat dance from the beginning. |

## Lyrics

| | | |
|---|---|---|
| I. | 1–2 | V-Shav-tem Mayim Bi-Sa-Son, Mi-ma-Yi-Wey Ha-Y'Shu-ah |
| | 3–4 | V-Shav-tem Mayim Bi-Sa-Son, Mi-ma-Yi-Wey Ha-Y'Shu-ah |
| II. | 5–6 | Ma-Yim Ma-Yim Ma-Yim, Ma-Yim, V-Ma-Yim Bi-Sa-Son |
| | 7–8 | Ma-Yim Ma-Yim Ma-Yim, Ma-Yim, V-Ma-Yim Bi-Sa-Son |
| III. | 1 | Hey! Hey! Hey! Hey! |
| | 2 | Mayim Mayim Mayim Mayim |
| | 3 | Mayim Mayim Bi-Sa-Son |
| | 4 | Mayim Mayim Mayim Mayim |
| | 5 | Mayim Mayim Bi-Sa-Son |

# *Ve' David*

## Israeli

The full title of Ve' David is Ve' David Y'Fey Enayim, meaning "And David of the Beautiful Eyes." It is a couple mixer choreographed by Rivkah Sturman.

***Dance A While* CD:** "Ve' David."
**CD:** High/Scope RM 3.
**Formation:** Double circle, couples facing counterclockwise. Woman to the right of partner, inside hands joined.
**Steps:** Walk buzz-step.
**Level:** Beginning 1

## Directions FOR THE DANCE

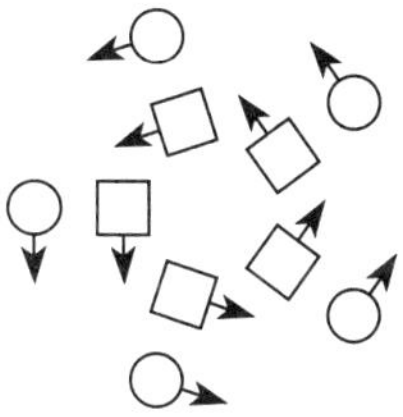

Meter 2/4

| *Measures* | *Counts* | |
|---|---|---|
| | | **PART I. (MUSIC A)** |
| | | Introduction (6 measures) |
| 1–2 | 1–4 | Beginning right, walk forward four steps. Couples turn to face center, join hands in a single circle on fourth step. Walk away from center four steps. |
| 3–4 | 5–8 | Beginning right, walk four steps to center and four steps away from center. |
| | | **PART II. (MUSIC B)** |
| 1–2 | 1–4 | Men clap hands, women walk four steps to center, and four steps back to place. |
| 3–4 | 5–8 | Men clap hands and walk four steps to the center, turn to the right and walk four steps away from the center to new partner. New partner is the woman to the right of original partner. |
| 5–6 | 1–4 | Hungarian-turn position: Partners stand right side to right side, right hands on partner's left hip, left hands curved overhead. Turn clockwise eight "buzz steps." |
| | | Repeat dance from the beginning. |

# Italy

ALB: Albania, BIH: Bosnia Herzegovina, HRV: Croatia, MKD: Former Yugoslav Republic of Macedonia, MNT: Montenegro, SVN: Slovenia

## Background

The Alps divide the Italian peninsula into two distinct climates. The north enjoys a temperate, moist climate and emerald-green landscapes, while the south features a dry, summerlike subtropical climate, producing a brown and yellow landscape. Over the centuries and even today, the northern area has been the most desirable and affluent part of Italy. The southern portion of the peninsula was mainly agrarian. The land was fertile and it was inhabited largely by Greek settlers along the southern and southeastern shores and Sicily.

During the Renaissance, Italy was home to several city-states ruled by strong families. The Visconti family and later the Sforza family ruled Milan. Florence was ruled by the de Medici family for sixty years. The city-states in the south were Tarantum, Syracuse, and Naples. By the beginning of the sixteenth century, Italy was ruled by five powerful states: the duchy of Milan, the republics of Venice and Florence, the Kingdom of Naples, and the states of the Church. The central portion of the country was occupied by the states of the Church. The general pattern of Church government was similar to that of other Renaissance governments; popes of this era made and broke treaties, hired soldiers (*condotteri*) for wars of conquest, and thus were hardly distinguishable from the leaders of other city-state governments.

### Influences on Dance

The Alps provided little barrier to invasion by European neighbors. The low-lying coastline also invited conquest by sea. Thus, the Romans were absorbed in military pursuits from the beginning of their settlement on the peninsula. In their role as invaders, the Romans assimilated the customs and folkways of the people they conquered over many centuries. It is not unusual, therefore, to find similarities to other cultures in the folklore and dance of Italy.

Although ancient chain and circle dances still exist, the couple dance seems to dominate the area, with much flirtation and bargaining between couples. Elements of the East can be found in the dance of the island provinces of Sicily, Sardinia, and Corsica. In the central portion of the country, the influence of the Church made dance somewhat circumspect, but that area did produce the lively and free-wheeling salterello. Dance movements in the northeast were similar to those of Yugoslavia. The many kinds of sword dances in the northwest were from Teutonic and Celtic influences. In the north, peasants copied their masters, who emulated provincial nobles; therefore, their dances displayed more dignity and courtly airs. In the south, the fiery tarantella was the favorite.

### Dance Characteristics

Italian dance steps are generally quite simple. They consist of skipping, waltzing, pivoting, and walking. The dance movements appear easy and almost lazy. Occasionally the dancers add clapping, stamping, balancing, and some mini-action. The sword dances depict the battles of the Crusaders.

### Preserving Folkways

The opera was and is the primary musical interest of the Italian people. The folk arias and dances were, on the other hand, a customary part of village life in the various provinces and thus were not widely known or appreciated. During the Mussolini era, an organization known as *Dopolavora* was charged with the task of fostering folk dance demonstrations and spectaculars to attract and entertain tourists. In more recent times, leading artists and writers have spearheaded a nationwide movement to preserve folkways in museums and universities. As a result, the government has stepped in to slow the loss of the folkways of Italy.

# Il Codiglione

Italian

IL CODIGLIONE MEANS "the cotillion" and is pronounced *eel koh-deel-YOH-neh.* Vyts Beliajus first saw this dance performed at Chicago's Hull House about 1928 by an Italian group of dancers, and he introduced it at Idyllwild in 1954.

***Dance A While* CD:** "Il Codiglione–Italian Cotillion."

**Formation:** Double circle of couples, Varsouvienne position, facing line of direction.

**Steps:** Walk, pas de basque.

**Level:** Beginning 2

## Directions FOR THE DANCE

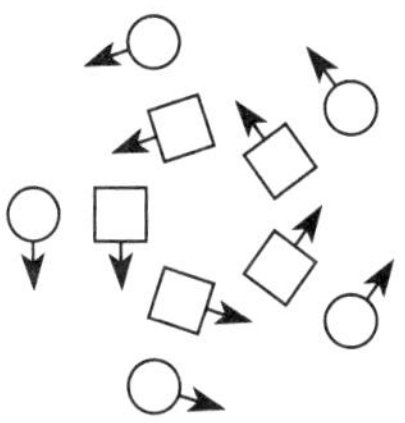

Meter 6/8

| ***Measures*** | |
|---|---|
| 1–4 | Introduction: No action. |
| | **PART I. WALK** |
| 1–16 | Beginning left, take 32 walking steps forward in line of direction. |
| 17–24 | All join hands to form a single circle and take 16 walking steps to right. Circle moves counterclockwise. |
| 25–32 | Take 16 walking steps to left. Circle moves clockwise. |
| | **PART II. TWO CIRCLES** |
| 1–8 | Women form circle and take 16 walking steps to left, circle moving clockwise. Men form circle around women and take 16 walking steps to right, circle moving counterclockwise. |
| 9–16 | Each circle moves in the opposite direction, women counterclockwise, men clockwise. |
| | **PART III. BASKET** |
| 1–8 | Men join hands and raise over and in front of women to form basket as women join hands. Woman remains to right of partner. Take 16 walking steps to right. Circle moves counterclockwise. |
| 9–16 | Women's hands remain joined. Men raise joined hands over women's heads, release hands, and reach under women's arms to rejoin hands in front of women and form basket again. Take 16 walking steps to left. Circle moves clockwise. |
| | **PART IV. WALK** |
| 1–16 | Repeat action of measures 1–16, Part I. |
| 17–24 | Men turn and walk clockwise single file in reverse line of direction while women continue to walk counterclockwise in line of direction. |
| 25–32 | Reverse. All turn half around and men walk counterclockwise while women walk clockwise. Women turn on the last measure to Varsouvienne position, facing line of direction. |

*continues on next page*

7

***Measures***

| | |
|---|---|
| | **PART V. WALK, PAS DE BASQUE, DO-SI-DO** |
| 1–3 | Varsouvienne position. Take six walking steps forward in line of direction. |
| 4 | Release hands. Partners turn to face and back away from each other two steps. End facing partner, man's back to center. |
| 5–8 | Snap fingers with arms outstretched above head and beginning right, take four pas de basque steps in place. |
| 9–12 | Lower arms to side and partners do-si-do, passing right shoulders first, taking eight steps. |
| 13–16 | Partners do-si-do, passing left shoulders first, taking eight steps and progress to new partner on left by moving diagonally left on last four steps. |
| 1–16 | Repeat action of measures 1–16. |
| | **PART VI. ENDING** |
| 1–2 | With feet slightly apart, take weight on right foot and clap hands (counts 1–3); pause (counts 4–6), step left and clap hands (counts 1–3); pause (counts 4–6). |
| 3–4 | Repeat action of measures 1–2. |
| 5–8 | Hook right elbow with partner and turn clockwise seven steps, then stop. Turn back on partner and clap hands overhead on last beat. |

## Style

There should be smooth transitions when changing directions. The walking steps are on the ball of the foot; a flat walk is heavy and ugly. The hands are joined shoulder high, elbows down, without an extended arm. The body is carried high. The success of this dance depends on the style of execution. The body is high and light.

# *Sicilian Tarantella*

## Italian

THE TARANTELLA IS PERHAPS Italy's most famous dance. It is depicted in famous paintings and has inspired writers like Goethe and composers such as Chopin. What began as a therapeutic remedy, inducing violent gyrations to exercise away the poison from a tarantula bite, has evolved into a charming dance, widely choreographed and enjoyed by dancers and spectators alike. The tarantella has taken many forms as each Italian province has imbued it with its own characteristics.

The Sicilian Tarantella is a flirtatious dance for four based on a number of typical Sicilian steps. Real tambourines add an exciting flavor to the dance. Snapping fingers and sharp hand claps may be substituted for shaking and hitting of tambourines.

***Dance A While* CD:** "Sicilian Tarantella."

**CD:** High/Scope RM 6.

**Music:** Herman, Michael, *Folk Dances for All*, p. 45.

**Formation:** Sets of two couples, partners facing. Men are side by side and women are side by side. Couple 1 is nearest the music. Couple 1 may be designated the "head couple," couple 2 the "foot couple."

**Steps:** Step-hop, run.

**Level:** Intermediate

## *Directions* FOR THE DANCE

Meter 6/8 • Directions are same for man and woman.

| *Measures* | *Counts* | |
|---|---|---|
| | | **PART I. STEP CLAP, HOP SWING** |
| 1 | 1–2 | All dancers step left, clap hands (count 1). Hop on left, swing right across (count 2). Striking tambourine or claps should be made in front of dancer, not overhead. |
| 2 | 3–4 | Repeat measure 1, beginning right, and swing left across. |
| 3–4 | 5–8 | Beginning left, four running steps in place. Men snap fingers, women shake tambourines or snap fingers. |
| 5–8 | 1–8 | Repeat measures 1–4. |
| 1–8 | 1–8 × 2 | Repeat Part I. |
| | | **PART II. RUNS FORWARD AND BACK** |
| 1–2 | 1–4 | Beginning left, four runs forward toward partner. Dancers begin bending low. Men snap fingers, women shake tambourines or snap. |
| 3–4 | 5–8 | Beginning left, four runs backward away from partner. Dancers slowly straighten up and raise arms upward. Men snap fingers, women shake tambourines or snap fingers. |
| 5–8 | 1–8 | Repeat measures 1–4. |
| 9–16 | | Repeat Part II. |

*continues on next page*

| ***Measures*** | ***Counts*** | |
|---|---|---|
| | | **PART III. RUN AND TURN** |
| 1 | 1–2 | Man 1 (head) and woman diagonally opposite (foot) run toward each other. |
| 2–3 | 3–6 | Hook right arms, turn once around. |
| 4 | 7–8 | Return to place. |
| 5–8 | 1–8 | Man 2 (foot) and woman 1 (head) repeat action of measures 1–4. |
| 9–16 | 1–8 × 2 | Repeat measures 1–8, turning with left arms. |
| | | **PART IV A. DO-SI-DO** |
| 1–4 | 1–8 | Man 1 (head) and woman diagonally opposite (foot) run toward each other; pass right shoulders, back to back; pass left shoulders, and dance backward to place. Do not fold arms across chest. Snap fingers as dancers pass each other. |
| 5–8 | 1–8 | Man 2 (foot) and woman 1 (head) repeat action of measures 1–4. |
| 9–16 | 1–8 ×2 | Repeat action, except pass left shoulders when moving forward and right shoulders when running backward to place. |
| | | **PART IV B. CIRCLE** |
| 1–4 | 1–8 | Dancers face a quarter-turn to the right; hands on hips, left shoulders to center of circle, move counterclockwise with eight skipping steps |
| 5–6 | 1–8 | Repeat measures 1–4, right shoulders to center of circle. |
| | | **PART V. STARS** |
| 1–4 | 1–8 | Dancers form a left-hand star and move counterclockwise with eight skipping steps. |
| 5–8 | 1–8 | Repeat measures 1–4, forming a right-hand star and moving clockwise. |

## Note

This arrangement is based on a piano score of 24 measures. Recordings may only have eight measures of music A and eight measures of music B. The dance may be done with only four parts to best fit the recording.

# Japan

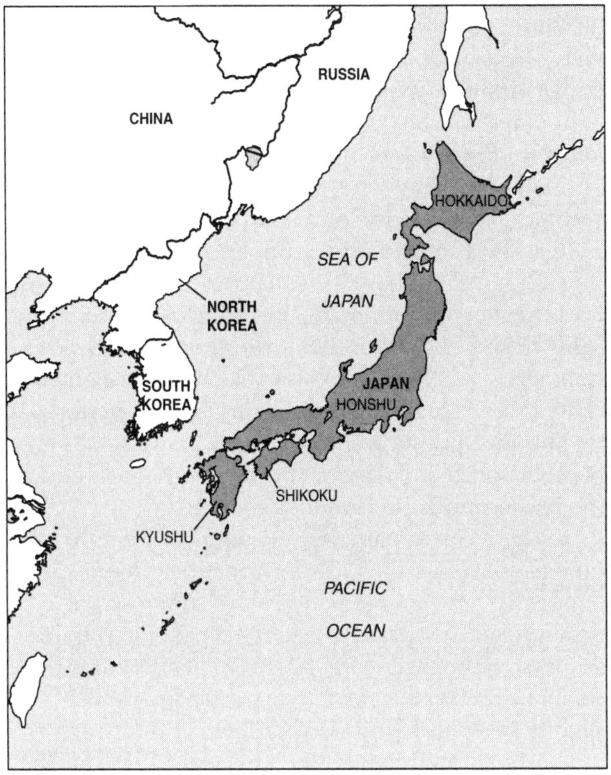


The three professional classic dance forms in Japan are Bugaku, Noh, and Kabuki. All three are performed by men, confirming Japanese society as indeed a man's world. Each represents an aspect of three different historical socioeconomic groups found in the cultural life of Japan. Bugaku was developed from dances brought from Asia for the imperial courts during the Heian period (794–1185). Noh was developed under the patronage of samurai rulers and aristocracy during the Muromachi period (1338–1573). Kabuki was a popular form among merchants and townspeople of Osaka and Edo (Tokyo) during the Todugawa period (1600–1867).

Folk dances in general occur as part of the three major religious festivals, Kaura, Ta Asobi, and Obaon. Kagura is the music (god music) and dance of Shinto, the indigenous pantheistic religion of Japan. It includes a wide variety of activities such as dances and ceremonies of the imperial shrines, dances of the Miko or shrine maidens, and numerous regional dance-dramas, martial arts, and animal dances. Ta Asobi or "rice paddy play" refers to a variety of agricultural rites dealing with the cultivation of rice from mid-winter to the fall harvest festivals. Bon dances are performed throughout Japan, generally on the grounds of Buddhist temples. Bon festivals are celebrations of the return of the souls of dead ancestors, who visit the earth once each year in mid-August. Noh performances are also given as a part of some festivals.

## Bugaku

Bugaku dance style emphasizes pure dance forms over the dramatic elements. Although dramatic elements exist in some dances, they become mostly topical and little or nothing of the story is communicated. Bugaku emphasizes symmetry of the basic movement patterns in solo dances and the frequent use of paired dancers. The dance setting is usually outdoors or in a simulated outdoor setting in a courtyard, shrine, temple, or the imperial household. The fixed repertoire is composed of some 60 pieces handed down from ancient times. The works are divided into two categories according to basic style and assumed place of origin. The Left Dance (Samai) includes dances from China, India, and Indochina, along with those from Japan in similar style. The movements are slow, gentle, and elegant. Dancers are costumed in reddish robes. The Right Dance (Umai) includes dances from Korea and compositions based on Korean dances. The movement is humorous and spirited. Dancers wear robes of a greenish color. In the Left Dance the dancers enter the stage from the left of a large drum located at the rear of the stage, or stage right. The Right Dancer enters the stage from the right of the drum, or stage left.

Bugaku dances are divided into four types based on content. They are ceremonial (hiramai), military (bumai), running (hashirimai), and children's (dodu) dances. Ceremonial dances are performed by two to four unmasked dancers wearing court or ceremonial robes. Military dances are performed in pairs. Dancers wear elaborate warrior robes and simulate battle action with swords and lances. Running dances are performed by solo masked dancers displaying a strong character. Children's dances are composed for and performed by children.

## Noh

Noh is held to be the greatest dance-drama tradition in human history. After appreciating the visual beauty and traditional conventions of Noh, those who make the effort will experience a powerful expression of the universal nature of man's spirit. The training and aesthetics of Noh were formulated by the writings of the famous performer, playwright, and philosopher Zeami in the mid-twelfth and early thirteenth centuries. His writings are still read by students, performers, and connoisseurs of the art, and his plays still form the core of Noh repertory.

A combination of the elegant world of the imperial court, Zen in the form of Buddhist meditation, and the code of ethics and conduct of the samurai were the main influences on the content of Noh dance-dramas. These three influences are seen in Noh plays in which samurai, nobles of the court, and Buddhist priests appear as characters.

Noh plays draw on the etiquette of Shintoism, including the carrying of the fan and the use of flute and drum, and on Kagura for ceremony. From Bugaku it drew its structure, namely the use of an introduction, development, and conclusion. Variety came from Sarugaku in the form of magic tricks, humorous skits, and acrobatics. Field music elements came from rice cultivation festivals. Dances performed by Buddhist priests (Ennem) at New Year festivals and popular songs and dances of the period are all part of the background and content of Noh theater.

Set movement patterns, meaning a form either in time or space, are the basis for construction of Noh dances. The movement patterns are composed of position and progression. The basic position requires the torso to be inclined and held in place with no rotation. The back is held in a straight line, knees slightly bent, and arms curved down and forward of the body, elbows slightly lifted to create a line for the large sleeves of the costume. The dancer imagines lines of force coming out of the center of the body to project his energy. This effort can be characterized as a level of high tension without being rigid. Concentration produces the effect of freedom coming from self-control.

Walking is the most characteristic movement. It is the progression that integrates the dance. In addition, it is the element by which the overall skill of the dancer is determined. The walk gives the impression that the dancer is gliding in space without effort. Stamping is also used and the resulting pattern of sound is augmented by placing clay pots under the stage to give resonance to this part of the performance.

The mechanics of turning and locomotion to various parts of the stage are highly codified in Noh. These movements are important to convey traveling to shrines, battlefields, or places in nature. Locale or the place depicted in Noh text is expressed primarily in movement, seldom with the aid of stage properties. Movements such as the activity of looking are depicted by a forward move, raising and pointing the fan, then backing away to add perspective. Some pantomime depicts praying, holding a shield, or riding a horse.

Noh dancing is not dynamic in that most movements are minimal and subtle. The goal is to express the highest ideals with the simplest means. Noh has been continued by generations of people who have a great sensitivity to all arts and a special talent for dance-dramas.

## Kabuki

Kabuki is one of Japan's most traditional and popular theater arts. Its beginnings date back to the latter part of the sixteenth century, a time when there was a rigid distinction between the warrior class and the commoners. Kabuki was cultivated by merchants who had become economically powerful but who remained socially inferior. The art of Kabuki was a means for expressing their resentment against the feudal system of the times. Kabuki themes were thus those of fundamental conflicts between humanity and the feudal system. It was the thematic content of Kabuki that endeared it to the public in its early development and even today.

In the beginning the players were women, but when they began to attract undue attention from their male audience, public officials banned their appearance in the theater. Male actors became the sole performers. During the 250 years that the ban on female dancers was enforced, male actors perfected the art of female impersonation or "onnagata." Onnagata became such an integral part of Kabuki that, if deprived of this element, the traditional quality of Kabuki could be lost forever.

Kabuki has incorporated parts of all preceding theater forms in its extensive and continuous evolution since the sixteenth century. It drew stage technique and repertoire from Noh. It adopted a comic element from Kyogen plays, which were interludes in Noh performances. It also drew from the puppet theater, which was developing at the same time. And finally, in the nineteenth century, it added literary realism.

Dance-drama constituted a segment of some 300 plays in the Kabuki repertoire. Actors danced to both vocal and instrumental music. Many of these dramas told complete stories; others were primarily dance. Historical dramas presenting accounts of warriors and nobles and domestic dramas depicting plebeian life constituted the remaining repertoire.

The aesthetic principle underlying Kabuki is formalized beauty. To prepare for their roles, actors study the style modeled by their predecessors. Over the years these model styles became highly formalized and symbolic even though they were intended to present realism. Thus in acting, gestures became more like dancing than acting, posture and poses placed more emphasis on statuesque beauty, vocal delivery became elocution accompanied by music and sets. Kabuki costumes and makeup are recognized as the most lavish and extravagant in the world. Audiences enjoy this spectacle of dazzling and superb color even if unconvinced by the plot of the story. Visual beauty sustains the popularity of Kabuki even today.

The modern Kabuki theaters are built largely in western style, but have retained some significant features of the traditional theater. Two of these are the flower-walk ramp and the revolving stage. The flower-walk ramp (*hanamichi*) is a passageway connecting the left side of the stage with the back of the hall. The ramp passes over the seats at head level with the audience. Actors enter and exit along the passageway and at the right and left exits on the stage. The passageway is part of the stage and often actors give important scenes of the play on the flower-walk. The revolving stage was invented in Japan some 300 years ago and is a major contribution to theater around the world.

Kabuki's greatness is primarily due to its actors, many of whom come from families of Kabuki actors that date back to the feudal era. To acquire all the skills needed, an actor must begin in childhood. The family system not only allows for early development but has made it possible to preserve the art of Kabuki.

The Kabuki actor of today no longer specializes in a particular role but has become more versatile. This is true except in the role of onnagata or female impersonation. In this role, specialization is still the rule. Formerly actors were popular among the masses but considered of low social status. Today actors are held in high esteem and many have been elected to the Academy of Art of Japan. Kabuki enjoys wide popularity in Japan today, although its content does not depict contemporary themes. The principle reason for its sustained popularity lies in the fact that it has become a crystallized art form and thus seems destined to retain the affection and pride of the nation.

# *Harukoma*

*(Town of Hachiman in Gifu Pref.)*

## Japanese

*Permission to use Harukoma courtesy of Ryoichi Oikawa, Japan.*

HARUKOMA, PRONOUNCED *Ha-ruh-KOH-ma* is a modernized dance created after World War II. It is a special favorite of all the dances from the Gujo area because of its rhythmical, dynamic movements and cheerful music. It is danced at the Bon festival. The name of this dance was changed from Saba (mackerel) to Harukoma. *Haru* means spring and *koma* means pony in Japanese.

**CD:** KICH 134, V20G-150
**Formation:** Single circle facing center.
**Level:** Beginning 1

## Directions FOR THE DANCE

Meter 2/4

| ***Measure*** | ***Counts*** | |
|---|---|---|
| 1–4 | 1–8 | Introduction: no action counts 1–7. Lift arms up in front and cross one wrist over the other, hands in a fist (arms are rounded, as if hugging someone), and point right foot back, count 8, preparing for first movement. |
| 1–2 | 1–4 | Point right foot diagonal, right forward, count 1. Point right foot back on count 2. Point right foot diagonal, right forward, count 3. Step right foot to side right and point left foot back on count 4.<br>Hands: Straight arms to side count 1. Bring them back to beginning position, count 2. Repeat for counts 3 and 4. |

| Measure | Counts | |
|---|---|---|
| 3–4 | 1–4 | Repeat measures 1–2 with opposite foot work. |
| 5–6 | 1–4 | Facing left diagonal forward, right foot steps forward; bending slightly over at the waist, count 1. Left foot steps side left, standing up straight, count 2. Hop on left foot, count 3. Right foot steps beside left, count 4. |
| | | Hands: Lower hands down on count 1, raise hands to chest level on count 2. Clap hands on count 3. Raise hands slightly above shoulder level, count 4. |
| 7–8 | 1–4 | Repeat with opposite foot work. Hands on count 4 returned to beginning position. |
| | | Repeat dance from the beginning. |

### Style

1. It is important to bounce rhythmically, using your knees.
2. Move left gradually while dancing.
3. Keep hands in a fist while dancing.
4. The point in measures 1–2 is accented.

### Translation of Lyrics

I grew up in the deep mountains in Gujo.

My husband and I do hard labor with horses and I spin thread.

Gujo is a famous place for horses.

That splendid horse, Surushumi, was also born in Kera village.

# *Tanko Bushi*

## Japanese

Tanko Bushi is pronounced *TAN-ko BUH-shee,* and is from the town of Tagawa in Fukuoka Prefecture. Tanko Bushi imitates the movements of workers in a coal mine. It is appreciated by people all over Japan. A special thank you to Ryoichi Oikawa for his clarifications of Tanko Bushi dance directions.

7



### Motifs

1. Nagame-Kazashi & Nagashi: Gaze at the moon while shading one's eyes with one hand (Nagame-Kazashi), the other diagonally down and backward (Nagashi).
2. Yama-Biraki: Hands open down at sides to outline a mountain shape.

***Dance A While* CD:** "Tanko Bushi." Also, many traditional Japanese music CDs contain Tanko Bushi.

**Formation:** Circle of solo dancers, traditionally traveling with the direction of the sun. Today, dancers may move clockwise or counterclockwise.

**Level:** Beginning 2

## *Directions* FOR THE DANCE

Meter 2/4

| *Measures* | *Counts* | |
|---|---|---|
| 1–8 | 1–36 | Dance moves counterclockwise. |
| | | Introduction: no actions; measure 1–7, counts 1–32. Clap hands three times with Cho Chon ga Chon, measure 8, counts 33–35. Hold count 36. Clapping rhythm is quick, quick, slow. (When using another musical arrangement, the introduction may be left out, starting the dance at any point). |
| | | **PART I. DIGGING** |
| 1–2 | 1–4 | Right foot points diagonal right forward on count 1. Lift right foot back and up, almost in front of left leg, count 2. Right foot repeats point, count 3. At the same time, stretch both hands diagonal right down, gesturing twice, as if digging coal with a shovel. Step with right foot where it was pointed and raise hands to chest level, count 4. |
| 3–4 | 5–8 | Repeat action of measure 1–2 with opposite footwork. |
| | | **PART II. THROWING THE COAL OVER THE SHOULDER** |
| 5 | 1–2 | Step right foot forward on count 1 while raising hands to right shoulder. Arm gesture as if throwing coal over the right shoulder on count 2. |
| 6 | 3–4 | Move left foot forward, but do not take weight count 3, hold count 4. Repeat opposite arm actions of measure 5. |
| | | **PART III. SHADE THE EYES FROM THE MOON (Nagami–Kazashi)** |
| 7 | 1–2 | Left foot points back count 1, take weight count 2. Hands perform right kazashi and left nagashi. |
| 8 | 3–4 | Point right foot back count 3 and take partial weight count 4. Repeat opposite hands from measure 7. |
| | | **PART IV. PUSHING THE CART** |
| 9–10 | 1–4 | Step right foot forward and hold, count 1–2. Step left foot forward and hold, count 3–4. Stretch both hands forward twice as if pushing a cart. |
| | | **PART V. Yama–Biraki + Clapping** |
| 11 | 1–2 | Right foot steps forward, count 1. Left foot steps back, count 2. |
| 12 | 3–4 | Bring right foot to left foot and step in place and clap hands together on count 3, hold count 4. |
| 13 | 1–2 | Clap hands on counts 1 and 2. |
| | | Repeat dance from the beginning. |

### Translation of Lyrics

The moon comes out over the coal mine in the town of Tagawa.
As the chimney is so high, the moon might be smoky.

# Lithuania

## Background

The Lithuanians have lived on the eastern shores of the Baltic Sea since the pre-Christian era. They were a peaceful people made up of farmers, fishermen, and friendly traders. During the first thousand years A.D., they and related tribes were invaded and nearly exterminated by the Crusaders. Over the centuries, Lithuania has been surrounded by enemies and repeatedly invaded by them. In brief periods of tenuous independence or absence of war, they were able to expand their territory and improve their cultural welfare. In the fourteenth and fifteenth centuries, they expanded their territory from the Baltic to the Black Sea. By not imposing their customs or culture on those they ruled, they were known as the "Vikings of the Continent."

From 1918 to 1940, free from adversaries, Lithuania had an opportunity to expand its educational institutions, book publishing, opera, theater, and ballet. This period was known as the Golden Age of Progress in culture and economics. However, that ended when Lithuania was dealt a triple blow by invasions from Russia, Germany, and Russia again between 1940 and 1944. Modern Lithuania is the result of a 1991 Russian coup that led to the formation of an interim government. At that time, Lithuania and 14 other Russian states declared independence and formed the Commonwealth of Independent States.

### Dance Characteristics

Lithuanian dance took second place to Lithuanian songs. The logic was that one can sing and work at the same time but one cannot work and dance at the same time.

Lithuanian life has centered largely around the farm, and therefore dancing was relegated to holidays and special occasions. Farm life was reflected in the actions of the dances. Dances often depicted farm chores and animals on the ground, in the sky, and in the water. No animal was too humble to be imitated in dance or heralded in song.

Lithuanians of the early Christian era danced dances of the "play party game" variety. There were also circle dances performed to the accompaniment of songs about nature and farm life. Emerging from the play party form, Lithuanian dances were slow and sedate. The polka appeared in Lithuania from Poland long before it was popularized in the western world, and Lithuanians gave it a distinct style. As a result of wearing wooden shoes called *Klumpes*, dancers were unable to lift their feet to any height or their shoes would drop off, so they danced a flat-footed polka. The style is still seen among old-timers who were raised in the peasant tradition. The polka has maintained its dominance as a social dance, and the waltz did not gain much recognition until later generations.

### Dance Heritage

During the period of independence between 1918 and 1940, the wealth of Lithuanian folk songs and dances was largely ignored. Fox-trots, tangos, and round waltzes were the fashion. An invitation to dance at the International Folk Festival in London ignited interest in "digging up" folk dances. With the help of the government, scouts were sent to every corner of the land to invite people who remembered the dances to demonstrate them. With the wealth of material contributed by older generations, Lithuanian dancers attended the London festival and captured highest recognition and returned home with great pride and appreciation for their dances.

# Kalvelis

Lithuanian

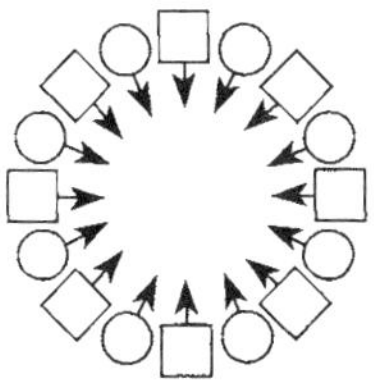

KALVELIS MEANS "the young blacksmith." The clapping action imitates the beating of the hammer on the anvil. The dance was introduced to the United States by Vytautas Finadar Beliajus, noted Lithuanian dance teacher.

***Dance A While* CD:** "Kalvelis."
**Formation:** Couples in a single circle facing center. Woman on man's right.
**Steps:** Polka, stamping, skips.
**Level:** Beginning 3

## Directions FOR THE DANCE

Meter 2/4

| ***Measures*** | |
|---|---|
| | **MUSIC A PART I. CIRCLE POLKA** |
| 1–8 | Circle counterclockwise with seven polka steps. End with three stamps on the eighth measure. |
| 1–8 | Repeat circling clockwise. |
| Music B | **CHORUS—CLAPS AND SKIPS** |
| 9 | Clap left hand onto right, right onto left. |
| 10 | Repeat left onto right and right onto left. |
| 11–12 | Hook right elbows with partner and turn once around with four skips. |
| 13–16 | Repeat claps, hook left elbow, and turn once around with four skips. |
| 9–16 | Repeat all of music B. |
| Music A | **PART II. TO CENTER AND BACK** |
| 1–4 | Women dance three polka steps to center, stamp three times. |
| 5–8 | Repeat back to place. |
| 1–4 | Men dance three polka steps to center, stamp three times. |
| 5–8 | Repeat back to place. (Note: Men's dance action should be vigorous.) |
| Music B | Repeat chorus. |
| Music A | **PART III. GRAND RIGHT AND LEFT** |
| 1–8 | Partners face, join right hands. Dance grand right and left for 16 polka steps to meet new partner. (Note: Music A is repeated.) |
| Music B | Repeat chorus with new partner. |

### Variations on Part III

Men stand in place as women weave to the right with 16 polka steps. Repeat chorus with new partner. Women stand in place as men weave around circle with 16 polka steps, ending, if all goes well, with partner. Repeat chorus with original partner. Instead of the grand right and left, take ballroom position with partner and dance 16 polkas around the circle. Repeat chorus.

Repeat dance from the beginning.

# *Klumpakojis*

## Lithuanian

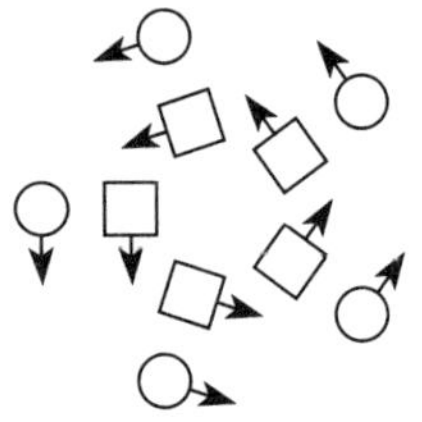

KLUMPAKOJIS MEANS "wooden footed" or "clumsy footed." It is frequently translated erroneously as "wooden shoes." It is a form of the finger polka-type folk dance found the world over. Notice its similarity to the Swedish Klappdans, the Dutch Hopp Mor Annika, and the Danish Siskind.

**CD:** Folkraft.

**Formation:** Double circle, couples side by side, inside hands joined, free hands on hips, facing line of direction.

**Steps:** Walk, stamp, polka.

**Level:** Beginning 2

## *Directions* FOR THE DANCE

Meter 2/4 • Directions are for man; woman's part reverse.

| ***Measures*** | |
|---|---|
| | **PART I. WALK** |
| 1–4 | Beginning left, take eight brisk walking steps in line of direction, turning toward partner to face reverse line of direction on last step. |
| 5–8 | Join inside hands, free hands on hips. Take eight walking steps in reverse line of direction. |
| 1–8 | Face partner, joining right hands, right elbow bent, left hand on hip. Partners take eight steps, walking around each other clockwise. Join left hands and take eight steps, walking counterclockwise. |
| | **PART II. STAMPS, CLAPS** |
| 1–4 | No action (counts 1 *and*, 2 *and*). Then stamp three times. No action (counts 1 *and*, 2 *and*). Clap own hands three times. |
| 5–8 | Shake right index finger, right elbow bent, at partner (counts 1–3), hold (count 4). Shake left finger, left elbow bent, at partner (counts 1–3), hold (count 4). Clap right hand of partner and turn solo counterclockwise in place once with two steps. Facing partner, stamp feet three times quickly. |
| 1–8 | Repeat action of measures 1–8, Part II. |
| | **PART III. POLKA** |
| 1–8 | Varsouvienne position. Beginning left, take 16 polka steps forward in line of direction. On last two polka steps, man moves forward to new partner. |

### Notes

1. Zest is added to the dance if dancers shout "hey hey" or "ya-hoo" spontaneously during the polka sequence.
2. This dance may be used to introduce either the two-step or the polka step.

# Mexico

## Dance in Mexico

*By Nelda G. Drury, Professor Emeritus, San Antonio College, San Antonio, TX.*

If you were to visit Mexico you would probably find a civil or religious celebration or parade in which dances are featured. Dance is an integral part of Mexican life. The costumes worn by the dancers add a high note of color to the occasion. Three phases in the history of the dance in Mexico become immediately apparent: pre-Hispanic, the period of conquest, and the dances of modern Mexico.

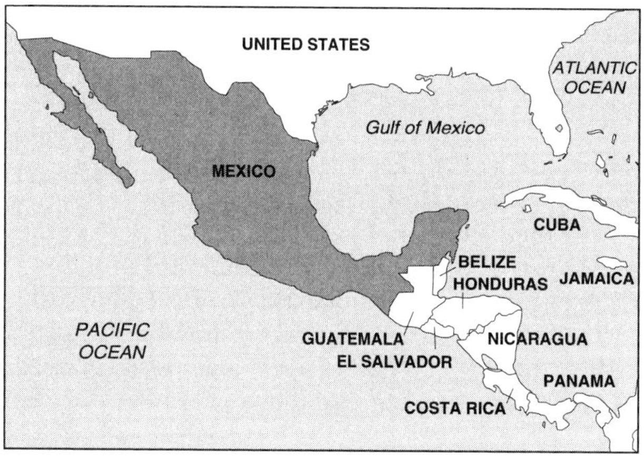


### Pre-Hispanic

The first inhabitants of Mexico were the Nahuas, Toltecas, Zapotecas, Mixtecos, Totonacos, and Mayas. Each group made dance a part of their existence. They taught their children to dance even before they attended school, for they believed it an essential part of growing into adulthood. Unfortunately, little is known about these ancient dances. Our knowledge of them is derived from ancient codices that have been discovered and from the writings of some of the priests who entered Mexico with Hernán Cortez.

These sources indicate the importance of dance to native Mexicans. They performed dances in their religious celebrations that often lasted several days. The dances were performed in concentric circles with the eldest of the group in the center directing the change of steps. Participants of higher rank were bestowed a place in the inner circle closer to the center. These dances had many similarities to those of ancient Egypt. Dances were performed before going off to war or as tribute to the god of rain or other gods as the occasion required. They were also performed in adoration of the sun or the moon. Some of the gods were bloodthirsty so human sacrifices were part of the rituals.

The Deer Dance is one of the few pre-Hispanic dances that has survived in its pure form over the centuries. It is a dance of the Yaquis from the states of Sonora and Sinaloa. It enacts the killing of a deer and is considered a classic of this era.

Dance accompaniment was predominantly by percussion instruments and woodwinds, such as flutes usually made of bamboo canes. These instruments were elaborately decorated and very colorful. A few instruments that have survived the ravages of time may be seen in the Museum of Anthropology and History in Mexico City.

### Period of Conquest

In the second phase of dance in Mexico a new lifestyle evolved with the arrival of the Spaniards. This period is characterized by astounding changes. The people were confronted with new customs, new ideologies, a new religion, new beliefs, and even a new language. Along with the Spanish conquistadors came evangelists bringing Christianity to the New World. When the new religious leaders realized the importance of dance in the life of the Indians and found that it could not be suppressed, they adapted the dances to Christian rituals. If the native Indians held a festival to honor one of their idols or gods, the priests would substitute a Christian saint in its stead. The Spanish introduced new dance rhythms and new string instruments.

The blending of the two cultures produced the *danza mestiza,* which rapidly spread to all the states of the republic. These dances were warlike reenactments of the conquest. One of the most famous dances of this type is La Danza de la Pluma (dance of the plumes). In the dance, from the state of Oaxaca, the performer dons a splendid headdress that is covered with feathers, beads, and mirrors in beautiful designs and breathtaking colors. The dance simulates the struggles between the Indians and the Spaniards. The choreography is simple, but the steps are quite difficult. The dance is performed by men only and is very popular even today.

Most of the dances of this era are of the same type. Examples are Moros y Cristianos (Moors vs. Christians) and the Danza de los Diablitos (devils). There are also dances of pre-Hispanic origin that have had their music and costumes embellished by European influence. Examples of these are La Danza de los Quetzales (quetzal is a bird) from the state of Puebla and La Danza de los Voladores from

Papantla, Veracruz. The latter is sometimes called the dance of the "Flying Indians."

Dances that depict the work ethic are demonstrated by such dances as Los Sonarjeros, a planting dance, and La Tortuga del Arenal, which reenacts the gathering of turtle eggs, an important part of the diet of the Juchitecas. Most of these dances were performed at fiestas and in the courtyard of the church, a custom that still exists. Every region has its own danzas mestizas, which correspond to its own way of life. Each embodies a reminder of what used to be and an acceptance of the new.

## Dances of Modern Mexico

The third phase of dance of Mexico evolved from the intermarriage of Spaniards and native Mexicans. As time went by, the children of this union, called *Mestizos*, began to acquire more and more of the Spanish customs and slowly discarded that which was purely indigenous. During the colonial period other nationalities also added their influence. The French who came with Maximilian brought the ballroom dances that were popular in the courts of Europe (*bailes de salon*) such as the polka, waltz, schottische, mazurka, and Varsouvienne. The Germans favored the northern part of Mexico and left their stamp on the music and dance of that region. Dance, however, took a new direction. Each region developed its own *zapateado* (footwork) and, with it, its own *jarabe*.

El Jarabe Tapatío is considered the national dance of Mexico. From the state of Jalisco, it is the most popular of all the jarabes. It is a dance of courtship and tells about the charro (young cowboy) who has taken a fancy to a beautiful "China" (young señorita) and decides to visit her and declare his passion. She shares the same feelings but does not want to seem overanxious. So she shyly repulses his advances. Dejected over the rejection, he goes off to a cantina where he imbibes a little too much tequila and proceeds to get a little tipsy. On coming to his senses, he decides to try once more to show his serious intentions. He throws his most prized possession, his sombrero, at her feet and allows her to dance in the brim. Upon observing the manifestation of his true love for her, as a gesture of acceptance, she picks up the hat and places it on her head, after which they dance a Diana, a dance of triumph.

The word *jarabe* actually means a syrup or sweet mixture of different herbs and sugars. In music it is a medley of different tunes and in dance it consists of steps characteristic of a particular region. These are truly Mexican dances, Indian in origin and influenced by the Spanish, giving them the true flavor of Mexico. The most popular, recognizable, and best known of the jarabes are Jarabe Tapatío, Jarabe de la Botella (Jalisco), Jarabe Michoacano, Jarabe Tlaxcalteco, and Jarabe Mixteco. Yucatan has produced the Jaranas; the Huapango is from Huastica; and the polkas are from the northern part of the country.

Music is also unique to each region. Jalisco, in the central part of Mexico, has mariachis or groups of strolling, singing musicians using the violin, different sized guitars, and more recently the trumpet. The typical musicians of Veracruz use the harp and violins and sing in a high pitch. The music of the north includes the guitar and accordion, often a button accordion, and in the south the marimba and the jaranas are common. Music has had a deep influence on dance and vice versa.

An added attraction is the colorful costumes worn in each of the different regions of Mexico. From the predominantly white costumes from the warm climates of Veracruz and Yucatan, to Jalisco's colorful and beribboned costumes, to the heavy woolen skirts of Michoacan, to the fringed leather garments of the vaquero (cowboy) of northern Mexico, there are more than 600 regional costumes. Dance in Mexico is the spontaneous manifestation of the feelings, the passions, and the pleasures of its people.

# El Jarabe Tapatío

## Mexican

*Directions by Nelda Drury, Professor Emeritus, San Antonio College, TX.*

El Jarabe Tapatío is often referred to as the Mexican Hat Dance and is considered the national dance of Mexico; see the previous page for background information. The more proficient dancer will add steps and flourishes; others will simplify the dance.

### Jarabe step

The basic step is like a very small two-step with accent on the first count. Example: step forward on right foot (count 1), step on left foot close to right instep (count 2), step forward on right foot. Repeat starting with left foot. This counts as two jarabe steps, six counts, one measure. There are many styles of jarabe step execution, such as: count 1 being done with just the heel, or the second count being done with the heel, rather than the whole foot. The steps should be very small since the music is very fast.

**CD:** Folkraft.

**Formation:** Any number of couples scattered informally around the dance area. Partners face each other or the front with inside hands joined, man's right holding woman's left.

**Steps:** Jarabe step, heel toe, stamp, run, buzz step, chug.

**Level:** Advanced

## Directions FOR THE DANCE

Meter 6/8 • Directions are the same for both man and woman.

| | |
|---|---|
| Roll of music | Introduction: Length of roll of music varies. The woman turns to her left under partner's joined hand, they release hands, and both move away from each other about three short steps. Man's hands are held low behind his back, woman holds skirt out to side. Body should lean forward slightly. |
| | **PART I.** |
| 8 measures | **A.** Beginning right, move toward partner using 14 basic jarabe steps. Stamp right foot and hold. At this point the couple should have right shoulder to right shoulder with partner. |
| 8 measures | Continue in same direction to partner's place with 12 jarabe steps, turning to right on steps 13 and 14, and stamp on right; now facing partner. **Cue:** Heel step, toe step |
| 8 measures | **B.** Step on right heel slightly in front of left foot, small step forward on left foot, step on right toe slightly back (but not behind) left foot, very small step forward on left foot. Use same floor pattern as **A** to partner (center) and stamp. Seven heel step, toe steps to the center and stamp. Continue across and turn to face partner and stamp. |
| 8 measures | Pass right shoulders and continue to own original place, seven more heel-toe steps, turn to right to face partner, and stamp. |
| 8 measures | **C.** Using 14 jarabe steps, go all the way to partner's place, turn and stamp right. |

*continues on next page*

7

El Jarabe Tapatío, *continued*

Meter 3/4

| | |
|---|---|
| | **PART II.** |
| 4 measures | Take 3 running steps toward partner (right, left, right), then cross left over right to do a full turn to right (in center, close to partner). Continue to opposite side, with three runs and cross left over right to a half-turn right to face partner. The running should be done lightly, like scissor kicks, straight legs lifting the free foot high from the hip. Pass by right shoulder. |
| 4 measures | **Turns:** Beginning right, take three buzz steps, turning right, stamp left. Turning left, repeat stepping left, stamp right. |
| 4 measures | Repeat turns to right and to left. The stamp should be done facing toward partner. |
| 12 measures | Repeat first 12 measures, runs and turns. |
| | **PART III. BORRACHITO (DRUNKEN) STEP** |
| | This is like a waltz step. Fall forward onto right foot (count 1), step on left close to (and behind) right ankle (count 2), step on right foot (count 3). Repeat, starting with left foot. Dip right shoulder slightly forward when falling onto right foot. Dip left shoulder when falling onto left foot. |
| 6 measures | Beginning right, take six borrachito steps, traveling to opposite side. Do not stop at center. |
| 2 measures | Cross right foot over left and dance six little rocking steps while turning to the right (clockwise) in place. End facing partner. |
| 8 measures | Repeat all, crossing back to original side. |
| Meter 2/4 | |
| | **PART IV. HOJAS DE TÉ** |
| | Hojas de té are the rhythmic words for practicing this step. This step is similar to Part I B; just add a chug to it. Step on right heel, step left. Step on right toe, step left, chug. |
| 8 measures | Beginning right, take seven of these steps to center and stamp. Right shoulder to right shoulder with partner. Continue to other side, step left, turning right, stamp right. Each should be in own original place, facing partner. |
| | **PART V.** |
| 6 measures | Run lightly forward, right, left, right, and cross left over right, do full turn (pivot) to right (clockwise), ending with right shoulder toward home. Beginning right, take four push steps back to place. Push step is similar to buzz step, without turning, but traveling in straight line. The number of push steps varies according to proficiency. |
| 6 measures | Repeat runs toward center; right, left, right, and cross left over right, do full turn, remain in center. Man throws hat on the floor at woman's feet during these push steps. Take 6 push steps, facing partner, leading with left shoulder, traveling around hat clockwise. |

**PART VI.**

| | |
|---|---|
| 8 measures | Left shoulder leading, stepping on left foot, dancers move around the hat with 16 push steps. |
| 8 measures | The man and woman travel around the hat in opposite directions: man clockwise, woman counterclockwise. End up at own side. |

*Woman* leaps lightly into brim of the hat, cross right over left and dance six rocking steps (weight onto right, lifting left heel, pointing left toe down, then transfers weight onto left, lifting right heel). During these rocking steps, maneuver to end up on woman's original side. Use last two measures to get out (step, jump, leap, whatever) of the hat, onto "her" side. Today the woman seldom leaps into the hat, because they want to save the hat.

*Man's* step like a polka. (Lunge or fall forward on right, lifting left heel high in back, step on ball of left, step on right. Repeat starting with left.

| | |
|---|---|
| 3 measures | **Interlude:** Woman sinks down, picks up hat with both hands, places hat on her head. Man swings right leg over her head, crosses right over left, pivots to left. Man extends his right hand to her left hand to help woman up, and she rises. They stand side by side facing front, inside hands joined. |

Meter 2/8

**PART VII.**

| | |
|---|---|
| 8 measures | Take four light running steps forward, four backing up to place. Repeat four forward, four back. |
| 8 measures | Hop on left, at same time place right heel out to right (count 1), hop on left, at same time cross right in front of left and touch right toe to floor (count *and*), hop on left, at same time place right heel to right (count 2), bounce lightly on both feet (count *and*). Repeat starting left. Repeat all. |
| 8 measures | Take four running steps forward, four backward. Skip in place. Raise joined inside hands, woman turns left under that arch. Man kneels on left knee, woman places left foot on man's right knee. Woman holds her skirt out to the side with right hand, man extends left arm out, and both lean away from each other and hold pose. |

# *La Cucaracha*

## Mexican

*Directions by Nelda Drury, Professor Emeritus, San Antonio College, TX.*

THE SONG THAT ACCOMPANIES the dance was popularized during the Mexican Revolution. There are many versions of La Cucaracha. An original version and an adapted version for recreational groups are presented.

***Dance A While* CD:** "La Cucaracha."

**Formation:** Couples scattered informally around the dance area. Partners face each other, man's left shoulder, woman's right shoulder toward the front. Man places thumbs in belt, woman holds skirt out to the side.

**Steps:** Walk, stamp.

**Level:** Beginning 3

*continues on next page*

## *Directions* FOR THE DANCE

Meter 3/4 • Footwork is the same for man and woman, both beginning right.

| *Measures* | *Counts* | |
|---|---|---|
| | | **PART I.** |
| 1 | 1 | Right foot, leaps diagonally left, across left foot. |
| | 2 | Step left in place. |
| | 3 | Step right in place. |
| 2 | 4–5 | Repeat measure 1 counts 1–2 with opposite footwork. |
| | 6 | Hold. |
| 3–4 | 1–6 | Spin to left with four steps (left, right, left, right). Hold (counts 5, 6). |
| 5–8 | 1–6 ×2 | Repeat measures 1–4, beginning with left foot, toward the right. |
| 9–16 | 1–6 ×4 | Repeat measures 1–8 facing front. |
| | | **PART II.** |
| 1–2 | 1–6 | Beginning right, walk forward diagonally left three steps (right, left, right). Stamp left twice (no weight). |
| 3–4 | 1–6 | Walk back to place (left, right, left). Stamp right foot twice (no weight). |
| 5–8 | 1–6 ×2 | Repeat measures 1–4 diagonally right. |
| 9–16 | 1–6 ×4 | Repeat measures 1–8 to partner's right shoulder and back to place, then to partner's left shoulder and back to place. |

### Variation (La Cucaracha, adapted)

**Formation:** Couples in a circle, facing center, both beginning right.

| *Measures* | |
|---|---|
| | **PART I.** |
| 1–8 | Action of measures 1–8 is original version, facing center of circle. |
| 9–16 | Repeat measures 1–8 facing partner. |
| | **PART II.** |
| 1–8 | Action of Part II measures 1–8 in original version to partner's right shoulder and back, then to left shoulder and back. |
| 9–10 | Weave the ring *three places:* Walk three steps to partner's right shoulder (right, left, right), stamp, stamp. |
| 11–12 | Continue forward to next person's left shoulder with three walks and two stamps. |
| 13–14 | Continue forward to next person's right shoulder with three walks and two stamps. This is a new partner. |
| 15–16 | Join both hands, walk four steps, turning three-quarter around and face center, woman to right of man, drop hands. |

# La Raspa

## Mexican

FREQUENTLY, LA RASPA IS CALLED Mexican Hat Dance by the public. The true Mexican Hat Dance, Jarabe Tapatío, is an entirely different dance.

**CD:** Folkraft CD 2911; High/Scope RM 3.
**Music:** Sedillo, Mela, *Mexican and New Mexican Folk Dances,* p. 36.
**Position:** Partners face, man holds clasped hands behind back, woman holds skirt, or two hands joined.
**Steps:** Bleking step, running or skipping step.
**Level:** Beginning 1

## Directions FOR THE DANCE

Meter 2/4

| | Measures | Counts | |
|---|---|---|---|
| | | | **PART I.** |
| A | 1–2 | 1–4 | Bleking step in place. Beginning right, hop (count *ah*), touch left heel forward, toe up (count 1) hold (count 2). Bringing left back to place, leap onto left (count *ah*), touch right heal forward, toe up (count 1) hold (count 2). |
| | 3–4 | 5–8 | With three quick changes, leap back onto right (count *ah*), touch left heel forward (count 1), leap back onto left (count *ah*), touch right heel forward, toe up (count 2), leap back onto right (count *ah*), touch left heel forward, toe up (count 1), hold (count 2). **Cue:** Left, right, left, hold. |
| | 5–8 | 1–8 | Turn slightly counterclockwise away from partner (right shoulder to right shoulder) and, beginning left, take one bleking step. |
| | 9–12 | 1–8 | Repeat action of measures 1–4, facing opposite direction (left shoulder to left shoulder). |
| | 13–16 | 1–8 | Repeat action of measures 1–4, facing partner. |
| | | | **PART II.** |
| B | 1–4 | 1–8 | Hook right elbows, left hands held high. Take eight running or skipping steps, clapping on eighth step. |
| | 5–8 | 1–8 | Reverse direction, hook left elbows. Take eight running or skipping steps, clapping on eighth step. |
| | 9–16 | 1–8 ×2 | Repeat action of measures 1–8, B. |

### Variation

Measures 1–8: Take 16 running steps, right elbows hooked. Measures 9–16: Reverse and take 16 running steps.

### Icebreaker

No partners, all stand in single circle. Turn slightly left and right for action of measures 1–16, A; run in line of direction and reverse line of direction for action of measures 1–16, B. Halfway through record, everyone may take a partner.

7

# La Varsoviana

## Mexican

*Directions by Nelda Drury, Professor Emeritus, San Antonio College, TX.*

La Varsoviana is a form of folk dance found in many countries. For example, there is the Swedish Varsouvienne, and the American Varsouvienne, also known especially in Texas as Put Your Little Foot, page 112. There is also a New England version, which differs from the Texas version. The mazurka type is the basic step. The Mexican form of the dance is perhaps the most involved, with many figures.

There are many versions of La Varsoviana, and it is usually done "freestyle," with sequence and styling according to individual dancers. In this case there are definite, prescribed figures for each sequence of music. This is a stately, ballroom-type folk dance with the peasant style bursting forth in Parts II, IV, and VII.

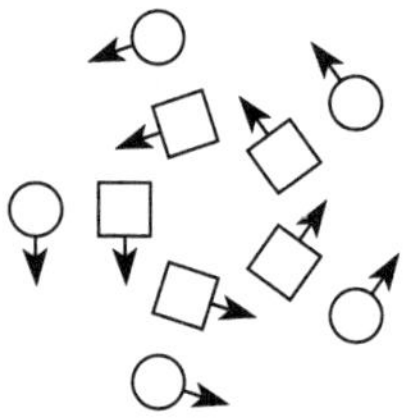

***Dance A While* CD:** "La Varsoviana."

**Formation:** After the couples bow, assume Varsouvienne position in a double circle, facing the line of direction.

**Steps:** Two-step, walk, run, waltz, hop, mazurka.

**Level:** Beginning 3

## Directions FOR THE DANCE

Meter 2/4 • Directions are the same for man and woman, except where noted.

| | |
|---|---|
| 4 measures | Bow. Assume Varsouvienne position. |
| | **INTRODUCTION** |
| 4 measures | Beginning left, take four two-steps, moving forward in the line of direction. |
| 4 measures | Drop left hands, take four two-steps, man progresses forward, woman turns clockwise once under man's right arm. |
| 4 measures | Repeat this whole sequence (8 measures) two times. The last time, the woman turns only three-quarters around to face partner. |
| Meter 3/4 | |
| | **PART I. VARSOVIANA** |
| | Partners facing, man's back to center of circle, take butterfly position, joined hands outstretched, man's left arm, woman's right are lower toward line of direction, man's right arm, woman's left are above shoulder; man begins left, woman right. |
| | Moving in the line of direction, take two mazurka steps. |
| 4 measures | *Man:* Lift right heel and bring left heel back toward right ankle (sweep) (count 1), step left (count 2), close right to left (count 3). Repeat (3 counts). Lift right heel and bring left heel back toward right ankle (sweep) and take four small walking steps forward and point left toe in front (6 counts).<br>*Woman:* Lift left heel and bring right heel back toward ankle (sweep), step right (count 2) and close left to right (count 3). Repeat (3 counts). Lift left heel, sweep right foot back, and turn clockwise under man's left arm, taking four walking steps and point right toe in front (6 counts). |
| 12 measures | Repeat three more times, ending in closed position. |

### Note

Man and woman lift their heels as they sweep. **Cue:** Sweep, step, close; sweep, step, close; sweep, turn woman around and step point

Meter 6/8

| | |
|---|---|
| | **PART II. "KICK UP YOUR HEELS"** |
| 1 measure | Closed position, man's back to center of circle. Couple exchange places: man beginning left, woman right, take three running steps (man steps back left, right, left, turning in place; woman moves right, left, right). Couple turns counterclockwise. Both put heels out to side, man's right, woman's left (6 counts). |
| 1 measure | Repeat this figure, man starts with right foot, woman left, man moves to his right, woman to her left, and finish with man's left heel out, woman's right heel out. Couple turns clockwise. |
| 2 measures | Repeat this whole figure. |

### Notes

1. Each time the heel is placed out to the side, the heel (or foot) is pointing in the line of direction.
2. In doing the running steps, heels are kicked up behind with exaggeration.

Meter 3/4

| | |
|---|---|
| | **PART III. VARSOVIANA** |
| 4 measures | Butterfly position, man's back to center of circle. Take two mazurka-type steps, moving in line of direction.<br>*Man:* Lift right heel, and beginning left, sweep, step, close, sweep, step, close, sweep, step left, right, left, point right foot to right (12 counts).<br>*Woman:* Lift left heel, and beginning right, do mirror image of man. Woman does not turn. |
| 12 measures | Repeat three more times. Move to reverse line of direction, then line of direction, then reverse line of direction. |

Meter 6/8

| | |
|---|---|
| | **PART IV. "KICK UP YOUR HEELS"** |
| 4 measures | Repeat action of Part II. |

Meter 3/4

| | |
|---|---|
| | **PART V. MAN KNEELS, WOMAN TRAVELS AROUND MAN** |
| 8 measures | Man kneels, woman places her left hand in man's right hand. Beginning right, woman travels counterclockwise around man, taking six waltz steps (continue to hold hands). On the fifth waltz step, man rises and twirls the woman clockwise under his right arm (6 counts), then kneels again. |
| 8 measures | Repeat action. After twirling woman under man's right arm, take butterfly position. |

*continues on next page*

**PART VI. VARSOVIANA IN AND OUT OF CIRCLE**

| | |
|---|---|
| 4 measures | Man facing line of direction, man begins left, woman right. Moving toward center of circle, repeat action of Part I, measures 1–4. Both point to side (man right, woman left). Both now face out. |
| 4 measures | Repeat the step away from center, man beginning right, woman left. Both point to side (man left, woman right). |
| 8 measures | Repeat action, moving toward and away from the center of the circle. |

Meter 6/8

**PART VII. JUMPING STEP**

| | |
|---|---|
| 1 measure | Man's back toward center, hands behind back; woman faces partner and holds skirt out to side. Man and woman extend right leg forward, toe pointed down, hop on left foot three times (counts 1 *and*, 2 *and*, 3 *and*). Quickly change feet so left leg, toe pointed down, is extended. Pause (counts 4 *and*, 5 *and*, 6 and). |
| 1 measure | Hop on right foot three times. Quickly change feet so left leg, toe pointed down, is extended. |
| 2 measures | Repeat above hopping action, left foot three times, then right only twice. Then cross left over right and do a full turn to right. |
| 4 measures | Repeat all again. |

Meter 3/4

**PART VIII. VARSOVIANA**

| | |
|---|---|
| 16 measures | Butterfly position, man begins left, woman right, repeat action of Part I. End with bow to partner. |

# *Las Chiapanecas*

## Mexican

*Directions by Nelda Drury, Professor Emeritus, San Antonio College, TX.*

LAS CHIAPANECAS IS A WOMAN'S DANCE from the state of Chiapas.

**Music:** Folkraft.

**Formation:** There are many options. As a couple dance, both on same foot, moving in the same direction, or opposite feet, moving in opposite direction. As a solo dance, dancers scattered, or group dance with a lot of choreography.

**Steps:** Waltz, three-step turn, stamp, step hop.

**Level:** Intermediate

## *Directions* FOR THE DANCE

Meter 3/4

| ***Measures*** | |
|---|---|
| | **PART I.** |
| 1 | Beginning left, step left in place (count 1), hop on left (count 2), step on right diagonally forward left, across left (count 3). |
| 2 | Step on left in place (count 1), hop on left (count 2), step backward on right (count 3). |
| 3–6 | Repeat measures 1 and 2 two more times. |
| 7–8 | Stamp four times, left, right, left, right (no weight on last stamp). |
| 9–16 | Repeat measures 1–8 to the right, starting with right. |
| 17–32 | Repeat measures 1–16. |
| | **PART II.** |
| 1–3 | Beginning right, turn to right with three-step turn or take three waltz steps. |
| 4 | Lean slightly to right and clap hands twice about shoulder high. |
| 5–8 | Repeat measures 1–4 to the left, beginning left. |
| 9–16 | Repeat measures 1–8. |
| | **PART IIIA.** |
| 1 | Beginning right, step to right (count 1), tap left heel close to right (count 2), step on left close to right (count 3). |
| 2–3 | Repeat measure 1 two more times (three times in all). |
| 4 | Two stamps, right, left (no weight on left). |
| 5–8 | Repeat measures 1–4 to left, starting with left. |
| 9–14 | Repeat measure 1 six times. |
| 15–16 | Do a pivot turn to right (step on right, cross left over right and turn). |
| | **PART IIIB.** |
| 17 | Beginning left, step to left on left (count 1), hop left and at same time lift right foot (keep it close to left ankle) (count 2), step on right close to left (count 3). |
| 18–32 | Repeat pattern of Part III A measures 2–16, to the left, substituting the "lift" instead of tapping heel. |

### Variation

Part I and/or Part III: Individuals may waltz around, turning, instead of suggested pattern.

# Philippines

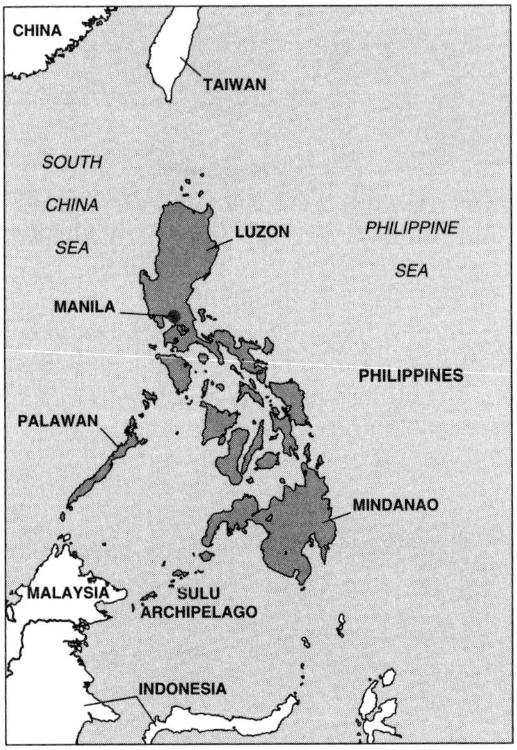


The Philippine archipelago lies some 500 miles off the southeast coast of Asia and is an integral part of the culture emanating from southeast India and China. Early inhabitants of the more than 7,000 islands came from south China and the Malay Peninsula. Some parts were occupied by the Indo-Malayan empire of Sri-Vishaya in the third century A.D. and later the Japanese empire of Madjapahit. In the fifteenth century, Arabs and Indians moved into Mindanao, bringing the Islamic and Hindu religions to this southernmost part of the country. The remote mountainous regions of the northern islands became the home of the earliest inhabitants, the pygmy tribes. These influences serve as a basis for a very diverse cultural beginning.

The colonial period began with the discovery of the islands by Ferdinand Magellan of Spain in 1521. The Spaniards brought Christianity to the islands, which was a strong and lasting influence for some 400 years. Today, except for the Muslim south and pagan north, the Philippines is the only Christian country in the Asian sphere.

In 1898 the United States took control and the American influence lasted for some 50 years. The Philippines became an independent country in 1946. Filipinos refer to their cultural heritage as "400 years in a convent and 50 years in Hollywood." Nevertheless, the Philippines are a rich mixture of Asian, European, American, and native cultures.

Although subdued by the missionary zeal of Christians and Muslims, cultural dance and drama are derived from four elements: Spanish, residual Filipino, Igorat (aboriginal), and Muslim. In most provinces local folk dance is Spanish in name as well as movement, for example, Polkabal, Mananguete, Surtido, and Los Bailes de Ayers. In the large city ballrooms, Filipinos execute rumbas, tangos, sambas, and paso dobles in a characteristically graceful Filipino style.

Among some of the remaining most conservative and aristocratic families, formal balls are still opened with the stately quadrille Regadon d'Honor. For the Regadon d'Honor ladies wear ternow or mestiza dresses with the renowned butterfly sleeves made of pineapple cloth, silk, satin, or brocade. The men wear black pants, shoes, socks, and the barong tagalog shirt made of fine linen or pineapple cloth with hand embroidery or ruffles and frills down the front. The Maria Clara, a minuetlike dance full of bows and curtsies, is also a popular replica of the past. The Maria Clara, popular toward the end of the Spanish rule, is often performed for formal occasions and as a part of historical stage dramas. The characteristic costume for the Maria Clara consists of a light blue dress with starched white long frilly sleeves, wide collars, and fans for the ladies and a velvet jacket and tight-fitting trousers for the men.

Two of the most well-known dances representing the residual or Filipino-derived dances are the Binusan Candle Dance and the world-renowned Tinikling. The Binusan dance consists of a series of virtuoso feats including a rollover on the floor while balancing lighted candles in a glass tumbler on the head. Historically, this feat appears in many dances from various provinces. The Pandaggo su Illaw, or dance of the lights, is a couple dance from Mindoro in which lighted oil lamps are balanced on the head and back of both hands. Tinikling is undoubtedly the most widely known dance associated with the Philippines. Its popularity makes it almost a national pastime. An early version or sighting described the dance as having four long bamboo poles and danced in 4/4 time by four dancers. The version most widely used, however, uses two bamboo poles struck together in 3/4 time. The latter version appears in *Philippine National Dances* by Francisca Reyes Tolentino, published in 1946.

Dances performed among the Igorat (aboriginal inhabitants or tribes of the northern Luzon) are authentically primitive. Dances occur during feasts, weddings, when conferring tribal title, at rice planting and harvesting festivals, when headhunting, and at moon- or star-worshipping ceremonies.

During U.S. control, headhunting was discouraged, except briefly during the Japanese occupation.

Now a nut from a fern tree or a carved wooden head serves the purpose. Headhunting dances are performed when a tribe member dies from an accident or lightning strike, or as a cure for illness. If all other remedies fail, dance is certain to cure the sick and ailing.

Tribal dances are performed by both men and women. They generally move clockwise in a circle accompanied by songs and gongs. Shouting, clapping, and stamping make these tribal dances more energetic and vigorous than those found in the lowlands. Costumes and dances vary among mountain tribes but all are colorful. Elaborate headdresses of native flowers, beads, turbans, and crowns made of bamboo adorned with rooster feathers are common. Necklaces of dog or pig teeth, colored beads, or metalwork highlight the costumes.

Dances among the Christian Filipinos center around fiestas held to honor patron saints. The Black Nazarene festival in Manila, a nine-day celebration, begins the year-round calendar of festivals. St. John's Day and St. Augustine's Day include colorful processions of people often led by dancers. In the province of Bulucan the Obando Dance is performed during celebration of the feast of Saint Clare. The dance is a fertility dance performed by childless married women who believe the dance prayer will give them children.

Harvest festivals are a time for singing, dancing, and eating. Courtship and wedding dances are the highlights of these most beloved Philippine festivities. Formal occasions such as inaugural balls for state and provincial officials or to entertain official guests are traditions carried on in cities and provinces. So it seems that Christians do, indeed, dance.

Perhaps the most important dancing in the Philippines, artistically and visually, is found among the Muslims or Moro (Mohammedans) in the southern part of the Sulu Archipelago, Mindanao, and Palawan. Dance among the Mohammedans is a curious phenomenon because traditionally their religion does not tolerate dance. The mix of cultures including Hindus, who foster dance, and perhaps the remoteness of the southern islands from the mainstream of Islam produces more tolerance of dance. Regardless of the reasons, the Muslim area of the south Philippines has more dance variety and quality than all other areas of the country. The dances are in fact vestigial remains of dances of India and Indonesia, with flowing movements of the arms, facial expressions, and extreme flexibility and use of the fingers. Ankle bells and fan manipulation complete the inheritance from southeast Asia.

The legacy of folk dance of the Philippines is found in the survival of the manuscript of the book *Philippine National Dances* by Francisca Reyes Tolentino, published in 1946 by Silver Burdett Company of New York. The manuscript was received in New York in 1941 but was not published until after the liberation of the Philippines from the Japanese in 1945. After the war, contact was reestablished with Mrs. Tolentino, who reported that all her resource materials, books and records, pictures, costumes, and musical instruments were burned or destroyed during the war.

The book contains 54 dances with brief historical notes, costume descriptions, and pictures, along with full piano scores for each dance. The piano scores are themselves of unique historical value. Mrs. Tolentino, who was physical education director of women students at the University of Philippines, was encouraged and supported in her original research of dances of less-developed regions of the country by the farsightedness of Dr. Jerge Bocobo, then president of the university. The first materials gathered between 1924 and 1926 were used for her master's thesis, which was later published in book form as *Philippine Folk Dances and Games*. Interest in Philippine dances was stimulated by the University of Philippines and the Bureau of Education as a valuable part of the curriculum of physical education classes in public schools. The result was a revival of interest and soon dance exhibitions and competitions were an integral part of school programs. The effect was an awakening of national pride.

As a result of this impetus, additional research was officially carried on by Lt. Antonio Buenaventura, Ramon P. Tolentino, Jr., and Mrs. Tolentino under the auspices of the University of Philippines President's Committee on Folk Songs and Dances. Costumes, music, and musical instruments were collected along with songs and dances. This research produced the manuscript that was published in 1946 as *Philippine National Dances*.

Many of the native dances show unmistakable Spanish influence; others reflect French, English, and Malayan influences to a degree. Performances over a long period of time, however, have given them the unmistakable stamp of Filipino interpretation, execution, and expression.

# *Tinikling*

## Filipino

TINIKLING, SOMETIME REFERRED TO as the Philippine Bamboo Dance, is danced by 1–4 dancers between two bamboo poles. The tinikling is a long-legged bird. The dance represents the tinikling stalking over long grass and tree limbs, trying to avoid a trap. The long poles used in the dance represent the trap.

**Requirements:** Two long bamboo poles, approximately 9 feet. Two pieces of a 2 × 4-board, about 30 inches long, are needed to strike the bamboo poles on.

***Dance A While* CD:** "Tinikling."

**Formation:** One couple facing each other, standing on the outside of the poles with their right hip towards the poles. One person per side.

**Steps:** Hop, leap, jump, run.

**Level:** Advanced

## *Directions* FOR THE DANCE

Meter 3/4

*Strikers/Pole rhythm:* One person kneels at each end of the poles. They hold the long bamboo poles and strike them together. On count 1 the poles come together (slide them along the boards, thumbs on top of the poles). Move (slide) poles to shoulder width and strike them down on the side board for counts 2 and 3 (lift them only ½ inch). The strikers need to keep the rhythm and should not watch the dancers. It may help the strikers to say, " In, out, out, in, out, out." Strikers should practice on their own a few times before trying to work with the dancers.

| ***Measures*** | ***Counts*** | |
|---|---|---|
| 1–7 | | Introduction: Strikers bow to each other, dancers bow to each other. |
| | | **PART IA. BASIC STEP (OUT IN IN, OUT IN IN)** |
| 1 | 1–3 | Hop on left foot on count 1. Leap with right foot to center of poles on count 2. Leap with left foot on count 3 in center of poles. |
| 2 | 1–3 | Leap out side of poles on right foot on count 1. Leap with left foot to center of poles on count 2. Leap with right foot on count 3 in center of poles. |
| 3–4 | 1-3 ×2 | Repeat the actions of measures 1 and 2. |
| 5–8 | 1-3 ×4 | Repeat measures 1–4. |

| Measures | Counts | |
| --- | --- | --- |
| | | **PART IB. STAR** |
| 9 | 1 | Hop on left foot toward partner and shake right hands, ending almost right side to right side. |
| | 2 | Leap with right foot to center of poles, keeping right side towards partner. Dancers are now parallel with the poles. |
| | 3 | Leap with right foot in center of poles. |
| 10 | 1 | Leap with right foot to outside of pole, ending with right side towards poles. Dancers are now on the opposite side from starting. |
| | 2 | Run in place right. |
| | 3 | Small run forward with left. |
| 11 | 1 | Run in place right. |
| | 2 | Leap with right foot to center of poles, keeping right side towards partner. Dancers are now parallel with the poles. |
| | 3 | Leap with right foot in center of poles. |
| 12 | 1 | Leap with right foot to outside of poles, right side towards poles, completing one full circle. |
| | 2 | Run left in place, releasing hand hold. |
| | 3 | Run right in place, staring to turn clockwise, putting left side to poles. |
| 13 | 1 | Run left in place, turning to face poles, while joining left hands. |
| | 2 | Leap with right foot to center of poles, keeping left side towards partner. |
| | 3 | Leap with right foot in center of poles. |
| 14 | 1 | Leap with right foot to outside of pole (opposite side from starting). |
| | 2 | Run in place right. |
| | 3 | Small run forward with left. |
| 15 | 1 | Run in place right. |
| | 2 | Leap with right foot to center of poles, keeping left side towards partner. |
| | 3 | Leap with right foot in center of poles. |
| 16 | 1 | Leap with right foot to outside of poles, completing one full circle. |
| | 2 | Run left in place, releasing hand hold. |
| | 3 | Run right in place turning to face poles. |
| | | **PART II. ROCKING STEP** |
| 1 | 1 | Facing poles, hop on left foot. |
| | 2 | Leap with right foot to center of poles. |
| | 3 | Hop on right foot in center of poles. |
| 2 | 1 | Leap with left foot to outside of poles (poles are now behind dancers). |
| | 2 | Reach right foot to center of poles and hop. |

*continues on next page*

| Measures | Counts | |
|---|---|---|
| | 3 | Hop on right foot again. |
| 3–4 | 1–3 ×2 | Reaching left foot back to outside of poles, repeat Part II, measures 1 and 2. |
| | | **TURNING THE ROCKING STEP** |
| 5 | 1 | Reaching left foot back to outside of poles, hop on left foot. |
| | 2 | Leap with right foot to center of poles. |
| | 3 | Hop on right foot, turning one-quarter clockwise, in center of poles. |
| 6 | 1 | Leap with left foot to outside of poles, turning one-quarter clockwise (ending with right side towards poles). |
| | 2 | Leap with right foot to center of poles, turning one-quarter clockwise. |
| | 3 | Hop on right foot, turning one-quarter clockwise, in center of poles. |
| 7–8 | 1–3 ×2 | Leaping with left foot to outside of poles on count 1, repeat Part II, measures 5 and 6. |
| 9–16 | 1–3 ×8 | Repeat Part II, measures 1–8. |
| 17–32 | 1–3 ×16 | Repeat Part II, measures 1–16. |
| | | **PART III. JUMPS** |
| 1 | 1 | Facing center (partner), jump and land with feet on outside of poles (straddling the poles). |
| | 2 | Jump with both feet to center of poles. |
| | 3 | Jump again in the center. |
| 2–4 | 1–3 ×3 | Repeat measure 1, three more times. |
| 5–8 | 1–3 ×4 | Repeat Part I, measures 1–4 (Basic Step). |
| 9–16 | 1–3 ×16 | Repeat Part III, measures 1–16. |
| | | **TO FINISH MUSIC** |
| 1–16 | | Repeat Part I, measures 1–8 (basic step and star). |
| 1–16 | | Repeat Part II, measures 1–8 (rocking step and turning rocking step). |
| 1–4 | | Repeat Part I, measures 1–4 (basic step). |
| 5–7 | | Repeat Part I, measures 9–10 (right hand star). |
| 8 | | Music slows down, bow toward partner. |

## Notes

1. Dancers should practice in stationary poles until comfortable with the steps. Tape or jump ropes laid out on the floor may also be used to practice with.
2. In Part III, doing a half turn clockwise on the second jump is a nice variation, but adds a level of difficulty.

## Style

Dancers may have free hands on hips. Lift feet a little higher than a normal step to avoid colliding with the poles.

# Poland

## Dances of Poland

*By Jacek Marek, Dedham, MA.*

Poland, a country roughly the size of New Mexico, is truly unique in the diversity reflected in its cultural inheritance. It is unlikely you will find anywhere in the world a comparable heritage, which includes some 15,000 folk songs, more than 1,000 dances, hundreds of carols, more than 200 folk costumes, and a distinctive range of ethnic customs and rites.

Folk culture and arts are vital components of Polish national heritage. They manifestly assert themselves in the unflagging popularity of folk song and dance groups and ensembles basing their work on folk motifs. Polish folk music determines its national musical style; Polish folk orchestration is among the richest in the world. One needs only to mention the names Chopin, Szymanowski, Moniuszko, and Wieniawski, and to remember the worldwide successes of the prominent Polish contemporary composers Gorecki, Lutoslawski, and Bacewicz. All are indebted to inspiration drawn from the inexhaustible resources of Polish musical folklore.

ALB: Albania, BIH: Bosnia Herzegovina, HRV: Croatia, MKD: Former Yugoslav Republic of Macedonia, MNT: Montenegro, SVN: Slovenia

### Dance Folklore

Our knowledge of Polish folk dance dates primarily back to the nineteenth century, although there are some brief dance references from the Middle Ages and the Renaissance. Some dance music also survives containing elements of rural tunes; there are seventeenth and eighteenth century paintings showing peasant dancing. Generally, however, few resources focus on peasant culture. To follow the development of folk dance in Poland one has to understand the historical context.

About the time that Christopher Columbus was discovering America, the Jagiello dynasty ruled most of east-central Europe. This was called the "Golden Age" in Polish history. Soon, however, privileges granted to the middle class gentry (szlachta) gradually weakened the state. Class egoism and shaky political structures eventually emptied the treasury, debilitated the standing army, and crippled the administration. As a result, Poland was partitioned between Russia, Prussia, and Austria and for a period of time (1795–1918) did not even exist on the political map of Europe.

Ironically, this contributed to the preservation of folk culture. The oppression of the partitioning powers–German and Russian especially–caused an unusual resistance in the Polish people, manifested in their attachment to native customs, family rites, music, dance, and costume. By wearing Polish folk dress, they kept alive the distinctive identity of their country even though it no longer existed on the political map. Strong occupants' reprisals provoked even more intense reactions. Poles struggled to preserve their cultural identity and to regain unity and political independence.

Toward the end of the eighteenth and at the beginning of the nineteenth century, a particular interest in peasant culture became evident. Individuals, societies, and groups began to turn to folk traditions as a repository of pure and untainted national values. They were also in hopes of gaining the support of the peasant masses for the independence movement and restoration of the Polish state. With the tendency of the mid-nineteenth century Romantic period to glorify aspects of rural life, privileged society began to introduce certain "folk" dances at sleighing parties, masquerades, and other courtly occasions. Especially popular were Krakowiak, Mazur, and Chodzony, later called Polonez. These dances in modified form first swept into drawing rooms at home and abroad and later, in even more modified form, were brought to the stage under the direction of the ballet masters of the day. For the first time, collectors of folklore also included dance. The marked development of social and economic structures gave rise to political changes within Polish society. The general economic development, though uneven in the three different administrations (Poland was partitioned at that time), strengthened democratic tendencies in all of Poland. The position of the peasantry was getting stronger, which led to a blossoming of folk culture. A reform giving freedom to the peasants led to the rise of an individual economy. A wealthy village society was established, and colorful costumes appeared all around the country. The second half of the nineteenth century was the period of the most exuberant flowering of traditional folk culture, which became the symbol of Polish national culture. Today's folk culture–and especially folk dance–is derived from the standards of that period.

The outbreak of World War I created a situation Poles had hoped for through three generations: The three co-partitioning powers were fighting among themselves. Upheaval in Russia swept away the tsarist regime, and the entry of the United States into the war gave Poland independence in 1918. After an independent Polish state was restored, national themes, including so-called folk dances (actually free expressions of folk dance themes by dancers and ballet masters), appeared on professional stages. The national repertoire began to grow. Organizations, societies, and institutes were created, aimed at the propagation and cultivation of traditional Polish folk culture. During the 1930s folk dance was introduced to the youth movement and to schools. Groups in folk costumes presenting folk dance, music, and customs performed at various state and local festive occasions. Also, some professional work was initiated in collecting peasant dances. Unfortunately, most of those works were destroyed in World War II.

After the war, well-organized ethnographic work on dance began. Publications appeared containing professional documentation of the entire dance folklore of many regions. In addition, research methods were established and results published.

Simultaneously, the progress of industrialization and urbanization of the Polish countryside substantially altered the ethnographic picture. Large-scale migration led to mixing of regional traditions. Traditional village dances, with some exceptions, have become only relics. Yet there were (and are) communities where traditional folk culture survives, although transformed in form and content. In some places the old traditions are treated with respect, if not reverence, and used to demonstrate national pride and patriotism.

## Dance Characteristics

Folk dance preserves the customs and rites of the family and community and is entertaining as well. There is a visible transition of dance heritage; dances were handed down from one generation to the next. The village names of the dances show a wide diversity. The same dance may have many names and variants. Youngsters learn dancing by imitation.

Five dances are currently identified as Polish national dances, which were originally known only in certain areas of Poland: Polonez (Polonaise), Krakowiak, Mazur, Kujawiak, and Oberek.

In addition to these, there are numerous others known as regional dances because they were performed in specific regions of Poland.

## Contemporary Situation

The historical wind of democracy, which in the fall of 1989 swept Communism away, simultaneously brought both new hopes and difficulties to the people in Eastern and Central Europe. For almost 50 years Poland had used folk groups as propaganda tools. Costumes, instructor's salaries, and free travel were provided for hundreds of amateur folk dance groups that traveled throughout the world. The government also subsidized hundreds of festivals throughout Poland.

Coincident with the disappearance of the Berlin Wall, a symbol of the so-called "Cold War," government funding for folk groups, and for all cultural activities, ended. By the early 1990s, more than half of the previously viable folk groups had disappeared from the folkloristic map of Poland due to the lack of funds. Among the survivors one may find not necessarily the most ethnographically valuable but more likely those able to adapt to the challenges of a free market. All must be self-supporting and thus constantly seeking financial aid.

Can we predict the future of the Polish folk dance movement? The Polish economy in recent years has been among the fastest growing in the developing countries. It is possible that by the end of the next decade, Poland may make up for a half century of Communist deprivation. The folk dance movement (at least in its recreational form) will probably recover. With more money in their pockets, people will be able to better afford participation in cultural activities–hopefully, including folk dance.

# Tramblanka—Polka Mazurka

## Polish

*Directions by Jacek Marek, Dedham, MA.*

TRAMBLANKA IS PRONOUNCED *tram-BLANK-ah* and is a couple dance from the region of Opoczno in the Mazowsze region in central Poland. Its most popular version was introduced for the first time by the State Ensemble "Mazowsze."

### Steps and Styling

1. *Mazurka Step:* 2 measure sequence:

   Measure 1: Hop on right foot (count 1); slide on left foot to the left (count 2); step on right closed to left foot (count 3).

   Measure 2: Three running steps in place, left, right, left foot.

   In measures 3–4, repeat action of measures 1–2 with opposite footwork and direction.

2. *Running Steps*: Steps are small, light, and bouncy. Do not kick feet up in back, but keep them close to the floor and don't prance. Body is held erect and proud. Occasionally man may typically move his head back and forth sideways rhythmically.

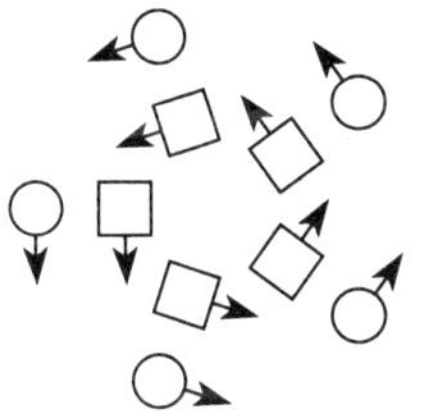

**CD:** "Dances of Poland."[1]

**Formation:** Couples around the circle in escort position, facing line of direction. Woman to the right of partner puts her left arm under man's folded right arm. Outside hands free.

**Level:** Intermediate

## *Directions* FOR THE DANCE

Meter 3/4 • Directions are for man; woman's part reverse.

| ***Measures*** | |
|---|---|
| 1–4 | Introduction: No action. |
| | **PART I. RUNNING ON THE CIRCLE** |
| 1–3 | Beginning with outside foot (man–left, woman–right), couple runs in line of direction, with three steps per measure, nine steps in all. At the same time outside fists move rhythmically forward/backward, with three movements per measure. |
| 4 | With three accented steps, couple turns counterclockwise in place (man backward, woman moves forward) to face reverse line of direction. |
| 5–7 | Another nine running steps, three per measure, in line of direction. |
| 8 | With three accented steps, couple makes one-quarter turn clockwise in place (man moves forward, woman backs up), end facing center. |
| 9 | Three running steps forward (toward center). |

*continues on next page*

1. CD available from Jacek Marek. See Appendix C.

| ***Measures*** | |
|---|---|
| 10 | Three accented steps in place, lean forward. |
| 11–12 | Three running steps backward, ending with two accented steps facing partner, woman's back to line of direction. |

**PART II. MAZURKA IN SEMI-OPEN POSITION**

| | |
|---|---|
| 1–3 | Leaning into direction of movement, do three sliding Mazurka steps (one per measure) toward center: man hops on right foot and slides on left, woman opposite. |
| 4 | Three accented steps in place (man: left, right, left; woman: right, left, right). Joined hands (man's left, woman's right) curved overhead. |
| 5–7 | Repeat action of measures 1–3 symmetrically, toward outside of the circle. |
| 8 | With three accented steps do couple turn one-quarter clockwise in place (man ends back to center). |
| 9–11 | Repeat action of measures 1–3 in line of direction. |
| 12 | Partners separate, take two accented steps away from partner. End with right hand on hip, and left arm bent with thumb up. |

**PART III. RUNNING DO-SA-DO**

| | |
|---|---|
| 1–3 | With nine running steps (three per measure) move diagonally forward to left, then make do-sa-do in clockwise direction around partner, passing right shoulders first and backing up passing left shoulders. Move left arms as in Part I. |
| 4 | Three accented steps in place. |
| 5–8 | Repeat action of measures 1–4 in counterclockwise direction, passing left shoulders first, then backing up passing right shoulders. |
| 9–12 | Hook right elbow with partner and turn once clockwise in place with nine running steps, both moving left arms as in Part I. On last measure, dance two stamping steps to end in closed position, man back to center. |

**PART IV. MAZURKA WITH HALF-TURNS**

| | |
|---|---|
| 1–2 | Leaning into line of direction, couple makes one sliding mazurka step, then makes half-turn clockwise in place with three running steps (woman ends back to center). |
| 3–4 | Repeat action of measures 1–2. |
| 5–8 | Repeat action of measures 1–4. End up in open position facing center of the circle. |
| 9–10 | Three running steps toward center, followed by three accented steps in place. |
| 11–12 | Three running steps backward toward outside of the circle, followed by two accented steps. |
| | Repeat whole dance from beginning two more times. |

# *Walczyk "Ges Woda"*

**Polish**

*Directions by Jacek Marek, Dedham, MA.*

WALCZYK "GES WODA," PRONOUNCED *VAL-chik GENSH VOH-dom*, is a couple dance in 3/4 meter from the Lublin region in eastern Poland. The name derives from the first words of the accompanying song, sang by the "Mazowsze" State Folk Ensemble. The suggested variant is done as a mixer with changing partners. Arrangement is by Jacek Marek. "Walczyk" is a soft meaning of the word *walc* = waltz.

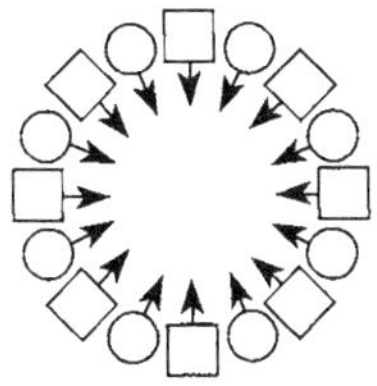

**CD:** "Dances of Poland."[1]

**Formation:** Single circle, partners facing center, joined hands, *W* position. Woman is to right of partner.

**Steps:** Step swing, walk, waltz.

**Level:** Beginning 2

## *Directions* FOR THE DANCE

Meter 3/4 • Directions are for both man and woman, except where noted.

| ***Measures*** | |
|---|---|
| 1–4 | Introduction: No action. |
| | **PART I. JOINED HANDS** |
| 1 | Step to right on right foot, swing left foot in front of right (bent knee) in direction of movement. |
| 2 | Step on left foot in line of direction, bend right knee. Keep knees close. |
| 3–4 | Repeat action of measures 1–2 one more time, except in measure 4 make one quarter counterclockwise turn on left foot. |
| 5–8 | Repeat action of measures 1–4, beginning right, travel in reverse line of direction, end in closed position, woman's back to line of direction. |
| | **PART II. COUPLE WALK, WALTZ** |
| 9–12 | Closed position, beginning with man's left foot, take four waltz-type steps in line of direction (step, step, close/no turns); man ends back to the center. |
| 13–16 | Beginning man left, woman right, take four waltz steps in line of direction, two full turns. |
| | **INTERLUDE: CIRCLE WITH PARTNER, CHANGE PLACES** |
| | Join both hands with partner. Take three waltz-type steps, couple turns one and a quarter times in place, then opens to face center position, man to the right of partner. |
| | Repeat dance from the beginning four more times; each time in measures 9–16 waltz with a new partner. |

1. CD available from Jacek Marek. See Appendix C.

# Romania

ALB: Albania, BIH: Bosnia Herzegovina, HRV: Croatia, MKD: Former Yugoslav Republic of Macedonia, MNT: Montenegro, SVN: Slovenia

## Background

The Roman Empire extended its influence in the northeast as far as Romania, and, despite a history of many ethnic influences (Slavic, Turkish, and Germanic), the language, based on Latin, has remained a unique feature of this Balkan country.

Romania is generally considered divided into six major folk regions: Oltania, Multania, Banat, Dobruja, Moldavia, and Transylvania. Each major region is, in turn, subdivided into several minor regions, all of which have their own unique folklore.

In general, the dances are quite fast, with intricate footwork, including heel-clicks and stamping in complex, rhythmic patterns. Traditionally, the men's movements in the dance are stronger than the women's.

Major dances done in a circle or a line include:

- Hora
- Bruil: Loosely translated as the "belt," usually done holding on to the neighbor's belt. Bruil was originally intended for men.
- Sirbia: Serbian-like, usually incorporates a lifting and a flicking of the foot.

The principal couple's dance is the Invirtitia (turning dance). This dance form has many patterns, and in a traditional setting, the man leads his partner in a way similar to American swing dance.

A notable characteristic of Romanian dancing is the shouts or "crying out" of the dancers during the dance. These vocalizations are known as strigaturi. A saying in Romania goes: "Those who dance and do not shout, they deserve a crooked mouth." Strigaturi are always shouted out in rhythmic harmony with the music. Some are simple, as "Hey *una*" (Hey, one), or as complex as a poem.

Traditional dancing in Romania is connected to many aspects of village life. The most prominent example occurs most Sundays. The Sunday dance event is referred to as the Hora, or Joc. People gather together to socialize and dance. In some areas, this event takes place in the village square. In northern Transylvania, a special structure, called the *ciuperca*[16] ("mushroom"), houses the dance event. As the influence of modernization has spread to the villages, attendance at the Hora has declined. For many, watching TV programs of Romanian football has replaced the traditional dance event.

Traditional dancing may still be performed in cities during wedding celebrations and other special events. Contemporary dances and traditional dances can be observed on the same dance floor to a mixture of popular and folk songs.

16. The shape of the roof resembles the top of a mushroom.

## Music

Traditional music of Romania has unique qualities for each of the major folklore regions. In Banat, many wind instruments are played; the most common is the taragot. In Multania a portable tambal, similar to a hammered dulcimer, is popular. In Dobruja, instruments display influences from Turkey and Bulgaria. The one instrument common to all regions is the violin. Several other stringed instruments are played in conjunction with the violin. The accordion, not a traditional instrument, is also played in most Romanian music today. The rhythms are frequently syncopated, in 2/4 meter.

# Alunelul

Romanian

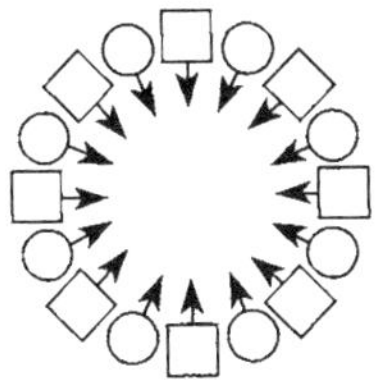

ALUNELUL, PRONOUNCED *ah-loo-NAY-loo,* means "little hazelnut."

***Dance A While* CD:** "Alunelul."

**Formation:** Single circle, all facing center, hands on shoulders of person on either side, arms straight. Small circles of eight to ten dancers are best.

**Steps:** Step, stamp

**Level:** Beginning 2

## *Directions* FOR THE DANCE

Meter 2/4

| *Measures* | *Counts* | |
|---|---|---|
| | | **PART I. FIVE STEPS** |
| 1–2 | 1–8 | Circle moves counterclockwise. Beginning right, take five steps sideward; step right to right side, step left behind right, step right to right side, step left behind right, step right to right side. Stamp left heel twice, close to right. Hold count 8. |
| 3–4 | 1–8 | Beginning left, repeat the action of measures 1–2. Circle moves clockwise. |
| 5–8 | 1–8 ×2 | Repeat actions of measures 1–4. |
| | | **PART II. THREE STEPS** |
| 1 | 1–4 | Beginning right, take three steps sideward; step right to right side, step left behind right, step right to right side. Circle moves counterclockwise. Stamp left heel once. |
| 2 | 5–8 | Beginning left, repeat the action of B, measure 1. Circle moves clockwise. |
| 3–4 | 1–8 | Repeat actions of measures 1–2. |
| | | **PART III. ONE STEP** |
| 5 | 1 | In place, step right. |
| | 2 | Stamp left heel close to right once. |
| | 3 | Step left. |
| | 4 | Stamp right heel close to left once. |
| 6 | 5 | Step right. |
| | 6–7 | Stamp left heel close to right twice. |
| | 8 | Hold. |
| 7–8 | 1–8 | Repeat action of Part III, measures 5–6, opposite footwork. |

### Notes

1. Dancers need to be light on their feet; use small, precise steps; and support weight of their own arms. Do not let arms sag, and hold heads erect.
2. The tempo of the music of some recordings accelerates at the end. The dancers enjoy the competitiveness of testing their agility of footwork with the musicians. A leader can adjust the speed of the music if using a variable-speed record player.

# Hora de Mina

Romanian

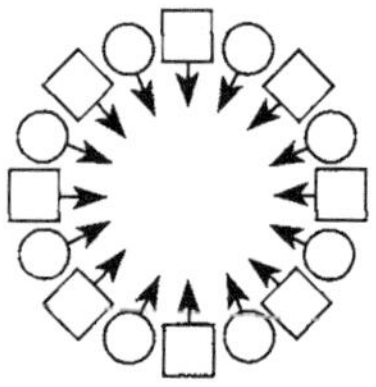

*Permission to use Hora de Mina courtesy of Mihai David, Los Angeles, CA.*

HORA DE MINA IS PRONOUNCED *Hoar-ah deh MU-nuh.* This dance was learned by Mihai David while a member of the Romanian State Folk Ensemble, 1965–1968.

**CD:** Gypsy Camp Vol. 3.[1]
**Formation:** Circle, hands joined, held at shoulder height, *W* position.
**Steps:** Walk, two-step.
**Level:** Beginning 3

## Directions FOR THE DANCE

Meter 2/4

| ***Measures*** | ***Counts*** | |
|---|---|---|
| 1–16 | | Introduction: No action. |
| | | **PART I. WALKS AND TOUCH (in and out of center)** |
| 1–2 | 1–4 | Beginning right, take three steps to the center, counts 1–3. On count 4 tap left foot next to right. |
| 3–4 | 5–8 | Beginning left, take three steps back, counts 5–7. On count 8 tap right foot next to left. |
| 5–16 | 1–8 × 3 | Repeat action of measures 1–4 three more times. |
| | | **PART II. WALK, TWO-STEP (travel in line of direction)** |
| 1–2 | 1–4 | Facing reverse line of direction, beginning right, take four steps moving back in line of direction. |
| 3–4 | 5–8 | Pivot on left foot, face line of direction, beginning with right, take two two-steps in line of direction. |
| | | Repeat action of measure 1–4 three more times; on last two-step, bring arms down. |
| | | **PART III. WALK, LIFT, WALK, STAMP (in and out of center)** |
| 1–2 | 1–4 | Beginning right, take four steps to the center, rising arms to *W* position by count 4. |
| 3 | 5–6 | Step side right with right, count 5, lift left leg (knee bent), count 6, |
| 4 | 7–8 | Step side left with left, count 7, lift right leg (knee bent), count 8. |
| 5–6 | 1–4 | Beginning right, take four steps back, lower arms down by count 4. |

1. CD available from Mihai David. See Appendix C.

| Measures | Counts | |
|---|---|---|
| 7 | 5–6 | Step side right with right, count 5, stamp left heel (no weight) next to right, count 6, lift arms to *W* on count 5. |
| 8 | 7–8 | Step side left with left, count 7, stamp right heel (no weight) next to left, count 8. |
| | | With count 7, lower arms down. |
| 1–8 | | Repeat action of measures 1–8, leaving arms in *W* on last count. |
| | | Repeat the dance from the beginning. |

# *Hora Pe Gheata*

Romanian

*Included by permission of Sunni Bloland, retired, University of California, Berkeley, CA.*

Hora Pe Gheata is pronounced *HOAR-ah pay GYAH-tsah* and means "the dance on the ice." It is a ballroom-type dance known in many of the villages of Multania (south-central Romania). Sunni Bloland, a Romanian dance specialist, learned this dance from Teodor Vasilescu.

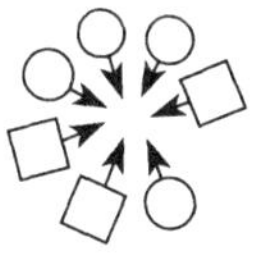

**CD:** High/Scope RM 4.
**Formation:** Broken circle, hands joined, held at shoulder height, *W* position.
**Step:** Walk.
**Level:** Beginning 1

## Directions FOR THE DANCE

Meter 2/4

| Measures | Counts | |
|---|---|---|
| | | **PART I.** |
| 1–2 | 1–4 | Face slightly right, right shoulder leading. Beginning right, take four steps, moving in line of direction. |
| 3 | 5–6 | Face center as stepping right to side right, bending right knee slightly, swaying to right, letting left leg come off floor slightly. |
| 4 | 7–8 | Transfer weight to left foot, swaying sideways left, right leg coming off floor slightly. |
| 5 | 1–2 | Step forward right, bending right knee slightly, upper torso rising to roll up in a forward direction (skating gesture) as left foot comes off floor slightly. |
| 6–8 | 3–8 | Moving backward, beginning left, take five small steps; alternately step left, twisting right heel and hip slightly to left, step right, twisting left. Stamp right in place (count 8) (weight remains on left). |

*continues on next page*

| Measures | Counts | |
|---|---|---|
| | | **PART II.** |
| | | Floor pattern zigs and zags as circle continues to move in line of direction, |
| 9 | 1–2 | Face slightly right, beginning right, take two steps forward. |
| 10 | 3–4 | Take one more step forward (right) and turn counterclockwise to face left on right foot. The turn is actually step lift, body rising as bent right knee straightens. The change of direction occurs on the step lift (count 4). |
| 11 | 5–6 | Take two steps backward (left, right). |
| 12 | 7–8 | Step backward left, turning clockwise to face right (step lift). |
| 13–16 | 1–8 | Repeat action of measures 9–12. |

### Style

The dancers move quietly and elegantly, as if skating on ice, reflecting the step pattern and the music.

# *Itele*

## Romanian

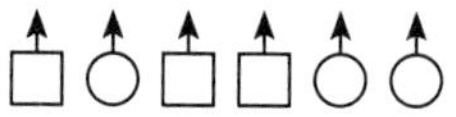

ITELE IS PRONOUNCED *it-el-lay*. This dance was learned by Mihai David while a member of the Romanian State Folk Ensemble, 1965–1968.

**CD:** Gypsy Camp Vol. 2.[1]
**Formation:** Short lines, belt hold, or hands joined in front basket hold.
**Steps:** Grapevine, stamp.
**Level:** Beginning 1

## *Directions* FOR THE DANCE

Meter 2/4

| Measures | Counts | |
|---|---|---|
| | | No Introduction. |
| | | **PART I. GRAPEVINE** |
| 1 | 1–2 | Beginning right, step right in front of left on count 1, step left to side on count (1 *and*), step right behind left on count 2, and step left to side on count (2 *and*). |
| 2–7 | | Repeat action of measure 1 six more times. |
| 8 | 1–2 | Step right foot in place on count 1, step left foot in place on count (1 *and*), step right foot in place on count 2. |
| 9–16 | | Repeat action of measures 1–8, with opposite footwork. |

1. CD available from Mihai David. See Appendix C.

| Measures | Counts | |
|---|---|---|
| | | **PART II. STAMPS IN PLACE** |
| 1 | 1–2 | Beginning right, stamp the right foot forward, taking weight, leaving the left foot in place, on count 1, step in place with left on count (1 *and*), step in place right on count 2, step in place left on count (2 *and*). |
| | 2–3 | Repeat action of measure 1 two more times. |
| | 4 | Step right foot in place on count 1, step left foot in place on count (1 *and*), step right foot in place on count 2. |
| | 5–8 | Repeat action of measures 1–4, with opposite footwork. |
| | 9–16 | Repeat action of measures 1–8. |
| | | Repeat dance from the beginning. |

### Note

Dancers need to be light on their feet, using small, precise steps.

# *Sirba Din Cimpoi*

## Romanian

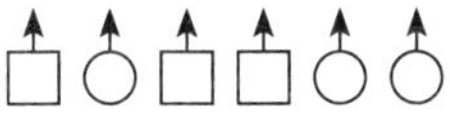

*Permission to use Sirba Din Cimpoi courtesy of Mihai David, Los Angeles, CA.*

SIRBA DIN CIMPOI IS PRONOUNCED *SIR-buh din Chim-poi.* This dance was learned by Mihai David while a member of the Romanian State Folk Ensemble, 1965–1968.

**CD:** Gypsy Camp Vol. 1.[1]

**Formation:** Medium length lines facing center with hands on shoulders of person on either side, arms straight.

**Steps:** Steps, stamp, leap.

**Level:** Intermediate

## *Directions* FOR THE DANCE

Meter 2/4

| Measures | Counts | |
|---|---|---|
| | | **PART I. STEP LIFT (SIRBA STEP), SIDE BEHIND** |
| 1 | 1 | Beginning right, step in place on count 1, hop on right foot while lifting left leg (knee bent) on count (1 *and*). |
| | 2 | Repeat action of count 1, with opposite footwork. |

1. CD available from Mihai David. See Appendix C.

*continues on next page*

| Measures | Counts | |
|---|---|---|
| 2 | 1 | Beginning right, step side right on count 1, step left behind right on count (1 *and*). |
| | 2 | Repeat action of count 1. |
| 3–16 | | Repeat action of measures 1–2 seven more times. |
| | | **PART II. SIRBA, STAMP, LEAP IN PLACE** |
| 1 | 1 | Beginning right, step in place on count 1, hop on right foot while lifting left leg (knee bent) on count (1 *and*). |
| | 2 | Repeat action of count one, with opposite footwork. |
| 2 | 1 | Repeat action of measure 1, count 1. |
| | 2 | Step left in place on count 2, stamp right foot next to left on count (2 *and*). |
| 3 | 1 | Step forward with right foot on count 1, bring left foot to right heel on count (1 *and*). Left knee is pointing slightly side left. |
| | 2 | Step back with left foot on count 2, stamp right foot next to left on count (2 *and*). |
| 4 | 1 | Step right in place on count 1, swing left leg in front on count (1 *and*). |
| | 2 | Leap onto left foot in place on count 2 (knee slightly bent), slap right foot in front with a straight leg on count (2 *and*). |
| 5–8 | | Repeat action of measures 1–4. |
| | | Repeat dance from the beginning. |

## Note

The sirba step is usually considered a step lift in place. Sometimes there is a quick flicking action of the foot during the lifting.

# Russia

## Dance Characteristics

A great variety of dance is found in Russia due to its rich and diverse cultural history. There are typical north Slavic dances: fast and slow, musical phrases of 6 or 8 measures, including many prysiadka (knee bend) variations for the men. The Western influence on Russian dance is limited to the Court Dances and contact with Poland.

Many of the dances favored by American folk dancers come from the Ukraine, where the Cossacks lived. Cossack dancing is reflective of the spirit of fearless soldiers and superb horsemen. It is exuberant, exciting, and characterized by fast running, leaping, and pas de basque steps and by the difficult knee bend or prysiadka steps, used by the men. Also characteristic are turning, spinning, stamping, and heel clicking. The Ukrainian dancers are unsurpassed for their vitality, competitive spirit, and endurance.

### Style

The Russian dances are characterized by emotional expressiveness. The movements are fluid in the warm countries and very vigorous in the cold countries. The Russian dances are not always set. On the inspiration and the mood of the dancer, the steps are changed.

### Music

The song-dances are sung by choirs with musical accompaniment. There are also ceremonial dances performed today with only vocal accompaniment. When Peter the Great tried to westernize the musical tastes of his people, native instruments were banned. The people then sang for the dancers. But, in the courts, imported classical instruments and Western Court Dances became very popular.

Russian music uses the pentatonic scale (five notes in an octave). The stretching or leaping that is followed by a sustained position in dance coincides with the characteristics of the pentatonic scale. During the latter part of the seventeenth century and the early part of the eighteenth century, peasant dances and folk songs became popular with all classes. The Russian minstrels are credited with making the balalaika popular. Eventually, even the aristocrats became interested in learning to play it.

7

# *Alexandrovska*

## Russian

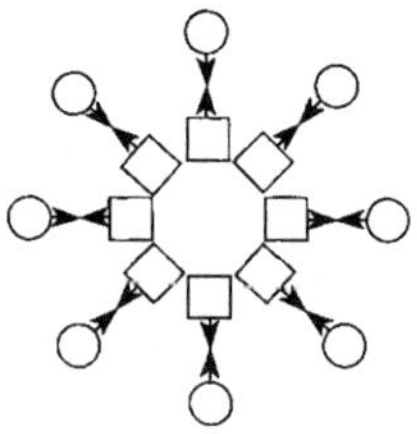

ALEXANDROVSKA IS A RUSSIAN BALLROOM DANCE, probably named in honor of Czar Alexander.

**CD:** Worldtone 004.

**Music:** Fox, Grace, *Folk Dancing in High School and Colleges,* p.10; Beliajus, V. F., *Dance and Be Merry,* Vol. 1, p. 22.

**Formation:** Double circle, man's back to center of circle. Partners face, two hands joined.

**Steps:** Waltz, draw step.

**Level:** Intermediate

## *Directions* FOR THE DANCE

Meter 3/4 • Directions are for man; woman's part reverse.

| ***Measures*** | |
|---|---|
| | **PART I. FACE TO FACE, BACK TO BACK** |
| 1 | Beginning left, take one draw step to left. |
| 2 | Step left to side (count 1), release man's left hand, woman's right, pivot on left back to back, swinging joined hands and right foot forward (counts 2–3). Join other hands shoulder high. Release right hand. |
| 3 | Beginning right, take one draw step in line of direction. |
| 4 | Step right to side, touch left to right, weight remaining on right. |
| 5–8 | Beginning left, repeat action of measures 1–4 in reverse line of direction. In measure 6, joined hands are swung down and back as partners pivot, bringing them face to face. |
| 9–16 | Repeat action of measures 1–8. |
| | **PART II. WOMAN'S TURN** |
| 1 | Partners face, inside hands joined, outside hands on hip. Beginning left, take one draw step in line of direction (counts 1–3). |
| 2 | Man repeats draw step to left as woman turns clockwise once with two steps (right, left) under man's right arm (counts 1–3). |
| 3–4 | Repeat action of measures 1–2, Part II. On last draw, man touches right to left, woman takes three steps in the turn (right, left, right). |
| 5–8 | Man beginning right, woman left, repeat action of measures 1–4, Part II, in reverse line of direction. |
| 9–16 | Repeat action of measures 1–8. |
| | **PART III. SKATING** |
| 1 | Promenade position. Beginning left, take one waltz step forward in line of direction. |
| 2 | Take one waltz step, turning toward partner to face reverse line of direction. Movement continues in line of direction. |

| Measures | |
|---|---|
| 3–4 | Take two waltz steps backward, moving in line of direction. |
| 5–8 | Repeat action of measures 1–4, Part III, in reverse line of direction. |
| 9–16 | Repeat action of measures 1–8, Part III. |
| | **PART IV. WALTZ** |
| 1–2 | Closed position. Beginning left, take one draw step to side, step left to side, touch right to left, weight remaining on left. |
| 3–4 | Beginning right, repeat action of measures 1–2, Part IV, to right side. |
| 5–8 | Take four waltz steps, turning clockwise, progressing in line of direction. |
| 9–16 | Repeat action of measures 1–8, Part IV. |

# *Korobushka*

Russian

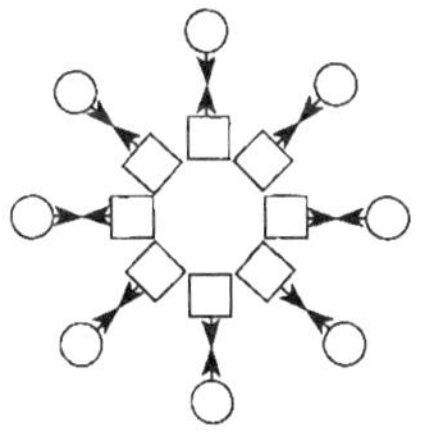

KOROBUSHKA, ALSO SPELLED KOROBOTCHKA, means "little basket" or "peddlar's pack." According to Michael Herman (1941), this dance originated on American soil among a group of Russian immigrants, following the close of World War I, to the Russian folk song, "Korobushka."

***Dance A While* CD:** "Korobushka."

**CD:** High/Scope RM 8.

**Music:** Beliajus, V. F., *Dance and Be Merry*, Vol. I, p. 20.

**Formation:** Double circle, partners facing, man's back to center. Two hands joined or man crosses arms on chest, woman places hands on hips.

**Steps:** Hungarian break step, schottische, balance, three-step turn.

**Level:** Beginning 3

## *Directions* FOR THE DANCE

Meter 2/4 • Directions are for man; woman's part reverse.

| Measures | Counts | |
|---|---|---|
| | | **PART I. SCHOTTISCHE STEP** |
| 1–2 | 1–4 | Beginning left, take one schottische step away from center of circle. |
| 3–4 | 5–8 | Beginning right, take one schottische step toward center of circle. |
| 5–6 | 1–4 | Repeat action of measures 1–2. |
| 7–8 | 5 | Hungarian break step: Jump and land with feet crossed. |
| | 6 | Jump with feet shoulder-width apart. |
| | 7–8 | Jump with feet together, hold on count 8. |

*continues on next page*

| ***Measures*** | ***Counts*** | |
|---|---|---|
| | | **PART II. THREE-STEP TURN** |
| 9–10 | 1–4 | Drop hands. Man and woman beginning with right foot, take one three-step turn to the right turning clockwise, hold and clap on count 4. |
| 11–12 | 5–8 | Beginning left, repeat three-step turn back to place. |
| 13–14 | 1–4 | Join right hands. Man and woman beginning right, balance together, balance back. |
| 15–16 | 5–8 | Man and woman beginning right, change places with four walking steps, woman turning counterclockwise under man's arm. |
| 17–24 | | Repeat action of measures 9–16, returning to original starting position. |

### Mixer

One may progress to a new partner on the last three-step turn, measures 19–20, by taking turn in place, balancing with a new partner, and changing sides. The man progresses to the woman in front of him at the completion of the three-step turn in place. Before dancers cross over, the man may identify his new partner as the next woman in the line of direction.

# *Troika*

## Russian

TROIKA MEANS "THREE HORSES." The dance symbolizes the three horses that traditionally drew sleighs for the Russian noble families.

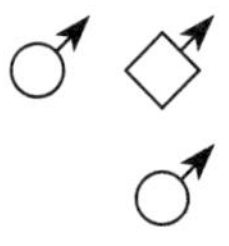

***Dance A While* CD:** "Troika."

**CD:** High/Scope RM 2.

**Music:** Herman, Michael, *Folk Dances for All,* p. 7; Neilson, N. P., and Van Hagen, W., *Physical Education for Elementary Schools,* 1954, p. 373.

**Formation:** Set of three, man between two women, facing line of direction, inside hands joined, outside hands on hip.

**Step:** Running step.

**Level:** Beginning 1

## *Directions* FOR THE DANCE

Meter 4/8

| *Measure* | *Counts* | |
|---|---|---|
| | | **PART I. RUN FORWARD** |
| 1 | 1–4 | Beginning right, take four running steps to diagonal right. |
| 2 | 5–8 | Four running steps to diagonal left. |
| 3–4 | 1–8 | Eight running steps, forward, in line of direction. |
| | | **PART II. ARCH** |
| 5–6 | 1–8 | Right-hand woman moves under arch made by raised arms of man and left-hand woman with eight running steps. Man runs in place and follows right-hand woman turning under his left arm. Left-hand woman runs in place. |
| 7–8 | 1–8 | Repeat with left-hand woman. |
| | | **PART III. CIRCLE** |
| 9–11 | 1–12 | Set of three join hands in circle, and beginning left, run 12 steps clockwise. |
| 12 | 13–16 | Stamp left, right, left, hold (count 16). |
| 13–16 | 1–16 | Repeat action of measures 9–12, moving counterclockwise, beginning right. |

### Style

The knees should be lifted high and the body and head held high.

### Mixer

The man may move forward to the next group of three as the stamps are taken in the last figure.

# Scandinavia

*By Gordon E. Tracie,* [1] *Seattle, WA.*

## Introduction

The native name for the part of Europe we call Scandinavia is *Norden,* literally meaning the North. It encompasses five nations: Denmark, Finland, Iceland, Norway, and Sweden; six cultures: Danish, Faroese, Finnish, Icelandic, Norwegian, and Swedish; seven flags: Denmark, the Faroe Islands, Finland, Iceland, Norway, Sweden, and the Aland Islands; and eight languages: Danish, Dano-Norwegian, Faroese, Finnish, Icelandic, Lappish, Neo-Norwegian, and Swedish. It is therefore not surprising that there is a wide diversity of cultures among the Scandinavians.

Geography, climate, history, lifestyle, and religion all have played a role in the development and acceptance of dance in a given culture. The flat islands of Denmark, the spectacular fjords and mountains of Norway, the rich farmlands and deep woods of Sweden, and the lakes and forests of Finland have all had an influence on the native music and hence on the traditional dance of the Nordic lands. Of equal if not greater importance is Scandinavia's proximity to other European countries. Germany and the British Isles seem to have been the ultimate source of much material, but Poland and France have also made significant contributions, as has been the case throughout Europe. The cold northern climate has dictated a need for heavy clothes, primarily wool, and for substantial shoes, both of which are reflected in Scandinavian folk costumes.

The pietistic movement of past generations had a devastating effect on dance and dance music in many parts of Scandinavia. Fortunately there were enough "folklore pockets," where musical traditions survived, to be able to pass on a remarkable heritage of true folk dances. Today, virtually all dancing in the Northlands is recreational in nature, rather than consciously ceremonial or ritualistic, although remnants of ancient seasonal rites do remain in the Midsummer and Yuletide serpentine dances and in the courting aspects of singing games. In contrast to folk dances in many other parts of the world, traditional Scandinavian dancing is almost exclusively coeducational in nature. With but a few exceptions, one always has a partner of the opposite gender with whom to dance. This is true in rings and other formations as well as in couple dances.

1. Gordon E. Tracie was founder and director of Skandia Folkdance Society, Seattle, and folklore consultant for the Smithsonian Institution, Washington, D.C.

ALB: Albania, BIH: Bosnia Herzegovina, HRV: Croatia, MKD: Former Yugoslav Republic of Macedonia, MNT: Montenegro, SVN: Slovenia

Perhaps the single most characteristic feature of Scandinavia's folklore-oriented dances is the predominance of couple rotation. Because this turning is usually relatively fast, factors not present in other types of dancing come into play. The focus is no longer on one or more independent persons, but on a single couple; hence counterbalance and momentum play a vital role. Furthermore, the need for a strong male lead is essential, for it is the man who must "start the wheel turning" and "steer."

It should go without saying that the single most important element in attaining authentic folk spirit in a dance is correct music. Lacking that, a folk dance is but a shell without a soul. Proper inspiration and motivation in a given dance can be assured only when the music approximates that with which the dance "grew up." From time immemorial, the dance music of Norway and Sweden has been played on bowed string instruments, usually without the aid of any percussion other than a tapping foot. Predecessors to the violin such as the bowed harp are named in Old Norse literature as far back as the 1300s, and many playing techniques used for instruments predating the violin are still extant in today's Norwegian and Swedish folk fiddling. Open strings characteristically serve as drones, a practice that generates legato rather than a staccato "drive" to the music. In Dalarna, Sweden's folklore district, fiddlers speak of "glued bowing," in which the bow seldom leaves the strings. Norway's Hardanger fiddle and Sweden's keyed fiddle "nyckelharpa" go a step further: Like the viola d'amore, they employ a set of unbowed understrings that vibrate in sympathetic resonance with the bowed strings, thus enhancing the instrument's sonority. All of this contributes to a sustaining legato quality in the music, which is in turn imparted to the dance itself.

The "town orchestra" tradition in Denmark, akin to that in many other parts of Europe, and the predominance of the accordion, an association with Imperial Russia in Finnish tradition, have produced a musical style considerably different from that of their Nordic neighbors. Inasmuch as dance naturally reflects music, the variance in dancing style between the Scandinavian countries can be illustrated by a continuum, as follows:

Legato, loose, "springy" (NORWEGIAN) to

Legato, more precise, lilting (SWEDISH) to

Quite precise, smooth (DANISH) to

Staccato, very precise, "crisp" (FINNISH)

The above differences are readily evident in the various schottische forms:

Norwegian "Reinlander"–Swedish "Schottis"–Danish "Rheinlaender"–Finnish "Jenkka"

and corresponding polka forms:

Norwegian "Polka," "Galopp"–Swedish "Polka"–Danish "Polka"–Finnish "Polkka"

The two most important holidays in Scandinavia are Christmas (Danish, Norwegian, Swedish: *Julen*; Finnish: *Joul*) and Midsummer (Danish, Norwegian: *Sankt Hans*; *Jonsok*; Swedish: *Midsommar*; Finnish: *Juhannus*). These are occasions to break out one's traditional folk dress if one is a fiddler, dancer, or participant in a procession, and the time to witness and participate in the most folk dancing short of a specific folk music or dance festival.

## Denmark

### Dance Characteristics

Through all Danish folk dance shines a distinctly light-hearted, often whimsical, quality that is consistent with the convivial Danish temperament. Not infrequently, an element of satire pervades, for the Dane is blessed with a great sense of humor.

The bulk of Danish folk dances bear a close kinship to the dances of the British Isles, with which Denmark has had both cultural and economic ties for centuries. Quadrilles, longways sets, and dances for two or three couples abound. The melodies often sound a lot like English or Scottish dance tunes, and they are obviously cognates. Denmark is the only one of the Nordic lands that has the rollicking Anglo-Celtic 6/8 rhythm, for example, and it has it in abundance. Danish folk dance instructions are organized geographically, the material having been meticulously collected from all parts of the land since around the turn of the twentieth century. A distinction is made between "folkedanse," folk dances, and "gamle danse," old-time dances. The latter (which include the nineteenth-century ballroom dances, waltz, polka, and mazurka) are not accorded the same reverence as the former. But the folk dances exist in Denmark today only through the efforts of organized folk dance societies, which limit their origin to the century between 1750 and 1850. Like Danish folk costumes, they are no longer a true living tradition.

During the past several years, there has been an effort, which has met with considerable success among young people's groups, to rekindle an interest in old-time dancing and its music, but in a modern setting (i.e., without "folk" costumes). The traditional folk dance ensemble of two violins, clarinet, and bass viol, still the norm for the formal folk dance movement, has been augmented by accordions, guitars, mandolins, and even bass saxophones. Needless to say, there is precious little cooperation between the advocates of these two approaches and what we in America lump together as folk dance.

## Norway

### Dance Characteristics

A folklorist's delight, Norway is without a doubt the most remarkable of the Scandinavian nations when it comes to the retention of native dance forms. In the remote valleys of this rugged land of fjords and mountains are to be found some of the oldest surviving dances in western Europe. Regional dances, "bygdedansar," such as the Gangar, Springar, Halling, and Pols, actively learned and danced today, have an unbroken tradition dating back to the sixteenth century. The formal folk dance movement recognizes two other forms: song-dance and figure dances. Song-dance, "songdans," a lyrical dance-song predominant during the Middle Ages, died out in Norway centuries ago but survived in the Faroe Islands. The form was reintroduced to Norwegian folk dancers around 1900 as an adjunct to the promotion of "Nynorsk," the Old Norse-based second language of the land. Figure-dances, "turdansar," consist of reels, contras, and sequence dances from the nineteenth century, many of ultimate foreign origin.

Because the Norwegians more than any other Scandinavians have retained the qualities of spontaneity and improvisation in their dancing, the folk dances of Norway are the most difficult for foreigners to emulate.

## Finland

### Dance Characteristics

The folk music and dance of Suomi/Finland reflects two distinct historical influences: the original Finno-Ugric linguistic heritage and the Scandinavian culture of Russia to the east. Finland is bilingual, with just under 10 percent of the population speaking Swedish. Hence there are two distinct folk dance movements, the pure Finnish and the Finland-Swedish, each with its own traditions.

The pure Finnish idiom is quite unlike that of the rest of Scandinavia. A different minor mode gives many Finnish tunes a seemingly melancholy quality. Yet the dance is very often brisk in character. The Finns display a great deal of verve and "snap" in their dancing, giving many folk dances an element of "fire." Steps are small and danced with a fast, even bounce. Frequently an abrupt change of tempo or rhythm occurs, making for added variety and interest.

## Sweden

### Dance Characteristics

"The Swedish forest," wrote a nineteenth-century naturalist, "sings in three-quarter time." A romantic but apt description, because the bulk of Sweden's native melodies are in triple meter, mostly "polska," a rhythmic form older than and unrelated to the waltz and not to be confused with the relatively modern polka. Long the national dance of Sweden, the "polska" has survived from the late 1500s right into the twentieth century, its most widely known form being the Hambo. Because the bowed strings of the fiddle have traditionally provided the music for Sweden's native dances, the interpretation is legato, a quality befitting the tranquil nature of the Swedish landscape and people. It has been said that the Swedes' distaste for excessive display of emotion likely accounts for the relative conservatism of Swedish folk dancing. Nevertheless, Swedish dance style is buoyant with the same lightness as is found in Denmark, but with an air of dignity and reserve that bespeaks a more serious nature.

The dances promulgated for over a century by the formal folk dance societies in Sweden are mainly the products of mid-nineteenth century national romanticism, and thus never actually danced by the "folk." It was not until around 1970, concurrent with a remarkable renaissance of interest in Swedish country fiddling, that true dances of the people became a part of the folk dance movement. Thanks to the work of a few devoted researchers, an unbelievable number of old dances, mostly "polska" types, were rescued from oblivion through interviews with elderly fiddlers and folks who had danced them when young. These "bygdedanser," regional dances, have at last reunited the folk dancer with the folk fiddler and the vibrant, unbroken tradition of native Swedish music.

# *Bitte Mand I Knibe*

## Danish

BITTE MAND I KNIBE means "little man in a fix." This is a very popular little dance, both in Denmark and all over the United States. *Knibe* means to be in a "spot" or "fix."

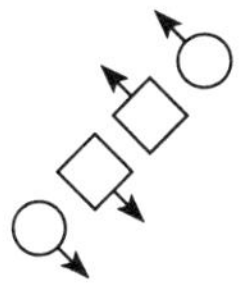

**CD:** Scandinavian Holiday.

**Music:** Burchenal, E., *Folk Dances of Denmark,* p. 44, and *Folk Dances from Old Homelands,* p. 62; LaSalle, D., *Rhythms and Dances for Elementary Schools,* p. 115.

**Formation:** Sets of two couples, woman to right of partner. Men hook left elbows and place right arm around partner's waist, women place left hand on man's left shoulder.

**Steps:** Running step, Tyrolian waltz, waltz.

**Level:** Intermediate

## *Directions* FOR THE DANCE

Meter 3/4 • Directions are same for man and woman, except when specially noted.

| ***Measures*** | |
|---|---|
| | **PART I. RUN AROUND** |
| 1–8 | Beginning left, take small running steps forward, moving counterclockwise. Couples lean away from pivot point. |
| 1–8 | As running steps are continued, men grasp left hands and raise left arms, holding women's left hand with their right, and two women move under arch and pass each other. Women turn counterclockwise to face center, men lower left arms, and women grasp each other's right hand on top of men's left-hand grasp. All four continue to take small running steps, moving counterclockwise. |
| | **PART II. TYROLIAN WALTZ** |
| 9–12 | Men release left hand, women right. The two couples turn back to back. Each couple takes couple position, inside hands shoulder height, outside arm relaxed at side. Man beginning left, woman right, take four Tyrolian waltz steps moving in the direction facing. Arms reach forward and draw back with each step. They do not swing forward. |
| 13–16 | Closed position. Man beginning left, woman right, take four waltz steps, turning clockwise, progressing anywhere. |
| 9–16 | Inside hands joined, find a new couple. Repeat action of measures 9–16. |

### Note

As the dance repeats, each couple dances with another couple. If a couple cannot find a couple for the first figure, they are *in a fix!* They go to the center and dance the running steps alone, with two hands joined. The next time the man will avoid being the *man in a fix* by hooking arms with another couple quickly for the first figure.

# *Den Toppede Høne*

## Danish

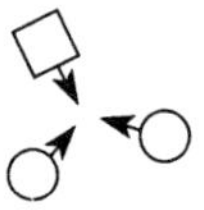

DEN TOPPEDE HØNE MEANS "the Crested Hen," referring to the fact that in Denmark the men wore red stocking caps with a tassel representing a rooster comb. The women added to the fun of the dance by trying to pull the man's cap off as he went through the arch. If successful, then the woman became the "crested" hen.

***Dance A While* CD:** "Den Toppede Høne."

**Music:** Burchenal, E., *Folk Dances of Denmark,* p. 49; LaSalle, D., *Rhythms and Dances for Elementary Schools,* p. 150. Neilson, N. P., and Van Hagen, W., *Physical Education for Elementary Schools,* p. 300.

**Formation:** Set of three, two women and a man, hands joined to form a circle.

**Step:** Step-hop.

**Level:** Beginning 1

## Directions FOR THE DANCE

Meter 2/4

| ***Measures*** | |
|---|---|
| | **PART I.** |
| 1–8 | Beginning left, step-hop around circle clockwise, taking a vigorous stamp on first beat. Dancers lean away from center as they circle. |
| 1–8 | Jump, bringing feet down sharply on first beat, step-hop around circle counterclockwise. |
| | **PART II.** |
| 9–10 | Continuing step-hop, women release joined hands, place free hand on hip, and right-hand woman dances through arch made by man and left-hand woman. |
| 11–12 | Man turns under his left arm, following right-hand woman through arch. |
| 13–14 | Left-hand woman dances through arch made by man and right-hand woman. |
| 15–16 | Man turns under his right arm, following left-hand woman through arch. |
| 9–16 | Repeat action of measures 9–16. |

### Mixer

The man may progress forward to the next group at the completion of Part II.

# Familie Sekstur

## Danish

FAMILIE SEKSTUR MEANS "family sixsome" and is pronounced *fa-MEEL-yeh SEKS-toor.* This Danish mixer is similar to American square dance figures and steps.

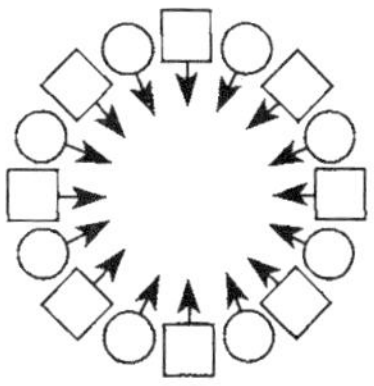

**CD:** RM 5.

**Music:** Farwell, Jane, *Folk Dances for Fun,* p. 20.

**Formation:** Couples in single circle, woman to right of partner, hands joined, held at shoulder height. Dancers stand close to each other.

**Steps:** Buzz step swing, walk.

**Level:** Beginning 2

## *Directions* FOR THE DANCE

Meter 6/8 • Directions are the same for man and woman except when specially noted.

| ***Measures*** | |
|---|---|
| 1–8 | Introduction. Beginning right, take 16 buzz steps to side (right crosses over left, right knee bending slightly). Circle moves clockwise. Take small light steps, keep circle small with elbows bent, and lean back slightly for better action. |
| | **PART I. IN AND OUT** |
| 9–10 | Beginning right, take four steps toward center, slowly extending joined hands above head. On fourth step, everyone nods head to greet everyone. |
| 11–12 | Beginning right, take four steps backward, to return to original formation, arms gradually lowering to original position (elbows bent, joined hands shoulder height). On fourth step, nod head to partner. |
| 13–16 | Repeat action of measures 9–12. |
| | **PART II. GRAND CHAIN** |
| 17–24 | Face partner and join right hands shoulder high, elbows bent, and continue around circle with grand right and left. Count out loud one to seven for each person met, keeping the seventh person for new partner. This keeps mixers in order. It is especially fun if counted in a Scandinavian language. Danish counting:<br>one–*en,* pronounced *enn*<br>two–*to,* pronounced *toe*<br>three–*tre,* pronounced *tray*<br>four–*fire,* pronounced *feer*<br>five–*fein,* pronounced *femm*<br>six–*sexs,* pronounced *sex*<br>seven–*syv,* pronounced *syou.* |

*continues on next page*

Familie Sekstur, *continued*

***Measures***

**PART III. SWING**

1–8 Swing position, with man's left arm, woman's right, extended straight out at shoulder level.

Swing new partner in place, taking 16 buzz steps, ending with woman on man's right. All join hands to form single circle.

Repeat action of Parts I–III, measures 9–24, 1–8, until end of record.

# *Familjevalsen*

## Swedish

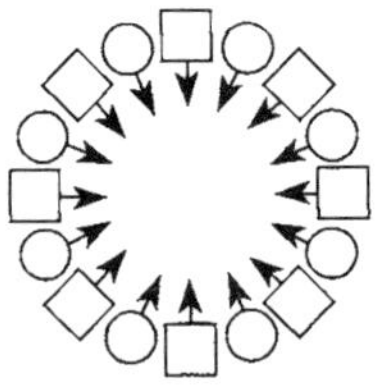

FAMILJEVALSEN MEANS "the family waltz" and is pronounced *fah-MIL-yeh-vahls-en.* Although this dance may be found throughout the Scandinavian countries, the Swedish version is described here as taught by Gordon E. Tracie, Seattle.

***Dance A While* CD:** "Family Waltz (Familjevalsen)"; any lively Swedish waltz.

**Records:** Viking Skandia Album 1

**Music:** Farwell, Jane, *Folk Dances for Fun.*

**Formation:** Couples in single circle, woman to right of partner, hands joined, held at shoulder height.

**Steps:** Waltz balance, waltz.

**Level:** Beginning 3

## *Directions* FOR THE DANCE

Meter 3/4 • Directions are for man; woman's part reverse.

***Measures***

**PART I. BALANCE**

1 Beginning left, take one waltz balance turning toward corner.

2 Beginning right, take one waltz balance turning toward partner.

3–4 Repeat action of measures 1–2.

**PART II. WALTZ**

5–8 Take closed position with corner. Arms, man's left, woman's right, are extended straight out, shoulder height. Man places left thumb against the palm of the woman's right hand and closes his hand around the back of her hand. Beginning left, take four waltz steps turning clockwise, progressing in line of direction. On last waltz step, form circle, man placing partner on right side. Repeat dance from beginning with new corner.

## Style

This should be a very smooth yet lively dance. Be sure to exchange smiles or greetings with corner and partner on the waltz balance. Remember that the body rises and lowers during a waltz balance. The waltz is light, graceful, and fast.

## Mixer

Skandia Folkdance Society, of Seattle, traditionally starts with partner on left, so that the first waltz in closed position (Part II) is with partners.

# *Fjäskern*

## Swedish

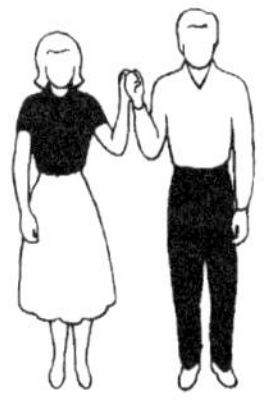

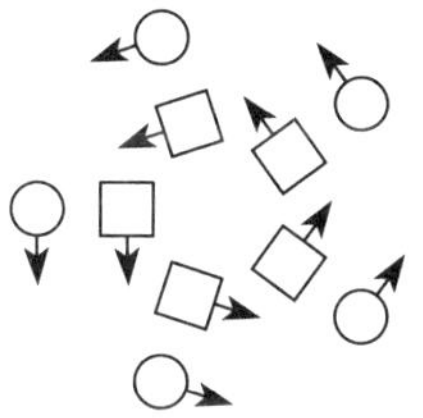

FJÄSKERN IS PRONOUNCED *FYESS-kehrn*. It is a simple mixer that appeals to beginners and old-timers as the music progresses from a very slow pace to almost too fast; thus, it may appropriately be called "Hurry-Scurry" in English. This dance was learned from Gordon E. Tracie, Seattle, Washington.

**CD:** RM 2.

**Piano:** Samkväms och gillesdanser, Svenska Ungdomsringen, Stockholm.

**Formation:** Double circle, couples facing line of direction. Inside hands joined and held at shoulders, outside hands on hips with fingers forward, thumbs back.

**Steps:** Walk, run.

**Level:** Beginning 1

## *Directions* FOR THE DANCE

Meter 4/4 • Directions are the same for man and woman.

| ***Measures*** | |
|---|---|
| | **PART I. FORWARD AND BACK** |
| 1–4 | Beginning left, take 16 walking steps, moving forward in line of direction. As music accelerates, these walking steps will become running steps. |
| 1–4 | Turn toward partner to face reverse line of direction and join inside hands, free hands on hips. Take 16 walking steps, moving forward in reverse line of direction. |
| | **PART II. KICK AND CHANGE PLACES** |
| 5 | Face partner, man's back to center of circle, hands on own hips. Beginning left, step left in place and kick right foot out, step right in place and kick left foot out. |
| 6 | Clap hands (count 1) and partners change places with four running steps, moving clockwise, always facing each other. |
| 7–8 | Repeat action of measures 5–6 to return to original position. |
| 5–8 | Repeat action of measures 5–8. Man then moves forward to next lady for a new partner. |
| | Repeat dance from beginning with new partner. |

# Hambo

## Swedish

THE HAMBO (ITS FULL NAME IS *Hambopolska*), often called the national dance of Sweden, is practiced far beyond the borders of its homeland. It is danced in neighboring Scandinavian countries and in Swedish national groups around the world; in the United States it is a top favorite among folk dancers.

The Hambo is the most common living example of the once all-popular Swedish "polska"—a distinctly Nordic music and dance form dating back to the sixteenth century. Because the Hambo is a living folk dance, yesterday's version is not the same as today's, according to Gordon E. Tracie. The form most common in the United States is a relatively old style called *nighambo*, referring to the characteristic "dip" on the first beat. It was brought to the United States by Swedish immigrants in the 1800s.

**Music:** Swedish Hambo music.

**Position:** Couple, inside hands joined at shoulder height, outside hands on hip, thumb pointing backwards fingers forward.

**Steps:** Step swing or waltz balance, polska.

**Level:** Advanced

## *Directions* FOR THE DANCE

Meter 3/4 • Directions are for man; woman's part reverse, except when specially noted.

***Measures***

**PART I. INTRODUCTION**

1 Beginning left, take one step swing (dal step) or waltz balance, turning body slightly away from partner, letting inside hands reach forward.

2 Take one step swing or waltz balance slightly forward, turning body slightly toward partner, drawing inside hands backward.

3 Take three steps or waltz step in line of direction.

**PART II. HAMBO (POLSKA) STEP**

4 Shoulder-waist position.

*Man's part:* Count 1, beginning right, step (with flat foot and bent knee) forward in line of direction with foot turned outward to start clockwise pivot. Place foot between partner's feet. Count 2, step left slightly forward in line of direction (almost in place) pivoting almost 360° clockwise. Body rises, coming up on ball of left foot. Count 3, touch ball of right foot firmly close behind left heel.

*Woman's part:* Count 1, beginning left, step almost in place pivoting 180° clockwise, bending left knee slightly. Count 2, right foot describes an arc, skimming floor, and touches toe close behind left heel. Body starts to rise. Count *and*, as body continues to rise, push slightly with left foot and leap into air. Count 3, complete 180° turn while both feet are in air, landing on right foot placed forward in line of direction between man's feet.

5–7 Repeat action of measure 4 three times.

8 Beginning right, take three steps almost in place. Take couple position, facing line of direction.

## Style

1. The Hambo is a very graceful, smooth-flowing dance. The music should be moderate speed, not fast. At the proper tempo, the dancers appear very relaxed and their movements effortless. Extra turns and twirls are to be discouraged.
2. The upper torso is always upright. The torso is lowered, or settles with the bending of the knee to accompany the primary accent (count 1). It rises on count 2. This body movement is subtle.
3. Both dancers should always be in control of their own body weight. The body is well "grounded" by planting each foot firmly in the step pattern. The touch of the man's right foot (count 3) acts to stabilize the body while pivoting. His weight is actually on both feet momentarily.
4. The woman should not let her right lower leg "fly up," or flick in the air, as it describes the arc (count 2).
5. The man guides the woman while in the air. He does not lift her, as she receives her impetus for height from her push (count and).
6. Once the basic footwork is learned, perfection and styling of the dance takes several years of regular practice and conscious effort.

## Suggestions for Teaching the Hambo (Polska) Step

1. Understand basic rhythm.

   Man: 3/4 Woman: 3/4

   | Step | Pivot | Touch | Step | Touch | Leap | Step |
   |---|---|---|---|---|---|---|
   | R | L | R | L | R | R | |
   | 1 | 2 | 3 | 1 | 2 | and | 3 |

2. Men stand single file, facing a wall; women single file, facing an opposite wall.
   a. Analyze basic step (without partner) for each group. Practice basic step in place.
   b. Analyze basic step (with turn) for each group. Emphasize exact placement of each foot in relation to line of direction and a specific wall. Face original wall with each Hambo step.
3. Double-file lines, couples in shoulder-waist position.
   a. Practice step with partner.
   b. Practice individually and then together, alternately.
4. Double circle, couples in shoulder-waist position.
   a. Practice step, progressing around room.
   b. Then analyze Introduction to Hambo and practice complete dance.

7

# Norwegian Polka

## Norwegian

THE NORWEGIAN POLKA IS also known as the *Scandinavian Polka, Seattle Polka,* and *Ballroom Polka.* Gordon E. Tracie suggests that the Americanized version may come from a simplification of the Norwegian dance Parisarpolka, meaning "Parisian Polka." The Norwegian immigrants probably brought the Parisarpolka to America, where it changed somewhat in form but retained the original Scandinavian Polka music.

**Music:** Any good Scandinavian Polka, eight-measure phrase.
**Position:** Couple, hands joined at shoulder height.
**Steps:** Walk, pivot turn.
**Level:** Intermediate

## Directions FOR THE DANCE

Meter 2/4 • Directions are for man; woman's part reverse.

| ***Measures*** | |
|---|---|
| | **PART I.** |
| 1–2 | Beginning left, take three walking steps in line of direction and stamp. |
| 3–4 | Beginning right, take three walking steps in reverse line of direction and clap, clap. |
| | **PART II.** |
| 5 | Beginning left, walk two steps in line of direction. Face partner on second step and take shoulder-waist position. |
| 6–8 | Beginning left, take a six-step pivot turn clockwise, progressing in line of direction. Partners should lean away from each other in turn. Man should end with back to center of room. |

### Variations

| | | |
|---|---|---|
| 1. | Measures 5–6 | Walk four steps in line of direction. |
| | Measures 7–8 | Four-step pivot turn clockwise. |
| 2. | Measures 1–2 | Take two steps in line of direction and a two-step in place, facing partner. |
| | Measures 3–4 | Repeat in reverse line of direction. |
| 3. | Measures 1–2 | Take three-step turn in line of direction. Clap at end of turn. |
| | Measures 3–4 | Repeat in reverse line of direction. |

### Teaching Suggestions

1. For help teaching the pivot turn see pages 46–47.
2. To simplify dance for the beginner, it is helpful to teach two walking steps in measures 5–8 in couple position, followed by two steps pivoting in shoulder-waist position and repeat. Gradually change the sequence to the regular four- or six-step pivot.

# Seksmannsril

## Norwegian

*Mrs. Helfrid Rudd, Norwegian folk dance authority, Oslo, Norway, taught this dance at the University of Washington, Seattle, WA, 1951.*

SEKSMANNSRIL MEANS "six persons' Reel" and is pronounced *seks-mahns-REEL.* It is classified as a formal folk dance. The dance comes from the region of Asker.

**CD:** Viking Skandia CD.

**Formation:** Three couples in single circle, woman to right of partner; hands joined with arms outstretched, shoulder height.

**Steps:** Step-hop.

**Level:** Beginning 2

## Directions FOR THE DANCE

Meter 2/4 • Directions are same for both woman and man, except where noted.

| | ***Measures*** | |
|---|---|---|
| | 1–4 | Introduction: No action. |
| | | **FIGURE I. RING** |
| A | 1–7 | Beginning left, take 14 step-hops to left, circle moving clockwise. |
| | 8 | Take three stamps (left, right, left), turning to face counterclockwise. |
| | 1–7 | Beginning right, take 14 step-hops to right, circle moving counterclockwise. |
| | 8 | Take three stamps (right, left, right), clapping hands once on first stamp. Partners face, joining two hands. Arms are outstretched with outside arms slightly higher than inside arms; body leans toward center of circle. Inside hands of all couples almost touch in center of circle. |
| | | **TWO-HAND HOLD** |
| B | 9–15 | Man beginning left, woman right, take 14 step-hops, moving in line of direction; man moves forward, woman backward. As couples are leaning slightly toward center of circle, body has banking effect as traveling. |
| | 16 | Clapping hands once, take three stamps, turning away from partner to face corner; man turns left, woman right, and join two hands with outstretched arms, still leaning toward center. |
| | 17–23 | Continuing to move in line of direction, repeat action of measures 9–15, woman moving forward, man backing up. |
| | 24 | Turning back to face partner (man turns right, woman left), repeat action of measure 16. |

*continues on next page*

| | ***Measures*** | |
|---|---|---|
| | | **CHAIN** |
| C | 25–32 | Giving right hand to partner, grand right and left around the ring, step-hopping (beginning left). Continue on meeting partner the first time. Second time facing partner, take three stamps and rejoin hands in single circle. |
| | | **FIGURE II. RING** |
| A | 1–8 | Repeat action of Figure I A, measures 1–8. |
| | | **HAND CLAPPING** |
| B | 9–24 | Repeat action of Figure I B, measures 9–24; instead of joining hands, clap hands on each step-hop. Action of arms while clapping is vertical: right hand swinging down, left up for clap, right hand coming up, left down for next clap, and alternating thereafter. |
| | | **CHAIN** |
| C | 25–32 | Repeat action of Figure I C, measures 25–32. |

### Notes

1. During Figure I A, some groups prefer to swing arms in and out while circling.
2. The Seksmannsril is a happy dance and must be danced quickly and with abandon. Stamps and claps are very precise. The dancers call "hey" or "ho" as they turn away or toward partners.

# *Snurrbocken*

## Swedish

SNURRBOCKEN, PRONOUNCED *SNOOR-book-en,* means "the whirl and bow." Like the Hambo, it is a form of Swedish polska. According to Gordon E. Tracie, the second (bowing) part of the dance is a bit of rustic satire in which the farm folk burlesqued the gentry and their affected mannerisms. Traditionally it was at just this point that the fiddler could have fun with the dancers by setting the timing and tempo of the bow sequence–often with long delays–and it was up to the dancers to follow the music.

**Music:** *Svenska Folkdanser och Sallskapsdancer*, Svendska Ungdomsringen, Stockholm.

**Position:** Shoulder-waist.

**Steps:** Polska, run.

**Level:** Advanced

## *Directions* FOR THE DANCE

Meter 3/4 • Directions are for man; woman's part reverse.

***Measures***

**PART I. POLSKA TURN**

1–8 Beginning left, take eight polska steps turning clockwise, progressing in line of direction. Analysis of polska step: *Man's part:* Count 1, step forward left, pivoting clockwise. Count 2, continue pivoting on left and place ball of right foot near left foot (weight remains on left foot, right foot helps to maintain balance). Count 3, step forward right. *Woman's part:* Count 1, step on both feet, preparing to pivot clockwise. Count 2, step right, pivoting clockwise. Count 3, step left, pivoting clockwise.

**PART II. RUN**

9–16 Conversation position, with free hand on hips (fingers forward, thumb back). Beginning left, take 24 light, small running steps forward in line of direction.

**PART III. BOWS**

17 Place hands on own hips fingers forward, thumbs back, and turn slowly toward partner, man with back to center, woman facing the center.

18 Slowly bow low to each other with dignity.

19 Each turn one half-turn, man counterclockwise, facing center, woman clockwise, facing outward.

20 Slowly bow while back to back.

21 Each turns one-half more to face each other. Take shoulder-waist position to repeat dance.

### Notes

This polska step, sometimes called delsbopolska, after a district in the province of Halsingland, is related to the Hambo step but begins with the man's *left* and has a pivot, whereas the Hambopolska begins with the man's *right* and has a "dip" (first beat) at the beginning of each step.

# *To Ting*

Danish

TO TING MEANS "two things." This refers to the two different rhythms, 3/4 and 2/4.

**Dance A While CD:** "To Ting."
**Music:** Herman, Michael, *Folk Dances for All,* p. 52.
**Position:** Inside hands joined, outside hands on hips.
**Steps:** Waltz, walk, pivot turn.
**Level:** Intermediate

## *Directions* FOR THE DANCE

Meter 3/4 • Directions are for man; woman's part reverse.

| *Measures* | |
|---|---|
| | **PART I.** |
| 1 | Moving forward, beginning left, take one waltz step, turning away from partner, swinging inside arms forward, hands at shoulder level. |
| 2 | Moving forward, take one waltz step, turning toward partner, swinging inside arms back. |
| 3–4 | Repeat action of measures 1–2. |
| 5–8 | Closed position. Beginning left, take four waltz steps, turning clockwise, progressing in line of direction. |
| 1–8 | Repeat action of measures 1–8. |
| Meter 2/4 | |
| | **PART II.** |
| 9–12 | Conversation position, outside hands on hips. Beginning left, take four walking steps forward. |
| 13–16 | Shoulder-waist position. Beginning left, turn clockwise with four steps in a pivot turn. |
| 9–16 | Repeat action of measures 9–16. |
| | **VARIATION** |
| 9–12 | The Danes skip four forward. |
| 13–16 | Turn with four step lifts (svejtril steps) in pivot turn. |

# Totur

## Danish

*This dance was arranged from the dance used in* The Folk Dancer, *Vol. 5, December 1945, pp. 10–11.*

TOTUR OR "TWO DANCE" IS a mixer from the district of Vejle in western Denmark. Dancers get new partners at the completion of the "chain" or grand right and left. It is customary to smile at each person you meet in the chain.

***Dance A While* CD:** "Totur."

**Formation:** Single circle, couples facing center, woman to right of partner, hands joined, held at shoulder level, W position.

**Steps:** Walk, two-step, polka.

**Level:** Intermediate

## Directions FOR THE DANCE

Music 2/4 • Directions are for man; woman's part reverse, except in the introduction.

| ***Measures*** | |
|---|---|
| | **INTRODUCTION** |
| 1–8 | Beginning left, take 16 walking steps, eight two-steps, or eight polka steps clockwise. |
| 1–8 | Repeat action of measures 1–8 counterclockwise. |
| | **FIGURE I.** |
| 9 | Single circle. Open position, men facing line of direction, joined hands toward center of circle. Beginning left, take one two-step toward center of circle. |
| 10 | Continue in same direction with two walking steps. |
| 11–12 | Beginning right, moving away from center, repeat action of measures 9–10 back to place in reverse open position or backout. |
| 13–16 | Beginning left, take four polka steps, turning clockwise, progressing in line of direction. |
| 9–16 | Repeat action of measures 9–16. |
| | **FIGURE II.** |
| 1–8 | Partners face, grasp right hands, and grand right and left around circle with walking, two-steps, or polka steps. |
| 1–8 | Continue grand right and left. (**Note:** At the end of this figure, dancers may have a new partner for repeat of the dance.) |
| | Repeat Figures I and II alternately for remainder of music. |

7

# *Vossarull*

## Norwegian

VOSSARULL IS FROM Voss, Vestlaudet, Norway.

***Dance A While* CD:** "Vossarull"
**Position:** Conversation.
**Steps:** Waltz, pivot turn, two-step.
**Sequence:** Walk, pivot turn, walk or two-step.
**Level:** Advanced

## *Directions* FOR THE DANCE

Meter 4/4 • Directions are for man; woman's part reverse.

**PART I. WALK**

Beginning left, walk forward in line of direction, outside arm swinging freely. Heel contacts floor first, transferring weight to sole of foot. The walk is light, springy, with a slight dip on each step.

**PART II. PIVOT**

Man initiates pivot at beginning of a phrase. Closed or shoulder-waist position. Beginning left, start pivot, heel contacting floor first, stepping on each beat, progressing in the line of direction. Pivot is very smooth. Refer to Pivot Turn, pages 46–47. The number of pivots varies for available floor space and skill of dancers.

**PART III. WALK OR TWO-STEP**

Man initiates next pattern. Two-step turning clockwise or change to conversation position, walk forward in line of direction.

Repeat dance, alternating walk or two-step and pivot.

## South America

# *Carnavalito*

## Bolivian

CARNAVALITO IS A DANCE from Bolivia. It was presented at the Maine Folk Dance Camp by Laura Zanzi de Chavarria from Uruguay.

Just before Lent, while some countries are celebrating Mardi Gras, Latin America is celebrating Tiempo de Carnaval. Several South American countries have their own Carnavalito. This is one of Bolivia's most popular dances. It is danced at many fiestas, but mainly during the Carnaval festivities, up and down the streets.

***Dance A While* CD:** "Carnavalito."

**Formation:** No partner. Lines facing forward, one person behind each other, hands joined.

**Steps:** Three walking steps forward and hold.

**Level:** Beginning 1

## *Directions* FOR THE DANCE

Meter 4/4

| *Measures* | *Counts* | |
|---|---|---|
| | | **PART I.** |
| | | Leader leads line in a serpentine figure. |
| 1 | 1–4 | Beginning right, take three steps forward and hold, bending forward at waist (right, left, right, hold–count 4). This step is like a schottische, but with a "hold" instead of a "hop." |

*continues on next page*

| ***Measures*** | ***Counts*** | |
|---|---|---|
| 2 | 5–8 | Take three steps forward and hold, body straightening up (left, right, left, hold). |
| 3–8 | | Repeat measure 1–2 three times. |
| | | **PART II.** |
| 1–4 | 1–16 | Leader leads line into a broken circle with 16 step-hops. |
| 5–8 | 1–16 | Take 16 step-hops in the opposite direction with the last person leading the line. |
| | | Repeat all in the original direction. In the last repeat, Part I is only half as long. |

# *Ranchera*

## Uruguayan

RANCHERA IS A COUPLE DANCE from Uruguay. It was presented by Laura Zanzi de Chavarria at the Maine Folk Dance Camp. Ranchera has been danced at all Uruguayan festivities since 1850. It is called "el limpia sillas"–the chair cleaner–because when this music is played, everyone gets up to dance. It is the most popular dance of Uruguay.

***Dance A While* CD:** "Ranchera."

**Formation:** Couples scattered, all facing *front,* side by side with woman to right of man, inside hands joined.

**Step:** Walk, waltz.

**Level:** Intermediate

## *Directions* FOR THE DANCE

Meter 3/4 • Directions are for man; woman's part is the reverse.

| ***Measures*** | |
|---|---|
| | **PART I.** |
| 1–4 | Starting with outside foot, take one waltz step forward. Drop hands, turn to face opposite direction with one waltz step. Join inside hands and take one waltz step toward the back wall, and one waltz step to face each other. |
| 5–8 | Balance to side, man's left, woman's right; balance to other side. Turning away from partner (all the way around) take two waltz steps and clap on count 5 (Counts: 1 – 2 – 3 – 4 – clap – 6). |

***Measures***

**PART II. THE SQUARE**

1–2 Semi-open position, couple moves forward with two waltz steps.

3–4 Closed position, take two waltz steps, turning clockwise three-fourths around to face left wall.

5–8 Repeat action of measures 1–4 to face back wall, alternating semi-open and closed position.

1–4 Repeat action of measures 1–4 to face right wall, alternating semi-open and closed position.

5–8 Repeat action of measures 1–4, alternating semi-open and closed position, but end up facing back wall, woman on man's left.

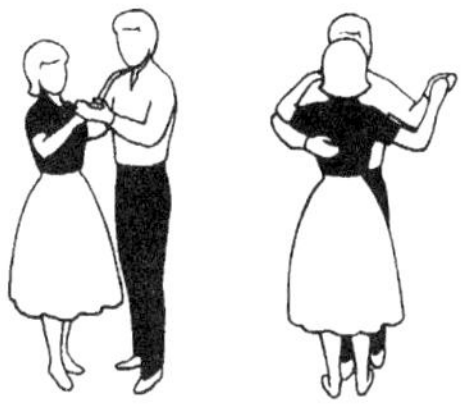

**PART III.**

1–8 Repeat action of Part I, toward back wall.

**PART IV.**

1–16 Closed position, take 16 waltz steps, turning clockwise, progressing freely around the floor.

**PART V.**

1–2 Man holding woman's right hand in his left, take one waltz step to change places, woman going under man's arm. Still holding hands, with one waltz step, balance away from each other.

**Cue:** Under and pull back.

3–8 Repeat movement of measures 1–2 three more times, ending in Varsouvienne position with woman on man's left.

**PART VI.**

1–8 Keeping woman in front, partners exchange sides with one waltz step; exchange sides again with one waltz step. Dancers look into partners' eyes as they cross sides. Repeat for a total of eight side to sides. This sequence is in place.

1–8 Repeat action of measures 1–8, moving forward while exchanging places. Move freely around the room.

**PART VII.**

1–8 Repeat action of Part I, inside hands joined.

# 8 SOCIAL DANCE

## INTRODUCTION

*Dance and music are not static forms. They mirror the culture in which they exist by reflecting the past, present, and any intercultural exchanges that have occurred. The everchanging human scene is absorbed and acted out in dance and music forms.*

The Renaissance of the fifteenth and sixteenth century in Italy and France saw the rebirth of interest in learning, literature, arts, and creative expression in general. The invention of printing made it possible for dance instruction and music notation to be widely distributed. Avid interest in dance and the creation of new musical forms swept through the courts of Europe. The period saw the establishment of dance teaching as a profession. New court dances were developed by professionals for the nobility. Courts used dance as an opportunity to educate courtiers in social graces and deportment. Queen Elizabeth I established social dance as an important part of court life. English country dance began to appear in court, and English dancing schools were in vogue. Dances in the latter part of Queen Elizabeth's reign were lively and extremely popular.

Because the dances of the court were performed in ballrooms, they became known as ballroom dances. These same elements from the court dances were part of elaborate cotillions and military balls in the early period of social dancing in America. The only dance to survive into the twentieth century from this period is the waltz. Other earlier dances—the polka, two-step, and minuet—have been replaced by a long line of changing dance forms that reflect current moods and trends.

## Phases of Social Dance

Since 1900, social dance has experienced ten distinct periods, each stimulated or motivated by a new style of music. Sometimes more than one dance was popular at the same time, depending on what part of the country you were in. The majority of new dances were ushered onto the ballroom floor with wild hysteria and daring, but throughout history those dances that were once shocking have, with time and refinement, evolved into an acceptable mode of expression.

### Ragtime Period: 1900–1920s

The Foxtrot had its beginning in 1914 as a fast, trotting step to a new jazz beat called "ragtime." The Foxtrot was one of many popular "animal" dances from that time period, and the only one to survive. The Wallaby Jump, Kangaroo Hop, Lame Duck, Bunny Hug, and the Grizzly Bear briefly rocked the population in an early dance revolution around the time of World War I. The animal dance craze was the most prolific era of dance in the twentieth century. In the 1930s, Fred Astaire and Ginger Rodgers changed the Foxtrot into a smooth dance. With each New York social season, new Foxtrot steps were introduced; in 1949, it was finally standardized by Arthur Murray.

### Tango

The tango first came to America in 1911. It was revised in 1925 and became the first revival dance. It has been restyled several times (now called the American tango), but remains a favorite social dance. In the 1990s, the original Argentine tango had a surge in popularity and it is still possible to see groups that utilize this style.

### Charleston Period: 1923–1928

Ushered in by the new sound of jazz, a huge dance fad accompanying the short haircut, the shorter skirt (revealing women's ankles and calves), and the whole flapper style of the roaring twenties, was the Charleston. Although strenuous and tricky to do, it reappears frequently due to its blend of syncopated beat and action. The Charleston is considered the number-one dance craze of all time.

### The Swing Era: 1930 into the mid-1950s

Swing was spearheaded by the big band music of the 1930s and 1940s. The music was called "swinging" and therefore the dance style was called "swing." In the 1930s, swing dancing was anything you danced to swing music, and several styles of swing developed in different parts of the country, but the first style that hit the dance floors was the Lindy Hop, which first emerged in Harlem in the late 1920s (refer to page 442 for more Lindy Hop history). By 1937, tour buses would stop in Harlem to watch the Lindy Hoppers. In 1939 the Lindy Hop went national.

In 1932 everyone was Shagging, a dance originally from North Carolina. There were single-, double-, and triple-time Shag steps, depending on how many hops you did. In 1936, the Big Apple appeared, and by the fall of 1937 it was a national dance craze. The Lambeth Walk, originally created for the musical, *Me and My Girl*, became popular in 1938. Single-, double-, and triple-time rhythms all enjoyed popularity.

### The Latin Dance Craze

A Cuban song, "The Peanut Vendor," came to America in 1930 with the rumba following it. In 1938 the second Latin dance arrived in America: the conga. The conga was originally a partner dance that had the same rhythm as the modern conga line dance. In 1950, the Mambo stirred up the dancing population, but was replaced by the cha cha around 1954. The bossa nova arrived in 1962. The salsa (Spanish for "sauce") was first done in the 1970s and in the late 1990s became very popular, with salsa dance venues appearing all over the country. In the spring of 2003, the first Salsa Dance Congress took place in Los Angeles, with participation by salsa dancers from all over the world.

### Rock and Roll

Rock and roll was first popularized in the mid-1950s with the song "Shake, Rattle and Roll" (Bill Haley and the Comets). Rock and roll music had a constant, driving beat that a dancer could pick up anytime. This was a noticeable departure from the 1940s, when the style and steps were in response to the melody and phrasing of the songs. Rock and roll dancing had a dropping action in the knees. There was a toe touch and then a step down, sometimes causing the hips to move. Each part of the country created its own style of rock and roll dance. It was not until *American Bandstand* became a national television program that steps became standardized. During the 1950s, while the young people were dancing to rock and roll, dance studios conceived of a swing dance style that was smooth and slow, created for the adult population. Most moves had the man staying in the middle with minimal movement, as the women passed back and forth in a slot. Marketed as sophisticated swing, this was the beginning of today's West Coast Swing.

### The Twist

In 1960, the Twist hit dance floors across the country. People didn't hold their partners, but stood close to them and moved in various free-style forms. The Twist was the second biggest dance craze in America.

Not only were teens dancing, but adults also danced the Twist. After the Twist, a series of dances came and went, including the Slop, the Mashed Potato, the Swim, the Monkey, the Pony, the Frug, the Hitchhiker, the Watusi, the Hully Gully, and the Jerk.

### Disco

In 1975, Van McCoy's song "The Hustle" became popular. Van McCoy wrote the song after hearing of a dance, the Bus Stop. Soon, most people referred to this dance as the Hustle. When the movie *Saturday Night Fever* was released, partner dancing became popular again. Disco—hustle partner dancing—was based on swing dancing.

### The 1980s and 1990s

Social dancing in the 1980s was characterized by a series of eclectic styles. Slam dancing, done mostly in clubs, and break dancing, performed on street corners, appeared early in the 1980s. Country western line dancing became mainstream with the popularity of the movie *Urban Cowboy* and the pop songs *Elvira* and *Swinging.* With M. C. Hammer's music, rap and hip-hop dance evolved. The 1990s started out with Madonna's song "Vogue," and the dance style Vogueing, and country western dancing was still going strong. In the mid-1990s, ballroom dancing started to become popular again.

### Swing Revival

In the mid-1990s, many new bands started to take on the style of music from the 1940s: swing music. With wonderful new live bands to dance to, swing dancing started making a big comeback. Older buildings with ballrooms that had been closed down for 40 years were reopened and renovated. In Portland, Oregon, the Crystal Ballroom had 600 people dancing swing every Sunday evening for several years. Frankie Manning, the grandfather of swing and Lindy Hop, was back, in his 80s, teaching around the world. After the 1998 Gap Khakis Swing commercial, swing dancing was back in full force. Swing dancers even performed alongside Big Bad Voodoo Daddy for half-time entertainment at the Super Bowl in 1999. Swing dancing is still very strong today, with younger people embracing the full experience by wearing retro clothing from the 1940s.

Social dance is part of an American heritage, to be borrowed, shared, and recreated. Each generation will continue to find its own way of relating to music and life through dance.

## Forms of Social Dancing

The term "social dance" covers a broad spectrum of dance forms generally executed with a partner. There are the formal ballroom dance forms, of which the most common are waltz, tango, Foxtrot, and Cha Cha. Today, there are also many other dance forms that are not always—but sometimes—included in the formal ballroom dance process. Salsa, Lindy Hop, and West Coast Swing are some examples. Ballroom dancing has two main forms, each overlapping. The main difference is the teaching approach or how the steps have been learned or passed on. People who learned in a strictly social environment might have learned from their parents, or at school, with no formal training. People who attend a ballroom studio to learn are introduced to steps by level. All the steps have been standardized across the world.

### Levels

There are three main levels of dance steps in formal ballroom dance training: bronze (beginning), silver (intermediate), and gold (advanced). Students can compete with other similarly skilled dancers at each of the three levels. Bronze dance steps provide a firm foundation in the basics. In the Foxtrot and waltz, bronze steps tend to finish with the feet together, whereas silver steps are more progressive, constantly traveling in a line of direction.

### Competition

Competition has long been a part of the history of ballroom dancing. In England an open Foxtrot competition was held in 1920. The most internationally renowned competition is the Blackpool Dance Festival in Britain. This started in 1930. The American equivalent to Blackpool is the Ohio Star Ball, which first started in 1977. Billed as "Championship Ballroom Dance," the Ohio Star Ball has been televised by the Public Broadcasting System since 1987. In the United States, ballroom dance competitions include two major divisions: American Rhythm and American Smooth. In the Rhythm division, competitors dance the Cha Cha, Rumba, East Coast Swing, Bolero, and Mambo. In the Smooth division, the dances are Waltz, Tango, Foxtrot, and Viennese Waltz. Internationally, the divisions are International Latin and International Standard, and the dances differ somewhat. The International Latin dances are the Cha Cha, Rumba, Samba, Jive, and Paso Doble. The International Standard dances are Waltz, Quickstep, Tango, Foxtrot, and Viennese Waltz.

World and national competitions make the ballroom scene one of beauty, skill, and exciting action enjoyed by dancers and spectators alike. In the past ten years, competitions for West Coast Swing, Lindy Hop, and Salsa have also emerged.

### Dancesport

*Dancesport* is the term given to ballroom dance competition held in the Olympics. It combines the theatrical performance elements of the activity with the aura of a sport. Like swimming, wind surfing, and ice skating, dancesport is an extension of a widely popular recreational activity.

The International Olympic Committee (IOC) provisionally recognized dancesport in June 1995 and gave it full Olympic status in 1998. The International Dance Sports Federation (IDSF) is a nonprofit, nonpolitical organization, founded in 1957, that controls 95 percent of all international competitions, including granting of events governed by IDSF rules. The International Body of Dance Teachers and Promoters controls the remaining group of fully professional dancers.

The worldwide flavor and involvement in IDSF is demonstrated by the fact that between general meetings the affairs are conducted by a presidium composed of members from Germany, Australia, England, Denmark, Japan, Switzerland, Scotland, Russia, and the United States. The formation of the IDSF has greatly increased the interest in dancesport throughout the world. Membership at present consists of 64 countries from five continents. The World Rock 'n' Roll Confederation (WRRC) is an associate member representing some 30 countries.

The five dances used in dancesport competition are: the Modern Waltz, Tango, Viennese Waltz, Slow Foxtrot, and Quickstep. All dances are performed by a couple using the closed hold position. Figures have been standardized and categorized into various levels for teaching. Vocabularies, techniques, rhythms, and tempos have been internationally agreed upon to make instruction uniform.

#### College and University Dance

Public awareness of ballroom dance has come about through the influence of a number of factors. Ice dancing uses ballroom dance forms, as does the skating in Ice Capades. Television, of course, has played an enormous role. Observances such as Ballroom Dance, sponsored by the New York Mayor's Office, and a move by Alabama dancers to have their senator help establish a National Ballroom Dance Week help build enthusiasm. College and university campuses have shown renewed interest in ballroom dance. Brigham Young University sports the largest ballroom dance program in the country, along with a touring performance group that travels and performs internationally. Other active centers are Wisconsin, Texas, University of California at Berkeley, and New York University. Several have very active dance teams. The attraction of ballroom dance seems to be that it allows a certain intimacy that produces a sense of pride, resulting in greater self-assurance for participants.

The reemergence of "touch dancing," or ballroom forms of the early 1900s, seems refreshing and widely welcomed. The likelihood, however, of its comeback matching its earlier popularity depends upon two circumstances: composers writing music for this type of dance and space to accommodate large groups of dancers. In earlier times there were major ballrooms, such as Roseland and the Rainbow Room in New York, especially designed for large crowds. At present there are no great moves by composers or promoters to support the renewed interest in these earlier dance forms.

## Teaching Social Dance

Dealing effectively with variables such as class size, available space, length of unit, and materials to be taught is of prime importance to both the teaching and learning processes. The following teaching techniques should be used carefully in relation to these variables.

### Trends in Vocabulary and Leading

The closed dance position is presently being referred to as the *frame*. The term conjures a body position of substance, firmness, or presence as opposed to "limp" or "just there." In addition, the terms "man and lady" or "man and woman" are being replaced by "lead" and "follow." In some cases, the traditional "women follow–men lead" notion is being reversed. The reversal is used to stimulate sensitivity to a partner's responsibilities. Switching roles, albeit temporarily, should improve a dancer's ability to lead or to follow.

### Formations

Beginning steps are often quickly and easily understood if the class is in line formation, all facing the same direction. This formation allows everyone to hear and see the demonstrated move. Partners should be side by side or opposite each other so they can quickly get together when needed. The teacher's position is in front of the line, facing the group when talking, and facing away from the group when demonstrating; see figure (a) on the next page. When the class is fortunate enough to have two teachers, a favorite formation is to have the leads standing in a line opposite their partners with the two teachers in between; see figure (b) on the next page

(a) Single lines facing one direction:

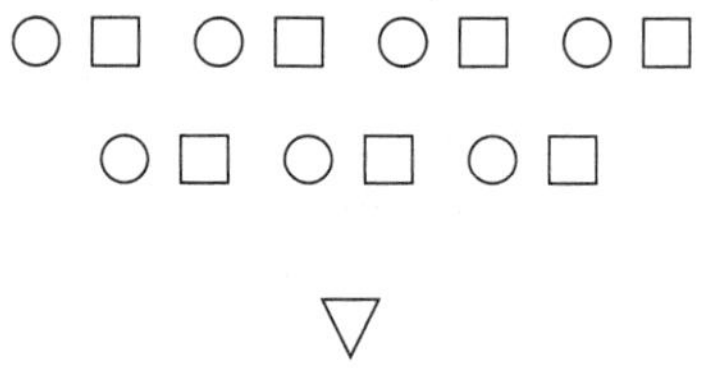

(b) Parallel lines with partners facing each other:

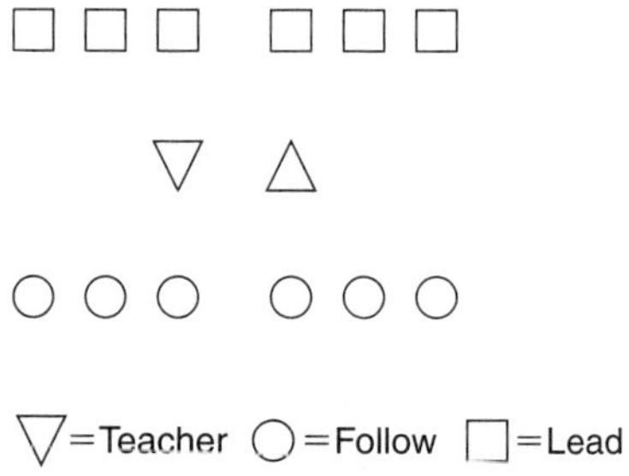


## Walk-Through

The teacher should be clearly seen and heard while demonstrating and analyzing the action of a step. On cue, the class should then follow through several times. The walk-through tempo should begin slowly and gradually increase until it is up to the tempo of the music to be used. The step should be tried first to music without a partner, then with a partner and music. A time free of instructional direction should be provided after the walk-through. During this time the teacher should circulate among the dancers giving individual assistance as needed.

## The Cue

The whole principle of unison practice to develop rhythmic awareness is contingent upon the accuracy of a system of cueing. A signal, such as "ready and," serves to start the dancers in unison. It is important that the cues be given rhythmically! This helps the student to feel the timing. A variety of cues are used to help the student remember the foot pattern and rhythm. For example:

| 4/4 | 1–2 | 3 | 4 |
|---|---|---|---|
| Rhythm cue: | slow | quick | quick |
| Step cue: | step | side | close |
| Direction cue: | turn | side | close |
| Style cue: | down | up | up |
| Warning cue: | "get ready for the break" | | |
| Foot cue: | right | left | right |

A good technique is to change from one cue to the other as needed. Cueing is a help, not a crutch, and should be abandoned as soon as the students appear to be secure in their execution. Cueing at any stage in the learning process is best when done over a sound system that amplifies the voice. Refer to Chapter 2, page 21 for more information on cueing.

## Demonstration

The advantages of demonstration are: (1) it hastens learning when students see what is to be learned; (2) it facilitates learning the style and flow of dance movement; and (3) teaching requires less talking, so that more practice is available. Demonstration is most helpful at the following times:

1. At the beginning of the lesson with partner and music to give a whole picture of the pattern. This is also a good motivational device.
2. When presenting a new step. Demonstrate the lead and follow parts separately, then the lead's as students take partners.
3. To teach style, lead and follow relationships, and timing.
4. Occasionally to demonstrate incorrect form followed by correct form.
5. To demonstrate for clarification.

## Unison versus Free Practice

The walk-through for a new step should be done in unison responding to teaching cues. The whole motion of the group assists in the learning process and allows the teacher the opportunity to spot problems. Teacher-directed unison practice should be abandoned as soon as a majority have learned the step. Free practice transposes the class into a "natural" situation, more akin to the way it is to be done as a leisure pursuit.

At every level of progress in the teaching and learning process, the student should be made aware of the importance of rhythm and the use of space when moving around the dance floor. Understanding rhythm means that the lead can more creatively combine and lead a variety of dance patterns to any given piece of music. Understanding space means that the lead can lead his partner around the dance floor in the traditional line of direction and at the same time employ steps and dance positions that allow him to steer his partner through and around other dancers without interrupting his or their movements.

## Dance Lesson Preparation

Teacher preparation should begin with selecting the basic step to be taught. Next analyze the underlying rhythm and know where the accent is placed in the music. Study the style of the movement used in the step and practice with the music so that it can be accurately demonstrated. If there is only one teacher, the teacher will need to know both the lead's and the follow's parts and be able to demonstrate them with a student from time to time. Two teachers demonstrating is a more ideal situation, but one well-prepared teacher can lead a good student after a class walk-through usually without out-of-class practice. In addition, the teacher should carefully analyze the position, leads, style, and teaching cues for both the lead's and follow's parts and develop routines for practicing the step forward, backward, or in place.

See Chapter 2 pages 13–16 for lesson plan and pages 19–20 for teaching progression.

# Style In Social Dance

Social-style ballroom dancing does not follow the rules of competition or dancesport. American ballroom dancing has borrowed steps and dances from many, many countries. Few of these are now done in the authentic style of any country. In most cases, it was the rhythmic quality that was fascinating and not its meaning. Therefore, only a semblance of the original style remains in the Latin American dances done on U.S. dance floors.

Particular consideration needs to be given to the importance of the individual as a person and the development of one's own style. Because all individuals are different, it is folly to try to get them all to perform exactly alike. The individual who likes to dance will work for the right feeling and take pride in the way it looks. The dance will gradually reflect an easy confidence and become part of the individual's personality.

At the beginning, few students realize the importance of good basic posture and footwork to the beauty and style of any dance. An easy, upright, balanced posture and motion of the feet in line with the body will make the dancer look good regardless of how limited the knowledge of steps. *Style* means the specific way of moving in any one dance as influenced by rhythmic qualities of the music, cultural characteristics of a country, or the current style of the movement. Styles of dances change from time to time with the rising popularity of a new star, a new band sound, or a new promotional venture by the popular dance studios.

## Footwork in Social Dance

*Footwork* is a term used to discuss the manner of using the feet in the performance of dance steps. With the exception of body posture, it has the most significant bearing on form and style. Far too often the placement of the feet and the action of the legs give a distorted appearance to the dance. The beauty, continuity, and balance of a figure may be lost entirely due to any comic and, at the same time, tragic caricature unintentionally given to the motion.

Some general principles are involved in the application of good footwork to good dance style.

1. The weight should be carried on the ball of the foot for easy balance, alert transfer of weight from step to step, and change of direction.
2. The feet should be pointing straight ahead. When moving from one step to another, they should reach straight forward or backward in the direction of the desired action and in line with or parallel to the partner's feet.
3. Any action will start with feet together. When moving, feet should pass as closely as possible. With a few exceptions, the feet should always come together before reaching in a new direction. This is known as a follow-through with the feet, and it is used in the Foxtrot, Waltz, and Tango.
4. The feet are never dragged along the floor from one step to another. There is a light connection to the floor as the foot is moved noiselessly into the next position. Occasionally, as in the tango, the foot glides smoothly into place and without a scraping sound on the floor.
5. The legs should reach forward or backward from the hip. The action is initiated by stabilizing the trunk and swinging the leg freely.
6. The faster the rhythm, the shorter the step. The slower the rhythm, the more reaching the step.
7. Changes of direction are more readily in balance and under control if initiated when the feet are close together rather than when they are apart.
8. For the specific actions of reaching with one foot forward or backward, as in a corté or a hesitation step, the arch of the foot should be extended and the toe pointed.
9. Turning and pivoting figures are most effectively executed from a small base of support with the action of the lead's and the follow's feet dovetailing nicely. This is possible when the action of the foot is a smooth turn on the ball of the foot with the body weight up, not pressing into the floor.
10. In accordance with the characteristic cultural style of a dance, the footwork will involve specific and stylized placement of the feet. This styling is described with each dance.

## Dance Walk

All smooth dances used to have a gliding motion with the ball of the foot. However, changes in style dictated a **dance walk** that is much like a regular walk when moving forward. It is a step forward on the heel of the foot, transferring the weight to the ball of the foot. This action is used by both lead and follow when they are moving forward. The backward step is a long reach to the toe, transferring the weight to the ball of the foot.

In closed dance position, the lead is reaching forward and the follow backward, simultaneously. There is a tendency for the lead to step sideways so as not to step on the follow's foot, but he should step forward directly in line with her foot. The follow consequently must reach backward into her step not only to avoid being stepped on but to give the lead room for his step. Master dance teachers have been quoted as saying, "If the follow gets her toe stepped on, it is her own fault." This reemphasizes the point that the dance walk is a long reaching step and both lead and follow must learn to reach out confidently. It is this reach that makes the style smooth and beautiful and provides contrast to other smaller steps. Taking all small steps gives the style a cramped, insecure feeling. The following points describe the mechanics of the forward dance walk.

1. The body sways forward from the ankles. The weight is on the ball of the foot.
2. The trunk is stabilized firmly. The leg swings forward from the hip joint. The reach results in a long step rather than a short, choppy step. An exaggerated knee bend will cause bobbing up and down.
3. The foot swings forward and the heel is placed on the floor first, followed by a transfer of weight to the ball of the foot. The feet never drag along the floor.
4. The legs are kept close together, with the feet passing closely together. The toes are facing straight ahead.
5. The lead and the follow dance on the same forward line. One should avoid letting one's feet straddle the partner's feet.

The backward dance walk is not an easy movement since one feels unstable moving backward. It should be practiced particularly by the follow since she will be moving backward a large part of the time.

1. The body weight is over the ball of the foot. Be careful not to lean forward or backward. The follow is pressing against the lead's hand at her back.
2. The trunk is stabilized firmly. The leg swings backward from the hip joint with a long, smooth reach. Avoid unnecessary knee bend of the standing leg.
3. The foot is placed backward on the toe with weight transferring to the ball of the foot. The weight remains on the ball of the foot, the heel coming down only momentarily during the next step.
4. The legs and feet pass as closely as possible and in a straight line. Avoid toeing out, heeling out, and swinging backward outside of the straight line.

# Dance Positions

Successful performance with a dance partner depends on learning how to assume the dance positions most often used in social dance: **closed position, semi-open position, left parallel position, right parallel (outside) position, swing out, cuddle,** and **side-by-side position.**[1] The closed position is the basic dance position; the others are adaptations of it. Dancers should learn how to assume the closed position as soon as they begin working with a partner. The results will lead to good balance, comfort, and confidence in leading and security in following.

## Closed Position

Each factor in the analysis of the closed position is significant. It is not a mere formality. Those who are learning dance will tend to form better dance habits if they understand specifically how the position aids the dance rather than being left to manage as best they can.

1. *Partners should stand facing each other, slightly offset to their left, with shoulders parallel.* The right foot of each partner should be placed between the partner's feet, near the front of the foot. When bending knees they should not knock together. A comfortable distance should be maintained. The body posture is in good alignment.
2. *The feet should be together and pointing straight ahead.* The weight is over the balls of the feet.
3. *The lead's right arm* is placed around the follow so that his arm *gives her security and support. The right hand is placed in the center of the follow's back, just below the shoulder blades.* The lead should keep his right elbow lifted to help support the follow's left arm.

1. Refer to the Glossary for descriptions of other positions. Illustrations of the various dance positions can be found on pages 49–53.

The fingers should be closed and the hand almost flat so that the lead can lead with the fingers or the heel of the hand. The lead's arm is extended away from his body with the elbow pointing slightly out to the right side. The lead's left hand should be no higher than the shortest person's shoulder level. A majority of leads are initiated by the lead's shoulders, right arm, and hand.

4. *The follow's left arm rests gently but definitely in contact with the lead's upper arm* and the hand should lie along the back of the lead's shoulder as is comfortable. The follow's ability to follow is often determined by her response to the action of the lead's arm.
5. *The follow should arch her back against the lead's right hand and move with it.* All pressure leads for change of step will come from the lead's right hand, and she will feel them instantly.
6. *The follow's free hand is raised sideways and the lead holds the follow's right hand in his left hand approximately between them at a level just above the follow's shoulder.* The lead may let her fingers rest on his upturned palm, or he may grasp lightly with his thumb against her fingers and close his fingers around the back of her hand. He should not push with his hand.
7. *Both the lead and follow should look at each other or over the partner's right shoulder.*
8. *Tone is essential.* A limp body or a limp hand is the surest indication of insecurity; a poor lead elicits a slow response. Dancers need to understand the difference between tension, which does not allow for easy moving along with one's partner, and relaxation, which cannot respond readily to change. An in-between state of body alertness, called *resistance,* is more desirable.

Some *common errors* in the use of closed position are the following:

1. Partner standing at an angle in a half-open position. This causes diagonal motion of the footwork and is uncomfortable.
2. Partner too far away.
3. Lack of support in the lead's right arm.
4. Lack of contact of the follow's left arm.
5. Primary use of lead's left hand to lead by a pushing or pumping action.
6. Lack of resistance by either lead or follow.
7. Lead's right hand too high on follow's back, pulling her off balance.
8. Follow's weight back on heels.
9. Lead leaning forward from the waist and thus off balance.
10. Lead pulling back with his left shoulder and hand, causing an awkward angle of motion.
11. Follow leaning heavily on partner's arm.

## Techniques of Leading and Following

Leading is done primarily by the use of the body, arms, and hands. The lead sets the rhythm, decides what steps are to be used, and controls the direction and progression around the floor. The follow is completely dependent upon her partner. Therefore, an alert yet easy posture should be assumed to allow dancers to move as a unit. The firmness of the lead's hand on the follow's back is an important pressure lead for changes in dance position and direction. Through the use of gentle yet firm leads, the lead can make dancing a mutually pleasant experience.

The follow's responsibility is to follow her partner and adapt to any rhythm or style. She should maintain an easy resistance to give the lead an alert, movable partner to lead. The follow should always maintain contact with her partner's upper right arm and shoulder and give firm resistance to his hand on her back. Should the lead be a poor leader, the follow must then pay close attention to his body movement, particularly the shoulders and chest, in order to follow. When in a position apart from a partner, following requires a firm controlled arm that responds to a lead by simultaneous action of the body. In the challenge position, the follow's only lead is visual. She must be alert and follow her partner's action by watching him. The general rules for following are listed on page 420–421.

### Specific Directions for Leading

1. *To lead the first step,* the lead should precede the step off with the left foot by an upbeat, forward motion of the body.
2. *To lead a forward-moving pattern,* the lead should give a forward motion in the body, including the right arm, which will direct the follow firmly in the desired direction.
3. *To lead a backward-moving pattern,* the lead should use pressure of the right hand. This will draw the follow forward in the desired direction.
4. *To lead a sideward-moving pattern in closed position,* the lead should use pressure of the right hand to the left or right to indicate the desired direction.
5. *To lead a box step,* the lead should use a forward body action followed by right-hand pressure and right-elbow pull to the right to take the follow into the forward sequence of the box. Forward pressure of the right hand followed by

pressure to the left side takes her into the back sequence of the box.

6. *To lead a box turn,* with slight pressure of the right hand, the lead should use the right arm and shoulder to guide or bank her into the turn. The shoulders press forward during the forward step and draw backward during the backward step.
7. *To lead into an open position,* or conversation position, the lead should use pressure with the heel of the hand to turn the follow into open position. The right elbow lowers to the side. The lead must simultaneously turn his own body, not just the follow, so that they end facing the same direction. The left arm relaxes slightly and the left hand sometimes gives the lead for steps in open position.
8. *To lead from open to closed position,* the lead should use pressure of the right hand and raise the right arm up to standard position to move the follow into closed position. She should not have to be pushed, but should swing easily into closed position as she feels the arm lifting. She should come clear around to face the lead squarely.
9. *To lead into right parallel position* (left reverse open position), the lead should not use pressure of his right hand, but rather should raise his right arm, rotating her counterclockwise one-eighth of a turn while he rotates counterclockwise one-eighth of a turn. This places the lead and the follow off to the side of each other, facing opposite directions. The follow is to the right of him but slightly in front of him. The lead should avoid turning too far so as to be side by side, as this results in poor style and awkward and uncomfortable motion. The lead's left hand may assist in the lead by pulling toward his left shoulder.
10. *To lead from right parallel position to left parallel position,* the lead should pull with his right hand, lowering the right arm, and push slightly with his left hand, causing a rotation clockwise about a quarter-turn until the follow is to the left of him but slightly in front of him. They are not side by side.
11. *To lead a hesitation step,* the lead should use pressure of the right hand on the first step and sudden body tension to control a hold of position as long as desired.
12. *To lead all turns,* the lead dips his shoulder in the direction of the turn, and his upper torso turns before his leg and foot turn.
13. *To lead into a pivot turn,* clockwise, the lead should hold the follow slightly closer, but with sudden body tension. Resistance is exerted outward by both the lead and follow leaning away from each other in order to take advantage of the centrifugal force of the circular motion. The right foot steps between partner's feet, forward on the line of direction, while the left foot reaches across the line of direction and turns on the ball of the foot about three-quarters of the way around.
14. *To lead into a corté* (dip) the lead should use firm pressure of the right hand with sudden increased body tension going into the preparation step. Then the lead should draw his partner forward toward him as he steps back into the dip. The left foot taking the dip backward should carry the weight, and careful balance of the weight should remain over that foot. Pressure is released as they recover to the other foot.
15. *Finger pressure leads and arm control* are important. Many times the lead's only contact with his partner is with one hand or changing from hand to hand. A soft, gentle handhold and a limp arm make it impossible to lead the variations of swing, cha cha cha, or rumba. It is necessary that the follow exert slight resistance to the lead's grasp so that pressure in any direction is reacted to instantly. Both the lead and follow should maintain elbow control by holding the arm firmly in front of the body with elbows down and always slightly bent. The arm is seldom allowed to extend in the elbow as this destroys the spring action needed to move out and in and under without jerking. The fingers often need to slip around the partner's without actually losing contact, in order to maintain comfortable action of the wrist and arm.
16. *To change the rhythm pattern,* the lead exerts extra pressure with the right hand and pushes a little harder from the chest.
17. *Visual lead.* When partners are apart, as in the shine position of cha cha cha, the follow watches her partner closely.

## Following

The follow's responsibility in dancing is to follow her partner and adapt to any rhythm or style he dances. She should maintain an easy resistance, not rigidity or tension, throughout the body. This is referred to as having *tone.* If there is no tone and the follow is too relaxed or stiff, leading becomes very difficult. The lead's ability to lead his partner will be enhanced when she has tone. In other words, it takes cooperation for two people to dance well, the same way it takes two people for a satisfactory handshake. The follow should always maintain contact with her partner's upper right arm and shoulder and give resistance against his hand at her back, moving with it as it guides her. If the lead is a poor leader, then the follow must pay close attention to his body movement, particularly his chest and shoulder movement, in order to follow. Following, when in an apart position, requires a firm, controlled arm that responds to a lead by simultaneous action of the body. A limp arm with no resultant body response makes leading difficult in swing, rumba, and Cha Cha. In the challenge position, the follow's only lead is visual. She must be alert and follow her partner's action by watching him. The good dancer will aim to dance with beauty of form. The follow can make a poor dancer look good or a good dancer look excellent. She can also cramp his style if she takes too small a step, has poor control of balance, dances with her feet apart, dances at an awkward angle, or leans forward.

### General Rules for Following

1. Keep the lead's rhythm.
2. Be alert to partner's lead.
3. Support one's own weight. Arch the back and move with the partner's hand.
4. Step straight backward with reaching motion so as to give the partner room to step straight ahead.
5. Pass the feet close together.
6. Know the basic steps and basic leads.
7. Try not to anticipate partner's action, just move with it.
8. Give careful thought to proper body alignment and good posture.

# SWING (JITTERBUG)

*Swing* IS AN UMBRELLA TERM for a wide variety of dances, such as West Coast Swing, East Coast Swing, Jive, Jitterbug, Shag, and Lindy Hop. With the advent of Dixieland jazz during the roaring twenties, a variety of dances appeared, including the Lindbergh Hop. Cab Calloway is credited with referring to the Lindy Hoppers as "jitterbuggers." The dance went through a fad period of being extremely eccentric, with its wild acrobatics inspired by the rising popularity of boogie woogie. The Big Apple, the Shag, and the swing were all products of that period. They changed after World War II to a more syncopated rhythm called rock and roll with the double-time swing pattern and to the swing with the smooth, sophisticated triple rhythm, which came in to vogue a short time later. All during the rock and roll period, both double- and triple-time swing could be seen on *American Bandstand.* A softer sound called boogie, but no relation to boogie woogie, has greater synthesization of electronic equipment.

Swing is danced to a wide variety of music and reflects the dance style of the particular music—big band music of the 1940s, rock and roll, rhythm and blues, salsa, reggae, country western, and Cajun—all written in 4/4 or cut time. Swing includes the rhythm of the Lindy Hop, single time, double time, and triple time. Some refer to these as the Jitterbug. The term *swing* is also applied to a myriad of figures as the couple covers a *circular space* in one area. There is wide variation in the footwork and figures in each style of swing. West Coast Swing is a more difficult and sophisticated dance. It is referred to as a **slot dance** because the couple moves back and forth in a narrow space, always the same space. The dance evolved in the 1950s. We will continue to use the term *swing* for single-, double-, and triple-time swing and circular space for swing dance.

Circular Space for Swing Dance

## *Swing* RHYTHM

Swing is written in 4/4 or cut time. It is extremely adaptable to fast or slow rhythm, or to 4/4 time from Foxtrot to hard rock. The Shag was actually the first dance to be called jitterbug, and its slow, slow, quick, quick rhythm set the pattern for all of the others. The single-time swing has the same rhythm.

| 4/4 | | | | | | | | |
|---|---|---|---|---|---|---|---|---|
| | / | | | | / | | | |
| | step | | step | | rock | step | | |
| | S | | S | | Q | Q | | |
| | 1 | 2 | 3 | 4 | 1 | 2 | | |

uneven rhythm

**Single Time**

Double time is very adaptable to slow or fast music. This style was very popular in the 1950s. Accent is on the offbeat.

| 4/4 | | | | | | | | |
|---|---|---|---|---|---|---|---|---|
| | | / | | / | | / | | |
| | dig | step | dig | step | rock | step | | |
| | Q | Q | Q | Q | Q | Q | | |
| | 1 | 2 | 3 | 4 | 1 | 2 | | |

even rhythm

**Double Time**

Triple time is more often danced to the slow, blues-style, sophisticated tempos.

| 4/4 | | | | | | | | | | |
|---|---|---|---|---|---|---|---|---|---|---|
| | / | | | / | | | / | | | |
| | step | close | step | step | close | step | rock | step | | |
| | Q | Q | S | Q | Q | S | S | S | | |
| | 1 | and | 2 | 3 | and | 4 | 1 | 2 | | |
| | | triple | | | triple | | | | | |

uneven rhythm

**Triple Time**

## Swing STYLE

Exciting styles and positions are used in swing. It is a matter of taste for the individual dancers whether they use a dig step, a step-hop, or a kick step. However, the basic rhythm must be maintained by both lead and follow to coordinate the pattern together, unlike discotheque (dancing apart), in which the step or rhythm pattern of each partner is unstructured. The lead is able to lead the dance because of the magnificent body alertness of both partners. A firm body and tone in the arms and fingers enable quick response in any direction. The space between partners is controlled by a spring tension in the elbow, which never extends fully but allows the pull away and the spring back to occur smoothly and with control. The follow uses her arm as a pivot center. The elbow is down and the hand is up for the underarm turns, and she turns around her arm but does not let it fly in the air. There should never be the appearance of arms flying loose or entangled. The fingers slip easily around one another without losing contact. Even the free arm is bent and remains close to the body.

Swing steps tend to cover a circular space in one area of the floor. The footwork is at all times small and close together, with rolling and turning on the ball of the foot. The turning action for beginner steps is always on the first step of the pattern when the follow is on her right foot and the lead is on his left. The rhythm pattern is generally the same over and over, but the changes of position and direction and the constant subtle smooth roll to offbeat rhythm generates a fabulous excitement for both dancer and observer.

# Single-Time Swing

Directions are for the lead; the follow's part is reversed, except when noted.

### Side-to-Side Basic

**Position:** Two hands joined
**Level:** Beginning 1

| STEPS | 4/4 COUNTS | RHYTHM CUE | STEP CUE |
|---|---|---|---|
| Step left in place | 1 | slow | left |
| Step right in place | 2 | slow | right |
| Step left backward, a little behind right heel, using ball of left foot | 3 | quick | rock |
| Step right in place | *and* | quick | step |

**Step Cue:** Left, right, rock step or side, in place, rock step.

**Partner Connection:** The dancers take two hands joined at approximately waist height, the lead's hands palm up. The elbow is down. The arms have tone in them and should not be limp. Fingers are together in a shape. Slightly angle fingers in partner's hands, so they do not dig into their palms. Exert a gentle pull against partner's fingers without squeezing! Lead's thumbs rest lightly on the follow's knuckles.

**Style:** The body takes a *slight* motion, leaning to the side from the waist and dipping the outside shoulder (lead's left, follow's right) on the first step. Take care not to exaggerate this motion. It is very subtle. The first step is a small step, approximately 12", or shoulder distance apart. Return to normal posture on the second step. Do not take the full body weight back on the rock step. On the rock step there is a spring tension in the arms that allows an apart-together action that is smooth and has arm control. The weight is carried on the balls of the feet and the steps are small throughout. There is a small amount of knee bend, depending on individual preference and style; however, the action should be smooth and not bouncy.

**Note:** Beginners should practice the foot pattern alone until they can move accurately with the rhythm. Then dancers take two hands and practice the footwork together.

**Lead:** The lead lowers his left arm down (a reverse curl action), while slightly dipping his left shoulder on the first side step. On the second step, the lead returns his arms to the starting position in preparation for the rock step. Arm cue: drop, recover, rock step.

The basic step is usually used to start dancing together and establish a connection with your partner. Once the connection is established, the lead begins to incorporate different variations, or steps. The following is a short list of swing dance steps.

## Single-Time Swing Variations

The lead's hands must be able to rotate easily in the follow's hands during any variation.

Arch and Trade
Inside Turn (Underarm Turn)
Walk Through (Brush Off)
Tuck Spin
Wrap (Cuddle)
Octopus
Hammerlock
Turning Basic (Collegiate)
Two Hands to Social Swing
Basic in Social Swing
Arch Out from Semi-Open

8

### Arch and Trade

**Position:** Two hands joined
**Level:** Beginning 2

The lead lifts his left arm up (forming the "arch"); the follow goes under the arch, trading places.

| STEPS | STEP CUE |
|---|---|
| Lead steps left forward while raising left arm up and slightly left<br>Follow steps right forward | forward |
| Lead step right, turning one-quarter counterclockwise<br>Follow, pivoting on right 180° clockwise, while turning under lead's arm, steps back left | side |
| Lead pivots one-quarter counterclockwise and rock steps<br>Follow rock steps | rock step |
| Finish move with an inside turn (see below) | |

**Step Cue:** Lift (lead's left arm), follow turn, rock step.

**Style:** Follow keeps right forearm at a right angle and right elbow at shoulder level. The follow turns around her own arm, not under it. Both take small steps, insuring that their arms have a slight bend in them for the rock step.

**Lead:** As the lead lifts his arm up, he gives a gentle pull back, guiding the follow under his arm. The lead's left arm is up and slightly left of them, allowing the follow a clear path to go under his arm.

**Note:** The lead lifts his arm up high enough so that the follow does not need to duck to go under, but the lead only lifts his arm as high as the follow's head. Lifting the arm too high above the follow will tend to pull her arm above a comfortable level.

### Inside Turn (Underarm Turn)

**Position:** Swing out
**Level:** Beginning 2

The lead and follow exchange places as the lead turns the follow counterclockwise across to his position and steps around to the follow's position.

| STEPS | STEP CUE |
|---|---|
| Lead steps left forward turning one-quarter clockwise, while raising left hand toward right shoulder, going over the follow's head | forward |
| Follow steps right forward turning one-quarter counterclockwise, moving under the lead's arm | |
| Lead continues to turn one-quarter clockwise, then steps back right, lowering left hand | behind |
| Follow continues turning counterclockwise and steps back left | |
| Both rock step. To perform a basic next, join both hands, or to repeat, stay in Swing out position | rock step |

**Step Cue:** Lift (lead's left arm), follow turns, rock step.

**Style:** Both turn halfway around on the first step, staying close together. They have exactly exchanged places after one complete pattern.

**Lead:** The lead turns his hand knuckles up, fingers down, so that the follow's fingers can slip around the lead's fingers.

8

**Note:** This underarm turn can be repeated over and over. It may serve as a connecting step to any other variation or can be used to return to the basic after ending in swing out position.

### Walk Through (Brush Off)

**Position:** Swing out, or if starting from two hands joined, the lead must release his right hand.
**Level:** Beginning 2

The lead and follow exchange places as the lead does a left turn while seemingly moving through his partner's arm.

| STEPS | STEP CUE |
|---|---|
| Lead steps diagonally left forward on left foot while turning one-quarter counterclockwise | diagonal |
| The lead's left hand pulls down toward his right hip, guiding the follow behind him | |
| Follow steps forward right | |
| Lead steps side on right foot, releasing his left hand on right side and moving his left hand to left side, (palm facing back) to reconnect with follow's right hand<br>Follow pivots one-quarter clockwise and steps side with left foot, lightly sliding right hand along partner's waist to reconnect with lead's left hand | side |
| Lead pivots on right foot one-quarter counterclockwise to face partner and rock step<br>Follow pivots on left foot one-quarter clockwise to face partner and rock step | rock step |
| Finish move with inside turn, page 424 | |

**Step Cue:** Lead turns, reconnect, rock step.

**Style:** As the lead turns, his free right hand must reach over his left arm.

**Lead:** The lead must turn his body sharply one-quarter counterclockwise, providing the follow a space to move through. If this turn is not done, the follow will bump into the lead's shoulder.

**Note:** At the end of this move, the lead's left hand will be palm down (opposite of normal). Do not try to flip the hand. While performing the inside turn, the hands will automatically rotate to the normal position.

### Tuck Spin

**Position:** Two hands joined
**Level:** Beginning 2

| STEPS | STEP CUE |
|---|---|
| Lead steps in place while moving both of the follow's hands to lead's right side (follow turns slightly to her left) | left |
| Lead steps right in place, pushing the follow in the opposite direction (releasing hands) with a quick flick, spinning the follow clockwise<br>Follow does a full turn clockwise, spinning on both feet | right |
| Rejoin hands for the rock step | rock step |

**Step Cue:** Tuck, spin, rock step.

**Style:** The follow must spin smoothly a full turn in place, standing tall, not losing her balance. Sliding the left foot to the right will facilitate spinning on both feet.

**Lead:** The lead must give a firm, quick lead, allowing the follow to respond with the proper timing.

**Note:** The lead may also spin at the same time, moving counterclockwise.

### Wrap (Cuddle)

**Position:** Two hands joined
**Level:** Beginning 2

| STEPS | STEP CUE |
|---|---|
| **Part I** | |
| Lead steps forward on left foot while lifting left arm, preparing to turn follow counterclockwise<br>Follow steps right foot forward and diagonally across left foot | left |
| Lead steps right in place while moving left hand in a counterclockwise circle in front of partner's face and continuing around his head<br>Follow pivots on right foot 180° counterclockwise and steps back on left foot, finishing with follow on lead's right side; hands are at the follow's waist level | right |
| Both rock step | rock step |
| **Part II** | |
| Lead steps forward on left foot while lifting left arm; a roll out is initiated with a gentle right forearm push on the follow's back<br>Follow steps forward on right foot | forward |
| Lead steps back (in place) on right foot<br>Follow pivots 180° clockwise on right foot, stepping back on left foot | back |
| Both rock step | rock step |
| The lead's left hand is slightly rotated after the follow rolls out; finishing this move with an inside turn, page 424, put the lead's hand in the upright position | |

**Step Cue:** Lift (lead's left arm), cuddle in, rock step, cuddle out, rock step.

**Style:** A smooth, continuous roll in (cuddle in) is important.

**Lead:** The lead must lift his left hand and circle (wrap) it around the follow's head. It is important to let the hands (lead's left, follow's right) rotate easily while performing this move.

**Note:** Once a couple is in the cuddle position, it is an option to stay there for a few extra beats. Foot work for both lead and follow is forward, in place (back), rock step. Another variation on the cuddle out (unwrap) is for the lead to release with his left hand and pull gently with his right hand, rolling the follow out to the lead's right side.

### Octopus

**Position:** Two hands joined
**Level:** Intermediate

| STEPS | STEP CUE |
|---|---|
| **Part I** | |
| Lead steps diagonally left forward on left foot<br>Follow steps diagonally left forward on right foot, ending right hip to right hip | diagonal |
| Lead steps in place right while swinging both arms up and over both heads<br>Both partners lower left hand behind their own head and right hand behind partner's head (Octopus position) | place |

| STEPS | STEP CUE |
|---|---|
| Lead releases both hands and slides right hand along follow's right arm, catching right hands. Both partners turn one-eighth right to catch right hand and perform rock step | rock step |
| **Part II** *(turn follow and change hands behind the lead's back)* | |
| Lead raises right elbow and turns follow counterclockwise under right arm while stepping left foot diagonally across right foot<br>Follow pivots 180° counterclockwise on left (turning under lead's arm) and steps back right | across |
| Lead lowers right arm behind his back putting the follow's right hand into the lead's left hand while stepping side right with right foot<br>Follow steps left foot back | side |
| Lead pivots on right foot 90° counterclockwise, moving left hand from behind back to front and faces follow for rock step | rock step |
| Finish move with inside turn, page 424 | |

**Step Cue:** Up and over, rock step.
Follow turns, changes hands, rock steps.

**Lead:** The lead must lift both hands high enough to go over both partners' heads, not just his own.

**Note:** Once the follow has the lead, she must let her arms float up and not pull down on the lead's arms.

## Hammerlock

**Position:** Two hands joined
**Level:** Beginning 3

This is just like the arch and trade, continuing to hold on to both hands. The follow ends up with her left arm folded behind her back in a Hammerlock (wrestling term) position.

| STEPS | STEP CUE |
|---|---|
| Lead steps forward left while raising left arm up and slightly left<br>Lead's right hand moves to his left side, giving a gentle pull, guiding the follow forward<br>Follow steps forward right, going under lead's left arm | forward |
| Lead steps right, turning 180° counterclockwise ending right hip to right hip, lowering left arm down in front of lead's body<br>Follow, pivoting on right 180° clockwise while turning under lead's arm, steps back left | side |
| Both rock step in hammerlock position | rock step |
| Using one full basic, reverse the pattern to return to two hands position | |

**Step Cue:** Lift (lead's left arm), turn (both lead and follow), rock step.

**Lead:** As the lead lifts his arm up, he gives a gentle pull back, guiding the follow under his arm. To reverse the hammerlock, the lead gives a *very gentle* pull with his right hand on the follow's left arm.

**Note:** On the reverse, the lead can spin the follow with his left hand (releasing the right hand) 1½ times back to two hands joined position. The spinning action is lead with the lead's wrist moving in a circular motion (counterclockwise) around the follow's head. The lead drops his arm back to waist height to stop the follow from spinning. The spin is done during the slow, slow, rejoining both hands for the rock step.

### Turning Basic (Collegiate)

**Position:** Two hands joined
**Level:** Beginning 3

During one basic, the couple will rotate 180°. This is an intermediate move.

| STEPS | STEP CUE |
|---|---|
| Lead steps diagonal left forward<br>Follow steps diagonal left forward with right foot, almost ending right hip to right hip | diagonal |
| Lead pivots on left foot 180° clockwise and crosses right foot behind left<br>Follow pivots on right foot 90° clockwise, steps side left | behind |
| Lead faces partner for rock step<br>Follow pivots 90° clockwise on left to face partner for rock step | rock step |

**Step Cue:** Side left, behind right (turn), rock step.

**Style:** This is a smooth, circular motion.

**Lead:** The lead must step strongly to diagonal left and drop left arm (reverse curl down) to give the follow the correct angle to step forward. The timing also must be sharp. If the lead is even a little late in leading this, the follow is already moving to the side.

**Variations:** (1) An optional lead is to reach sideways with each hand shoulder high on the first step and bring the hands back together on the second step. This creates a butterfly turn effect. (2) A second and more advanced option has the lead pivoting to right parallel position (right hip to right hip) on the first slow and to left parallel position (left hip to left hip) on the second slow.

### Two Hands to Social Swing

**Position:** Two hands joined
**Level:** Beginning 2

| STEPS | STEP CUE |
|---|---|
| Lead and follow step toward each other, the lead pulling his left hand downward and placing right hand on follow's back, rib level | forward |
| Both step backward a short step in semi-open position | turn |
| Rock step in same position | rock step |

**Step Cue:** Pull down, come together, rock step.

**Style:** The steps are small.

**Lead:** The lead pulls down on the follow's hand, guiding the follow into semi-open position.

### Basic in Social Swing

**Position:** Social swing
**Level:** Beginning 2

| STEPS | STEP CUE |
|---|---|
| Lead steps left forward | forward |
| Lead steps right backward | back |
| Rock step in place | rock step |

**Step Cue:** Forward, back, rock step.

**Style:** Dancers remain in social swing position throughout. All steps are small. The hand grasp is low with a straight elbow (not hyperextended), held in close to the body. The lead's fingers reach around the little-finger side of the follow's hand.

**Note:** This is a good rest step, or what is commonly used during a *dance jam*.

### Arch Out from Semi-Open

**Position:** Social swing
**Level:** Beginning 2

The lead takes the entire step pattern in place as he turns the follow out under his left arm to face him.

| STEPS | STEP CUE |
|---|---|
| Lead steps left forward, lifting left arm up<br>Follow steps right forward | forward |
| Lead steps in place right, giving the follow a gentle push on her back, turning her under the lead's left arm<br>Follow pivots 180° on right foot (to face partner), stepping back with left foot | back |
| Rock step in place | rock step |

**Step Cue:** Lift, follow under, rock step.

**Style:** Follow keeps right forearm at a right angle and right elbow at shoulder level. The follow turns around her own arm, not under it. Both take small steps, ensuring that their arms have a slight bend in them for the rock step.

**Lead:** As the lead lifts his left arm up, he gives a gentle push with his right hand on the follow's back, guiding the follow under his arm.

**Note:** The lead lifts his arm up high enough so that the follow does not need to duck to go under, but the lead only lifts his arm as high as the follow's head. Lifting the arm too high above the follow will tend to pull her arm above a comfortable level.

**Variation:** Instead of lifting the arm on the first slow, the lead can tuck (see tuck spin, page 425) the follow in on the first slow, then arch and spin the follow under arm on the second slow.

# *Triple Time Swing*

TRIPLE TIME IS LOVELY and pleasant to do to a nice swingy Foxtrot or blues song. It should be smooth and relaxing.

Directions are for the lead; the follow's part is reversed, except when noted.

### Triple Rhythm

**Position:** Social swing
**Level:** Beginning 3

8

| STEPS | 4/4 COUNTS | RHYTHM CUE |
|---|---|---|
| Step left forward | | |
| Close right to left, take weight right | 1 *and* 2 | quick quick slow |
| Step left forward | | |
| Step right backward | | |
| Close left to right, take weight left | 3 *and* 4 | quick quick slow |
| Step right backward | | |

**Step Cue:** Triple step, triple step, rock step.

**Style:** The triple rhythm should be small shuffling steps, keeping the feet close to the floor. Weight is on the ball of the foot. Refer to basic swing style, page 422.

**Lead:** The lead cues the follow for the triple steps by increasing the tension in his right hand as he starts the shuffle step forward.

**Variations:** Any of the variations for single-time swing can be done in triple rhythm.

## Triple-Time Swivel Step

**Position:** Social swing position and traveling in line of direction, forward; rhythm pattern changes

**Level:** Beginning 3

| STEPS | 4/4 COUNTS | RHYTHM CUE |
|---|---|---|
| **Lead's Part** (follow's part is the reverse) | | |
| Step left forward | | |
| Close right to left | 1 *and* 2 | quick quick slow |
| Step left forward | | |
| Step right forward | | |
| Close left to right | 3 *and* 4 | quick quick slow |
| Step right forward | | |
| Pivot on right foot to face partner, and bring left foot alongside of it, shifting weight to left foot | 1 | slow |
| Pivot on left foot to face open position, bring right foot alongside of it, shifting weight to right foot | 2 | slow |
| Repeat pivot on right foot | 3 | slow |
| Repeat pivot on left foot | 4 | slow |
| Step left forward | | |
| Close right to left | 1 *and* 2 | quick quick slow |
| Step left forward | | |
| Step right backward | | |
| Close left to right | 3 *and* 4 | quick quick slow |
| Step right backward | | |
| (turning follow out clockwise in an underarm turn) | | |
| Rock step (in swing out position) | 1, 2 | slow slow |

**Step Cue:** Triple step, triple step
swivel 2 3 4
triple step, triple step, rock step.

**Style:** The swivel steps are tiny, crisp, and neatly turning, just a quarter-turn on each pivot. The body turns with the foot closed, open, closed, open.

**Lead:** The lead must lead the swivel step by turning the follow from open to closed, and so forth.

**Note:** The couple progresses along the line of direction as the pivot turn is being done in four slow steps.

## *Swing* COMBOS

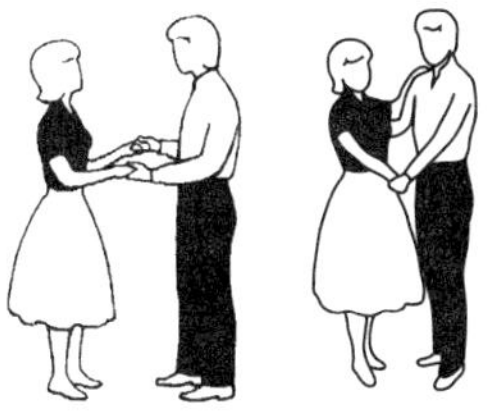

The swing routines are combinations for practice, which are listed from simple to complex. They may be used for either single time or triple time. (Two hands joined or social swing position, unless otherwise indicated.)

1. *Basic Swing Out and Close*
   1 basic
   single underarm break
   break to original position
2. *Basic, Swing Out, Underarm Turn, Close*
   1 basic
   single underarm break
   break to original position
3. *Swing Out, Collegiate*
   2 basics
   single underarm break
   3 collegiate steps
   underarm turn
   original position
4. *Swing Out, Brush Off*
   2 basics
   single underarm break
   brush off
   underarm turn
   original position
5. *Collegiate, Brush Off*
   2 basics
   single underarm break
   underarm turn
   3 collegiate steps
   underarm turn
   brush off
   underarm turn
   original position
6. *Collegiate, Tuck, Spin*
   2 collegiate steps
   tuck spin
   underarm turn
7. *Collegiate, Wrap*
   2 collegiate steps
   wrap
   unwrap
8. *Wrap, Unwrap Spin*
   2 collegiate steps
   wrap
   unwrap
   tuck spin
   underarm turn

# *West Coast Swing*

## *West Coast* SWING RHYTHM

West Coast swing rhythm is 6 or 8 beats. It is usually danced to a slower rhythm than triple time swing (120–130 BPM).

| 4/4 | | | | | anchor step | | | | |
|---|---|---|---|---|---|---|---|---|---|
| | step | step | touch | step | step | step | step | | |
| | S | S | S | S | Q | Q | S | | |
| | 1 | 2 | 3 | 4 | 1 | & | 2 | | |
| | 1 | 2 | 3 | 4 | 5 | & | 6 | | |
| | | | | | triple | | | | |

uneven rhythm—6 count

| 4/4 | | | | | | | | |
|---|---|---|---|---|---|---|---|---|
| | | | | | | anchor step | | |
| | step | step | step step step | | | step step step | | |
| | S | S | Q | Q | S | Q | Q | S |
| | 1 | 2 | 3 | & | 4 | 1 | & | 2 |
| | 1 | 2 | 3 | & | 4 | 5 | & | 6 |
| | double | | triple | | | triple | | |

uneven rhythm—6 count

| 4/4 | | | | | | | | | | | |
|---|---|---|---|---|---|---|---|---|---|---|---|
| | | | | | | | | anchor step | | | |
| | step | step | step step step | | | step | step | step step step | | | |
| | S | S | Q | Q | S | S | S | Q | Q | S | |
| | 1 | 2 | 3 | & | 4 | 1 | 2 | 3 | & | 4 | |
| | 1 | 2 | 3 | & | 4 | 5 | 6 | 7 | & | 8 | |
| | double | | triple | | | double | | triple | | | |

uneven rhythm—8 count

## *West Coast* SWING STYLE

West Coast Swing is referred to as a slot dance because the couple moves back and forth repeatedly in the same narrow space. The dance evolved in the 1950s on the West Coast in small clubs where dance space was limited.

The follow's step is different from the lead's; partners do not mirror each other. The step is like the Cuban walk (page 502). Little kicks and toe touches on the beat give flair for a sophisticated look. The anchor steps (quick, quick, slow) occur at the end of the slot.

### Sugar Push (Basic step variation)

**Position:** Two hands joined
**Level:** Intermediate

| STEPS | COUNTS | STEP CUE |
|---|---|---|
| **Lead's Part** | | |
| Step back left | 1 | step |
| Step right to left | 2 | together |
| Touch left | 3 | touch |
| Step forward left | 4 | step |
| Step right behind left (hook) in place and release lead's right, follow's left hand (swing out position) | 5 | hook |
| Step left in place, pushing off | *and* | step |
| Step right in place | 6 | step |
| **Follow's Part** | | |
| Step forward right | 1 | step |
| Step forward left | 2 | step |
| Touch right to left instep | 3 | touch |
| Turning right toward partner, step back right (continue to travel in slot) | 4 | step |
| Step left behind right (hook) and release follow's left, lead's right hand | 5 | hook |

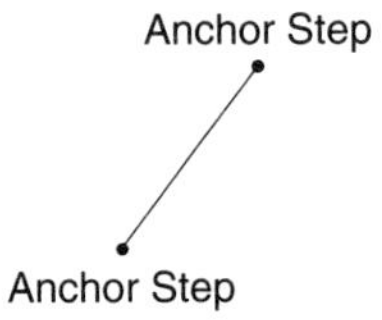

**Narrow Space for West Coast Swing Dance**

| STEPS | COUNTS | STEP CUE |
|---|---|---|
| Step right in place | *and* | step |
| Step left in place | 6 | step |

**Step Cue:** The cue "walk" may be used for counts 1, 2, 4.

**Style:** The footwork and hips are like the Cuban walk. Dig, pressing the foot into the floor while moving forward.

**Lead:** The arms need to be firm (give weight) as the follow moves forward, the lead pulling toward himself. On count 3 the follow leans a little more forward, body rising to receive the *push*. On count 4 the lead *pushes* as the follow moves backward. Both dancers must offer resistance. The lead initiates the *pull* and *push*.

**Note:** The steps on counts 5 and 6 are the "anchor steps." The follow may choose to do a "coaster step" for counts 5 and 6. Coaster step is step back left, close right to left, step forward left.

**Variation:** Triple step. Counts 3, 4 become "3 and 4" (QQS). Instead of touch step, lead steps left, right, left, follow steps right, left, right.

## West Coast Swing Variations

### Underarm Turn

**Position:** Swing out
**Level:** Intermediate

The follow passes the lead's right side, turns under her arm to face opposite direction.

| STEPS | COUNTS | STEP CUE |
|---|---|---|
| **Lead's Part** | | |
| Moving to left side, step left | 1 | step |
| Step forward right | 2 | step |
| Moving toward slot, step left, pivoting clockwise | 3 | side |
| Step right, still turning | *and* | step |
| Raising left arm, step left into the slot (now facing opposite direction) | 4 | step |
| Step right behind left | 5 | hook |
| Step left | *and* | step |
| Step right in place | 6 | step |
| **Follow's Part** | | |
| Step forward right | 1 | step |
| Step forward left | 2 | step |
| Take 3 running steps (right, left, right) to the end of slot, turning counterclockwise under right arm, on count 4 | 3 *and* 4 | run, run, turn |
| Step left behind right | 5 | hook |
| Step right | *and* | step |
| Step left in place | 6 | step |

**Lead:** Lead pulls the follow forward, left hand down, raises arm for turn on count 4.

**Note:** Alternate one sugar push sequence with one underarm turn. Follow may use "coaster step" for counts 5 and 6.

8

## Left Side Pass

**Position:** Swing out position
**Level:** Intermediate

Follow passes lead's left side.

| STEPS | COUNTS | STEP CUE |
|---|---|---|
| **Lead's Part** | | |
| Moving to right side, step left across right | 1 | step |
| Pivoting counterclockwise on left, step right near left (now facing slot) | 2 | step |
| Following the follow, take 3 steps (left, right, left) | 3 *and* 4 | step, step, step |
| Facing opposite direction, step right behind left | 5 | hook |
| Step left | *and* | step |
| Step right in place | 6 | step |
| **Follow's Part** | | |
| Step forward right | 1 | step |
| Step forward left | 2 | step |
| Passing partner (lead's left side), traveling in the slot, take 3 short running steps (right, left, right), pivoting counterclockwise on last run | 3 *and* 4 | run, run, turn |
| Facing opposite direction, step left behind right | 5 | hook |
| Step right | *and* | step |
| Step left | 6 | step |

**Note:** The left side pass is usually preceded by one sugar push.

**Style:** The follow holds left arm, elbow bent, to chest as she passes partner and turns.

**Lead:** On count 4 lead drops left shoulder, pulls his left hand down as follow passes.

## Whip

**Position:** Swing out position
**Level:** Intermediate

Starting in swing out position, couple moves into closed position, makes one complete turn clockwise as a couple at the center of the slot, separates into swing out position, and ends in original position.

| STEPS | COUNTS | STEP CUE |
|---|---|---|
| **Lead's Part** | | |
| Step back left | 1 | step |
| Moving to left side, step right across left and move into closed position | 2 | cross |
| Step left forward, pivoting clockwise as a couple | 3 | turn |
| Continuing to turn, step right in place | *and* | and |
| Step left across slot (left and right feet straddle slot) | 4 | step |
| Step right behind left (hook), continuing to turn as a couple | 5 | hook |
| Releasing lead's right, follow's left hand and separating, step left forward into slot. Now facing original direction | 6 | step |
| Step right behind left, step left, step right in place | 7 *and* 8 | hook, step, step |

| STEPS | COUNTS | STEP CUE |
|---|---|---|
| **Follow's Part** | | |
| Step forward right toward partner | 1 | step |
| Moving into closed position, step left, pivoting clockwise to face partner | 2 | pivot |
| Step back right | 3 | back |
| Close left to right | *and* | together |
| Step right forward between the lead's feet | 4 | step |
| Continuing to turn clockwise as a couple, step left | 5 | step |
| Release follow's left, lead's right hand and step back right | 6 | step |
| Step left behind right, step right, step left in place | 7 *and* 8 | hook, step, step |

**Note:** Follow's part, counts 3 and 4, is an *anchor step*. It may be cued as "an-chor step" (3 *and* 4) (QQS).

# *Hustle*

Disco stands to the 1970s as rock and roll stood to the 1960s. *Disco* comes from the word *discotheque,* which in France is a place where records and disques are stored. In the United States, a **discotheque** is a place where records are played and one can listen or dance to rock music. **Disco dance** has become a descriptive term that encompasses a wide variety of dance steps to many musical rhythms. Originally, the partners did not touch and the patterns were simple, characterized by (1) a stationary base, (2) response to a steady beat–predominantly 4/4 time, (3) action in the upper torso (this is styling of hands and movement of body above the hips), and (4) not following the lead of a partner.

What began as fury and inspiration became fashion. How to keep the momentum going became a major concern as record sales declined and disco attendance dropped. Two events occurred that increased the desire of the whole nation for dance. Studio 54 in New York City proved that a discotheque could work on a grand scale. People wanted an opportunity to exhibit themselves. Gone were the glitter balls; they were replaced by video screens with computer graphics. The disc jockey continued to be in the driver's seat. The dance floor was more spacious. The music and the atmosphere for overstimulation was shared with a profusion of lights, sound, rhythm, and spectacles that could be interpreted as the formula for "pleasure and high times."

The other event was the movie *Saturday Night Fever.* John Travolta strutted and presented a virile young man's need to be assertive, seeking a stage on which to perform.

"Touch dancing" was the new phrase for holding one's partner. The Hustle is credited with bringing people together again on the dance floor. One of the common tunes for dancing was "Feelings"; the dance included body contact, dancing in one spot, responding to the music, and a 4/4 rhythm.

Clubs reopened and new ones arrived to meet the new disco interest. With the Hustle, partners touching once again, the dance studios were back in business. Many of the old forms, like the Lindy and the Latin dances, and the closed dance position or variations, reappeared.

## *Hustle* WITH PARTNER

THE PARTNER HUSTLE WAS POPULAR during the disco dance era in the late 1970s. In the mid–1990s, the partner hustle resurfaced as part of several "night club" dance styles. Music ranging from 160–190 beats per minute (BPM) may be used.

| 4/4 | rock | step | step | | step | | | |
|---|---|---|---|---|---|---|---|---|
| | 1 | 2 | 3 | 4 | 1 | 2 | | |

Directions are for the lead; the follow's part is reversed, except when noted.

### Basic Step

**Direction:** Clockwise
**Position:** Two hands joined, lead's hands palm up
**Level:** Intermediate

| STEPS | 4/4 COUNTS | RHYTHM CUE | STEP CUE |
|---|---|---|---|
| Step left backward, a little behind right heel | *and* | quick | rock |
| Step right in place | 1 | quick | step |
| Step forward left, pivot clockwise 180° forward | 2 | slow | step |
| Step back right | 3 | slow | step back |

**Note:** Four basic steps equals three measures of music.

**Style:** Keep steps small.

**Lead:** The lead pulls down with both hands on count 2, to initiate the partner turn.

**Style:** The forward and back steps are almost in a straight line. The style is very smooth; be careful not to bounce with the "rock step."

### Social Basic Step

**Direction:** Counterclockwise
**Position:** Social swing position with follow at right angle to partner, lead left hand lowered. Lead is pointing left foot to side, follow is pointing right foot forward.
**Level:** Intermediate

| STEPS | 4/4 COUNTS | RHYTHM CUE | STEP CUE |
|---|---|---|---|
| **Lead's Part** | | | |
| Step left side | *and* | quick | side |
| Step right in place | 1 | quick | check |
| Step forward left, crossing in front of right, pivot counterclockwise 90° | 2 | slow | cross |
| Step back right, pivoting counterclockwise 90° | 3 | slow | back |
| **Follow's Part** | | | |
| Step right back, next to left | *and* | quick | together |
| Step left forward, pivot counterclockwise 90° | 1 | quick | forward |
| Step right side, pivot counterclockwise 90° | 2 | slow | side |
| Step left back | 3 | slow | back |

**Lead:** On count 2 in the lead's part, the lead's crossing step is placed in between the follow's feet. He follows her around.

### Throw Out

**Position:** Social swing position to swing out position
**Level:** Intermediate

| STEPS | 4/4 COUNTS | STEP CUE |
|---|---|---|
| **Lead's Part** | | |
| Step left side | *and* | side |
| Step right in place | 1 | check |
| Step left forward, crossing in front of right, pivot counterclockwise 90°, releasing follow with right hand | 2 | cross |
| Small step right back | 3 | back |
| **Follow's Part** | | |
| Step right back, next to left | *and* | together |
| Step left forward | 1 | forward |
| Pivot counterclockwise 90° on left, step right side on right | 2 | side |
| Pivot counterclockwise 90° on right, step back on left | 3 | back |

**Style:** It is common for both the lead and the follow to point their free arms in the air, similar to John Travolta's famous point pose in *Saturday Night Fever*. At the end of the throw out, the lead should adjust, if necessary, to face the follow squarely.

**Lead:** On count 2, the lead pulls down with his left hand, guiding the follow out.

**Note:** The throw out may be used as a prep step for many variations, or the couple may return to social swing position.

### Returning to Social Swing Position

**Level:** Intermediate

| STEPS | 4/4 COUNTS | STEP CUE |
|---|---|---|
| **Lead's Part** | | |
| Step left back, next to right | *and* | together |
| Step right in place | 1 | place |
| Pivot on right 45° clockwise, side step left on left foot | 2 | side |
| Step right in place | 3 | place |
| **Follow's Part** | | |
| Step right back, next to left | *and* | together |
| Step left forward | 1 | forward |
| Step right forward | 2 | forward |
| Pivot on right 180° clockwise, step left back | 3 | turn |

**Lead:** The lead pulls down with his left hand to guide the follow next to him. The lead replaces his right hand on the follow's back by count 3.

### Lead's Underarm Pass

**Position:** Swing out position
**Level:** Intermediate

The lead veers to the left while he goes under the follow's arm, as the follow passes behind.

| STEPS | 4/4 COUNTS | STEP CUE |
|---|---|---|
| **Lead's Part** | | |
| Step left back, next to right | *and* | together |
| Step right forward | 1 | forward |
| Step diagonal forward left on left | 2 | under |
| Pivot on left 180° counterclockwise, step right back | 3 | back |
| **Follow's Part** | | |
| Step right back, next to left | *and* | together |
| Step left forward | 1 | forward |
| Step right forward | 2 | forward |
| Pivot on right 180° clockwise, step left back | 3 | turn |

**Style:** The free arms are extended out to the side as the lead goes under the arm.

**Lead:** The lead lifts his left arm and gently guides the follow behind him as he goes under her arm.

**Note:** This move is usually done two times in a row.

# *Charleston*

THE ROARING TWENTIES SAW the advent of Dixieland jazz and the Charleston. Definitely a fad dance, the Charleston comes and goes, only to reappear again. The dance, with its fancy footwork and carefree abandon, is a challenge to young and old. Black dock workers of Charleston, South Carolina, are credited with performing the dance steps eventually referred to as the Charleston. In 1923, the Ziegfeld Follies popularized the dance in a show called "Running Wild." Teachers toned the kicking steps down and interspersed them with the Two-step and Foxtrot, and the United States had a new popular dance. The Varsity Drag was one of many dances that incorporated the basic Charleston step. The dance permitted individuals to express their ability with many Charleston variations, independent of their partner.

## *Charleston* RHYTHM

The Charleston rhythm is written in 4/4 time. The bouncy quality of the music occurs in the shift of accent, becoming a highly syncopated rhythm.

| | | | | | | | | | |
|---|---|---|---|---|---|---|---|---|---|
| | / | / | | / | | / | | / | / |
| 4/4 | Q | Q | Q | Q | Q | Q | Q | Q | Q |
| | & | 1 | & | 2 | & | 3 | & | 4 | & |

The rhythm is an even beat pattern of quicks counted "*and* 1, *and* 2, *and* 3, *and* 4." The knee bends on the *and* before the step. It is the *and* that gives the Charleston its characteristic bounce. Rhythmically, the beats are:

4/4 

The accent shifts from the first beat to the eighth note tied to the third beat, which gives punch to the rhythm. The rhythm is jerky, staccato, and syncopated.

## *Charleston* STYLE

The twisting of the feet and the bending of the knees before each step, then the straightening of the leg, are basic. The arms move in opposition to the feet: For example, step left, point right and swing both arms across to the left, step right, point left, and swing arms across right. The Charleston may be danced as a solo; in a line with a group; or with a partner, side by side, on the same foot, or facing each other, hands joined or closed position.

## *Teaching* SUGGESTIONS

1. Practice rhythm first. Feet slightly apart and parallel, bend knees (*and*), straighten legs (count 1). Repeat the action of "*and* 1, *and* 2, *and* 3, *and* 4." Then add the music.
2. Practice pivot on balls of feet. Heels out (*and*), heels in (count 1). Repeat.
3. *Charleston Twist.* Combine items 1 and 2 above. Bend knees and heels out (*and*), straighten legs and heels in (count 1). Repeat.
4. Add arm movement, swinging arms in opposition to feet. Swinging arms helps to maintain balance.
5. If balance and timing are difficult, try sitting on the edge of a chair to establish the rhythm; then stand behind the chair, holding onto the back for support.
6. Teach all figures in place. Then move forward and backward. Practice without music, slowly. If the music player has variable speed, introduce music as soon as possible. Gradually increase tempo until the correct tempo is reached.

## *Fundamental* CHARLESTON STEPS

**CD:** ASU Living Era, Tracks 1 and 4.
**Music:** Twelfth Street Rag or any good recording of the 1920s.
**Formation:** Free formation, all facing music.
**Level:** Beginning 3

### Point Step

(Feet together, weight on right)

| STEPS | 4/4 COUNTS | STEP CUE |
|---|---|---|
| Bend right knee | *and* | *and* |
| Step forward left | 1 | step forward |

*continues on next page*

Point Step, *continued*

| STEPS | 4/4 COUNTS | STEP CUE |
|---|---|---|
| Bend left knee | *and* | *and* |
| Point right toe forward, straighten knees | 2 | point forward |
| Bend left knee | *and* | *and* |
| Step back right | 3 | step back |
| Bend right knee | *and* | *and* |
| Point left toe back, straighten knees | 4 | point forward |

**Arms:** Swing arms in opposition to legs. Right toe forward, left arm swings forward, right arm swings back; left toe forward, right arm swings forward, left arm swings back.

### Single Kick Step

(Feet together, weight on right)

| STEPS | 4/4 COUNTS | STEP CUE |
|---|---|---|
| Bend right knee | *and* | *and* |
| Step forward left | 1 | step forward |
| Bend left knee | *and* | *and* |
| Kick right leg forward, straighten knees | 2 | kick forward |
| Bend left knee | *and* | *and* |
| Step back right | 3 | step back |
| Bend right knee | *and* | *and* |
| Kick left leg back | 4 | kick back |
| Straighten knees | *and* | *and* |

**Arms:** Swing arms in opposition to the kick. Kick right leg forward, left arm swings forward, right arm swings back; kick left leg forward, right arm swings forward, left arm swings back.

## Variations

1. *Double Kick.* Step forward left; kick right forward, then backward; step right in place. Repeat kicking left forward, then backward; step left.
2. *Single Diagonal Kick.* Step sideward left, kick diagonally forward across left leg, step sideward right, kick diagonally forward across right leg.

### Charleston Twist

(Weight on the balls of both feet, heels touching, toes pointing out)

1. The twist comes from pivoting on balls of feet, heels turned out, then pivoting on balls of feet, heels turned in. Heels are slightly off the floor to allow the pivot action.

| STEPS | 4/4 COUNTS | STEP CUE |
|---|---|---|
| Bend knees, pivot in on balls of feet | *and* | heels out |
| Pivot out, straighten knees | 1 | heels in |
| Repeat over and over | | |

2. Twist and snap (heels touching, toes pointing out, weight on right).

| STEPS | 4/4 COUNTS | STEP CUE |
|---|---|---|
| Bend right knee, pivot in on ball of foot, lifting left leg up, knee turned in | *and* | heels out |
| Pivot out on ball of right foot; straighten knees; place left foot by heel of right, toe pointed out; left takes weight | 1 | heels in |
| Bend left knee; pivot in on ball of foot, lifting left leg up, knee turned in | *and* | heels out |
| Pivot out on ball of left foot, straighten knees, place right foot by heel of left, toe pointed out; right takes weight | 2 | heels in |

### Jump

| STEPS | 4/4 COUNTS | STEP CUE |
|---|---|---|
| Bend both knees together | *and* | bend |
| Jump forward diagonally left, both arms swing left, at shoulder height | 1 | jump |
| Bend both knees | *and* | bend |
| Jump back, both arms swing down | 2 | jump |
| Repeat jump and arms forward and back | *and* 1 *and* 2 | |
| Bend both knees together | *and* | |
| Jump forward diagonally right, both arms swing right at shoulder height | 1 | jump |
| Bend both knees together | *and* | |
| Jump back, both arms swing down | 2 | jump |
| Repeat jump and arms forward and back | *and* 1 *and* 2 | jump |
| Alternately jump left, right, left, right; arms swing left, right, left, right | 2 | |

## Charleston with Partner

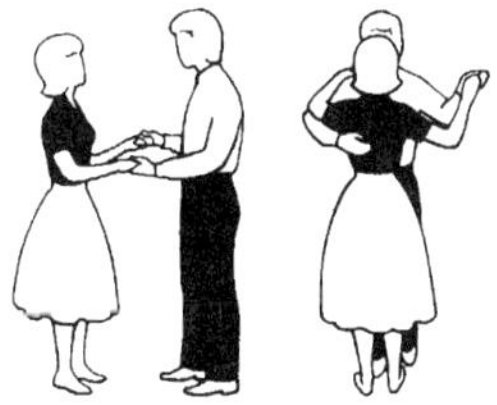

Partners may be (1) side by side, on the same foot, (2) facing each other, hands joined, or (3) in closed position. The lead is visual. The lead starts with his left, follow right. Any step changes start with lead's left. Lead and follow stop together.

### Swivel

Weight on heels, pivot toes right (count *and*); weight on toes, pivot heels right (count 1). Continue to move right, heel, toe, heel, toe. Arms swing left and down, repeating with heel, toe. Travel on counts *and* 1 *and* 2. Reverse movement to travel left.

### Suzy Q

Pivot on left heel and right toe simultaneously (count *and*), then pivot on left toe and right heel simultaneously (count 1). Continue alternating, traveling right. Hands in front of chest, elbows out as heels are apart; drop elbows as toes are apart; alternate elbows out and dropped with foot movement. Reverse footwork to travel left.

# *Lindy Hop*

THE LINDY HOP EMERGED in the late 1920s to a sound of a new style of music being played in Harlem. The African American jazz musicians of that day called this new rhythm "swinging the beat" (Wagner 1997, 8). The music was swinging and so were the dancers. The name Lindy Hop came from a dancer named Shorty Snowden. During a dance marathon in the 1920s, a reporter asked him what he was doing, and in honor of Charles Lindbergh's recent "hop" over the Atlantic, he said, "Lindy Hop." The Lindy Hop is considered the granddaddy of all the American swing forms.

The Lindy Hop incorporated many moves from a previous dance fad, the Charleston. Many other steps, often theatrical, were created for dance contests in Harlem. An example is Air Steps, or putting the women in the air with a flip.

The Lindy Hop's popularity was driven by many events of the day. Whitey's Lindy Hopper, a dance troupe from Harlem, toured the United States and Europe. Popular movies, such as *A Day at the Races* and *Hellzapoppin,* included Lindy Hop dance scenes. These factors helped the Lindy Hop continue to gain popularity as it moved into middle-class America. A *Life* magazine article in 1943, marking a high point of popularity, called the Lindy Hop "America's true folk dance." After World War II, the Lindy Hop's popularity declined.

In the mid-1980s, dancers from California (Erin Stevens and Steve Mitchell), Sweden (founding members of the Rhythm Hot Shots), and England (the Jiving Lindy Hoppers) went to New York seeking the guidance of some original Lindy Hoppers. These people wanted to learn more than what they had seen in old movies or magazines (Erin Stevens, personal communication). Frankie Manning, an original member of Whitey's Lindy Hoppers, had just started dancing again, after retiring from the post office. These dancers worked with Frankie and other original Lindy Hop dancers and used this new knowledge to revive the Lindy Hop.

More recently, the Lindy Hop has exploded onto the dance scene. Movies like *Swing Kids* and *Malcolm X* have Lindy Hop dance sequences. TV commercials are using the Lindy Hop (the most notable is the spring 1998 Gap Khakis "swing" ad campaign). Bands are playing music in the style of the 1930s and 1940s swing bands (e.g., Big Bad Voodoo Daddy). The Lindy Hop revival is in full swing!

**Style:** Knees are bent and there is a constant gentle bounce throughout the movements. Bend over slightly from the waist. Follows are slightly more upright than the leads. Self-expression is encouraged.

**Music:** Normal tempo is 140–160 BPM.

**CD:** Really Swingin', LTM 0695

## Full Lindy Basic

**Position:** Swing out–Lindy position

**Level:** Intermediate

Starting in swing out–Lindy position, couple moves into closed position, makes one complete turn clockwise as a couple, and separates into swing out position.

| STEPS | COUNTS | STEP CUE |
|---|---|---|
| **Lead's Part** | | |
| Step back left, bending slightly forward, look at partner<br>Leave right foot in place | 1 | rock |
| Step in place right | 2 | step |
| Pivoting one-quarter clockwise, step forward left | 3 | three |

| STEPS | COUNTS | STEP CUE |
|---|---|---|
| Right hand moves to social position | | |
| Pivoting one-eighth clockwise, step right behind left (leave left foot in place) | *and* | and |
| Pivoting one-eighth clockwise, step left in place, left knee bent | 4 | four |
| **Face-Off Position** | | |
| Step right behind left (hook) in place, release right hand | 5 | hook |
| Pivoting one-quarter clockwise on right, step side left on left | 6 | step |
| Pivoting one-quarter clockwise on left, step back right | 7 | step |
| Step left in place | *and* | in |
| Step right in place | 8 | place |
| **Follow's Part** | | |
| Step swivel right, wave left hand in the air | 1 | swivel |
| Step swivel left, wave left hand in the air | 2 | swivel |
| Step forward right | 3 | three |
| Pivoting one-quarter clockwise, step side left with left (leave right foot in place) | *and* | and |
| Pivoting one-quarter clockwise, step right in place | 4 | four |
| **Face-Off Position** | | |
| Pivoting one-quarter clockwise, step side left | 5 | run |
| Remove left hand from lead's shoulder | | |
| Step side left with right, crossing right in front | 6 | run |
| Step side left with left | 7 | step |
| Pivoting one-quarter clockwise, step right in place | *and* | in |
| Step left in place | 8 | place |

**Style:** Always keep eye contact with partner. On counts 1 and 2, the lead is mimicking "bowing down" to the follow. On counts 1 and 2, the follow may vary her arm movement.

**Lead:** On count "3 *and*," lead leans forward with left shoulder. The lead releases right hand on count 5, allowing the follow to move away.

**Variations:** On counts 1 and 2, either the lead or the follow may change their footwork: for example, a heel drop or a kick away may be substituted. These variations are executed independently of the partner.

## Lindy Hop Variations

### Basic to a Jockey

**Position:** Swing out–Lindy position
**Level:** Intermediate

Starting in swing out–Lindy position, lead makes one complete turn clockwise (follow, one and a half), bringing the follow to his right side, ending in the jockey position.

| STEPS | COUNTS |
|---|---|
| Repeat counts 1–4 for full Lindy basic | |
| **Lead's Part** | |
| Step in place right. Do not release right arm as in the basic; with right arm, reach around to partner's right side, starting to bring her into the jockey position. | 5 |

Basic to a Jockey, *continued*

| STEPS | COUNTS |
|---|---|
| Pivoting one-half clockwise on right, step side left | 6 |
| Step back right | 7 |
| Step left in place (next to right) | *and* |
| Step back right | 8 |
| **Follow's Part** | |
| Pivoting one-quarter clockwise on right, step side left | 5 |
| Pivoting one-quarter clockwise on left, step forward right | 6 |
| Pivoting one-quarter clockwise on right, step side left | 7 |
| Step right in place (next to left) | *and* |
| Pivoting one-quarter clockwise on right, step back left | 8 |

## Lindy Charleston

**Position:** Jockey position
**Level:** Intermediate

Directions are for the lead. The follow's footwork is reversed.

| STEPS | COUNTS | STEP CUE |
|---|---|---|
| Step back left | 1 | rock |
| Step in place right | 2 | step |
| Kick left forward | 3 | kick |
| Step left | 4 | step |
| Kick right forward | 5 | kick |
| Swing right foot back to place | 6 | and |
| Kick right back | 7 | kick |
| Step right | 8 | step |

**Note:** This step is usually repeated two to three times.

**Style:** Lead releases his left hand, follow's right hand. Free arms swing forward and back during the Charleston footwork. A constant bounce is maintained during the step.

## Jockey to a Swing Out

**Level:** Intermediate

| STEPS | COUNTS | STEP CUE |
|---|---|---|
| **Lead's Part** | | |
| Repeat the footwork of Lindy basic | 1–8 | |
| **Follow's Part** | | |
| Step back right | 1 | rock |
| Step left in place | 2 | step |
| Step right forward | 3 | step |
| Step left together | *and* | together |
| Step right forward (now in face-off position) | 4 | step |
| Repeat counts 5–8 of Lindy basic, ending in Swing out–Lindy position | 5–8 | |

**Lead:** Lead rejoins his left hand with follow's right hand on counts 7 and 8 of the previous measure. By count 4, the lead's right hand has returned to the middle of the follow's back.

### Shine

**Position:** Swing out–Lindy position
**Level:** Beginning 3

The lead stays in place, bringing his knees together and apart as the follow swivel steps clockwise around him, waving her left hand in the air; this is called *shining*.

| STEPS | COUNTS | STEP CUE |
|---|---|---|
| **Lead's Part (wobbly knees)** | | |
| With feet together, both knees go to the side | *and* | and |
| Step in place left and bring knees together | 1 | in |
| Both knees go to the side | *and* | and |
| Step in place right and bring knees together | 2 | in |
| Repeat counts: *and* 1 *and* 2 | *and* 3–8 | |
| Repeat counts 1–8 | | |
| **Follow's Part** | | |
| Starting with right, take 16 swivel steps to move clockwise around the lead | | |

**Style:** The follow is trying to attract attention, waving and smiling as she moves around the lead.

**Lead:** On approximately count 5 of a basic, the lead would say "Hey Baby, do you want to shine?" During the next basic he waits for a yes or no answer from the follow. When he hears a "yes," at the end of that basic, the shine starts. He continues to hold on to the follow's right hand with his left as she moves around him.

## LINE DANCE

LINE DANCE AS A SPECIFIC DANCE form has become widely popular. It flourishes with equal enthusiasm in schools, dance halls, clubs, and senior centers. Its chief attraction lies in the fact that since a partner is not required, everyone can participate. Formations are equally unencumbered, ranging from dancers simply scattered about the floor all facing one direction to lines and circles.

Line dancing, or nonpartner dance, has enjoyed an extensive and rich history. In addition to its longevity as a dance form, line dancing also facilitates beginning dance instruction. Its value is particularly apparent when starting a unit with line dances and *then* moving to partner dances. The major benefits of line dancing are:

- Everyone is dancing.
- Dancers have a chance to learn and practice uninhibited by a partner.
- Many basic movements may be introduced to students as a line dance.

Many of the popular novelty and fad dances of the past, such as Bunny Hop, Big Apple, and Hokey Pokey, are nonpartner line dances. If all the nonpartner dances from various world cultures were added to this mix, we would have to say, without a doubt, that the line dance is the grand dame of dance!

## *Teaching* TIPS FOR LINE DANCING

1. When applicable, having students move to the colored lines on the gym floor helps organize the class.
2. Students need to be an "arm's distance" apart. This allows them enough space to move and discourages roughhousing.
3. When facing the class, the instructor's movement should be a mirror image to the students' movement. When the students move to their right, the instructor should move to the left.
4. Rotate lines often. The front row moves to the back, and all other lines move forward. Rotating lines provides several benefits:
   - All students will have a chance to be in the front row with a clear view of the instructor and the demonstration of steps.
   - The instructor has an equally good view of all student reactions and progress.
   - Rotation prevents troublemakers from lingering in the back row and creating a disruption.
5. In a large class, the instructor can watch one line at a time and assist as needed. For this technique, after a line has been reviewed by the instructor, the students sit down while maintaining their lines.
6. Many line dances face a different direction or wall on each repetition and are known as *four-wall line dances.* When the dance is repeated facing a new direction, the instructor should move to maintain a position in front of the students. This effort tends to reduce student disorientation. Once the class knows the dance, cueing the steps should be sufficient.

Line dances can be flexible enough to fit a variety of musical tastes and trends catered to class interest. In the mid-1990s line dancing was generally a country western phenomenon, though not all line dancing has a country western character. Dances such as the Macarena gained popularity well beyond country western dancers.

## *Line* DANCE STYLE

The dance reflects the style of music played: country western, disco, rap, or pop. In country western line dancing, when the hands are free, the thumbs are hooked near the belt buckle or both hands are overlapped behind the back with palms facing out.

### Line Dances

| | | |
|---|---|---|
| All Shook Up | Freeze | Electric Slide |
| The Continental | Hip Hop Dance | Slappin' Leather |
| Cowboy Boogie | Saturday Night Fever (line dance) | |

For more line dances in American folk style, see Chapter 4, pages 91–96.

# *All Shook Up*

ALL SHOOK UP WAS PRESENTED at Brainerd, Minnesota, in June 1999 by Gary E. Sanders, University of Missouri–Kansas City, Missouri.

**Meter:** 4/4 • Directions presented in beats.

**Music:** *Slow:* "Two of a Kind" by Garth Brooks, "You Ain't Much Fun" by Toby Keith, "All I Want Is A Life" by Tim McGraw.

*Full Speed:* "All Shook Up," *Honeymoon in Vegas* soundtrack. The dance starts exactly 16 beats into the song.

**Formation:** Lines of dancers all facing front, four-wall style.

**Patterns:** There are two patterns

Wall 1 Patterns 1 and 2
Wall 2 Patterns 1 and 2
Wall 3 Patterns 1 and 2
Wall 4 Pattern 2
Wall 5 Patterns 1 and 2
Wall 6 Pattern 2
Wall 7 Patterns 1 and 2
Ending

**Level:** Intermediate

| COUNTS | STEPS |
|---|---|
| | **Pattern 1** |
| 1–2 | Cross right over left, stepping down on the toe, then heel |
| 3–4 | Step out on left, stepping down on the toe, then heel |
| 5–6 | Cross right over left, stepping down on the toe, then heel |
| 7–14 | Traveling slightly to the right, kick right foot, ball change, four times |
| | **Pattern 2** |
| 1–2 | Point right toe to the side, cross over left |
| 3–4 | Point left toe to the side, cross over right |
| 5–6 | Point right toe to the side, cross over left |
| 7–8 | Point left toe to the side, cross over right |
| | **Snap Kicks** |
| 9–10 | Kick right foot out in front and to the side |
| 11–12 | Step side right on count 11, step left next to right on count 11 and, step side right on count 12 |
| 13–14 | Kick left foot out in front and to the side |
| 15–16 | Step side left on count 15, step right next to left on count 11 and, step side left on count 16 |
| | **Swivel** |
| 17–18 | Swivel to the right: heels, toes, heels, toes |
| 19–20 | Put right toe out in front, pivot one half-turn to left |
| 21–22 | Put right toe out in front, pivot one half-turn to left |
| 23–24 | Right one quarter-turn, stomp right and hold (one count) |
| 25–26 | In place stomp left (feet together) and hold (one count) |
| 27–30 | Bump hips right, left, right, left |
| 1–2 | Ending<br>Roll hips twice |

8

# The Continental

THE CONTINENTAL was a popular line dance done in the 1960s. It was one of the many dances performed in the original movie *Hairspray*.

**Meter:** 4/4
**Music:** The Continental or any pop song
**Formation:** Line of dancers
**Level:** Beginning 1

| COUNTS | STEPS |
|---|---|
| | **Walk Side, Turn Side** |
| 1–4 | Right foot steps side right count 1. Left foot crosses over right foot and step side right on count 2. Right foot steps side right on count 3. Clap hands on count 4. |
| 5–8 | Three step turn counterclockwise. Left foot steps side left, turning 90° on count 1. Pivoting on left foot 90°, right foot steps side right on count 2. Pivoting on right foot 180° (ending facing original direction) left foot steps side left on count 3. Clap hands on count 4. |
| | **Points** |
| 1–4 | Right foot steps side right on count 1. Left foot points diagonal right (across right foot) on count 2. Left foot points side left on count 3. Left foot points diagonal right (across right foot) on count 4. |
| | **Turn and back up** |
| 5–8 | Pivot on right foot 90° clockwise, left foot steps back on count 1. Right foot steps back on count 2. Left foot steps back on count 3. Clap hands on count 4. |

**Style:** When stepping, the feet may be slightly swiveled. On the points, there is a slight tilt of the upper body away from the pointing direction. Backing up, add hips.

# Cowboy Boogie

COWBOY BOOGIE, also called Country Boogie, is a country western line dance.

**Meter:** 4/4, medium to fast. Directions are presented in beats.
**Music:** "Friends in Low Places," or popular 4/4 country western tune.
**Formation:** Scattered, all facing music.
**Level:** Beginning 2

| COUNTS | STEPS |
|---|---|
| 1–4 | Grapevine. Beginning right, step sideward, cross left behind right, step sideward right, scuff left heel forward and clap |
| 5–8 | Repeat grapevine beginning left |
| 9–10 | Step right in place, scuff left heel |
| 11–12 | Step left in place, scuff right heel |
| 13–16 | Moving backward, step right, left, right, and lift left knee up (hitch) |
| 17–18 | Rock forward left, touch right in back |
| 19–20 | Rock backward right, touch left in front |
| 21–24 | Rock forward left, rock back right, rock forward left, pivoting on left foot, one-quarter turn left and swing right knee up (hitch) |

# *Freeze*

FREEZE IS A COUNTRY WESTERN line dance.

**Meter:** 4/4, medium fast. Directions presented in beats.
**Music:** Suggested tunes: "Tulsa Line," "Swingin'," "Elvira."
**Formation:** Line of dancers, all facing forward.
**Level:** Beginning 1

| COUNTS | STEPS |
|---|---|
| 1–4 | Grapevine: beginning left, step left sideward; step right behind left; step sideward left; lift right knee turned out, crossing right heel in front of left, then kick right foot out |
| 5–8 | Grapevine: beginning right, repeat action of measures 1–4 to the right |
| 9–12 | Traveling backward, step back left, right, left; lift right knee turned out, crossing right heel in front of left, then kick right foot out |
| 13–14 | Rock; step forward right, touch left to right; step backward left, touch right to left |
| 15–16 | Turning one quarter-turn right, pivot on right foot with left knee bent, foot off the floor, touch left to right; weight remains on right; left foot is free |

## Variations

1. Funky or hip hop music. Use upper body and arms, turning shoulders left and right. Lift knees high.
2. Zydeco music. Upper torso quiet, footwork subtle. Merengue step and body action.

# *Hip Hop Dance*

THE HIP HOP DANCE presented here has two versions, both choreographed by Kelly Mucha, Portland, Oregon. The beginner version has also been adapted for students with disabilities. The advanced version has more similarity to traditional hip hop styling. Because both versions use the same music, students with or without disabilities are able to dance side by side.

**Meter:** 4/4
**Music:** "Getting Jiggy Wit It" by Will Smith.
**Formation:** Lines of dancers, all facing front.
**Level:** Beginning 2

## Beginning Hip Hop Dance

| COUNTS | STEPS |
|---|---|
| | **Step Touch Forward** |
| 1–2 | Beginning right, step forward right, touch left. |
| 3–4 | Step forward left, touch right. |
| 5–8 | Repeat last 4 counts. |
| | **Look** |
| 9–10 | Turn head and shoulders to the right, place hands near right hip and snap on beat. |
| 11–12 | Repeat on left side. |
| 13–16 | Repeat last 4 counts. |
| | **Step Touch Back** |
| 1–2 | Beginning right, step back right, touch left. |
| 3–4 | Step back left, touch right. |
| 5–8 | Repeat last 4 counts. |
| | **Look (same as above)** |
| 9–10 | Turn head and shoulders to the right, place hands near right hip and snap on beat. |
| 11–12 | Repeat on left side. |
| 13–16 | Repeat last 4 counts. |
| | **Grapevine** |
| 1–8 | Beginning right, step to the right counts 1–2, step left behind right counts 3–4, step side right with right counts 5–6, and touch with left counts 7–8. |
| 9–16 | Repeat starting left. |
| | **Step Together** |
| 1–4 | Beginning right, step to the right, touch left, step left, touch right. |
| 5–8 | Repeat last 4 counts. |
| | **Walk Around** |
| 9–12 | Walk in a small circle counterclockwise 360° plus another 90° to face a new wall. |
| | **Hold** |
| 13–16 | Hold 4 counts before repeating dance. |

**Adaptation:** If students have difficulty with the grapevine, have them step to the side, step together, step to the side, then touch (remove the cross behind).

## Teaching Tips

1. Students with disabilities are easily integrated into a general physical education class because all good teaching should be adaptive teaching. Regardless of whether the students have a disability or not, students should be offered a variety of options when performing the movements to incorporate all students into the class.
2. Start with one section of the body. (For example, show the feet and practice the steps. As the students catch on, introduce the upper body into the dance.)
3. Start with the basic steps; as students demonstrate that they know the steps, introduce more complex steps or invite the students to add their own style (e.g., strut like Will Smith instead of just walking, move hips or shoulders with the beat).
4. As an instructor, be willing to get into the dance. If you just walk through the steps your students will, too. Show them that they are in a safe environment and should let go and enjoy moving!

### Intermediate Hip Hop Dance

**Level:** Intermediate

| COUNTS | STEPS |
|---|---|
| | **Strut Forward** |
| 1–4 | Beginning right, step forward right, left, right, place left foot even with right foot shoulder width apart. |
| | **Look** |
| 5–6 | Turn head and shoulders to the right, place hands near right hip and snap on beat. |
| 7–8 | Repeat on the left side. |
| | **Sailor Shuffle Back** |
| 9–10 | Beginning right, step right foot back, placing the ball of the right foot a bit behind the left heel (count 9), step left in place (count *and*) step right to right (count 10). |
| 11–12 | Repeat, beginning left; step left foot back, placing the ball of the left foot a bit behind the right heel (count 11), step right in place (count *and*), step left to left (count 12). |
| 13–16 | Repeat counts 9–12. |
| | **Out, In, Cross, Turn** |
| 1–2 | Jump up landing with feet slightly apart, then jump and bring feet together (like a jumping jack). |
| 3 | Cross right foot in front of left so right toe just touches the ground and legs are twisted. |
| 4–8 | Push right heel to the ground, slowly turning counterclockwise 360°. (Students can add wiggling hips to the turn as they master the move.) |
| | **Military Groove** |
| 9–12 | Beginning right, step forward right, leaving some weight on left foot; step back right, leaving some weight on left foot; step forward right and bring left foot in to meet right. |
| 13–16 | Repeat (leading with the right again). |
| | **Groove Up, Groove Down** |
| 1–2 | Beginning right, step side right with right foot; at the same time move right arm to right with thumb out (like a hitchhiker), touch left foot to right. |

*continues on next page*

Intermediate Hip Hop Dance, *continued*

| COUNTS | STEPS |
|---|---|
| 3–4 | Step side left with left foot, hitchhike with left thumb, touch right foot to left. |
| 5–6 | Step side right with right foot, hitchhiking with right thumb, and bring left foot to right, transferring weight to both feet. |
| 7–8 | Push knees apart and both thumbs move out at same time, bring knees back together on last count. |
| 9–16 | Repeat counts 1–8 above. |
| | **Turn Back** |
| 1–4 | Step right foot back, turning (clockwise) right shoulder back, continue turning clockwise, stepping left, right, left (should turn 360° and finish with feet shoulder width apart). |
| | **Out, In, Down, Up** |
| 5–6 | Jump up landing with feet slightly apart, then jump and bring feet together (repeating the jumping jack move). |
| 7–8 | Bend knees, placing hands on the ground in front of feet; hold on count 8. |
| 9–12 | Stand up slowly. |
| | **Jump Turn, Hold** |
| 13–16 | Jump and turn 90° to the left, hold three counts before repeating dance. |

# *Saturday Night Fever (line dance)*

THIS LINE DANCE CONTAINS MANY of the disco dance steps that were made popular by the movie *Saturday Night Fever.*

**Meter:** 4/4
**Music:** "Staying Alive."
**Formation:** Lines of dancers, all facing front.
**Level:** Beginning 2

| COUNTS | STEPS |
|---|---|
| | **Walk Forward and Back** |
| 1–4 | Walk back; beginning right, step back right, left, right, touch left foot to right and clap. |
| 5–8 | Repeat walking forward, beginning left. |
| 9–16 | Repeat actions of counts 1–8. |
| | **Walk Side, Turn Side** |
| 1–4 | Walk side; beginning right, walk to the right, right, left, right, touch left foot to right and clap. |
| 5–8 | Repeat walking left, beginning left. |

| COUNTS | STEPS |
|---|---|
| 9–12 | Three step turn to the right; beginning right, turn 90° to right, step forward right, pivoting 90° clockwise, on right foot, step side left on left (end facing back wall); pivoting 180° clockwise on left foot, step side right on right; end facing front; touch left foot to right and clap. |
| 13–16 | Three step turns to the left; repeat action of counts 9–12 to the left. |
| | **Roll It** (feet are shoulder width apart) |
| 1–2 | With hands at waist level, roll them around in a counterclockwise motion. |
| 3–4 | Reach behind the back and clap twice. |
| 5–8 | Repeat actions of counts 1–4. |
| | **Point** |
| 1 | Lift right arm, side high right, pointing up with index finger. |
| 2 | Cross the right arm in front of the body, pointing side left low. |
| 3–6 | Repeat action of counts 1 and 2 twice. |
| | **Funky Chicken** |
| | Arms are raised, with hands in a fist by shoulders, elbows are dropped to the side, in a "wing-flapping" motion on counts 7 and 8. |
| 7 | Rise up on balls of the feet, toes together and heels out; click heels together. |
| 8 | Repeat action of count 7. |
| | **Heel-Toe** |
| 1 | Touch right heel in front. |
| 2 | Repeat. |
| 3 | Touch right toe behind. |
| 4 | Repeat. |
| 5 | Touch right heel in front. |
| 6 | Touch right toe behind. |
| 7 | Step forward on right (leaving left in place). |
| 8 | Pivoting on right foot 90° counterclockwise, slide left foot to right. |

**Style:** Roll It: Move hips to the right on counts 1–2 and left on counts 3–4.

## *Adaptations* FOR STUDENTS WITH DISABILITIES

Students who use wheelchairs may need to refer to the adaptations listed in Chapter 3 for the basic locomotor movements, pages 33–38. Students with visual disabilities may benefit from the guidance of a peer tutor.

### Walk Forward and Back

Allow students to start movement on whatever side is natural to them (e.g., step with left or right; just move forward). This allows them to concentrate on moving with the beat, and eliminates a potential obstacle. Remember that for safety, you will want all students moving in the same direction (forward, back, right, left).

### Walk Side, Turn Side

Some students who use wheelchairs may have difficulty turning the chair to one side, then the other, in four counts. Invite these students to perform a sweeping motion with their arms in the direction of the dance step (refer to slide variation, Chapter 3, page 37). Invite students who have difficulty in completing the turn to continue the previous step walking to the side and add the turn when they are ready for a challenge.

### Roll It

Students with limited range of motion can clap in front of their body or tap their legs. Students with motor impairment may have difficulty rolling their arms; they can push their hands forward or up (raise-the-roof motion) two times on the beat in place of the rolling motion.

### Point

Simplify this movement by not specifying a side of the body or direction of the point. Students need enough space between them to prevent contact with other students.

### Funky Chicken

Allow students to perform either the foot motion or the arm motion; then add in the other when they are ready for a challenge.

### Heel-Toe

Students who use wheelchairs may perform the heel and toe taps by rolling their chair slightly forward (heel) and back (toe) on the beat. Students who have difficulty performing this step can simply turn on counts 1–4 and hold for counts 5–8.

# *Electric Slide*

ELECTRIC SLIDE WAS FIRST DANCED in 1990 to a pop song, "Electric Boogie." Soon after, the Electric Slide also gained popularity in country western line dance circles.

**Meter:** 4/4, medium to fast. Directions are presented in beats.
**Music:** "Electric Boogie" or any popular song.
**Formation:** Lines of dancers, all facing front.
**Level:** Beginning 1

| COUNTS | STEPS |
|---|---|
| 1–4 | Beginning right, step sideward right, close left to right, step sideward right, close left to right, step touch. |
| 5–8 | Repeat same action to left. |
| 9–12 | Moving backward, step right, close left to right, step right and touch left heel to right foot. |
| 13–14 | Rock forward left, touch right (dig) in place; may swing right arm in arc, bending over, and touch floor in front of left foot on the "dig." |
| 15–16 | Rock backward right, touch left (dig) in place. |
| 17–18 | Step left (count 1), pivoting on left one quarter-turn left and brush right foot forward (count 2). |

8

## Variations

| COUNTS | STEPS |
|---|---|
| 1–4 | Take three fast slides to right, letting left foot drag, step right, touch left. Repeat to left. |
| 1–4 | Or grapevine right (right, left, right), touch left heel. Repeat left. |

**Style:** Bend knees on grapevine.

### Electric Slide to Funk Music

**Music:** Any popular funk tune.

**Style:** Bring knees up high. Bend elbows and work arms like a hammer alternately. On the rock, twist shoulders and torso forward and back. Add hops at every opportunity. Whole body makes exaggerated moves to the music.

# *Slappin' Leather*

SLAPPIN' LEATHER IS A COUNTRY WESTERN line dance choreographed by Gayle Brandon.

**Meter:** 4/4, medium to fast. Directions presented in beats.

**Music:** Suggested tunes: "Elvira," "Tulsa Times," "Swingin'," "Baby's Got Her Blue Jeans On."

**Formation:** Line of dancers, all face front.

**Level:** Beginning 2

| COUNTS | STEPS |
|---|---|
| | **PART IA** |
| 1–4 | Swivel, weight on balls of feet; spread heels apart, heels together; spread heels apart, heels together. |
| | **PART IB** |
| 1–4 | Touch right heel forward, step right in place; touch left heel forward, step left in place. |
| 5–8 | Repeat action of counts 1–4. |
| | **PART II** |
| 1–2 | Tap right heel in front twice, foot turned out. |
| 3–4 | Tap right toe in back twice. |
| 5–8 | Star: Touch right toe forward, to right side, behind left, and to right side. |
| 1 | Slap leather: Weight remains on left; swing right foot behind left and slap right boot with left hand. |
| 2 | While turning a quarter-turn left (pivot on left foot), swing right foot to right side and slap right boot with right hand. |
| 3 | Swing right foot in front of left and slap right boot with left hand. |
| 4 | Swing right foot to right side and slap right boot with right hand. |

*continues on next page*

8

| COUNTS | STEPS |
|---|---|
| | **PART III** |
| 1–4 | Grapevine: Beginning right, step right, step left behind right, step sideward right, chug (scoot) right, lifting left knee up (hitch), and clap hands. |
| 5–8 | Beginning left, repeat action of counts 1–4 to the left. |
| 1–4 | Traveling backward, step right, left, right, chug (scoot) right, lifting left foot behind right leg and slap left heel with right hand. |
| 5–6 | Step forward left, close right next to left; weight on both feet. |
| 7–8 | Step forward left, stomp on right foot next to left, weight on both feet. |

# *Foxtrot*

The Foxtrot, as a present-day form, is of relatively recent origin. The only truly American form of ballroom dance, it has had many steps and variations through the years. The Foxtrot gets its name from a musical comedy star, Henry Fox, of the years 1913–1914 (Hostetler 1952), who danced a fast but simple trotting step to ragtime music in one of the Ziegfeld shows of that time. As an additional publicity stunt, the theater management requested that a star nightclub performer, Oscar Duryea, introduce the step to the public but found that it had to be modified somewhat, because a continuous trotting step could not be maintained for long periods without exhausting effort. Duryea simplified the step so that it became four walking steps alternating with eight quick running steps. This was the first Foxtrot.

Since that time, under the influence of Vernon and Irene Castle and a series of professional dancers, the Foxtrot has been through a gradual refining process and has developed into a beautifully smooth dance. It claims considerable popularity today.

Music from ragtime through the blues on down to modern jazz and swing has had its effect on the Foxtrot. The original Foxtrot was danced to a lively 2/4 rhythm. Its two parent forms were the one-step, 2/4 –––– quick, quick, quick, quick rhythm; the other was the two-step, 2/4 |–––|–––| quick, quick, slow or step-close-step. Both of these forms are danced today but have given way to a slower, smoother 4/4 time and a more streamlined style. The Foxtrot is danced in three tempos (slow, medium, and fast) and can be adapted to almost any tempo played in the music.

The basic Foxtrot steps can be used together in any combination or sequence. A dancer who knows the basic steps and understands the fundamentals of rhythm can make up his or her own combinations easily and gradually develop the possibilities for variation in position, direction, and tempo.

## *Foxtrot* RHYTHM

The modern Foxtrot in 4/4 time, or cut time, has four quarter-beats or their equivalent to each measure. Each beat is given the same amount of time, but there is an accent on the first and third beats of the measure. When a step is taken on each beat (1-2-3-4), these are called *quick beats.* When steps are taken only on the two accented beats (1 and 3), they are twice as long and are called *slow beats.*

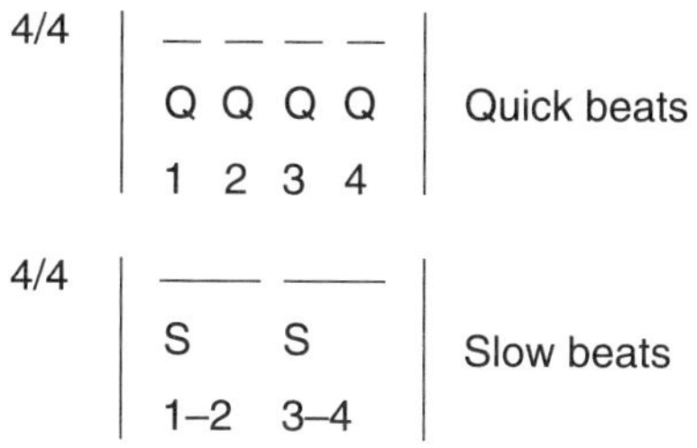


A use of these quick and slow beats and a combination of them into rhythm patterns form the basis for all of the modern Foxtrot steps. There are two patterns used predominantly: the magic step and the Westchester box step.

## Magic Step (Bronze Basic)

The magic step pattern represents broken rhythm, as it takes a measure and a half of music and may be repeated from the middle of the measure. It is an uneven rhythm pattern: slow, slow, quick, quick.

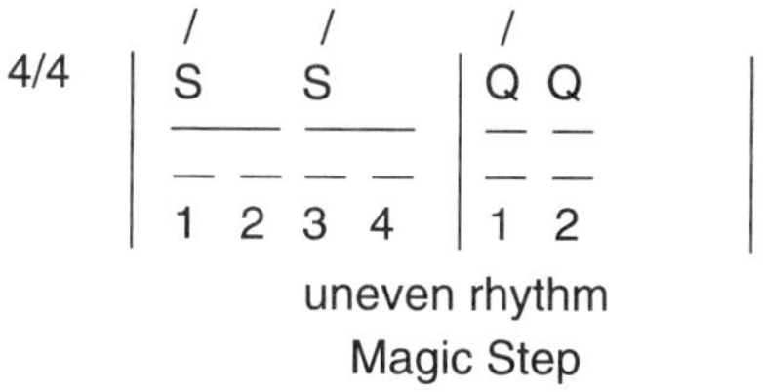


## Westchester Box Step

The Westchester box step is a one-measure pattern, but it takes two measures to complete the box. The rhythm is uneven: slow, quick, quick. The rhythm may also be played in cut time, but it is still slow, quick, quick. Beats 1 and 2 are put together to make one beat. Beats 3 and 4 are put together to make one beat. The time signature for cut time is ¢. It is played faster and feels very much like 2/4 time.

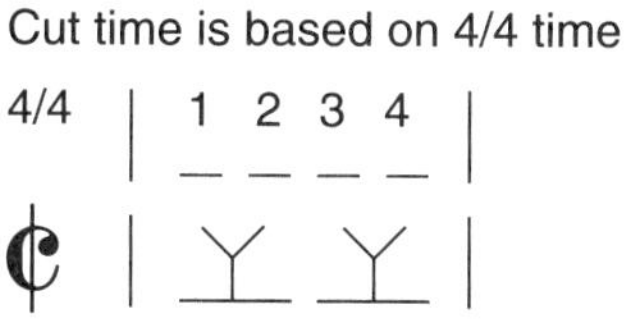


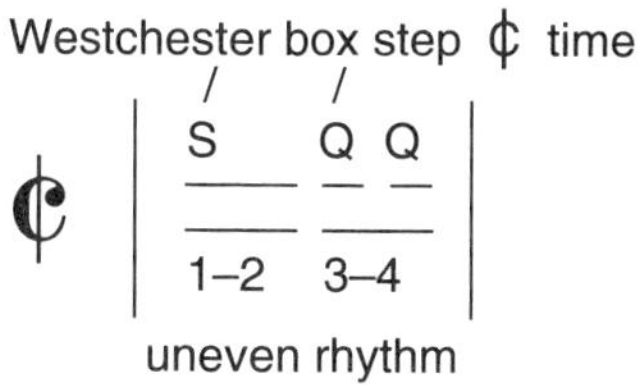


## *Foxtrot* STYLE

Foxtrot style truly reflects its American origin. It is the least affected of any of the ballroom dances. Completely without stylized or eccentric arm, foot, head, or torso movement, the Foxtrot is a beautifully smooth dance. The body is held easily erect and follows the foot pattern in a relaxed way with little up and down or sideward movement. The good dancer glides normally along the floor and blends the various steps together without bobbing or jerking. This effect is accomplished by long, reaching steps with only as much knee bend as is needed to transfer the weight smoothly from step to step. It gives the Foxtrot a streamlined motion and a simple beauty of form that can be enjoyed without strain or fatigue, dance after dance. As one becomes more and more skillful at putting together steps for the Foxtrot, there will be increasing joy derived from the tremendous variety of quick and slow combinations.

## Magic Step Series

| | | |
|---|---|---|
| Magic Step (Basic Step) | Promenade with an Arch | The Conversation Pivot |
| Open Magic Step (Promenade) | Rock, Recover | The Corté |
| Magic Left Turn | Right and Left Parallel | |

The magic step series was created by Arthur Murray (1954). It is called by this name because it can be varied in a surprising number of ways. The pattern is uneven rhythm and requires a measure and a half for one basic step. This is called broken rhythm.

### Magic Step (Basic Step)

**Position:** Closed
**Level:** Beginning 2

| STEPS | 4/4 COUNTS | RHYTHM CUE |
|---|---|---|
| Step left forward | 1–2 | slow |
| Step right forward | 3–4 | slow |
| Step left sideward, a short step | 1 | quick |
| Close right to left, take weight on right | 2 | quick |

**Step Cue:** forward, forward (long steps) side, close (short steps)

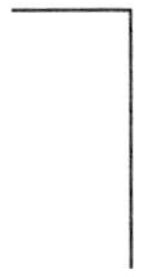

Start
Floor Pattern

**Style:** The forward steps should be long, smooth, walking steps, straight ahead. The follow, moving backward, takes a long step reaching from hip to toe.

**Lead:** Body and right arm lead forward.

**Variations:** The following three techniques are used for maneuvering in a closed dance position.

1. Forward or backward–the lead may maneuver forward or backward if he is aware of the traffic around him. The lead to move backward is a pressure lead at the follow's back during the quick, quick beats and then a step into the backward direction on the next slow beat. Generally the lead will not have room to move backward more than one or two consecutive patterns.
2. Right or left–the lead may maneuver to the right or to the left to go around another couple. He will change direction on the quick, quick beats by use of a pressure lead with his right hand and turn his body at the same time one-eighth of a turn to the right so as to travel diagonally outward or one-eighth turn to the left so as to travel diagonally inward beginning with the next slow beat. The right turn is particularly handy in leading a partner out of a crowded situation away from the center of the floor. Closed position is retained throughout.
3. Dance in place–used on a crowded dance floor. Closed dance position.

| STEPS | 4/4 COUNTS | RHYTHM CUE |
|---|---|---|
| Step sideward left, slide right to left, no weight change | 1–2 | slow |
| Step sideward right, slide left to right, no weight change | 3–4 | slow |
| Step sideward left | 1 | quick |
| Close right to left, take weight right | 2 | quick |

**Step Cue:** Slide, slide, step together.

**Style:** The steps are very small.

**Lead:** Increase pressure with the right hand to keep the follow from stepping back. Indicate sideward action.

**Note:** The lead may maneuver this in-place pattern into a turn counterclockwise by the use of the right hand and elbow.

## Open Magic Step (Promenade)

**Position:** Closed

**Level:** Beginning 2

| STEPS | 4/4 COUNTS | RHYTHM CUE |
|---|---|---|
| Step left forward | 1–2 | slow |
| Step right forward | 3–4 | slow |
| Step left forward a short step, turning to semi-open dance position | 1 | quick |
| Close right to left, take weight right | 2 | quick |
| Step left forward in semi-open position | 3–4 | slow |
| Step right forward | 1–2 | slow |
| Step left forward a short step | 3 | quick |
| Close right to left, take weight right | 4 | quick |
| Step left forward | 1–2 | slow |
| Step right forward | 3–4 | slow |
| Step left forward a short step, turning to closed position | 1 | quick |
| Close right to left, take weight right | 2 | quick |

**Step Cue:** Forward, forward, step, close.

**Style:** It is a heel lead on the slow beats in open position for both the lead and follow.

**Lead:** To lead into a semi-open position or promenade, the lead should use pressure with the heel of the right hand to turn the follow into semi-open position. The right elbow lowers to the side. The lead must simultaneously turn his own body, not just the follow, so that they end facing the same direction. The left arm relaxes slightly and the left hand sometimes gives the lead for steps in the semi-open position.

**Lead:** To lead from semi-open to closed position the lead should use pressure of the right hand and raise the right arm up to standard position to move the follow into closed position. The follow should not have to be pushed but should swing easily into closed position as she feels the arm lifting. She should move completely around to face the lead squarely.

**Lead:** The lead may wish to return to closed position on the quick beats following the first two slows in open position.

**Note:** It is possible to maneuver when going into semi-open position so that the couple opens facing the line of direction and afterward closes with the lead still facing the line of direction, starting from closed position as follows:

## Magic Left Turn

**Level:** Beginning 3

| STEPS | 4/4 COUNTS | RHYTHM CUE |
|---|---|---|
| Step left forward | 1–2 | slow |
| Step right forward | 3–4 | slow |

Magic Left Turn, *continued*

| STEPS | 4/4 COUNTS | RHYTHM CUE |
|---|---|---|
| Step left, right moving around the follow on the left side while turning her halfway around to semi-open position | 1–2 | quick, quick |
| Step left forward in semi-open position, moving in line of direction | 3–4 | slow |
| Step right forward | 1–2 | slow |
| Step left, right in place, bringing the follow around to face the closed dance position | 3–4 | quick, quick |

**Step Cue:** Forward, forward, come around, forward, forward in place.

**Style:** The follow must be sure to swing around, facing the lead, into a correct closed dance position while taking two quick beats.

**Lead:** The lead must start bringing his right elbow up to indicate to the follow that he is going into closed position on the first quick beat.

**Note:** Any number of open magic steps may be done consecutively when traveling in the line of direction without fear of interfering with the dancing of other couples.

### Promenade with an Arch

**Position:** Semi-open-promenade
**Level:** Beginning 2

Starting in promenade position, the lead arches the follow under his arm, ending in closed position.

| STEPS | RHYTHM CUE |
|---|---|
| Lead steps left forward, lifting left arm up | slow |
| Follow steps right forward | |
| Lead steps right forward, giving the follow a gentle push on her back, turning her under the lead's left arm | slow |
| Follow steps right forward, pivoting 270° (3/4 turn) to face partner | |
| Lead steps left forward, turning to closed position | quick |
| Close right to left, take weight right | quick |

**Step Cue:** Forward, forward, side, close.

### Rock, Recover

**Position:** Closed
**Level:** Beginning 2

| STEPS | 4/4 COUNTS | RHYTHM CUE |
|---|---|---|
| Step left forward a short step | 1–2 | slow |
| Step right backward, toe in and turn counterclockwise one-quarter | 3–4 | slow |
| Step in place left, toeing out left, and turning one-quarter counterclockwise | 1 | quick |
| Step right to left, take weight right, and finish the one-half turn | 2 | quick |
| Repeat to make a full turn | | |

**Step Cue:**

| | | | |
|---|---|---|---|
| Rock | rock | step | close. |
| S | S | Q | Q |

**Style:** The slow steps forward and backward are like short rocking steps, but the body is straight, not leaning.

**Lead:** The lead must strongly increase pressure at the follow's back on the first step so that she will not swing her left foot backward. Then he uses his firm right arm to turn her with him counterclockwise. As the follow reacts to these two leads, she will step in between the lead's feet and pivot on her left foot as he guides her around.

**Note:** The pattern may be reduced to a quarter-turn at a time, or it may be increased to make a full turn at a time. This variation provides a means of turning in place or of turning to maneuver into position for another variation or for recovering the original line of direction. Because of this, it is often used to tie together all types of Foxtrot variations.

## Right and Left Parallel Magic Step

**Position:** Closed
**Level:** Intermediate

This is a delightful variation involving right and left parallel position.

| STEPS | 4/4 COUNTS | RHYTHM CUE |
|---|---|---|
| Step forward | 1–2 | slow |
| Step right forward | 3–4 | slow |
| Step left sideward a short step, turning to right parallel position | 1 | quick |
| Close right to left, take weight on right | 2 | quick |
| Step forward left, diagonally in right parallel position | 3–4 | slow |
| Step forward right | 1–2 | slow |
| Step in place left, turning in place one-quarter clockwise into left parallel position | 3 | quick |
| Close right to left, take weight on right | 4 | quick |
| Step forward left in left parallel position | 1–2 | slow |
| Step forward right | 3–4 | slow |
| Step in place left, turning to right parallel | 1 | quick |
| Close right to left, take weight on right | 2 | quick |
| Step left forward in right parallel position | 3–4 | slow |
| Step right forward | 1–2 | slow |
| Step left in place, turning to closed position | 3 | quick |
| Close right to left, take weight on right | 4 | quick |

**Step Cue:** Forward, forward, step turn.

**Style:** The follow in parallel position must reach back parallel to the lead's forward reach.

**Lead:** To lead into right parallel position, the lead should not use pressure of his right hand but rather should raise his right arm, rotating the follow counterclockwise one-eighth of a turn while he rotates counterclockwise one-eighth of a turn. This places the lead and follow off to the side of each other, facing opposite directions. The follow is to the right of the lead but slightly in front of him. The lead should avoid turning too far so as to be side by side, as this results in poor style and awkward and uncomfortable motion. The lead's left hand may assist the lead by pulling toward his left shoulder.

**Lead:** To lead from right parallel position to left parallel position, the lead should pull with his right hand, lowering the right arm, and push slightly with his left hand, causing a rotation clockwise about a quarter of a turn until the follow is to the left of him but slightly in front of him. They are not side by side.

**Note:** The couple should move forward in a zigzag pattern, down the floor, changing from one parallel position to the other. The lead must be careful to take the quick beats in place as he is changing position in order to make a smooth transition. A more advanced use of this variation is to make a half-turn clockwise in place on the quick beats as the lead changes from right parallel position to left parallel position, such that the lead would then travel backward in the line of direction and the follow forward. A half-turn counterclockwise in place would then turn the couple back to right parallel position. Innumerable combinations of this variation will develop as dancers experiment with changes of direction.

### The Conversation Pivot

**Position:** Semi-open
**Level:** Intermediate

| STEPS | 4/4 COUNTS | RHYTHM CUE |
|---|---|---|
| Step left forward | 1–2 | slow |
| Step right forward | 3–4 | slow |
| Step left around the follow clockwise going into closed position | 1–2 | slow |
| Step right between follow's feet and pivot on the right foot, turning clockwise | 3–4 | slow |
| Step left forward a short step, taking semi-open position again | 1 | quick |
| Close right to left, taking weight right | 2 | quick |

**Note:** Two extra slow beats have been added for this variation, S S S S Q Q.

**Step Cue:** Step, step, pivot, pivot, quick, quick.

**Style:** Couples must hold the body firmly and press outward to move with the centrifugal force of the motion on the pivot turn. The follow will step forward in between the lead's feet on the third slow beat and then around him with her left foot on the fourth slow beat, followed by a quick, quick to balance oneself in place.

**Lead:** See lead indication above. The pivot turn is only the third and fourth slow beats. Then the lead will lead into semi-open position and take the quick beats.

**Note:** Following this variation it is usually wise to dance one more magic step in open position before leading into the basic closed position. Note details on pivot turn, pages 467–468.

### The Corté

**Position:** Closed
**Level:** Intermediate

A fascinating dip step in magic step rhythm.

| STEPS | 4/4 COUNTS | RHYTHM CUE |
|---|---|---|
| Step left forward | 1–2 | slow |
| Step right forward | 3–4 | slow |

| STEPS | 4/4 COUNTS | RHYTHM CUE |
|---|---|---|
| Step left sideward a short step | 1 | quick |
| Close right to left, take weight on right | 2 | quick |
| Dip left backward | 3–4 | slow |
| Transfer weight forward onto right foot | 1–2 | slow |
| Step left sideward, a short step | 3 | quick |
| Close right to left, take weight right | 4 | quick |

**Step Cue:** Forward, forward, side close, (preparation beats) dip (corté) recover, quick, quick. (weight forward)

**Style:** *Lead*–The weight is transferred onto the left foot as the lead steps backward into the dip. The left knee is bent, the back is straight, the right toe extends forward. *Follow*–Her weight is transferred onto the right foot as she steps forward into the dip. The right knee is bent and directly over her foot. The back is arched, keeping her straight up and down. The left leg is extended strongly from the hip through the knee to the pointed toe. Her head should be turned left to glance at the extended foot. For additional style details, see the corté, page 474.

**Lead:** To lead into a pivot turn clockwise, the lead should hold the follow slightly closer, but with sudden body tension. Resistance is exerted outward by both the lead and follow leaning away from each other in order to take advantage of the centrifugal force of the circular motion. The right foot steps between partner's feet, forward on line of direction, while the left foot reaches across the line of direction and turns on the ball of the foot about three-quarters of the way around. The lead must take care not to step too long backward or to dip too low, as it is difficult for both lead and follow to recover in good style.

**Note:** The exciting part about the corté is that it may be used as a variation in the dance or it may be used as a finishing step at the end of the music. It is perfectly acceptable to end a beat or two in advance and hold the position to the end of the music. It is also acceptable to corté after the music has finished. There is no pressure to get the corté on the last note of the music.

## Box Step Series—Westchester

| | | |
|---|---|---|
| Westchester Box Step | Bronze Twinkle | Grapevine Step |
| Box Turn | Twinkle Step (Cross Over) | |

The Westchester box is based on slow, quick, quick rhythm in 4/4 or cut time. It is a one-measure pattern–but it takes two measures to complete the box–with uneven rhythm in a smooth style. It is a combination of dance walk and side close.

### Westchester Box Step

**Position:** Closed
**Level:** Beginning 2

| STEPS | 4/4 COUNTS | RHYTHM CUE |
|---|---|---|
| Step left forward | 1–2 | slow |
| Pass right alongside of left, no weight change | | |
| Step right sideward | 3 | quick |
| Close left to right, take weight on left | 4 | quick |
| Step right backward | 1–2 | slow |
| Pass left alongside of right, no weight change | | |
| Step left sideward | 3 | quick |
| Close right to left, take weight on right | 4 | quick |

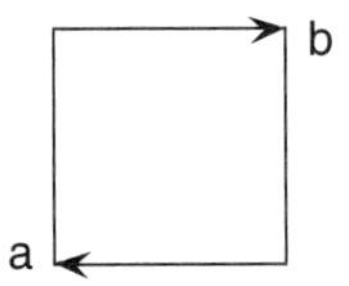


Floor Pattern

**Step Cue:**

| | | | |
|---|---|---|---|
| (a) | Forward | side | close. |
| | S | Q | Q |
| (b) | Backward | side | close |
| | long steps | short | steps. |
| | S | Q | Q |

**Style:** The forward step is a heel step. Both forward and backward steps should be long reaching steps. Dancers must not lose a beat by pausing as they slide alongside the standing foot.

**Lead:** To initiate a box step, the lead should use a forward body action followed by a side body action, using his firm right side connection (dance frame). Pressure from the lead's right hand toward himself, and then a side body action, takes the follow into the back sequence of the box.

**Note:** The lead must understand the concept of the forward side close as being the forward sequence of the box and the backward side close as being the back sequence of the box. It is important because this terminology will be used in future patterns and leads.

## Box Turn

**Position:** Closed
**Level:** Beginning 2

| STEPS | 4/4 COUNTS | RHYTHM CUE |
|---|---|---|
| Step left forward, toe out; turn one-quarter to left | 1–2 | slow |
| Step right sideward | 3 | quick |
| Close left to right, take weight on left | 4 | quick |
| Step right backward, toe in; turn one-quarter to left | 1–2 | slow |
| Step left sideward | 3 | quick |
| Close right to left, take weight on right | 4 | quick |
| Step left forward, toe out; turn one-quarter to left | 1–2 | slow |
| Step right sideward | 3 | quick |
| Close left to right, take weight on left | 4 | quick |
| Step right backward, toe in; turn one-quarter to left | 1–2 | slow |
| Step left sideward | 3 | quick |
| Close right to left, take weight on right | 4 | quick |

**Step Cue:** Turn side close, turn side close.

**Style:** The follow is taking the reverse of this pattern except that, when the follow steps forward with her left foot, instead of toeing out as described for the lead, she steps forward between lead's feet. This style for the follow greatly facilitates the turn.

**Lead:** Refer to lead indications above. A cue for the lead might be bank side close, draw side close.

**Note:** The lead may use this turn to maneuver himself into any direction he may wish to use next.

## Twinkle, Bronze

**Position:** Closed
**Level:** Beginning 3

This is a simple but pretty step, turning to semi-open dance position momentarily on the forward sequence.

| STEPS | 4/4 COUNTS | RHYTHM CUE |
|---|---|---|
| Step left forward | 1–2 | slow |
| Step right sideward, turning to open position | 3 | quick |
| Close left to right, take weight on left | 4 | quick |
| Step right forward in semi-open position | 1–2 | slow |
| Step left forward, turning on left foot to face partner in closed position | 3 | quick |
| Close right to left, take weight right | 4 | quick |

**Step Cue:** Forward side close, cross side close.

**Style:** The lead and follow do not open up to a side-to-side position, but open just enough to step forward on the inside foot, which feels like a crossing step. It should be accented by a long reaching step on the heel but not a dipping knee or body action.

**Lead:** To lead into a semi-open position or conversation position, the lead should use pressure with the heel of the right hand to turn the follow into open position. The right elbow lowers to the side. The lead must simultaneously turn his own body, not just the follow, so that they end facing the same direction. The left arm relaxes slightly and the left hand sometimes gives the lead for steps in the open position.

**Lead:** To lead from open to closed position, the lead should use pressure of the right hand and raise the right arm up to standard position to move the follow into closed position. She should not have to be pushed but should swing easily into closed position as she feels the arm lifting. She should move completely around to face the lead squarely.

**Note:** It is possible to go into this step when the lead is facing out so that the cross step may travel into the line of direction.

### Twinkle Step (Cross Over)

**Position:** Closed
**Level:** Beginning 3

This is a slow, quick, quick rhythm using right and left parallel positions, led from the forward sequence of the box pattern.

| STEPS | 4/4 COUNTS | RHYTHM CUE |
|---|---|---|
| Step left forward | 1–2 | slow |
| Step right sideward | 3 | quick |
| Close left to right, take weight on left | 4 | quick |
| Step right diagonally forward in right parallel position | 1–2 | slow |
| Step left sideward, turning from right parallel to left parallel position | 3 | quick |
| Close right to left, take weight on right | 4 | quick |
| Step left diagonally forward in left parallel position | 1–2 | slow |
| Step sideward right, turning from left parallel to right parallel position | 3 | quick |
| Close left to right, take weight on left | 4 | quick |
| Step right diagonally forward in right parallel position | 1–2 | slow |
| Step left sideward, turning to closed position | 3 | quick |
| Close right to left, take weight on right | 4 | quick |

**Step Cue:** Diagonal turn together.

**Style:** The quick steps are small. Changing from one parallel position to the other is done in a very smooth, rolling manner. The follow needs lots of practice alone to learn the back side close pattern because it is on the diagonal backward parallel to the lead.

**Lead:** To lead into right parallel position the lead should not use pressure of his right hand, but rather should raise his right arm, rotating the follow counterclockwise one-eighth of a turn while he rotates counterclockwise one-eighth of a turn. This places the lead and follow off to the side of each other facing opposite directions. The follow is to the right of the lead but slightly in front of him. The lead should avoid turning too far so as to be side by side, as this results in poor style and awkward and uncomfortable motion. The lead's left hand may assist the lead by pulling toward his left shoulder.

**Lead:** To lead from right parallel position to left parallel position, the lead should pull with his right hand, lowering the right arm, and push slightly with his left hand, causing a rotation clockwise about a quarter of a turn until the follow is to the left of him but slightly in front of him. They are not side by side.

**Note:** Progress is a zigzag pattern down the floor. The parallel part of the steps may be repeated as many times as desired before going back to closed position.

### Grapevine Step

**Position:** Closed
**Level:** Beginning 3

It is a beautiful pattern in slow, quick, quick time with four quick steps added to make the grapevine design, using parallel position.

| STEPS | 4/4 COUNTS | RHYTHM CUE |
|---|---|---|
| Step left forward | 1–2 | slow |
| Step right sideward, turning into right parallel position | 3 | quick |
| Close left to right, take weight on left | 4 | quick |
| Step right diagonally forward in right parallel position | 1 | quick |
| Step left sideward, turning to left parallel position | 2 | quick |
| Step right diagonally backward in left parallel position | 3 | quick |
| Step left sideward, turning to right parallel position | 4 | quick |
| Step right forward in right parallel position | 1–2 | slow |
| Step left sideward, turning to closed position | 3 | quick |
| Close right to left, take weight on right | 4 | quick |

| **Step Cue:** | Forward, side, turn | forward, side, back, side | forward, side, close |
|---|---|---|---|
| | forward sequence of box | grapevine pattern | transition back to closed position |

**Style:** Practice on the grapevine step alone will help dancers get this pattern smoothly and beautifully. Cue lead: forward, side, back, side (right, left, right, left) on the grapevine step. Cue follow: back, side, forward, side (left, right, left, right) on the grapevine step.

**Lead:** To lead into right parallel position, the lead should not use pressure of his right hand, but rather should raise his right arm, rotating the follow counterclockwise one-eighth of a turn while he rotates counterclockwise one-eighth of a turn. This places the lead and follow off to the side of each other, facing opposite directions. The follow is to the right of the lead but slightly in front of him. The lead should avoid turning too far so as to be side by side, as this results in poor style and awkward and uncomfortable motion. The lead's left hand may assist the lead by pulling toward his left shoulder.

**Lead:** To lead from right parallel position to left parallel position, the lead should pull with his right hand, lowering the right arm, and push slightly with his left hand, causing a rotation clockwise about a quarter of a turn until the follow is to the left of him but slightly in front of him. They are not side by side.

**Lead:** The lead is from the forward sequence of the box.

**Note:** The lead should maneuver to face out before he starts this step so that the grapevine step may travel in the line of direction. He may maneuver into this by use of a three-quarter turn or a hesitation step.

## The Pivot Turn

The continuous pivot turn is a series of steps turning clockwise as many beats as desired. The lead should be careful that he has room to turn, as the pivot turn progresses forward in the line of direction if done properly, and he should not turn so many steps as to make his partner dizzy. The principle involved in the footwork is the dovetailing of the feet, which means that the right foot always steps between partner's feet and the left foot always steps around the outside of partner's feet. The pivot turn described here has two slow beats as a preparation followed by four quick beats turning and comes out of it into the box step.

### The Pivot Turn

**Position:** Closed
**Level:** Intermediate

| STEPS | 4/4 COUNTS | RHYTHM CUE |
|---|---|---|
| Step left forward | 1–2 | slow |
| Step right forward, starting to turn the body clockwise and increasing the body tension | 3–4 | slow |
| Step left, toeing in across the line of direction and rolling clockwise three-quarters of the way around on the ball of the left foot | 1 | quick |
| Step right, between partner's feet forward in the line of direction, completing one turn | 2 | quick |
| Step left, toeing in and reaching forward but across the line of direction, turning clockwise three-quarters as before | 3 | quick |
| Step right, between partner's feet forward in the line of direction, completing the second turn | 4 | quick |
| Step left forward in the line of direction, not turning but controlling momentum | 1–2 | slow |
| Step right sideward | 3 | quick |
| Close left to right, take weight on left | 4 | quick |
| Step right backward | 1–2 | slow |
| Step left sideward | 3 | quick |
| Close right to left, taking weight right | 4 | quick |

**Step Cue:** Step ready
S S
turn turn turn turn
Q Q Q Q
forward side close
S Q Q
back side close
S Q Q

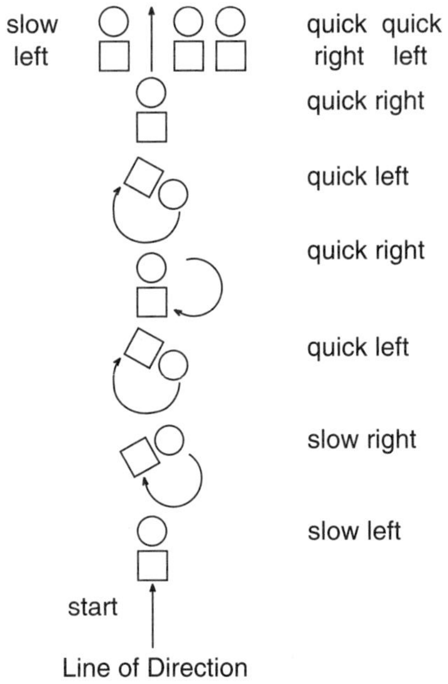


**Follow:** On the second slow beat, the follow receives the lead as the lead increases body tension. She does the same. Then, on the first quick beat, she has been turned far enough to place her right foot forward in between his feet on the line of direction, left foot across the line of direction, right foot between, left across, and into the box step.

**Style:** They both must lean away, pressing outward like "the water trying to stay in the bucket." The concept of stepping each time in relation to the line of direction is what makes it possible to progress while turning as a true pivot turn should do.

**Lead:** To lead all turns, the lead dips his shoulder in the direction of the turn and his upper torso turns before his leg and foot turn.

**Lead:** To lead into a pivot turn clockwise, the lead should hold the follow slightly closer, but with sudden body tension. Resistance is exerted outward by both lead and follow leaning away from each other to take advantage of the centrifugal force of the circular motion. The right foot steps between partner's feet, forward on line of direction, while the left foot reaches across the line of direction and turns on the ball of the foot about three-quarters of the way around.

## *Foxtrot* COMBOS

The Foxtrot routines are listed here merely as examples to show how the various steps can be used in combination for practice routines. They are listed from simple to complex. (Closed position unless otherwise indicated.)

1. *Magic Step*
   2 magic steps
   2 open magic steps
   conversation pivot
2. *Magic Step, box*
   2 magic steps
   1 box step
   2 magic steps (open)
3. *Magic Step, Corté*
   1 magic step (open or closed)
   corté (recover)
   1 side close
   1 box turn
   corté (recover)
4. *Advanced Combo*
   1 magic step
   1 single twinkle to open
   1 single twinkle to left parallel
   1 single twinkle to open
   1 single twinkle to close

8

# *Tango*

THE TANGO BEGAN AS A RAW, sensuous dance born on the Rio de la Plata in Buenos Aires amid the slums in a multiracial setting. In its earliest form, the name *tangoo,* an onomatopoetic rendition of the sounds of drums, strongly suggests its African origin. As with all dance forms, the tango has passed through many evolutions. During its formative stages, it was a combination of *Candombe,* a syncopated African dance, the *Habanera,* an eighteenth-century European dance, and the *Milango,* an indigenous Argentine dance.

The tango and its music was introduced to Paris and the Riviera by wealthy South Americans after World War I. It became the rage of Paris, and it is from this setting and refinement that it spread throughout Europe and came to North America.

The 1990s became the new age of the tango. *Tangueros* are found in major cities around the world. Devotees attend workshops, organize weekly dances, and practice to improve their skills while exchanging feelings and excitement about dancing the Argentine tango. While maintaining its smooth, sophisticated, and suave style, the tango's new charm lies in its improvised nature that relies on communication between partners rather than executing prelearned step routines.

## *Tango* RHYTHM

The modern tango is written in both 2/4 and 4/4 time. Here it will be presented 2/4 time.

| 2/4 | / | / | / | / | / |
|---|---|---|---|---|---|
| | S | S | Q | Q | S |
| | 1 | 2 | 1 | and | 2 |

uneven rhythm

Basic Tango Rhythm

| 2/4 | / | / | |
|---|---|---|---|
| | S | Q | Q |
| | 1 | 2 | and |

uneven rhythm

Box Step Rhythm

| 2/4 | / | | / |
|---|---|---|---|
| | Q | Q | S |
| | 1 | and | 2 |

uneven rhythm

Twinkle Rhythm

The tango rhythm is a deliberate accented beat that is easily distinguished. Few dancers have trouble following the tango rhythm. There is a calculated contrast between the slow promenade beats of the first measure and the staccato of the tango break in the second measure.

## *Tango* STYLE

The tango is characterized by a deliberate glide, not sliding the foot on the floor, but a long reach from the hip with a catlike smoothness and placement of the ball of the foot on the floor. The knees remain straight. The break, which is quick, quick slow, is a sudden contrast ending in the subtle draw of the feet together. It is this combination of slow gliding beats and the sharp break that makes the tango distinctive. Restraint is achieved by the use of continuous flow of movements and a controlled, stylized break presenting disciplined and sophisticated style, instead of a comic caricature. The dancer should strive to effect the idea of floating. Care should be taken to avoid the look of stiffness. In the long reaching glide, the feet should pass each other close together. The draw in the tango close is executed slowly, taking the full length of the slow beat to bring the feet together and then sweep quickly into the beginning of the basic rhythm again. The follow should synchronize the action of her drawing step with that of the lead. The body and head are carried high and the follow's left hand, instead of being on the lead's shoulder as in other dances, reaches around the lead at his right shoulder-blade level. The fingers of the hand are straight, and the arm is in a straight line from the elbow to the tip of the fingers.

Once in a while, deliberately move the shoulders forward in opposition to the feet. For example, stepping left, the right shoulder moves forward. The fan steps, most glamorous of all tango patterns, turn, whip, or swirl in an exciting, subtle way. The fan style is described in detail with the variations used.

## *Fundamental* TANGO STEPS

Directions are for the lead, facing the line of direction; the follow's part is reversed, except as noted.

### Basic Tango Step

**Position:** Closed
**Level:** Beginning 3

A combination of the promenade or walking step and the break.

| STEPS | 2/4 COUNTS | RHYTHM CUE |
|---|---|---|
| Step left forward | 1 | slow |
| Step right forward | 2 | slow |
| Step left forward | 1 | quick |
| Step right sideward abruptly | *and* | quick |
| Draw left to right, weight remains on right | 2 | slow |

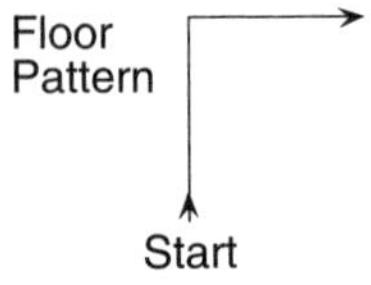


**Step Cue:** Forward, forward, tango close.
S S QQ S

**Style:** The slow beats are long, smooth, gliding steps. The feet pass each other closely. The break–quick, quick, slow–is in place or slightly forward.

**Lead:** Lead must draw to the right with right hand and elbow to guide the follow in the break step.

**Note:** This step repeats each time from the lead's left foot, because there is no change of weight on the draw. This pattern will tend to carry the couple outward toward the wall. It immediately becomes necessary to know how to vary the step in order to counteract this action. Open position, right parallel position, or quarter-turn all may be used for this purpose.

### Tango Step Variations

- Promenade
- Right Parallel Basic Tango
- Quarter-Turn
- Cross Step and Quarter-Turn
- Half-Turn Counterclockwise
- Half-Turn Clockwise
- Double Cross
- The Box Step
- The Corté
- Preparation Step

### Promenade

**Position:** Closed
**Level:** Beginning 2

| STEPS | 2/4 COUNTS | RHYTHM CUE |
|---|---|---|
| Step left into open position, turning abruptly | 1 | slow |
| Step right forward, in open position | 2 | slow |

| STEPS | 2/4 COUNTS | RHYTHM CUE |
|---|---|---|
| Step left forward, a short step, pivoting on left foot abruptly to face partner in closed position | 1 | quick |
| Step right sideward, in closed position | *and* | quick |
| Draw left to right, no change of weight | 2 | slow |

**Step Cue:** Open, step, close, side, draw.

**Style:** The abrupt turning to open position on the first slow step and the turn back to closed position are sharp and only a firmness in the body can accomplish this.

**Lead:** Refer to directions for leading, numbers 7 and 8, page 419–420. The lead is sudden and on the first slow beat.

### Right Parallel Basic Tango

**Position:** Closed
**Level:** Beginning 3

| STEPS | 2/4 COUNTS | RHYTHM CUE |
|---|---|---|
| Step left diagonally into right parallel position, turning abruptly | 1 | slow |
| Step right forward | 2 | slow |
| Step left, a short step forward, turning abruptly to closed dance position | 1 | quick |
| Step right sideward | *and* | quick |
| Draw left to right, no change of weight | 2 | slow |

**Step Cue:** Parallel, step, close, side, draw.

**Style:** Right parallel travels diagonally forward; follow's foot reaches parallel to lead's left foot. The second slow is an exaggerated reaching step forward.

**Lead:** To lead into right parallel position (left reverse open position) the lead should not use pressure of his right hand, but rather should raise his right arm, rotating the follow counterclockwise one-eighth of a turn while he rotates counterclockwise one-eighth of a turn. This places the lead and follow off to the side of each other facing opposite directions. The follow is to the right of the lead, but slightly in front of him. The lead should avoid turning too far so as to be side by side, as this results in poor style and awkward and uncomfortable motion. The lead's left hand may assist the lead by pulling toward his left shoulder.

### Quarter-Turn

**Position:** Closed
**Level:** Beginning 3

| STEPS | 2/4 COUNTS | RHYTHM CUE |
|---|---|---|
| Step left forward | 1 | slow |
| Step right forward | 2 | slow |
| Step left, turning one-quarter counterclockwise | 1 | quick |
| Step right sideward | *and* | quick |
| Draw left to right, no change of weight | 2 | slow |

### Cross Step and Quarter-Turn

**Position:** Closed
**Level:** Intermediate

| STEPS | 2/4 COUNTS | RHYTHM CUE |
|---|---|---|
| Step left sideward | 1 | slow |
| Step right across in front of left, take weight right | 2 | slow |
| Step left sideward, turn toe out, turn one-quarter counterclockwise | 1 | quick |
| Step right sideward | *and* | quick |
| Draw left to right, no change of weight | 2 | slow |

**Step Cue:** Side, cross, turn, side, close.

**Style:** All of this pattern is taken in closed position. The turn actually begins by a pivot on the crossing foot at the end of the second slow beat.

**Lead:** Refer to directions for leading, number 12, page 420.

### Half-Turn Counterclockwise

**Position:** Closed
**Level:** Beginning 3

| STEPS | 2/4 COUNTS | RHYTHM CUE |
|---|---|---|
| Step left into semi-open position, turning abruptly | 1 | slow |
| Step right forward, a short step, pivoting one-quarter counterclockwise on the right foot; bring up right arm and turn the follow around the lead a three-quarter turn to closed position | 2 | slow |
| Step left bringing left foot next to right foot | 1 | quick |
| Step right sideward | *and* | quick |
| Draw left to right, no weight change | 2 | slow |

**Step Cue:** Step, pivot, break, side, draw.

**Style:** The follow pivots counterclockwise on her left foot (second slow beat) around the lead a three-quarter turn into closed position. The follow's step on this beat is a longer step than the lead's, giving her freedom to pivot. She must bring her first quick step with right foot alongside of left foot.

**Lead:** Lead must bring up his right arm and elbow firmly, almost lifting her so that she can pivot easily on her left foot on the second slow beat.

### Half-Turn Clockwise

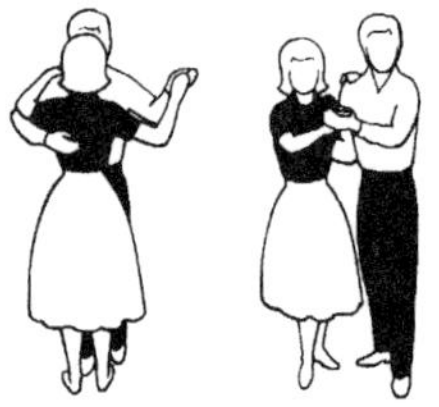

**Position:** Closed
**Level:** Beginning 3

| STEPS | 2/4 COUNTS | RHYTHM CUE |
|---|---|---|
| Step left into semi-open position, turning abruptly | 1 | slow |
| Step right forward, a long step, pivoting one-half clockwise on the right foot around the follow into closed position | 2 | slow |

| STEPS | 2/4 COUNTS | RHYTHM CUE |
|---|---|---|
| Step left sideward, a short step apart from where right foot is at the end of the pivot | 1 | quick |
| Step right sideward | *and* | quick |
| Draw left to right, no weight change | 2 | slow |

**Step Cue:** Step, pivot, break, side, draw.

**Style:** The lead smoothly pivots on his right foot clockwise about halfway around the follow. The follow turns clockwise in place on her left foot. This step is very easy for the follow.

**Lead:** Refer to directions for leading, numbers 7 and 8, pages 419–420, for open and closed position. The main lead is increased resistance in hand, arm, and body as the lead pivots halfway around the follow.

### Double Cross

**Position:** Closed, in twinkle rhythm
**Level:** Intermediate

| STEPS | 2/4 COUNTS | RHYTHM CUE |
|---|---|---|
| Step left sideways | 1 | slow |
| Step right across in front of left | 2 | slow |
| Point left sideways, take weight slightly | 1 | quick |
| Pivot hips to right with a slight push off with left, take weight right | *and* | quick |
| Swing left across in front of right, take weight left | 2 | slow |
| Point right to side | 1 | quick |
| Pivot hips to left with slight push off with right, take weight left | *and* | quick |
| Swing right across in front of left, take weight right | 2 | slow |

**Step Cue:** Side cross pivot and cross pivot and cross.
S S Q Q S Q Q S

**Style:** Stay in closed position throughout. Follow crosses in front, also.

**Lead:** Firm body and arm control are needed to hold closed position.

**Note:** Finish with break, side, draw, quick, quick, slow. This could also be done with the follow crossing behind.

### The Box Step

**Position:** Closed
**Level:** Beginning 3

The rhythm of the tango box step is like that described in the Foxtrot—slow, quick, quick—forward side close, back side close. The tango gliding action will be used on the first slow beat. The box step variations for Foxtrot may also be used here, including the box turn (page 464) and the grapevine step (page 466).

### The Corté

The corté is a dip, most often taken backward on the lead's left or right foot. It is a type of break step used to finish off almost any tango variation and is used as an ending to the dance. The skilled dancer will learn to use the corté in relationship to the music of the tango so that the feeling of the corté will correspond to the climax or the phrase of the musical accompaniment.

The left corté will be described here. A right corté may be taken by starting on the right foot and reversing the pattern. A preliminary step is nearly always used as a preparation for going into the corté. It is described here as a part of the rhythm of the corté.

### Preparation Step

| STEPS | 2/4 COUNTS | RHYTHM CUE |
|---|---|---|
| Step forward left, a short step | 1 | quick |
| Shift weight back onto right | *and* | quick |

### Corté

**Level:** Intermediate

| STEPS | 2/4 COUNTS | RHYTHM CUE |
|---|---|---|
| Step left backward, take weight, and bend left knee slightly | 2 | slow |
| Recover forward, take weight right | 1 | slow |
| Step left in place beside right | 2 | quick |
| Step right in place beside left | *and* | quick |

**Step Cue:** Rock and dip recover step step.
Q Q S S Q Q

**Style:** As the *lead* steps backward into the corté, the weight is all taken on the standing foot with a bent knee. The lead should turn his bent knee slightly outward so that the follow's knee will not bump his as they go into the dip. His left shoulder and arm move forward (the left leg and left shoulder are in opposition). His back should remain straight. He should avoid leaning either backward or forward. His right foot should be extended (arched) so that the toe is only touching the floor.

The *follow* should step forward on the right, arch her back, and place all of her weight over the forward right foot. The right knee is bent. The left leg is extended behind and should be a straight line from hip to toe. A bent line makes the whole figure sag. The left arch of the foot should be extended so that the toe is pointed and remains in contact with the floor. If the follow steps forward too far or does not bend the forward knee, she will be forced to bend at the waist, which destroys the form of the figure. She may look back over her left shoulder. The execution of the dip should be as smooth as any slow backward step.

The lead should avoid leaping or falling back into the dip.

**Lead:** The left shoulder leads forward as the lead goes into the preparation step on the first beat. There is an increase of tension of the lead's right arm and hand also on the first beat, plus general resistance throughout the upper body. The lead will draw the follow with his right arm when stepping into the dip and release on the recovery step. The lead is essential for the corté as the pattern cannot be executed correctly unless both lead and follow are completely on balance and ready for it.

**Note:** The recovery step is followed by two quick steps left right, which finish on count 2 and complete the measure of music. These may be omitted when they follow a variation that takes up those extra counts. Learn the footwork first, then work on the style.

## Fan Step

The *fan* is a term used to describe a manner of executing a leg motion, in which the free leg swings in a whiplike movement around a small pivoting base. This should not be a large sweeping movement in a wide arc but rather a small subtle action initiated in the hip and executed with the legs close together. The balance is carefully poised over the pivoting foot at all times. When the lead and follow take the fan motion, the action is taken parallel to partner; that is, the right leg, which is free, swings forward. When it reaches its full extension, just barely off the floor, the right hip turns the leg over, knee down, while pivoting on the standing foot to face the opposite direction. The right leg then swings through forward and the weight is taken on the right foot. This action usually is done in slow rhythm. Accompanying the hip action there is also a lift and turn on the ball of the standing foot. This lift permits the free leg to swing through gracefully extended and close in a beautiful floating style.

### Open Fan

**Position:** Open
**Level:** Intermediate

| STEPS | 2/4 COUNTS | RHYTHM CUE |
|---|---|---|
| Step left forward | 1 | slow |
| Step right forward | 2 | slow |
| Step left in place, releasing right arm around follow, and turn halfway around to the right to a side-by-side position with follow on lead's left | 1 | quick |
| Step right sideward, a short step | *and* | quick |
| Draw left to right, no weight change (the lead's left hand is holding the follow's right) | 2 | slow |
| Step forward left | 1 | quick |
| Swing the right leg forward, pivoting on left foot while fanning the right, coming halfway around to open position | *and* | quick |
| Step forward right in open position | 2 | slow |
| Step left forward, pivoting toward the follow into closed position | 1 | quick |
| Step right sideward | *and* | quick |
| Draw left to right, no weight change | 2 | slow |

**Step Cue:** Forward, forward, open, side, draw, fan, through, break, side, draw.

**Style:** When the lead releases his arm around her, the follow turns halfway around to the left. On the fan, the follow steps right, swings left leg forward, hip turns over, knee faces down. Foot is kept close to the floor and sweeps through, pivoting clockwise to open position, and weight is transferred forward onto left foot. She then goes into break step with partner.

**Lead:** The lead drops his right arm and pulls away from the follow to side-by-side position. Then, with his left hand, he pulls in as he fans through to open position and from there lifts his right arm into closed position for tango close.

**Note:** This is an easy step in fan style for beginners and gives them the thrill of the tango.

### Grapevine Fan

**Position:** Start in open position; end in closed.
**Level:** Intermediate

| STEPS | 2/4 COUNTS | RHYTHM CUE |
|---|---|---|
| Step left forward | 1 | slow |
| Rock forward and back right, left | 2 *and* | quick, quick |
| Step right backward, rising on right toe and lifting left leg just off the floor | 1 | slow |
| Step left backward, turning toward partner | 2 | quick |
| Step right sideward, turning to face reverse open position | *and* | quick |
| Step left forward in reverse open position | 1 | quick |
| Fan right leg forward and through to open position | *and* | quick |
| Step right forward, in open position | 2 | slow |
| Step left forward, a short step, turning to closed position | 1 | quick |
| Step right sideward | *and* | quick |
| Draw left to right, no weight change | 2 | slow |

**Step Cue:** Step rock and back grapevine step fan through break side close.
S Q Q S Q Q Q Q S Q Q S

**Style:** The couple should not get too far apart or lean forward to maneuver this grapevine pattern. They should stand upright and keep carefully balanced over standing foot. The fanning leg swings in line with the traveling and facing action, not in a side arc. The legs are kept close together.

**Lead:** This is a pattern lead and follow must know together but the lead cues the follow by use of both hands and use of his body in turning from one position to another.

**Note:** This is a beautiful pattern when used following the forward and open rock.

### Parallel Fan

**Position:** Start in closed position; fan style in parallel position.
**Level:** Intermediate

| STEPS | 2/4 COUNTS | RHYTHM CUE |
|---|---|---|
| **Lead's Part:** Starts and ends in closed position Starting left, take one basic tango step, slow, slow, quick, quick, slow | | |
| Step left forward | 1 | slow |
| Step right sideward, turning to open position | 2 | quick |
| Step left to right, taking weight left | *and* | quick |
| Step right forward, turning follow to right parallel position | 1 | slow |
| Rock backward onto left, turning follow to open position | 2 | slow |
| Rock forward onto right, turning follow to right parallel position | 1 | slow |
| Rock back onto left, turning follow to open position | 2 | slow |
| Step right forward turning follow to closed position | 1 | slow |
| Take tango close step, turning to closed position | 2 *and* 1 | quick, quick, slow |

| STEPS | 2/4 COUNTS | RHYTHM CUE |
|---|---|---|
| **Follow's Part:** Starting right, take one basic tango step, slow, slow, quick, quick, slow | | |
| Step right backward | 1 | slow |
| Step left sideward, turning to open position | 2 | quick |
| Step right to left, taking weight on right | *and* | quick |
| Step left forward (fan), pivoting to right parallel position | 1 | slow |
| Step right forward (fan), pivoting to open position | 2 | slow |
| Step left forward (fan), pivoting to right parallel position | 1 | slow |
| Step right forward (fan), pivoting to open position | 2 | slow |
| Step left forward, turning to closed position | 1 | slow |
| Take tango close | 2 *and* 1 | quick, quick, slow |

**Step Cue:** With slow and quick rhythm except for the fan: rock, rock, rock, rock/forward break, side, draw.

**Style:** The steps are small in the fan part of the step so that the follow may turn without reaching for the step. The lead in the fan part of the step rocks forward, back, forward, back in place, as he turns the follow. She takes her fan, pivoting alternately on the left, right, left, right, swinging the free leg forward a short distance until the toe just clears the floor and then turning the hip with her pivot to the new direction and reaching through for the next step. The follow should rise slightly on her toe as she pivots. This smooths out the turn and makes one of the most beautiful movements in the tango.

**Lead:** The lead's first lead will be to lower right arm into open position. He then guides her forward with his right hand, moving her alternately from right parallel position to open position until the end, when he raises his right arm and turns her to closed position.

**Note:** A corté may be added to this figure instead of the tango close by stepping through to open position on the right (count 1), turning the follow quickly to closed position, rocking forward and back (counts 2 *and*); corté (count 1), recover onto the left foot (count 2), and finish with tango close (counts 1 and 2).

## *Tango* COMBOS

The tango routines are combinations for practice, listed from simple to complex. (Closed position, unless otherwise indicated.)

1. *Basic*
   2 basics
   1 promenade
2. *Basic, Cross Step*
   2 basics
   4 cross steps and quarter-turn
3. *Box, Basic, Cross Step*
   2 box steps
   1 basic
   1 cross step and quarter-turn
4. *Basic, Cross, Corté*
   2 basics
   1 cross step, quarter-turn
   1 corté
5. *Advanced Combo*
   2 box steps
   1 basic
   1 cross step
   open fan
6. *Advanced Combo*
   2 basics
   open fan
   half-turn clockwise
   corté
   1 basic

# Waltz

ALTHOUGH A MAJORITY OF the middle European countries lay some claim to the origin of the waltz, the world gives credit for its rise mainly to Germany and Austria, where the great waltz was made traditional by the beautiful music of Johann Strauss and his sons. It has a pulsating, swinging rhythm, which has been enjoyed by dancers everywhere, even by those who dance it only in its simplest pattern, the waltz turn. Its immediate popularity and its temporary obscurity are not unlike other fine inheritances of the past, which come and go with the ebb and flow of popular accord. Early use of the waltz in America was at the elegant social balls and cotillions. Its outstanding contribution to present-day dancing is the waltz position. Even in its early stages, it was quite some time before this position was socially acceptable. Now the closed position is universally the basic position for ballroom dancing.

The waltz music is played in three different tempos—slow, medium, and fast. The slow or medium waltz is preferred by most people. However, the fast waltz is a favorite of those who know the Viennese style. The slower American style is danced for the most part on a box pattern, but the use of other variations has added a new interest.

## Waltz RHYTHM

The waltz is played in 3/4 time. It is three beats per measure of music, with an accent on the first beat. The three beats of waltz time are very even, each beat receiving the same amount of time. The three movements of the waltz step pattern blend perfectly with the musical tempo or beat of each measure. The tempo may be slow, medium, or fast.

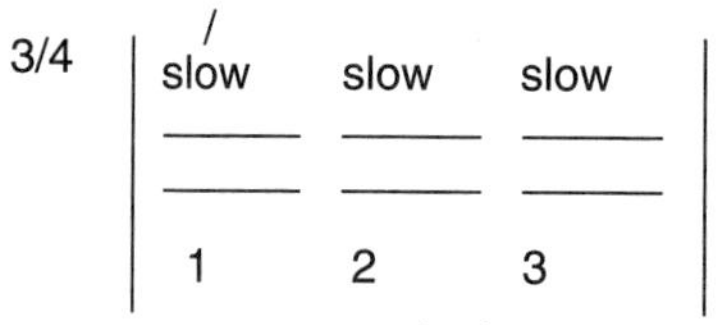


even rhythm

Slow Box Rhythm

**Canter rhythm** in waltz time is a means of holding the first and second beats together so the resultant pattern is an uneven rhythm, or slow, quick, slow, quick. It is counted 1, 3, 1, 3.

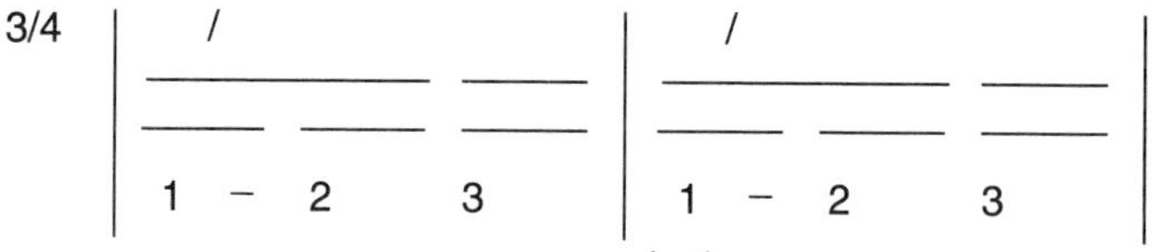


uneven rhythm

Canter Rhythm

The Viennese waltz is an even three-beat rhythm, played very fast. It is a turning pattern. There is only one step on the first beat of the measure and a pivot of the body on that foot for the two remaining counts of the measure.

3/4 | step (/) pivot | 1 2 3 |

even rhythm

Viennese Rhythm

## *Waltz* STYLE

The waltz is a smooth dance with a gliding quality that weaves an even pattern of swinging and turning movement. The first accented beat of the music is also accented in the motion. The first step of the waltz pattern is the reaching step forward, backward, sideward, or turning. Because it is the first beat that gives the dance its new impetus, its new direction, or a change of step, there evolves a pulsating feeling, which can be seen rather markedly and is the chief characteristic of the beauty of the waltz. This should not be interpreted as a rocking or bobbing motion of the body. Starting with knees slightly bent (as if just finishing count 3), on count 1, the lead steps forward; on count 2, his body rises, stepping on the ball of the foot; on count 3, his feet come together and his body lowers. The "rise and fall" action of the body can be seen in every waltz step. The footwork is most effective when the foot taking the second beat glides past the standing foot as it moves into the sideward step. The feet should never be heard to scrape the floor, but should seem to float in a silent pattern.

## *Fundamental* WALTZ STEPS

Directions are for the lead, facing line of direction; follow's part is reversed, except as noted.

### Box Step

**Position:** Closed
**Level:** Beginning 2

| STEPS | 3/4 COUNTS | STYLE CUE |
|---|---|---|
| Step left forward | 1 | level |
| Step right sideward, passing close to the left foot | 2 | rise |
| Close left to right, take weight left | 3 | lower |
| Step right backward | 1 | level |
| Step left sideward, passing close to the right foot | 2 | rise |
| Close right to left, take weight right | 3 | lower |

Floor Pattern

**Step Cue:** Forward side close, back side close.

**Style:** The forward step is *on the heel.* Follow through on the second beat, moving the free foot closely past the standing foot, but do not lose a beat by stopping. Body rises on count 2 as stepping on ball of foot, and lowers on count 3. The floor pattern is a long narrow rectangle rather than a square box.

**Lead:** To initiate a box step, the lead should use a forward body action followed by a side body action, using his firm right side connection (dance frame). Pressure from the lead's right hand toward himself, and then a side body action, takes the follow into the back sequence of the box.

**Note:** The lead must understand the concept of the forward side close as being the forward sequence of the box and the backward side close as being the back sequence of the box. This terminology will be used in future patterns.

## Box Turn

**Position:** Closed
**Level:** Beginning 2

| STEPS | 3/4 COUNTS | STYLE CUE |
|---|---|---|
| Step left forward, toe out, turning one-quarter left | 1 | level |
| Step right sideward, gliding past the left foot | 2 | rise |
| Close left to right, taking weight left | 3 | lower |
| Step right backward, toe in, turning one-quarter left | 1 | level |
| Step left sideward, gliding past the right foot | 2 | rise |
| Close right to left, taking weight right | 3 | lower |
| Step left forward, toe out, turning one-quarter left | 1 | level |
| Step right sideward, gliding past the left foot | 2 | rise |
| Close left to right, taking weight on left | 3 | lower |
| Step right backward, toe in, turning one-quarter left | 1 | level |
| Step left sideward, gliding past the right foot | 2 | rise |
| Close right to left, taking weight right | 3 | lower |

**Step Cue:** Turn side close, turn side close.

**Follow:** The follow is taking the reverse pattern, except that, when the follow steps forward with the left foot, instead of toeing out as described for the lead, she steps forward between the lead's feet, her left foot next to the instep of the lead's left foot. This style greatly facilitates the turn.

**Lead:** A common error is that the lead tries to step around his partner. The follow must be directly in front of her partner.

**Style:** Accent the first step by reaching with a longer step. However, the lead must be careful not to overreach his partner. There is no unnecessary knee bending or bobbing up and down.

**Lead:** To lead a box turn with slight pressure of the right hand, the lead should use the right arm and shoulder to guide or bank the follow into the turn. The shoulders press forward during the forward step and draw backward during the backward step.

**Note:** For the right turn, start with the right foot. Follow the same pattern with opposite footwork.

## Traveling Box

**Position:** Closed
**Level:** Beginning 2

Use this step to travel around the dance floor in the line of direction.

| STEPS | 3/4 COUNTS | STYLE CUE |
|---|---|---|
| Step left forward | 1 | forward |
| Step right side | 2 | rise |
| Close left to right, taking weight left | 3 | lower |

| | | |
|---|---|---|
| Step right forward | 1 | forward |
| Step left side | 2 | rise |
| Close right to left, taking weight right | 3 | lower |

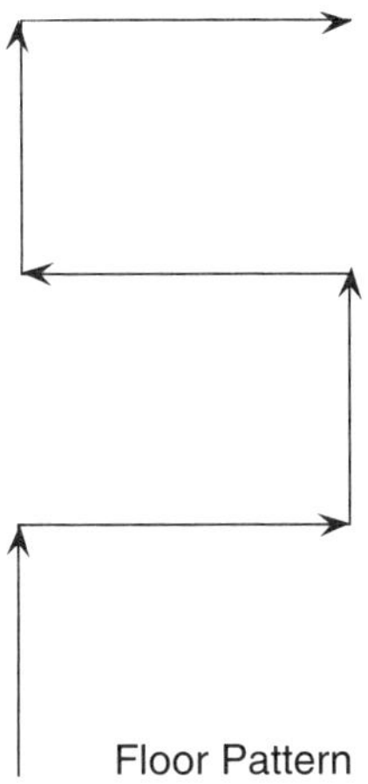

Floor Pattern

**Style:** The first three counts are exactly like the basic box step. On count 2 of the second part, the lead must step forward, in between the follow's feet, not outside.

**Lead:** The lead has a forward body action on count 1 of the second part, guiding the follow in line of direction. If the lead hesitates, the follow will start to move in the back sequence of the box step.

## Teaching Strategy for Changing Leads from Turn Right to a Turn Left

It is important to learn to turn counterclockwise and clockwise. The foot must be free to *lead* in the direction of the turn: left lead for left turn; right lead for right turn. There are several ways to change the lead. With the left, step balance or a hesitation step, then start the box with the right foot (right side close, left side close). Another is to take two waltz steps forward, take the third waltz step backward; right foot is now free to turn right. To return to the left lead, either step (right) balance or take two waltz steps forward and the third one backward; then the left foot leads again. Once the student can turn left and right, the teacher should present a definite routine that drills this change. When students learn this concept for the waltz, they will be able to transfer the principle to other rhythms.

## Waltz Step Variations

| | | |
|---|---|---|
| Hesitation Step | Weaving Step | Streamline Step |
| Cross Step | Twinkle Step | Viennese Waltz |

### Hesitation Step

**Position:** Closed
**Level:** Beginning 3

| STEPS | 3/4 COUNTS | STYLE CUE |
|---|---|---|
| Step left forward | 1 | level |
| Bring right foot up to the instep of left and hold, no weight change | 2, 3 | rise |
| Step right backward | 1 | level |
| Bring left foot up to the instep of right foot, no weight change | 2, 3 | rise |

**Step Cue:** Step close hold.

**Style:** Smooth.

**Lead:** To lead a hesitation step, the lead dips his shoulder in the direction of the turn, and his upper torso turns before his leg and foot turn.

**Note:** As in the Foxtrot, a beautiful combination is to dance two hesitation steps, then the first half of the box turn, two more hesitation steps, and then the second half of the turn. The hesitation step repeated may also be done turning either counterclockwise or clockwise and may be useful in maneuvering for the next step.

### Cross Step (Bronze Twinkle)

**Position:** Closed
**Level:** Beginning 3

| STEPS | 3/4 COUNTS | STYLE CUE |
|---|---|---|
| Step left forward | 1 | level |
| Step right sideward, turning to semi-open position | 2 | rise |
| Close left to right, taking weight left | 3 | lower |
| Step right forward, in semi-open position | 1 | level |
| Step left forward, turning on left foot to face partner in closed position | 2 | rise |
| Close right to left, taking weight right | 3 | lower |

**Step Cue:** Forward side close, cross side close.

**Style:** The position is closed to semi-open position, just enough to step forward on the inside foot, which feels like a crossing step. It should be accented by a long, smooth, reaching step on the heel, not a dipping or bobbing action.

**Lead:** To lead into a semi-open position or conversation position, the lead should use pressure with the heel of the right hand to turn the follow into semi-open position. The right elbow lowers to the side. The lead must simultaneously turn his own body, not just the follow, so that they end facing the same direction. The left arm relaxes slightly, and the left hand sometimes gives the lead for steps in the semi-open position.

**Lead:** To lead from semi-open to closed position, the lead should use pressure of the right hand and raise the right arm up to standard position to move the follow into closed position. The follow should not have to be pushed but should swing easily into closed position as she feels the arm lifting. She should move completely around to face the lead squarely.

**Note:** When the lead is facing out in closed position, he can go into this step and the cross pattern will travel in the line of direction.

### Weaving Step

This step is the same as the Cross Step, only the crossing is from side to side.

**Position:** Closed
**Level:** Intermediate

| STEPS | 3/4 COUNTS | STYLE CUE |
|---|---|---|
| Step left forward | 1 | level |
| Step right sideward, turning to semi-open position | 2 | rise |
| Close left to right, taking weight left | 3 | lower |
| Step right forward in semi-open position | 1 | level |
| Step left forward, turning to side-by-side position facing the reverse line of direction | 2 | rise |
| Close right to left, taking weight right | 3 | lower |
| Step left forward, in side-by-side position | 1 | level |
| Step right forward, turning to open position | 2 | rise |
| Close left to right, taking weight left | 3 | lower |
| Step right forward in open position | 1 | level |

| | | |
|---|---|---|
| Step left forward, turning to closed position | 2 | rise |
| Close right to left, taking weight right | 3 | lower |

**Step Cue:** Forward side open, cross side reverse, cross side reverse, cross side close.

**Style:** Reach into crossing step on the heel. It is a long reaching step on the accented beat.

**Lead:** Turn follow to semi-open position for first cross step and then drop right arm and lead through with the left hand to side-by-side position, facing the reverse line of direction. Next time, as they reverse direction, the lead puts his arm around her in open position and follows standard procedure for returning to closed position.

**Note:** The weave pattern may be repeated back and forth, crossing as many times as desired, but should go back to closed position as described above.

## Twinkle Step

**Position:** Closed
**Level:** Intermediate

It is led from the back sequence of the box step.

| STEPS | 3/4 COUNTS | STYLE CUE |
|---|---|---|
| Step left forward | 1 | level |
| Step right sideward, turning into right parallel position | 2 | rise |
| Close left to right, taking weight left | 3 | lower |
| Step right, diagonally forward in right parallel position | 1 | level |
| Step left sideward, turning from right parallel to left parallel position | 2 | rise |
| Close right to left, taking weight right | 3 | lower |
| Step left diagonally forward in left parallel position | 1 | level |
| Step right sideward, turning from left parallel position to right parallel position | 2 | rise |
| Close left to right, taking weight on left | 3 | lower |
| Step right diagonally forward in right parallel position | 1 | level |
| Step left sideward, turning to closed position | 2 | rise |
| Close right to left, taking weight on right | 3 | lower |

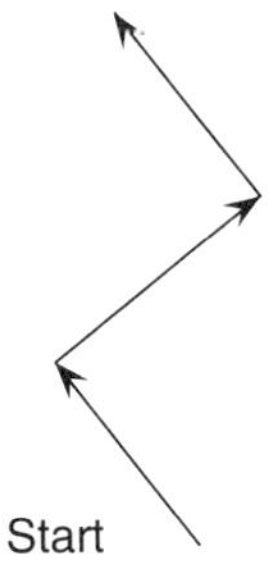

Floor pattern

**Step Cue:** Step turn close. The second beat has a short step and a smooth roll from one position to another. The follow reaches parallel to the lead's step, except that she is stepping diagonally backward, which takes a lot of practice to do well.

**Lead:** To lead into right parallel position the lead should not use pressure of his right hand, but rather should raise his right arm, rotating the follow counterclockwise one-eighth of a turn while he rotates counterclockwise one-eighth of a turn. This places the lead and follow off to the side of each other facing opposite directions. The follow is to the right of the lead but slightly in front of him. The lead should avoid turning too far so as to be side by side, as this results in poor style and awkward and uncomfortable motion. The lead's left hand may assist the lead by pulling toward his left shoulder.

**Lead:** To lead from right parallel position to left parallel position the lead should pull with his right hand, lowering the right arm, and push slightly with his left hand, causing a rotation clockwise about a quarter of a turn until the follow is to the left of him but slightly in front of him. They are not side by side.

**Note:** Progress is in a zigzag pattern down the floor in the line of direction and may repeat over and over as desired.

## Suggestions for Variations

Any student or teacher who has followed these directions this far should be prepared to make use of the corté (page 462–463), advance twinkle (pages 464–465), and pivot turn (pages 467–468) described in the Foxtrot section by transposing a slow, quick, quick in 4/4 time into slow, slow, slow in 3/4 time.

### Viennese Waltz

**Level:** Advanced

The rhythm is three even, quick beats instead of slow ones. The Viennese waltz music is fast and it is hard to keep one's balance on the pivot step when it is slowed down, so that students get discouraged learning the step. An experiment of a half-Viennese has proved successful in getting students to learn the pivot step by doing it first on the right foot and then taking a regular waltz step on the left sequence.

| 3/4 | step | side | cross | step | pivot | |
|---|---|---|---|---|---|---|
| | 1 | 2 | 3 | 1 | 2 | 3 |
| | quick | quick | quick | right | pivot | |

Half-Viennese Step

**Half-Viennese Step:** Both lead and follow need to practice this pattern alone, traveling down the line of direction.

| STEPS | 3/4 COUNTS | RHYTHM CUE |
|---|---|---|
| Step left forward, turning one-quarter counterclockwise | 1 | quick |
| Step right sideward, turning one-quarter counterclockwise | 2 | quick |
| Slide the left foot, heel first, in across right to the right of the right foot. Transfer weight to left foot. Both toes are facing the reverse line of direction, feet are crossed | 3 | quick |
| Step right backward and pivot one-half counterclockwise on the right foot | 1 | quick |
| Bring the left foot up to the instep of the right foot and with the left toe help balance on the right foot | 2, 3 | quick, quick |
| Closed position, the lead facing the line of direction. | | |
| Starting left, the lead takes the step side cross while the follow, starting right, takes the back pivot | 1, 2, 3 | all quick |
| Starting right, the lead takes the back pivot while the follow, starting left, takes step side across | 1, 2, 3 | all quick |

**Style:** The couple remains in closed position throughout. The steps are small, as the follow is turning on a small pivot base while the lead takes step side cross. Because the lead turns one-quarter on his forward step, his second step is in the line of direction, a small step, and cross on third beat. Then he steps back a short step and pivots while the follow takes the step side cross. The dancers always progress in the line of direction. Use two waltz steps for one complete turn. The body resistance is firm for both lead and follow. They must lean away, pressing outward but keeping the center of gravity over the pivoting feet. The shoulders tilt slightly in one direction and then the other; tilt left as the left foot leads, right as the right foot leads. Do not resist the momentum of body weight, but rather give into the momentum.

**Lead:** Firm body and arms in correct position. The momentum comes from the rapid transfer of the body forward in the line of direction every time on count 1.

**Cue:** 1, 2, 3, 1, 2, 3.

**Viennese Step:** The true Viennese with a step pivot repeated over and over is in closed dance position. Lead starting left forward, follow right backward.

| STEPS | 3/4 COUNTS | RHYTHM CUE |
|---|---|---|
| Step left forward, pivoting on the ball of the foot one-half counterclockwise; the right foot coming up to the instep of the left and with the right toe, helps to balance on the left foot | 1, 2, 3 | all quick |
| Step right backward, pivoting on the ball of the foot one-half counterclockwise; the left foot coming to the instep of the right helps to balance on the right foot | 1, 2, 3 | all quick |

**Step Cue:** Step pivot, step pivot.

**Style:** There is a lift of the body going into the pivot, which lifts the body weight, momentarily allowing the feet to pivot with less weight. Take care not to throw the weight off balance.

**Lead:** Same as above.

**Variations:** The hesitation step as given under the box pattern is very helpful in giving a rest from the constant turning. Also, by using an uneven number of hesitation steps, the right foot is free and the whole Viennese turn may be changed to a clockwise turn, starting with the right foot and applying the pattern with opposite footwork.

## *Waltz* COMBOS

These waltz routines are combinations for practice, listed from simple to complex. (Closed position, unless otherwise indicated.)

1. *Balance, Box*
   2 balance steps (forward, backward)
   4 box steps
2. *Waltz, Box*
   1 box step
   2 forward waltz steps
   1 box turn
3. *Cross Step, Box Turn*
   2 cross steps
   1 box turn
4. *Hesitation and Box Turn*
   2 hesitation steps (forward, backward)
   1 box turn
5. *Cross Step, Weaving*
   2 cross steps
   1 weaving step
6. *Advanced Combo*
   1 box turn
   4 twinkle steps
   2 hesitation steps
   2 pursuit waltz steps
   1 corté
   1 forward waltz step
7. *Advanced Combo*
   6 streamline steps (18 beats)
   2 twinkle steps
   4 streamline steps
   2 hesitation steps

# Cha Cha

A CUBAN INNOVATION of the old basic Latin form (danson), the cha cha is said to be a combination of the mambo and American swing. A close look shows its rhythm to be that of a triple mambo, its style that of the rumba, and its open swingy variations that of the triple time swing. It does not have as heavy a quality or as large a foot pattern as the mambo; nor has it the smooth sophistication or the conservative figures of the rumba. It reflects a light, breezy mood, a carefree gaiety, and a trend in the challenge steps for dancers to ad-lib variations to their hearts' content. Consequently one sees variations in almost every known position.

## *Cha Cha* RHYTHM

In 4/4 time, the catchy rhythm and delightful music of the cha cha have brought dancers and musicians alike a new treat in the undeniably Latin flavor. The rhythm has been a controversy. Originally it was done on the offbeat of the measure, and then there was a widespread acceptance of the onbeat rhythm, which is the easier way, but the current trend is to go back to the offbeat rhythm. Analysis in this edition will be done with the offbeat rhythm.

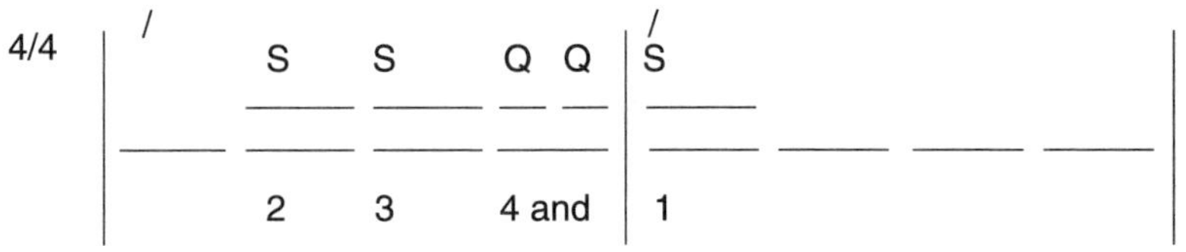


uneven rhythm

The rhythm is an uneven beat pattern of slow, slow, quick, quick, slow and will be counted 2 3 4 *and* 1, with the 4 *and* 1 being the familiar cha cha cha triple. Rhythmically, the beats are as follows:

Note that the last beat of the triple is a quarter note, not an eighth note as is sometimes misinterpreted.

## *Cha Cha* STYLE

The cha cha is seen danced in a variety of positions as it moves in and out of the variations. However, the three basic positions are Latin social, two hands joined, and the challenge. Beginners usually prefer the two hands joined position. In this position, both lead and follow hold their forearms firm, so that the lead can push, pull, or turn the follow. The follow responds with body motion in the direction of the lead, rather than using arm or shoulder motions. The arms and hands, when free, are held up and parallel to the floor. Intermediate and advanced dancers use the challenge position to demonstrate their Cuban motion (hip action) and expressive arm gestures.

The cha cha, with its light bouncy quality, is delightfully Latin as it carries with it some of the subtleness of the rumba movement. The forward foot should be placed nearly flat on the floor. The knee is bent over the stepping foot. The back step (instead of a flat step that tends to give the appearance of a sag) is a toe step, holding the body firmly so as to avoid the sag. The cha cha triple is taken with small steps, keeping contact with the floor. The upper body is held comfortably upright and the head focuses on one's partner in a typical gracious Latin manner. The eye contact brings the dance to life.

## *Fundamental* CHA CHA STEPS

The cha cha has two primary basic steps: the back and forward basic (sometimes referred to as the Slot Cha Cha because it moves back and forward in a narrow space) and the Latin basic, which uses Latin social position.

Directions are for the lead; the follow's part is reverse, except as noted.

### Back Basic Step

**Position:** Challenge or two hands joined
**Level:** Beginning 3

| STEPS | 4/4 COUNTS | RHYTHM CUE |
|---|---|---|
| Step left sideways (preliminary step) | 1 | slow |
| Step right backward | 2 | slow |
| Step left forward in place | 3 | slow |
| Step right in place next to left | 4 | quick (cha) |
| Step left in place | *and* | quick (cha) |
| Step right in place | 1 | slow (cha) |

**Note:** There is a side step on the accented first beat to begin the dance only, and it is not used again.

### Forward Basic Step

**Level:** Beginning 3

| STEPS | 4/4 COUNTS | RHYTHM CUE |
|---|---|---|
| Step left forward | 2 | slow |
| Step right back in place | 3 | slow |
| Step left in place next to right | 4 | quick (cha) |
| Step right in place | *and* | quick (cha) |
| Step left in place | 1 | slow (cha) |

**Step Cue:** Back, forward, cha cha cha; forward, back, cha cha cha.

**Style:** The back basic has the toe step, the forward basic has the flat style (see "Cha Cha Style"). Dancers have a tendency to pound the feet on the floor for the cha cha cha. It should be neither a pounding nor scuffing sound.

**Lead:** The lead leads by pulling with his right hand going into the back basic or pushing with the left hand going into the forward basic. If arm and elbow are firm, finger resistance aids in getting the message across. The body should respond by moving backward or forward.

**Position:** The basic cha cha may be done in facing or challenge position.

**Note:** This is the basic step of cha cha. The forward half is also called the "forward break"; the back half is the "back break."

## Latin Basic in Latin Social Position

This cha cha step travels to the side, rather than forward and back.

**Level:** Intermediate

| STEPS | 4/4 COUNTS | RHYTHM CUE |
|---|---|---|
| Step left sideways (preliminary step) | 1 | slow |
| Step right backward | 2 | slow |
| Step left forward | 3 | slow |
| Step right side right | 4 | quick (cha) |
| Step left next to right | *and* | quick (cha) |
| Step right side right | 1 | slow (cha) |
| Step left forward | 2 | slow |
| Step right backward | 3 | slow |
| Step left side left | 4 | quick (cha) |
| Step right, next to left | *and* | quick (cha) |
| Step left side left | 1 | slow (cha) |

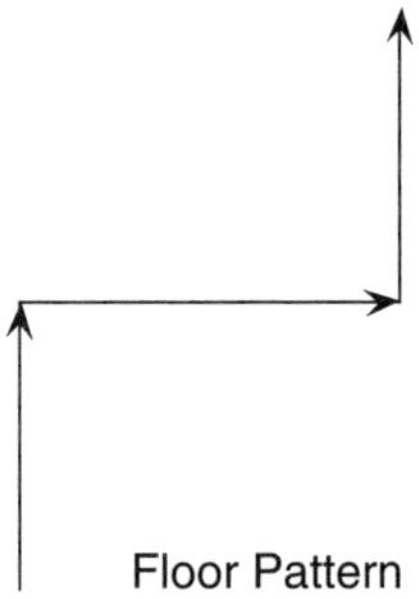

Floor Pattern

**Step Cue:** Side, rock step, cha cha side, rock step, cha cha side.

**Lead:** Following the rock step forward or backward, you can lead into the side cha cha steps with a side body action using a firm right side connection (dance frame) to take the follow to the side.

## Cha Cha Step Variations

| | | | |
|---|---|---|---|
| Open Break | Return to Basic | Full Turn | Shadow |
| Right Break | Cross Over Turn | Jody Break | Kick Swivel |
| Cross Over | Chase Half-Turn | Reverse Jody | Kick Freeze |

### Open Break

**Position:** Two hands joined or Latin social
**Level:** Intermediate

The purpose of the break is to change position from face to face to side by side. The couple may open to either right or left. The right break is described next.

### Right Break

**Level:** Intermediate

| STEPS | 4/4 COUNTS | RHYTHM CUE |
|---|---|---|
| Step right backward, releasing right hand hold with follow | 2 | slow |
| Step left forward in place | 3 | slow |

| | | |
|---|---|---|
| Step right in place, turning one-quarter clockwise to face right in a side-by-side position | 4 | quick |
| Step left in place | *and* | quick |
| Step right in place | 1 | slow |

**Step Cue:** Break, open, turn, cha cha cha.

**Style:** The released hand and arm remain up in place and turn with the body.

**Lead:** The lead releases right hand for right turn, left hand for left turn, and guides through to the side-by-side position with the other joined hand. As the lead does this, the follow should exert slight resistance against his arm with her arm or wrist to facilitate following forthcoming leads in side-by-side position.

**Note:** The left break will start forward with the left foot and turn one-quarter left.

### Cross Over

**Position:** Side-by-side, having taken the open break to the right. Lead's left is holding follow's right hand. Start with the inside foot (lead's left, follow's right).

**Level:** Intermediate

| STEPS | 4/4 COUNTS | RHYTHM CUE |
|---|---|---|
| Step left forward | 2 | slow |
| Step right back in place | 3 | slow |
| Step left in place, turning to face follow, and release her right hand | 4 | quick |
| Step right in place, still turning on around, take follow's left hand | *and* | quick |
| Step left in place, finishing a half-turn to face opposite direction in side-by-side position | 1 | slow |
| Repeat, starting with the inside foot (lead's right, follow's left) and turning back to starting position | | |

**Step Cue:** Forward, turn, cha cha cha.

**Style:** On the forward step, the inside foot should step straight ahead. The body is upright and the head is looking over the inside shoulder at partner. The free hand is up. Avoid bouncing, leaning forward, turning back on partner, or looking at the floor.

**Lead:** The lead's inside hand guides forward into the forward step and pulls back to start the turn. If the arms of both lead and follow remain up when turning, the arms are ready to receive the lead when changing from one hand to the other.

**Note:** If the open break was taken to the left side, then the cross over step will begin with the inside foot (lead's right, follow's left). The cross over step may be repeated from side to side any number of times.

### Return to Basic

**Position:** Side-by-side, facing right, starting with the inside foot

**Level:** Intermediate

| STEPS | 4/4 COUNTS | RHYTHM CUE |
|---|---|---|
| Step left forward | 2 | slow |
| Step right backward in place, turning to face partner | 3 | slow |

Return to Basic, *continued*

| | | |
|---|---|---|
| Step left, right, left in place, taking both of the follow's hands | 4 *and* 1 | quick, quick, slow |
| With right foot now free, go into a back basic | | |

**Lead:** If the lead uses pressure against the follow's fingers of the hand he holds just before he takes both hands, she will recognize the intent to go back to basic and will facilitate the transition.

## Cross Over Turn

**Position:** Side by side, facing left, starting with the inside foot (lead's right, follow's left)

**Level:** Intermediate

| STEPS | 4/4 COUNTS | RHYTHM CUE |
|---|---|---|
| Step right forward, turning counterclockwise away from the follow about halfway around | 2 | slow |
| Step left in place, continuing to turn counterclockwise, completing the turn around to face the follow | 3 | slow |
| Bring feet together and hold | 4 *and* 1 | quick, quick, slow |
| Free the left foot and step into a forward basic on count 2 | | |

**Step Cue:** Out around *hold,* cha cha cha; forward step, cha cha cha.

**Style:** A smooth spin on the ball of the foot is taken on counts 2 and 3 and then a sudden hold during the cha cha cha part gives this variation a bit of special pizazz. It is necessary to count the timing carefully so as to step forward into basic again on count 2. The follow is turning clockwise.

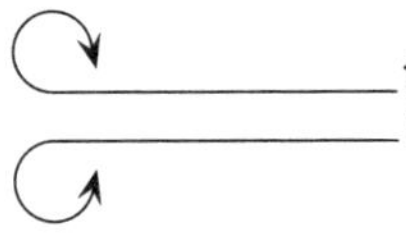


**Lead:** The lead, knowing he is going into the cross over turn, will not grasp the follow's hand as he comes through from the other side but will place the heel of his hand against the back of her hand and push out slightly into the turn. He must then direct her into a back basic as he steps into his forward basic.

**Note:** Of course, the turn may be taken from either side. The lead may use this variation as a lead into challenge position, in which case he will not rejoin hands with partner but will remain apart, facing partner.

## Chase Half-Turn

**Position:** Challenge or two hands joined

**Level:** Beginning 3

It is a turning figure in which the lead is always one turn ahead of the follow. He will start the turn while she takes a back basic. On her next forward basic she starts the turn. After the desired number of turns he will finish with a forward basic while she completes her last turn to face him. Use alternating feet for all turns in the forward break.

| STEPS | 4/4 COUNTS | RHYTHM CUE |
|---|---|---|
| **Lead's Part** | | |
| Step left forward, turning clockwise on both feet halfway around with back to follow | 2 | slow |
| Take weight on right foot | 3 | slow |
| Step left, right, left in place | 4 *and* 1 | quick, quick, slow |

| | | |
|---|---|---|
| Step right forward, turning counterclockwise a half-turn, on both feet, to face follow's back | 2 | slow |
| Take weight on left foot | 3 | slow |
| Step right, left, right in place | 4 *and* 1 | quick, quick, slow |
| **Follow's Part** | | |
| Step right backward | 2 | slow |
| Step left forward in place | 3 | slow |
| Step right, left, right in place | 4 *and* 1 | quick, quick, slow |
| Step left forward, turning clockwise on both feet halfway around with back to lead | 2 | slow |
| Take weight on right foot | 3 | slow |
| Step left, right, left in place | 4 *and* 1 | quick, quick, slow |

**Step Cue:** Turn about, cha cha cha.

**Style:** The turn about is called a swivel turn and is done with both feet in an apart position. The step is forward, the swivel turns toward the back foot, with the weight on the balls of the feet. There is a cocky manner as lead and follow look over the shoulder at partner.

**Lead:** The lead drops both hands when stepping forward on left foot, and the rest is a visual lead for the follow. She keeps turning if he does. When the lead wishes to go back to basic, he will take a forward basic while she does her last turn and then rejoin hands and go into a back basic on the right foot.

**Note:** The half turn may be done again and again. A familiar styling is to tap partner's shoulder when facing partner's back.

### Full Turn

**Position:** Challenge
**Level:** Beginning 3

Step left forward, pivoting clockwise a half-turn. Step right in place, again pivoting clockwise a half-turn. Take cha cha cha in place, facing partner.

**Lead:** The lead is a visual one, having let go of hands to start the turn and taking the hands to finish it.

**Style:** The manner is a bit cocky as each looks over the shoulder at partner. The pivoting steps are small and on the ball of the foot for good balance and smoothness.

**Note:** The lead will make a complete turn while the follow does a back basic, and then she follows with a complete turn while he does a back basic.

### Jody Break

**Position:** Two hands joined
**Level:** Intermediate

| STEPS | 4/4 COUNTS | RHYTHM CUE |
|---|---|---|
| **Lead's Part** | | |
| Step left backward, at the same time changing hands from a two-hand grasp to a right-hand grasp | 2 | slow |
| Step right forward, and at the same time pull with the right hand to guide the follow into a counterclockwise turn | 3 | slow |

*continues on next page*

Jody Break, *continued*

| | | |
|---|---|---|
| Take cha cha cha (left, right, left) in place, guiding the follow into Varsouvienne position | *4 and* 1 | quick, quick, slow |
| Step right backward in Varsouvienne position | 2 | slow |
| Step left forward in place and, at the same time, release the left hand and guide the follow with the right hand to turn clockwise | 3 | slow |
| Take cha cha cha (right, left, right) in place, guiding the follow back out to original position, facing lead completing half-turn clockwise | *4 and* 1 | quick, quick, slow |

**Follow's Part**

| | | |
|---|---|---|
| Starting right foot into regular back break. | | |
| Step right backward, allowing lead to change from two-hand grasp to a right-hand grasp | 2 | slow |
| Step left forward, toeing out and pivoting on left counterclockwise, being guided by lead's lead toward Varsouvienne position | 3 | slow |
| Take cha cha cha (right, left, right), finishing the turn into Varsouvienne position beside the lead | *4 and* 1 | quick, quick, slow |
| Step left backward in Varsouvienne position | 2 | slow |
| Step right forward, toeing out and pivoting on the right clockwise, being guided by the lead's lead toward the original facing position | 3 | slow |
| Take cha cha cha (left, right, left) in place, finishing the turn to face partner | *4 and* 1 | quick, quick, slow |

**Step Cue:** Back, forward, cha cha cha.

**Note:** This may be repeated over and over without changing the right-hand grasp. When the lead desires to go back to regular basic, he will change to two-hand grasp and forward basic when the follow returns to facing position.

**Style:** Both lead and follow should keep steps small and not get too far apart. Large steps and big movement spoil the beauty of this lovely figure and make it awkward to maneuver.

**Lead:** Arm tension control makes it possible for the lead's lead to guide the follow smoothly in and out of Varsouvienne position.

## Variations of Jody Position

(Also called Varsouvienne position)

**Level:** Intermediate

### Reverse Jody

While in Varsouvienne position, both break back on the inside foot, and while stepping forward turn one-half clockwise in place to reverse Varsouvienne, with the follow on the left of the lead, and take cha cha cha in place. Repeat, starting with the inside foot, and turn counterclockwise to end up in original position. This may be repeated any number of times. Steps are very small. Both partners are using back break continuously.

### Shadow

While in Varsouvienne position, both break on the inside foot, then releasing the Varsouvienne grasp, step forward, the lead guiding the follow across in front of him. Take the cha cha cha, finishing the cross over, and catch inside hands. Follow is to left of lead.

Repeat, starting with the inside foot and crossing the follow in front of the lead to a hand-grasp position on his right. This may be repeated any number of times. Return to Varsouvienne position with the follow on the right when ready to go back to a facing position and back to a regular basic.

**Style:** In the Shadow, couples do not get farther apart than a bent-elbow control. The footwork in the apart position changes on count 2 to a back-cross style; that is, the inside foot crosses behind the standing foot. The action of the changing sides with partner is done on the cha cha cha beats like a running motion.

**Step Cue:** Cross step, cha cha cha.

**Lead:** The lead leads with his fingers, pulling follow on count 4.

**Note:** The lead may lead the follow across in front of him or in back of him.

### Kick Swivel

**Position:** Two hands joined
**Level:** Intermediate

| STEPS | 4/4 COUNTS | RHYTHM CUE |
|---|---|---|
| Step left sideward | 2 | slow |
| Kick right across in front of left | 3 | slow |
| Put both feet together and swivel both toes to the right and then both heels to the right | 4 *and* 1 | slow, slow |
| Repeat stepping right sideward | 2 | slow |
| Kick left across in front of right | 3 | slow |
| Put both feet together and swivel both toes to the left and then both heels to the left | 4 *and* 1 | slow, slow |
| Return to basic from either side by using the free foot, if left to lead a forward basic, if right to lead a back basic | | |

**Step Cue:** Step, kick, swivel, swivel.

**Style:** Dancers should take small steps. Keep the kick low and take the swivel steps with the feet and knees close together. One may bend the knees slightly. The lead and follow kick in the same direction.

**Lead:** The lead pulls both of the follow's hands in the direction of the step kick, and then he puts the hands close together and gives a push-pull action for the swivel. Part of the lead the follow picks up visually.

**Note:** The two swivel steps take the place of the three cha cha cha steps and are even rhythm, being the equivalent of counts 4 and 1.

### Kick Freeze

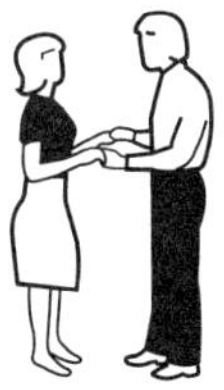

**Position:** Facing or Latin social
**Level:** Intermediate

| STEPS | 4/4 COUNTS | RHYTHM CUE |
|---|---|---|
| Step left sideward | 2 | slow |
| Kick right across in front of left | 3 | slow |
| Touch right foot sideward to the right in a stride position (no weight change); count 4–hold count 1 | 4, 1 | slow, slow |

Kick Freeze, *continued*

| | | |
|---|---|---|
| Step right, left, right, moving to the right without changing position | *2 and 3* | quick, quick, slow |
| Repeat on the same foot | 4, 1, 2, 3, 4, *and* 1 | |

**Step Cue:** The posture on the freeze straightens to be extra firm and holds with the leg extended sideward. Arms extend sideward to butterfly position. The body may turn slightly to the right during the cha cha cha but should end up facing partner.

**Lead:** The lead pulls both of the follow's hands in the direction of the kick and then suddenly increases tension as arms and legs swing to freeze position. They hold the position one beat. Then he releases pressure and leads sideward for the quick, slow beats.

**Note:** The freeze is on counts 4 and 1. These are two extra counts added to the regular pattern. It is best to take the kick freeze twice to make it fit rhythmically with the music. Return to basic by leading into a back basic with the right foot.

## *Cha Cha* COMBOS

The cha cha routines are combinations for practice, listed from simple to complex. (Partners facing, unless otherwise indicated.)

1. *Open Break, Cross Over*
   2 forward and back basics with open break
   4 cross overs
2. *Cross Over with Turn*
   2 basics with open break
   3 cross overs and turn
   repeat
3. *Cross Over, Freeze*
   2 basics with open break
   2 cross overs
   2 freezes
   1 cross over and turn
4. *Basic, Chase*
   2 basics
   4 half-turns
   2 full turns
5. *Basic, Jody*
   2 basics
   4 jody breaks
6. *Jody Variations*
   2 basics
   jody break
   2 double jodys
   2 shadows
7. *Basic, Kick Freeze*
   2 basics (closed position)
   2 kick freezes

# *Mambo*

THE MAMBO IS A CUBAN DANCE that appeared on the ballroom scene in the United States shortly after World War II. It is a very free dance, allowing for individual interpretation and innovation. Probably due to its difficult rhythm, it became less popular in the 1950s than the cha cha. However, it did survive and finds renewed interest among dancers in the United States, especially the advanced dancer. Over the years it has become more sophisticated and conservative. It is most often done in closed position.

## *Mambo* RHYTHM

The rhythm is difficult and has spurred controversy as to whether the rhythm is off-beat or onbeat, that is, quick, quick, slow or slow, quick, quick. Because of its highly syncopated beat, it has been a difficult rhythm to learn. The rhythm pattern described here will be in 4/4 time, that is, quick, quick, slow.

| 4/4 | | | | |
|---|---|---|---|---|
| | ___ | ___ | ___ | ___ |
| | 4 | 1 | 2 | Hold |

A preparation step on the first two beats of the measure is helpful in getting started with the mambo beat.

| 4/4 | | | | | | | |
|---|---|---|---|---|---|---|---|
| ___ | ___ | ___ | | ___ | ___ | ___ | ___ |
| 1 | 2 | Hold | | 4 | 1 | 2 | Hold |
| Preparation | | | | Mambo Rhythm | | | |

## *Mambo* STYLE

The sultry rhythm and oddly accented beat gives the dance a heavy jerky quality, which may be interestingly thought of as a "charge." Basically, the style is rumba movement, but as one steps forward on the accented fourth beat, it is with the suddenness of a quick lunge but immediately pulling back for the second quick beat, giving the jerky quality to the dance. The "charge" movement is further accented by a slightly heavier step and the action of the shoulders, which move forward alternately in opposition to the stepping foot. The arms and hands are carried in a bent-elbow position parallel to the floor, palms down. The arms move the shoulders, and thus the mambo presents a more dynamic body movement than any of the other Cuban dances.

## *Fundamental* MAMBO STEPS

Only the basic step will be given here since all variations may be taken from the cha cha. The relationship between the mambo and the cha cha will also be noted. See pages 488–494 for cha cha variations. Directions are for the lead; follow's part is reversed, except as noted.

### Preparation Step

Used only at the beginning of the dance to get started on the mambo beat.

| STEPS | 4/4 COUNTS | RHYTHM CUE |
|---|---|---|
| Step left in place | 1 | quick |
| Step right in place | 2 | quick |
| Hold | 3 | hold |

8

### The Basic Step

**Level:** Intermediate

| STEPS | 4/4 COUNTS | RHYTHM CUE |
|---|---|---|
| Step left diagonally forward to right | 4 | quick |
| Step right back in place | 1 | quick |
| Step left sideward left | 2 | slow |
| Hold, closing right to left | 3 | no weight change |
| Step right diagonally backward to left | 4 | quick |
| Step left back in place | 1 | quick |
| Step right sideward right | 2 | slow |
| Hold closing left to right | 3 | no weight change |

**Step Cue:** Cross back side, cross back side.

**Style:** Dancers should avoid taking too large a step. The sideward step tends to increase the size of the total pattern and may look very awkward if taken too wide. The quality is sultry.

**Lead:** The lead's lead is a sharp shoulder action as his shoulder moves forward in opposition to the stepping foot. The follow should merely follow the action of his leading shoulder and not try to figure out which shoulder to move.

**Position:** Latin social position.

**Note:** The first half of this step is referred to as the "forward break" and the back half as the "back break." It may be used as in the cha cha.

## Mambo Variations

These variations are fully described in the cha cha found on pages 486–494. Also refer to Cha Cha Combos on page 494.

| | | |
|---|---|---|
| Open Break | Cross Over with Turn | Shadow |
| Cross Over | Jody Break | |

# *Merengue*

THE MERENGUE THAT IS POPULAR today in trendy salsa clubs evolved from a folkloric dance of the Caribbean. It is now widely considered to be the national dance of the Dominican Republic. The music is a peppy, pert, marchlike rhythm, and the dance patterns are the most simple of all the Latin dances. There are two styles: the original "limp step" from the Dominican Republic and the more even, smooth Haitian style. The Haitian style will be described here.

## Merengue RHYTHM

In 4/4 time, there is a very pronounced beat of the music, which has an exciting uneven beat in the rhythm pattern, but the dance follows the basic beats of the measure and is in even rhythm.

| 4/4 | Q (accent /) | Q | Q | Q |
|---|---|---|---|---|
| | 1 | 2 | 3 | 4 |

even rhythm

## Merengue STYLE

Perhaps merengue style could be described as a combination of the rumba movement and a majorette swagger step. The feet are placed flat, but the weight is on the ball of the foot for easy balance. It is a controlled hip movement resulting from the bent-knee action with each step as in the rumba, but it has the almost sassy quality and breezy manner of the majorette. A slight rock sideways with the shoulders to accompany the foot pattern is optional. It is not meant to be an exaggerated body movement, but the lively music and the character of the step give this dance a delightful touch of humor.

With a simple step, the footwork must be disciplined or it may look sloppy. The feet face squarely forward and close tightly together. The step is small.

## Fundamental MERENGUE STEPS

Directions are for the lead; the follow's part is reversed, except as noted.

### Basic Side Step

**Position:** Latin social
**Level:** Beginning 2

| STEPS | 4/4 COUNTS | RHYTHM CUE |
|---|---|---|
| Step left sideward | 1 | quick |
| Close right to left, take weight on right | 2 | quick |
| Step left sideward | 3 | quick |
| Close right to left, take weight on right | 4 | quick |

**Step Cue:** Side close.

**Style:** Steps are small, head high, focus on partner. Rock body left, right with the step.

**Lead:** To lead a sideward-moving pattern in closed position, the lead should use pressure of the right hand to the left or right to indicate the desired direction.

**Note:** Could travel sideways any number of side steps. Should travel in line of direction.

## Box Step

**Position:** Latin social
**Level:** Beginning 2

| STEPS | 4/4 COUNTS | RHYTHM CUE |
|---|---|---|
| Step left forward | 1 | quick |
| Close right to left, take weight on right | 2 | quick |
| Step left backward | 3 | quick |
| Close right to left, take weight on right | 4 | quick |

**Step Cue:** Forward together, back together.

**Style:** The same foot leads each time. The shoulders lead the rock from side to side.

**Lead:** To lead a box step the lead should use a forward body action, followed by right-hand pressure and right elbow pull to the right to take the follow into the forward sequence of the box. Forward pressure of the right hand followed by pressure to the left side takes the follow into the back sequence of the box.

## Box Turn

**Position:** Latin social
**Level:** Beginning 2

| STEPS | 4/4 COUNTS | RHYTHM CUE |
|---|---|---|
| Step left, toeing out to a left one quarter-turn counterclockwise | 1 | quick |
| Close right to left, take weight on right | 2 | quick |
| Step left backward | 3 | quick |
| Close right to left, take weight on right | 4 | quick |

**Step Cue:** Turn close, back close.

**Style:** A shoulder rock on the turn makes it very easy to lead.

**Lead:** See directions for leading, number 6, page 419.

**Note:** Repeat three times to make a full turn.

## Cross Step

**Position:** Latin social
**Level:** Beginning 3

| STEPS | 4/4 COUNTS | RHYTHM CUE |
|---|---|---|
| Step left sideward, turning to open position | 1 | quick |
| Step right forward, in open position | 2 | quick |
| Step left sideward, turning to closed position | 3 | quick |
| Close right to left, take weight on right | 4 | quick |

**Step Cue:** Open step side close.

**Style:** Each step must be precisely taken in the closed or open position. If the footwork is not square with each position, the merengue loses all of its distinctive character.

**Lead:** To lead into an open position or conversation position, the lead should use pressure with the heel of the right hand to turn the follow into open position. The right elbow lowers to the side. The lead must simultaneously turn his own body, not just the follow, so that they end facing the same direction. The left arm relaxes slightly and the left hand sometimes gives the lead for steps in the open position.

**Lead:** To lead from open to closed position, the lead should use pressure of the right hand and raise the right arm up to standard position to move the follow into closed position. The follow should not have to be pushed but should swing easily into closed position as she feels the arm lifting. She should move completely around to face the lead squarely.

**Variation:** The flick is like the cross step, except that there is a *leap* onto the left foot in open position, bending the right knee and flipping the right foot quickly up in back, and then right foot steps forward and side close as above. The lead raises his right elbow as he turns to open position into the leap.

### Swivel

**Position:** Open and closed, traveling in line of direction
**Level:** Beginning 3

| STEPS | 4/4 COUNTS | RHYTHM CUE |
|---|---|---|
| Leap left forward in open position, flick right foot | 1 | quick |
| Step right forward in open position | 2 | quick |
| Pivot on right foot to face partner, bringing left foot alongside of right, shift weight to left | 3 | quick |
| Pivot on left foot to open position, bringing right foot alongside of left, shift weight to right | 4 | quick |
| Repeat pivot on right | 1 | quick |
| Repeat pivot on left | 2 | quick |
| Step left, turning to closed position | 3 | quick |
| Close right to left, taking weight right | 4 | quick |

**Step Cue:** Leap step, swivel, swivel, swivel, swivel, side close.

**Style:** Steps are tiny and neat, turning exactly a quarter-turn each time. The body turns with the foot.

**Lead:** To lead into an open position or conversation position, the lead should use pressure with the heel of the right hand to turn the follow into open position. The right elbow lowers to the side. The lead must simultaneously turn his own body, not just the follow, so that they end facing the same direction. The left arm relaxes slightly and the left hand sometimes gives the lead for steps in the open position.

**Lead:** To lead from open to closed position, the lead should use pressure of the right hand and raise the right arm up to standard position to move the follow into closed position. The follow should not have to be pushed but should swing easily into closed position as she feels the arm lifting. She should move completely around to face the lead squarely.

### Ladder

**Position:** Latin social
**Level:** Beginning 3

| STEPS | 4/4 COUNTS | RHYTHM CUE |
|---|---|---|
| Step left sideward | 1 | quick |
| Close right to left, take weight on right | 2 | quick |

Ladder, *continued*

| STEPS | 4/4 COUNTS | RHYTHM CUE |
|---|---|---|
| Step left forward | 3 | quick |
| Close right to left, take weight on right | 4 | quick |

**Step Cue:** Side close, forward close.

**Style:** Footwork is small and neat. Face partner squarely.

**Lead:** Moving squarely into position helps lead the body. Because there are a lot of direction changes in the merengue, the follow must be extremely alert to the action of the lead's right arm and shoulder.

### Side Close and Back Break

**Position:** Latin social

**Level:** Beginning 3

| STEPS | 4/4 COUNTS | RHYTHM CUE |
|---|---|---|
| Step left sideward | 1 | quick |
| Close right to L, take weight on right | 2 | quick |
| Step left sideward | 3 | quick |
| Close right to left, take weight on right | 4 | quick |
| Step left sideward | 1 | quick |
| Step right, in place, turning to open position | 2 | quick |
| Step left backward, in open position | 3 | quick |
| Step right, in place, turning to closed position | 4 | quick |

**Step Cue:** Side close, side close, side open, back step.

**Style:** There is a rather sudden swing to open position on count 2 of the second measure and then immediately back to closed position on count 4.

**Lead:** The lead uses his left hand to push the follow out quickly to open position.

## *Merengue* COMBOS

1. 4 basic steps
   4 box steps
   4 basic steps
   4 box turns
2. 4 basic steps
   4 cross steps
   8 box steps
3. 4 basic steps
   4 box turns
   4 swivels
4. 4 basic steps
   4 ladder steps
   4 box turns
   4 side close and back breaks

# Rumba

THE RUMBA IS A Cuban dance (along with the mambo, bolero, and cha cha), but it has enjoyed greater popularity than any of the others, probably because of its slower, more relaxed, smoother style. The music is usually identified by the tantalizing rhythms of the percussion instruments known as the maracas, which carry the continuous quick beat, and the sticks or bongo drum, which beat out the accented rhythm of the dance.

## Rumba RHYTHM

The rumba is written in 4/4 time and is played both fast and slow. Many Americans prefer the slower bolero-type tempo, but actually in the Latin American countries the rumba is danced considerably faster. The rhythm is tricky, as it is a 1 2 3, 1 2 3, 1 2 count in 4/4 time.

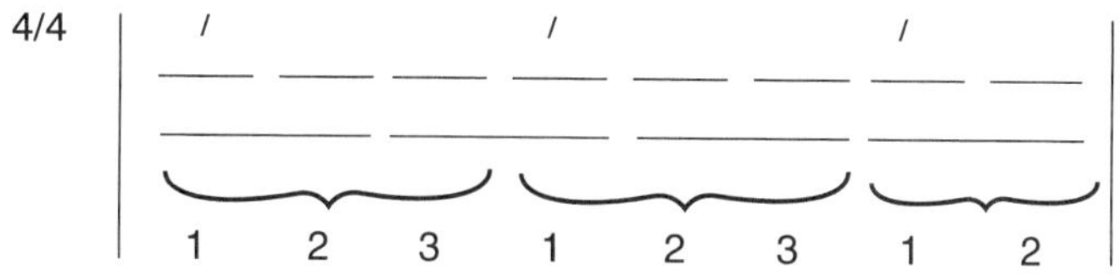


It was taught in the United States for many years as a quick, quick, slow rhythm, but it has gradually shifted over to a slow, quick, quick beat with the accent on the first and third beats of the measure. This is the rhythm that will be used in this text.

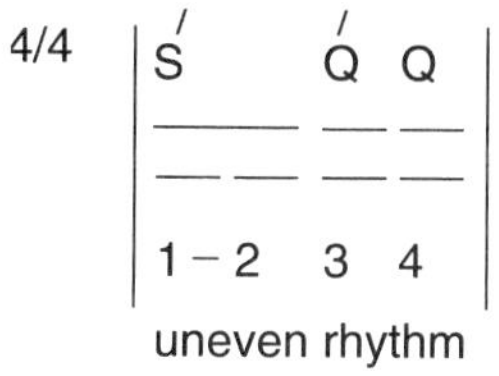


Rumba music has a subtle, beautiful melody with a rolling quality that requires the subtle rolling rumba movement. It is seldom mistaken for cha cha or mambo music because of its smoothness and continuity.

## Rumba STYLE

Naturally, in the transition, the rumba lost a lot of its original character. The style has been greatly exaggerated and distorted at times. Some people dance it like the foxtrot, without attempting to get any of the Cuban flavor. It is hoped that dancers will feel sufficiently challenged to put in a little extra time to get the feeling of the subtle, continuous, rolling motion. Three characteristics make it different from other dances:

1. The action is in the feet and the knees.
2. There is a delayed shift of weight.
3. The upper body is upright and quiet, with a focus on one's partner.

The step itself is comparatively short and flat-footed, with the knee leading. The weight tends to be maintained over the heel of the foot more than in any other dance. The Cuban rumba movement is a springlike action, resulting from placing the left foot on the floor first, without taking weight but with a bent knee. This is followed by pressing the weight into the floor and straightening the left knee. Accompanying this press into the floor, a smooth roll of the weight is shifted to that left foot. The right knee begins to bend and leads the right foot, then free of weight, into its new position. The roll is completed as the weight is transferred gradually to the newly placed right foot. Then the entire action is repeated by pressing the weight into the right foot and straightening the right knee, rolling smoothly. As the left foot is freed of weight, the knee leads, shifting the left foot to its new position with the weight coming over it, completing the roll.

The knees should be bent directly over the foot, and the feet should be placed with the toes pointing straight ahead. A pigeon-toed effect should be avoided. As the feet pass each other, the steps are small and close together, with the toes pointed straight ahead in the line of direction. The movement of the hips is merely the subtle result of the specific action of the feet and the knees. There should be no intentional swinging of the hip from side to side. There needs to be a stabilization of the upper trunk at the waist to keep it easily upright and the shoulders straight.

The head is held with the focus constantly on one's partner. The arm and hand, when free from partner, are held in a bent-elbow position at waist level, palm down. The lead does not hold his partner close. There is seldom any body contact.

The rumba, with its open and encircling patterns, is generally danced within a small space and reflects a dignified, although flirtatious, quality.

### Teaching Suggestions for Rumba Style

First, practice the motion described above, moving forward in a slow, slow rhythm, working to achieve the feeling of the roll. Practicing in front of a mirror is usually helpful. Second, practice the same motion forward in a slow, quick, quick rhythm (Cuban walk). Third, practice the motion as in the box step. Finally, practice with a partner in closed dance position.

## *Fundamental* RUMBA STEPS

Directions are for the lead, facing line of direction; follow's part is reversed, except as noted.

### Cuban Walk

**Level:** Intermediate

| STEPS | 4/4 COUNTS | RHYTHM CUE |
|---|---|---|
| Place left forward, roll weight slowly onto left | 1–2 | slow |
| Place right forward, roll weight quickly onto right | 3 | quick |
| Place left forward, roll weight quickly onto left | 4 | quick |

**Step Cue:** Place roll roll roll.
1 – 2 3 4

8

**Style:** The roll is the springlike action of pressing into the floor. The knee of the free foot bends and leads the foot into its new position, followed by the transfer of weight to that foot.

**Note:** The Cuban walk step is used for all moving variations when not in closed position. It may move forward, backward, or in a circle.

### Box Step

**Position:** Latin social
**Level:** Beginning 3

| STEPS | 4/4 COUNTS | RHYTHM CUE |
|---|---|---|
| Place left forward, roll weight slowly onto left | 1–2 | slow |
| Place right sideward, roll weight quickly onto right | 3 | quick |
| Place left close to right, roll weight quickly to left | 4 | quick |
| Place right backward, roll weight slowly onto right | 1–2 | slow |
| Place left sideward, roll weight quickly onto left | 3 | quick |
| Place right close to left, roll weight quickly onto right | 4 | quick |

**Step Cue:** Forward side close, back side close.

Floor pattern

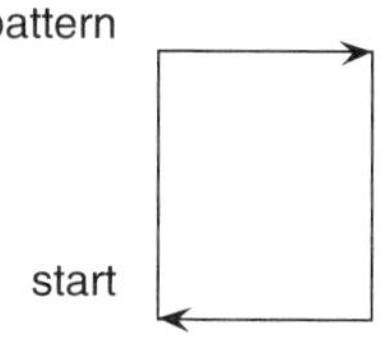


**Style:** The knee leads each step. The feet are placed flat on the floor, in a small box pattern.

**Lead:** To lead a box step, the lead should use a forward body action followed by right-hand pressure and right elbow pull to the right to take the follow into the forward sequence of the box. Forward pressure of the right hand followed by pressure to the left side takes the follow into the back sequence of the box.

**Note:** Students need to understand that this forward, side, close constitutes the forward sequence or forward basic and that back, side, close constitutes the back sequence or back basic. These will be referred to in the variations.

## Rumba Step Variations

- Box Turn
- Flirtation Break
- Side by Side
- Circular Turn
- Parallel Turn
- Bolero Break
- Bolero Break Walk Around
- Parallel Turn
- Bolero Break Parallel Turn
- Bolero Break Circular Turn
- Varsouvienne Break

### Box Turn

**Position:** Latin social
**Level:** Beginning 3

The rumba box step is the same foot pattern as the Westchester box step in the Foxtrot. The box turn will follow the same pattern as the Foxtrot box turn, page 464. The style is different and one needs to shorten the step and add the Cuban movement.

### Flirtation Break

**Position:** Latin social
**Level:** Beginning 3

Starting from Latin social position, dancers will change to flirtation position and travel with the Cuban walk either forward or backward.

| STEPS | 4/4 COUNTS | RHYTHM CUE |
|---|---|---|
| Step left forward | 1–2 | slow |
| Step right sideward | 3 | quick |
| Close left to right, roll weight left | 4 | quick |
| Step right backward, a larger step, changing to flirtation position, removing lead's right arm from around partner | 1–2 | slow |
| Step left sideward | 3 | quick |
| Close right to left, roll weight to right | 4 | quick |
| Step left forward | 1–2 | slow |
| Step right forward | 3 | quick |
| Step left forward | 4 | quick |
| Step right forward | 1–2 | slow |
| Step left forward | 3 | quick |
| Step right forward | 4 | quick |

**Step Cue:** Forward side close, separate side close, walk walk, walk, walk, walk walk.

**Style:** In flirtation position, the dancers use the Cuban walk step, all forward or all back. The lead steps back a little larger step when he is changing to flirtation position. Finger pressure and arm control are essential, as they are the only way the lead has to lead. The free arm is held up, elbow bent, parallel to the floor.

**Lead:** To lead all turns, the lead dips his shoulders in the direction of the turn and his upper torso turns before his leg and foot turn. The lead's left-hand position changes to palm up, finger grasp in flirtation position. Lead may lead with fingers to push the follow backward, or to pull to bring her forward. Pressure should come on the quick beats, so that change of direction actually occurs on the next slow.

**Note:** The lead may lead as many steps in either direction as desired. To return to closed position and the basic rumba box step, the lead will be moving the follow forward in flirtation position. During a back sequence on the right foot, the lead will go into closed position as follows:

| STEPS | 4/4 COUNTS | RHYTHM CUE |
|---|---|---|
| Step right backward, pulling the follow into closed position | 1–2 | slow |
| Step left sideward, changing left-hand position | 3 | quick |
| Close right to left, roll to right | 4 | quick |
| Step left forward into the forward sequence | | |

### Side by Side

**Position:** Flirtation
**Level:** Beginning 3

Starting from flirtation position with the couple traveling either forward or backward in flirtation position, the lead turns one-quarter to the right (follow to the left), to side-by-side position, follow on the lead's left.

**Lead:** On the quick, quick beats, his left hand guides her into side-by-side position. She must then press with her arm against the lead's arm or wrist to follow the leads in this position. The lead may direct them forward or backward in this position, changing on the quick beats.

### Circular Turn

**Position:** Side-by-side
**Level:** Beginning 3

Starting from side-by-side position, the couple is traveling forward. The lead on the quick beats will change his direction so as to move backward, pulling with his lead hand toward himself to direct the follow to continue forward. This will result in a turn clockwise, side by side. They should focus on each other over the shoulder.

a. Side-by-side position 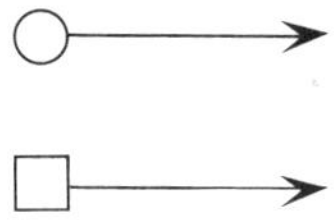

b. Circular turn (lead moves backward) (follow moves forward) 

○ = Follow; □ = Lead

**Note:** The lead may return to basic box when he is on a back sequence with the right foot by facing the follow, taking Latin social position, guiding into the quick, quick beats sideward left, and starting the forward sequence on the left foot.

### Parallel Turn

**Position:** Starting from circular turn
**Level:** Beginning 3

When traveling in circular turn, the lead backward, the follow forward, the lead on the quick beats will turn suddenly one-half counterclockwise into right parallel position and, turning clockwise, both lead and follow will be moving forward, around each other. Return to basic box as noted above.

a. Circular turn: lead moving backward, follow forward 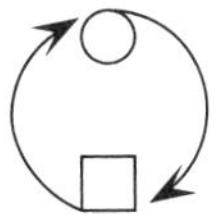

b. Parallel turn: both lead and follow move forward 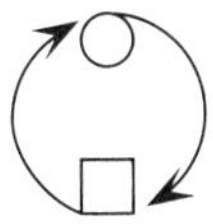

### Bolero Break

**Position:** Latin social
**Level:** Beginning 3

Starting in closed dance position, the dancers execute the forward sequence of the box step. Then, as the lead starts the back sequence, he turns the follow clockwise under his left arm. The lead continues to take the box step in place while the follow travels in a circular pattern clockwise until she faces him again at arm's distance. He has maintained hand contact (his left, her right) during this time and he finally guides her forward toward him back into Latin social position.

**Step Cue:**

| Lead: | Follow: |
|---|---|
| Forward, side, close | Back, side, close |
| Back, side, close | Forward, turn under |
| Forward, side, close | Forward, forward, forward (in a tight circle) |
| Together (as partners), side, close | Together (as partners), side, close |

**Style:** The follow will use the Cuban walk when moving around clockwise and keep the lead's rhythm until back in closed position. She should keep the body upright, outside arm up, and focus on her partner.

a. 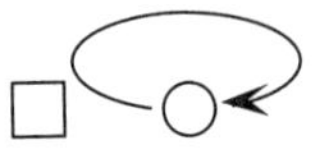

b. 

**Lead:** The lead gives the lead by lifting his left hand high enough so that the follow does not have to duck her head to get under his arm. He also guides her under with his right hand. His left hand guides her around clockwise and finally draws her toward him to Latin social position.

**Note:** Any number of basic sequences (slow, quick, quick) may be taken, and, if the partners both keep the pattern going, they can move right back into the box step when they come together in closed position.

## Variations of Bolero Break

**Level:** Intermediate

### *Walk Around*

As the follow comes around from bolero break, instead of going into closed position, the lead with his left hand will lead the follow toward his right side and past his right shoulder, bringing her around behind him and toward his left side. He then turns one-half left to face her, and they move into Latin social dance position.

**Step Cue:** Starting at the end of the bolero break: back (follow to the side), side, close (follow behind lead), diagonal (turn to face follow), side, together.

**Style:** The follow will use Cuban walk and keep her circle in close to the lead. The lead will keep the box step going until she passes his right side, and then he will go into the Cuban walk on a forward sequence and come around to his left to meet her. Both focus on each other. From closed position:

a. Bolero break 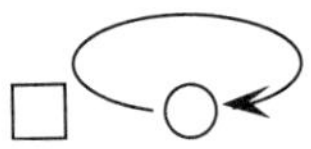

b. Walk around 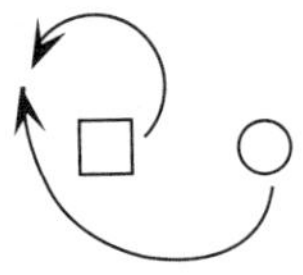

**Lead:** The lead should raise his left arm high enough so that he does not have to duck his head as the follow goes around. He will move under his own left arm and turn left to meet the follow.

**Note:** When the lead and follow meet, they should go back into Latin social position and box step on whichever foot is free.

### *Parallel Turn*

As the follow comes around in her wide arc at arm's distance, the lead will move in toward her, coming into right parallel position, and they will turn clockwise as far as desired. The lead may then lead the follow to closed position or twirl the follow clockwise once around in place to finish in Latin social position. The lead for the twirl should come as the lead steps into the forward basic sequence with the left foot, so that the follow may turn on one basic step starting with her right foot. They finish together in the back part of the box step in Latin social position.

**Step Cue:** Forward, step, step.

**Style:** Use the Cuban walk. Focus on each other.

a. Bolero break

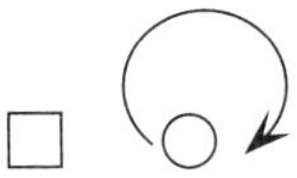

b. Lead moves forward to parallel position

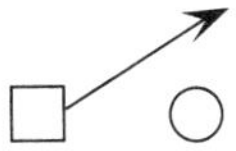

c. Parallel turn

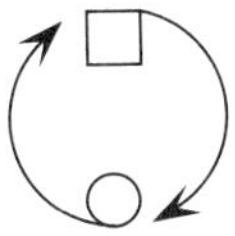

### *Circular Turn*

Immediately after the lead turns the follow under his left arm to start the bolero break, the lead brings his left arm down to a pressure position against the follow's right elbow and turns one-quarter right to be in a side-by-side position. Then the lead moves backward, the follow forward, turning in place clockwise. To get out of this turn, the lead turns to face the follow and steps back with his right foot into the back basic sequence, taking closed dance position.

**Step Cue:** Back, step, step.

**Style:** They must be in a tight side-by-side position. They will use the Cuban walk. Focus should be on the partner, outside arm up.

**Lead:** Firmness in the arm is necessary to the lead and response to this firm pressure is needed by the follow.

### Varsouvienne Break

**Position:** Latin social
**Level:** Intermediate

This is a delightful series of turns with the couple rolling from one side of partner to the other side, all the while keeping the basic Cuban walk rhythm–slow, quick, quick–going in the feet. There are four changes of position that should be practiced before the rhythm is added.

1. *Turn into the Varsouvienne position:* The lead releases the follow's right hand and reaches across in front of the lead's right shoulder to take her left hand, pulling it across in front of him, causing the follow to turn clockwise a half-turn until she is by his right side, facing in the same direction. The lead now holds the follow's left hand in his left and has his right around her waist to take her right hand at her right side. They circle clockwise one complete turn. To do this effectively, the lead moves forward, the follow backward to turn in place.

8

2. *Turn into reverse Varsouvienne position:* The lead releases the follow's right hand and turns to his own right, bringing their joined left hands across in front of follow as she turns left until she is by his left side and slightly behind him, facing in the same direction. The follow reaches around behind the lead with her right hand to take his right hand at his right side. They continue to circle clockwise another complete turn, the lead now moving backward, the follow forward.

3. *Return to Varsouvienne position:* The lead releases the follow's right hand and, turning to his left, brings their joined left hands across in front of him, turning the follow halfway around clockwise until she is to his right. The lead's right arm is around her waist, holding her right hand. They continue turning clockwise, the lead again moving forward, the follow backward, one full time around.
4. *Turn back to Latin social position:* The lead releases the follow's left hand and by pulling with his right toward him, he turns the follow clockwise halfway around into closed dance position. The lead changes her right hand into his left and the lead leads into the basic box step, usually on the back sequence, with his right foot.

**Step Cue:** Change, step, step.

**Style:** Although this is described in four parts, the transitions into each part should be smooth so as to make the entire maneuver blend into one figure rather than four disconnected parts. There is no set number of Cuban walk steps to be taken for each part. The couple should turn continuously clockwise throughout the figure. Dancers should be careful to maintain good rumba style throughout.

## Rumba COMBOS

The rumba routines are combinations for practice, listed from simple to complex.

1. *Cuban Walk, Box*
   4 Cuba walks
   2 box steps
2. *Box, Bolero Break*
   2 box steps
   bolero break
3. *Box, Flirtation Step*
   2 box steps
   flirtation break forward and back
4. *Bolero Break, Walk Around*
   2 box seps
   bolero break
   walk around
5. *Bolero Break, Parallel Turn*
   2 box steps
   bolero break
   parallel turn
6. *Flirtation Break, Reverse Turn*
   2 box steps
   flirtation break
   side by side
   parallel turn

# Salsa

THE TERM *SALSA* REFERS TO A MIXTURE OF STYLES that came together to create a dance form that is now popular around the world. It is wildly diverse, energetic and rich with culture and history.

Although there is a lot of debate as to the origin of salsa, most agree the term was first used in the 1970s by young musicians such as Hector Lavoe, Willie Colon, Larry Harlow, and Ray Barreto to describe a hot, powerful sound coming out of the barrios of New York. The dance itself evolved out of Cuban Son, which became popular in Cuba in the 1940s and 1950s.

The diversity of the world has had an influence on the development of this style. In the United States alone there are four to five recognized styles of salsa (New York "On 2," Los Angeles "On 1," Ballroom, Casino, Miami-Style). Each salsa music hot spot (New York, L.A., Miami, Cuba, Puerto Rico, and Colombia) took their own cultural flavors and infused them into the musical basics of what makes salsa. Because the music sounded differently in each of these regions, the dance adopted styles to fit the music. However, one thing remained—the centerpiece or heartbeat of salsa—the Clave.

Whether it's a Son Clave or a Rumba Clave, this rhythm exists in all music that is considered salsa. And to any dancer—whether they dance New York, L.A., Cuban, Colombian, or Puerto Rican style—the Clave is the soul or connection to the music.

In the last two decades salsa has exploded on a whole new level. Thanks to promoters such as Albert Torres and the late David Melendez, salsa addicts get their dance fix at salsa congresses. Just about every weekend, there's a salsa congress somewhere in the world. These events have workshops from top-level instructors, performances by amazing teams and dancers, and live bands to help connect new generations of dancers with the music.

The salsa is written in 4/4 cut time. The rhythm is quick, quick, slow. It is counted 1 and 2 of the cut time beat.

¢ | Q Q S |
  | 1 & 2 |

Cut Time

## *Salsa* STYLE AND FLAVOR

The style is hard to define for salsa because of the variety involved. New York is described as smooth, elegant, powerful with intricate turns and patterns. L.A. is defined as glitzy and with a pop to it. Cuban is raw, energetic, and complex. It's a fast dance that is centered on individual style with an emphasis on Afro-Cuban movement. Each style can take years, maybe even decades, to master, which makes salsa highly addictive. The following steps are done with a general ballroom style.

## *Fundamental* SALSA STEPS

Directions are for the lead, follow's part reversed, except as noted.

## Basic Step

**Position:** Latin social
**Level:** Beginning 3

| STEPS | COUNTS | RHYTHM CUE |
|---|---|---|
| Step left forward | 1 | quick |
| Step right backward | *and* | quick |
| Step left beside right | 2 | slow |
| Step right backward | 1 | quick |
| Step left forward | *and* | quick |
| Step right beside left | 2 | slow |

Use basic step to turn left or right in place.

## Side Step

**Position**: Latin Social
**Level**: Beginning 3

| STEPS | COUNTS | RHYTHM CUE |
|---|---|---|
| Step sideways left | 1 | quick |
| Close right to left | *and* | quick |
| Step sideways left | 2 | slow |
| Reverse to right | 1 *and* 2 | quick, quick |

## Cross Step

**Position**: Two hands joined
**Level**: Beginning 3

| STEPS | COUNTS | RHYTHM CUE |
|---|---|---|
| Cross left over right (with exaggeration) | 1 | quick |
| Step back right | *and* | quick |
| Step left close to right | 2 | slow |

Repeat crossing right.

## Throw Out

**Position:** Latin social
**Level:** Beginning 3

Two basic steps (left right left, right left right).

Lead releases his right hand, gives the follow a slight push, and takes 2 more basic steps in place.

The follow moves away from partner (right, left, right) and comes back (left, right, left) to closed position.

8

## Open Break

**Position**: Latin Social
**Level**: Beginning 2

This move opens the couple to swing-out position and is used as a prep step for many other moves. Follow's foot work is a normal basic.

| STEPS | COUNTS | RHYTHM CUE |
|---|---|---|
| Lead steps back with his left foot | 1 | quick |
| Lead steps right in place | 2 | quick |
| Lead step left in place | 3 | slow |

| **Step Cue:** | Back | in | place |
|---|---|---|---|
| | Q | Q | S |

**Style:** On count 1, the lead's right arm and the follow's left arm float out to the side as space on the dance floors permits.

**Lead:** On count 1, the lead releases his right hand from the follow back, while lowering his left hand to her waist, level continuing to hold hands.

## Right Turn

**Position:** Closed Latin
**Level:** Beginning 2

This moves beginnings with an Open Break, with a special prep for the right turn on count 3. On counts 5–7 the follow makes a full clockwise turn, ending facing her partner.

| STEPS | COUNTS | RHYTHM CUE |
|---|---|---|
| Lead steps back with his left foot | 1 | quick |
| Lead steps right in place | 2 | quick |
| Lead step left in place | 3 | slow |
| Follow steps with right foot to diagonal right | | |
| Lead steps side right with right foot | 4 | quick |
| Follow, pivoting on right foot, crosses left foot over making 180° turn clockwise, her back is to her partner | | |
| Lead steps left in place | 5 | quick |
| Follow, pivoting on left turn 180° clockwise to face her partner and step right foot in place | | |
| Lead step right in place | 6 | slow |
| Follow steps left in place. | | |

| **Step Cue:** | Op | en | Break | Follow | a | round |
|---|---|---|---|---|---|---|
| | Q | Q | S | Q | Q | S |

**Style:** Follow does a tight turn, staying close to lead. She turns with the power of her legs and not by the lead cranking her around from the top. When the lead lifts his left arm, it is a suggestion, and hopefully, she will follow through with the turn.

**Lead:** On count 3, the lead lifts his left hand up a bit higher than the follow face, and allows the follow's hand to rotate in his, so they are palm to palm. On counts 5–6 he gently guides the follow in a clockwise circle. Joining back into Latin social on counts 7–8.

8

## Cross Body Lead

**Position**: Latin Social
**Level**: Beginning 3

This move brings the follow across in front of the lead and allows them to trade place while still in social position. It is also used as a prep for many other moves.

| STEPS | COUNTS | RHYTHM CUE |
|---|---|---|
| Step left foot forward | 1 | quick |
| Step right in place | 2 | quick |
| Lead: Lower left arm to follows waist level, staying connected . Pivot on right foot, 1/4 counterclockwise and side step with left foot to left. The lead and the follow are not at a 90° angle to each other. This is referred to as opening the door. | 3 | slow |
| Follow: The follow does a normal forward basic | | |
| Lead: Steps in place | 5 | |
| Follow: Step forward | | |
| Lead: Pivoting on right foot, turn counter clockwise 90°, cross left foot slightly in front of right foot and step | 6 | |
| Follow: Pivoting on left foot, turn 180° counterclockwise (the follow is now facing her partner) and step back on right foot | | |
| Lead: Right foot steps in place | 7 | |
| Follow: Left foot steps back | | |

| **Step Cue:** | Open | the | door | Follow | a | round |
|---|---|---|---|---|---|---|
| | Q | Q | S | Q | Q | S |

**Lead:** On count 5 the lead pushes gently with his right hand on the follow back to guide her across in front of him. He does not pull with his left hand.

## Left Turn

**Position**: Latin Social
**Level**: Beginning 3

This begins with a cross body lead and on the second half, the follow turns 1½ times in place.

| STEPS | COUNTS | RHYTHM CUE |
|---|---|---|
| Follow the directions for the first half of a cross body lead | 1–6 | quick, quick, slow |
| Lead: Cross body lead foot work for count 7 | 7 | |
| Follow: Pivoting on right foot, continue to turn counterclockwise 180° (Follow's back is to the lead) and step left in place | | |
| Lead: holding | 8 | |
| Follow: Continues to pivot on left foot counter-clockwise to face lead | | |

| **Step Cue:** | Open | the | door | Spin | the | follow |
|---|---|---|---|---|---|---|
| | Q | Q | S | Q | Q | S |

**Style:** By the end of count 8, both the lead and the follow flow back into Social Latin position to begin a basic.

**Lead:** By count 5, the lead releases his right hand from the follow's back. He brings his left hand in-between himself and the follow on count 6. On count 7 he continues to turn her counterclockwise.

# *Samba*

THE SAMBA, FROM BRAZIL, is the most active of the Latin American dances. It was introduced to the United States about 1929. It is interesting to discover how similar it is to some of the native dance rhythms of Africa. The samba is sensitive and smooth. The music is fiery, yet lyrical; and the dance is characterized by tiny, light footwork, and the rise and fall of the body (always turning and at the same time swaying back and forth at a most deceiving pendular angle).

## *Samba* RHYTHM

Samba is written in 4/4 cut time and may be either slow or fast, although it is generally preferred at the faster tempo. The rhythm is slow, quick, slow, an uneven rhythm pattern. It has a double accent, one on each of the two major beats, and these downbeats are represented by the down movements of the dance. It will be counted as 1 *ah* 2 of the cut-time beat.

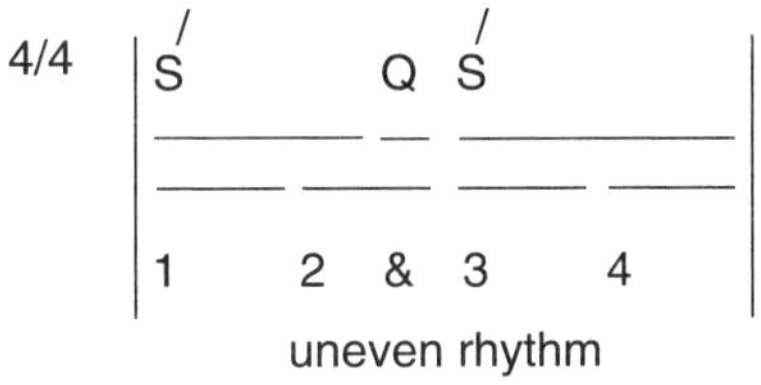


The execution of the up, down weight change is the secret to the smooth, springing rhythm. There is a change of weight from one foot to the other on each of the three beats, down up down, but a preliminary uplift of the body on the upbeat of the music sets the rhythmical swing in motion. The music is fast and lighthearted.

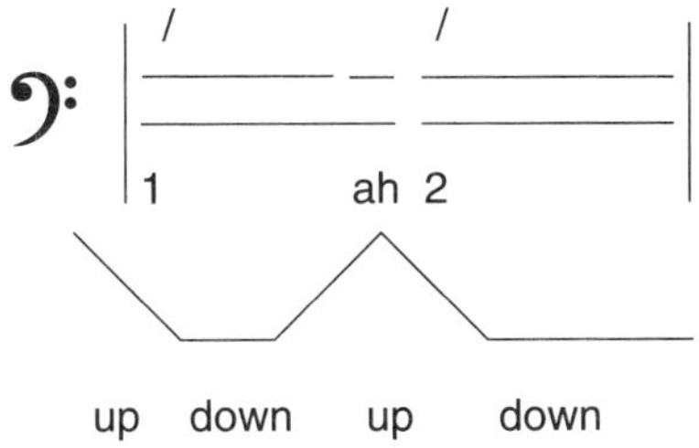

## *Samba* STYLE

In contrast to the rumba, which has a lower body movement, the samba has a total body action. The easy springing motion comes from the ball of the foot, the flexible ankle, and the easy relaxed knees. The upper body is held firmly poised, never sagging, and it seems to sway forward and back about an axis that centers in the pelvic area. The arm, when not in contact with partner, is held out from the body, a little above waist level, bent at the elbow, parallel to the floor, palm down. The first accented step, count 1, is the largest of the three steps, the other two being like a quick-change weight step. It has been called a "step-ball-change" in the language of tap dancing. It is important to get the correct rhythm and foot pattern before working on the body sway. However, having that mastered, the body sways backward as the feet take the forward basic and forward as the feet take the back basic. Always the pattern is small and on the ball of the foot.

## *Fundamental* SAMBA STEPS

Directions are for the lead; the follow's part is reversed, except as noted.

### Basic Step

**Position:** Latin social
**Direction:** Forward and back
**Level**: Beginning 3

| STEPS | 4/4 COUNTS | RHYTHM CUE |
|---|---|---|
| Step left forward | 1 | slow |
| Step right forward next to left | *ah* | quick |
| Step left in place | 2 | slow |
| Step right backward | 1 | slow |
| Step left backward beside right | *ah* | quick |
| Step right in place | 2 | slow |

**Step Cue:** Forward, change weight, back, change weight.

**Style:** The steps are small. Feet are close together on the change step. The rise and fall of the body begins on the upbeat with the rise of the body. This is the preparatory motion for each step. With the first step, the down motion is executed on the first slow beat, followed by an up motion on the quick beat and down again on the slow beat. The body is controlled. It does not bend at the waist.

**Lead:** With the increased pressure of his right hand, the lead sways backward slightly when stepping forward with his left foot and sways forward when stepping backward with his right foot. The follow sways forward when the lead sways backward, backward when he sways forward, so that the appearance is a rocking action parallel to each other.

## Samba Step Variations

- Basic Turn
- Forward Progressive Step
- Slow Side Close
- Sideward Basic
- Copa Step

### Basic Turn

**Position:** Latin social
**Direction:** Counterclockwise
**Level**: Advanced

| STEPS | 4/4 COUNTS | RHYTHM CUE |
|---|---|---|
| Step left forward, turning one-quarter counterclockwise | 1 | slow |
| Step right forward beside left | *ah* | quick |
| Step left beside right | 2 | slow |
| Step right backward, toe in, and turn one-quarter counterclockwise | 1 | slow |
| Step left backward beside right | *ah* | quick |
| Step right beside left | 2 | slow |

**Step Cue:** Turn, step, step.

**Style:** Keep the down, up, down motion going. Sway backward and then forward.

**Lead:** Bank right arm in direction of turn, and pull into the back step.

**Note:** It is important to turn on a small base, turning on the ball of the foot, not trying to step sideward around partner.

### Forward Progressive Step

**Position:** Latin social
**Level**: Advanced

| STEPS | COUNTS | RHYTHM CUE |
|---|---|---|
| Step left forward | 1 | slow |
| Step right beside left | *ah* | quick |
| Step left beside right | 2 | slow |
| Step right backward, changing from closed position to two hands joined with partner | 1 | slow |
| Step left beside right | *ah* | quick |
| Step right beside left, drop left hand | 2 | slow |
| **Into Forward Progressive Step (side-by-side position)** | | |
| Step left forward and diagonally outward to the left (follow right) | 1 | slow |
| Step right beside left | *ah* | quick |
| Step left beside right | 2 | slow |
| Step right forward and diagonally inward toward partner (follow left) | 1 | slow |
| Step left beside right | *ah* | quick |
| Step right beside left | 2 | slow |

*continues on next page*

Forward Progressive Step, *continued*

| STEPS | COUNTS | RHYTHM CUE |
|---|---|---|
| **Back to Latin Social Position** | | |
| Step left, turning diagonally outward | 1 | slow |
| Step right beside left | *ah* | quick |
| Step left beside right | 2 | slow |
| Step right, turning diagonally inward, and take Latin social position | 1 | slow |
| Step left beside right | *ah* | quick |
| Step right beside left | 2 | slow |
| Into basic, step forward on the left foot | | |

**Step Cue:** Forward step, step change step step; out step step, in step step; out step step, close step step; forward step step, back step step.

**Style:** The couple turns only diagonally away from each other and back, not back to back. When they come in, the outside hand, which is up turning with the body, touches partner's hand, palm to palm. Arm when free stays up.

**Lead:** The lead's right hand controls the motion and the diagonal position by reaching forward and back with the hand as he turns.

**Note:** The diagonal step should reach in the line of direction each time, so that the couple will progress down the floor. The progressive step may be repeated over and over as desired.

### Slow Side Close

**Position:** Latin social
**Level**: Advanced

A resting step.

| STEPS | COUNTS | RHYTHM CUE |
|---|---|---|
| Step left sideward | 1 | slow |
| Close right to left, take weight right | 2 | slow |

Repeat three times, moving left. The last time, do not take weight right, but be ready to go back the other direction. Take four side close steps to the right.

**STEP CUE:** Side close, side close.

**STYLE:** The sway of the samba is discontinued, as is the down, up, down motion. The rhythm is an even-beat step close.

**LEAD:** Following a basic samba step forward and back, the lead has his left foot free. Stopping the sway and motion by control of his body and right arm, he steps left sideward into the pattern. Check directions for leading, number 4, page 419.

**NOTE:** Many beginners find the samba basic step very tiring, so this step may be used to permit the dancers a resting variation.

### Sideward Basic

**Position:** Latin social
**Level**: Advanced

| STEPS | COUNTS | RHYTHM CUE |
|---|---|---|
| Step left sideward | 1 | slow |
| Step right behind left heel | *ah* | quick |
| Step left in place | 2 | slow |
| Step right sideward | 1 | slow |
| Step left behind right heel | *ah* | quick |
| Step right in place | 2 | slow |

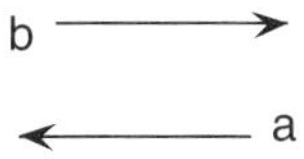

Floor Pattern

**Step Cue:** Side back step, side back step.

**Style:** Both lead and follow may rock the body and turn the head in the direction away from the leading foot. The steps are small. A long step is awkward.

**Lead:** The lead directs the sideward step with his right arm, but the body leans in the opposite direction.

**Note:** For variation, the lead may (1) turn the follow one-quarter counterclockwise as he steps to the left side, so that she turns her back on the direction they are traveling. As he repeats the step to the right, he turns her a half-turn clockwise. (2) They may both turn from reverse open position to open position.

## Copa Step

**Position:** Open
**Level:** Advanced

| STEPS | COUNTS | RHYTHM CUE |
|---|---|---|
| Step left forward | 1 | slow |
| Step right back in place on ball of foot, leaving the left foot forward | *ah* | quick |
| Drag left foot back half the distance, taking weight on left | 2 | slow |
| Step right forward | 1 | slow |
| Step left back in place on ball of foot, leaving right foot forward | *ah* | quick |
| Drag right foot back half the distance, taking weight right | 2 | slow |

**Step Cue:** Down, up, drag.

**Style:** The left step forward is flat, with the knee bending, and the body leans backward slightly. The right step backward on the ball of the foot is accompanied by a raise of the body, which stays up during the drag of the left foot backward.

**Lead:** The lead leads into the open position on the back right sequence of the basic step and then starts the copa with the left foot in open position. The lead leads the copa action by a back lean and down, up, up action in the body.

**Note:** Dragging the foot only halfway back allows the copa step, when repeated over and over, to progress forward in open position. If the lead opens in reverse open position, the copa will begin on the inside foot.

## *Samba* COMBOS

The samba routines are combinations for practice, listed from simple to complex. (Latin social position, unless otherwise indicated.)

1. *Basic Slow, Side Close*
   8 basic (forward ad backward)
   8 side close (4 left, 4 right)
2. *Basic Step, Turn*
   4 basic steps
   4 turning left
   8 side close (4 left, 4 right)
3. *Basic: Forward and Sideward*
   8 basic (forward and backward)
   4 sideward steps
4. *Basic Turn, Copa*
   4 basic turns
   4 slow side close
   4 copa steps
5. *Advanced Combo*
   4 basics
   4 sideward basic
   8 forward progressive
   8 copa steps (open)
6. *Advanced Combo*
   4 basic
   8 copa steps
   8 basic turns
   4 slow side close

# Periodicals

APPENDIX A

The following periodicals are of two types. The first type is an association or federation publication dealing with news and current dance events aimed at a particular geographic area. The second type is a more traditional publication that specializes in one dance form and gives in-depth coverage of the social and cultural background of that particular dance form.

***Amateur Dancers.*** The official membership publication of the United States Ballroom Dancers Association, Inc. Editorial Offices: Robert Meyer, Editor East, 1427 Gibsonwood Rd., Baltimore, MD 21228; Phone and Fax: (410) 747-7855; http://www.usabda.org

***The American Dance Circle.*** Enid Cocke, 2924 Hickory Court, Manhattan, KS 66503; (913) 539-6306. The Lloyd Shaw Foundation quarterly.

***Ballroom Dancing Times.*** Clerkenwell House, 45–47 Clerkenwell Green, London, England ECIR OEB. www.dancing-times.co.uk/ballroomdt.html

***Bridges.*** Lithuanian American News Journal, c/o Ramas Pliūra, 1927 West Boulevard, Racine, WI 53403; http://javlb.org/bridges_en.php

***Clog Today*** (formerly ***FlopEared Mule).*** www.geocities.com/kloggirl/clogging/clogging.html

***Country Dance and Song Society News.*** Country Dance and Song Society, 132 Main Street, P.O. Box 338, Haydenville, MA 01039; (413) 268-7426; Fax (413) 268-7471; e-mail: office@cdss.org; http://www.cdss.org

***The Dance Gypsy.*** Publishes monthly calendar and sponsors dance events in northern New England; www.thedancegypsy.com

***Dancesport Magazine.*** P.O. Box 13, Boca Raton, FL 33429-0013; (800) ADO-8211. Publication of the American Dancesport Organization; http://www.dancesportmagazine.com

***Dancing USA.*** 200 N. York Road, Elmhurst, IL 60126; (800) 290-1307

***The Double Toe Times.*** Jeff Driggers, Ed. Monthly. P.O. Box 1352, St. Albans, WV 25177-1352; (304) 727-9357; Fax (304) 727-9568; http://www.doubletoe.com

***Ethnomusicology.*** Society of Ethnomusicology, Morrison Hall 005, Indiana University, Bloomington, IN 47405; (812) 855-6672; Fax (812) 855-6673. Good folklore and music dealing with dance; http://www.ethnomusicology.org

***Folk Dance Scene.*** Published monthly by the Folk Dance Federation of California South, Inc., Phone/Fax: (310) 478-6600; www.socalfolkdance.org

***Folklife Center News.*** American Folklife Center, The Library of Congress. 101 Independence Avenue, S.E.Washington, DC 20540-4610. Abundant American folklife information.

***Footnotes.*** Square and Folk Dance Federation of Washington, P.O. Box 2420, Walla Walla, WA 99362-0370; (509)-522-2716; http://www.squaredance-wa.org/footnote.htm

***Let's Dance.*** Folk Dance Federation of California, Inc., Box 561, Sauslito, CA 94966; (415) 332-1020; http://www.folkdance.com

***Northern Junket.*** Ralph Page, editor and publisher 1949–1984. Contre and square dance. No longer published. See Ralph Page Collection, Appendix B.

***Northwest Folkdancer.*** c/o Linda Caspermeyer, 1023 NE 61st St., Seattle, WA 98115-6601; www.scn.org/arts/nfdi

***The Orff Echo.*** The quarterly journal of the American Orff-Schulwerk Association; www.aosa.org

***Slovakia.*** A Slovak Heritage newsletter of the Slovak Heritage and Folklore Society of North America, 151 Colebrook Dr., Rochester, NY 14617-2215; (716) 342-9383.

***Sets In Order: The Magazine of Square Dancing.*** 1949–1963. Changed to *Square Dancing*. 1963–1985. No longer published. Check local libraries for back issues.

***Spotlight on Dance.*** National Dance Association, 1900 Association Dr., Reston, VA 20191; www.aahperd.org/nda

***Step-In-Time.*** Texas Clogging Council. Quarterly. Ethel E. Wilmesmier, ed., 410 Highland Mist Circle, Houston, TX 77015; e-mail: clogdance@ix.netcom.com; http://www.texas-clogging.com/stepintime.htm

***The Texas Clogger.*** Texas Clogging Council. Quarterly; Bobbi Boyce, editor. 12711 Quail Cove, Buda, TX 78610; (512) 312-0201; cloggerbee@austin.rr.com; http://www.texas-clogging.com/TexasClogger.htm

***Viltis.*** Vytautas (Vyts) F. Beliajus, editor and publisher. International Folk Dance. No longer published. Check local libraries for back issues 1944–1994. Index available from L. DeWayne Young, 359 S. Cleveland Ave., Blackfoot, ID 88221.

# Organizations and Resources

APPENDIX B

**American Callers Association**
P.O. Box 2406
Muscle Shoals, AL 35662
(256) 383-7585
www.AmericanCallers.com

**BYU Sports and Dance Camps (Ballroom Dance Camps)**
147 Harman Continuing Education Building
Provo, UT 84602
(801) 378-4851; for registration press option 1; for camp information press option 2.
http://ce.byu.edu/cw/cwdance

**CALLERLAB**
467 Forrest Avenue, Suite 118
Cocoa, FL 32922
(321) 639-0039
Fax (321) 639-0851
Callerlab@aol.com
www.callerlab.org/

**Center for Traditional Music and Dance**
(formerly the Ethnic Folk Arts Center)
200 Church Street, Room 303
New York, NY 10013-3831
(212) 571-1555
Fax (212) 571-9052
www.ctmd.org

**College Ballroom Dance Association**
Suzanne Zelnik-Geldys
Health, Physical Education, Recreation and Dance Department
Eastern Michigan University
318 Porter
Ypsilanti, MI 48197
(734) 487-7120 x2729

**Congress in Research in Dance (CORD)**
www.cordance.org.

**Contralab**
International Association of Contra Callers
Glen Nickerson
606 Woodland Way
Kent, WA 98031

**Country Dance and Song Society (CDSS)**
152 Main Street (Route 9)
P.O. Box 338
Haydenville, MA 01039-0338
Fax (413) 268-7471
e-mail: sales@cdss.org
www.cdss.org.

Promotes the preservation of American Country Dance; English Country Dance also included. Publishes *Country Dance and Song Society News* six times a year, books, and a *Group and Membership Directory;* produces records; sells records, cassettes, videos, books; sponsors dance camps.

**Country Dance and Song Society Library and Archives**
This is part of the New Hampshire Special Collection of Traditional Music and Dance; *see* the Ralph Page Collection.

**Dance Notation Bureau (DNB)**
Uses symbols called Labanotation.
www.dancenotation.org.

**East European Folklife Center (EEFC)**
P.O. Box 12488
Berkeley, CA 94712-3488
(510) 549-2124
www.eefc.org

**Farnum Hill Productions**
David Millstone
176 Farnum Hill Road
Lebanon, NH 03766
603-448-2950
millstone@valley.net

**Flying Cloud Academy**
P.O. Box 628113
Cincinnati, OH 45262-8113
(513) 981-7131
www.vintagedance.net

**Folk Alliance**
962 Wayne Ave., Suite 902
Silver Spring, MD 20910-4480
(301) 588-8185
Fax (301) 588-8186
www.folk.org

**Folk Arts Center of New England**
42 West Foster St.
Melrose, MA 02176
(781) 662-7475
www.facone.org

**Folk Dance Association**
P.O. Box 300500
Brooklyn, NY 11230-0500
(888) 321-1023
e-mail: director@folkdancing.org
www.folkdancing.org

**Folk Dance Federation of California**
Box 561
Sausalito, CA 94966
(415) 332-1020
www.folkdance.com

**Folklife Center News**
American Folklife Center, The Library of Congress
101 Independence Avenue
S.E.Washington, D.C. 20540-4610
Abundant American folklife information.

**Folk Moot**
112 Virginia Avenue
P.O. Box 658
Waynesville, NC 28786
(828) 452-2997; toll free (877) 365-5872
Fax (828) 452-5762
www.folkmoot.com

**International Folk Culture Center**
(located at Our Lady of the Lake University)
411 S.W. 24th Street
San Antonio, TX 78207-4689
(210) 436-8888
Fax (210) 436-8889 (weekdays)
e-mail: infolkcultu@aol.com
www.ifcchouseconcerts.com

**Library of Congress**
101 Independence Ave., SE
Washington, D.C. 20540
(202) 707-5000 (General Information)
e-mail: lcweb@loc.gov
www.loc.gov

Largest collection of dance books in the United States.

1. American Folklife Center. Goal is to preserve and present programs relating to folklife and cutural heritage in the United States. Published quarterly newsletter. (202) 707-5510.
2. Archive of Folk Culture. Founded by the Lomaxes in 1978. Archives include dance material in tape recordings, documentaries. Available for research. (202) 707-5510.
3. Research: www.loc.gov/rr

**The Lloyd Shaw Foundation**
Preserves and promotes American square and round dance. The Lloyd Shaw Foundation publishes the *American Dance Circle,* quarterly. For more information about becoming a member or information on the archives, contact:

Dr. William M. Litchman, President
1620 Los Alamos SW
Albuquerque, NM 87104
(505) 247-3921
www.lloydshaw.org

**The Lloyd Shaw Archives and Collection**
Carson-Brierly Dance Library in the Penrose Library at the University of Denver
www.penlib.du.edu/About/collection/SpecialCollections/index.cfm

**The National Clogging Organization, Inc.**
(formerly the National Clogging and Hoedown Council, NCHC)
David and Susan Phillips, Executive Directors
3054 Ashly Pines Drive
Snellville, Georgia, 30078-4550
(770) 985-5557
Fax (603) 925-0967
e-mail: clog@clog.org
www.clog.org

**National Dance Education Organization**
Jane M. Bonbright, Executive Director
4948 St. Elmo Avenue, Suite 301
Bethesda, MD 20814-6013
(301) 657-2880
http://ndeo.org

**National Dance Association, Division of AAHPERD**
1900 Association Drive
Reston, VA 22091-1502
(800) 213-7193 x464
www.aahperd.org/nda

**National Folk Organization of the USA**
NFO Membership Services
15221 N. Country Road 400
East Eaton, IN 47338
www.nfo-usa.org

**National Recreation and Parks Association**
22377 Belmont Ridge Road
Ashburn, VA 20148-4501
(703) 858 0784
Fax (703) 848-0794
www.nrpa.org

**National Square Dance Directory**
P.O. Box 880
Brandon, MS 39043
(601) 825-6831 or (800) 542-4010.
www.folkdancing.org/fd_directory.html

Directory includes 10,000 square, round, clogging, and contra dance clubs in the United States, Canada, and around the world.

**New England Folk Festival Association (NEFFA)**
PMB 282, 1770 Massachusetts Ave.
Cambridge, MA 02140
(781) 662-6710
Fax (781) 662-6730
www.neffa.org

**New York Public Library for the Performing Arts Dance Collection**
Lincoln Performing Arts Center
111 Amsterdam Avenue
New York, NY 10023
(212) 870-1630
e-mail: dance@nypl.org
www.nypl.org

Holdings include 40,000 books, plus films, videotapes, oral history tapes. The *Complete Catalogue of Dance Collections of the New York Public Library* is available.

1. Published directory in reference section of large libraries.
2. CD-ROM copy of disc at large libraries.

**North American Federation of German Folk Dance Groups**
Karin P. Gottier, Editor
48 Hilltop Road
Tolland, CT 06084
www.germandance.org/NAFGFDG/workshops.html

**Orff-Schulwerk Association**
P.O. Box 391089
Cleveland, OH 44139-8089
(440) 543-5366
www.aosa.org

National association that promotes the Orff-Schulwerk approach to understanding rhythm.

**Ralph Page Collection**
Special Collections Room
Dimond Library
University of New Hampshire
Durham, NH 03824
(603) 862-2714

Ralph Page's personal collection of dance and music books is available for research at www.izaak.unh.edu/nhltmd/pagehome.htm.

**Smithsonian Institution**
1000 Jeferson Drive, S.W.
Washington, D.C. 20560
General information: (202) 633-1000
www.si.edu

1. The Smithsonian Center for Folklife Programs and Cultural Studies promotes the understanding and continuity of contemporary grassroots cultures in the United States and abroad. Produces Smithsonian Folklife Festival, Smithsonian Folkways Recordings, exhibitions, documentary films, videos, etc.

P.O. Box 37012
Victor Building, Suite 4100
MRC 953
Washington, D.C. 20013-7012
(202) 275-1150
Fax (202) 275-1119
e-mail: folklife-info@si.edu.
www.si.edu/collections/folklife.htm
www.folkdlife.si.edu

**Society of Folk Dance Historians**
2100 Rio Grande Street
Austin, TX 78705-5513

Publishes *Folk Dance Phone Book*, sponsors dance opportunities, and preserves history and practice of international folk dancing.

**United States Amateur Ballroom Dance Association**
Central Office
P.O. Box 128
New Freedom, PA 17349
(800) 447-9047
Fax (717) 235-4183
www.usabda.org

# Record, CD, Cassette, and Video Sources—Distributors and Producers

APPENDIX C

## MUSIC, DVD, AND VIDEO SOURCES

The sources listed are of two types: producers who make recordings and distributors who supply retailers. Ordering from a nearby distributor is not only convenient and timesaving but, more important, it alerts the distributor to the dance records and supplies most commonly used in that area. Producers can supply catalogs of their products and suggest sources from which they may be obtained.

**Ardey Allotey.** Music from Africa, especially Ghana. P.O. Box 19006, Portland, OR 97219.

**American Alliance for Health, Physical Education, Recreation and Dance (AAHPERD).** Publications, products, and services catalogs. Country western and line dance books and videos. Order from AAHPERD, 1900 Association Dr., Reston, VA 20191-1598; (800) 213-7193. www.aahperd.org

**Amuse-A-Mood Co.** Catalogue of books, manuals, instructional tapes, and videos. Booklets covering dance steps (beginner to advanced), history of swing and music fundamentals. 128 Hancock Place N.E., Leesburg, VA 22075.

**Andy's Front Hall.** Folk, traditional, acoustic music store. Books, records, cassettes for American country dance, including contra, New England, and West Virginia squares, English country dance. Many folk instruments. P.O. Box 307, Voorheesville, NY 12186; (518) 765-4193; (800) 759-1775; Fax (518) 765-4344; www.andysfronthall.com

**Country Dance and Song Society, Inc.** 132 Main Street, P.O. Box 338, Haydenville, MA 01039-0338; (413) 268-7426; Fax (413) 268-7471; www.cdss.org

**Andor Czompo.** Hungarian dance notes, music and videos. 100 Gleneagles, Williamsburg, VA 23188.

**Dance Plus.** Over 500 strict-time ballroom CDs. New releases and music list available. 22A Dorchester Ave., Toronto, Ontario, Canada, M87 4W3; (888) 844-4122; www.danceplus.com

**Dance Trax International.** CDs for International style, American style, and showcase dancing. 2217 N. Woodbridge, Saginaw, MI 48602; Phone/Fax (517) 799-0349; Orders: (800) 513-2623.

**Dance Vision USA.** Catalogue of instructional videos, tapes, and CDs. 9081 West Sahara Avenue, Las Vegas, NV, 89117-5745; (800) 851-2813; Fax (702) 256-4227; www.dancevision.com

**Dancing Times Limited.** Extensive stock of Ballroom Dancing Times books and videos. 45–47 Clerkenwell Green, London, EC1R OEB, England.

**Mihai David.** Romanian dance music. 2940 West Lincoln Blvd., Suite D, Anaheim, CA 92801.

**Educational Frontiers.** Distributes software, filmstrips, videos, records, cassettes, and CDs. 132 West 21st Street, Suite 5, New York, NY 10011; (800) 753-6488; www.educational-frontiers.com

**Festival Records.** Foreign and folk dance records, cassettes, videos, books, and folklore imports. 2773 West Pico Boulevard, Los Angeles, CA 90006; (323) 737-3500; Fax (323) 737-3500; www.festivalrecords.com.au

**Floyd's Record Shop.** Cajun mail order. P.O. Box 10, 434 E. Main Street, Ville Platte, LA 70586 (318) 363-4893; (800) 738-8668; www.floydsrecordshop.com

**Folk Arts Center of New England.** Distributors of folk dance records, CDs, cassettes, videos, sheet music, and books; 42 West Foster St., Melrose, MA 02176; (781) 622-7475

**Folk Dancer Record Center.** Distributing center for The Michael Herman Record Series. Single records, 45s, 33-10, and albums. CDs also available. 6290 Olin Road, Brandenburg, KY; (800) 446-1209; www.folkdancer.org

**Folkraft Records, Compact Discs, Tapes, and Books** (sublabel of Syncoopshop www.syncoop.com/syncoopshop/enter.html). Contact Folkraft-Europe, Rue Sant-Norbert, BE-1090 Brussels, Belgium; e-mail: rhfe@usa.net

**Folkstyle Productions.** Folk dance CDs, videos, and workshops by Sanna Longden. 1402 Elinor Place, Evanston, IL 60201; (800) 894-4378; Fax (847) 328-5241; www.FolkStyle.com

**Gold Star Video Productions.** Square, round, ballroom videos. P.O. Box 1057, Sisters, OR 97759; (541) 549-4302

**Great Meadow Music.** Produces and distributes contra music. P.O. Box 4, Westmoreland, NH 03467; (603) 399-8361; www.greatmeadowmusic.com

**Grenn, Inc.** Producer of Grenn Records for recreational dancing: square, round, line, and clogging. 2775 Yellow Creek Road, Akron, OH 44333; (330) 836-5591.

**Hanhurst's Music Review Source.** Distributors of vast collection of music for square and round dance on 45 RPM vinyl, CDs, and MP3 files that can be downloaded on the web. Square and round dance publications, videos, DVDs. 2818 Highway 44 East, Shepherdsville, Kentucky 40165; (800) 328-3800; Fax: (800) 227-5420; www.Dosado.com

**Hendrickson Group.** Country Dance books, music, and cassettes. P.O. Box 766, Sandy Hook, CT 06482; (205) 426-1165.

**High/Scope.** Produces High/Scope books, records, CDs, cassettes, and videos. 600 N. River Street, Ypsilanti, MI 48198-2898; (734) 486-6660; Fax (734) 485-0704.

**Hilton Audio Products, Inc.** 1033 E. Shary Circle, Concord, CA 94518; (925) 682-8390; Fax (925) 682-8497; e-mail: HiltonAudio@aol.com; www.hiltonaudio.com.

**Hoctor Products for Education.** Produces and retails CDs, records, cassettes, and videos. P.O. Box 38, Waldwick, NJ 07463; (201) 652-7767; Fax (201) 652-2599; www.hoctordance.com

**Human Kinetics Publishers.** Social dance cassettes. P.O. Box 5076, Champaign, IL 61825-5076; (800) 747-4457; Fax (217) 351-1549; www.humankinetics.com

**International Folk Rhythms, Ltd.** Folk dance records, CDs, cassettes, ethnic and educational music and books, electronic equipment, imported clothing and specialties. P.O. Box 1402, Northbrook, IL 60065; (847) 564-2880; Fax (847) 564-2868; www.folkrhythms. com

**John Music Education Catalog.** Dance records, cassette, videos, books, and instruments from around the world. 4501 Interlake N. #9, Seattle, WA 98103. (206) 548-0916; (800) 473-5194; Fax (206) 548-0422.

**Kentucky Dance Foundation.** Folk Dancer Record Center. 6290 Olin Road, Brandenburg, KY 40108; (502) 422-3655; (800) 446-1209; Fax (502) 422-3655; www.folkdancer.org

**Kimbo Educational.** Producers of a wide variety of dance and musical play activities, videos, cassettes, and records for school and recreational use. P.O. Box 477, Long Branch, NJ 07740; (908) 229-4949; Fax (908) 870-4440; (800) 631-2187; Fax (732) 870-3340; www.kimboed.com

**Lamon Records.** Singing calls, hoedowns, round dances, clogging, waltz, line dancing. Lamon Studios, P.O. Box 23625, Charlotte, NC 28227; (877) 280-6346; www.lamonrecords.com

**Christy Lane.** 225 N. El Cielo Rd., Suite 366, Palm Springs, CA 9222; (800) 555-0206; www.christylane.com

**Lloyd Shaw Foundation, Inc.** P.O. Box 11, Macks Creek, MO 65786; (573) 363-5868; Fax (573) 363-5820; e-mail: Audio@mail.usmo.com; www.lloydshaw.org.

**Jacek Marek.** Dance music from Poland. 200 Highland Street, Dedham, MA 02026; (781) 326-2460; e-mail: jacekmarek@comcast.net

**Melody House Publishing Co.** World of Fun records and cassettes. Collection includes American play party games, American square dances, and many international dances. 819 N.W. 92nd Street, Oklahoma City, OK 73114; (405) 840-3383; Fax (405) 840-3384.

**Modern Music Center.** Cajun mail order: P.O. Box 856, 413 N. Parkerson, Crowley, LA 70526; (318) 783-1601.

**Musical Services.** Helmut Licht-Variety cassettes and CDs of ballroom favorites. 409 Lyman Avenue, Baltimore, MD 21212; (410) 323-0866; www.ballroom music. com

**National Association of Country Dances.** P.O. Box 9841, Colorado Springs, CO 80932.

**Norsk, Ltd.** Carries Scandinavian folk music, primarily Norwegian and Swedish. LP, CDs, and cassettes. Jofrid Sodal, 770 Linden Avenue, Boulder, CO 80304; (303) 442-6452; Fax (303) 440-8303; www.csd.net/~sodaling

**Northwest Dance Network.** Music for swing, zydeco, vintage, Cajun, and more. http://nwdance.net

**Perry's Place Records and Supplies, Inc.** P.O. Box 69, 1155 Lexington Road, Nicholasville, KY 40340; (800) 884-9440; www.perrysplace.com

**Princeton Book Company, Publishers.** Source for dance books and videos. P.O. Box 831, Hightstown, NJ 08520; (609) 426-0602; (800) 220-7149; Fax (609) 426-1344; www.dancehorizons.com

**Putumayo World Music CDs.** www.putumayo.com

**Ravenna Ventures.** Eric Chappelle's Music for Creative Dance and Brain Dance Music. www.RavennaVentures.com

**Reeves Records, Inc.** Square, round, clogging,
**Roper Records.** Produces a wide variety of social dance records, 45s, LPs, and cassettes. CDs include ballet, tap, jazz for class use. 45-15 21st Street, Long Island City, NY 11101; (718) 786-2401.

**Savoy's Music Center.** Cajun mail order. 4413 Highway 190, Eunice, LA 70535; (337) 457-9563.

**Marilyn M. Smith.** Dance music from France. 1560 Yardley Street, Santa Rosa, CA 95403.

**Square Dance Record Roundup.** Dealer in square, folk, line, round, and clogging records. 957 Sheridan Boulevard, Denver, CO 80214; (303) 238-4810.

**Starlight Dance Studio.** Ballroom dance videos; 6506 El Cajon Boulevard, San Diego, CA. 92115; (619) 287-9036.

**Supreme Audio, Inc.** Distributor of square dance and round dance records. Source for audio equipment for instructors. P.O. Box 50, Marlborough, NH 03455-0050; (800) 445-7398; Fax (603) 876-4001; www.supremeaudio.com.

**Volksmusik Oberer Neckar.** German folk dance music. Webmaster @ v-o-n.de

**Wagon Wheel Records and Books.** Excellent source for folk, square, and clogging dance records, cassettes, and teaching materials. Paul James, 16812 Pennbrook Lane, Huntington Beach, CA 92649; Phone or Fax (714) 846-8169; www.wagonwheelrecords.net

**Wagon Wheel/Windsor Records.** Records and CDs. P.O. Box 2546, Toluca Lake, CA 91610; (206) 722-4747.

**Worldtone Music, Inc.** Distributes folk, square, ballroom, jazz, contra, clogging. Producers of Worldtone Folk Music. 230 Seventh Avenue, New York, NY 10011; (212) 691-1934; Fax (212) 691-2554.

## VIDEO SOURCES

**Best Film and Video Corp.,** Great Neck, NY 11021.

**Country Dance and Song Society.** 132 Main St., P.O. Box 338, Haydenville, MA 01039-0338; (413) 268-7426; www.cdss.org

**Flower Films and Video.** 10341 San Pablo Avenue, El Cerrito, CA 94530; (510) 525-0942, www.lib.berkeley.edu/MRC/Flowerfilm.html

**High/Scope Videos.** 600 N. River Street, Ypsilanti, MI 48198-2898; (734) 485-2000, Fax (734) 485-0704; www.highscope.org

**Hoctor Products for Education.** P.O. Box 38, Waldrick, NJ 07463; (201) 652-7767; Fax (201) 652-2599; www.dancecaravan.com

**International Dance Discovery.** Folk/Ethnic Dance Videos Catalogue. 1025 South Minor Road, Bloomington, IN 47041.

**PPI Parade Video.** 88 St. Francis St., Newark, NJ 07105; (800) 272-4214; www.peterpan.com

# Instructional Aids—Music and Videos

APPENDIX D

*See Appendix C for distributors' addresses and contact information where available.*

## AMERICAN COUNTRY DANCE

***American Country Dances*** (1775–95). Eight Tunes. Cassette. George A. Fogg. Order from Hendrickson Groups.

***Dances from Appalachia,*** Series I, II, III. Berea College, Box 287, Berea, KY 40404.

## CAJUN

***Allons Dancer!*** Randy Speyrer, P.O. Box 15908, New Orleans, LA 70175-5908; (504) 899-0615. ***Cajun Dancing, Step by Step Instruction.*** Waltz, two-step, one-step, Cajun jitterbug. ***Introduction to Cajun Dancing, Vol. I & II.*** (Video) Speyrer, Cynthia, and Randy Speyrer. Gretna, LA: Pelican Publishing Co., 1993.

***Floyd's Record Shop.*** Cajun mail order.

***Louisiana Catalog.*** Cajun mail order.

***Modern Music Center.*** Cajun mail order.

***Savoy's Music Center.*** Cajun mail order.

## CLOGGING

Any musical selection with a 2/4 time signature may be used for clogging. Square dance music without calls (hoedown music) is a good choice when the tempo is appropriate for the skill level of the dancers. Many musical selections can be made more appropriate if the instructor uses a variable-speed player. The following are examples of records with music of a moderate tempo.

***Appalachian Clog Dance Steps*** (Video). Duke Publishing Co.

***Bar Clogging in St. Louis*** (Video). Rush McAllister, 1109 S. Taylor Avenue, St. Louis, MO 63110.

***Chinese Breakdown/Rockabout,*** Sets In Order 2123. ***Phase Craze/Pavalon Stomp,*** Sets In Order 2114.

***Clog Dancers' Choice,*** Old-time fiddle tunes for clogging practice. Bob Dalsemer. Cassette.

***Clogging Appalachian Free-Style Techniques*** and ***Line Dancing Video for Seniors*** (Videos). Video Vacation.

***Clogging and Buck Dancing, Dances of the World: Appalachia.*** Clogging groups with history and commentary. ***Talking Feet,*** Solo Southern Dance, Buck Flatfoot and Tap by Mike Seeger and Ruth Pershing. Country Dance and Song Society.

***Dixie on My Mind,*** Rhythm Records RR 157. ***I'm Just a Redneck in a Rock and Roll Bar;*** Rhythm Records RR 118. ***Trucking Fever,*** Rhythm Records RR 151.

***Dueling Banjos/Pitter Patter,*** Wagon Wheel WW 125. ***Rain/Timber,*** Wagon Wheel WW 134.

***Gladys Stomp/Clogging Down Yonder,*** Red Boot Records RB 301.

***Louisiana Saturday Night,*** Chaparral Records C-311.

***Melody Hoedown,*** Lamon Records LR 10076.

***Minstrel Man,*** Jay-Bar-Kay Records JBK 6018.

***Ragtime Annie/Sasafrass,*** Blue Star BS 1612.

***Talking Feet,*** Flower Films and Video, Country Dance and Song Society.

***Ten Toe Percussion: Clog, Tap, and Step Dancing*** (Irish step dancing, French-Canadian step dancing, Cape Breton step dancing, Appalachian flatfooting, English clogging, and rhythm tap dancing). Ira Bernstein, 179 Flint Street, Asheville, NC 28801; (704) 255-9393; Fax (704) 255-9291; e-mail: IraTenToe@aol.com.

## CONTRA

***Airdance; Flying on Home; Cloud Nine,*** three CDs by Rodney Miller and Airdance, high energy and musical virtuosity. Great Meadow Music.

***Alive in Prague!*** The Percolators. American and French-Canadian dance tunes for squares and contras. Yodel-Ay-Hee #058

***Any Jig or Reel,*** well-phrased dance-length tunes by Andy Davis, accordion; Becky Tracy, fiddle; Keith Murphy, piano, guitar, and foot percussion. New England Dancing Masters #07-02.

***Best of Wild Asparagus,*** Great Meadow Music. CD #2013.

***Canterbury Country Dance Orchestra.*** Selections from several Canterbury LPs. F&W Records #CD-01-FW8.

***Chimes of Dunkirk,*** Teaching Dances to Children. Peter Amidon, New England Dancing Masters, Brattleboro, VT. Note: This is a CD, video, and book; www.dancingmasters.com

***Choose Your Partners!*** Contra dance and square dance music of New Hampshire. Smithsonian Folkways CD #LC9628.

***The Civil War Ballroom,*** Spare Parts, dance-length cuts with rich orchestration of period tunes. Bill Matthiesen, 33 Stormview Road, Lanesboro, MA 01237.

***Contra Connections.*** DVD contains two videos, ***Paid to Eat Ice Cream: Bob McQuillen and New England Contra Dancing*** (70 min.) and ***What's Not To Like? A Community Contra Dance*** (20 min.). David Millstone, 2001, 2003.

***Contra Music: The Sound of New England,*** sampler from twelve different albums, mostly traditional sound, Great Meadow Music #2012.

***Contra Roots and Branches,*** sampler of 14 different bands, more contemporary sounds. Great Meadow Music #2017.

***Domino,*** lively French-Canadian tunes with piano, fiddle, accordion. #DOMCD101, available from Great Meadow Music.

***Eight American Contras and Squares*** as called by the dean of New England callers. Cassette. George A. Fogg, 40 Gray Street, Boston, MA 02116-6210.

***Farewell to the Hollow,*** New England Tradition. Historic recording of powerful trio (Bob McQuillen, April Limber, Pete Colby). Great Meadow Music #2014.

***Faster than a Walk,*** The Moving Violations play both traditional New England tunes as well as some from Scandinavia and Eastern Europe. Great Meadow Music #2009.

***Fiddledance,*** featuring Frank Ferrel, fiddle; excellent selection of Irish tunes and others for contra dance. Great Meadow Music #2018.

***Hand It Down!*** Laurie Andres, accordion; Cathie Whitesides, fiddle; Bob McQuillen, piano, playing selections from the more than 1,200 dance tunes composed by McQuillen.

***Listen to the Mockingbird,*** More Great Dances for Children, Schools & Communities. New England Dancing Masters, Brattleboro, VT. CD and book.

***New England Chestnuts, Vol. 1 & 2,*** Randy and Rodney Miller. Tunes for New England contras. Great Meadows Music, CD #2005.

***Notorious,*** Eden MacAdam-Somer, fiddle; Larry Unger, guitar and banjo. Tunes from many traditions plus original compositions, played by a duo that tours extensively. Black Socks #26.

***Old New England, ONE:TWO,*** and ***ONE:III,*** features Bob McQuillen, piano; Jane Orzechowski, fiddle; Deanna Stiles, flute; traditional New England sound. Available from Great Meadow Music.

***The Other Way Back:*** Dancing with Dudley (DVD). David Millstone, 2007.

***Paid to Eat Ice Cream: Bob McQuillen and New England Contra Dancing*** (Video). David Millstone, 2001. Contracopia.

***A Portland Selection: Contra Dance Music in the Pacific Northwest.*** Susan Songer, Portland, OR; www.theportlandcollection.com

***Pure Quill,*** Rodney Miller, fiddle, and Bob McQuillen, piano and accordion; two of the best-known New England musicians. Great Meadow Music #2004

***Ralph Page and His Orchestra,*** Kentucky Dance Foundation, CD, Folk Dancer #42

***Sleeping on a Rock,*** The Latter Day Lizards. Upbeat and jazzy tunes by popular trio. Canis #005.

***Together In Time: A Story of New England Contra Music and Dance*** (Video/DVD). Steve Alves, Great Meadow Music, #2011.

***What's Not To Like? A Country Contra Dance*** (Video). David Millstone, 2003.

## COUNTRY WESTERN

***Kicker Dancin' Texas Style: How to Do the Top Ten Country and Western Dances like a Texas Cowboy.*** 1982. Rushing Productions, 5149 Blanco Road, #214, San Antonio, TX 78216.

***National Association of Country Dances.*** Country Dance Music.

***Texas Dance Styles*** by Valerie Moss and Scott Schmitz. ***Texas Two-Step, Down and Dirty*** (Jerk, Twist, Stroll, Monkey, Hustle, etc.) PPI Parade Video.

***Texas Two-Step.*** Coffey Video Productions.

***28 Country Swing Moves and Combinations.*** National Association of Country Dances.

## FOLK DANCE

Single records are recommended as a primary music source for instruction. Multiband, long-playing records arranged in a series are useful and economical. Records or cassettes packaged in series form offer a variety of basic steps, nationalities, and formations. They are usually graded easy to difficult; thus they are adaptable to all ability levels. These would also be suitable for One-Night Stands. Single records or audio cassettes make it less expensive to upgrade dance selections, thus keeping dance materials current.

***Dance A While CD, Vols. 1 & 2.*** Kentucky Dance Foundation.

***Easy American Dances #105*** and ***Easy Israeli Dances,*** Yehuda Emanuel of Israel.

***Favorite Folk Dances of Kids and Teachers,*** Sanna Longden.

***High-Scope Dances.*** Phyllis Weikart. Worldtone Music, Inc.

***Easy Folk Dance Lessons for Children,*** Dancecraft Cassette Series. A series of six cassettes supervised by Jack Geddes, lecturer at MacMaster University School of Physical Education (Canada). The series contains graded dances from a number of nationalities based on locomotor skills. Dance directions accompany each cassette. Series numbers are DC 387, 487, 587, 687, 787, 887.

***Folk Dances from 'Round the World,*** Merit Audio Visual. A seven-album series containing twelve or more dances each from the United States and abroad. Each album presents steps for dancers of increasing ability. Well-illustrated manuals of dance instructions accompany each album. It is especially useful to beginning folk dance teachers. (Formerly the RCA Victor Series supervised by Michael and Mary Ann Herman.)

***Folkdances 1, 2, 3, 4.*** High/Scope Videos.

***International Dance Discovery.*** Publishes a Folk/Ethnic Dance Video catalogue. 1025 South Minor Road, Bloomington, IN 47401; (313) 485-0704; Fax (313) 485-2000.

***Michael Herman Record Series.*** Folk Dancer Record Center.

***Pericles in America.*** Video of Greek dance and Pericles Halkias, Greek clarinet player. ***Salute to Immigrant Cultures.*** Film, three days of folk dance in Manhattan. Ethnic Folkarts Center (EFAC), 325 Spring Street, Room 314, New York, NY 10013; (212) 691-9510.

***Wagon Wheel Records, Folk Dance Now!*** and ***Dances for Fun and Fitness.***

## LINE DANCE

***Country Line Dancing for Kids. Country Line Dancing. More Country Line Dancing.*** Diane Horner. Quality Video, Inc., 7399 Bush Lake Road, Minneapolis, MN 55439.

***Fun and Funky Freestyle Dancing. Line Dancing. Line Dancing, Vol. 2. New Line Dancing.*** Christy Lane.

***Line Dancing, New Line Dancing Fun and Funky Freestyle Dancing.*** Brentwood House Video.

***Line Dancing for Seniors, Vol. I.*** Grant F. Longley. New England Caller, Inc., P.O. Box 8069, Lowell, MA 01853.

## SOCIAL DANCE

Music for social dance or ballroom dance is subject to the particular "sound" in vogue in each generation. "Standards" are records that are recognized by musicians and public alike as favorites and do, indeed, survive several generations. In addition to local distributors, the four most extensive sources are: Grenn, Hoctor, Roper, and Windsor. Refer to Appendix C for distributors.

***Amuse-A-Mood Co.*** Catalogue of books, manuals, instructional tapes, and videos. Booklets covering dance steps (beginner to advanced), history of swing and music fundamentals.

***Arthur Murray Dance Magic Series: Waltz, Tango, Swing, Samba, Merengue, Night Club, Rumba, Salsa, Cha Cha, Dancin' Dirty, Fox Trot, Mambo.*** Princeton Book Company.

***B & M Dance Productions (AD).*** American social dance instructional videos–beginner to advanced. "How-to" tapes teach beginner to advanced steps.

***Charleston. Hip Hop.*** Hoctor Products for Education.

***Club Salsa, Vol. 1.*** Moves for salsa and mambo, variations with turn combinations. Video, 46 minutes. ***Club Salsa, Vol. 2.*** Longer turn combinations, added step patterns, tips on leading and following. Video, 54 minutes. ***Dance Time.*** Video, 45 minutes. ***Dance with Me, Vol. 1.*** Fox-trot, waltz, tango, and rumba. ***Dance with Me, Vol. 2.*** Mambo, cha-cha, and swing. ***Let's Lindy Hop, Vol. 1.*** Video, 45 minutes. ***Let's Lindy Hop, Vol. 2.*** Video, 51 minutes. Mad Degrees Productions, P.O. Box 2945, Beverly Hills, CA 90213-2945; (800) 326-4997.

***Complete Guide to Party Dance.*** Christy Lane's new video of most requested party dances: Electric Slide, YMCA, Macarena, Chicken Dance, Stroll, Conga, Hand Jive, Swing, etc. National Dance Association, Attn: Millie Puccio, 1900 Association Drive, Reston, VA 20191-1598.

***Dance Lovers.*** VHS videos, music, and tapes. P.O. Box 7071, Asheville, NC 28802.

***Dance Plus,*** Over 500 strict ballroom CDs. New releases and music list available.

***Dancing Times Limited.*** Extensive stock of Ballroom Dancing Times books and videos.

***Dance Trax International,*** CDs for international style, American style, and showcase dancing.

***Dare to Dance Music CD,*** Christy Lane.

***Fred Astaire Dancing: Ballroom*** (fox-trot, waltz), ***Latin*** (cha cha, salsa). Best Film and Video Corp.

***Musical Services.*** Helmut Licht–Variety of cassettes and CDs of ballroom favorites.

***Not Strictly Ballroom: Social Dance Library of Video Tapes.*** Eight tapes cover fox-trot, waltz, tango, Viennese waltz, rumba, cha cha, East Coast swing, samba, mambo, merengue, West Coast swing and country western dances: two-step, waltz, polka, cha cha, Eastern swing, Western swing, country line dances, the "B.C." Vance Productions, c/o Colortech Video Productions, 4501 College Boulevard, Suite 110, Shawnee Mission, KS 66211-9989.

***Pattern Ballroom Dances for Seniors.*** Video of 27 dances, 1992. Mary J. Sarver, 1224 S.W. Normandy Terrace, Seattle, WA 98166.

***Pro Dance.*** CDs for class practice or home use all in international dance rhythm.

***Rhythm Dances*** (Polka and regional dances, samba, merengue, swing, mambo, cha cha and rumba). ***Smooth Dances*** (fox-trot, waltz, tango). Myrna Martin Schild, SIU Box 1126, Edwardsville, IL 62026.

***Roll up the Rug, Triple Time Swing, Volumes I and II. Really Swingin', Frankie Manning's "Big Band Favorites." Cascade of Tears,*** 15 romantic dances, popular vintage dances, Cajun music, zydeco music, living traditions.

***Savoy-Style Lindy Hop, Levels 1, 2, 3*** (Video). ***Shim Sham*** (Video). Swing/Tap line from the 1930s and 1940s. Other videos, CDs and cassettes. Living Traditions.

***Tango–Argentine Style.*** Instructional video by Alberto Toledano and Loreen Arbus. Tanguero Productions, 5351 Corteen Place, Code AD11, North Hollywood, CA 91607.

***West Coast Swing: International Dancing in America Series.*** Skippy Blair. R & R Video–International Dancing in America Series.

## SQUARE DANCE

Records without calls should be chosen for musical key, beat, and overall good phrasing. Callers and teachers who specialize in patter calls will find a wealth of instrumentals or hoedowns available. Instructors should listen to and select their own background music.

Records with calls are excellent supplementary instructional aids. Videos add a visual as well as an auditory dimension during the beginning learning stages.

***All Join Hands!*** Cowan Creek Mountain Music School. Dance-length cuts of traditional Appalachian tunes. Cowan Community Center, 81 Sturgill Branch, Whitesburg, KY 41858 (606 633-3187 June Appal #JA0083CD.

***Scope SC-303:*** Upstart/hoedown.

***Sets In Order*** CD-001. Two CDs wtih 30 minutes of hoedowns recorded by Bob Osgood. Kentucky Dance Foundation.

***Shindig in the Barn,*** Ralph Sweet's All-Stars. 12 classic singing squares with calls from a master caller. Available from www.sweetheartflute.com

***Smoke on the Water,*** 10 singing squares, available with calls (TC 123C, Bob Dalsemer) or without (TC 124C). Hanhurst's Tape & Record Service. www.Dosado.com/Music.

***When the Work's All Done,*** 10 singing squares, generally easier than above, available with calls (TC 125C, Bob Dalsemer) or without (TC 126). Hanhurst's Tape & Record Service. www.Dosado.com/Music.

***Square Dance Party for the New Dancer, No. 1.*** Bob Ruff, Wagon Wheel Cassette or LP 1001. Includes eight singing calls, 1 contra, and 1 hoedown. Callerlab movements 1–22.

***Square Dance Party for the New Dancer, No. 2.*** Bob Ruff, Wagon Wheel Cassette or LP 1002. Includes eight singing calls, 1 contra, 1 hoedown. Callerlab movements 1–34.

***Wagon Wheel ww–121: Billy John/Freddie's Fancy.***

## GENERAL DANCE

Amazon and iTunes also offer a large variety of dance music for each genre.

# Music on the Dance A While CD

*Dance A While* is accompanied by a CD that has the following musical selections available:

| Track | Name | Page | Track | Name | Page |
|---|---|---|---|---|---|
| 1 | Alunelul | 381 | 25 | Misirlou | 276 |
| 2 | Boil 'Em Cabbage Down | 84 | 26 | Nobody's Business | 76 |
| 3 | Carnavalito | 409 | 27 | Pljeskavac Kolo | 278 |
| 4 | Den Toppede Hone (Crested Hen) | 396 | 28 | Polka | 107 |
| 5 | D'Hammerschmeidsg'selln | 252 | 29 | Pravo Horo | 277 |
| 6 | Die Alte Kath (Zwiefacher) | 264 | 30 | Rag Time Annie | 84 |
| 7 | Doudlebska Polka | 313 | 31 | Ranchera | 410 |
| 8 | Ersko Kolo | 270 | 32 | Savila Se Bela Loza | 280 |
| 9 | Family Waltz (Familjevalsen) | 398 | 33 | Schottische, Bummel (Texas) | 101,103 |
| 10 | Gie Gordons | 294 | 34 | Schottische | 99 |
| 11 | Grand March | 78 | 35 | Siamsa Beirte | 297 |
| 12 | Hineh Ma Tov | 340 | 36 | Sicilian Tarantella | 349 |
| 13 | Il Codiglione (Italian Cotillion) | 347 | 37 | Spinnradl zu Dritt | 261 |
| 14 | Irish Washerwoman (Virginia Reel) | 80 | 38 | St. Anne's Reel (Ninepin Reel) | 85 |
| 15 | Kalvelis | 357 | 39 | Syrtos | 283 |
| 16 | Korobushka | 389 | 40 | Tancuj | 315 |
| 17 | Krüz König | 256 | 41 | Tanko Bushi | 354 |
| 18 | La Bastringue | 304 | 42 | Tinikling | 372 |
| 19 | La Cucaracha | 363 | 43 | To Ting | 406 |
| 20 | La Varsoviana | 366 | 44 | Totur | 407 |
| 21 | Lesnoto | 274 | 45 | Troika | 390 |
| 22 | Man in the Hay | 258 | 46 | Tropanka | 284 |
| 23 | Mayim | 343 | 47 | Ve' David | 345 |
| 24 | Miller's Reel | 200 | 48 | Vossarull | 408 |

# Bibliography


## GENERAL DANCE HISTORY

Basso, Keith H. *The Gift of Changing Woman.* Anthropological Papers, No. 76. Smithsonian Institute, Bureau of American Ethnology. U.S. Government Printing Office, Washington, D.C., 1966.

Bauer, Marion, and Ethel R. Peyser. *Music Through the Ages: An Introduction to Music History.* 3rd ed. Revised by Elizabeth E. Rogers, ed. New York: G.P. Putnam's Sons, 1967.

Bowers, Faubion. *Theatre in the East, A Survey of Asian Dance and Drama.* New York: Thomas Nelson & Sons, 1956.

Chapline, Claudia. "Dance and Religion," *Journal of Health, Physical Education and Recreation,* vol. 28, no. 8, November 1957, p. 39.

Damon, S. Foster. *The History of Square Dancing.* Barre, MA: Barre Gazette, 1957.

Fisher, James S. *Geography and Development, A World Regional Approach,* 4th ed. New York: Macmillan Publishing Company, 1992.

Kennedy, Douglas. *English Folk Dancing Today and Yesterday.* London: G. Bell and Sons, 1964.

Kraus, Richard. *History of the Dance in Art and Education.* Englewood Cliffs, NJ: Prentice-Hall, 1969.

Lawler, Lillian B. *The Dance in Ancient Greece.* Middletown, CT: Wesleyan University Press, 1964.

Meerloo, Joost A. M. *The Dance: From Ritual to Rock and Roll—Ballet to Ballroom.* New York: Chilton Co., 1960.

Sachs, Curt. *World History of the Dance.* New York: W.W. Norton and Co., 1937.

Van Zile, Judy. *Dance in Africa, Asia, and the Pacific.* New York: MSS Information Corporation, 1976.

## MOVEMENT AND RHYTHM

Bennett, John Price, and Pamela Coughenour Riemes, *Rhythmic Activities and Dance,* Champaign, IL: Human Kinetics, 1995.

Burton, Elsie C. *Introduction to Movement Fundamentals.* Minneapolis, MN: Bureau of Artistry, 1971.

Cusimano, Barbara E. "Teaching Tips: Rhythmic Activities," *Journal of Health, Physical Education and Recreation,* vol. 60, no. 4, April 1989, p. 11.

Gilbert, Anne Green. *Creative Dance for All Ages.* Reston, VA: American Alliance for Health, Physical Education, Recreation and Dance, 1992.

H'Doubler, Margaret. *Dance: A Creative Art Experience.* Madison, WI: The University of Wisconsin Press, 1957.

Lockhart, Aileen, and Esther E. Pease. *Modern Dance Building and Teaching Lessons.* Dubuque, IA: Wm. C. Brown Co., 1966.

Murray, Ruth Lovell. *Dance in Elementary Education: A Program for Boys and Girls.* New York: Harper & Row, 1963.

Pangrazi, Robert P. *Dynamic Physical Education for Elementary School Children,* 14th ed. San Francisco: Benjamin Cummings, 2004.

Winnick, Joseph P., *Adapted Physical Education and Sport,* 3rd ed., Champaign, IL: Human Kinetics, 2000.

## AMERICAN DANCE SAMPLER

Bannerman, Glenn Q., and M. Neil Pugsley, *Recreation with Dance, Movement and Music.* Montreat, NC 28757: Self Published 1999.

Baron, Marshall. *Minuets, Cotillions and Early American Country Dances.* New York: Country Dance and Song Society, 1990.

Botkin, B. A. "The Play-Party in Oklahoma," *Follow the Drinkin' Gou'd.* J. Frank Doble, ed. Publications of the Texas Folk-Lore Society, no. VII. Austin, TX: Texas Folk-Lore Society, 1928.

Boyd, Neva. L., and Tressie M. Dunlavy. *Old Square Dances of America.* Chicago: H.T. Fitzsimmons Co., 1932.

Brewster, Mela Sedillo. *Mexican and New Mexican Folk Dances.* Albuquerque: University of New Mexico Press, 1938.

Burchenal, Elizabeth. *American Country Dances.* New York: G. Schirmer, 1918.

Casey, Betty. *Dance Across Texas.* Austin, TX: University of Texas Press, 1985.

Craddock, John R. The Cowboy Dance," *Coffee in the Gourd.* J. Frank Doble, ed. Publications of the Texas Folk-Lore Society, no. II. Austin, TX: Texas Folk-Lore Society. (Reprint edition, 1935.

—. *Contradictations.* New York: Country Dance and Song Society, 1997.

—. *Legacy: 50 Years of Dance and Song.* New York: Country Dance and Song Society, 2002.

Czarnowski, Lucille. *Dances of Early California Days.* Palo Alto, CA: Pacific Books, 1950.

—. "Spanish Mexican Dance: California and the Southwest," *Focus on Dance VI.* Jane Harris Erickson, ed.

Washington, D.C.: American Association of Health, Physical Education and Recreation, 1972, p. 23.

Damon, S. Foster. *A History of Square Dancing.* Barre, MA: Barre Gazette, 1957.

Demille, Agnes. *The Book of the Dance.* New York: Golden Press, 1963.

Duggan, Anne Schley, Jeanette Schlottmann, and Abbie Rutledge. *Folk Dances of the United States and Mexico.* The Folk Dance Library, vol. 5. New York: Ronald Press, 1948.

Duke, Jerry. *Dance of the Cajuns.* San Francisco, CA: Duke Publishing Co., 1987.

——. *Clog Dance in the Appalachians.* San Francisco, CA: Duke Publishing Co., 1984.

Ericson, Jane Harris (ed.). *Focus on Dance VI.* Washington, D.C.: American Association for Health, Physical Education and Recreation, 1972.

Emery, Lynne Fauley. *Black Dance in the United States from 1619 to 1970.* Palo Alto, CA: National Press Books, 1972.

Evanchuk, Robin. "Cajun Sight, Sound and Movement." *Ethnic and Recreational Dance: Focus on Dance VI.* Dance Division of American Association for Health, Physical Education, and Recreation, Washington, D.C., 1972, pp. 43–46.

Ferrero, Edward. *The Art of Dancing.* New York: Dick Fitzgerald, 1859.

Ford, Henry, and Mrs. Henry Ford. *Good Morning,* 4th ed. Dearborn, MI: Dearborn Publishing Co., 1943.

Greene, Hank. *Square and Folk Dancing.* New York: Harper and Row, 1984.

Hendrickson, Charles Cyril. *Early American Dance and Music: John Griffiths, Dancing Master. 29 Country Dances.* 1788. No. 1 in the Series. Sandy Hook, CT: The Hendrickson Group, 1989.

Hendrickson, Charles Cyril, and Kate Van Winkle Keller. *Social Dances from the American Revolution.* New York: Country Dance and Song Society, 1992.

Hoffman, Erik. *The Contrarians.* Oakland, CA: Erik Hoffman, 2001.

Keller, Kate Van Winkle. *If the Company Can Do It!: Techniques in Eighteenth-Century American Social Dance.* Sandy Hook, CT: The Hendrickson Group, 1990.

Keller, Kate Van Winkle, and Genevieve Shimer. *The Playford Ball. 103 Early Country Dances 1651–1820 As Interpreted by Cecil Sharp and His Followers.* Chicago: Country Dance and Song Society, 1990.

Keller, Kate Van Winkle, and Ralph Sweet. *A Choice Selection of American Country Dances of the Revolutionary Era.* New York: Country Dance and Song Society, 1975.

Keller, Robert. *Dance Figures Index: American Country Dances, 1730–1810.* Sandy Hook, CT: The Hendrickson Group, 1989.

Kraus, Richard. *History of the Dance in Art and Education.* Englewood Cliffs, NJ: Prentice-Hall, 1969.

——. *Dance Figures Index: Eighteenth-Century English Country Dances, 1708–1800.* Sandy Hook, CT.

——. *British-American Country Dance Title Index.*

Longley, Grant F. *Line Dance Manual, Vol. I.* Lowell, MA: New England Caller, Inc., 1987.

——. *Solo (Line) Dance Manual, Vol. II.* Lowell, MA: New England Caller, Inc., 1979, 1985.

——. *Solo (Line) Dance Manual, Vol. III.* Lowell, MA: New England Caller, Inc., 1990.

Mason, Kathleen Griddle (ed.). *Focus on Dance VII.* Washington, DC: American Association for Health, Physical Education and Recreation, 1974.

Mayo, Margot. *The American Square Dance.* New York: Sentinel Books, 1948.

McDowell, William. *Tennessee Play Party.* Delaware, OH: Cooperative Recreation Service, 1960.

McIntosh, David Seneff. *Singing Games and Dances.* New York: Association Press, 1957.

Melamed, Lanie. *All Join Hands: Connecting People Through Folk Dance.* Montreal: Lanie Melamed, 1977.

Meyers, Rick. *Traditional American Dance Book.* Published 1983. Available from: Rick Meyers, 1827 S.E. 76th, Portland, OR 97215.

Millar, Jolen Fitzhugh. *Country Dances of Colonial America.* Williamsburg, VA: Thirteen Colonies Press, 1990.

Morrison, James. *Twenty-Four Early American Country Dances, Cotillions and Reels.* New York: Country Dance and Song Society, 1976.

Nevell, Richard. *A Time to Dance: American Country Dancing from Hornpipes to Hot Hash.* New York: St. Martin's Press, 1977.

Ray, Ollie M. *A Fun Encyclopedia of Solo and Line Dances: The Steps That Came and Stayed.* Whitewater, WI: Siddall and Ray Research Foundation, Publications for Dance, 1987.

Rohrbough, Lynn. *Handy Play Party Book.* Delaware, OH: Cooperative Recreation Service, 1940.

Rose, Marian. *Step Lively: Dances for Schools and Families.* Vancouver, B.C. VSN 1H7 Canada, 1998.

——. *Step Lively 2: Primary Dances.* Vancouver, B.C. VSN 1H7 Canada, 2003.

——. *Play Party Games of Pioneer Times.* Delaware, OH: Cooperative Recreation Service, 1939.

——. *Quadrilles, Thirty American Square Dances.* Delaware, OH: Cooperative Recreation Service, 1941.

Ryan, Grace L. *Dances of Our Pioneers.* New York: A. S. Barnes Co., 1939.

Sedillo, Mela Brewster. *Mexican and New Mexican Folk Dances.* Albuquerque: University of New Mexico Press, 1948.

Shaw, Lloyd. *Cowboy Dances.* Caldwell, ID: Caxton Printers, 1939.

——. *The Round Dance Book.* Caldwell, ID: Caxton Printers, 1948.

Spalding, Susan E. and Jane H. Woodside. *Communities in Motion: Dance, Community, Traditions in America's Southeast and Beyond.* Westport, CT: Greenwood Publishing Group, 1995.

Spizzy, Mable Seeds, and Hazel Gertrude Kinscella. *La Fiesta: A Unit of Early California Songs and Dance.* Lincoln, NE: The University Publishing Co., 1939.

Stearns, Marshall Winslow, and Jean Stearns. *Jazz Dance.* New York: Macmillan Pub. Co., 1968.

Theriot, Marie del Norte, and Catherine Blanchet. *Les Danses Rondes: Louisiana French Folk Dances.* Abbeville, LA: R. E. Blanchet, distributor, 1955.

Thorpe, Edward. *Black Dance.* New York: Overlook Press, 1989–90; Reprint, 1994.

Tolman, Beth, and Ralph Page. *The Country Dance Book.* Weston, VT: Countryman Press, 1937. Brattleboro, VT: The Stephen Greene Press, 1976.

Wakefield, Eleanor Ely. *Folk Dancing in America.* New York: J. Lowell Pratt and Co., 1966.

Wallace, Carol McD., et al. *Dance: A Very Social History.* New York: The Metropolitan Museum of Art, 1986.

Werner, Robert. *The Folklore Village Saturday Night.* Dodgeville, WI: Folklore Village Farm, Inc., 1981.

Youmans, John Green. "History of Recreational and Social Dance in the United States," University of Southern California, Ph.D. dissertation (Microcard), 1966.

## CONTRA DANCE

Armstrong, Don. *Contra.* Lakewood, CO: The Lloyd Shaw Foundation, 1960.

—. *The New Century Collection: Don Armstrong's Favorite Dances.* Macks Creek, MO: The Lloyd Shaw Foundation, 2002.

—. *The Caller-Teacher Manual for Contras.* Los Angeles: American Square Dance Society, 1973.

Briggs, Dudley T. *Thirty Contras from New England.* Burlington, MA: Dudley T. Briggs, 1953.

Brundage, Al, and Reuben Merchant. *Contras Are Fun.* 1952.

Burchenal, Elizabeth. *American Country Dances.* New York: G. Schirmer, 1918. *Community Dance Manual.* Numbers 4 (1954) and 5 (1957). New York: Country Dance Society, Inc.

Dart, Mary. *Contra Dance Choreography: A Reflection of Social Change.* New York: Garland Publishing, Inc., 1995.

Fix, Penn. *Contra Dancing in the Northwest.* Spokane, WA: Penn Fix, 1991.

Ford, Henry, and Mrs. Henry Ford. *Good Morning,* 4th ed. Dearborn, MI: Dearborn Publishing Co., 1943.

Fuerst, Michael, ed. *Midwest Folklore, A collection of Contras, Squares, and other. Dances from Expanded Midwest.* Urbana, IL: Michael Fuerst, 1992.

Gadd, May. *Country Dances of Today:* Vol. 2. New York: Country Dance Society of America, 1951.

Gaudreau, Herbie. *Modern Contra Dancing.* Sandusky, OH: American Square Dance Magazine, 1971.

Hamilton, Bruce. *Notes on Teaching Country Dance.* Haydenville, MA: Country Dance and Song Society, 2005.

Hendrickson, Charles Cyril. *A Colonial Dancing Experience: Country Dancing for Elementary School Children.* Sandy Hook, CT: The Hendrickson Group, 1989.

—. *Early American Dance and Music: John Griffiths, Dancing Master, 29 Country Dances, 1788.* Sandy Hook, CT: The Hendrickson Group, 1989.

Hinds, Tom. *Dance All Night and Dance All Night 2.* Arlington, VA: Tom Hinds, 1991.

—. *Dance All Night III.* Arlington, Virginia: Tom Hinds, 1992.

—. *Dance All Day, Too.* Arlington, Virginia: Tom Hinds, 1995.

Hoffman, Erik. *Old-Time Dance Calling For Weddings, Parties, and One-Night Stands.* Oakland, CA: Erik Hoffman, 2001.

Holden, Rickey. *The Contra Dance Book.* Newark, NJ: American Squares, 1956, 1997.

Hubert, Gene. *Dizzy Dances Volumes I and II.* Bethesda, MD: Gene Hubert, 1986.

—. *More Dizzy Dances: Volume III.* Bethesda, MD: Gene Hubert, 1990.

Hutson, James, and Jeffery Spero. *(Southern) California Twirls: A Collection of Contra Dances and Three Community Histories.* Haydenville, MA: Country Dance and Song Society, 1996.

Jennings, Larry. *Give-and-Take.* Cambridge, MA: The New England Folk Festival Association, 2004.

—. *Zesty Contras.* Cambridge, MA: The New England Folk Festival Association, 1983.

Kaynor, David A. *Calling Contra Dances for Beginners by Beginners.* Montague Center, MA: David A. Kaynor, 1991.

Keller, Kate Van Winkle, and George A. Fogg. *Country Dances from Colonial New York.* Boston: Country Dance Society, Boston Centre, 2000.

_____. *"No Kissing Allowed in School!" A Virginia Dancing School in 1784.* Annapolis, MD: The Colonial Music Institute, 2006.

Keller, Kate Van Winkle, and Ralph Sweet. *A Choice Selection of American Country Dances of the Revolutionary Era, 1775–1795.* New York: Country Dance and Song Society, 1976.

Kelley, Owen. *How the Friday Night Dance Came to Glen Echo Park.* Greenbelt, MD: Owen Kelley, 2002.

Kennedy, Douglas, ed. *Community Dance Manual, Books 1–7, 130 Traditional English and American Contras, Squares, Big Circles, Mixers, Waltzes, Polkas, and Marches.* Princeton, NJ: Princeton Book Co. Publishers, 1986.

Kitch, Jim. *To Live Is To Dance: A Collection of Uncommon and Enjoyable Contra Dances.* Phoenixville, PA: Jim Kitch, 1995.

Knox, Roger, ed. *Contras as Ralph Page Called Them.* Ithaca, NY: Roger Knox, 1990.

McQuillen, Bob. *Bob's Notebooks: Jigs, Reels and Other Tunes.* Volumes 1–11. Petersborough, NH: Bob McQuillen, 1982–1997.

Nevell, Richard. *A Time to Dance. American Country Dancing from Hornpipes to Hot Hash.* New York: St. Martin's Press, 1977.

Page, Ralph. *An Elegant Collection of Contras and Squares.* Denver, CO: The Lloyd Shaw Foundation, Inc., 1984.

—. *Heritage Dances of Early America.* Colorado Springs, CO: The Lloyd Shaw Foundation, 1976.

—. *The Ralph Page Book of Contras.* London: English Folk Dance and Song Society, 1969.

Parkes, Tony. *Contra Dance Calling, A Basic Text.* Bedford, MA: Hands Four Books, 1992.

—. *Shadrack's Delight.* Bedford, MA: Hands Four Books, 1988.

—. *Son of Shadrack.* Bedford, MA: Hands Four Books, 1993.

Pimental, Joseph, et. al. *The Cardinal Collection.* Columbus, OH: Joseph Pimentel, 2004.

Quirey, Belinda. *May I Have the Pleasure? The Story of Popular Dancing.* England: Vine House, 1976, 1993.

Richardson, Mike. *Crossing the Cascades, Contra Dances and Tunes from the Pacific Northwest.* Seattle, WA: Mike Richardson, 1992.

Sannella, Ted. *Balance and Swing.* New York: Country Dance and Song Society, Inc., 1982.

—. *Calling Traditional New England Squares* (includes a CD with Tad Sannella calling squares). Haydenville, MA: Country Dance and Song Society, 2005.

—. *Swing the Next.* Northampton, MA: Country Dance and Song Society, 1996.

Shacklette, Stew. *Contra Calling Made Easy.* Brandenburg, KY: Kentucky Dance Institute, 1980.

Sher, Ruth, ed. *"And Everyone Would Sashay": The Remembrances of the Ed larkin Contra Dancers.* VT: The Ed Larkin Old Time Contra Dancers, 1989. West Topsham VT: Gibbey Press.

Smukler, David, ed. *Syllabus of the Ralph Page Dance Legacy Weekend.* Annual edition. Cambridge, MA: New England Folk Festival Association.

Thompson, Allison, ed. *Legacy: 50 Years of Dance and Song.* Haydenville, MA: Country Dance and Song Society, 2002.

Tolman, Beth, and Ralph Page. *The Country Dance Book.* Brattleboro, VT: Stephen Greene Press, 1976 reprint of 1937 edition.

Tolman, Newton F. *Quick Tunes and Good Times: Authentic New England Square Dance Music and Stories of Its Players.* Dublin, NH: William L. Bauhan, 1972.

Twork, Eva O'Neal. *Henry Ford and Benjamin B. Lovett: The Dancing Billionaire and the Dancing Master.* Detroit: Harlo Press, 1982.

## INTERNATIONAL FOLK DANCE

Beliajus, V. F. *Dance and Be Merry.* Vols. I and II. Evanston, IL: Summy-Birchard Co., 1940.

—. *The Dance of Lietuva.* Clayton F. Summy Co., 1951.

—. "Folk Dance and Costume of Czechoslovakia." *Viltis,* March 1960.

Beliajus, Vyts. "Jews from Bukhara." *Viltis,* May, 1962.

—. "The Story of Jewish Dance." *Viltis,* October–November 1968.

Bergquist, Nils W. *Swedish Folk Dances.* Cranbury, NJ: Thomas Yoseloff, 1928.

Berk, Fred. *Ha-Rikud, The Jewish Dance.* American Zionist Youth Foundation, Union of American Hebrew Congregations, United States of America, 1972, 1975.

Brehthnach, Breandan. *Folk Music and Dances of Ireland.* Dublin, Ireland: Mercier Press, 1986.

Bryans, Helen L., and John Madsen. *Scandinavian Dances.* Toronto: Irwin Clarke and Co., 1942.

Burchenal, Elizabeth. *Folk Dances from Old Homelands,* 1922; *Folk Dances and Singing Games,* 1922; *National Dances of Ireland,* 1929; *Folk Dances of Germany,* 1938; *Folk Dances of Denmark,* 1940. New York: G. Schirmer, Inc.

Butenhof, Ed. *Dance Parties for Beginners.* Mack Creek, MO: The Lloyd Shaw Foundation, 1990.

Callens, Philippe. *Antwerp Antics.* Lovendegem, Belgium: Anglo-American Dance Shop, 2004.

—. *Belgian Boutades.* Lovendegem, Belgium: Anglo-American Dance Shop, 2004.

—. *Continental Capers.* Lovendegem, Belgium: Anglo-American Dance Shop, 1999.

Casey, Betty. *International Folk Dancing U.S.A.* Garden City, NY: Doubleday & Co., Inc., 1981.

Cavalier, Debbie, Ed. *Canadian Folk Dances.* Miami, FL: Warner Bros. Publications, Inc., 1995.

Chapru, Doleta. *A Festival of the English May.* Dodgeville, WI: Folklore Village Farm, Inc., 1977.

Cwieka, R. *The Great Polish Walking Dance, Volume I; The Polish Running Dance, Volume II; The Polish Figure Dance Book, Volume III: The Krakowiak Dance Workbook, Volume IV; The Kujawiak Dance Workbook, Volume V; The Oberek Dance Workbook, Volume VI; The Zakopane Mountain Dance Workbook, Volume VII.* Copyright © 1983. Order from R. Cwieka, 1375 Clinton Avenue, Irvington, NJ 07111-1442.

Czompo, Andor. *Hungarian Recreational Folk Dances* (Video), 1998. Williamsburg, VA 231898: Andor Czompo Producer.

Dalsemer, Bob. *Folk Dance Fun for Schools and Families.* Brasstown, NC: John C. Campbell Folk School, 1995.

Duggan, Anne Schley, Jeanette Schlottmann, and Abbie Rutledge. *The Teaching of Folk Dance, Volume I; Folk Dances of Scandinavia, Volume II; Folk Dances of European Countries, Volume III; Folk Dances of the British Isles, Volume IV; Folk Dances of the United States and Mexico, Volume V.* The Folk Dance Library. New York: Ronald Press, 1948.

Dunlay, Kate, and David Greenberg. *Traditional Celtic Violin Music of Cape Breton.* Mississauga, Ontario, Canada: DunGreen Music, 1996.

Dunsing, Gretel, and Paul Dunsing. *A Collection of the Descriptions of Folk Dances,* 1972; Second Collection, 1976; Third Collection, 1977.

—. *German Folk Dances.* Vol. 1, Leipzig: Verlag Friedrick Hofmeister, 1936.

—. *Dance Lightly.* Delaware, OH: Cooperative Recreation Service, 1946.

Dziewanowska, Ada. *Polish Folk Dances and Songs.* New York: Hippocrene Books, Inc., 1987.

Eisenberg, Helen, and Larry Eisenberg. *The World of Fun Series of Recreation Recording.* Nashville, TN: Board of Education of the United Methodist Church, 1970.

*English Country Dances of Today.* Delaware, OH: Cooperative Recreation Service, 1948.

The English Folk Dance and Song Society. *Community Dance Manual, Books 1–7.* Princeton, NJ: Princeton Book Co., 1986.

Farwell, Jane. *Folk Dances for Fun.* Delaware, OH: Cooperative Recreation Service, n.d.

—. *The Folklore Village Saturday Night Book.* Dodgeville, WI: Folklore Village Farm, Inc., 1981.

Fillafer, Klaus, Rudi Hoi, and Mario Kanavc. *Tänze aus Kärnten.* Villach: Klagenfurt, 1997.

Flett, J.P., and T. M. Flett. *Traditional Dancing in Scotland.* Boston: Routledge and Kegan Paul, 1986.

Folklore Village Farm. *Folk Dances and Music.* Booklets Vol. 1, 1975; Vol. 2, Dodgeville, WI: Folklore Village Farm, Inc., 1976.

Gault, Ned and Marian. *Half a 100 and 1 More Easy Folk Dances.* 17632 Via Sereno, Monte Sereno, CA, 1983.

—. *100 and 1 Easy Folk Dances.* 17632 Via Sereno, Monte Sereno, CA, 1980.

*Gauzeitung.* Wilhelm Banzaf, Ed. Jeanette, PA: Gauverband Nordamerika, Inc. Vol. 10 #2 1996.

Giurcheacu, Anca, and Sunni Bloland. *Romanian Traditional Dance.* Mill Valley, CA: Wild Flower Press, 1995.

Goldschmidt, Anne. *Handbuch des deutschen Volkstanzes.* Wilhelmshaven, Germany: Heinrichshofen's Verlag, 1981.

Grau, Dr. Andrée. *Dance.* London: Dorling Kindersley, 2000.

Grieco, Rose. "Tarantella." *Viltis,* December 1979.

Guilcher, Yves. *La Danse Traditionnelle en France.* France: Librairie de la Danse, 1998.

Hamilton, Bruce. *Notes on Teaching Country Dance.* Haydenville, MA: Country Dance and Song Society, 2005.

Harris, Jane A. *File O'Fun.* Minneapolis: Burgess Publishing Co., 1970.

Haskins, Samuel. *African Image.* London: The Bodley Head, 1967.

Hendrickson, Charles Cyril. *English Dances for the Dutch Court: Recueill de 24 Contredances Angoloise les Plus Usité, 1755 by G. Willsim.* Sandy Hook, CT: The Hendrickson Group, 1996.

Herman, Michael. *The Folk Dancer,* vol. 1. April 1941. Folk Dance House, P.O. Box 2305, North Babylon, NY 11703.

—. *Folk Dances for All.* New York: Barnes and Noble, 1947.

Hinman, Mary Wood. *Group Dances, Gymnastics and Folk Dancers.* Vol. IV. New York: A.S. Barnes and Co., 1930.

Holden, Rickey, and Mary Vouras. *Greek Folk Dance.* Newark, NJ: Folkraft Press, 1965.

Holy, Ladislav. *The Art of Africa: Masks and Figures from Eastern and Southern Africa.* London: Paul Hamlyn, 1967.

Jackson, Rich, and George A. Fogg. *A Choice Collection of Country Dances: As Printed and Sold by John & William Neal in Christ Church Yard, Dublin, c. 1726.* Boston: Country Dance and Song Society, 1990.

Jankovic, Ljubica, and Danica Jankovic. *Dances of Yugoslavia.* New York: Crown Publishers, 1952.

Jensen, Mary Bee, and Clayne R. Jensen. *Folk Dancing.* Provo, UT: Brigham Young University Press, 1973.

Joukowsky, Anatol M. *The Teaching of Ethnic Dance.* New York: J. Lowell Pratt and Co., 1965.

Katzarova-Kukudova, Raina, and Djener, Kiri. *Bulgarian Folk Dances.* Sophia, Bulgaria: The Science and Art State Publishing House, 1958.

Keller, Kate Van Winkle, and Genevieve Shimer. *The Playford Ball, 103 Early English Country Dances.* North Hampton, MA: Country Dance and Song Society, 1990.

Kennedy, Douglas. *English Folk Dancing Today and Yesterday.* London: G. Bell and Sons, 1964, p. 112.

Kennedy, Douglas, ed. *Community Dance Manual, Books 1–7.* London: English Folk Dance and Song Society, 1991.

—. *English Folk Dancing Today and Yesterday.* London: G. Bell and Sons, Ltd., 1964.

Khumer, Gertrude, and Eliot Khumer. *The Golden Gate Book of Original Solo/Line Dances.* Vol. I. 1324 Bay View Place, Berkeley, CA.

Kraus, Richard G. *Folk Dancing: A Guide for Schools, Colleges, and Recreation Groups.* New York: Macmillan Pub. Co., 1962.

Krause, Richard. "Mexican Moriscas: A Problem in Dance Acculturation." *Journal of American Folklore,* vol. 62, no. 244, April–June 1949, pp. 87–106.

Lapson, Dvora. *Dances of the Jewish People.* New York: The Jewish Education Committee of New York, 1954.

LaSalle, Dorothy. *Rhythms and Dances for Elementary Schools,* New York: Ronald Press, 1951.

Lawson, Joan. *European Folk Dance: Its National and Musical Characteristics.* New York: Pitman Publishing Co., 1953.

Leeming, Joseph. *The Costume Book for Parties and Plays.* Philadelphia: J. B. Lippincott Co., 1938.

Lidster, Miriam D., and Dorothy H. Tamburini. *Folk Dance Progressions.* Belmont, CA: Wadsworth Publishing Co., 1965.

Lloyd, A. L. *Dances of Argentina.* London: Max Parrish and Co., n.d.

Lobley, Robert and Priscilla. *Your Book of English Country Dancing.* London: Faber and Faber, Ltd., 1980.

Longden, Sanna H., and Phyllis S. Weikart. *Cultures and Styling in Folk Dance.* Ypsilanti, MI: High/Scope Press, 1998.

Marek, Jacek, and Bozena Marek. *Dance Poland.* Mansfield, MA: Jacek and Bozena Marek, 1997.

Martin, Phil. *Across the Fields. Traditional Norwegian-American Music from Wisconsin.* Dodgeville, WI: Folklore Village Farm, Inc., 1982.

Milligan, Jean C. *Won't You Join the Dance.* Available from: The Royal Scottish Country Dance Society, 12 Coates Crescent, Edinburgh, Scotland, EH3 7AF.

Mooney, Gertrude X. *Mexican Folk Dances for American Schools.* Coral Gables, FL: University of Miami Press, 1957.

Mynatt, Constance V., and Bernard D. Kaiman. *Folk Dancing for Students and Teachers.* Dubuque, IA: William C. Brown and Co., 1968.

*The New Brunswick Collection of Scottish Country Dances.* Fredericton, N.B., Canada: The Fredericton Scottish Country Dance Group, 1984.

O'Keefe, J. G. *A Handbook of Irish Dances.* Dublin: M. H. Gill and Sons, 1944.

Parrinder, Geoffrey. *African Mythology.* London: Paul Hamlyn, 1967.

Petrides, Ted P. *Greek Dances.* Athens, Greece: Lyeabettus Press, 1975.

Petrides, Theodore, and Elfleida Petrides. *Folk Dances of the Greeks.* New York: Exposition Press, 1961.

Pinon, Roger, and Henri Jamar. *Dances of Belgium.* London: Max Parrish and Co., 1953.

Playford, John. *The English Dancing Master: Or, Plaine and Easie Rules for the Dancing of Country Dances, With the Tune to Each Dance.* Reprinted Princeton, NJ: Princeton Book Co., 1986.

Rohrbough, Lynn. *Treasures from Abroad.* Delaware, OH: Cooperative Recreation Service, 1938.

Rose, Marian. *Step Lively: Dances for Schools and Families.* Vancouver, B.C., V5N 1H7: Community Dance Project, 1998.

Ross, F. Russel, and King, Virginia. *Multicultural Dance,* Box 18227, Cleveland Heights, OH: Russel & King, 1984.

Sedillo, Mela Brewster. *Mexican and New Mexican Folk Dances.* Albuquerque: University of New Mexico Press, 1948.

Segy, Ladislas. *African Sculpture.* New York: Dover Publications, Inc. 180 Varick Street, 1958.

Shambaugh, Mary Effie. *Folk Festivals for Schools and Playgrounds.* New York: A.S. Barnes and Co., 1932.

Sharp, Cecil J., and Maud Karpeles. *The Country Dance Book.* London: Novello and Co., 1918. (Reissued, 1946.)

Sharp, Cecil J., and A. P. Oppé. *The Dance, An Historical Survey of Dancing in Europe.* London: Halton and Truscott Smith, Ltd.: New York: Murton, Balch and Company, 1924. (Republished EP Publishing, Ltd., 1972.)

Spiesman, Mildred C. *Folk Dancing.* Philadelphia: W.B. Saunders Co., 1970.

Thompson, Allison, ed. *The Blind Harper Dances: Modern English Country Dances Set to Airs by Turlough O'Carolan.* Pittsburgh, PA Squirrel Hill Press.

Thurston, Hugh. "History of Scottish Dancing," *Viltis*, March 1964, p. 5.

Tierou, Alphonse. *Doople, The Eternal Law of African Dance*. Translated from the French by Deirdre McMahon. USA: Harvard Academic Publishers, 1992.

Van Clef, Frank C. *24 Country Dances from the Playford Editions*. Princeton, NJ: Princeton Book Co., 1986.

Wang, Kefen. *The History of Chinese Dance*. Translated into English by Ke Ruibo. Beijing, China: Foreign Languages Press, 1985.

Weikart, Phyllis S. *Teaching Movement and Dance*. Ypsilanti, MI: High/Scope Press, 1982, 2003.

——. *Teaching Intermediate Folk Dance*. Ypsilanti, MI: High/Scope Press, 1982, 2003.

Werner, Bob. *Scandinavian Folk Dances and Tunes. A Compilation*. Dodgeville, WI: Folklore Village Farm, 1981.

Witzig, Louise. *Dances of Switzerland*. New York: Chanticleer Press, 1949.

## TUNE BOOKS

Barnes, Peter, ed. *The Barnes Book of English Country Dance Tunes, Volume Two*. Greenfield, MA: Peter Barnes, 2005.

——. *English Country Dance Tunes*. Massachusetts: Peter Barnes, 1986, 1996.

——. *A Little Couple-Dancemusik, 400 Waltzes, Polkas, Tangos, Hambos, Zwiesfachers, and Other Traditional Dance Tunes*. Massachusetts: Peter Barnes, 1992.

Blay, Robert, and Randy Miller. *New England Fiddler's Repertoire*. 2nd edition. 2003.

Borggreen, John, ed. *Right to the Helm*. Cape Breton Square Dances. 2002.

Brody, David. *The Fiddler's Fakebook*. Oak Publications, 1983.

Cahn, David. *A Dozen Waltzes*. Seattle, WA: 1992.

Cole, M. M. *One Thousand Fiddle Tunes*. 1940, 1991.

Edelman, Larry. *Timepieces: Vintage Originals*. Baltimore, MD: Larry Edelman, 1989.

Geisler, Richard. *The Bulgarian Collection, The International Collection, The Yugoslav Collection*. The Village and Early Music Society, 15181 Ballantree Lane, Grass Valley, CA 95949.

Grossman, Dorothy. *An Index to Printed Sources of Folk Dance Tunes from the United States & British Isles*. Berea, KY: North American Imprints, 1995.

Kennedy, Peter, Ed. *The Fiddler's Tune Book: 200 Traditional Airs: Traditional Dance Music of Britain and Ireland*. 1994.

McQuillen, Bob. *Bob's Note Books: Jigs, Reels, and Other Tunes. Volumes 1–12*. Petersborough, NH: Bob McQuillen, 1982–1997.

Miller, Randy, and Jack Perron. *Irish Traditional Fiddle Music*. 1977.

——. *The New England Fiddler's Repertoire*. East Alstead, NH: Fiddlecase Books, 1983, 1986.

Songer, Susan, ed. *The Portland Collection, Contra Dance Music in the Pacific Northwest*. Portland, OR: Susan Songer, 1997.

Sweet, Ralph. *The Fifer's Delight*. Hazardville, CT: Ralph Sweet, 1964, 1981.

Williams, Vivian, ed. *Brand New Old Line Fiddle Tunes, Vols. 1, 2, 3*. Seattle, WA: Voyager Recordings & Publications, 1992.

## SQUARE DANCE

Beck, Donald H. *Out of Sight*. Stowe, MA: Donald H. Beck, 176 West Acton Road, 1983.

Burleson, Bill. *Square Dance Encyclopedia*. 2565 Fox Avenue, Minerva, OH 44657.

Casey, Betty. *The Complete Book of Square Dancing and Round Dancing*. Garden City, NY: Doubleday, 1976.

Clossin, Jimmy, and Carl Hertzog. *West Texas Square Dances*. El Paso, TX: Carl Hertzog Printing, 1949.

Dalsemer, Bob. *New England Quadrilles and How to Call Them*. Baltimore, MD: Bob Dalsemer, 1985.

——. *Smoke on the Water, Square Dance Classics*. Baltimore, MD: Traditional Caller Productions, 1989.

——. *West Virginia Square Dances*. New York: Country Dance and Song Society, 1982.

——. *When the Work's All Done: A Square Dance Party for Beginners and Old Hands*. Baltimore, MD: Traditional Caller Productions, 1990.

Damon, S. Foster. *The History of Square Dancing*. Barre, MA: Barre Gazette, 1957.

Durlacher, Ed. *Honor Your Partner*. New York: Devin-Adair Co., 1949.

Edelman, Larry. *Square Dance Caller's Workshop*, 4th ed. Baltimore, MD: D & R Productions, 1991.

Everett, Bert. *Fifty Canadian Square Dances*. Toronto: Can-Ed Media, 1983.

Ford, Henry, and Mrs. Henry Ford. *Good Morning!* 3rd ed. 1941. 4th ed. 1943. Dearborn, MI: Dearborn Publishing Co.

Greene, Hank. *Square and Folk Dancing. A Complete Guide for Students, Teachers and Callers*. New York: Harper & Row, 1984.

Greggerson, Herbert F. *Herb's Bluebonnet Calls*. H. F. Greggerson, Jr., 1946.

Gunzenhauser, Margot. *Square Dancing at School*. Virum, Denmark: Square Dance Partners, 1991.

——. *The Square Dance and Contra Dance Handbook*. 1996.

Holden, Rickey. *The Square Dance Caller*. Newark, NJ: American Squares, 1951.

Howard, Carole. *Just One More Dance: A Collection of Old Western Square Dance Calls*. Chelsea, MI: Book Crafters, 1989.

*The Illustrated Basic and Mainstream Movements of Square Dancing*. Handbook Series. Official Publication of Sets In Order American Square Dance Society, 426 North Robertson Blvd., Los Angeles, CA 90048.

*The Illustrated Plus Movements of Square Dancing*. Handbook Series. Official Publication of Sets In Order American Square Dance Society, 426 North Robertson Blvd., Los Angeles, CA 90048.

Jensen, Clayne R., and Mary B. Jensen. *Square Dancing*. Provo, UT: Brigham Young University Press, 1973.

Kemper, Bob, and Janette Kemper. *Handbook for Square Dance Leaders*. Oak Ridge, TN: Bob and Janette Kemper.

Kraus, Richard G. *A Pocket Guide of Folk and Square Dances and Singing Games for Elementary School*. Englewood Cliffs, NJ: Prentice-Hall, Inc., 1966.

——. *Square Dances of Today and How to Call Them*. New York: Ronald Press, 1950.

Linnell, Rod, and Louise Winston. *Square Dances from a Yankee Caller's Clipboard*. Nowell, MA: The New England Square Dance Caller, 1974.

Lyman, Frank Jr. *One Hundred and One Singing Calls.* Woodbury, NJ: American Squares, 1951.

Mayo, Jim. *Step by Step Through Modern Square Dance History.* Bloomington, IN: 1st Books Library, 2003.

Nevell, Richard. *A Time to Dance: American Country Dancing from Hornpipes to Hot Hash?* New York: St. Martin's Press, 1977.

Owens, Lee, and Viola Ruth. *Advanced Square Dance Figures of the West and Southwest.* Palo Alto, CA: Pacific Books, 1950.

Page, Ralph. "A History of Square Dancing," *Square Dancing.* vol. XXVI, no. 1–5. 1974.

Pete, Piute. *Piute Pete's Down Home Square Dance Book.* New York: Grosset & Dunlap, 1977.

Ryan, Grace L. *Dances of Our Pioneers.* New York: Ronald Press, 1939.

Sharp, Cecil J., and Maud Karpeles. *The Country Dance Book, Part I–V, Running Set Part V.* London: Novello and Co., 1918 (Reissued, 1946).

Shaw, Dorothy. "The Story of Square Dancing: A Family Tree," *Sets In Order,* vol. XIII, no. 11, 1961, pp. 33–48.

Shaw, Lloyd, *Cowboy Dances.* Caldwell, ID: Caxton Printers, 1939.

Stultz, Sandra J. *Contemporary Square Dance.* Minneapolis: Burgess Publishing Co., 1974.

Sumrall, Bob. *Do-Si-Do.* Abilene, TX: Bob Sumrall, 1942.

——. *Fifty-One Square Dance Calls.* Abilene, TX: 1948.

——. *Thirty-Five Square Dance Calls.* Abilene, TX: 1948.

Sweet, Ralph. *Let's Create "Old Type" Square Dancing.* Hazardville, CT: Ralph Sweet, 1966.

Trimmer, Gene. *Singing Thru Mainstream.* Marlborough, NH: Supreme Audio, Inc., 1995.

## SOCIAL DANCE

Aldrich, Elizabeth. *From the Ballroom to Hell, Grace and Folly in Nineteenth-Century Dance.* Evanston, IL: Northwestern University Press, 1991.

Ancelet, Barry Jean. *Cajun Music: Its Origins and Development.* Lafayette, LA: University of Southwest Louisiana, 1989.

Bottomer, Paul. *Line Dancing.* New York: Anness Publishers, 1996.

Bottner, Paul. *Dance Crazy Series.* New York: Lorenz Books.

Boven, John. *South to Louisiana. The Music of the Cajun Bayous.* Gretna, LA: Pelican Publishing Co., 1992.

Boyd, Neville. *New Vogue Sequence Dancing.* North Star Publishers, 1989.

Buckman, Peter. *Let's Dance: Social, Ballroom and Folk Dancing.* New York and London: Paddington Press Ltd., 1978.

Casey, Betty. *Dance Across Texas.* Austin, TX: University of Texas Press, 1985.

Clark, Sharon Leigh. "What Do You Dance, America?" *Focus on Dance VI.* Jane Harris Ericson, ed. Washington, D.C.: American Association for Health, Physical Education and Recreation, 1972, pp. 51–55.

Collier, Simon, Artemis Cooper, Maria Susana Azzi, and Richard Martin. *Tango, The Dance, The Song, The Story.* London: Thames & Hudson Ltd., 1995.

Collies, Simon. *Tango.* London; New York: Thames & Hudson, Ltd., Inc. 1995.

Conrad, Glenn R. *The Cajuns: Essays on their History and Culture.* Lafayette, LA: University of Southwest Louisiana, 1983.

Daniel, Yvonne. *Rumba Dance and Social Change in Contemporary Cuba.* Bloomington IN: Indiana University Press, 1995.

Dow, Allen, with Mike Michaelson. *The Official Guide to Ballroom Dancing.* Northbrook, IL: Domus, 1980.

——. *The Official Guide to Latin Dancing.* Northbrook, IL: Domus, 1980.

Driven, Ian. *A Century of Dance: Waltz to Hip Hop.* London: Octopus Publishing Group, Limited; First Cooper Square Press/Hamlya, 2000.

Duke, Jerry. *Social and Ballroom Dance Lab Manual,* San Francisco: Duke Publishing Co., 1988.

——. *Dance of the Cajuns.* San Francisco: Duke Publishing Co., 1987.

Elfman, Bradley. *Breakdancing.* New York: Avon Books, 1984.

Evanchuk, Robin. "Cajun Sight, Sound and Movement." *Ethnic and Recreational Dance: Focus on Dance VI.* Washington, D.C.: Dance Division of the American Association for Health, Physical Education and Recreation, 1972, pp. 43–46.

Fischer-Munstermann, Uta. *Jazz Dance and Jazz Gymnastics Including Disco Dancing.* New York: Sterling Publishing Co., Inc., 1978.

Franks, A.H. *Social Dance: A Short History.* London: Routledge and Kegan Paul, 1963.

Fresh, Mr., and the Supreme Rockers. *Breakdancing.* New York: Avon Books, 1984.

Fry, Macon, and Julie Posner. *Cajun Country Guide.* Gretna, LA: Pelican Publishing Co., 1992.

Goldman, Albert. *Disco.* New York: Hawthorn Books, Inc., 1978.

Gould, Philip. *Cajun Music and Zydeco.* Baton Rouge, LA: Louisiana State University Press, 1992.

Green, Jairus, and David Branwell. *Hip Hop Handbook: Break Dance Volume 1.* Olympia, WA: Steel Style Publications LLC, 2003.

Gwynne, Michael. *Sequence Dancing.* London: A. & C. Black Publishers, 1985.

Hager, Steven. *Hip Hop: The Illustrated History of Break Dancing, Rap, Music, and Graffiti.* New York: St. Martin's Press, 1984.

Hampshire, Harry Smith, and Doreen Casey. *The Viennese Waltz.* Brooklyn, NY: Revisionist Press, 1993.

Heaton, Alma, and Israel Heaton. *Ballroom Dance Rhythms.* Dubuque, IA: William C. Brown Co., 1961.

Heaton, Alma. *Disco with Donny and Marie, Step by Step Guide to Disco Dancing.* CA and MT: Osmond Publishing Co., 1979.

——. *Techniques of Teaching Ballroom Dance.* Provo, UT: Brigham Young University Press, 1965.

——. *Techniques of Teaching Ballroom Rhythms.* Dubuque, IA: Kendall/Hunt Publishing Co., 1971.

——. *Fun Dance Rhythms.* Provo, UT: Brigham Young University Press, 1976.

Hostetler, L. A. *Walk Your Way to Better Dancing.* Rev. ed. New York: A. S. Barnes and Co., 1952.

Javna, John. *How to Jitterbug.* New York: St. Martin's Press, 1984.

Kilbride, Ann, and Angelo Algoso. *The Complete Book on Disco and Ballroom Dancing.* Los Alamitos, CA: Hwong Publishing Co., 1979.

Lane, Christy. *Complete Book of Line Dancing.* Champaign, IL: Human Kinetics, 1995.

Laird, Walter. *Technique of Latin Dancing: International Dance.* London: Book Service. New edition 1988. Reprint 1992.

——. *The Ballroom Dance Pack.* London: Dorling Kindersley. Publisher: Houghton Mifflin Co., 1994.

Livingston, Peter. *The Complete Book of Country Swing and Western Dance and a Bit About Cowboys.* Garden City, NY: Doubleday & Co., Inc., 1981.

Lustgarten, Karen. *The Complete Guide to Disco Dancing.* New York: Warner Books, Inc., 1978.

——. *The Complete Guide to Touch Dancing.* New York: Warner Books, Inc., 1979.

Marlow, Curtis. *Break Dancing.* Cresskill, NJ: Sharon Publications, Inc., 1984.

Monte, John. *The Fred Astaire Dance Book.* New York: Simon and Schuster, 1978.

Moore, Alex. *Ballroom Dancing: with 100 Diagrams and Photographs of the Quickstep, Waltz, Foxtrot, Tango.* London: A. & C. Clark Publishers, 1986.

National Association of Country Dancers. *Country and Western Dance Manual.* P. O. Box 9841, Colorado Springs, CO 80932.

Needbar, Maureen. *I See American Dancing,* Selected Reading 1685–2000. Urbana, Chicago: University of Illinois Press, 2002.

Osborne, Hilton. *Line Dancing: Run to the Floor for Country Western.* Glendale, CA: Griffin Publishers, 1994.

Pener, Degen. *The Swing Book.* Boston, New York, London: Back Bay Books, Brown & Company, 1999.

Plater, Ormonde, Cynthia Speyrer, and Randy Speyrer. *Cajun Dancing.* Gretna, LA: Pelican Publishing Co., 1993.

Ray, Ollie Mae. *Encyclopedia of Line Dances.* Reston, VA: National Dance Association, American Alliance for Health, Physical Education, Recreation and Dance, 1992.

Rushing, Shirley, and Patrick McMillan. *Kicker Dancin' Texas Style.* Winston-Salem, NC: Hunter Textbooks, 1988.

Schild, Myrna Martin. *Social Dance.* Dubuque, IA: Wm. C. Brown, 1985.

Silvester, Victor. *Modern Ballroom Dancing: The Maestro's Manual.* London: Book Service, 1971.

Stephenson, Richard M., and Joseph Iaccarino. *The Complete Book of Ballroom Dancing.* New York: Doubleday, 1980.

Taylor, Julie. *Paper Tangos.* Durham and London: Duke University Press, 1998, 2001.

Villacorta, Aurora S. *Step by Step to Ballroom Dancing.* Danville, IL: Interstate Printers and Publishers, Inc., 1974.

——. *Charleston, Anyone?* Danville, IL: Interstate Printers and Publishers, Inc., 1978.

Wagner, Michael. "Swing Dance," *Viltis,* vol. 57, no. 5, September–October, 1997, p. 8.

White, Betty. *Teen Age Dance Book.* New York: David McKay Co., 1952.

——. *Teen Age Dance Etiquette.* New York: David McKay Co., 1956.

——. *Latin American Dance Book.* New York: David McKay Co., 1958.

——. *Ballroom Dance Book for Teachers.* New York: David McKay Co., 1962.

Wright, Judy Patterson. *Social Dance: Steps to Success.* Champaign, IL: Leisure Press, 1992.

# Glossary

**Above** Contra dance term. Refers to the next couple or the couples up the set from the actives.

**Accent** The stress placed on a beat that makes it stronger or louder than the others. The primary accent is on the first beat of the measure. Sometimes there is more than one accent per measure. Some dance steps have the accent on the off-beat, which makes the rhythm syncopated.

**Active Couple** Relating to square dance and Quadrilles, refers to lead couple. Relating to contra dance, refers to every other couple (1, 3, 5, and so forth) or every third couple (1, 4, 7, and so forth). Same as first couple, head couple, or top couple.

**Affective Domain** Deals with feelings, attitudes, and values the students receive and develop in the classroom.

**Air Steps** A dance move that places the women in the air. Most often seen in swing and Lindy Hop dance styles.

**Alamo Style** A square dance term. A variation of grand right and left. All eight dancers do an allemande left, hold on to the corner, but shift to a hands-up position and take partner by the right, making a complete circle with the men facing in and the ladies facing out. Dancers balance forward and back. They release the left hand halfway around so that the men now face out and the ladies face in. They join hands as before and repeat balance. Dancers release with the right hand and turn with the left hand halfway around. They join hands as before and repeat balance and right-hand turn. They repeat balance and left-hand turn and meet partner.

**All Around Your Left-Hand Lady** A square dance term. Corners move one time around each other in a loop pattern, the man starting behind the corner, continuing on around her and moving back to place. The woman starts in front of the man and continues on around him and back to place. As they move, both partners always remain facing the center of the square. This completes half of the loop. "See-saw your partner" is a similar action around partner that completes the other half of the loop.

**All Eight** A square dance term. Refers to all eight members in set.

**Allemande Left** (1) *Square dance:* Corners take a left-forearm grasp and turn each other once around and go back home. Left elbow is bent, and dancers pull away from each other to take advantage of the centrifugal force. (2) *Contra:* Corners take a pigeon-wing handhold.

**Allemande Right** A square dance term. Man and woman designated take a right-forearm grasp and turn each other once around. Right elbow is bent, and dancers pull away slightly as in allemande left.

**Allemande Thar** A square dance term. A star formation involving all four couples in the set. Dancers go allemande left, return to partner, give a right hand, pull by, and take the next with a left-forearm grasp. The man then turns this woman about a half-turn counterclockwise until he can put his right hand into the box star position with all the other men. The men travel backward in the star; the women travel forward. To "shoot the star," the men release the box star position, turn the women on their left halfway around so that the women are facing clockwise and the men are facing counterclockwise. They release arm position, move forward to the next person, give a right hand, pull by, and take the next with a left-forearm grasp. The men turn as before into another box star, backing up. They shoot the star once more, pulling around to meet original partner.

**All Jump Up and Never Come Down** A square dance term. All jump into the air; usually followed by partner swing.

**Along the Line** A square dance term. This refers to the persons in the same line. If the call is "ladies chain along the line," each side of the line turns to face the other couple in the line and chains the women.

**Anchor Step** West Coast swing term. Step right behind left (hook) (count 1), step left in place (count *and*), step right in place (count 2). Usually danced at the end of the slot.

**Anticipatory Set** Telling the students what the objectives of the new material are (what they should be able to do as a result of this lesson). This helps to focus students on the task.

**Arch in the Middle** A square dance term. The two persons in the center of a line take hands and make an arch for others to duck under. After the arch is made, the couple, if facing out, turns a California twirl to face the center of the set. Also called "make an arch."

**Arm Around** *See* Cast Off.

**Around One or Two** A square dance term used following split the ring, pass thru, or cross trail thru. Couples separate; one goes right, the other left around the outside of the set, just passing one person. They come into a line or into the middle of the set. Sometimes the call is "come around two," meaning the person going on the outside passes two persons before coming in.

**Back Break** A move performed in several styles of Latin dances. From Latin social position the man steps back from the woman, releasing his right hand.

**Back Cross Position** Man and woman stand side by side, the woman on the right. Arms are crossed behind them so that the woman's left arm is behind him and her left hand holds his left hand at his left side; his right arm is behind her and his right hand holds her right hand at her right side.

**Back to Back** *See* Face to Face.

**Back Track** A square dance term referring to a double turn back from a grand right and left. *See also* Single-File Turn Back; Turn Back.

**Balance**
(1) *Contra:* The following is suggested.
(a) (4 counts). Preceding a swing, two dancers take right hands or both hands and step forward toward each other, back from each other, and then directly into the swing. Over the years this figure has developed to the right foot moving forward and slightly to the right of the partner lifting the free left foot in a kicking or swinging motion, followed by rising on the ball of the right foot. Weight is then transferred by stepping on the left foot, backing up slightly, and moving to left of partner. The right foot swing in front is followed by rising on the ball of the left foot. Often the stepping on the right and left foot is accompanied by heavy stomps.
(b) Refer to folk dance balance in 2/4 time.
(2) *Folk Dance:* The balance may be done forward, backward, or sideward.
(a) *3/4 Time:* Step left (count 1); touch right to left, rising on balls of both feet (count 2); and lower heels in place (count 3). Repeat same movement, beginning right.
(b) *2/4 Time:*
(1) Step left (count 1); touch right to left, rising on balls of both feet (count *and*); lower heels (count 2); and hold (count *and*). Repeat, beginning right.
(2) Or step left (count 1) and touch right to left (count 2). Repeat same movement, beginning right. Omit the pronounced lift of the heel in this analysis. However, there should be a slight lift of the body as the movement is executed.
(c) *English Country Dance:* 3/4 Time. Balance forward. Step forward onto right, bring left close to right, step back on left (3 counts). Balance back. Step backward onto left, bring right close to left, step forward onto left. *Note:* Change of weight allows moving forward into a traveling figure (3 counts).
(3) *Square Dance:* Partners face, inside hands joined; or man may hold woman's left hand in his right.
(a) Each takes two steps backward, dipping back on second step; then two steps forward to original position.
(b) Or man rocks back on left, taking weight on left, pointing right front (counts 1–2); then steps forward right to original position (counts 1–2). Woman's part reverse.
(4) *Social Dance:* Same as the folk dance balance described above.

**Balance in Line** A contra dance term. Four in line, hands joined at shoulder height, elbows bent. Beginning right, balance to the right, then left. Look at the person with whom you are balancing.

**Banjo Position** *See* Right Parallel Position.

**Bar** Same as measure. Used in European dance descriptions.

**Baskethold Grasp** A square or folk dance term. Usually involves four or more people. Each puts the right hand into the center, and they all face left, one behind the other, and put the right hand on the wrist of the person in front of them.

**Becket Formation** Contra dance formation, but couples stand side by side with partner. Each couple faces an opposite couple. Couples 1, 3, and 5 start as active on the women's line; couples 2, 4, and 6 start as inactive on the men's line.

**Beguine** A step from a South American dance in Bolero rhythm (2/4).

**Below** Contra dance term. Usually refers to the next couple or the couples down the set from the actives.

**Bend the Line** A square dance term. From any line of even numbers (four, usually), the line breaks in the middle, the ends move forward, and the centers back up, so that one half of the line now faces the other half.

**Bleking Step** 2/4 time. A quick change of the feet, moving in place, in an uneven rhythm. Hop right (count *ah*); touch left heel forward (counts 1–2); leap onto left, bringing it back into place (count *ah*); touch right heel forward (counts 1–2); leap onto right in place (count *ah*); touch left heel forward (count 1); leap onto left in place (count *ah*); touch right heel forward (count 2); leap onto right in place (count *ah*); touch left heel forward (counts 1–2). The *ah* count comes on the pickup beat, and the heel touch on the accented beat of the music.

**Bolero Break** A dance move performed in the rumba.

**Boogie** A term used to replace the word "dance" in the late 1970s through the early 1990s.

**Bossa Nova** A social dance from Brazil.

**Bottom of Set** In contra and longway sets, the end of the set farthest from the caller and musicians.

**Bow** A square and folk dance term. In square dance, it is the term that has replaced "honor." It is a slight turn to face partner while shifting the weight to the outside foot and pointing the inside foot toward partner. One may dip slightly as the weight shifts and one nods to partner.

**Bow and Swing** A square dance term. Bow, then step forward into swing position and swing once around. *See* Bow; Swing, item 3.

**Box Star Position** Also referred to as Pack Saddle Star and Basketweave Grasp. Each person places right (left) hand on wrist of the person in front to form a star.

**Box the Flea** A square dance term. Similar to box the gnat, except that both man and woman use the left hand instead of the right. The woman is turned clockwise under the man's left arm; the man walks around her counterclockwise. They end up facing each other, as they started, but they have exchanged places. Also called "swat the flea."

**Box the Gnat** A square dance term. A man and woman face each other, take right hands, and exchange places, the woman turning counterclockwise under the man's right arm while he walks around her clockwise. They end up facing each other, but they have exchanged places.

**BPM** Beats per minute. This is the measurement of tempo for dance music. Based upon the beats per minute, the instructor can quickly determine the best dance for a particular piece of music.

**Break** Drop clasped hands.

**Break and Form a Line** A square dance term. This occurs when two couples are in a circle. The lead man drops his left hand and pulls the others into a line square with the visited position. If first couple leads out to second couple, the man circles about two-thirds of the way to the left and breaks to form a line in the second position.

**Break and Swing** Drop clasped hands and partners swing with a waist swing.

**Break and Trail Along that Line** A square dance term. Drop hands, turn and face in opposite direction, move in single file to home position; the woman leads, the man follows.

**Bridge Position** *See* Yoke Position.

**Broken Circle** A single circle of dancers in which all hands are joined except two.

**Bronze Level** Fundamental steps and technique used to introduce ballroom dance to beginners. Bronze steps usually finish with feet together.

**Bronze Twinkle** A waltz and fox-trot term where a couple moves from closed position to semi-open.

**Brush** A clogging term. The Brush is a toe movement (*see* Toe Movement) occurring on the upbeat (count *and*). The leg performing the movement swings forward as the ball of the foot brushes the floor. No weight change occurs in the Brush. Brushes also may cross in front of the body or swing out to the side. Less frequently they are performed brushing backward. Both legs are straight on the Brush; on the following downbeat (accent), both knees bend slightly while performing the next movement.

**Butterfly Position** Couple faces, arms extended shoulder high and out to the sides, hands joined. In this position, couple may dance forward and backward or to the right or left, and in the line of direction and reverse line of direction.

**Buzz Step** A turning step used in contra, folk, square, and social dance. Done alone or with a partner, turning clockwise or counterclockwise in swing or shoulder-waist position. Buzz step may be used to travel sideways. The rhythm is uneven (long, short).
(1) *Clockwise turn:* Step right (turn toe right), pivoting clockwise on ball of foot (long); push with ball of left foot placed slightly to side of right (short). Repeat as required. Reverse footwork for counterclockwise turn. *Note*: The weight remains on the right or pivot foot; the impetus for turn is given by left foot.
(2) *Sideways:* Step left sideways (long); push with right foot as it moves to the left, displacing left foot (short). *Note:* The turning action of the pivot foot is omitted.

**Buzz-Step Swing** A contra and square dance term. Use swing position for contra and square dance. Folk dance position as directed. Step right on long count into swing position; the left foot takes the short count in a pushing-off motion to propel the turn. Couples generate centrifugal force by pulling away of upper torso. *Note:* Contra swings are usually eight measures; square dance swings are usually two turns and open up to face center of set.

**California Twirl** A square dance term. Used by couples to change or reverse direction without changing relation of couple position. Woman's left in man's right, man walks around woman clockwise as woman executes a left-face turn, moving under raised right arm of man. If partners began movement side by side, facing center of set, they now are side by side, facing away from center of set. A repeat of the movement puts dancers in original position. Also referred to as "Frontier Whirl" a square and contra term.

**Canter Rhythm** An uneven pattern in 3/4 time, resulting from a long beat (counts 1–2) followed by a short beat (count 3). A step is taken on count 1 and held over on count 2. Another step is taken on count 3. The three-step turn in canter rhythm is step left (count 1); pivot on left a half-turn counterclockwise (count 2); step right (count 3), pivoting almost a half-turn counterclockwise; step left (count 1), completing the turn; and hold (counts 2–3). Close right to left (count 3), but keep weight on left. It may be done clockwise by starting with the right foot.

**Cast** Refers to English country dance and contra dance. Partners turn away from each other and move outside the set to a new position; other dancers move up or down as indicated.

**Cast Down** A contra dance or English country dance term. Cast down means first or active couple face up, separate, and travel down the outside of the set one place.

**Cast Off** A contra dance term. Refers to one of the following ways to progress in the set:
(1) *Walk Around:* Active couple separates, walks around the inactive and finishes below inactive, facing partner. Inactives do not turn.
(2) *Arm Around:* Active couple separates and the inactive faces up the set; the active and nearest inactive put their nearest arm around each other's waist. May be same sex. The inactive person acts as a pivot or backs up, turning as the active moves forward, the two turning side by side. The active ends one position below, both facing partner.
(3) *Unassisted, Two Dancers:* Like the arm around, the two dancers stand side by side, shoulders close together, but they do not touch. They turn as a unit, active ends one position below, with both facing partner.
(4) *Hand Cast-Off:* Coming up in a line of four, joined hands shoulder height, elbows down, active couple separates, active and inactive turn forward. The inactive acting as a pivot, the two turn; active ends one position below, with both facing their partners. Or active couple separates and joins hands with inactive, as in an allemande, and the two turn.
(5) *Two Couple:* Active couple leads up the set, followed by inactive. Active couple separates and travels in a small circle to one position below inactive. The inactive couple separates and turns almost in place, backing into the line above the active couple.
(6) *Separately:* Sometimes one person casts off, as in a star figure, and the other person casts off in the next figure.

**CCW** Abbreviation referring to counterclockwise. *See* Counterclockwise.

**Center** The space in the middle of the square (set) or circle formed by dancers.

**Centrifugal Force** The force exerted outward from the center that is created by dancers rotating as in a buzz step swing or pivot turn.

**Cha Cha** A Latin dance from Cuba.

**Chain** A type of dance in a line. Contra, folk, square dance term. See Ladies Chain, Grand Right and Left.

**Challenge Position** A social dance term. The man faces the woman at approximately arm's distance. Hands are not joined. Also called Shine position.

**Charleston Step** A step in 4/4 meter, accent on count *and*. Put weight on right bent knee, left foot in the air. Flip left foot up behind (count *and*); step forward left (count 1); bend left knee and flip right foot up behind (count *and*). Point right toe forward; straighten knees (count 2); bend left knee and flip right foot up behind (count *and*). Step back on right (count 3); bend right knee and flip left foot up behind (count *and*); point left toe behind and straighten knees (count 4).

**Chassé** A series of sliding steps; one foot displaces the leading one, moving forward, backward, or sideward. In square dance, called sashay.

**Chug Step** Move forward or backward on one or two feet or sideward on one foot. Moving backward on left foot, with weight on left foot and right foot slightly off the floor and knee flexed, the left foot pulls (drags) backward as the left knee straightens (count *and* 1). Body bends forward slightly with action.

**Circle** Four, six, eight, or more dancers join hands in a circle and move left or right as directions of the call or dance indicate. In a contra or square dance call, if the direction is not indicated, circle left.

**Circle to a Line–Line of Four** Couples 1 and 3 lead to the right, join hands and circle three-quarters around, lead men (men 1 and 3) drop left hands with left-hand woman to form lines of four dancers. Couples 1 and 3 will be on the end of the line opposite their home position. Lines will be facing across the set from the side couples' (couples 2 and 4) position. Also done with side couples 2 and 4, leading out to couples 1 and 3. Lines will be formed, facing from the head couple position.

**Circle Wide** Dancers join hands and circle left. In a square dance call, it may also mean that dancers enlarge circle as they circle left.

**Clockwise** Refers to the movement of dancers around a circle in the same direction as the hands of a clock move or to a turning action of one dancer or couple as they progress around the floor. In directional terms, clockwise is to the left (e.g., "circle to the left").

**Close** Free foot is moved to supporting foot. Weight ends on free foot. Begin weight on left, move right (free foot) to left, and take weight on right.

**Closed Position** Partners stand facing each other, shoulders parallel and toes pointed directly forward. Man's right arm is around the woman and the hand is placed on the small of her back. Woman's left hand and arm rest on man's upper arm and shoulder. Man's left arm is raised sideward to the left, and he holds her right hand in his palm.

**Cognitive Domain** Teaching students to understand and apply knowledge.

**Contra Corners Turn (16 counts)** Contra corners are diagonally across the set for each person. The *first contra corner* is diagonally right and the *second contra corner* is diagonally left. For the call "turn contra corners," active partners crossing set take right hands, turn halfway, take left hand of *first contra corner*, turn all the way around, take right hand of partner, turn three-quarters around in middle of set, take left hand of *second contra corner*, turn all the way around and return to center of set and await next call. The actives use their right and left hands alternately; the corners always use their left hands. Each turn is 4 counts.

**Contra Dance Formation** Parallel lines, men in one line or on one side and women in other line or on opposite side. Head or top of set to man's left, woman's right. Foot or bottom of set to man's right or woman's left when couples face partner. In longway or contra sets, dancers may face partners across lines; all dancers may face top or head of set; or couples 1, 3, and 5 may change sides or lines to put odd-numbered couples facing each other on opposite sides of set.

**Contra Set** *See* Longway Set.

**Conversation Position** As described for open position, but with the forward hand released and arm (man's left, woman's right) hanging at the side.

**Copa Step** A dance move performed in the samba.

**Corner** The woman on the man's left. Also called left-hand lady. The woman's corner is the man on her right.

**Corners** An English country dance term. In duple minor formations; the *first corners* are the first man and second woman, *second corners* are the first woman and second man.

**Corner Swing** Square dance term. A waist swing or buzz-step swing with left-hand woman.

**Corté** Step back on foot indicated, taking full weight and bending the knee. The other leg remains extended at the knee and ankle, forming a straight line to the floor. The toe remains in contact with the floor. Also called a Dip.

**Counter Balance** While holding on to one or both hands, partners lean away from each other with equal force.

**Counterclockwise** Refers to the movement of dancers around a circle in opposite direction from the movement of the hands on a clock or to a turning action of one dancer or couple as they progress around the floor. In directional terms, counterclockwise is to the right (e.g., "circle to the right").

**Country Dance** A category that consists of round, square, or longways dances. It involves a pair of dancers who interact with a series of other couples. The Americans and English use this term.

**Couple** A man and a woman. Woman stands at man's right.

**Couple Position** Partners stand side by side, woman on man's right, inside hands joined, both facing in same direction. Also referred to as strolling, side-by-side, or open position, or inside hands joined.

**Courtesy Turn** A contra dance and square dance term. A couple is standing side by side, with the woman on the right of the man. They turn counterclockwise. The man takes the woman's left hand in his left. He puts his right arm around her waist and guides her forward as he moves backward. It is a spot turn in place.

**Cross** An English country dance term. Actives go directly across the set to the other side, passing right shoulders or as directed.

**Cross Over** A contra dance term. Two facing dancers exchange places, passing right shoulders.

**Cross-Over Position** Social dance term for cha cha. The couple is side by side, with inside hands joined.

**Cross Trail Thru** A square dance term. Active couples meet, pass right shoulder to right shoulder, woman then crosses in front of partner to her left, man crosses behind woman to his right. Wait for caller's direction.

**Cowboy Arch** The man lifts up his left arm (forming an arch) and goes under as the woman goes behind him, trading places.

**Cowboy Cross Position** The man lifts up both hands keeping them together; he leads the woman to his right side going under his hands, ending with arms in a "crossed position."

**Cuban Walk** A style of walking, accenting the hips.

**Cuddle or Cowboy Cuddle** The man leads the woman into a cuddle, or wrap position. *See* Wrap Position.

**Curtsey** The term used occasionally to refer to the action of honors in which the woman nods her head to partner, at the same time shifting her weight to the outside foot as she turns to face partner. Usually accompanied by a smile. *See also* Bow.

**Cut Step** Step left (count 1); bring right quickly up to left and step right displacing left (count 2). Used in Mazurka.

**Cut Time** A rhythm that comes from 4/4 time.

**CW** Abbreviation referring to clockwise. *See* Clockwise.

**Dal Step** A Swedish step in 3/4 time. Step left (count 1), swing right across in front of left (count 2), raise left heel from floor as weight rolls to ball of left foot, and complete swing of right across left (count 3). Repeat movement, beginning right.

**Dance Walk** A social dance term that describes the basic walking step. May move forward, backward, or sideward in fox-trot, waltz, or tango.

**Dig Step** Place slight weight on the ball of one foot; usually followed by stepping on the foot.

**Dip (Corté)** Step back on foot indicated, taking full weight and bending the knee. The other leg remains extended at the knee and ankle, forming a straight line from the hip. The toe remains in contact with the floor.

**Disco Dance** A descriptive term that encompasses a wide variety of dance steps to many rhythms of recorded music.

**Discotheque** A French word referring to a place where records (disques) are stored. In common usage, it describes a place for contemporary dancing to records as opposed to live music.

**Dive Thru** A square dance term. Active couple duck under an arch made by the couple they are facing. If the arching couple then faces the outside of the square, they turn a California twirl to reverse direction and end facing in.

**Docey Doe** A square dance term. *See* Do-Si-Do, Shaw Style.

**Do Paso** A square dance term. Starting position is a circle of two or more couples. Partners face, take a left-forearm grasp, and turn each other counterclockwise until facing corner. They turn corner with right-forearm grasp until facing partner and take partner with the left hand. Man turns woman with a courtesy turn.

**Do-Sa-Do** A square dance term. The man and woman face, pass each other right shoulder to right shoulder, move around each other back to back, and return to original position. In contra dance, this is the correct action for the call "do-si-do."

**Do-Si-Do**
(1) *Contra Dance:* The call is the same as defined by "do-sa-do" above.
(2) *Shaw Style* (for two couples in a circle): A square dance term. Form a circle of four and release hands; women pass left shoulders, turn left, and give left hand to partner. As the women move around behind partner, the men do (a) or (b).

(a) Always facing partner and moving forward and backward to minimize the amount of space that the woman must travel, man releases partner's hand and gives right to opposite woman, who moves around behind him once.
(b) Partners pass back to back; man releases partner's hand, gives right to opposite woman, and turns once around until the partners again pass back to back. Then man takes partner's left hand and turns woman with a courtesy turn.

(3) *Texas-Southwest Style* (for two or more couples in a circle): A square dance term. Partners face, join left hands, and turn once around to face corner; corners join right hands. Turn once around to face partner. Dancers describe a figure-eight pattern as they execute the figure. The Texas-Southwest style do-si-do is generally repeated until the caller calls "one more change and promenade." The last time the man turns his partner, the man puts his right arm around the woman's waist and turns her counterclockwise into place to promenade.

**Double Pass Thru** Starting position. Couple 1 stands with backs to couple 4; couple 3 stands with backs to couple 2. All couples move forward, passing right shoulders with two dancers (men pass two men; women pass two women), to end facing away from center of set. Couples 1 and 3 can get into starting position by circling couple 4 in center until backs are to designated couples. Danced also with couples 2 and 4 circling into positions with couples 1 and 3.

**Double Pass Thru Formation** Parallel lines. Outside couples face in or down the line. Inside couples face each other.

**Double Progression** A contra dance term. Each couple moves two positions within one dance sequence. *See* Progression.

**Double-Toe** A clogging term. The Double-Toe is a toe movement (*see* Toe Movement) occurring on the upbeat (count *and*). The foot performing the movement makes two clicking sounds with the ball of that foot. A small brushing movement of the ball of the foot forward and a small brushing movement backward occur during the "and-ah" count. No weight change occurs in the Double-Toe. The knee of the supporting leg is straight; the knee of the leg performing the movement straightens on the small brushing movement forward and relaxes on the small brushing action backward. On the following downbeat (accent), both knees bend slightly while performing the next movement.

**Double Turn Back from Grand Right and Left** A square dance term. Dancers meet partner on grand right and left, take forearm grasp, turn halfway around to face reverse direction. Go grand right and left in reverse direction to meet partner for the second time, then turn halfway around to face original direction. Go grand right and left in original direction to meet partner for the third time. A promenade usually follows. Also called Back Track.

**Down** Contra dance term. Refers to the foot of the set and away from the music.

**Downbeat** The first beat of a measure or grouping of measures (musical phrase).

**Drag** A clogging term. The Drag is a toe movement (*see* Toe Movement) occurring on the upbeat (count *and*). A weight-bearing movement that may be performed on both feet simultaneously or on one foot. Similar to a chug step, the Drag is a movement that scoots *backward* a few inches as the weight is shifted to the balls of the feet. Heels skim the floor during the movement. Both knees are straight (not stiff) on the Drag; on the following downbeat (accent), both knees bend slightly while performing the next movement.

**Draw Step** In 2/4 time, step sideward on left (count 1) and draw right to left, transferring weight to right (count 2). To draw, the foot is dragged along the floor. In 3/4 time, step sideward on left (counts 1–2) and draw right to left (count 3).

**Drop the Gate** A square dance term. Called to form one circle of eight from two circles of four. Men of active couples release hands with corner woman in circle of four and join hands with original corner women to form a circle of eight.

**Duple Minor** A contra set is divided into minor sets, two couples each.

**Eight Chain Thru** A square dance term. For starting position, first and third couples take the opposite person and face the side couples. Four couples are lined up across the floor. Two are on the outside facing in, while two are on the inside facing out. The action is like a grand right and left across the set and back, using a right and left thru when facing out.

**Eight Chain Thru Formation** Parallel lines. Outside couples face down the line; inside couples face to outside. Example: Couple 1 faces couple 2 and couple 3 faces couple 4.

**Elbow Swing** Hook right elbows (or left) with person indicated and turn once around.

**Ends Turn In** A square dance term. Starting position is two lines of four, facing out. The two persons in the center of the line form an arch; the two persons on the ends of the line drop hands, walk forward, and go together under the arch, moving into the center of the square. The arching couple does a California twirl.

**Escort Position** Couple faces line of direction, woman to man's right. The woman slips her left arm through the man's right arm, which is bent at the elbow so that her left hand may rest on his right forearm. Free arm hangs to side.

**Even Rhythm** When the beats in the rhythm pattern are all the same value, the rhythm is said to be even.

**Face Off Position** A position used in the Lindy Hop. Partners are facing each other in closed position, bending slightly forward with the man's left foot forward and right foot back. Woman's footwork is opposite.

**Face to Face, Back to Back** A pattern of movement used by a couple moving in the line of direction or reverse line of direction. Partners face, inside hands joined. The basic steps most generally used to effect this movement are the two-step, polka, or waltz. For example, in the two-step, the man would begin left, the woman right. They would take the first two-step in the line of direction, turning toward each other. Inside joined hands are swung back and arms are extended. They would take the second two-step in the line of direction, turning away from each other. Inside joined hands are swung forward, and arms are extended. Repeat pattern.

**Facing Position** *See* Two Hands Joined Position.

**Fan** A term used to describe a manner of executing a leg motion, in which the free leg swings in a whiplike movement around a small pivoting base. Should be a small, subtle action initiated in the hip.

**File** A type of formation. Dancers stand one behind the other, all facing the same direction.

**First Four** Refers to the first and third couples in the set. Also called the head couples, first two couples, or heads.

**First Position** One of five basic positions of the feet used in classical ballet. The heels remain touching as the feet are rotated 180° to form one line.

**First Two Couples** Refers to the first and third couples in the set. Also called head couples, first four, or heads.

**Flare** An exaggerated lift of the foot from the floor accompanying a knee bend. It is often used in the rock step of the tango.

**Flirtation Position** Also called Swingout Position. Partners are facing; man's left hand and woman's right hand are joined. The arms are bent and are firm so as to indicate or receive a lead.

**Foot Four** In longway sets, refers to the last two couples.

**Foot of Set** In contra and longway sets, the end of the set farthest from the caller and musicians.

**Forearm Turn** A square dance term. Partners grasp each other by the forearm just below the elbow with either right or left hand, as directions indicate. They press the palm of the hand against the person's forearm, pulling back slightly and keeping the elbow bent as the two people turn each other around. Avoid grasping with the fingers and thumb. This grasp is used in square dance for all arm turns, particularly for allemande left, back track, do paso, do-si-do, and allemande thar.

**Form a Ring** Join hands and circle left.

**Forward and Back** Move forward four steps and back four steps into place.

**Four Gents Star** A square dance term. All four gents go into the center, take a box star position with their right hand (or left hand), and turn the star as far as designated by the caller.

**Four Sides** A square dance term referring to all four couples in the set.

**Four-Step Turn** One complete turn is made in four steps. The turn may be made to the left (counterclockwise) or to the right (clockwise). To right, step right to side (count 1); pivot clockwise on right and step left to face opposite direction (count 2); pivot clockwise on left and step right to side to face original direction (count 3); and step left across right in line of direction (count 4).

**Foxtrot** An American social dance.

**Frame** Posture and tone of the upper body while in a dance position.

**Frontier Whirl** *See* California Twirl.

**Full Turn 'Round** A square dance term meaning one full turn around from where the turn was started.

**Funky Chicken** A disco dance move, characterized by flapping the arms like a chicken.

**Funky Music** Popular music from the late 1970s to the 1980s.

**Gallop** A basic form of locomotion in uneven rhythm, moving forward diagonally with a step, close, step, close pattern (slow, quick, slow, quick).

**Gents Turn Back** A square dance term. When couples are promenading in a circle, this call indicates that the man will drop promenade position, turn to his left, take four steps around to the next woman behind him, and take promenade position with her. It is a good means of changing partners quickly.

**Get Outs** Short calls that allow action in the square to be culminated with an allemande left to return couples to original positions. Typically used when the call sequence ends with the "key" couples out of sequence, i.e., not with partner or in position to move to home position.

**Glide** To move smoothly and continuously.

**Gold Level** Advanced steps and technique used in ball room dancing.

**Grand Right and Left** A square and folk dance term. Partners take right hands, move past partner, take next with the left hand, move past, take next with the right hand, move past, and so on until partners meet. In European folk dance, the term *chain* indicates the same movement.

**Grand Square** A square dance term. This is a no-patter, geometric figure that keeps all dancers in the set active at the same time. First and third couples have one action, while second and fourth couples have a different action.

**Grapevine** Step left to side (count 1), step right behind left (count 2), step left to side (count 3), and step right in front of left (count 4). Bend knees, let hips turn naturally, and keep weight on balls of feet.

**Grapevine Schottische** Beginning right, step right to side, step left behind right, step right to side, and hop right.

**Gypsy (8 counts)** Two dancers face each other and continuing to face each other with eye contact, move clockwise around each other once. "Left gypsy" travels counterclockwise.

**Half Promenade** Opposite couples take promenade position, pass each other to the right in the middle of the set (men pass left shoulders), and turn as a couple in the opposite position.

**Half Right and Left** A contra dance term. Same as right and left thru. Couples cross over with a courtesy turn but *do not* return.

**Half Sashay** *See* Sashay Halfway Around; Roll Away With a Half Sashay.

**Half Square Thru** A square dance term. *See* Square Thru.

**Halfway Around** Move in one direction, left or right, halfway around the circle (180°). In a circle of four couples, move left or right until on the opposite side of circle from original position.

**Hammerlock Position** Woman will be in the Hammerlock. Partners stand side by side with right hips together, facing opposite directions. Woman's left arm is behind her back at waist level. The woman's left hand is holding on to the man's right hand. The woman reaches in front of the man to hold his left hand with her right. This may be reversed to put the man in a Hammerlock.

**Hand Cast-Off** *See* Cast Off.

**Head Couple** Refers to first and third couples in a set of four couples. In contra and longway sets, head couple is the first couple (man's left shoulder is to top or head of the set).

**Head Four** Refers to first and third couples in a square.

**Head of Set** In longway (contra) sets, the end of the set closest to the caller and musicians.

**Heads** Refers to first and third couples in the set. Also called head four.

**Heel** A clogging term. The Heel step is a weight-bearing heel movement (*see* Heel Movement) occurring on the downbeat (accent). Weight is shifted from the ball of the foot to the heel as it snaps to the floor.

**Heel and Toe Polka** Moving to the left, hop right (count *and*), place left heel close to right instep (count 1), hop right (count *and*), place left toe close to right instep (count 2), and take one polka step to the left (counts *and* 1 *and* 2). Repeat beginning hop on left, moving to the right.

**Heel and Toe Schottische** Moving to the left, place left heel close to right instep (counts 1–2), place left toe close to right instep (counts 3–4), and take one schottische step to the left (counts 1–4). Repeat, beginning right.

**Heel Movement** A clogging term. The heel movements in clogging (step, slide, heel) take place on the downbeat (accent) of the music. Both legs are slightly bent. Heel movements are accented as the weight is transferred to the entire sole of the foot.

**Hesitation** A social dance step that cues "step hold, step hold."

**Hey for Four** An English dance figure, also used in contra dance. Four dancers in a line, center two facing, weave without touching hands, moving in a figure-eight pattern with an additional loop at end.

**Hip Hop** A form of dancing developed in the 1990s. Originally performed by young males in the inner cities to rap music. Today it is a common part of a jazz dance class.

**Hitch** A country western dance term. Swing right (left) knee almost waist height as one step hops on the other foot, slight chug back. Step hop is subtle.

**Home Position** Original position of each dancer or couple in the set.

**Honey** Partner.

**Honors** Man bows to woman, woman curtseys to man. "Honors right" means bow to partner; "honors left" means bow to corner. *See also* Bow.

**Hop** A basic form of locomotion in even rhythm. It is a transfer of weight by a springing action from one foot to the same foot.

**Hub Flies Out, Rim Flies In** A square dance term called from star promenade position. The man, starting in the center, breaks the star and, with arm around partner, wheels counterclockwise around one full turn and a half more to put the woman into the center to form the star (rim flies in).

**Hungarian Break Step** (cross apart together). Hop left, touching right toe in front of left (count 1); hop left in place, touching right toe to right side (count 2); draw right foot to left, clicking heels together (count 3). Hold (count 4).

**Hungarian Turn** Partners face in opposite directions with right side to right side. Right hands on partner's right hip, left arm curved overhead. Turn using a push step, buzz step, or hop-step-step. Lean weight away from partner during turn. Reverse position for counterclockwise turn.

**Hustle** A style of dance developed during the "disco" dance era (late 1970s), with a strong revival in the 1990s in the ballroom dance world.

**Improper** A contra dance term. Refers to contra dances in which the active couples cross over (partners exchange places).

**Inactive Couple** In contra dance, refers to 2, 4, or 6 couples in duple minor dances; 2, 3, 5, 6, 8, or 9 in triple minor dances.

**Indian Style** A square dance term. *See* Promenade Single File.

**Inside Hands Joined Position** Partners stand side by side, woman on man's right, inside hands joined, both facing same direction. Also referred to as side-by-side, open, or strolling position.

**Inside Out, Outside In** A square dance term. When two couples are facing, the couple designated by the call ducks under an arch made by the other couple. Immediately after they get under the arch, they stand up, make an arch, and back up, letting the other couple duck and move backward under that arch to starting position.

**Jitterbug** An American social dance done to jazz or swing music. *See* Lindy.

**Jockey Position** Partners stand side by side in open position. Man holds woman's right hand in his left hand at waist level. Knees are bent and couple is slightly bending over from the waist, mimicking the position of a jockey riding a horse.

**Jody Position** *See* Varsouvienne Position.

**Jump** A basic form of locomotion in which one or both feet leave the floor, knees bending; both return to the floor together, landing toe-heel with an easy knee action to catch body weight. Spring off the floor on the upbeat of the music and land on the beat.

**Kolo Step** Moving right: hop on left foot, leap onto right foot, step on left foot behind right, step on right in place, and hop on right foot. Moving left: hop on right foot, leap onto left foot, step on right foot behind left, step on left in place, and hop on left foot.

**Ladder** Refers to a step that moves sideward, then forward, sideward, and forward, as in the merengue.

**Ladies Chain**
(1) *Two Ladies Chain:* A contra and square dance term. Women meet in center, clasp right hands, pass right shoulders, and give left hand to opposite man. Man puts his right arm around woman's waist and turns her with a courtesy turn. Women return to partner in the same manner.
(2) *Four Ladies Chain:* A square dance term. All four women place right hands in the center, forming a star as they catch hands, and move to the left around circle to opposite man. He turns woman with a courtesy turn. Women return to partner in the same manner.
(3) *Three-Quarters Chain.* A square dance term. Women chain three-quarters of the way around the ring instead of half of the way. Finish with a courtesy turn.

**Lady by Your Side** A square dance term. Left-hand woman, corner, or woman on man's left.

**Lady Go Gee. Gent to Haw** A square dance term. Woman goes to right, man goes to left.

**Latin Social Position** Partners are in closed position with man's left elbow touching the woman's right elbow.

**Lead** A physical signal to alert the follow of the next move.

**Lead Couple** In square dancing, refers to the couple indicated to *move* (lead out) and progress through a figure. If two couples are requested to lead out, there are two lead couples. Also called active couple.

**Leap** A basic method of locomotion involving a transfer of weight from one foot to the other foot. Push off with a spring and land on the ball of the other foot, letting the heel come down; bend the knee to absorb the shock.

**Left-Face Turn** Dancer turns individually one full turn to the left, or counterclockwise.

**Left-Hand Mini-Wave** Couples face in opposite direction. Left hands held above shoulders.

**Left-Hand Two-Faced Line** Line of four dancers. Couples face in opposite direction. Center couples have left shoulders adjacent.

**Left Parallel Position** *See* Parallel Position.

**Left Square Thru** A square dance term. Same as square thru (full), except begin with left-hand grasp instead of right.

**Lindy** An American social dance done to jazz or swing music in 4/4 or cut time. There are three Lindy rhythms: single, double, and triple.

**Lindy Hop** An American social dance first done in the late 1920s in Harlem.

**Line** A type of formation. Dancers stand side by side, all facing in the same direction.

**Line of Direction** Refers to the direction of movement of dancers around the circle *counterclockwise.*

**Little Windows Position** Partners stand side by side with right hips together, facing opposite directions. Right arms are in front with a 90° bend at the elbow. The elbow is next to the partner's shoulder. Partners hold right hands on top and shake left hands in the window created by the right arm.

**LOD** Abbreviation for *l*ine *o*f *d*irection.

**Long Lines, Join Hands** Along the line, join hands with neighbor.

**Longway Set** Couples stand in a double line (file or parallel lines), men in one line and women in opposite line. Partners face in a double line or partners face head of set in a double file. This is also known as Contra.

**Magic Step** A social dance term. A basic step of the American fox-trot.

**Major** A contra dance term. The whole contra set is referred to as the major set. The major set is divided into minor sets.

**Make an Arch** A square dance term. Any two dancers facing the same direction make an arch by raising their joined inside hands. The next call will be for someone to duck under, so arching couples need to separate slightly and make room for that, so that people do not bump each other. Also, if short people are making the arch, they may release hands in the arch in order to allow more room for the ducking couple to go under.

**Mazurka** Step left (slight stamp), bring right up to left with a cut step displacing left, and hop right while bending knee so that left foot approaches right ankle.

**Measure** One measure encloses a group of beats made by the regular occurrence of the heavy accent. It represents the underlying beat enclosed between two adjacent bars on a musical staff. *Bar* is another term for measure.

**Men's Line** A contra dance term. When a contra set is formed, the men are to the right of the caller. Even though they may cross over, this term refers to the original side.

**Meter** Refers to time in music or group of beats to form the underling rhythms within a measure.

**Minor or Minor Set** A contra set is divided into smaller sets that dance together. Two couples dancing together is called duple minor; three couples dancing is called triple minor.

**Minuet Position** Man extends right arm forward about waist high or to accommodate woman, bending elbow slightly and with palm down and fingers straight. Woman places her left hand, palm down, lightly upon his, keeping her forearm gracefully extended to side, palm down and fingers softly straight. Arms are horizontal; partners are side by side.

**Motifs** A short step pattern, for example, two-step. Several patterns (motifs) may be combined. Refer to Hungarian dances.

**Neighbor** A contra dance term. Same as the opposite person (different sex) or corner. It is not your partner.

**Neutral Couple** Relating to contra dance. A couple waiting out at either end of the set is called the "neutral couple."

**Note Values** A term used to refer to the relative value of the musical notes or beats that make up the rhythmic pattern.

**Ocean Wave** A square dance and contra dance term. A line of dancers–usually four, facing in alternate directions–join hands and balance (e.g., step or rock, forward and back). Count 1–2 for forward movement, counts 3–4 for backward movement.

**Octopus Position** With two hands joined, partners stand side by side with right hips together, facing opposite directions. The man's left hand is behind his head and his right hand is behind his partner's head.

**Open Position** Partners stand side by side, woman on man's right, facing in the same direction. Man's right arm is around woman's waist. Woman's left hand rests on man's right shoulder. Man holds woman's right hand in his left. Arms extend easily forward.

**Opposite** The person standing in opposite position across the set.

**Outside Position** *See* Parallel Position.

**Parallel Position** Refers to right or left parallel position. Right parallel is a variation of closed position, in which both man and woman are turned one-eighth turn counterclockwise to a position facing diagonal. The woman is slightly in front of but to the right of the man. Also referred to as Banjo Position. In left parallel position, man and woman are turned clockwise to face diagonally on the other side. Woman is in front of and to the left of the man.

**Parallel Two-Faced Lines** Parallel lines. Couples in each line face in opposite direction. Each line is in a right-hand two-faced line.

**Partner** Woman to immediate *right* of man and man to immediate *left* of woman. Also called taw and honey.

**Pas de Basque**
(1) *3/4 Time.* Leap to side on left foot (count 1), step right in front of left (count 2), and step left in place (count 3).
(2) *2/4 Time.* Leap to side on left (count 1), step right in front of left (count *and*), step left in place (count 2), and hold (count *and*).

**Pas de Bourrée** Step forward on left (count 1), step on right beside left or slightly forward of left (count 2), step on the left slightly forward (count 3). Step alternates. This step can be done in place.

**Pass Thru** A square dance and contra dance term. Two couples face. They move toward each other, each passing his opposite by the right shoulder, and then wait for the next call.

**Pedagogy** The teaching skills an instructor uses to reach his/her learner. The lesson delivery, verbal cues, and modeling all aid the student in learning.

**Phrase** A musical term that represents a short division of time comprising a complete thought or statement. In dance, it is a series of movements considered as a unit in a dance pattern. It is a group of measures, generally four or eight, but sometimes 16 to 32.

**Pickup Beat** The beat immediately preceding and leading to the "downbeat" or the first beat of a measure or grouping. The less formal version of "upbeat." Usually counted out as "and."

**Pigeon-Wing Handhold** A handhold used in allemande for contra dances. Man and woman face each other and place their forearms, held vertically, close together. The palms are held together, open and upright, and elbows are almost touching.

**Pirouette** A turn clockwise or counterclockwise. To go clockwise, step right foot across left and turn, pivoting on the balls of both feet halfway around until feet are uncrossed.

**Pivot** Turn clockwise or counterclockwise on balls of one or both feet.

**Pivot Turn** Closed or shoulder-waist position. Step left, pivoting clockwise (count 1); continuing in same direction, step right (count 2); step left (count 3), and step right (count 4). Make one complete turn progressing in line of direction. May also be done counterclockwise.

**Pivot Turn Dip** Step left, turn clockwise (count 1); step back on right, continuing turn (count 2); step left, facing forward (count 3); dip back on right foot, still facing forward (count 4).

**Polka** Hop right, step left forward, close right to left, and step forward left. Repeat, beginning hop left.

**Posture** The position of the body. An easy, upright standing position is a tremendous advantage in helping one to move efficiently in dance.

**Pressure Lead** A lead in which extra pressure is exerted by the fingers, arm, or body frame of the man in order to lead the lady into a particular position or step.

**Pretzel** A three-part move usually done in cowboy swing.

**Progression** A contra dance term. Refers to the movement of each couple to new positions during the dance. Active couples move down the set, inactive move up the set. A new minor set forms for each time through the dance. For most contras, each couple progresses only one position.

**Promenade** Couples move counterclockwise around the set or large circle in promenade position. *See* Promenade Position. In square dance, the man may give his partner a finishing whirl, bow, and/or swing before resuming ready position facing the center of the set. *See also* Twirl.

**Promenade But Don't Slow Down** A square dance term. Couples continue promenading until caller gives the next call. They do not stop in home position.

**Promenade Eight** A square dance term. All four couples promenade once around the set and return to home position.

**Promenade Inside Ring** A square dance term. Promenade counterclockwise around the inside of the square.

**Promenade Outside Ring** A square dance term. Promenade counterclockwise around outside of square.

**Promenade Position, Ballroom Style** Semi-open position in the fox-trot and tango is often referred to as promenade.

**Promenade Position** Partners stand side by side, facing line of direction. The woman stands to the right of the man. The man holds the woman's right hand in his right and her left in his left. The man's right arm is crossed above the woman's left arm. In some sections of the country, it is customary for the man to cross his right arm underneath the woman's left arm. The promenade position is also referred to as the skater's position.

**Promenade Single File** A square dance term. Promenade one behind the other in single file, woman in front, man behind. The line may move clockwise or counterclockwise or down the middle of the set. May also be referred to as Indian style.

**Proper** A contra dance term. Refers to contra dances in which the men and women remain on the original sides on which they started the dance.

**Psychomotor Domain** Seven primary areas of focus for physical educators.

**Push Step** Moving to the left, beginning left, step (chug) to the side (count 1); bring right toe close to left instep; and push right foot away from body (count *and*). Repeat pattern. The push step is similar to a buzz step, except that the action is taken to the side instead of in a turning or circling movement.

**Q** Symbol for Quick. Used for rhythm cue. For example, QQSS is quick, quick, slow, slow.

**Quadrille Formation** *See* Square.

**Quick** A rhythm cue. For example, 4/4 time, 4 quarter beats to each measure; each beat is given the same amount of time, an accent on the first beat of the measure. When a step is taken on each beat (1-2-3-4), these are called *quick* beats. When steps are taken only on 1 and 3, they are twice as long and are called *slow* beats.

**Red Hot** A square dance term. Executed during a promenade by all four couples. Man releases woman's right and walks partner to center with left forearm grasp. Man moves forward to meet right-hand woman, with right forearm turns once around to meet partner, turns partner with left once and a half counterclockwise, faces corner, turns corner with the right once clockwise, moves back to partner with a left, and turns once around counterclockwise. Wait for caller's directions.

**Reel**
(1) A lively Scotch and Irish dance, usually in 4/4 or 2/4 time. A reel for 8 or 4 is sometimes called a hey (hay). Dancers do not touch hands.
(2) A figure used in longway dances like the Virginia Reel. Head couple meets in middle of set and hooks right elbows, turns once and a half around. Man faces women's line, woman faces men's line. Couple separates and head man hooks left elbows with second woman in line; head woman hooks left elbows with second man in line and turns once around. Head couple returns to middle of set.

They hook right elbows, turn once, and return to respective lines to swing third dancer. Repeat the "reeling action" until head couple reaches the foot of the set.

**Re-Sashay** After having done a half sashay (*see* Half Sashay), dancers retrace steps to original position. Often the call "go all the way around," is given following a re-sashay. To "go all the way around" dancers, beginning in original positions, encircle each other once and go back to position. Men generally move behind partner first. Dancers usually face center of set while traveling on any variation of a sashay.

**Reverse Line of Direction** Refers to the direction of movement of dancers around the circle *clockwise*. Dancers move in the opposite direction from the line of direction.

**Reverse Open Position** From an open social dance position, facing line of direction, partners turn in toward each other to face reverse line of direction but do not change arm or hand positions.

**Reverse Varsouvienne Position** Couples are standing almost side by side, with the woman on the left side of the man. She is slightly behind him. The man reaches across in front of the woman to hold her left hand in his left. Her right arm is around his shoulders and her right hand grasps his right hand at shoulder level. For social dance, the right arm is sometimes extended behind partner at waist level and grasps his hand at the waist. Still a different concept of reverse Varsouvienne position is merely to turn half about from Varsouvienne position. Now woman is on man's left side but slightly in front of him, and his left arm is around her shoulders. Her right arm is across in front of him.

**Rhythm Pattern** The rhythm pattern in dance is the grouping of beats for the pattern of a dance step. The rhythm pattern must correspond to the underlying beat of the music.

**Right and Left Eight** *See* Grand Right and Left.

**Right and Left Four** *See* Right and Left Thru.

**Right and Left Thru** A contra and square dance term. Two couples are facing each other. Both man and woman, using the right hand, pass by the opposite person on the right side and then immediately give the left hand to their own partner. The man, putting his right arm around his partner, turns her halfway around (courtesy turn) to face the same couple. The two couples have exchanged places.

**Right-Face Turn** Dancer turns individually one full turn to the right, or clockwise.

**Right Hands Across** Men and/or women join right hands in center and turn clockwise. Usually followed by the call "back with the left," which means break with the right, join left hands in the center, and turn counterclockwise.

**Right-Hand Lady** A square dance term. The woman in the couple on the right, not partner.

**Right-Hand Mini-Wave** Couples face in opposite direction, right hand held above shoulders.

**Right Hand Star** Four dancers extend their right hand, grasping the wrist of the dancer in front of them. The group revolves clockwise.

**Right-Hand Two-Faced Line** Line of four dancers. Couples face in opposite direction. Center dancers have right shoulders adjacent.

**Right Parallel Position** *See* Parallel Position.

**Ringing** Circle formed by two or more dancers joining hands, usually moving left, unless otherwise indicated.

**RLOD** Abbreviation for reverse line of direction. *See* Reverse Line of Direction.

**Rock** A clogging term. The Rock is a toe movement (*see* Toe Movement) occurring on the upbeat (count *and*). A weight-bearing movement in which the weight is taken on the ball of the foot. Both knees are straight (not stiff) on the Rock; on the following downbeat (accent) of the music, both knees bend slightly while performing the next movement.

**Rock** A dance term used when the dancer steps forward (or backward) a short step and then backward (or forward) a short step. With the body weight shifting forward and backward over the foot, this creates a rocking motion. The term is used in social dance and in American round dance and folk dance.

**Rock-and-Roll** When the second and fourth beats are accented in country western and folk blues music, it is referred to as rock-and-roll music. Contemporary fad dances are done to rock-and-roll music. Rock-and-roll is a rhythm; but the term *Rock Dance* is used.

**Roll Away with a Half Sashay** A square dance term. Partners are side by side, facing the same direction, woman on the man's right. The woman rolls across in front of the man to his left side. As she rolls, she makes one complete turn counterclockwise. The man guides the woman across with his right hand and simultaneously steps to his right so that they end up having exchanged places.

**Roll Back** A square dance term. From a star promenade position with the woman on the outside, the woman is released. She rolls out and around once to meet the man who is behind her. If the star is turning counterclockwise, she will roll back clockwise. If the star is turning clockwise, she will roll back counterclockwise.

**Roll Promenade** A square dance term. A man and woman meet with the left hand. The man rotates to face the same way as the woman with her on his right in promenade position. They wheel around until they face standard promenade direction.

**Round Dance** An American term that refers to couple dances like the schottische, polka, Salty Dog Rag. The term probably started in the 1950s in the Southwest to refer to couple dances moving counterclockwise "around" the dance floor as opposed to square dances.

**Rumba** A Latin American dance from Cuba in 4/4 time.

**Run** A basic form of locomotion in fast, even rhythm. It is similar to a walk, except that the weight is carried forward over the ball of the foot with a springlike action.

**Running Step** A light, bouncy, dignified half-walk, half-run as in English dances. *See* Run.

**Running Waltz** A step used in European folk dance. Take three tiny running steps with the accent on the first beat, three beats to each measure.

**Russian Polka** The customary polka hop is omitted. Step left (count 1), close right to left (count *and*), step left (count 2), and hold (count *and*). Repeat, beginning right.

**S** Symbol for slow. Used for rhythm cue. For example, SSQQ is slow, slow, quick, quick.

**Samba** A Latin American dance from Brazil in 4/4 or cut time.

**Sashay** Dancers move once around each other. Man moves sideways to the right and behind the woman and the woman moves sideways to the left and in front of the man. Dancers face center of circle throughout the sashay.

**Sashay Halfway Around** *See* Roll Away with a Half Sashay.

**Schottische** Step left (count 1), step right (count 2), step left (count 3), and hop left (count 4). Repeat, beginning right.

**Scissor Kick** Kick the left leg (stiff-legged) forward (count 1) and exchange by kicking the right leg forward and left back to place (count *and*). Continue action.

**Scoot** A country western dance term. *See* Chug Step.

**Scuff** A country western dance term. A brush of the heel forward.

**Second Corners** An English country dance term. Refer to Corners.

**See Saw** A square dance term. Man moves to his right around behind and then in front of partner and back to home position.

**Semi-Open Position** A social dance position halfway between open and closed position.

**Separate** A square dance term meaning to turn one's back on the partner and do what the next call says. Couples frequently separate to go around the outside ring (man goes left, woman right) until they meet each other. Wait for next call.

**Separate, Go Around One** Couple 1 moves into center, man goes left between couple 4 and around woman 4 and back to place; woman 1 goes right between couple 2 and around man 2 and back to place. Also done with two couples facing. Example: Couple 1 leads out to couple 2, couple 1 moves between couple 2, man moving around woman, and back to place as woman 1 moves around man 2 and back to place.

**Set** An English country dance term. Setting steps are done either in place, or advancing toward or retiring from another dancer. A single set is to the right and the left. Dancer springs lightly on right, usually to side, steps onto left, then back onto right with a quick change of weight. Repeat to the left. (Slow, quick, quick, slow, quick, quick.)

**Set** Refers to a group formation for square, contra, and longway formations. The term *set* is also used to describe a group of three people (i.e., "set of three").

**Shine Position** A social dance term. The man faces the woman at approximately arm's distance. Hands are not joined. Also called the Challenge Position.

**Shoulder Hold** A position in folk dancing where people extend their arms to the person next to them and gently hold on to their shoulders.

**Shoulder-Waist Position** Partners stand facing each other, shoulders parallel and toes pointed directly forward. The man extends his arms in a "barrel shape" around the woman; both hands are placed below the woman's shoulder blades. Woman's raised arms rest gently on man's arms; her hands, folding over his shoulders, point slightly toward each other. The woman supports the weight of her arms and give a firm pressure with her hands. Both lean slightly away from each other against the firm hand support of the other.

**Shuffle** An easy, light one-step; the ball of the foot is kept in contact lightly with the floor.

**Sicilian Circle** A double circle with *couples facing*, woman to man's right. Couples may be numbered 1, 2, 3, and so forth. All *even*-numbered couples face line of direction, while all *odd*-numbered couples face reverse line of direction.

**Side** Refers to second and fourth couples.

**Side-by-Side Position** *See* Inside Hands Joined Position.

**Side Car Position** *See* Left Parallel Position; Parallel Position.

**Side Couples** Refers to second and fourth couples in a set of four couples.

**Side Four** Refers to second and fourth couples.

**Side Step** Step to the left with the left foot (count 1). Close right to left, take weight on right (count 2).

**Side Two Couples** Refers to second and fourth couples in the set. Also called side four.

**Silver Level** Intermediate steps and technique used in ballroom dancing. Silver steps are progressive, constantly traveling in the line of direction.

**Single-File Promenade** *See* Promenade Single File.

**Single-File Turn Back** A square dance term. From a single-file promenade, traveling counterclockwise, either man or woman may be designated by the caller to step out of the circle, about-face to the right, and go the other way, making another circle on the outside, traveling clockwise.

**Skater's Position** Couple is standing side by side with the woman on the right side. The man reaches across in front of the woman to hold her right hand in his right. Her left arm is in front of his waist, grasping his left hand. Also called Promenade Position.

**Skip** A basic form of locomotion in uneven rhythm. The pattern is a step and a hop on the same foot in slow, quick, slow, quick rhythm.

**Slide** A basic form of locomotion in uneven rhythm. The movement is sideward. It is a step, close, step, close pattern (slow, quick, slow, quick).

**Slide** A clogging term. The Slide is a heel movement (*see* Heel Movement) occurring on the downbeat (accent). A weight-bearing movement that may be performed on both feet simultaneously or on one foot. Feet scoot *forward* a few inches as weight is shifted from balls of feet to heels. Heels skim along the floor. Both knees are slightly bent on the Slide; on the following upbeat (count *and*), both knees straighten while performing the next movement.

**Slipping Step** An English country dance term. Spring sideways to the right (or left) (count 1); bring trailing foot up, taking weight (count *and*); spring again to right (or left).

**Slot Cha Cha** When the cha cha is performed moving straight back and forth, in a slotted space.

**Slot Dance** The West Coast swing is referred to as a slot dance because the couple moves forward and backward in a narrow, slotted space.

**Slow** A rhythm cue. *See* Quick.

**Social Swing Position** A social dance position similar to "semi-open." Man's right arm is around the woman and the right hand is placed in the center of the woman's back, just below the shoulder blades. The woman's left arm rests gently but definitely in contact with the man's upper arm and the hand should lie along the back of the man's shoulder. Man's left, woman's right hands are joined with man's palm up and woman's palm down, arms lowered.

**Split the Ring** A square dance term. From square formation, the lead-off couple joins hands and goes between the couple they are facing, splitting them apart. After going through, they wait, facing out, for the next call.

**Square** The formation for square dancing. A square is composed of four couples, each standing on the imaginary sides of a square, facing the center. Each couple stands with their backs to one side of the room. Also called a set.

**Square Sets** A square dance term. At home: Man has his partner on the right and they are standing side by side, inside hands joined. Away from home: After a swing or promenade, man is on the left, woman is on the right, inside hands joined. The couple faces the center of the set.

**Square Thru (full)** A square dance term. The square thru is executed when two couples are facing. Couples move forward, take opposite's right hand, pull by; do quarter-turn to face partner, join left hands, pull by; do quarter-turn to face original opposite again, join right hands, pull by; make quarter-turn to face partner, join left hands, pull by; and wait for caller's directions.

**Square Thru (half)** A square dance term. The half square thru is executed when two couples are facing. Couples move forward, take opposite right hand, pull by; do quarter-turn to face partner, join left hands, pull by; do quarter-turn to face partner, join left hands, pull by; and wait for caller's directions. This is one half of a full square thru.

**Square Thru (three-quarters)** A square dance term. The three-quarters square thru is executed when two couples are facing. Couples move forward, take opposite's right hand, pull by; do quarter-turn to face partner, join left hands, pull by; do quarter-turn to face original opposite again, join right hands, pull by; and wait for caller's directions. This is three-quarters of a full square thru.

**Stamp** Place the ball of one foot firmly on the floor, accenting the placement. The weight is not usually transferred to the foot taking the stamp; however, in some instances, it does take the weight.

**Star Contra** Three or more dancers extend their right or left hand, grasping the wrist of the dancer in front of them, The group revolves clockwise or counterclockwise depending on the call.

**Star Promenade** A square dance term. Either man or woman may be on the inside of the set, forming a star (box star position). The free arm is around partner, who travels in the same direction. If right hand forms the star, it will travel clockwise with left arm around partner. If left hand forms the star, it will travel counterclockwise with right hand around partner.

**Star Thru** A square dance term. When two couples are facing, each person works with the opposite. The man takes the woman's left hand in his right hand and turns her a quarter-turn counterclockwise as he walks around her one-quarter of the way clockwise. They end up side by side. This woman is now his new partner and is on his right.

**Step** A basic form of locomotion. A transfer of weight from one foot to the other, the weight rolling forward from the heel to the ball of the foot and toes. A step may be in place, forward, sideward, or backward. If backward, the toe will lead.

**Step** A clogging term. The Step is a weight-bearing flat-footed heel movement (*see* Heel Movement) occurring on the downbeat (accent). Both knees are slightly bent on Step; on the following upbeat (count *and*) both knees straighten.

**Step Close** Step sideward left (count 1), and close right to left, take weight on right (count 2). The right foot does not draw along the floor, but moves freely into place beside left.

**Step-Hop** Step on the left foot (count 1) and hop on the same foot (count *and*). Even rhythm.

**Strathopey Traveling Step** A step used in Scottish reels and country dancing. 4/4 meter, the rhythm is slower than reel music. Beginning right, step forward closing left to right, step right forward, lifting right heel slightly as left foot swings through and reaches forward for next step. Alternate leads.

**Stride Position** A social dance term. Legs straight, feet apart.

**Strut** Walk forward, upper torso high and leading, left knee slightly bent, toe pointed, preparing to step. Step on *ball of foot first* and then lower heel gently.

**Suzy Q** Moving sideward, toes are together, heels apart, "pigeon-toed." Weight on both feet, shift weight to left heel, right toe simultaneously, pivoting to "pigeon-toed" position; shift weight to left toe, right heel, pivoting to toes out, "roach-toed." Alternating toe heel, heel toe, move sideward.

**Sweep** Cue word for Varsouvienne and country western line dances as left heel swings across in front of right instep. Same as wing.

**Sweetheart Position** Country western dance position. Same as Varsouvienne.

**Swing**
(1) *Right- or Left-Hand Swing:* The woman and man clasp right (or left) hands and swing around clockwise. Forearm grasp may be used.
(2) *Two-Hand Swing:* The woman and man face each other, join both hands, and one-step or walk once around clockwise. The elbows are held in close to the body.
(3) *Waist Swing:* Couples move into swing position (right parallel position) and turn clockwise as a unit with a walk

or two-step (even rhythm) or buzz step (uneven rhythm). Both dancers step right toward each other on the first beat; walking or two stepping dancers are side by side; buzz step, right toes are almost touching, hips are almost parallel and shoulders are parallel; dancers lean back slightly from the waist as momentum increases. Buzz step, the right toes act as a pivot on the long count, the left foot pushes on the short count. Refer to Buzz Step Swing for more details.

**Swing Out Position** Also called Flirtation Position. Partners are facing; man's left hand and woman's right hand are joined. The arms are bent and are firm so as to indicate or receive a lead.

**Swing Out Position–Lindy Style** Partners are facing; man's left hand and woman's right hand are joined. Man's left foot is extended behind his right with bent knees. Woman's knees are bent and both feet swivel to her right or woman has the option of a right foot rock step.

**Swing Position** The man and woman step into right parallel position; the woman and man are almost right side to right side. The man's right arm is around the woman's waist, and his right hand is firm at her waist so that she may lean back against it. The woman places her left hand on his right shoulder. His left hand holds her right hand. The couple look at each other and lean back as they move around in a clockwise direction.

**Swing the Right-Hand Lady** A square dance term. The women all stay in home position. The men pass in front of partner on the inside and move to the right to swing right-hand lady twice around and square the set in that position.

**Swing Thru** A square dance term. From an ocean wave position, the two on each end of the line turn each other with right arm halfway around. Then the two in the center of the line turn each other with left arm halfway around. All balance forward and back and follow the next call.

**Swing Your Opposite** A square dance term. The women stay in home position. The men move straight across the inside of the set to the opposite woman, but the man must allow the man in the couple to his left to cross in front of him. He swings the opposite woman twice around and opens up to square the set from that new position. Another call to swing the opposite will take him back to his own original partner, but the caller may choose to get him back to his partner in another way.

**Swivel** Toes and heels move sideward, either weight on toes, pivoting heels, or weight on heels, pivoting toes. Also called Suzy Q. Or, pivoting on one toe and one heel simultaneously, then pivoting on the other toe and heel, alternating toe heel, heel toe, moving sideward; or, in place by shifting weight, feet are "pigeon-toed," then heels together, toes pointed out, "roach toed."

**Swivel Turn** In one spot, a complete turn on the ball of one foot, either direction. Free foot may be lifted, bending knee, or close to other heel.

**Syncopation** A temporary displacement of the natural accent in music. For instance, shifting the accent from the naturally strong first and third beat to the weak second and fourth beat.

**Tango** A Latin American dance from Argentina.

**Tempo** Rate of speed at which the music is played, or the speed of the dance.

**Three-Quarter Chain** *See* Ladies Chain.

**Three-Step Turn** One complete turn made in three steps. The turn may be made to the left (counterclockwise) or to the right (clockwise). To turn right (clockwise), step right to side (count 1), pivot clockwise on right, and step left to face opposite direction (count 2); pivot clockwise on left and step right to side to face original direction (count 1). Hold the last count of 2/4 or 4/4 music. For 3/4 time, *see* Canter Rhythm.

**Throw Out** A move in the hustle, in which the man sends the lady from closed position to swing out position.

**Time Signature** A symbol indicating duration of time. Example: In 2/4 time, the upper number indicates number of beats per measure, while the lower number indicates the note value that receives one beat.

**Tip** A square dance term. One completed square dance call (sequence).

**Toe** A clogging term. The Toe step in clogging is a weight-bearing toe movement (*see* Toe Movement) occurring on the upbeat (count *and*). Weight is placed on the ball of the foot, followed by a Heel step.

**Toe Movement** A clogging term. The toe movements in clogging (rock, drag, toe, double-toe, brush) occur on the upbeat (count *and*) of the music. Both legs are straight (but not stiff).

**Tone** Firm, yet not resistant, state of muscles while dancing.

**Top of Set** In contra (longways) sets, the end of the set closest to the caller and musicians.

**Touch** A clogging term. The Touch is a variation of the Toe step. The Touch step involves no change of weight. The ball of the foot touches the floor on the upbeat (count *and*) and lifts on the downbeat (accent).

**Traveling Box** Using the basic waltz box step to travel forward in the line of direction.

**Triple Allemande** A square dance term. Men turn corner women with a left allemande and send them to the center. Women form a right-hand star and move star clockwise, while men walk counterclockwise around star. Men again turn corners with left allemande one full turn, move to center, and form a right-hand star. Star moves clockwise, as women walk counterclockwise, around star. Men again, third time, turn corners (original always) with left allemande one full turn and move into a grand right and left or wait for caller's directions.

**Triple Minor** A contra set is divided into minor sets, three couples each.

**Triple Set** A set of three couples.

**Turn** Dancers may move around individually clockwise or counterclockwise or with a partner. With a partner, dancers join right, left, or both hands as directed and move around clockwise (or counterclockwise).

**Turn as a Couple** A contra dance term. Hands may or may not be joined. Partners, side by side, turn as a unit counterclockwise, the woman moving forward, the man pivoting almost in place.

**Turn Back** A square dance term.

(1) Sometimes used as "gents turn back and swing the girl behind you."
(2) May be used as a single-file turn back.
(3) *See* Back Track.

**Turn Contra Corners** *See* Contra Corners Turn.

**Turn Single** An English country dance term. One dancer turns clockwise (or counterclockwise) individually, taking four walking steps.

**Turn Thru** A square dance term. Two dancers are facing each other. They take a right forearm grasp and turn each other around clockwise 180°, so as to end up facing the direction they had their backs to when they started.

**Turning Basic (collegiate)** A swing dance term. Rotating clockwise, while performing the basic single-time swing step.

**Twinkle** A ballroom variation based on box rhythms for both fox-trot and waltz.

**Twinkle Step** A movement that takes three steps, with the first step crossing in front of the other foot. It may be done in either direction.

**Twirl** In square dance, the twirl may be used to move into and out of a promenade. To move into a promenade, partners face and join right hands. The man lifts his right hand, twirling the woman clockwise one time around under his right arm. As she comes around, he takes her left hand underneath the right and they are ready to promenade. To move out of a promenade at home position, the man, as he nears his home position when promenading, releases with the left hand and raises the right hand, twirling the woman clockwise under one half-turn into her home position. Then they both face the center of the set. In some areas of the country, this twirl out is followed by a swing. To go from a swing into a promenade, the man, as he completes the swing, will not open out to face center but will come around to face the line of direction. He raises his left hand and twirls the woman clockwise under his left hand once around. As she comes around, he puts her right hand in his right and reaches underneath for her left hand. This needs practice so that the woman can be moving in the line of direction while twirling under because the total movement should be continuous.

**Two-Hand Swing** *See* Swing.

**Two-Hand Turn** *See* Swing, Two-Hand Swing.

**Two Hands Joined Position** Partners stand facing each other, shoulders parallel, and toes pointed directly forward. Two hands are joined, man's palms up, his thumbs on top of her hands. The elbows are bent and held close to the body.

**Two-Step** Step left (count 1), close right to left (count 2), step left (count 3), and hold (count 4).

**Tyrolian Waltz** A series of waltz steps taken in the line of direction. Beginning left, step diagonally forward left on first waltz step, step diagonally forward to the right on the second waltz step. Repeat pattern. Partners tend to face away from and toward each other, with alternate steps, as they *glide* forward.

**Unassisted, Two Dancers** *See* Cast Off.

**Underarm Pass** A West Coast swing dance term. The woman moves under the man's arm passing next to his side.

**Underlying Beat** The duration of time becomes established by the beat or the pulse. As the beat is repeated, it is referred to as the underlying beat.

**Uneven Rhythm** When the beats in the rhythm pattern are not all the same value but are a combination of slow and quick beats, the rhythm is said to be uneven.

**Upbeat** An unaccented beat that precedes the downbeat.

**U Turn Back** Either a single dancer or a couple turn around in place 180°, ending facing in opposite direction.

**V Position** A folk dance hold in which people standing next to each other are holding hands with the person next to them, arms down.

**Varsouvienne Position** Couple faces in line of direction, woman in front and slightly to the right of man. Man holds woman's left hand in his left at shoulder level. Man's right arm extends back of woman's shoulders and holds woman's raised right hand in his right. In social dance, this is sometimes called jody position.

**W Position** A folk dance hold, where people standing next to each other are holding hands with the person next to them at shoulder level with elbows pointing down.

**Walk** A basic form of locomotion in even rhythm. Steps are from one foot to the other, the weight being transferred from heel to toe. The walk is used in contra and square dancing.

**Walk Around** *See* Cast Off.

**Walk Through/Brush Off** A swing dance term. In two-hand position, the man releases his right hand and moves to his left, turning his back to the woman. The man releases his left hand to pass through the woman's left arm. The man rejoins his right hand to the woman's left hand.

**Walking Waltz** 3/4 time. Traveling forward, step on each beat.

**Waltz** Step forward left (count 1), step sideward right (count 2), close left to right, and take weight left (count 3).

**Waltz Balance** *See* Balance, 3/4 time.

**Weave the Ring** A square dance term. Same as grand right and left, except that dancers *do not* touch hands in passing each other.

**Wheel Around** A square dance term that is also used in contra. From the promenade position, couples wheel around as a unit to face in opposite direction. Men back up, women move forward around men. Dancers retain the promenade position handhold.

**Whip** A variation of the West Coast swing. Usually an eight-count move.

**Whirl** Term used for waist swing in square dance. Also refers to several rather rapid individual right- or left-face turns.

**Whirlaway with a Half Sashay** *See* Roll Away with a Half Sashay.

**Women's Line** A contra dance term. When a contra set is formed, the women are to the left of the caller. Even though they may cross over, this term refers to the original line.

**Wrap Position** The woman is at the right of the man. His right arm is around her waist and his right hand holds her left hand. His left hand is holding her right hand in front.

**Yemenite Step** In 4/4 meter. Begin left, with flexed knees, and step to left (count 1); step right behind left (count 2); step left in front of right (count 3); and hold (count 4).

**Yoke Position** Couple is standing side by side with the woman on the right side of the man. Man holds woman's left hand in his left hand, behind his shoulder. Man's right arm extends back of woman's shoulders and holds woman's raised right hand in his right hand.

**Zydeco** A Cajun dance and music. A combination of Cajun, rhythm and blues with a Carribean musical pulse.

# Index Contents

INDEX OF MIXER AND NONPARTNER DANCES, 556

CLASSIFIED INDEXES

Chapter 4: American Dance Sampler, 557

Chapter 5: Square Dance, 560

Chapter 6: Contra Dance, 562

Chapter 7: International Folk Dance, 564

Chapter 8: Social Dance, 568

SUBJECT INDEX, 573

# Index of Mixer and Nonpartner Dances

## MIXER

All-American Promenade 114
La Bastringue 304
Bingo 66
Brown-Eyed Mary 67
Captain Jinks 68
Den Toppede Høne 396
D'Hammerschmiedsg'selln 252
Doudlebska Polka 313
Familie Sekstur 397
Familjevalsen 398
Fjaskern 399
Glowworm Mixer 115
Gong Xi 310
Jiffy Mixer 116
Korobushka 389
Levi Jackson Rag 90
Looby Loo 70
Mexican Mixer 118
Ninepin Reel 85
Nobody's Business 76
Oh Johnny 88
Oslo Waltz 215
Patty-Cake Polka 117
Paul Jones Your Lady 84
Red River Valley 89
Square Dance Mixers 178
  Big Circle Mixers 179
  Methods for Squaring Up 179
  Methods for Changing Partners 180
Tennessee Wig Walk 119
Teton Mountain Stomp 108
Texas Schottische for Three 103
Totur 407
Troika 390
Ve' David 345

## NONPARTNER

Admiring the Moon 308
All Shook Up 447
Amos Moses 91
Borborbor 246
Branle d'Ossau 320
Carnavalito 409
Charleston 438
Cherkessiya 337
Las Chiapanecas 368
The Continental 448
Cotton-Eyed Joe (Line Dance) 92
Cowboy Boogie 448
Electric Slide 454
Ersko Kolo 270
Freeze 449
Gahu 247
Harukoma 353
Hasápikos 271
Hineh Ma Tov 340
Hip Hop Dance 450
Hora 341
Hora De Mina 382
Hora Pe Gheata 383
The Hukilau 143
Itele 384
Jessie Polka 93
Kahuli Aku Kahuli Mai 145
Kocanska Gada 273
Lesnoto 274
Ma Na'avu 342
Mayim 343
Misirlou 276
Mon Père Avait un Petit Bois 321
Pata Pata 249
Pljeskavac Kolo 278
Popcorn (Alley Cat) 94
Pravo Horo 277
Pupu Hinuhinu 147
Ranchera 410
Rondeau de Garein 323
Sarajevka Kolo 279
*Saturday Night Fever* Line Dance 452
Savila Se Bela Loza 280
Šetnja 281
Sirba Din Cimpoi 385
Slappin' Leather 455
Syrtós 283
Tanko Bushi 354
Ten Pretty Girls 94
Tropanka 284
Twelfth Street Rag 95

## CLASSIFIED INDEX FOR CHAPTER 4: AMERICAN DANCE SAMPLER

### Beginning 1


| NAME OF DANCE | PAGE | TYPE | FORMATION | MIXER |
|---|---|---|---|---|
| Alabama Gal | 75 | Play Party | Longway set | |
| Amos Moses | 91 | Novelty Dance | Nonpartner | |
| The Bear Went Over the Mountain | 74 | Play Party | Circle, couples | |
| Bingo | 66 | Play Party | Circle, couples | X |
| Brown-Eyed Mary | 67 | Play Party | Circle, couples | X |
| Cajun Jitterbug | 123 | Social, partner | Scattered, couples | |
| Cajun One-Step | 122 | Social, partner | Scattered, couples | |
| Captain Jinks | 68 | Play Party | Circle, couples | X |
| Glowworm Mixer | 115 | Mixer | Circles, couples | X |
| Grand March | 78 | March | Couples | |
| Heel and Toe Polka | 107 | Round Dance | Couples | |
| Jiffy Mixer | 116 | Mixer | Circles, couples | |
| Looby Loo | 70 | Play Party | Circle | |
| Nobody's Business | 76 | Play Party | Circles, couples | X |
| Oh Johnny | 88 | Mixer | Circles, couples | X |
| Patty-Cake Polka | 117 | Mixer | Circles, couples | X |
| Popcorn | 94 | Novelty Dance | Nonpartner | |
| Pop Goes the Weasel | 71 | Play Party | Circles, couples | X |
| Sandy Land | 72 | Play Party | Circles, couples | |
| Shoo Fly | 73 | Play Party | Circles, couples | X |
| Skip to My Lou | 74 | Play Party | Circles, couples | X |
| Tennessee Wig Walk | 119 | Mixer | Circles, couples | X |
| Ten Pretty Girls | 94 | Line Dance | Nonpartner | |
| Teton Mountain Stomp | 108 | Mixer | Circles, couples | X |
| Virginia Reel | 80 | Contra | Longway set | |
| Zydeco Two-Step | 123 | Social, partner | Circles, couples | |

## CLASSIFIED INDEX FOR CHAPTER 4, *continued*

### Beginning 2

| NAME OF DANCE | PAGE | TYPE | FORMATION | MIXER |
|---|---|---|---|---|
| All-American Promenade | 114 | Mixer | Circles, couples | X |
| Boston Two-Step | 106 | Round Dance | Couples | |
| Cajun Two-Step | 122 | Social, partner | Circle | |
| Cajun Waltz | 121 | Social, partner | Circle | |
| Cotton-Eyed Joe (line dance) | 92 | LInedance | Nonpartner | |
| Country Waltz | 138 | Social, partner | Circle | |
| Garden Waltz | 111 | Round Dance | Sets of threes | |
| The Hukilau | 143 | Traditional | Lines or scattered | |
| Jessie Polka | 93 | Round Dance | Two or More | X |
| Mexican Mixer | 118 | Mixer | Circles, couples | X |
| Ninepin Reel | 85 | Square Dance | Square | X |
| Paul Jones Your Lady | 84 | Mixer | Circles, couples | X |
| Portland Fancy | 87 | Progressive | Four couples | |
| Red River Valley | 89 | Mixer | Two sets of threes | X |
| Salty Dog Rag | 104 | Round Dance | Couples | |
| Schottische | 99 | Round Dance | Couples | |
| Ten-Step | 135 | Round Dance | Couples | |
| Texas Schottische for Three | 103 | Mixer | Circle | X |
| Traditional Country Western Swing | | Social, partner | Scattered, couples | |
| Basic Step | 126 | | | |
| Cowboy Cuddle | 128 | | | |
| Traditional Two-Step | 132 | Social, partner | Couples, circle | |
| Twelfth Street Rag | 95 | Novelty Dance | Nonpartner | |
| Varsouvienne | 112 | Round Dance | Couples | |

## Beginning 3

| NAME OF DANCE | PAGE | TYPE | FORMATION | MIXER |
|---|---|---|---|---|
| Hula Fundamentals | | Traditional | Lines or scattered | |
| Hela (Reach Tap) | 142 | | | |
| Kaholo (Vamp) | 142 | | | |
| Lewa (Sway) | 142 | | | |
| Traditional Country Western Swing | | Social, partner | Scattered, couples | |
| Cowboy Arch | 127 | | | |
| Cowboy Cross | 127 | | | |
| Walk Through (Brush Off) | 129 | | | |
| Traditional Two-Step | | Social, partner | Couples, circle | |
| Varsouvienne | 133 | | | |
| Yoke | 134 | | | |

## Intermediate

| NAME OF DANCE | PAGE | TYPE | FORMATION | MIXER |
|---|---|---|---|---|
| Cotton-Eyed Joe (couple dance) | 109 | Round Dance | Couples | |
| Grand Square Quadrille | 82 | Quadrille | Square | |
| Kahuli Aku Kahuli Mai | 145 | Traditional | Scattered, facing front | |
| Levi Jackson Rag | 90 | Mixer | Five couples | X |
| Pupu Hinuhinu | 147 | Traditional | Scattered, facing front | |
| Texas Schottische Variations | 101 | Round Dance | Couples | |
| Traditional Country Western Swing | | Social, partner | Scattered, couples | |
| Octopus | 129 | | | |
| Traditional Two-Step | | Social, partner | Couples, circle | |
| Little Windows | 134 | | | |
| Traveling Cha Cha | 136 | Round Dance | Circle, couples | |

## Advanced

| NAME OF DANCE | PAGE | TYPE | FORMATION | MIXER |
|---|---|---|---|---|
| Traditional Country Western Swing | | Social, partner | Scattered, couples | |
| Pretzel | 130 | | | |

## CLASSIFIED INDEX FOR CHAPTER 5: SQUARE DANCE

### Beginning 1


| PATTER CALLS | PAGE |
|---|---|
| Bird in the Cage: Seven Hands 'Round | 182 |
| Promenade the Ring | 186 |
| Sally Goodin' | 186 |
| Split the Ring | 187 |


### Beginning 2


| PATTER CALLS | PAGE |
|---|---|
| Arkansas Traveler | 182 |
| Bend It Tight | 182 |
| Catch All Eight | 183 |
| Cowboy Loop | 183 |
| Easy Bend the Line | 184 |
| Ends Turn In | 184 |
| Forward Up Six | 184 |
| Gents Star Right | 185 |
| Promenade the Outside Ring | 186 |
| The Route | 186 |
| Split the Ring and Around Just One | 188 |
| Texas Star | 188 |


### Beginning 3


| PATTER CALLS | PAGE |
|---|---|
| Another Trail | 182 |
| Forward Up and Back | 184 |
| Inside Arch and Outside Under | 185 |

## Intermediate

| PATTER CALLS | PAGE |
|---|---|
| Arkansas Traveler with a Cross Trail Thru | 182 |
| Box the Gnat: Pull By | 182 |
| Duck Then Wheel | 183 |
| Easy Square Thru | 184 |
| Gnat and Flea | 185 |
| Go the Route | 185 |
| Half Square Thru | 185 |
| New Star Thru | 185 |
| Ocean Wave | 186 |
| Sides Divide | 186 |
| Star Thru: California Twirl | 188 |
| Star Thru Square Thru Combo | 188 |

## Advanced

| PATTER CALLS | PAGE |
|---|---|
| Spinning Wheel | 187 |
| Texas Whirlwind | 188 |

| SINGING CALLS | PAGE | BASIC MOVEMENTS INVOLVED | LEVEL |
|---|---|---|---|
| Alabama Jubilee | 189 | Sashay, promenade, allemande left, grand right and left | Beginning 2 |
| Gentle on My Mind | 189 | Right and left thru, roll away, weave the ring, ladies chain, pass thru | Beginning 3 |
| Houston | 189 | Allemade left, weave the ring, pass thru, star right, swing, do paso | Beginning 3 |
| Just Because | 190 | Allemande left, allemande right, grand right and left, ladies chain, see saw star | Beginning 1 |
| Smoke on the Water | 190 | Allemande left, star, grand right and left, turn back, sashay, pass thru | Beginning 3 |

## CLASSIFIED INDEX FOR CHAPTER 6: CONTRA DANCES

### Beginning 1

| NAME OF DANCE | PAGE | TYPE | FORMATION |
|---|---|---|---|
| Aw Shucks! | 204 | Duple | Improper/cross over |
| Broken Sixpence | 207 | Duple | Improper/cross over |
| Easy Does It | 214 | Duple | Improper/cross over |
| Lady of the Lake | 218 | Duple | Improper/cross over |
| The Nova Scotian | 220 | Duple | Improper/cross over |
| So When Was the Wedding? | 229 | Duple | Improper/cross over |
| Supernova Scotian | 231 | Duple | Improper/cross over |
| The Tourist | 234 | Duple | Improper/cross over |

### Beginning 2

| NAME OF DANCE | PAGE | TYPE | FORMATION |
|---|---|---|---|
| Contra for Margie | 211 | Duple | Improper/cross over |
| Jed's Reel | 218 | Duple | Improper/cross over |
| Salmonchanted Evening | 226 | Duple | Improper/cross over |
| Small Potatoes | 228 | Duple | Improper/cross over |

### Beginning 3

| NAME OF DANCE | PAGE | TYPE | FORMATION |
|---|---|---|---|
| Chain the Swain | 209 | Duple | Improper/cross over |
| Delphiniums and Daisies | 214 | Duple | Improper/cross over |
| Roll in the Hey | 224 | Duple | Improper/cross over |
| Stars of Alberta | 230 | Duple | Improper/cross over |
| Symmetrical Force | 232 | Duple | Improper/cross over |
| Thorn Street Gypsy | 233 | Duple | Improper/cross over |

## Intermediate

| NAME OF DANCE | PAGE | TYPE | FORMATION |
|---|---|---|---|
| Becket Reel | 205 | | Becket |
| Chorus Jig | 210 | Duple | Proper/not cross over |
| Dance Gypsy | 212 | | Becket |
| Hills of Habersham | 215 | Duple | Proper/not cross over |
| More Again | 219 | Duple | Improper/cross over |
| Roadblock Reel | 223 | Duple | Improper/cross over |
| Shadrack's Delight | 227 | Duple | Improper/cross over |
| Weave the Line | 235 | Duple | Improper/cross over |
| With Thanks to the Dean | 236 | Duple | Improper/cross over |

## Advanced

| NAME OF DANCE | PAGE | TYPE | FORMATION |
|---|---|---|---|
| Brimmer & May Reel | 206 | Duple | Improper/cross over |
| CDS Reel | 208 | Duple | Improper/cross over |
| Dancing Sailors | 213 | Duple | Proper/not cross over |
| Hull's Victory | 217 | Duple | Proper/not cross over |
| The Other Mary Kay | 221 | Duple | Becket |
| Petronella | 222 | Duple | Proper/not cross over |
| Rory O'More | 225 | Duple | Proper/not cross over |

| SPECIAL FEATURES | PAGE |
|---|---|
| Becket Formation | |
| Becket Reel | 205 |
| Dance Gypsy | 212 |
| The Other Mary Kay | 221 |
| Contra Corners | |
| Chorus Jig | 210 |
| Dancing Sailors | 213 |
| Rory O'More | 225 |
| Double Progression | |
| Contra for Margie | 211 |
| Thorn Street Gypsy | 233 |
| Weave the Line | 235 |
| With Thanks to the Dean | 236 |
| Hey for Four | |
| Dancing Sailors | 213 |
| Delphiniums and Daisies | 214 |
| The Other Mary Kay | 221 |
| Roll in the Hey | 224 |
| Stars of Alberta | 230 |

## CLASSIFIED INDEX FOR CHAPTER 7: INTERNATIONAL FOLK DANCE

### Beginning 1

| NAME OF DANCE | PAGE | NATIONALITY | FORMATION | MIXER |
|---|---|---|---|---|
| Branle D'Ossau | 320 | French | Circle, nonpartner | |
| The Bridge of Athlone | 289 | Irish | Longways sets | |
| Carnavalito | 409 | Bolivian | Line | |
| Cherkessiya | 337 | Israeli | Line | |
| Den Toppede Høne | 396 | Danish | Set of three | X |
| Ersko Kolo | 270 | Serbian | Line | |
| Fjäskern | 399 | Swedish | Couples in circle | |
| Harukoma | 353 | Japanese | Scattered, nonpartner | |
| Hava Nagila | 338 | Israeli | Couples in circle | |
| Hora | 341 | Israeli | Circle, nonpartner | |
| Hora Pe Gheata | 383 | Romanian | Broken circle, nonpartner | |
| Itele | 384 | Romanian | Short line | |
| Lesnoto | 274 | Macedonian | Line | |
| Man in the Hay | 258 | German | Four couples | |
| Pata Pata | 249 | South African | Scattered, nonpartner | |
| Pljeskavac Kolo | 278 | Serbian | Broken circle, nonpartner | |
| Pravo Horo | 277 | Bulgarian | Broken circle, nonpartner | |
| La Raspa | 365 | Mexican | Couples | |
| Rondeau de Garein | 323 | French | Line, nonpartner | |
| Savila Se Bela Loza | 280 | Serbian | Line, nonpartner | |
| Troika | 390 | Russian | Set of three | |
| Ve' David | 345 | Israeli | Couples in circle | |

## Beginning 2

| NAME OF DANCE | PAGE | NATIONALITY | FORMATION | MIXER |
|---|---|---|---|---|
| Admiring the Moon | 308 | Chinese | Circle | |
| Alunelul | 381 | Romanian | Circle | |
| Borborbor | 246 | Ghanaian | Circle | |
| Il Codiglione | 347 | Italian | Couples in circle | |
| A Crossing Bourrée in Two Time | 318 | French | Longways | |
| Familie Sekstur | 397 | Danish | Couples in circle | X |
| Hasápikos | 271 | Greek | Line | |
| Hineh Ma Tov | 340 | Israeli | Broken circle | |
| Klumpakojis | 358 | Lithuanian | Couples in circle | |
| Ma Na'avu | 342 | Israeli | Circle | |
| Mayim | 343 | Israeli | Circle | |
| Mon Père Avait un Petit Bois | 321 | French | Circle | |
| Road to the Isles | 296 | Scottish | Couples in circle | |
| Sarajevka Kolo | 279 | Bosnian | Broken circle, nonpartner | |
| Seksmannsril | 403 | Norwegian | Couples in circle | |
| Šetnja | 281 | Serbian | Broken circle, nonpartner | |
| Spinnradl zu Dritt | 261 | Austrian | Set of three | |
| Syrtós | 283 | Greek | Broken circle, nonpartner | |
| Tancuj | 315 | Czech | Couples in circle | |
| Tanko Bushi | 354 | Japanese | Circle | |
| Three Meet | 298 | English | Sets of three | |
| Walczyk "Ges Woda" | 379 | Polish | Couples in circle | |
| Willow Tree | 301 | English | Longways set | |

## CLASSIFIED INDEX FOR CHAPTER 7, *continued*

### Beginning 3

| NAME OF DANCE | PAGE | NATIONALITY | FORMATION | MIXER |
|---|---|---|---|---|
| La Bastringue | 304 | Canadian | Couples in circle | X |
| Butterfly Hornpipe | 291 | English | Longways set | |
| Csárdás Palócosan | 332 | Hungarian | Couples | |
| La Cucaracha | 363 | Mexican | Couples | |
| D'Hammerschmiedsg' selln | 252 | German | Two couples | |
| Doudlebska Polka | 313 | Czech | Couples | X |
| Dr Gsatzlig | 254 | Swiss | Couples | |
| Familjevalsen | 398 | Swedish | Couples | |
| Gahu | 247 | Ghanaian | Circle | |
| Gong Xi, Happy New Year | 310 | Chinese | Circle | |
| Hora de Mina | 382 | Romanian | Circle | |
| Kalvelis | 357 | Lithuanian | Couples in circle | |
| Kiskanásztánc | 334 | Hungarian | Scattered, nonpartner | |
| Kocanska Gada | 273 | Roma | Broken circle, nonpartner | |
| Korabushka | 389 | Russian-American | Couples in circle | X |
| Misirlou | 276 | Greek-American | Broken circle, nonpartner | |
| Oslo Waltz | 295 | Scottish-English | Couples in circle | X |
| Tropanka | 284 | Bulgarian | Short lines | |
| Ugrós | 335 | Hungarian | Scattered, nonpartner | |
| La Varsoviana | 366 | Mexican | Couples in circle | |
| The White Cockade | 299 | Scottish | Longways set | |

## Intermediate

| NAME OF DANCE | PAGE | NATIONALITY | FORMATION | MIXER |
|---|---|---|---|---|
| Alexandrovska | 388 | Russian | Couples | |
| El Baile del Palo | 324 | Guam | Couples | |
| Bitte Mand I Knibe | 395 | Danish | Two couples | |
| Las Chiapanecas | 368 | Mexican | Couples | |
| Flowers of Edinburgh | 292 | Scottish | Longways set | |
| Gie Gordons | 294 | Scottish | Couples in circle | |
| Krüz König | 256 | German | Set of three | |
| Norwegian Polka | 402 | Scandinavian | Couples | |
| Ranchera | 410 | Uruguayan | Couples | |
| The Saint John River | 305 | Canadian | Four couples, longways set | |
| Siamsa Beirte | 297 | Irish | Couples | |
| Sicilian Tarantella | 349 | Italian | Longways set | |
| Sirba Din Cimpoi | 385 | Romanian | Line | |
| Sonderburg Doppelquadrille | 260 | German | Four Couples | |
| Tramblanka–Polka Mazurka | 377 | Polish | Couples in circle | |
| To Ting | 406 | Danish | Couples | |
| To Tur | 407 | Danish | Couples in circle | X |

## Advanced

| NAME OF DANCE | PAGE | NATIONALITY | FORMATION | MIXER |
|---|---|---|---|---|
| Die Alte Kath (Zwiefacher) | 264 | German | Couples | |
| Hambo | 400 | Swedish | Couples | |
| Holderbeerli (Zwiefacher) | 265 | German | Couples | |
| El Jarabe Tapatío | 361 | Mexican | Couples | |
| Snurrbocken | 404 | Swedish | Couples | |
| Tinikling | 372 | Filipino | One or two couples | |
| Vossarull | 408 | Norwegian | Couples | |

## CLASSIFIED INDEX FOR CHAPTER 8: SOCIAL DANCES

### Beginning 1


| NAME OF DANCE | PAGE |
|---|---|
| *The Continental | 448 |
| *Electric Slide | 454 |
| *Freeze | 449 |
| Swing, Single Time | |
| Side to Side Basic | 423 |


### Beginning 2


| NAME OF DANCE | PAGE |
|---|---|
| *Cowboy Boogie | 448 |
| Foxtrot | |
| Box Turn | 464 |
| Magic Step (Basic Step) | 458 |
| Open Magic Step (Promenade) | 459 |
| Promenade with an Arch | 460 |
| Rock, Recover | 460 |
| Westchester Box Step | 463 |
| *Hip Hop Dance (Beginning) | 450 |
| Merengue | |
| Basic Side Step | 497 |
| Box Step | 498 |
| Box Turn | 498 |
| Salsa | |
| Open Break | 511 |
| Right Turn | 511 |
| *Saturday Night Fever | 452 |
| *Slappin' Leather | 455 |
| Swing, Single Time | |
| Arch and Trade | 424 |
| Arch Out from Semi-Open | 429 |
| Basic in Social Swing | 428 |
| Inside Turn (Underarm Turn) | 424 |
| Tuck Spin | 425 |
| Two Hands to Social Swing | 428 |
| Walk Through (Brush Off) | 425 |
| Wrap (Cuddle) | 426 |


*indicates nonpartner dances

## Beginning 2, *continued*


| NAME OF DANCE | PAGE |
|---|---|
| Tango | |
| Promenade | 470 |
| Waltz | |
| Box Step | 479 |
| Box Turn | 480 |
| Travel Box | 480 |


## Beginning 3


| NAME OF DANCE | PAGE |
|---|---|
| Cha Cha | |
| Basic, Forward and Back | 487 |
| Chase, Half Turn | 490 |
| Full Turn | 491 |
| Charleston | |
| Charleston Twist | 440 |
| Jump | 441 |
| Partner Charleston | 441 |
| Point Step | 439 |
| Single Kick Step | 440 |
| Suzy Q | 441 |
| Swivel | 441 |
| Foxtrot | |
| Grapevine Step | 466 |
| Magic Left Turn | 459 |
| Twinkle, Bronze | 464 |
| Rumba | |
| Bolero Break | 505 |
| Box Step | 503 |
| Box Turn | 503 |
| Circular Turn | 505 |
| Flirtation Break | 504 |
| Parallel Turn | 505 |
| Side by Side | 505 |
| Variations of Bolero Break | 506 |


*indicates nonpartner dances

## CLASSIFIED INDEX FOR CHAPTER 8, *continued*

### Beginning 3, *continued*


| NAME OF DANCE | PAGE |
|---|---|
| Salsa | |
| Basic Step | 510 |
| Cross Body Lead | 512 |
| Cross Step | 510 |
| Left Turn | 512 |
| Side Step | 510 |
| Throw Out | 510 |
| Samba | |
| Basic Step | 514 |
| Swing, Single Time | |
| Hammerlock | 427 |
| Swing, Triple Time | |
| Triple Rhythm | 429 |
| Triple Time | 430 |
| Tango | |
| Basic Tango Step | 470 |
| Box Step | 473 |
| Cross Step and Quarter Turn | 472 |
| Half-Turn Counterclockwise | 472 |
| Half-Turn Clockwise | 472 |
| Quarter Turn | 471 |
| Right Parallel Basic Tango | 471 |
| Waltz | |
| Hesitation Step | 481 |
| Cross Step (Bronze Twinkle) | 482 |


*indicates nonpartner dances

## Intermediate

| NAME OF DANCE | PAGE |
|---|---|
| *All Shook Up | 447 |
| Cha Cha | |
| Basic in Latin Social Position | 488 |
| Cross Over | 489 |
| Cross Over Turn | 490 |
| Jody Break | 491 |
| Kick Freeze | 493 |
| Kick Swivel | 493 |
| Open Break | 488 |
| Return to Basic | 489 |
| Right Break | 488 |
| Variations of Jody | 492 |
| Foxtrot | |
| Conversation Pivot | 462 |
| Corte | 462 |
| Pivot Turn | 467 |
| Right and Left Parallel Magic Step | 461 |
| Twinkle Step (cross over) | 465 |
| *Hip-Hop Dance (Intermediate) | 451 |
| Hustle | |
| Basic Step | 436 |
| Lead's Underarm Pass | 438 |
| Returning to Social | 437 |
| Social Basic Step | 436 |
| Throw Out | 437 |
| Lindy Hop | |
| Basic to a Jockey | 443 |
| Full Lindy Basic | 442 |
| Jockey to a Swing Out | 444 |
| Lindy Charleston | 444 |
| Shine | 445 |
| Mambo | |
| Basic | 496 |
| Rumba | |
| Cuban Walk | 502 |
| Varsouvienne Break | 507 |

*indicates nonpartner dances

## CLASSIFIED INDEX FOR CHAPTER 8, *continued*

### Intermediate, *continued*

| NAME OF DANCE | PAGE |
|---|---|
| Swing, Single Time | |
| Octopus | 426 |
| Turning Basic (Collegiate) | 428 |
| Swing, West Coast | |
| Left Side Pass | 434 |
| Sugar Push (Basic Step Variation) | 432 |
| Underarm Turn | 433 |
| Whip | 434 |
| Tango | |
| Corté | 474 |
| Double Cross | 473 |
| Grapevine Fan | 476 |
| Open Fan | 475 |
| Parallel Fan | 476 |
| Waltz | |
| Twinkle Step | 483 |
| Weaving Step | 482 |

### Advanced

| NAME OF DANCE | PAGE |
|---|---|
| Samba | |
| Basic Turn | 515 |
| Copa Step | 517 |
| Forward Progressive Step | 515 |
| Slow Side Close | 516 |
| Sideward Basic | 516 |
| Viennese Waltz | 484 |

*indicates nonpartner dances

# Subject Index

Note: Page numbers followed by *f* indicate a figure and by n. indicate a note.


Acadian dance, 120–121
accent, 29
acoustic requirements, 7
activity lesson plan, 13
Adaptations, Special Needs, 15, 18
  cognitive disabilities, 18
  hearing impairments, 18
  inclusion, 17–18
  visual impairment, 18
African Americans
  Lindy Hop music played by jazz musicians, 442
  unique contributions of, 61–62
African folk dance, 244–249
  background, characteristics, 244–245
  folk dances, 246–249
Age of Enlightenment, 61
Allotey, Ardey, 246, 247
Alpine region folk dance, 250–265
  background, characteristics, 250–251
  folk dances
    Austrian, 261
    German, 252, 256, 258, 260, 263–265
    Swiss, 254
Alumbaugh, "Doc," 108, 114
Alumbaugh, Winnie, 114
American Callers Association (ACA), 155
*American Bandstand* (TV show), 421
American folk dances
  cotillion, 61, 192
  dances of the people, 62–63
  dress appropriate for, 63–64
  folk traditions revived in, 63–64
  european sources, 60–61
  historic development of, 00
  melting pot vs. ethnic identity elements in, 64–65
  music used in, 63
  social dance, 60
  social occasions for, 64
  sources and types of, 59
  Spanish-Mexican influence on, 62
  unique contributions of African Americans to, 62
  *See also* dance style
American Folk Dance Society, 240
*American Morris Newsletter*, 286
amplifier, 8
Anderson, Kathy, 235
Appalachian clog dances, 60, 160
Appalachian square dance, 194
Arabs, 338
Arbeitsgremeinschaft der Sing-Tanz-und Spielkreise, 265
Armstrong, Don, 195, 207
*The Art of Dancing* (Ferrero), 61
artistic dance, 4
"Arts Alliance Plan" (Callerlab), 155
assemblé, 36
assessing group variables, 13
Association of Folk Dance Groups, 251

Baal Shem, Israel, 336
Badgers Gavotte, 61
*bailes*, 62, 193
*Balance and Swing* (Sannella), 208
*bal chantée* practice, 316
Balkan countries folk dance, 267–284
  background, characteristics, 267–269
  folk dances
    Bosnian, 279
    Bulgarian, 277, 284
    Greek, 271, 276, 283
    Macedonian, 274
    Roma, 273
    Serbian, 270, 278, 280, 281
ballet performances, 4
Ballroom Dance (New York), 415
*bals clandestins*, 316
*bals folks* (the folk ball), 317
*La Bamba*, 62
banjer, 63
Bannerman, Glen, 160
Barnes, Peter, 196
Barreto, Ray, 509
basic dance steps
  mazurka, 41
  polka, 39
  schottische, 38
  shuffle, dance walk, or glide, 37, 425
  teaching, 40–41
  two-step or triple-step, 37
  waltz, 38–39
basic dance turns
  pivot, 46–47
  polka, 39
  schottische, 39
  two-step, 43, 44
  waltz, 45–46
basic movements
  contra dance figures, 200–201
  square dance, 164
  square dance standardization of, 155
  wheelchair adaptations, 32–38
  *See also* locomotor movements
beat
  African American development of syncopation, 61
  defining, 28
  listening to the, 54–55, 350
  *See also* rhythm
Becket formation, 198, 205
Beliajus, Vytautas Finadar, 234, 336, 347, 357
Berea College, 194
Berk, Fred, 239, 336
biblical times, 336
Big Apple, 413
Big Circle Square Dance, 159–163
the Bile, 245
Blackpool Dance Festival, 414
Bloland, Sunni, 383
Blue Bonnet Set, 92, 153
Bolivian folk dance, 409
"Book of Odes" (Wang), 308
Bosnian folk dance, 268–269, 279
Bon festival, dances, 351, 353
Boxell, Dennis, 279
Brandon, Gayle, 455
Breunig, Fred, 200
Brigham Young University
  ballroom dance, 415
  International Folk Dance Ensemble, 240
Brimmer & May School, 206
British Isles fold dance
  background, characteristics, 285–288
  English folk dance, 291, 298, 301
  Irish folk dance, 289, 297
  Scottish folk dance, 292, 294, 295, 296, 299

British National Committee on Folk Arts, 239
Brownee, 84
Buenaventura, Antonio, 371
Bugaku dance style, 351
Bukhara Jewish dance, 336
Bulgarian folk dance, 269, 277, 284
bulletin boards, 24
Burchenal, Elizabeth, 60, 85, 198, 240
Burkhardt, Ludwig, 256
El Burro, 62
Buschmann, Friedrick, 242
Butterfly dance, 11
Buzzard Lope, 61

El Caballo, 62
Cajun dance, 63, 120–124
Cake Walk, 62
Callerlab, 155, 164
California Folk Dance Federation, 239
calling
contra dance, 199–200
square dance, 151, 157
described, 157–159
prompt, 158
use of prerecorded calls, 159
sequence of, 158
sight, 158–159
singing, 158, 181
traditional vs. modern western, 159
Calloway, Cab, 421
Canadian folk dance, 306
background, characteristics, 303
folk dance, 304, 305
Canterbury Country Orchestra, 195
canter rhythm, 40, 478
Cape Breton, 303
card file, 200
cassette tape decks, 9
carole, song dances, 2
CD players, 8–9
cha cha, 486–494
combos, 494
chain dance formation, 2, 2*f*, 267
Championship Ballroom Dance, 414
Chang's International Dancers, 239
Chang, Soon, 239
Charleston, 438–441
Twelfth Street Rag, 95–96
Charleston period (1923–1928), 413
de Chavarria, Laura Zanzi, 409, 410
The Cheyenne Mountain Dancers, 153
Chicago Barn Dance Company, 232
Chicago's Hull House, 351
Chinese folk dance, 307–311
background, characteristics, 307–308
folk dances, 308, 310
Christmas Country Dance School, 196
Circle Two-Step, 84
class grading, 23
class projects, 23–24
clave, 509
clogging, 160
closure lesson plan, 14
clothing
American dances
appropriate for, 63
costume, 243
international folk dance, 238; *see also* individual country
Glowworm Garotte, 61
clubs, 239
cognitive disabilities, 18
Collette, Fred and Mary, 215
colored tags for grading, 23
Colon, Willie, 509
combos. *See* social dance
community resources, 23–24
competitive ballroom dance, 421
Conga, 413
content selection, 13
contra dance
active couple, 197, 201
basics, 197–198
basic figures, 200–201
basic step, 200
caller, 199
card file, 199–200
dances, 204–237
dance structure, 197–198
"Dudley Dancers," 195
formation, 197–198
history, 192–197
levels of dance, 202
music, 193, 195, 196, 198
sources, 200
tunes, Ralph Page, 203
neutral couple, 198
Northern Junket, 195
numbering off, 197
progression, 198
Ralph Page Dance Legacy Weekend, 195
research, 196
teaching, 201–202
timing, music, 198
*La Contradanza*, 193
contradanse, Acadian, 121
*Contredanse Française*, 60, 192
*contredanses* (English country dances), 60
costumes. *See* clothing
cotillion, 61, 150, 192
Cotton-Eyed Joe, 109
counting rhythm, 32
*The Country Dance Book* (Page and Tolman), 194
*The Country Dance Book* (Sharp and Karpeles), 151
Country Dance and Song Society, library/archives (University of New Hampshire), 143
Country Dance and Song Society (CDSS), 194, 208, 211, 239
*Country Dance and Song Society News*, 142
country dances, English, 60, 192, 193, 186–287
country dancing, 59, 64
country western dance
dances, 126–139
described, 63
etiquette, 125
style of, 125
*Cowboy Dances* (Shaw), 153, 194
Crampton, C. Ward, 240
Creoles, 120
Crum, Richard George, 239, 270, 280, 281
the cue, 151, 152, 416
cueing techniques, 21–22
culminating activities, 24
cutting in (dance class), 17
Czarnowski, Lucille, 193n.3
Czech Republic and Slovakian folk dance, 312–313
background and characteristics, 312–313
folk dances, 313, 314
Czompo, Andor, 329, 331, 332, 334, 335

D'Acres, S. C., 217
daily planning instruction, 12
Dalsemer, Bob, 223
dance
artistic, 4
beginning history of, 1–2
cultural significance of, 238
forms of, 2
history of music and, 2–3
purpose of, 6–7
religion, 3
recognizing music for specific, 49
social recreation, 5
theatrical, 4
in today's world, 4–5
traditional, 5
worship, 1
dance class orientation
etiquette, 16
first class meeting, 19
fun with cutting in, 17
setting the stage, 16
social aids, 17
teaching students with special needs, 17–18
dance class procedures
enrichment activities, 24–25
evaluation, 23
general teaching points, 20–21
practical test, 23
review, 23
selecting material and presentation, 19–20
teaching a specific dance, 21–22
written test, 23–24
dance culture
in form of fertility rites, 4
historical role in education by, 3–4
historical role in health, 4
as part of religion, 3
dance directions, 54, 243
dance hall etiquette, 000
dance education
history of, 3–4
music, recordings and live, 9–11
planning instruction for, 11–16
purpose of, 6–7
*Dance Education—What Is It? Why Is It Important?* (National Dance Association), 6–7

dance facilities
  acoustic requirements for, 7
  floor requirements for, 7
dance formations, 48
dance fundamentals
  analysis of a basic rhythm, 28–31
  basic dance steps, 38–42
  dance formations, 48
  dance positions, 49–53
  dance style, 56–59
  locomotor movements/wheelchair adaptations, 32–38
  music in relation to dance, 54–56
  rhythm and meter, 28–32
  turns, 42–47
dance instruction
  adaptations, special needs, 17–18
  assessing group variables, 13
  basic dance steps and turns, 40–42
    teaching, 41–47
  class procedure, 19–27
    cue cards, 21–22
    evaluation, 23
    grading, 24
    practical test, 23
    review, 23
    selecting material, 19
    teaching specific dances, 21–22
    written test, 23
  contra dances
    dance levels and progression of teaching, 202
    suggestions for teaching, 201–202
  using live music, 10, 11
  organizing special activities, 25–27
  orientation to dance class, 16–17
  planning, 12–16
  using recordings, 10
  setting stage, 4
  social dance
    the cue, 416
    demonstration, 416
    formations, 415–416
    line dance, 455
    style, 417
    trends in vocabulary and leading, 415
    unison versus free practice, 416
    walk-through, 416
  square dances, Big Circle Square Dance, 151–152, 156–181
  for teaching style, 51–52
dance instruction planning
  assessing group variables, 13
  content selection, 13
  daily, 12
  dance unit, 12
  of lesson plan, 13–16
  objectives/student outcome, 12–13
  social dance, 415–417
  total dance program, 11–12
dance lesson plans
  five sections of, 13
  procedure and organization of, 16
  *Saturday Night Fever* line dance example of, 14–15
  social dance, 416–417
dance positions, 49–53
  social dance
    closed position, 418–419
    following, 420–421
    leading, 419
the dancer
  dance style of beautiful, 56–57
  listening to the beat, 54–55
dancesport, 415–445
dance steps. *See* basic dance steps
dance structure, 13
dance style
  achieving appropriate, 57–58
  American dance
    Big Circle Square Dance, 151
    County Western, 122
    Square Dance, 157
  of beautiful dancer, 56
  ear and ankle alignment, 57
  folk dance. See international fold dance, background, dance characteristics
  good posture for balance/control, 50
  social dance
    cha cha, 486–487
    Charleston, 439
    fox-trot, 457
    line dance, 446
    mambo, 495
    merengue, 497
    rumba, 501–502
    salsa, 509
    samba, 514
    swing (jitterbug), 422
    tango, 469–470
    waltz, 479
    West Coast swing, 432
  teaching, 58–59
Dance Theater of Harlem, 4
dance timeline, 5
dance, traditional, 5
dance unit
  defining, 12
  establishing goals for, 12
  planning instruction for, 12
dance walk
  described, 33, 38
  social dance, 418
*The Dancing Master* (Playford), 151, 226
Danish folk dance, 395, 396, 397, 406, 407
Danish Folk Dance Society, 239
*danserond*, 121
David, Mihai, 382, 384, 385
Davis, Margie, 211
*A Day at the Races* (film), 442
Death Dance, 5
Derschmidt, Hermann, 261, 262
devil dances, 4
Dieckelmann, Heinrich, 256
Diggle, Roger, 224
Dillingham, Uncle Dave, 109
disabled students. *See* special needs students
disability dance adaptations
  Hip Hop dance, 450
  Saturday Night Fever, line dance, 452
disco dance, 414, 435
discotheque, 435
*Dopolavora* (Italy), 346
Dorsch, Brunhilde, 276
dress. *See* clothing
drums, 238, 240
Drury, Nelda G., 118, 359, 361, 363, 366, 368
Dunsing, Paul and Gretel, 260
Duquesne University, 276
Duryea, Oscar, 456

ear/ankle alignment, 57
Edward, Prudence, 305
Electric Slide to funk music, 454
*An Elegant Collection of Squares and Contras (Page)*, 194
English country dances (*contredanses*), 60, 152, 286, 412
English Dancing Master (Playford), 63, 192
English folk dance, 291, 295, 298, 301
English Folk Dance and Song Society, 000
English Folk Dance Society, 301
English sword dance, 194, 239
English longway sets, 2
enrichment activities
  bulletin boards, 24
  class projects, 24
  community resources, 24
  culminating activities, 24
  teacher resources, 24
equipment requirements, 7–9
  amplifier, 8
  care of turntable and records, 8
  microphones, 8
  music playing devices, 8
    CD players, 8
    MP3, 8
  sound system, 7
  speakers, 8
  video recorder, 9
Ericson, Jane Harris, 154
escort position, 53
ethnic identity, 64
ethnic/traditional folk dance, 236
etiquette
  dance class orientation on, 16–17
  dance hall, 122
  dancing masters, 64
evaluation, 23–24
Evageline country, 120
extracurricular opportunities, 12

facilities, 7
*fais-dodo* ("go to sleep") gatherings, 120
family dances, 25
*el fandangos*, 62
farandole dance formation, 2
Farwell, Jane, 103, 240, 254
Feddy, Beatric, 246, 247
Feild, Fred, 232
Feis tradition, 287
Ferrero, Edward, 61
festivals. *See* holidays
fertility rite dances, 4
fiddle (violin) music, 63
*fiestas*, 62

Fink, Klaus, 265
Finnish folk dance
background, characteristics, 394
first class meeting, 19
Fitzgerald, Dick, 61
Fix, Louise, 219
Fix, Penn, 197, 218, 219
floor, 7
Fogg, George A., 286, 291
Folk Dance House (New York City), 239, 313
folk dance, 65
*See also* international folk dance
The Folk Dancer, 407
folk dancing, value, 242
Folk Festival Councils, 239, 240
Folklore Village, 189, 196
following techniques, 420
footwork (social dance), 417
Ford, Henry, 61, 194
Ford, Iran W., 104
formations, dance, 48
Fox, Henry, 456
fox-trot, 456–468
combos, 468
free practice, 416
French Canadian, 151
French folk dance, 323
background, characteristics, 316–317
folk dances, 318–323
Fresh Fish, 226
Friends of Swedish Folk Dance, 239

Gadd, May, 194, 198
gallop, 36
Gaudreau, Herbie, 205
the Gbon, 245
gender-based instruction, 21
"ghost partner," 17
Gibson, M. M., 292, 299
Gilmore, Ed, 184
Gillette, Mary, 194
Giouba, African, 62
glide, 38
*Glowworm Gavotte*, 61
Golden, Kristina Waller, 17
*Good Morning!* (Ford), 151
*Good Morning* (Lovett), 194
good posture, 57
Gottier, Karin, 250, 256, 261, 263
Gow, Nathaniel, 222
*Grand March*, 78
"Great Unity of the People" (Tiananmen Square), 307
Greek dancing, 4*f*
background, folk dance characteristics, 267–268
folk dances, 267–268, 271, 276, 283
Greek folk dance, 266–267
Greene, Madelynne, 321
Greggerson, Herb, 94, 97, 101, 153
Greggerson, Pauline, 94, 153
Griffiths, John, 193
group variables assessment, 13
*Der grüne Heinrich* (Keller), 247
Guam fold dance, 324–328
Guerrero, Juan C., 324
Gulick, Luther, 194
gypsy dance. See Roma
gypsy music, 330

*Hairspray* (movie), 448
Harlow, Larry, 509
Harris, Jane, NO PAGE NUMBERS PROVIDED
Harry Ransom Division Library, 143
Hawaiian folk dance, 140–149
Hazelius, Arthur, 239
headhunting dances (Philippines), 370–371
health/dance rites, 4
hearing impairments, 18
Hebert, Donna, 196
"heel burners," 193
*Hellzapoppin* (film), 442
Helt, Jerry and Kathy, 116
Hempel, Graham, 233
Henneger, Maurice, 220
Herbert, Victor, 235
*Herb's Blue Bonnet Calls* (Greggerson and Greggerson), 153
*Heritage Dances of Early America* (Page), 194
Herman, Mary Ann, 234
Herman, Michael, 239, 278, 279, 313, 389
Hill, Becky, 209
Hinds, Tom, 221
Hinman, Mary Wood, 240
Hip Hop Dance
beginning, 450
intermediate, 451
hoedown, 62
Hoffman, Erik, 229
Hofman, Huig, 252
Hofstra, Warren, 224
Ho, Jimmy, 308
Holden, Rickey, 143, 176, 187, 188, 194
holidays
festivals, 194
religious, 238
Hoolyeh Folk Dance Festival (1998), 246, 247
hop, 35
Hopi Indians, 4
Hornpipe, 4
Hubert, Gene, 212
Hull House, Chicago, 347
Hull, Isaac, 217
Hungarian folk dance, 330–335
background, characteristics, 33
folk dances, 332–335
motifs, 331–332
*Hungarian Recreational Folk Dances* (video), 330
Hurok, Sol, 239
Hustle, 239

Idyllwild, 347
improvisation, 245
inclusion concept, 17–18
instruction. *See* dance instruction
instructional inclusion, 18
instructor, effective, 6
Intercollegiate Outing Club Association (IOCA), 194
International Association of Square Dance Callers, 155
International Congress of Popular Arts (1928), 239
International Dance Federation (IDSF), 415
international folk dance
countries
Africa, 244–249
Alpine region (Swizterland, Austria, Germany), 250–265
Balkan countries, 267–284
Bulgaria, 269
Greece, 267–268
Roma culture, 269
Serbia, Macedonia, and Bosnia, 268–269
British Isles, 285–302
England, 285–287
Ireland, 287–288
Scotland, 288
Canada, 303–306
China, 307–311
Czech Republic and Slovakia, 312–315
France, 316–323
Hungary, 330–335
Guam, 324–328
Israel, 336–345
background, characteristics, 336
folk dances, 337
Italy, 346
Japan, 351–355
background, characteristics, 351–352
folk dances, 353–355
Lithuania, 356–358
Mexico, 359–364
Philippines, 370–374
Poland, 375–379
Romania, 380–386
Russian, 000
Scandinavia, 392–408
Denmark, 393
Finland, 394
Norway, 393–394
Sweden, 394
South America
Bolivia, 409
Uruguayan, 410
definition, 238
development in industrialized society, 238
movement of
folk dance camps, 240
future of, 236
history in American education, 240
performing groups, 240
preserving folk dancing, 239
research and advanced studies as part of, 241
three main styles today, 242
in the United States, 239–240
value of folk dancing, 242–243
teaching approaches, 243
reading dance directions, 243

using musical recordings for, 9
understanding folkways to enhance
costumes, 243
eastern and western culture, 241
geography and climate, 241
holidays, festivals, and special occasions, 243
music, 241–242
religion, 241
International Folk Dance Festival (1939), 234
international folk dance performing groups, 235
International Olympic Committee (IOC), 415
international, teaching approaches, 243
Irish folk dance
background, characteristics, 281–288
folk dances, 289, 297
Israeli folk dance, 336–345
background, characteristics, 336
folk dances, 337–345
Italian folk dance, 346
background, characteristics, 346
folk dances, 347–350
Ivory Cross Competition, 000

Jacobites, 292
Japanese folk dance, 351–355
background, characteristics, 351–353
El Jarabe, 62
Jazz Age, 194
Jiang Quing, 308
jitterbug (swing), 421–422
John C. Campbell Folk School, 196
Jones, Fenton, "Jonesy," 188
Juba, 64
jump, 34

Kabuki theater, 352-353
Karpeles, Maud, 151
Kassel, Bärenreiter Verlag, 256
Keller, Gottfried, 250
Keller, Kate Van Winkle, 286
Kennedy, Douglas, 285
Kitch, Jim, 228
*Kneveler, das Tanzbuch mit "Krüz-König"* (Kassel), 250
the Koou, 245
Kopp, Carol, 204

LaFarge, Rod, 142
Lambeth Walk, 413
lancer, 151
Lapson, Dvora, 338, 343
Latin Dance Craze, 413
Laufman, Dudley, 195
Lavoe, Hector, 509
leading
specific directions for, 419–420
trends in, 45
leap, 34
Lee, Earl, 310
Legacy (square dance), 154
Legacy survey (1990), 154
Legacy Weekend (contra dance), 195
lesson plan example, 16–17
lesson reflection plan, 13–16
Library of Congress, 241
Library of Traditional Music and Dance, 196
*Life* magazine, 442
Lindbergh, Charles, 442
Lindy Hop, 413, 442
Line dance, 445–446
line values, 30
Lira vase, 2
Lithuanian folk dance, 000
background, characteristics, 256
folk dances, 357–358
live music, 10–11
teaching with, 11
Lloyd Shaw Archives (University of Denver), 143
Lloyd Shaw Foundation, 154, 196, 214
locomotor movements, 32–38
assemblé, 36
exercises for fundamental, 38
gallop, 36
hop, 35
jump, 34
leap, 34
run, 33
sissone, 35
skip, 38
slide, 37
special need students, 17
walk, 23
*See also* basic movements; wheelchair adaptations
Long, Jere, 187
Long Sword dance, 286
Lover, Samuel, 225
Lovett, Benjamin B., 194

McCullough, Paul, 211
McDermid, "Shadrack" and Betty, 224
Macedonian folk dance, 000–000
McLeod, Kenneth, 296
McQuillen's Squeezebox (contra dance tune), 263
mainstream, 143
*Malcolm X* (film), 442
mambo, 494–496
Manning, Frankie, 442
Marek, Jacek, 375, 377, 379
May Day Rounds, 139
Mayo, Margot, 142
Mayo, Monty, 276
Maypole Dance, 152, 286
Maypoles, 241
mazurka, 49
measure, 29
Melender, David, 509
melting pot, 64
Mendocino Folk Lore camp, 321
Merce Cunningham Dance Company, 4
merengue, 496–50
combos, 500
Messager, Jeanne, 321
meter, 29
Mexican folk dance, 361–369
background, characteristics, 359–360
folk dances, 361–369
microphone, 8
Mi'Kmaq Indians, 303
Miller, Rodney and Randy, 195–196
Millstone, David, 192
military dance, 329
*Minuet*, 62
Mitchell, Steve, 442
Morris dance, 241, 285–286
Morris Ring, 285–286
Mountain Folk Festival, 90
Mountain Folk School, 121
mouth harp, 63
Mucha, Kelly, 18, 450
music
American dance
Cajun dance, 120–121
traditionally used in, 62
contra dance
sources of, 193, 195, 196, 198
timing and,198
tunes composed by Ralph Page, 203
fundamentals of dance and
how to recognize music for dance, 55–56
listen to the beat, 54
rhythm training and appreciation, 56
history of dance and, 2–3
international folk dance
African, 245
Balkan countries
Bulgaria, 269
Greece, 268
Serbia, Macedonia, and Bosnia, 269
Canadian, 303
Chinese, 307
Czech Republic and Slovakia, 313
English country dances, 287
French, 317
Guam, 324
Hungarian, 330
Irish, 288
Israeli, 36
Mexican, 360
overview of, 241
Romanian, 380
Russian, 387
Scottish, 288
lancer, 151
using live, 10–11
using recordings of, 9–10
social dance, 10
square dance, 9
musical accompanist, 11
musical instruments
African folk dance, 245
Bulgarian fold dance, 269
Canadian fold dance, 303
contra, 188
Czech and Slovakian folk dance, 313
English country dances, 287
folk dance, 241–242

French folk dance, 317
Greek folk dance, 268
Guam folk dance, 324
Hungarian folk dance, 330
Irish folk dance, 288
Mexican folk dance, 359–360
Romanian folk dance, 380
Russian folk dance, 392
Scottish folk dance, 288
Serbia, Macedonia, Bosnia, 269
Swedish fold dance, 394

National Ballroom Dance Week, 415
New England Chestnuts, 200
Chorus Jig, 210
Hull's Victory, 217
Lady of the Lake, 318
Petronella, 222
Rory O'More, 225
New England Folk Festival Association (NEFFA), 194, 196, 239
new material lesson plan, 13, 16
New School of Social Research, 235
New York City Ballet, 0
Noh dance style, 351–352
Nordiskz Museet (Northland Museum), 234
North American Federation of German Folk Dance Groups, 265
*Northern Junket* magazine, 194
Norwegian folk dance, 402, 403, 408
note values, 29
Novak, Jeannette, 313

Oaks, Dick, 277
objectives (instruction), 12–13
objective test, 23–24
O'Farrell, Sian and Una, 297
Oglebay Folk Dance Camp, 276
Oglebay Institute, 240
Ohio Star Ball, 414
Olson, Al, 213
One-Night stands, 25–26
*On the Trail of Negro Folksongs* (Scarborough), 109
Open Foxtrot Competition, 414
Orff-Schulwerk process, 56
orientation. *See* dance class orientation
Ormand, Carol, 230
Osgood, Bob, 155
Owens, Jack, 143
*Oxford Minuet*, 61

Page, Ralph, 214, 220, 234, 236
Palestinian, 336
Parkes, Tony, 196, 227
Patriot's Jig (contra dance tune), 203
patter calling. *See* square dance
Pearl, Dan, 206
performance folk dance, 242
*Philippine National Dances* (Tolentino), 370, 371
Philippines folk dance
background, 370
folk dance, 372–374
"Phoenix Plan" (Callerlab), 155
physical inclusion, 17–18
pick-up beat, 32
Pigeon Wing, 61
Pilobolus, 4
Pittman, Anne, 154, 324
Playford, John, 63, 152, 192–193, 286
Playground and Recreation Association of America, 240
Playground Association of America, 194
play party games, 62, 65–76, 356
Polish folk dance, 380–381
background, characteristics, 375–376
folk dances, 377–379
polka, 39
positions, dance, 49–53
posture, 57
practical test, 23
presentation, 19
prerecorded calls, 145
Processional Court Dance, 2
the processional dance formation, 2
progression figure, 192
*Promenade* (Mayo), 142
prompter, 151, 158
proper formation, 000
Prudhomme, Chef Paul, 120
purpose of dance, 7'
*Put Your Little Foot*, 112

*quadrilles*
history of, 137, 150, 192
Grand Square Quadrille, 82–83
*Lancer*, 151
New England development of, 138

Ragtime period (1900–1920s), 143, 194
*The Ralph Page Book of Contras* (Page), 194
Ralph Page Collection (University of New Hampshire), 196
rap and hip hop, 414
Rapper dance style, 286
recordings, 9–10
Cajun music, 121
using live music instead of, 10–11
using prerecorded calls, 145
teaching with, 10
records
care of, 9
turntables of, 9
recreational folk dance, 5, 242
*redowa*, 151
religion
African folk dance and spiritual world of, 245
international folk dance and, 241
religious dance, 3
religious holidays. *See* holidays
research, 235–236
review. *See* instruction
rhythm
analysis of basic, 32
analysis of basic dance step, 38–42
canter, 40, 478
counting, 32
cueing and, 423
defining, 28
even, 31
folk dancing and, 241–242
social dance
cha cha, 486
Charleston, 438
fox-trot, 456
hustle, 436
mambo, 495
merengue, 497
rumba, 501
salsa, 509
samba, 513
swing (jitterbug), 421
West Coast Swing, 431
tango, 469
waltz, 478
training and appreciation of, 56
uneven, 30–31
*See also* beat
rhythm and meter fundamentals
accent, 29
counting rhythm, 32
even rhythm, 31
line values, 30
measure, 29
meter, 29
note values, 29
phrase, 30
rhythm, 27
rhythm pattern, 28, 31
tempo, 30
time signature, 30
underlying beat, 28
uneven rhythm, 31
rhythm pattern, 31
Riafati, Sani, 273
Rippon, Hugh, 301
Robinson, Alfred, 193
rock and roll, 413, 421
Roma folk dance, 269, 273
Romanian folk dance
background, characteristics, 380
folk dances, 381–386
Romanian Folk Ensemble, 382, 384, 385
Rotenberg, Tanya, 214
*Round Dance Book* (Shaw), 153
round and novelty dances, 62
round eight, 152
*rounds*, 150
Royal Scottish Country Dance Society, 292, 299
Rudd, Helfrid, 403
Ruff, Bob, 189
rumba, 501–508
combos, 508
run, 33
running set dance form, 138–139, 151
running waltz, 40, 42
"Running wild" (Ziegeld Follies show), 447
Russian folk dance
background, characteristics, 387
folk dances, 388–391
Russian Moiseyev Dance Ensemble, 239

salsa, 413, 509–512
samba, 513–518
combos, 518
Sanders, Gary E., 447
Sanders, Olcutt, 193
Sannella, Ted, 194–165, 208, 211, 213, 234

*Saturday Night Fever* (film), 435, 452
*Saturday Night Fever* line dance lesson plan, 14–15
Scandinavian folk dance
background, characteristics, 392
Denmark, 393
Finland, 394
Norway, 393
Sweden, 394
folk dances, 395–408
Scarborough, Dorothy, 109
schottische, 39
Schützenberger, Erna, 261
Scottish folk dance
background, characteristics, 288
folk dances, 292, 294–296, 299
Senior Dances, 27
Sephardic Jews, 341
Serbian folk dance
background, characteristics, 268–269
folk dances, 270, 278, 280, 281
*Seven Brides for Seven Brothers*, 4
Sharp, Cecil J., 151, 193, 194, 239, 285, 287
Sharples, Philip, 194
Shaw, Dorothy, 141, 153, 194
Shaw, Ed, 213
Shaw, Lloyd, 153, 194
Shaw, Pat, 90
shuffle, 38
Sicilian circle, 48, 201
sight call, 158–159
singing calls
described, 158, 181
examples of, 180–186
singing quadrille, 151
sissone, 35
skip, 38
slide, 37
slot dance, 421
Slovakian folk dance. *See* Czech Republic and Slovakian
Smith, Marilyn M., 320, 323
Smith, Frank, 194
Smithsonian Institution, 241, 392
Smukler, David, 231
snap, 288
Snowden, Shorty, 442
social aids (dance class), 15
social dance, 60, 412
combos
cha cha, 494
foxtrot, 468
merengue, 500
rumba, 508
samba, 518
swing, 431
tango, 477
waltz, 485
competition history of, 414
dance positions
closed position, 418–419
leading and following, 419–421
dances
cha cha, 486–494
Charleston, 438–441
foxtrot, 456–468
hustle, 435–437
Lindy hop, 442
line dances, 445–456
mambo, 494–496
merengue, 496–500
rumba, 501–508
salsa, 509–513
samba, 503–518
swing, 421–435
tango, 469–477
viennese waltz, 484
waltz, 478–485
historic phases of, 412–414
using musical recordings for, 10
style of
dance walk, 418
described, 417
footwork in, 417
levels of, 424–425
teaching, 415–416
vocabulary
frame, 415
lead and follow, 415
social events, 25–27
social/recreational dance, 5
sound system, 9
Spanish dance, 62
speakers, 8
special activities
family dances, 25
One-Night Stand, 25–26
Senior Dances, 26
special parties, 26
theme parties, 26
special needs students
with cognitive disabilities, 18
general adaptations for teaching dance to, 18–19
with hearing impairments, 19
inclusion of, 17–18
with visual impairments, 18
*See also* wheelchair adaptations
special parties activities, 26
spin, 47
*Spinnradlunser Tanzbuch. Spinnradl* (Derschmidt and Schützenberger), 261, 262
Spivak, Joseph and Rajah, 345
square dance
American Callers Association (ACA), 155, 164
"Arts Alliance Plan," 155
basic step, 152, 157
basic movements, 155, 165–177
caller, 151, 157
prompter, 151
callerlab, 155, 164
calls
calling, 157
calling methods, 158–159
patter, 177–181
singing calls, 181
cue, 151
cue cards, 159
history, 150–156
instruction, 157. *Also see* teaching approaches
Legacy, 154
magazines, 155
mainstream, 155
methods of changing partners, 178
planning units and lessons, 157
"Phoenix Plan," 155
records with calls, 159
research, 155
style, 157
teaching approaches, 156
Big Circle, 156
changing partners, 179–180
mixers, 178
organizing squares, 178–180
progression, 164–173
set/square, 156
United States postal stamp, 154
Square Dance Week, 142
*Square Dancing Magazine*, 155
Star Championship, 421
stepping
Cape Breton, 303
English Sword Dance, 286
Stevens, Erin, 442
Stockton Folk Dance Camp, 297
Sturman, Rivka, 340, 345
style, 56–59
folk dance, 242. *Also see* specific country
social dance, 417. *Also see* specific dance
subjective rating, 23
Swedish folk dance, 339
background, characteristics, 392, 394
folk dances, 398, 399, 400, 404
Swenson, Marlys Waller,
Swing Era (0000 to mid-1950s), 413
swing (jitterbug), 414–415
*Swing Kids* (film), 442
*Swing the Next* (Sannella), 208
Swiss Costume Association, 251
sword dance, 241, 286
*The Sword Dances of Northern England*, 286
syncopation, 60

tango, 413, 469–477
combos, 477
tape deck, 7
Tamburitzans, 240
teacher resources, 25
teaching and methods. *See* dance instruction
tempo, 30
Texas Folk Dance Camp (TFDC), 234
Texas square dance, 140
TFDC (Texas Folk Dance Camp), 234
theatrical dance, 4
theme parties, 26–27
Thurston, Hugh, 285
time signature, 30
Tolentino, Francisca Reyes, 370, 371
Tolentino, Ramon P., Jr., 371
Torres, Albert, 509
total dance program
extracurricular opportunities, 12
program curriculum for, 11–12
"touch dancing," 415, 435
Tracie, Gordon E., 392, 398, 399, 400, 402, 404
traditional country western swing. *See* Country Western Dance

traditional dance, 5
traditional/ethnic folk dance, 242
*Traditional Music of America* (Ford), 109
Traditional Two-Step movements. *See* Country Western Dance
Travolta, John, 444
triple-step, 39
Trip Time steps, 413
triplet notes, 28
Trygg, Harry and Dia, 119
"tunks," 193
Turkey Trot, 61
turns
  basic dance, 42
  pivot, 46–47
  polka, 44
  progressive two-step, 42
  schottische clockwise, 42
  two-step clockwise, 43
  waltz, 45–46
turntables, care of records, 9
twirl, 47
the Twist (1960s), 413
two-step, 39

underlying beat, 28
uneven numbers, 5
uneven rhythm, 31–32
unison walk-through, 423
United States Amateur Ballroom Dance Association, 421
United States Ballroom Championships, 421
United States postal stamp, 154
University
  Duquesne, 276
  of Denver, 143
  of Texas, 43
  of New Hampshire, 143, 196
  of Pacific Folk Dance Camp, 154
  of Philippines, 371
  of Washington, 103

variable speed turntables, 9
VCR/camcorder, 9
Viltis, 519
violin (fiddle) music, 63
Virginia Reel, 62, 80
visual impairments, 18
"V" position handhold, 57

walk
  analysis, 32
  contra, 200
  social dance, 418
  square dance, 157
Waller, Marlys Swenson, 142, 154
walk-through, 423
waltz, 478–485
  combos, 485
  style of, 000
  turns, 00–00
warm-up activities, 13
West Coast Swing, 413, 431–435
*West Texas Square Dances* (Greggerson and Greggerson), 153
wheelchair adaptations
  assemblé, 36
  gallop, 36
  hop, 35
  jump, 34
  leap, 34
  run, 34
  Saturday Night Fever (line dance), 452
  sissone, 35
  skip, 38
  slide, 37
  walk, 33
  *See also* locomotor movements; special needs students
Whitehead, Professor, 109
Wills, Bob, 120
Witzig, Luise, 251
World Rock 'n Roll Confederation (WRRC), 422
Works Progress Administration (WPA), 64
Wright, Christina, 317, 318
written tests, 23–24

YWCA, Boston, 194

Zakon, Steve, 226, 236
*zydeco*, 120, 123–124
zwiefacher, 263